APOLLOS OLD TESTAMENT
COMMENTARY

16

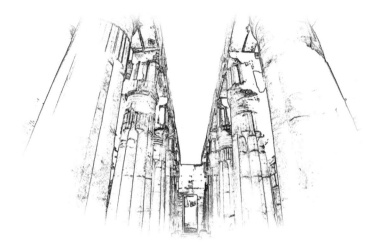

ECCLESIASTES &
THE SONG OF SONGS

Series Editors
David W. Baker and Gordon J. Wenham

DANIEL C. FREDERICKS
& DANIEL J. ESTES

Apollos
Nottingham, England

InterVarsity Press
Downers Grove, Illinois 60515

InterVarsity Press, USA
P.O. Box 1400
Downers Grove, IL 60515-1426, USA
World Wide Web: www.ivpress.com
Email: email@ivpress.com

APOLLOS (an imprint of Inter-Varsity Press, England)
Norton Street
Nottingham NG7 3HR, England
Website: www.ivpbooks.com
Email: ivp@ivpbooks.com

InterVarsity Press®, USA, is the book-publishing division of InterVarsity Christian Fellowship/USA® <www.intervarsity.org> and a member movement of the International Fellowship of Evangelical Students.

Inter-Varsity Press, England, is closely linked with the Universities and Colleges Christian Fellowship, a student movement connecting Christian Unions throughout Great Britain, and a member movement of the International Fellowship of Evangelical Students. Website: www.uccf.org.uk

USA ISBN 978-0-8308-2515-8
UK ISBN 978-1-84474-413-8

First published 2010
Set in Sabon 10/12pt
Typeset in Great Britain by CRB Associates, Potterhanworth, Lincolnshire
Printed and bound in Great Britain by MPG Books Group

Library of Congress Cataloging-in-Publication Data

Fredericks, Daniel C.
  Ecclesiastes & the Song of Songs / Daniel C. Fredericks & Daniel J. Estes.
    p. cm.—(Apollos Old Testament commentary ; 16)
  Includes bibliographical references and index.
  ISBN 978-0-8308-2515-8 (cloth: alk. paper)
  1. Bible. O.T. Ecclesiastes—Commentaries. 2. Bible. O.T. Song of Solomon—Commentaries. I. Estes, Daniel J. II. Title. III. Title: Ecclesiastes and the Song of Songs.
  BS1475.53.F74 2010
   223'.8077—dc22

2009046563

British Library Cataloguing in Publication Data
A catalogue record for this book is available from the British Library.

P	20	19	18	17	16	15	14	13	12	11	10	9	8	7	6	5	4	3	2	1
Y	27	26	25	24	23	22	21	20	19	18	17	16	15	14	13	12	11	10

CONTENTS

EDITORS' PREFACE

The Apollos Old Testament Commentary takes its name from the Alexandrian Jewish Christian who was able to impart his great learning fervently and powerfully through his teaching (Acts 18:24–25). He ably applied his understanding of past events to his contemporary society. This series seeks to do the same, keeping one foot firmly planted in the universe of the original text and the other in that of the target audience, which is preachers, teachers and students of the Bible. The series editors have selected scholars who are adept in both areas, exhibiting scholarly excellence along with practical insight for application.

Translators need to be at home with the linguistic practices and semantic nuances of both the original and target languages in order to be able to transfer the full impact of the one into the other. Commentators, however, serve as interpreters of the text rather than simply its translators. They also need to adopt a dual stance, though theirs needs to be even more solid and diversely anchored than that of translators. While they also must have the linguistic competence to produce their own excellent translations, they must moreover be fully conversant with the literary conventions, sociological and cultural practices, historical background and understanding, and theological perspectives of those who produced the text as well as those whom it concerned. On the other side, they must also understand their own times and culture, able to see where relevance for the original audience is transferable to that of current readers. For this to be accomplished, it is not only necessary to interpret the text; one must also interpret the audience.

Traditionally, commentators have been content to highlight and expound the ancient text. More recently, the need for an anchor in the present day has also become more evident, and this series self-consciously adopts this approach, combining both. Each author analyses the original text through a new translation, textual notes, a discussion of the literary form, structure and background of the passage as well as commenting on elements of its exegesis. A study of the passage's interpretational development in Scripture and the church concludes each section, serving to bring the passage home to the modern reader. What we intend, therefore, is to provide not only tools of excellence for the academy, but also tools of function for the pulpit.

David W. Baker
Gordon J. Wenham

ABBREVIATIONS

TEXTUAL

Akk.	Akkadian
Arab.	Arabic
Bab.	Babylonian
Aram.	Aramaic/Aramaism
Egypt.	Egyptian
Eth.	Ethiopic
Gr.	Greek
HB	Hebrew Bible
Hebr.	Hebrew
Hellen.	Hellenistic
Lat.	Latin
Mes.	Mesopotamian
MS(S)	Manuscript(s)
Pers.	Persian
Pesh.	Peshitta
Phoen.	Phoenician
Sans.	Sanskrit
Sum.	Sumerian
Syr	Syriac
Tg(s)	Targum(s)
Ug.	Ugaritic
Vg	Vulgate

HEBREW GRAMMAR

abs.	absolute	m.	masculine
art.	article	ni.	niphal
const.	construct	pi.	piel
f.	feminine	pl.	plural
hiph.	hiphil	po.	poel
hith.	hithpael	pol.	polel
hoph.	hophal	Q	Qere (the Hebrew text to be
K	Kethibh (the written		read out)
	Hebrew text)	sg.	singular

MISCELLANEOUS

ANE	ancient Near East(ern)
ASV	American Standard Version
AV	Authorized (King James) Version
ET	English translation
Hebr.	Hebrew
JB	Jerusalem Bible
JPS	Jewish Publication Society
LD	Lectio divina
lit.	literally
LXX	Septuagint
MT	Masoretic Text
NASB	New American Standard Bible
NEB	New English Bible
NIV	New International Version
NLT	New Living Translation
NT	New Testament
OT	Old Testament
RSV	Revised Standard Version
v(v).	verse(s)

JOURNALS, REFERENCE WORKS, SERIES

AARCCS	American Academy of Religion Cultural Criticism Series
AB	Anchor Bible
ABD	*The Anchor Bible Dictionary*, ed. David Noel Freedman, 6 vols., New York: Doubleday, 1992
ACCSOT	Ancient Christian Commentary on Scripture: Old Testament
ACW	Ancient Christian Writers
AJBA	*Australian Journal of Biblical Archaeology*
AJSLL	*American Journal of Semitic Languages and Literature*
AJT	*Asia Journal of Theology*
AMT	Athenäum Monografien Theologie
AnBib	Analecta biblica
ANE	Ancient Near East
ANES	*Ancient Near Eastern Studies*
ANET	*Ancient Near Eastern Texts Relating to the Old Testament*, ed. J. B. Pritchard, 3rd ed., Princeton: Princeton University Press, 1969
AOAT	Alter Orient und Altes Testament
AOS	American Oriental Series
ATD	Das Alte Testament Deutsch
ATR	*Anglican Theological Review*

AUSS	*Andrews University Seminary Studies*
BA	*Biblical Archaeologist*
BASOR	*Bulletin of the American Schools of Oriental Research*
BAT	Die Botschaft des Alten Testaments
BBET	Beiträge zur biblischen Exegese und Theologie
BCOTWP	Baker Commentary on the Old Testament Wisdom and Psalms
BDB	F. Brown, S. R. Driver and C. A. Briggs, *A Hebrew and English Lexicon of the Old Testament*, Oxford: Clarendon, 1907; repr. Peabody: Hendrickson, 2005
BEATAJ	Beiträge zur Erforschung des alten Testaments und des antiken Judentums
BeO	*Bibbia e oriente*
BETL	Bibliotheca ephemeridum theologicarum lovaniensium
BGBE	Beiträge zur Geschichte der biblischen Exegese
BHQ	*Biblia Hebraica Quinta*, ed. A. Schenker et al., Stuttgart: Deutsche Bibelgesellschaft, 2004
BHS	*Biblia Hebraica Stuttgartensia*, ed. K. Elliger and W. Rudolph, Stuttgart: Deutsche Bibelgesellschaft, 1967–83
Bib	*Biblica*
BibInt	*Biblical Interpretation*
BIS	Biblical Interpretation Series
BJS	Brown Judaic Studies
BKAT	Biblischer Kommentar, Altes Testament
BLE	*Bulletin de littérature ecclésiastique*
BN	*Biblische Notizen*
BO	*Bibliotheca orientalis*
Brev	*Bible Review*
Bsac	*Bibliotheca sacra*
BST	The Bible Speaks Today
BT	*Bible Translator*
BTB	*Biblical Theology Bulletin*
BZ	*Biblische Zeitschrift*
BZAW	Beihefte zur Zeitschrift für die alttestamentliche Wissenschaft
CBC	Cambridge Bible Commentary
CBQ	*Catholic Biblical Quarterly*
CC	Continental Commentaries
CH	*Church History*
CJT	*Canadian Journal of Theology*
CurTM	*Currents in Theology and Mission*
DBI	*Dictionary of Biblical Imagery*, ed. Leland Ryken, James C. Wilhoit and Tremper Longman III, Downers Grove: IVP, 1998
DSB	The Daily Study Bible Series

EBC	*The Expositor's Bible Commentary*, ed. F. E. Gaebelein, 12 vols., Grand Rapids: Zondervan, 1984
EJ	*Evangelical Journal*
ErIsr	*Eretz-Israel*
ERT	*Evangelical Review of Theology*
ET	English translation
ETL	*Ephemerides theologicae lovanienses*
ETR	*Etudes théologiques et religieuses*
ExpTim	*Expository Times*
FAT	Forschungen zum Alten Testament
FCB	Feminist Companion to the Bible
FCBSS	Feminist Companion to the Bible, Second Series
GBS	Guides to Biblical Scholarship
GKC	*Gesenius' Hebrew Grammar*, ed. E. Kautzsch, 2nd ed. (enlarged), Oxford: Clarendon, 1910
GTJ	*Grace Theological Journal*
HAR	*Hebrew Annual Review*
HAT	Handbuch zum Alten Testament
Hor	*Horizons*
HS	*Hebrew Studies*
HTR	*Harvard Theological Review*
HTS	*Hervormde Teologiese Studies*
HUCA	*Hebrew Union College Annual*
IDB	*The Interpreter's Dictionary of the Bible*, ed. G. A. Buttrick, 4 vols., Nashville: Abingdon, 1962
IEJ	*Israel Exploration Journal*
Imm	*Immanuel*
Int	*Interpretation*
ITC	International Theological Commentary
ITQ	*Irish Theological Quarterly*
JAAR	*Journal of the American Academy of Religion*
JAAS	*Journal of Asia Adventist Seminary*
JANES	*Journal of the Ancient Near East Society*
JATS	*Journal of the Adventist Theological Society*
JBL	*Journal of Biblical Literature*
JBQ	*Jewish Bible Quarterly*
JEA	*Journal of Egyptian Archaeology*
JETS	*Journal of the Evangelical Theological Society*
JNES	*Journal of Near Eastern Studies*
Joüon	Paul Joüon, *A Grammar of Biblical Hebrew*, rev. ed., 2 vols., SubBi 14, ET Rome: Pontificio Istituto Biblico, 1996 (French original 1995)
JPOS	*Journal of the Palestine Oriental Society*
JQR	*Jewish Quarterly Review*
JR	*Journal of Religion*

Jsem	*Journal for Semitics*
JSJ	*Journal for the Study of Judaism in the Persian, Hellenistic, and Roman Periods*
JSNTSup	Journal for the Study of the New Testament, Supplement Series
JSOT	*Journal for the Study of the Old Testament*
JSOTSup	Journal for the Study of the Old Testament, Supplement Series
JSPSup	Journal for the Study of the Pseudepigrapha, Supplement Series
JSS	*Journal of Semitic Studies*
JTS	*Journal of Theological Studies*
JTT	*Journal of Translation and Textlinguistics*
KAT	Kommentar zum Alten Testament
KBANT	Kommentare und Beiträge zum Alten und Neuen Testament
KHAT	Kurzer Hand-Kommentar zum Alten Testament
NAC	New American Commentary
NCBC	New Century Bible Commentary
NIB	*The New Interpreter's Bible*, ed. L. E. Keck, 12 vols., Nashville: Abingdon, 1993–2002
NIBCOT	New International Biblical Commentary on the Old Testament
NICOT	New International Commentary on the Old Testament
NIDOTTE	*New International Dictionary of Old Testament Theology and Exegesis*, ed. W. A. VanGemeren, 5 vols. (Carlisle: Paternoster; Grand Rapids: Zondervan, 1996)
NIVAC	New International Version Application Commentary
NSBT	New Studies in Biblical Theology
NV	*Nova et vetera*
OBO	Orbis biblicus et orientalis
OBT	Overtures to Biblical Theology
OTE	*Old Testament Essays*
OTG	Old Testament Guides
OTL	Old Testament Library
OtSt	Oudtestamentische Studiën
Parab	*Parabola*
PEQ	*Palestine Exploration Quarterly*
Proof	*Prooftexts: A Journal of Jewish Literary History*
RB	*Revue biblique*
RTR	*Reformed Theological Review*
SATAO	Studien zum Alten Testament und zum Alten Orient
SBL	Society of Biblical Literature
SBLDS	Society of Biblical Literature Dissertation Series
SBLMS	Society of Biblical Literature Monograph Series
SBLSymS	Society of Biblical Literature Symposium Series

SBLSS	SBL Semeia Studies
SCH	Studies in Church History
Scr	*Scripture*
ScrHier	Scripta hierosolymitana
SHR	Studies in the History of Religions (supplement to *Numen*)
SEÅ	*Svensk exegetisk årsbok*
SJOT	*Scandinavian Journal of the Old Testament*
Spec	*Speculum*
SR	*Studies in Religion*
STAC	Studies and Texts in Antiquity and Christianity
SubBi	Subsidia biblica
TB	Theologische Bücherei
TD	*Theology Digest*
TDOT	*Theological Dictionary of the Old Testament*, ed. G. Johannes Botterweck and Helmer Ringgren and H.-J. Fabry, 15 vols., Grand Rapids: Eerdmans, 1974–2006
Them	*Themelios*
ThR	*Theologische Rundshau*
TJ	*Trinity Journal*
TOTC	Tyndale Old Testament Commentaries
TWOT	*Theological Wordbook of the Old Testament*, ed. R. Laird Harris and Gleason L. Archer, Jr., 2 vols., Chicago: Moody, 1980
TynB	*Tyndale Bulletin*
TZ	*Theologische Zeitschrift*
UBS	United Bible Societies
UF	*Ugarit-Forschungen*
USQR	*Union Seminary Quarterly Review*
VoxEv	*Vox Evangelica*
VT	*Vetus Testamentum*
VTSup	Supplements to *Vetus Testamentum*
Waltke	Bruce K. Waltke and M. O'Conner, *An Introduction to Biblical Hebrew Syntax*, Winona Lake: Eisenbrauns
WBC	Word Biblical Commentary
WTJ	*Westminster Theological Journal*
YJS	Yale Judaica Series
ZAH	*Zeitschrift für Althebräistik*
ZAW	*Zeitschrift für die alttestamentliche Wissenschaft*
ZTK	*Zeitschrift für Theologie und Kirche*

ECCLESIASTES

Dedicated to you pastors and teachers
who serve your disciples in their profound,
yet transient, lives by challenging and
consoling them with God's perfect wisdom.

AUTHOR'S PREFACE

Biblical commentary is based on the commentator's presuppositions on canonicity. Whether the biblical book under review is considered to be only a catalyst for the reader's free associative musings about some aspect of life, whether the book is read solely as an artefact of an unfathomable authorial mind, whether it is read as an independent but lucid verbalization of an individual's response to history, personal experience and the spiritual, whether the book is seen in harmony or dissonance with any concentric circles of *context* that may be said to surround it – regardless, a judgment about canonicity is imposed on that commentary. Questions have always risen about the extent to which Ecclesiastes relates to these contexts, including its historical milieu, its relationship to Hebrew wisdom literature or any broader theological understanding of the Hebrews during the OT or even intertestamental times. Seldom is the book mentioned in the contexts of NT history or theology.

The presupposition of this commentator is that Ecclesiastes is found in the canon because it plays a significant role in a cumulative theology of the Old and New Testaments. How probable, cohesive or comprehensible any cumulative theology is, again depends on a commentator's view of biblical theology. However, I believe that once Ecclesiastes' thematic words and phrases are allowed to speak with their Hebrew voices and are listened to carefully and with the benefit of the doubt, the listener begins hearing familiar ideas with the rest of the OT, and even the NT. By this intensive listening, Ecclesiastes is allowed to add depth and texture to the rest of the canon.

Consequently, this commentary shows Ecclesiastes' affinity with the breadth of OT legal, poetic, wisdom and prophetic writings as well as the teachings of Christ and the apostles. Some might say this is an overestimation of a book that has for centuries been on the margins of biblical theology because of its challenging message of bald realism, pragmatism and frustrated confessions. But Ecclesiastes should not be coddled as if it were a precocious and embarrassing threat to the family of biblical literature, nor should it be humoured as if it were the doddering ramblings of a bitter old uncle in that family. Rather, Ecclesiastes demands respect with a moderating voice of realism and composure within biblical discussions of life's challenging, even overwhelming, circumstances. A goal of this commentary is a more regular inclusion of Ecclesiastes in the preaching and teaching of the church as it deepens the thought and faith of its congregations. This commentary intends to build trust in Ecclesiastes that has been lacking because it has not been heard while calling us to urgent, responsible biblical living in the marketplace and in the kingdom. This commentary is dedicated to you pastors and teachers who accept your calling to bless and console your disciples in their precious, profound, yet transient, lives.

Two dear friends have been most helpful in this labour. Thank you, Rose Mary Foncree for being a constant encouragement and a principled grammarian for my drafts who has made my muddled thoughts cogent. Thank you too Chris Cullnane for applying your librarian skills unfailingly to find every document I have requested. Furthermore, I appreciate the opportunity, guidance and patience of IVP, and its Apollos editors, Gordon Wenham, David Baker and, most notably, Philip Duce. This is a labour I have thoroughly enjoyed because of you all.

Daniel C. Fredericks

INTRODUCTION

1. WHAT IS MAN?

When I observe your skies, the work of your fingers,
The moon and stars which you have placed.
What is man that you are concerned about him?
The son of man that you care for him?

How majestic is your name in all the earth!

(Ps. 8:4, 9)

O Lord, *what is man* that you acknowledge him?
What are the sons of men that you even take them into
    account?
Man is like a breath, his days as a brief shadow!

(Ps. 144:3–4)

Leave me alone, for *breath*like are my days.
What is man that you set your mind to honour him?

(Job 7:16–17)

What is your life? You are like a mist that appears
For a little while, then it is gone!

(Jas 4:14)

If we were left simply to our intuition about our significance in God's vast and almost timeless universe, we would conclude that we are worthless – exactly David's first impression when he ponders human significance in Ps. 8. He is struck by his own infinitesimally minute value compared to God's infinite self-expression in his creation. When contemplating God's immense creation, we wonder why we have any meaning in God's gigantic and eternal cosmic order. Only the naively arrogant person ambles through life ignoring the profound order and beauty of the surrounding creation which soundly challenges his chaotic, grotesque pride. On the other hand, when the faithful appreciate and accept God's loving care and ample gifts for an enjoyable life, they are lifted to those same heavenly and daunting heights which for a moment dwarfed them. David's reflections, then, are personal, emotional, and eventually, worshipful: 'O LORD, the majesty of your name fills the earth!' (Ps. 8:1, 9).

Overcome by God's stunning creative genius and power, and so humbled by his sovereign care, David is driven to ask, 'Why should you care about me?' But the answer is so much more wonderful than the questioner could even anticipate: not only does God care for us; he entrusts the entire earth to us as his governing assistants! David remembers God's primary commission of Gen. 1:26–28, 'Fill the earth and subdue it, be masters . . . ' But he also notices the irony of having authority over God's creation yet being totally dependent on the Lord's care as his sovereign servant. In this short psalm lies the seeds of a full biblical theology – our sovereign creator blesses his commissioned sovereign humanity with his shepherding care.

This commissioned authority of humanity over the world is a permeating theme in OT and NT theology. Guided by God's legal and wisdom axioms, humanity is expected to fulfil its purpose by managing the earth in a godly fashion. Our purpose in God's cosmic order is to be his ruling servants 'under the sun', as Ecclesiastes refers to the whole world. Even Christ's saving incarnation, as well as his glorious return to continue reigning as the divine king, have this same fundamental purpose – to fulfil the primary commission of godly ruling of earth. This dominant theme of the first book's first chapter, Gen. 1, reverberates clearly throughout the scriptures in places such as Ps. 8 and Heb. 2, and culminates in the last book's last chapter in Rev. 22:5.

The role of the OT wisdom literature, including Ecclesiastes, is to reflect this commissional theology by describing more fully our function as managers of God's earth. In the wisdom literature, we find the resources for knowledge and discernment to order our life's personal daily schedules and to order our surroundings according to the standards of Scripture. In the OT, the primary commission is expanded for the Israelite community in the legal literature, but is described in just as much detail for the individual in the wisdom literature. A substantial portion of the wisdom literature gives very practical instructions for the daily subduing of the apparently random challenges we face between waking and sleeping. These instructions in turn are synchronized with God's sovereign administration of the planet through his built-in physical, social, psychological and spiritual principles.

Ecclesiastes is an intense exhortation along these lines. But what throws us off in this speech called Ecclesiastes is its uncensored, bottom-line assessment of reality based on an exploration autonomous from special revelation. Furthermore, the book is not palatable to those steeped in theological platitudes and whose theology never travels a block past Justification Street. Yet those who thirst for the required wisdom for holistic sanctification will listen exhaustively to the teachings of this biblical sage.

2. WHAT IS THE ADVANTAGE?

The voice in Ecclesiastes is similar to that of David's in Pss 8 and 144. There is the same sigh of awe at the order and mystery of creation; for example, in Eccl. 1:5–7; 3:11; 11:5. But Ecclesiastes' question about human significance is not compared with the vastness of the cosmos, a *spatial* concept. Rather, human significance is questioned on the basis of a *temporal* concept. Like Ps. 144, where this exact question rises, it is the issue of human transience that challenges one's sense of value in God's creation, not human bodily dimensions. As a momentary shadow, a mere fleeting breath, how is it that God should give to us the daily care and joy we experience as those good in his sight? In fact, not only one's *life*, but also everything *done during life* under the sun is temporary. Transience of life itself, and the transience of our labours and joys – these are significant themes of this speech. But these realities of a fallen world are not licence for negativity. *Coping* with, and *thriving* within, this transient life is the compensatory theme in Ecclesiastes. This coping, in the way James and Peter see it, matures our wisdom and persistence (Jas 1:2–5; 1 Pet. 1:6–7).

Though we appreciate the wisdom in patiently weathering the storm during trials and tragedies, it is hard when our fragile souls are hammered with crises and fears, even if for only a short season. During these ordeals, we are debilitated in making right judgments. Our once simple, optimistic faith is crushed by our human limitations and weakness in withstanding such testing. These limitations are what frustrate our speaker in Ecclesiastes, compelling him to ask in various ways, 'Why should we even be wise, righteous or hard working?' One can explain the *cause* of the sorrow and hard work experienced in life from Gen. 3:17–19: 'Cursed is the ground because of you, in grief you will eat from it ... By the sweat of your face you will eat food until you return to the ground.' But the understandable question is whether there is any advantage in working with, or even against, that curse: 'What is the advantage in all one's laborious labour under the sun?' (1:3; 2:22; 3:9; 5:11, 16; 6:8).

Creation in all its power, order, diversity, consistency, beauty, and yet in its dependency on the Creator, teaches us the importance of wisdom. We share these same attributes of the natural world in order to manage it! We are made of the same dust and elements, but created higher than the rest of creation to steward it. This is the call to a biblical sense of 'world domination'. It does not come through violence, abuse, murder of the innocent, but from routine, daily obedience to God's written Word as we apply it in the marketplace, relationships and in the world of ideas. But, if our life purpose is to rule this planet in godliness, what advantage can there be in our efforts when we are limited so significantly in how we can manage our own life and its contents? Examples of our limitations are found throughout Ecclesiastes: we remember little about the past, are unable to discover enough about the present, and it is impossible to predict much about the future. We cannot change the status quo, whether it is determined by God, our superiors or impersonal forces such as weather or wealth.

Within all the frustration in the book, however, the question is not one of desperation about whether there is any *purpose* in life. Rather, after one's investment of time and effort in being wise, Ecclesiastes evaluates whether there is any advantage to the labour involved. The emphasis in Ecclesiastes is not about human meaning; it is about labour's benefits. Over sixty times words are used meaning *deeds* explicitly (*ma'ĕśeh*), and the book frequently asks, '*māh yitrôn?*', literally 'What remains?' We will find that the answer to 'What remains?' is that indeed there are profound, good and enjoyable benefits to one's wise conduct, though admittedly the downside to the answer is that there are no *lasting* advantages, since everything is temporary under the sun.

The overriding interest of Ecclesiastes about human limitations and challenges to responsible living is our very temporary and brief lifespan, and the brief impact of even our wisest accomplishments. This is why the theme of transitoriness has its own formulaic phrasing and expressions pervading the speech, and why the theme is chosen to introduce and conclude the speech in extreme articulations (1:2; 12:8). Compared to the eternal existence of God in the 'past' and 'future', our very recent appearance on earth limits our knowledge, and certainly our experience, of everything that occurred before us. Furthermore, our mere seventy years of life is a negligible blip in the planet's history.

But, there is consolation in the parallel concerns of David in Ps. 8. As David says, the proportion of our size compared to the vast universe is not indicative of our importance in God's kingdom. Ecclesiastes tells us this as well but not in the context of the *spatial* universe. Instead, we are told that there is meaning to our life in spite of our personal *temporal* limitations. Both limitations of humanity and our purpose – our smallness and brevity – can discourage us from taking our full responsibility for managing the planet as described in Genesis' primary commission. But Ecclesiastes counters this by assuring us that the God who created the awesome universe has provided more than adequate resources to us so that we can subdue our portion of the earth.

Though our life is temporary, that does not negate the value of our life and wise labour. Eventually Ecclesiastes' initial and pervasive question 'What advantage . . . ?' will be answered with encouragements for the hearer to cherish the satisfaction, shalom, of a profound, deep-flowing joy (e.g. 2:24–26; 5:20)! The question of 'advantage' is not answered by 'There is no advantage.' On the contrary, it is answered by numerous explanations of what is 'good', 'advantageous' and what one's 'portion' is that comes from God's generosity.

3. BUT IS EVERYTHING TEMPORARY?

We saw above that Ps. 144:3–4 questions the possibility of any human significance in the light of our transience: 'O LORD, what is man that you acknowledge him? . . . *Man* is like a *breath* . . . A *brief shadow*.' In the middle and pivotal point in Ecclesiastes, the same question is asked using very similar words: 'Who knows what is good for *man* while he lives the *few days* of his *breath*like life which he spends as a *shadow*?' (6:12). We should add Job's same question from 7:16–17. His question has the edge of the afflicted in it, yet echoes the same thoughts:

> Leave me alone, for *breath*like are my days.
> What is man that you set your mind to honour him?

This theme of the brevity of life permeates Ecclesiastes through many other words, phrases and pervasive themes as well.

This word for 'breath' in Ps. 144 and Ecclesiastes is the Hebrew word *hebel*. It is this very word that introduces and concludes the speech in Ecclesiastes and appears many times in between. The phrase *hăbēl hăbālîm . . . hăbēl hăbālîm, hakkōl hābel* is the beginning and ending thought of this speech we call Ecclesiastes. The Hebraic phrasing for the superlative is the same as the 'King of kings' or 'Lord of lords' used in the NT to show the pre-eminent position of Christ. This phrasing is used to introduce and close Ecclesiastes, by expressing superlative truth that everything is merely *hebel*, or 'breath'.

The fundamental meaning of this metaphor, *hebel* or 'breath', in the OT is 'temporary', so the opening comments in Ecclesiastes are intended to announce this key frustration of humanity: 'Everything is Temporary!' I will explain later how the more popular translation of *hebel* in Ecclesiastes as 'vanity', 'futility' or 'meaninglessness' is due in large part to the inadequate LXX and Vg translations.

3.1. The Ancient Near East on brevity in life

Ecclesiastes, of course, is not alone in highlighting the transience of human life and its activities. It is a concern of all ages including that of the ANE:

> Whatsoever men do, does not last forever, humanity and their
>   achievements alike come to an end.
>   (A Mesopotamian sage; Lambert 1975: 109)

> The dragon-fly leaves its shell,
>   that its face might but glance at the sun.
> Since the days of yore there has been no permanence.
>   (Epic of Gilgamesh; *ANET* 92)

> The life of mankind does not last forever.
>   (Poet from Emar; Lambert 1975: 39–40)

> As for the duration of what is done on the earth, it is a kind of
>   dream.
>   (Egyptian harper; *ANET* 34)

> Behold, there is not one who departs who comes back again.
>   (Egyptian harper; *ANET* 467)

> Life is a transitory state, and even trees fall.
>   (Egyptian sage, third millennium; Faulkner 1956: 27)

Even in Far Eastern culture, the Tibetan monks still create elaborate sand paintings, mandalas, each one taking several days of work by several artists. Quickly after its completion, the painting is destroyed as a metaphor for life's transience. Japanese culture has an aesthetic view of reality, *wabi-sabi*, which accepts and seeks to appreciate the impermanence built into everything.

3.2. The Old Testament on brevity in life

The OT, like Egyptian and Mesopotamian cultures, also laments the limitations transience imposes on life and its activities. It, of course, has a whole theology of the curse of transience from the Fall onwards. Rather than allowing humanity to live endlessly, God drove them out of the Garden to live out the few days of their remaining lives. Ecclesiastes uses the word *mispar* for an extremely limited number, *a few*, as quoted above in 6:12 in reference to the *few* days of one's temporary life. The same word is used to express our short number of days in 2:3 and 5:17. But Job 14:5

also uses this word to describe the short span of life God determines for our lives: 'You have determined his days and his *few* months...' Job had just referred to his life as a fleeting *shadow* as well in v. 2. And again in Job 16:22 he grieves that 'After a *few* (*mispar*) years I will go the way from where I will never return.' Earlier Job 10:20 had said literally, 'Are not my days little (*mě'at*)?'

There are many other examples of the biblical concern about our shortness of life. Ps. 90:5–6, 10, 12 speaks of God's discernment as the reason for our transience:

> You sweep people away like dreams that disappear,
>   or like grass that springs up in the morning.
> In the morning it blooms and flourishes,
>   but by evening it is dried and withered...
> Seventy years are given to us,
>   some may even reach eighty,
> But even the best of these years are filled with pain and trouble;
>   Soon they disappear and we are gone.
> Teach us to realize the brevity of life,
>   so that we may grow in wisdom.

But Ps. 103:15–17a goes on to console us even in the wake of this transience:

> Our days on earth are like grass;
>   Like wild flowers we bloom and die.
> The wind blows and we are gone –
>   As though we had never been.
> But the love of the LORD remains for ever for those who fear
>   him.

Isa. 40:6b, 7, 24 repeats the imagery of transient life of Pss 90 and 103, and Peter endorses it in the NT (1 Pet. 1:24):

> Shout that the people are like the grass that dies away.
> Their beauty fades as quickly as the beauty of flowers in a field.
> The grass withers and the flowers fade beneath the breath of the
>   LORD.
> And so it is with people...
> They hardly get started, barely taking root,
> When He blows on them and they wither.

Excerpts from Job show his clear awareness of human transience:

> My days are swifter than a weaver's shuttle...
> Remember that my life is but breath...

Man, born of woman, is short-lived and full of trouble.
Like a flower he comes forth and withers
He also flees like a shadow and does not remain...

(7:6–7; 14:1–2)

Hosea speaks of disobedient Ephraim with four similes of brevity:

So, they will be like the morning cloud, and
Like dew disappearing early,
Like chaff blown off the threshing floor, and
Like smoke out of a window.

(13:3)

The 'wisdom book' of the NT also portrays our transience: 'Your life is like the morning fog – it is here a little while, then it is gone' (Jas 4:14).

In addition to Ecclesiastes, there are four passages that use our word *hebel* to convey the meteoric nature of our life. I have already mentioned Ps. 144 and Job 7. But two other Psalms passages use *hebel* in this way. Ps. 78:33 says in reference to the nation of Israel:

So he made their days vanish like a *breath*,
    and their years in haste.

But the idea is elaborated much more fully for the individual in Ps. 39. Like Job, the psalmist is morbidly counting on his *hebel*-ness to bring an end to his agony. By using other words and phrases denoting transience along with *hebel* in vv. 4–6, the poet anticipates his short-lived future:

LORD, remind me how *brief* my time on earth will be.
Remind me that my *days are numbered*, and that my *life is fleeing* away.
My life is *no longer than* the width of my hand.
An entire lifetime is *just a moment* to you; human existence is but a **breath**.
Surely man travels as a *shadow*.
Surely, for a **breath** they are in turmoil;
one heaps up but does not know who will gather.

The psalmist then concludes in vv. 12–13 that he is only a momentary presence on earth:

For I am your guest, a traveller *passing through*, as my fathers were.
Spare me so I can smile again, before I am *gone and exist no more*.

Not only is life *itself* temporary, according to the OT, but the results of our labours are also only fleeting in length. Twice, for instance, using the word *hebel*, Proverbs discounts passing wealth as an end in itself:

Wealth from fast (*hebel*) schemes quickly disappears;
   wealth from hard work grows.

(13:11)

Wealth achieved by lying is a *fleeting breath* (*hebel*)
   for those seeking death.

(21:6)

We find in Ecclesiastes many statements similar to these that attribute only a temporary value to those activities and accomplishments in our ephemeral lives.

ANE and OT thought provide an ample context within which Ecclesiastes expands on both the curses and the blessings of a fleeting life and its activities. Furthermore, it is particularly in the wisdom and poetic books where we find an interest in the transience of life and its activities expressed by *hebel* and other words, namely Psalms, Job, Proverbs and Ecclesiastes. It should not be a mystery at all why the canon includes a book devoting itself entirely to the realistic assessment of how we should live our lives as wise sovereign managers of God's earth, even in spite of our very short opportunity to do so.

3.3. Metaphorical uses for *hebel*

Hebel is used seventy-eight times in the OT. Surprisingly, in only three instances is the word's literal meaning, *breath*, intended (Ps. 63:9; Prov. 21:6; Isa. 57:13). However, Ecclesiastes uses the term metaphorically thirty-eight times out of those seventy-eight to convey temporariness. The term is used in the OT to describe the insubstantiality of an action related to false religion and idolatry or the feeble attempts to substitute misleading human wisdom for God's ways. These autonomous attempts at worship and wisdom are frequently referred to as *hebel*. This meaning is derived from another characteristic of breath: its weightlessness. Not only is a breath momentary; it is weightless, or insubstantial. However, the two biblical uses are not simply to be combined, and most commentators see the metaphor being applied in the OT judiciously and most often separately. For instance, Abel's name is identical to *hebel*, and he may have been named *Hebel* because Cain cut his life short. However, he probably would not have been so named because people considered him to be meaningless or insignificant, since Abel was actually considered the righteous sufferer – and the example of the true faith – to his own end (see

E. Dor-Shav 2008: 216–217). When one uses the simile 'He is like a rock', one does not mean that the same person is solid and dependable as well as dense and stubborn simultaneously, though both meanings are uses of the metaphor.

It may at first seem curious that a metaphor is used to express this most critical assessment of everything 'under the sun' as temporary. Yet, why it was chosen makes sense when one realizes that (at least in the OT Hebrew vocabulary) there are only metaphorical words for transience.

3.4. A biblical constellation of words describing transience

We have seen already that the biblical wisdom and poetic writings include a constellation of words that converge at times to describe transience. Eccl. 6:12, Pss 39:5 and 144:4 use 'breath' and 'shadow' (*ṣēl*) together ('shadow' denotes transitoriness in 1 Chr. 29:15; Pss 102:12; 109:23; Job 8:9; 14:2; 17:7). Eccl. 2:3, 5:17 and 6:12 use 'a few days', as does Job 16:22. And again, Eccl. 6:12 combines 'shadow' and 'a few days' just as in Job 14:2, 5.

'Wind' (*rûaḥ*) is also combined with the concept of transience in the OT. Job 7:6–7 groans, 'My days are swifter than a weaver's shuttle ... remember my life is *rûaḥ*.' Isa. 57:13 warns about the brevity of physical idols:

> The *rûaḥ* will carry them off,
>   a breath (*hebel*) will take them away.

The psalmist's recounting of Israel's fleeting past is included in 78:33, 39, 'He made their days vanish like a breath (*hebel*) ... a passing *rûaḥ* that does not return.'

Ecclesiastes also regularly puts these two words together and creates a poetic refrain from them that is repeated seven times: 'all is *hebel* and as the *whim of the wind* (*rûaḥ*)' (1:14; 2:11, 17, 26; 4:4, 16; 6:9). This phrase 'whim of the wind' is translated very differently throughout the commentaries, and the lexical and grammatical reasons for my translation will be provided later. Suffice it for now to propose that since this particular pairing of *hebel* and *rûaḥ* is paralleled elsewhere in poetic or wisdom texts to denote transience, its pairing in Ecclesiastes probably does so as well.

3.5. Significance of time in Ecclesiastes

The intense interest in the concept of time in Ecclesiastes is obvious when one looks at the list of some other temporal topics, words and phrases that reference it.

3.5.1. Repetitiveness

The concept of repetitiveness in Ecclesiastes accentuates the brevity in life, since repetitiveness implies the transience of the constituent parts that are repeated. Though breathing is repetitive, each breath in breathing is temporary. For instance, even though generations always exist, they do so by reproducing themselves and replacing their own short lives with other equally short lives of their children and grandchildren – generations come and go, and do nothing new under the sun, since anything can only be repeated because it has already been done by previous generations (1:4, 9–10; 2:12, 18; 3:15). The rivers also simply repeat their cycles, as do the clouds eventually after each rainfall (1:7; 12:2). We will later look in detail at Ecclesiastes' three poetic sections (1:4–11; 3:1–8; 12:2–7) and how each deals with the cycles within life and the brevity of its parts (Fredericks 1993: 24–28; Azize 2003: 135, 138).

3.5.2. Timing

It is clear in Ecclesiastes that one's wisdom is shown in the perfect timing of one's activities. Circumstances and opportunities provide the setting for the wisest decisions and actions. Since the windows of opportunity are only temporary, one must have the ability to discern the advantageous time. The poem found in 3:1–8 about the seasons of wise conduct begins with the advice that there is a right time for anything done (3:1). The poem implies that only a temporary stint is appropriate for each activity, since it must give way eventually to its opposite. The word *'ēt* (opportune time) alone occurs forty times in Ecclesiastes and accentuates that there is only a relatively brief time when actions are appropriate. We simply need to be wise now! As God's earthly stewards we are responsible for applying and enjoying his principles of community and personal management to his kingdom work while we are able to do so (3:22; 10:14). For a fine study of 'timing' in Ecclesiastes, see Schultz 2005.

3.5.3. Past and future

Given our merely temporary existence, there is a severe limitation of understanding reality in its fullness. In spite of having that intuition of *infinity* created within us, we still have only a seriously incomplete view of creation's history from beginning to end (3:11). Even if at one point in time something were to be known, Ecclesiastes has little hope of it being remembered (1:11; 2:16; 9:15). Its transience buries it in obscurity. Regarding the past, God chooses to repeat it (3:15). This is the paradox that motivates us to live responsibly in the ever-renewed transience of the present. God's ways can be found through observing the past, but since we do not know the future we cannot know what circumstances, blessings, crises and opportunities are to come.

3.5.4. *Death and subsequence*

The fact of death is a frequent concern in Ecclesiastes, which carries the obvious implication, even intensification, of human transience (2:16; 3:2– 3, 19–21; 5:15–16; 6:3–6; 7:1–4, 15, 17; 7:26; 8:8, 13; 9:3–6, 10; 12:7). In this sense, Ecclesiastes is the memento mori of the Bible. From the passing of generations (1:4) to the passing of the individual (12:7), death looms as an impetus to work wisely and enjoy life while one can. Furthermore, several times the speech refers to what follows a person's brief life (2:12, 18; 3:22; 6:12; 7:14; 10:14), though never implying nor denying an afterlife.

3.6. The extent of temporariness in our lives

When Ecclesiastes pronounces everything to be temporary, it qualifies this in two ways. First, clearly the claim does not apply to God and all of his actions: they exist for ever (3:14). For example, God's created earth exists relatively for ever (1:4), and even transient humanity carries a divinely implanted intuition of the eternal (3:11). Secondly, the book frequently qualifies what is temporary by locating it 'under the sun', 'under heaven' or 'on the earth'. Clearly, human life and its activities are encompassed by the claim that all is temporary. Ecclesiastes makes a firm distinction between the life of mortals and the acts of God, comparable to Isaiah's pronouncement about human life and the acts of God: 'The grass withers, and the flowers fade ... so it is with people ... but the word of our God stands for ever' (Isa. 40:7–8).

What Ecclesiastes considers explicitly to be temporary, calling them *hebel*, are the following:

Every effort	1:14; 2:11, 15, 17, 19
Any fruit of our labours	2:21, 26
Pleasure	2:1, 23
Life	3:19; 6:4, 12; 7:15; 9:9
Youth	11:10
Success	4:4
Wealth	4:7–8; 5:10; 6:2
Desire	6:9
Frivolity	7:6
Popularity	4:16; 8:10

Injustice	8:14
All future events	11:8
Everything!	1:2; 12:8

4. AUTHOR AND DATE

So far I have referred to the book as 'Ecclesiastes', its Greek title meaning a 'member of an assembly', and used in the NT to describe Christians. Consequently, 'ecclesiastical' is the most frequent English derivative used with any frequency. However, we cannot reason backwards from the NT, as many do, and presume that this title for the book denotes any specific religious gathering as the occasion for the speech. The actual Hebrew word is *qōhelet*, an abstract f. noun describing a position or role in the Hebrew establishment, but not with any inherent religious function. Thus the Hebrew title of the book is simply extracted from the title for the position of 'Assembler, Gatherer' or, in more contemporary language, the 'Convener' or 'Chair'. Consequently, it is a misleading anachronism to identify the speaker as 'The Preacher' with a heavy ecclesiastical or liturgical denotation. The gathering is simply a meeting where the convener chooses to speak at some length.

Whoever put this speech we call 'Ecclesiastes' into writing clearly intended to attribute it to Solomon either because Solomon was the one who actually gave the address or because they wanted these words attributed to him. The prima facie evidence points to Solomon. Combining 1:1, 12 and 2:9, Qoheleth is a son of David, a king who ruled Israel from Jerusalem, and one whom no previous king was greater than. A few posit that 'son of David' does not necessarily mean an immediate son but perhaps some generation of grandson. But, as Seow (1997: 97) concludes, the phrase does always mean an immediate son in the OT, especially regarding David and Solomon. Furthermore, Solomon was the only son of David to have ruled Israel's twelve tribes from Jerusalem. No other person could make these claims than Solomon. So the absence of Solomon's name is hardly important, since everything short of that is announced – the editor simply chooses not to state the obvious. The emphasis is that Solomon here is 'Qoheleth' (assembler), the one who assembles audiences.

However, most scholars have thought the theory of a pseudonymous writer to be preferable, because Ecclesiastes' alleged lateness in its language and theology precluded Solomon as the author, and the work is then estimated to be 400–700 years later than the great king. However, the language of Ecclesiastes is either vernacular in dialect or transitional in the history of the Hebrew language (see discussion below, pp. 56–61). If transitional, it appears to be more transitional from early Biblical Hebrew to later Biblical Hebrew than between later Biblical Hebrew to the still later Mishnaic Hebrew Therefore, no later than an eighth- or seventh-century BC date for the current text is probable, as we have it, if the language is not vernacular. If it is an example of a more vernacular dialect, then it could be earlier yet. Of course this does not mean the words are not those of a creative writer other than Solomon, just that the Hebrew dialect itself does not necessarily preclude him, especially if what we have is a crystallization of oral tradition. Transmission of this speech through the writing process could have modernized the language to the extent that it looks somewhat later than early written Hebrew (see Longman 1998: 10).

The book is also thought to be late by many who believe it to be pessimistic and indicative of a later, unorthodox wisdom literature. The speaker supposedly reflects the inevitable hopelessness of a degenerating socio-economic environment, an individual who speaks in a cynical tone about wisdom, work and joy. As we have seen above, this theory depends wholly on the meaning of *hebel* in Ecclesiastes to be 'vanity, meaningless'. If, however, the meaning of *hebel* is 'temporary', this devolutionary view of the wisdom literature is in total inaccurate. Despite a Qumran fragment, Whitley (1978: 148) suggested a mid-second century BC date. The third century BC is favoured by Whybray (1989: 4–12), Lohfink (2003: 4–5) and Krüger (2004: 19). Seow (1997: 21–35) prefers the fifth to early fourth centuries BC. Because of linguistic peculiarities and controversy, others remain agnostic on the weight of those arguments alone (Eaton 1983: 24; Longman 1998: 9–10; Shields 2006: 23) apart from a strong consensus among almost all that the book is post-exilic.

There is a growing interest however in a pre-exilic date for Ecclesiastes. It is being asked whether the political milieu described in Ecclesiastes is consistent with the state of affairs in the later political and sociological configurations of Israel. A kingly perspective is pervasive, since kings, rulers and princes are mentioned no fewer than twenty-six times in Ecclesiastes. This royal perspective indicates personal kingly experience, rather than mere observations of someone who has never ruled but attempts to simulate what it would be like if one had!

The exilic and post-exilic periods of Israel's history would hardly have been a fruitful time for any extensive wisdom speeches offered by Qoheleth, whoever he might be, about court life within a monarchy. There was no monarchy! Even if one runs the date up as late as the Ptolemaic and Seleucid kingdoms, there is no situation in which, and to which, a Jewish Qoheleth could speak with any authority or practicality about how Jews should live their lives in the royal court. Young (1993: 146–147, 157) and Anderson (1997: 80–95) emphasize this point in their arguments for a pre-exilic date for Ecclesiastes, Anderson proposing the eighth or seventh centuries BC. A post-exilic situation would have all the upper echelons of society dispersed throughout the Babylonian Empire, leaving no such audience for Qoheleth to address about court life and leadership. Perhaps a pre-exilic monarchic setting would be less contrived and more natural, since attempts to make Qoheleth feel at home in the Persian era's socio-economic situation or

Greek setting fall short in reconstructing a suitable audience for 'Qoheleth'. The theory of a fictional king implies a theory of a fictional audience as well as a fictional sociopolitical environment.

Krüger speaks of a *Corpus Salomonicum* made up those writings ascribed to Solomon: Proverbs, Ecclesiastes and Song of Solomon (2004: 27–28). Among other connections, he emphasizes the convergence of three themes common to all three books: 'seeking and finding', 'women' and 'wisdom' (Prov. 2:4–5; 3:13; 4:22; 7:15; 8:9, 12, 17, 35; 31:10; Eccl. 7:24–29; 8:17; 12:10; Song 3:1–4; 5:6–8; 6:1; 8:1). We might add to these books the Solomonic traditions in the histories, particularly 1 Kings. Many other common conceptual and linguistic characteristics are found within this expanded corpus. If Ecclesiastes is a speech by a pseudonymous writer who wishes to use Solomon's traditional wisdom reputation, then the writer is an exceptional success. His vocabulary and phrasing draws frequently and effortlessly from a rich fabric of pre-existing literature connected to Solomon in one significant way or another.

1. The Hebrew root for Qoheleth is *qāhāl*, 'an assembly' or 'a gathering', and often describes the assembled Israelites for various reasons, whether civil, religious or military. Solomon assembled the Israelites for the conse- cration of the new temple (1 Kgs 8; 2 Chr. 5) and found foreign dignitaries assembled before him, including the Queen of Sheba (1 Kgs 4:34; 10:1). Perhaps one of these occasions was the setting for this particular lecture we call Qoheleth or Ecclesiastes. The international flavour of the speech (including Aramaic and Persian words), its universality in philosophical subject matter, its theme of the administration of justice by officials, all would fit this setting. This is certainly consistent with the philosophical and cosmopolitan style of the speech. See below 'Genre'.

2. During Solomon's reign, Israel was 'eating, drinking and rejoicing' (1 Kgs 4:20) – precisely the activities and words to express those activities that compose Qoheleth's enjoyment refrain for his listeners.

eating	*'ākal*	Eccl. 2:24–25; 3:13; 5:18–19; 8:15; 9:7
drinking	*šātâ*	Eccl. 2:24; 3:13; 5:18; 8:15; 9:7
rejoicing	*śāmaḥ*	Eccl. 2:26; 3:12, 22; 5:19–20; 8:15(twice); 9:7

This does not include the equivalent phrase for rejoicing; that is, 'see good': 2:1, 24; 3:13; 5:18; 6:6; 9:9. This phraseology is more than coincidental. It is a thematic description of life under Solomon as well as king Qoheleth's primary desire for his audience.

3. 1 Kgs 4 goes on to explain the accomplishments of Solomon in 4:21– 28, setting the backdrop for the accomplishments of Qoheleth in Eccl. 2:4–8. When Israel was in its golden years of peace after David had established his empire, Solomon had time to devote to cultural manage- ment. Rather than a goal of expanding the borders, or simply protecting his nation, he enhanced it culturally with material prosperity and profound

literature. Solomon's greatness was seen in his many accomplishments, including those in international commerce, diplomacy, agriculture as well his construction of cities, edifices and fortresses. Furthermore, the book of Proverbs, his many songs, and this speech in particular, prove his ability to stabilize a nation through art, ethics, philosophical reflection and discussion. Rather than warring and alienating other nations, Solomon engaged them and their literature and redeemed those modes of cultural expression within Israel's own chosen relationship with their God. His failures are well documented, but what he accomplished with his God-given wisdom should not be discounted as meaningless. We will see later, at 2:4–8, the designed parallels of Qoheleth and Solomon regarding their achievements as king.

4. The Solomonic biography in 1 Kgs 4:33 also highlights the king's knowledge and pronouncements on botanical and zoological subjects. The writer of Song of Songs composes with reference to flora, fauna and the terrain, as does Qoheleth, contributing these components of a creation theology to a *Corpus Salomonicum*. Qoheleth's interest in nature forms poetic inclusios in 1:4–8 and 12:1–8 and is found interspersed throughout the intervening speech: sun, wind, rivers, gardens, fruit trees, forests, silver, gold, stones, beasts, thorn bushes, dogs, lions, oil, fish, birds, flies, horses, serpents, winged creatures, waters, clouds, rain, fetuses, moon, stars, almond trees, grasshoppers and the caperberry bush.

5. The epilogue's comments about Qoheleth bring Solomon to mind immediately; for example, he sought out and arranged proverbs and taught with satisfying words.

6. Solomon saw himself as a 'child' (*nā'ar*) in 1 Kgs 3:7 because he was unwise: he was immature in wisdom – exactly the word and nuance in Eccl. 10:16.

7. God tells Solomon in 1 Kgs 3:12 that he has given the king a wiser and more discerning heart than all those before him, exactly what Qoheleth says of himself in Eccl. 1:16. God says he will make Solomon wiser than all those who succeed him as well, setting the scene for Qoheleth's cathartic expression of frustration about who his successor will be (Eccl. 2:18–21). And in Eccl. 2:4, 8–9, Qoheleth mentions he increased in material ways beyond his predecessors, just as 1 Kgs 10:23 describes Solomon's wealth.

8. D. Johnston, in an all but lost manuscript (1880), delineates many conceptual and linguistic parallels between the 'Solomonic' works of Proverbs, Song of Songs, Ecclesiastes and the Solomonic histories. The strongest of Johnston's parallels are listed in the table below. Through the course of this commentary, many proverbial parallels will be noted, most of which are expected thematic parallels. The first seven of the parallels (see the table below), however, are especially close in thought and reflect a common tradition permeated with characteristic vocabulary and phraseology. Many of these examples are words or phrases used exclusively by the Solomonic literature, but the rest show the preponderant use by Solomonic literature.

	Word/Phrase/Thought	Qoheleth	Proverbs	Song of Songs	Solomonic History	Other
1	Foolish hand-folding for rest	4:5	6:10; 24:33			
2	A good name is worth more than wealth	7:1	22:1			
3	Wisdom gives life	7:12	8:35			
4	There is no person who does not sin	7:20			1 Kgs 8:46	
5	Solomon's vineyards	2:4–5		8:11		
6	Ensnaring women	7:26	5:3–14; 7:25–27; 9:13–18			
7	Happily married	9:9	5:15–19			
8	bašûq (in the street)	12:4–5	7:8	3:2		
9	ta'ănûg (delight)	2:8	19:10	7:7		Mic. 1:16; 2:9
10	pardēs (park)	2:5		4:13		Neh. 2:8
11	môtār (advantage)	3:19	14:23; 21:5			
12	'aṣlâ (laziness)	10:18	19:15			
13	ḥābaq (embrace)	3:5; 4:5	4 times	twice		6 times
14	mātôq (sweet)	twice	3 times	once		5 times
15	kĕsîl (fool)	18 times	49 times			3 times
16	lēb ḥākām (heart of a wise man)	8:5; 7:4; 10:2	16:23		1 Kgs 3:12	
17	pega' (occurrence)	9:11			1 Kgs 5:4	
18	ba'al kānāp (having wings)	10:20	1:17			
19	lēb bĕnē hā'ādām (heart of the sons of man)	8:11; 9:3	15:11		1 Kgs 8:39; 2 Chr. 6:30	
20	yāda' lēb (knowing heart)	1:17; 7:22; 8:5, 16	14:10		1 Kgs 2:44	3 times
21	šĕ (which)	68 times		32 times		39 times

	Word/Phrase/ Thought	Qoheleth	Proverbs	Song of Songs	Solomonic History	Other
22	ʿad šĕ/ʾăšer (until)	2:3; 12:1–2, 6		1:12; 2:7, 17; 3:4–5; 4:6; 8:4		
23	nātan hāʾĕlohîm ʾošer, ûnĕkāsîm, kābôd (God gives riches, wealth, glory)	5:19; 6:2			1 Kgs 3:13; 2 Chr. 1:11–12	
24	Posterior pronoun (see 'Notes' at 1:16)	20 times		twice		3 times

The explicit reference to the one who spoke this speech refers to a son of David who ruled Israel from Jerusalem and who was preceded by no one greater. That could only mean Solomon. The official title given to this son is a name that denotes what Solomon's history tells us about him: he was a convener, assembler, a Qoheleth. The sociopolitical scenario implied in Ecclesiastes fits into the Solomonic age rather than the post-exilic era. Finally, the sheer number of linguistic affinities in this *Corpus Salomonicum* goes far beyond simply any traditional ascriptions of authorship for Proverbs, Ecclesiastes and the Song of Solomon. Believing the Solomonic allusions are fictional commends the writer for writing this speech in a style and vocabulary so similar to Solomon's traditionally ascribed texts and narratives about him. This pseudonymous writer, depending on how late in Israel's history he has composed this work, has also recreated the setting with great precision.

5. OTHER THEMES

5.1. Wisdom generally

The wisdom literature is the second moral focal point in the OT. The Law addresses how one is to relate to one's community in the context of the centralized government, whether tribal or national. It emphasizes the formal structures within a society. Wisdom literature, on the other hand, emphasizes the informal structures in a society and one's responsibilities to manage one's life morally in the routines of daily life. Of course, the two moral sources overlap, but the latter allows for the reflection, grappling and apologetic for moral living in a cursed world where justice does *not* always prevail in the legal system, nor, immediately, in God's overall schema. This is obvious in Job and Ecclesiastes. Finite human knowledge limits one's certainty and subsequent arrogance, and forces the wise to trust in the mercy of an overseeing and fair God. This is not the patient conviction of Qoheleth alone – it is the faith of Joseph (von Rad 1961: 434), that of Proverbs (16:1–2, 9; 19:21; 20:24; 21:30–31; 27:1; 30:2–4; Murphy 1981: 236) and of course that of the psalmists and prophets who await a final personal and covenantal vindication from their Lord. This commentary will demonstrate a fundamental agreement between Qoheleth with the Testaments about wisdom, justice, reverence and God's sovereignty.

Greater wisdom is Qoheleth's goal for his listeners since it has vast advantages over folly (2:13), including protection and safety (7:11–12) and success (10:10). It is the strongest of possessions (7:19; 9:16, 18). But his view of wisdom includes and implies the moral righteousness of Proverbs and Job, though one is not encouraged to anticipate immediate rewards. I will review the many attempts by leading commentators to remove this moral incentive from Qoheleth's injunctions, but they fail to mitigate his clear statements about the superiority of doing right and not sinning. Though it is a problematic verse that will be addressed later, 7:16 equates wisdom and righteousness, just as he does wickedness and folly (7:17). His moral imperatives are given within the context of traditional wisdom sayings and conclusions. As preposterous as it might sound to those holding to the traditional negative view of the term *hebel*, and thus all of Ecclesiastes, wisdom and righteousness are as interwoven in Ecclesiastes as they are in Proverbs and Job. Qoheleth affirms in 3:12 that there is nothing better than 'doing good', just as the psalmist expresses it in Hebrew (Pss 14:1; 34:14), though Qoheleth acknowledges no one is righteous all the time (7:20). Qoheleth warns against 'doing evil' (5:1; cf. 8:11). The phrase 'do evil' is used freely by him (4:3; 5:1; 8:11–12). The one who is good is contrasted with the sinner, 2:26 and 7:26. The sinner is criticized in 5:5, 7:20 and 9:18. God's judgment is explained in traditional OT theological terms in 3:16–17, 8:10–13 and 11:9. The fool and his folly will be frequent targets of judgment (2:13–14; 4:5; 5:2–3; 7:17; 10:1, 12, 14–15).

Nonetheless, regardless of Qoheleth's basic consistency with OT morality, there is an honesty to Qoheleth that insults the proud. Think you are wise? You'll die. Think you are discerning? Prove it by your grief. Do you have fine things? They will be destroyed. Done great things? They will pass. Qoheleth has no goal to encourage one to feel that one has arrived at a perfect state of shalom, anymore than Christ wanted an inexperienced and naive young man to believe he really had fulfilled the whole law (Matt. 19:16–24). Until Christ returns, the world of even the most devout is fraught with destabilizing experiences that almost unbearably challenge one's wisdom. God challenges our finitude with his infinity, but here is a limited reward, even abundant at times, which the individual enjoys because of God's grace. However, even that assigned blessing is limited in its span: it is only temporary here under the sun.

5.2. Advantages in life

It is often assumed that Qoheleth is attempting to answer the ultimate question of the 'meaning of life'. Evidently, because his statements include generalizations of the highest order, there is the temptation to overestimate what Qoheleth is trying to explain. But the issue in Ecclesiastes is not the meaning of life, nor is it intended to be an assessment of the human condition as a whole. This speech is more precisely focused than that – it is an answer to the very particular question of difficult toil. It is a deep investigation into the importance of diligence and wise action in one's routine daily labour. It is not a search for permanence or impermanence either. It is a speech designed to address not *the* question, but *a* question of the ages; that is, 'Why should one work so hard and wisely?' Qoheleth confirms clearly in 2:13, 7:11–12 and 10:10 that there are advantages to wise conduct, even the advantage of actually enjoying this arduous toil that is in question (3:13, 22; 5:18).

There is a constellation of words and phrases that form the fabric of his positive response to this question about labour, just as there is a collection of words that assist Qoheleth in his pronouncements about 'transience'. That there are 'advantages' to wise labour (*yitrôn, kišrôn*) is plainly said: 2:13, 21; 5:9; 7:11–12; 10:10–11. Though it may not be *lasting* profit (2:10; see 'Comments' there) because all is temporary (2:11). The 'Nothing-is-better-than' statements are also answers to this 'advantage' question. Most of the pleasure refrains are introduced in this way (2:24; 3:12–13, 22; 5:18; 8:15). That one has a 'reward' for one's labour is also a recurrent thought (*ḥeleq*; 2:10, 21; 3:22; 5:18–19; 9:9; 11:2; *śākār*; 4:9). In 9:9, together with *hebel*, these constructs affirm labour by identifying its advantages, but within the realism of transience. Advantages are found in certain situations over others, apart from labour as well (4:3, 6, 9, 13; 6:3, 9; 7:1–3, 5, 8; 9:4, 16, 18).

5.3. Joy and pleasure

The primary advantage to one's labour is the privilege to enjoy the labour itself as well as its fruit, as God blesses. The Refrains of Enjoyment punctuate Qoheleth's speech, and apart from the *hebel* refrains are the most pervasive phrasings of the speech: 2:24–26; 3:12–13, 22; 5:18–19; 8:15; 9:7–9; 11:9–10. They compose the 'shalom' theme of satisfaction of the OT – the sign of a fulfilled covenant nation – eating, drinking and rejoicing (1 Kgs 4:20). Astonishingly, however, joy is suppressed as a significant positive theme of the book by those who cannot square it with 'meaninglessness', essentially marginalizing it even though it persistently appears as a key conclusion to Qoheleth's observations. Yet there are those who hear Qoheleth and his resonant call to joy; for example, Klopfenstein (1972), R. K. Johnston (1976), Witzenrath (1979), Whybray (1982, 1989), Ogden (1987) and, a bit more tentatively, Pinçon (2008).

Qoheleth recounts many joys in his own life in addition to those he encourages his audience to enjoy. Eating and drinking are only metonyms for all other pleasures: music (2:8), the feminine form (2:8), food and drink (2:24; 9:7), laughing and dancing (3:4), embracing (3:5), love (3:8), doing good (3:12), rest (4:6; 5:12), wealth (5:19; 7:11–12), a good reputation (7:1), prosperity (7:13), wine (9:7), spouse (9:9), the light (11:7), youth (11:9–10) and, actually, for the wise who use discretion, everything one's eyes and heart desire (2:10; 11:9–10) is to be a source of joy.

5.4. Wise, enjoyable effort

The thematic advantage question is *asked* in reference to what is the advantage 'in' one's labour, using the prepositional *bēt* (1:3; 2:22; 3:9). The identical phrase is used to *answer* the advantage question – the advantage is the enjoyment 'in' one's labour (2:24; 3:13, 22; 4:9; 5:18–19; 8:15; 9:9). In other words, the thematic question is phrased in a way that sets up the parallel positive answer found in the Refrains of Enjoyment and elsewhere. Qoheleth leaves no uncertainty as to a positive answer to whether there are advantages in hard, even afflicting, toil, when he asks in 2:22–24:

> Surely, *what is there for a man in all his labour* and heart's desire for which he labours under the sun since grief and sorrow are his affliction all his days? Even at night his heart has no rest. Also this is temporary. *Nothing is better for one than to eat and drink and for his soul to enjoy the good in his labour.*

This enjoyment in work itself, not only in its fruits of pleasure, is a creation blessing. The Garden was a place of work before the Fall. Still, even now, the curse having subjected the earth and humanity to an intense struggle with each other, there can be satisfaction in wise work. As Brown (2000: 90) explains, '[joy] is more than an antidote for toil, since Qoheleth finds enjoyment and intrinsic value in work itself ... within the context of rest, refreshment, and fellowship'. So Qoheleth recommends pursuing one's work with all one's might (9:10), since planning wisdom and action are not possible from the grave. This was apparently his incentive for his accomplishments recounted in 2:4–8 and his instructions to his audience about wisdom and diligence.

For Qoheleth, focused efforts, done with all one's might, define the lifestyle of the vigilant and wise. Laziness is denigrated (4:5; 8:11; 10:18), as is frivolity and carousing (2:1–2; 7:2–6; 10:16–17, 19). Foolish communication (5:5; 6:11; 7:10, 20–21; 10:12–15, 20; cf. 3:7b) is denounced as it is in the plurality of aphorisms in Proverbs. Many other traditional wisdom topics are mentioned, such as teachableness (4:13; 7:5; 9:17), bribery (7:7) and anger (7:9, 21–22; 10:4).

5.5. God's sovereignty

The theme of the sovereignty of God permeates Ecclesiastes and is treated as it generally is in the rest of the OT. This sovereignty is often described by what God 'gives'. He gives a tragic affliction in letting us know too much about this world, either experientially or by observation (1:13, 18; 3:10). But he is also the one who gives us the pleasures of food, drink, work, wisdom and knowledge, riches and wealth (2:24–26; 3:13; 5:19–20; 6:2). He gives the very days and years we live (5:18; 8:15; 9:9) as the Creator who gives the common breath of life to humans and animals (3:18–19; 7:29; 12:1, 7). God gives us the sense of the infinite with which we can only faintly identify with him (3:11), so his actions are ultimately beyond our comprehension both by his infinite nature and by his intent (3:11–15; 7:14; 11:5). He is the one who in judgment takes blessings from the sinner (2:26) and in his own timing judges all, whether 'righteous or wicked' (3:17; 5:6; 12:14; 8:13; 9:7, 9). He is to be revered in and out of the sanctuary (3:14; 5:2, 7; 7:18, 26; 8:2, 12–13; 12:13) and his ways are unchangeable (3:14; 7:13).

Implicit in Ecclesiastes, however, is the same synergy of divine sovereignty and human responsibility. Qoheleth is no more deterministic than are the rest of the words we have in the OT. Indeed, human responsibility is the starting point from which wisdom and discretion must be pursued in every moral direction to which Qoheleth pushes his audience. The Poem of the Seasons (3:1–8) is not a poem of resignation to the determined fate for every act under the sun. Instead, it challenges the discerning to determine from their own wisdom what the best timing is for each of their preferences.

5.6. Realism

His theology of God's sovereignty is what spawns Qoheleth's realism which offends many. His realism relentlessly reveals his conclusions about a fallen world that can be described in no other terms than full of trouble and affliction. This realism does not agree to hide the tragic instances of human folly and its debilitating influence on the individual and his community. But unfortunately, few commentaries hear the extent of Qoheleth's resonance with biblical realism, because of an errant interpretation of *hebel*. Qoheleth's realism, therefore, is distorted as a radical cynicism, since beyond bearable transience everything is considered meaningless. Qoheleth is not shy to state the negative realities as he sees them, since they do not render wisdom and its pursuit useless. Instead, they challenge the wise to even higher levels of wisdom.

Proverbs and Job show the world for its fallenness, and what can happen even to the faithful *under* the sun when those *above* it are in controversy. Human folly and injustice, supplemented with God's mysterious allowance of the Enemy's torturous interference in the divine eternal purposes, contribute to a world that could not be reviewed and summarized any less morbidly or severely than it is by Qoheleth. That students of Qoheleth find similar assessments in the cultures to his south-west or north-north-west is not an indication of their influence; rather, it is an indication of the universal plight of humanity when it loosens itself from revealed truth and embarks on a journey where the travellers eventually abuse and cannibalize themselves, if they have not already succumbed to the other dangers along the way. Injustice is forced on victims by personal relationships (4:1–2, 4; 7:7, 21–22; 9:16), the government (3:16; 5:8; 8:11; 10:5–7, 16) or just one's circumstances (2:18–19; 7:15; 8:14; 9:1–3, 11–12, 18; 10:1), including others' poor memory (1:11; 2:16; 9:5, 15).

Qoheleth's realism is most often based on either an implicit or explicit realization of humanity's finite limitations. The art of wisdom is to succeed in spite of those limitations. The most prevalent example of human limitation in Ecclesiastes is one's lack of reliable foresight. Qoheleth has at least three different types of expressions for the fact that we do not know what the future brings, and 10:14b contains them all:

> No one knows what will be (8:7; 9:1, 12; 10:14; 11:2)
> No one can say what will be (3:22; 6:12; 8:7; 10:14)
> No one knows what will come after them (2:19; 6:12; 7:14; 10:14)

Finally, death is a reality so ominous and immediate that it informs much of what Qoheleth's main thrusts are in his speech. Death is a most significant reason for all under the sun being temporary. If one's life is temporary, then its activities and accomplishments cannot be stewarded indefinitely. This is precisely the reason for Qoheleth's catharsis in 2:15–21. Since it is death that terminates our breath and activity, we would expect a speech that emphasizes our transience to speak to the issues of mortality (2:16, 18, 21; 3:2, 4, 19–21; 4:2; 5:15–16; 6:3–6; 7:1–4, 15, 17; 8:8, 10, 13; 9:3–6, 10; 12:1–7).

6. HISTORY OF INTERPRETATION

6.1. Overview

Eccl. 12:10 concludes the book with a complimentary description of the speaker as one who sought to write pleasing words of truth. By most interpretations of Ecclesiastes through the centuries, however, it was hardly a resounding success if one were to use pleasantness as the standard. Though clearly the book is presented as truth, if the history of interpretation is to be followed, one could hardly consider Ecclesiastes' words pleasing! According to the consensus of interpretation, regardless of the number of diversified approaches, everything is vanity or meaningless.

The three significant areas of agreement among most commentators, both Christian and Jewish, until nearly the twentieth century were that (1) Solomon was the author, (2) a key message is that everything is 'vanity', and (3) the book is inconsistent with the OT in its presentation of that message (Murphy 1992: xlix–l). The following surveys are used in this analysis of the history of Ecclesiastes, and the reader is referred to them. They are listed in order of progressively greater detail of coverage: Murphy 1992: xlviii–lvi; Barton 1908: 18–31; Bartholomew 1998: 32–51; 68–81; 1999; Spangenberg 1998; Fox 1999: 6–26. Ginsburg paraphrases over seventy-five commentators prior to his 1861 commentary.

The Mishnah and Talmud saw contradictions in Ecclesiastes' presentation of pleasing and truthful words, and the issue was part of the debate on whether to recognize the book as canonical. At Jamnia, c. AD 90, the typical partisanship between the Jewish Shammai and Hillel persuasions led to disagreements about Ecclesiastes' appropriateness in the canon. However, eventually it remained in the canon of both Jews and Christians despite concerns of its apparent inconsistency with itself and with the OT. Its undeniable orthodoxy in some sections and the presumption of Solomonic authorship were the two critical arguments that won the day.

Of course, the subsequent centuries of biblical commentary found a litany of interpreters intoxicating themselves with habitual allegorical interpretation of all the books of the OT. This dulled the pain from the perceived inconsistencies and biting theology of Ecclesiastes, allowing interpreters to escape into the surreal, free-association method of allegorical commentary. This allegorical approach by Jerome and Ambrose was perpetuated in the church until its rejection as the main rubric by the more literal hermeneutic of the Reformation.

6.2. Conservative interpretation

In the redemptive-historical vein of theology, where continuity between the OT and NT is sought, a key NT interpretation of Ecclesiastes is thought to be found in Rom. 8:20, where we are told by Paul that all of creation was subjected to vanity. For those believing that *hebel* in Ecclesiastes means 'vanity', the verbal similarity is convincing enough for them to see a NT allusion to Ecclesiastes and therefore to see the book as a precursor to the full revelation of a Saviour who delivers the world from its vanity. Consequently, the presumed message of futility in Ecclesiastes is a truth consistent with progressive revelation (e.g. Shank 1974; Kidner 1976; Anderson 1997: 230–236; Iovino 2001). However, one clearly does not deny the truth of Rom. 8:20 if contending that Ecclesiastes is not itself saying that everything is vanity. The book's message is clearly about *transience*, not minimal purposefulness. If there is a NT passage that is closest to the spirit of Ecclesiastes' message of brevity', it is that found in Jas 4:14, 'For your life is like the morning fog – it is here for a little while, then it is gone!'

A better NT parallel to Ecclesiastes' message is found in Paul's comment on the temporary and eternal in 2 Cor. 4:18. In reference to those things that are seen (since they are in the light under the sun) he encourages the Corinthians, 'we do not look at the things that are seen, but the things that are not; for the things that are seen are temporal, but the things that are not are eternal'. This is the distinction in Ecclesiastes – things under the sun are transient, while God's ways (beyond the sun) are eternal.

Another errant connection is made between Ecclesiastes' frequent encouragement to enjoy eating and drinking (e.g. 2:24) and the poor priorities of the fool in Luke 12:16–21. In Luke, the fool says, 'I'll sit back, take it easy, eat, drink and be merry because I am going to die anyway.' However, there really is no parallel here, since avoiding work and taking it easy are not the conclusion in Ecclesiastes, whereas diligence certainly is. Being merry is not a conclusion for Ecclesiastes either; frivolity and merriment are a curse, whereas profound joy is a gift from God. This fool in Luke is condemned for his materialism; in Ecclesiastes, the diligent and wise are commended for their effective labour.

By this interpretation, the believer is encouraged to enjoy life under the sun (until Christ returns) and to fear God and remain holy as the epilogue commands (12:13–14). However, given the repetitive and weighty description of the world and life as meaningless, even conservatives find little in Ecclesiastes to absorb into sermons and the life of the church. Often, the book is explained as if the text were spoken by a shallow Zophar or Bildad, thus worthy only of correction by a fuller and higher theology of a Job or Elihu. Obviously, it is the book most avoided in the theology of the church. The typical redemptive-historical theologies prove inadequate to engage substantively much of the wisdom literature at all, and Ecclesiastes in particular. If one surveys published Christian theologies, one will find that though little is incorporated from the wisdom literature anyway, Ecclesiastes is especially skirted like the plague. Usually any indexes will include little more than a reference to the summary verses 'Everything is *hebel*', and even then only to use the book as a foil with which to compare the otherwise consistent theology of the OT and NT. This is unfortunate, since the biblical translation of *hebel* as 'temporary' would eliminate the need for any such circuitous and dismissive approaches to Ecclesiastes and would instead look to the book for mature conclusions about life in a cursed world.

6.3. Critical interpretation

The historical-critical era of interpretation has applied to Ecclesiastes its various methodologies. For example, source criticism atomized the book into fragmented sources; for example, Siegfried (1898), Barton (1908) and Rose (1999). Form criticism groups its sources by genre and categories that are either obvious or too elaborate for what is clearly just a speech or a portion of a speech; for example, 'independent sentences', Galling (1969); 'royal testament', von Rad (1972); 'reflections', Ellermeier (1967); this also includes the currently popular 'Frame Narrative' theory of Fox (1977) and Longman's 'fictional autobiography' category (1991). Though Ecclesiastes has successfully eluded all attempts to find a unified rhetorical form (apart from the attempt by Wright 1968, 1980), intricate structures have been found in the book which we will observe in this study, and which may eventually some day compound to reveal an overall order.

Various influence theories are proposed for Ecclesiastes, including Greek, Egyptian and Mesopotamian, particularly Gilgamesh for the latter. However, it is primarily Greek influence that has won most attention. A combination of presumptions of a late language, historical allusions and evidence of various schools of Greek thought has been the source of this perspective throughout the history of Ecclesiastes interpretation. Many parallels are proposed from Levy (1912) to Braun (1973), Schwienhorst-Schönberger (1994) and Rudman (2001), with Whitley (1978) and Lohfink (1980) itemizing specific philosophers and their influence. Philosophies as diverse as Epicureanism and Stoicism are allegedly found in this one speech as well as influence from Euripides (Lohfink 1980), Heraclitus (de Savignac), Hesiod and Phokylides (Ranston 1925), Homer and Menander (Braun 1973). Others are less specific in finding influencers, per se, and simply see a 'spirit' of Hellenism (Zimmerli 1962; Scott 1971; Hengel 1974). On the other hand, strong reaction against these identifications also abound (Loretz 1964; Aziz 2000). Nonetheless, after all parallels are considered, Ecclesiastes ideas are neither late nor Greek; as with the universal awareness of the brevity of life, discussed above, this speech voices the intuitive concerns and astute observations of all cultures.

Since all commentators would admit that there are at least some orthodox statements in the speech, the insistence that its central message is negative forces most to resort to harmonization theories to account for these obvious statements of conventional Hebrew wisdom. Because the speech is said to be fraught with statements inconsistent within itself as well as with Hebrew orthodoxy, there are those who would simply delete some positive statements in order to achieve a better balance; for example, Barton (1908: 108, 150, 185) and Crenshaw (1987: 102, 155, 184). This 'procrustean bed' approach tortures the text and, of course, is unnecessary if there is an internal consistency based on the biblical meaning of *hebel* that does not require such drastic measures. Though quotations are not always presented in order to refute them, when there is an apparent contradiction, the cynic is seen to quote traditional wisdom as foolishness compared to his enlightened cynicism. This 'quotation theory' is represented by Gordis (1968), Whybray (1981) and Michel (1988).

The prevailing critical theory claims that the wisdom movement ended in disillusionment with any faith in a loving, covenant God who rewards wisdom. Starting with the clear faith of Proverbs and wisdom psalms (that wise acts will result in blessed consequences for the wise), Israel's trust in that moral system soured after the exile until a sceptical disenchantment set in, represented by this speech called Ecclesiastes. Earlier wisdom supposedly promised a mastery of life that was a source of shalom. Then OT theology spiralled down to a cynical pessimism, which finally sighed that everything is vanity, and thus futile. This 'crisis' in Hebrew wisdom literature also appears in Job, though there is the consoling ending to that book. But Ecclesiastes is said to portray a 'tired, intellectual pessimism' (Lauha 1954: 188). Such a consensus would be deeply disturbed if Ecclesiastes indeed said that all was only temporary, not meaningless, because there would be no such plummet from orthodox wisdom theology.

Even some recent commentators, though, cannot deny an obvious emphasis on joy; for example, R. K. Johnston (1976), Ogden (1979) and Whybray (1982). Though they are generally marginalized, their lauding of Ecclesiastes as a book of qualified joy, though rare, is evidence that even modernity cannot stifle the clear theme and refrains of pleasure in the book.

Needless to say, the implications of reinterpreting *hebel* along the lines of *transience* affect dramatically one's view of Ecclesiastes as a whole. First, the book describes the human condition as being limited in its duration and in the duration of its human efforts. Yet it does so without emptying life of true, though temporary, value. Secondly, the book consoles rather than disturbs the realist. It reminds him of his transience in this intimidating world with its pressing and tragic problems, while at the same time comforting humanity with the knowledge that evil itself is temporary in its impact on life. Both Peter and Paul confirm this in their letters:

> So after you have suffered a little while, he will restore, support and strengthen you, and he will place you on a firm foundation. (1 Pet. 5:10)

> For our present troubles are small and won't last for very long.
> (2 Cor. 4:17a)

This realism is in line with at least one theme in the wisdom literature outside Ecclesiastes: How does one cope in a world where wickedness and folly surround every part of life, apparently outweighing all current righteousness and wisdom? The advice of Qoheleth, then, is that true wisdom will recognize the temporality of virtually all that is experienced and will accept the fact that our experience of a fallen world and the evil within it is soon to pass. Though it will lead to a substantially different interpretation of the book than if either 'vanity' or 'absurd' is seen to be the thrust of *hebel*, it is consistent linguistically and contextually to prefer this temporal nuance of the word. Ecclesiastes profoundly and accurately presents to the reader the challenges involved in living in a world characterized by transience, but does so with adequate consolations and guidance on how to cope.

If Qoheleth is disenchanted with the human condition to the extent that for him everything is futile or absurd, then he is indeed naive and superficial to commend joy and wise behaviour as often as he does. This picture of Qoheleth as a self-contradicting, incoherent thinker, who concludes that life is both meaningless and yet an enjoyable gift of God, does not so much portray *his* thought and disorientation as it does that of his interpreters. Without wishful thinking, it is the best of both worlds to maintain a legitimate Biblical Hebrew connotation to *hebel* in most cases in the book and to receive in return a more coherent, edifying Hebrew sage.

6.4. Interpretation of *hebel*

The history of interpretation of Ecclesiastes, however, is a history mainly of its meaning of *hebel*. Some Greek translations simply render *hebel* in its literal sense of 'breath' and are unhelpful in deciding if in fact translations carry weight as opposed to the certain biblical meanings found in the lexicons; for example, Symmachus, Aquila and Theodotion. The LXX translates *hebel* as *mataiotēs*, which has a similar breadth of meaning as *hebel*, including 'emptiness', 'futility' and 'transience' (Bertram 1952). Thereafter, until the middle of the twentieth century, the only meaning ever considered by commentators for *hebel* was that of 'vanity', because the Latin Vg errantly translated the Hebrew word as *vanitas*. In English, 'vanity' means 'hollow, empty, worthless, pointless, without any real value', at most, 'trivial'. Jerome's choice to translate *hebel* by the one connotation pertaining to value rather than transience cast the book's future for centuries. Since the Vg was given unquestioned authority to determine Christian theology and exegesis until the Reformation, and since the Hebrew text and the LXX were considered virtually unnecessary, the presumption of interpreters, then, was that *hebel* meant 'vanity' (Holm-Nielsen 1974: 174–177; Farmer 1991: 144; see Lavoie 2006: 219–249 for a historical-cultural survey of *hebel*'s interpretation). But even after the Reformation, the long-standing traditional interpretation reigned until the 1940s, virtually without competition. Simply put, conservative interpretations tended towards, 'Yes, everything is vanity, that is, apart from a life devoted to God.' Critical interpretations took vanity to its logical conclusion: 'Yes, everything is vanity, and therein lies Ecclesiastes' radical, heretical break with OT theology.' And moderates find a *via media* in 'Yes, everything is vanity, but go ahead and enjoy life anyway.'

6.4.1. Hebel *as 'vanity' or 'meaningless'*

The positive case for *hebel* meaning 'transience' has been made above. However, there are several reasons for serious doubt that *hebel* means 'vanity' or 'meaninglessness' in Ecclesiastes. First, whereas we find numerous words, phrases and contexts that form a constellation of references in Ecclesiastes that emphasizes life's ephemerality, even independently from the word *hebel*, no such lexical or contextual constellation exists for the concept of vanity or futility (Fredericks 1993: 28–29; Lys 1977: 88). For those advocating that *hebel* means 'vanity', *hebel* alone must carry their burden of proof throughout the book. This is because nowhere to be found in the book are the words that occur nearly a hundred times elsewhere in the OT as synonyms for 'futility':

'ayin	'nothing, naught'
rēq	'empty, worthless'
rîq	'emptiness, vanity'
šāwě'	'emptiness, vanity'
tōhû	'empty, worthless'

When the meaning of a word in a text is to be decided between two different biblical meanings, and the surrounding contexts, words and phrases support one over the other exclusively, it can be only tenuously held that the unsupported meaning be preferred over the cumulative voices of the other linguistic evidences. Consequently, since Ecclesiastes' emphasis throughout the speech is on life's ephemeral destiny, *transience* should be adopted as the biblical meaning for its key word, *hebel*. If the contexts where *hebel* is found were to be removed, leaving the rest of the speech to form its message, 'futility' or 'absurdity' would not be the natural conclusion, whereas 'brevity' would.

A second reason for discounting the meaning of *hebel* to mean 'futility' or 'vanity' is its pairing with those aspects of life that even the most cynical and sceptical could not dismiss as inconsequential. That some aspects of life are *hebel*, as well as severely evil (2:21; 6:2) and afflicting (4:8), speaks against 'vanity', 'meaninglessness'. In fact, these evils are so grievous that we are fortunate that they are solved or mitigated only by transience. As Ogden (1987: 49) concludes, 'the word *hebel* can be applied to either negative ... or positive ... situations, indicating clearly that the traditional rendering "vanity" is most inappropriate'.

A third reason lies in the contradictory reasoning of those who accuse Qoheleth himself of being self-contradicting; for example, Gordis, Fox, Loader, Longman, Michel and Koh. The predominant view, that Qoheleth claims *everything* is vain, meaningless or absurd, requires us to believe that when he makes comparisons like 'nothing is better than' and '*x* is better than *y*', he is making qualitative distinctions *within* the categories of 'meaningless' and 'absurd'. However, can something be more meaningless than something else, if all is indeed meaningless? Can something be more absurd than the next when everything has been deemed absolutely absurd? Qoheleth's thought becomes muddled only when commentators bring their own confusion to bear on his speech. With the presupposition of *hebel* meaning 'meaningless, futile, vanity or absurd', comes a tangled task of determining how the text can be made meaningful. In this process, one of the most profound minds in all literature is reduced to a confused philosopher, embittered by his milieu and his inability to make sense of even his own convictions. However, the coherence in Qoheleth's thought is clear when he is heard to say, along with OT and other ancient thinkers, that all is temporary.

Fourthly, it would take only a perverse authority figure to perpetrate a grand sham to pretend there was significance to one's acts when indeed the authority was convinced all those efforts were meaningless or absurd. It is one thing to say that Qoheleth is confused or conflicted, or that he has some design to deconstruct conventional wisdom; it is quite another to describe him as a bully, mocking those who are under his leadership. If there is ultimately no meaning to one's activities, or if any activity is absurd in the end, telling one to do what one wants 'with all your might' (9:10) is at least a mischievous sending of one on a fool's journey. Industriousness and diligence, convictions of Qoheleth that he drives home to his hearers, are hardly to be played upon if the one giving the orders knows it will eventually be utterly futile.

It cannot be presumed that the transitory must by nature be meaningless or inconsequential. The temporary can have great value – eternality is not the only criterion of meaning. Immediately equating the temporariness of breath with futility would be a serious non sequitur. This reasoning is basically Gnostic in its dismissal of the transient physical creation as inherently bad when temporality was built into the cosmos and deemed 'good' at creation. That there are temporary seasons for all wise activities is exactly the point in 3:1–8, where daily activities are surveyed, some of which would be performed whether there had been a fall from grace at the beginning of time or not. It is natural and critical, then, to keep temporality separate from any sweeping and pervasive cynical conclusions about the lack of value or meaning of life or actions.

6.4.2. Non-biblical meanings for hebel

Relatively new in the history of interpreting Ecclesiastes, especially the latter part of the twentieth century, are the *extra-biblical* translations offered for *hebel*. For the proponents of creating a new, non-biblical meaning for the word, much is said of lexicology not being the only way to determine the meaning of a word, and that the context needs to be considered as well. However, lexicology is the primary way linguists determine meanings of words unless it leads to an insoluble challenge ending in near or actual nonsense. The translation process, then, includes as basic this sequential methodology starting with lexicology, *then* resorting to contextual exploration if necessary. It is unreasonable to play lexicology simultaneously against contextuality, unless lexicology has proven ineffective. It is even less reasonable to place contextual innovations *over* lexicology.

The disillusionment of the twentieth-century Jewish and Christian traditions in respect to epistemology and the knowableness of God and his creation reveals itself when dealing with the translation and interpretation of Ecclesiastes and its key word. Staples (1943) suggests *hebel* means 'incomprehensible, unknowable'. His line of reasoning, which includes a mixture of considering the regional cognates and the contexts within which *hebel* is found in Ecclesiastes, is an example of the new approach which emphasizes the contextual use of the word, as opposed to its etymological and biblical meanings. This trend in translating *hebel* to convey that which challenges reason or is contrary to it, surfaces in one way or another in the interpretations of many translators since Staples's work. Good (1981) induces 'irony' as the meaning for *hebel*, and Ogden (1987) follows with 'enigmatic'.

Fox (1986) tries to distance himself from this trend with his anachronistic, existentialist translation of *hebel* as 'absurd'; nevertheless, his epistemologically negative bent is certainly consistent with Staples by going outside biblical meanings for *hebel*. He strains an argument that though Qoheleth is linguistically unable to express the concept of 'meaningful', he can somehow express a concept of the 'absurd' through a metaphor used nowhere else in Hebrew (1998: 226). Also, Fox does not understand the philosophy of existentialism and its claim of cosmic absurdity. Existentialism is based on the presupposition that any metaphysical truths are pure myth, placing the sole value in life only on fragmentary acts of the will. The bishops of modern existentialism, Sartre and Camus, could hardly live in that type of world themselves, making political choices in their lives which by their own world view had no

moral basis for such preferences. Besides, Fox's Qoheleth is a firm
believer in metaphysical reality, better, theological truths about God and
humanity and the practical, moral derivations from them. His parallels
with ANE literature also do not reveal those thinkers to be any more
than disenchanted souls seeking answers, and hardly draw existentialist
conclusions.

The danger of moving outside etymological considerations unnecessarily
is succinctly shown by Miller (2002: 5):

> there are quite a number of abstract terms which are plausible for
> *hebel*, and it is difficult to adjudicate the superiority of one
> proposed term over another. By the same process used to offer
> 'incomprehensible,' 'vain,' or 'absurd' for *hebel*, one might argue
> just as well for 'bizarre' or 'frustration.'

In other words, if it were simply a matter of determining what makes sense
in the context, quite independent of lexicology, one might add as candidates
for *hebel*'s meaning, 'nuts', 'profound' or 'whatever'. Crüsemann (1979)
proposes the German equivalent for the profane four-letter word for
'excrement' in English as a translation for *hebel*. This is a crass but logical
conclusion to the misdirected methodology that elevates only plausible
contextual estimations of word meanings over sensible, proven, biblical
etymological determinations.

Another example of proposing non-biblical meanings for *hebel* is that
suggested by Miller himself. He can go only to the rabbinic writers to find
'foulness' as a meaning (2002: 15, 51, 97, 189; followed by Frydrych 2002:
45). But stepping outside the OT realm of meanings to translate the word is
equally unnecessary as are the other imaginative creations of *hebel*'s
meaning by recent commentators.

6.4.3. Hebel *basically means 'temporary'*

Multiple meanings for *hebel* in Ecclesiastes has its proponents as well.
Biblical translations as well as commentators usually find some places
where *hebel* actually means 'temporary'. In fact, some find several meanings for the word in Qoheleth's one speech (Meek 1960: 331; Whitley
1978: 172–173; Whybray 1989: 36; Miller 2002; Ingram 2006: 91–129;
Rudman 2007: 134–140). Their inability to find an adequate single
meaning for *hebel* throughout the book leads them to make sense out of
the passages by ascribing different meanings to the word depending on the
context. Such analysis encourages them to include 'temporary' as a meaning at times, but only occasionally, along with other meanings. For
instance, Krüger (2004: 42–44) draws an artificial distinction between
the human lifespan (where *hebel* means 'fleeting') and the events and

values in life (where *hebel* means 'futile'). The separation between these distinct meanings can be as few as 10–12 words in 6:11–12.

Though this multiple-meaning approach may appear in its flexibility to solve the enigma of *hebel*, it ignores the poetic consistency and grammatically *formulaic* presentation of *hebel* in almost every instance where it occurs in Ecclesiastes. When one acknowledges the obvious intention in the speech to ascribe a consistent thematic conclusion to its several observations, it becomes clear that there should also be a consistent interpretation as one, singular meaning in all similar contexts. *Hebel* is almost invariably the third word in Qoheleth's Hebrew formulaic refrains; for example, 1:14, *wehinnēh hakkōl hebel*, 'really, it is all temporary'; 2:1, *wehinnēh gam-hû' hebel*, 'but really it was also temporary': that is, sixteen out of nineteen times, apart from the *hebel* clusters in 1:2 and 12:8. It becomes unnecessarily obscure to take 'everything is breath' and have any number of options for interpretation in each context. Fox is correct to criticize this pick-and-choose approach (1999: 36):

> If [Ecclesiastes] were saying, 'X is transitory; Y is futile; Z is trivial,' then the summary, 'All is *hebel*' would be meaningless. . . . To do [Ecclesiastes] justice we must look for a concept that applies to all occurrences, or, failing that to the great majority of them.

6.4.4. *Singular meaning throughout*

The case for *hebel* meaning 'temporary' has been made extensively before (Fredericks 1993: 11–32). No substantive objection has been made against such a proposal; instead, there has been mainly a very telling passive resistance. To entertain the belief that *hebel* means 'transience' would essentially destroy the current predominant views of OT theology and its development especially within the wisdom literature. Most commentary on Ecclesiastes sees it to be near the close of Israel's devolving continuum towards cynicism about the covenantal theology of hope and faithfulness towards, and from, God. The conventional correlation between righteous wisdom and God's blessings and between evil folly and God's discipline has supposedly dissolved into a theology of moral disillusionment. However, if *hebel* means 'temporary' and not 'futile' or 'absurd', this popular approach is no longer valid.

Attempts such as that by Fox (1999: 30) to dismiss 'temporary' as the viable, pervasive meaning for Ecclesiastes are inadequate, to say the least. In reference to 8:14 and its obvious description of frustration with the inversion of justice for the righteous and the wicked, Fox reasons in a circular fashion that the *hebel*-ness of this particular travesty could not possibly mean that it is 'fleeting', because that would be a good thing! If injustice is only temporary, that would be a positive truth in this world. But since Fox assumes Ecclesiastes never describes any *hebel* situation as good, only 'absurd', transience cannot be considered. Incidental and dismissive comments such as Shields's (2006: 120) 'this interpretation is overly strained and ultimately unconvincing' are no longer adequate to answer a thoroughly coherent and more sensible reading of Ecclesiastes based on *hebel* meaning 'temporary'.

The fact that by the use of *hebel* Ecclesiastes describes the fleeting nature of life and its activities is not a novel idea. Other commentators have opted for *hebel* to mean 'temporary', though significant linguistic analysis has admittedly been lacking. D. B. Macdonald (1936: 87) found in the juxtaposition of the eternality of God and the ephemerality of humanity the foundation on which to translate *hebel* consistently as 'temporary':

> [The speaker's] philosophy was the philosophy of a realist, of a man who, for himself, had looked steadily at life in all its manifestations and who brought over nothing from the past save the one devastating certainty that behind the passing phenomena of life there was an eternal and personal Absolute...

Farmer (1991: 145), while citing other OT passages where *hebel* means 'transitory', argues the case that the message of Ecclesiastes refers to transience rather than meaninglessness or worse:

> When we look closely at the ways in which the word is used in other parts of the OT, it becomes clear that the essential quality to which *hebel* refers is lack of permanence rather than lack of worth or value. A breath, after all, is of considerable value to the one who breathes it. However, it is not something one can hang on to for long. It is air like, fleeting, transitory, and elusive rather than meaningless.

Since the publications of Farmer (1991) and Fredericks (1993), understanding *hebel* to mean 'temporary' in Ecclesiastes has gained momentum. Perdue (1994: 206–208) also proposes that, at least in the key passages in Ecclesiastes, *hebel* connotes evanescence and ephemerality. Webb (2000: 100), Provan (2001: 57), Schultz (2005: 266) and Bolin (2005: 245–259) also prefer 'transience'. Seow (1997: 112) splits the difference by concluding that *hebel* 'does not mean "vain" in the sense of being meaningless or worthless, but that it is ephemeral and unreliable'. In the sense of 'ephemeral' he is correct, but as far as 'unreliable', that would be a misreading of 1:4–7. Recently, Dor-Shav (2008: 217) concludes that *hebel* in Ecclesiastes refers 'strictly to mortality and the fleeting nature of human life ... Without the negative connotations of "vanity," we discover in Kohelet one who is tormented not by the meaninglessness of life, but by how swiftly it comes to an end.'

In only one case, noticeably in the section dedicated to inappropriate worship, 5:1–7, does *hebel perhaps* mean what it means in cultic passages in the OT, namely 'vanity' (5:6). Furthermore, this exceptional use is not found in the usual formulaic phrase of Qoheleth; rather, in 5:6 it is couched in its own unique phrasing. Consequently, the audience would not have been surprised to hear *hebel* as 'vanity' in this passage, and without confusion over its otherwise pervasive meaning in the speech as 'temporary'. In fact, however, even in this context 'temporary' is the probable meaning.

One additional linguistic point that supports my rendering of *hebel* in Ecclesiastes needs clarification. A frequent companion to *hebel* is the phrase *rĕ'ût rûaḥ*. Seven times the phrase, translated by many as 'desiring the wind', 'chasing the wind' or some similar denotation of futility occurs in Ecclesiastes. In this case, the Hebrew syntax of the noun sequence of construct–absolute would be seen as the objective genitive. However this syntax just as easily recommends the subjective, possessive genitive, as some commentators interpret the phrase, including Staples (1955: 45) and Perdue (1994: 207). I translate *rĕ'ût rûaḥ* accordingly as 'the wind's desire' or 'the whim of the wind', connoting the brevity of life and its experiences, which are like the unpredictable wind's desire. The wind periodically changes from north to south, east to west, downward, upward, around, and even temporarily becomes absolutely still.

The history of the liturgical use of Ecclesiastes is instructive as well for what the message of the book intends. The festival of Booths (Sukkot) includes in its ceremony the reading of Ecclesiastes. The feast celebrates the blessings of God through the year, and, of course, as a feast it is a time of joy. The emphasis Ecclesiastes puts on enjoying one's life, food and drink as well as enjoying the harvesting work is a very appropriate part of Sukkot (thus Lys 1977: 79–80; Farmer 1991: 198–199). But the feast's name itself refers to the tents the Israelites had to live in while wandering the Sinai wilderness. Temporary shelters were all they had, just as temporary blessings are all any person has in one's life under the sun. Hardly would the message of cynicism and pessimism of an Ecclesiastes governed by themes of vanity and futility encourage the joy and festivities of a celebration as much as an Ecclesiastes that genuinely encourages great joy in the face of one's temporary life.

This realism is in line with at least one theme in the wisdom literature outside Ecclesiastes: how one copes in a world where wickedness and folly surround every part of life, apparently outweighing all current righteousness and wisdom. The advice of Qoheleth, then, is that true wisdom will recognize the temporality of virtually all that is experienced and will accept the fact that our experience of a fallen world and the evil within is soon to pass. Though it will lead to a substantially different interpretation of the book than it would if either 'vanity' or 'absurd' is seen to be the thrust of *hebel*, it is consistent linguistically and contextually to prefer this temporal nuance of the word. Ecclesiastes profoundly and accurately presents to the reader the challenges involved in living in a world characterized by temporariness, but does so with adequate consolations and guidance on how to cope.

The greatest exegetical gymnastics are seen in the attempt to reconcile the assumption that Qoheleth says that everything is vain, futile or absurd, with his repeated orthodox statements about fearing God, enjoying life, pursuing wisdom and working responsibly. Portraying Qoheleth as a con-fused observer and interpreter of reality is understandable if for one reason or another one fails to apply the biblical meaning of 'temporary' for *hebel*. But since this is such an unnecessary error, one would hope that Qoheleth's inclusion in the Canon will increasingly be seen to be due to his cohesive, profound thought rather than because of a first-century concession to authorship alone.

7. GENRE

At least six characteristics of Ecclesiastes' genre make the book unique in the OT and consequently an edifying challenge to understand and enjoy. The first five can be appreciated in the English; the sixth is evident only in the Hebrew grammar and vocabulary.

7.1. Philosophical

It is clear when reading Ecclesiastes that the speaker is sharing philo-sophical reflections from the experiences and observations of his life. His interests are global; his generalizations describe all of humanity's history and future; his observations leave no category of reality untouched. The key components of any world view (viz. the nature of God, humanity and society; the issues of ethics, economics and politics) are all addressed in generality as well as in particular. Without the 'Thus says the LORD' of the prophets, Ecclesiastes' philosopher draws conclusions consistent with them but with the much greater specificity and edgy relevance of the wisdom culture. Schoors (1998b: 39) shows that the four most frequent words in Ecclesiastes (*'ādām, hāyāh, rā'â, tôb*) inundate the speech with words dealing with humanity, being, observation and the good. Other very frequently used words or phrases (such as 'heart', 'time', 'season', 'eternity', 'temporary', 'there exists', 'know', 'wise', 'explanations', 'sons of men', 'wisdom', 'fool', 'all', 'under the sun', 'under heaven', 'memory', 'joy', 'death' and 'toil') confirm that the nature of Ecclesiastes' contents is unique in the OT. An example of the grammatical implications of this genre is the virtual absence of the waw consecutive, which has as its main function to describe the historical, narrative sequence of events. Our philosopher is not so much interested in history's sequence as he is in its principles. Morphologically speaking, word endings denoting the conceptual and abstract are as frequent in Ecclesiastes as they are in other proverbial literature. As Schoors (1992: 175–176) claims, the frequentative or habitual use of the imperfect in Ecclesiastes is consistent with the wisdom genre (see also Isaksson 1987: 55, 190).

7.2. Cosmopolitan

There is an intentional avoidance of ethnocentric terminology or phrasing in Ecclesiastes, including any distinctive cultic descriptions. It is only the editor's identification of the speaker as a son of David and resident of Jerusalem that locates this speech in time and space. The speaker himself, on the contrary, studiously eludes any such pinpointing, choosing thus not to limit the universal applicability of his conclusions. This is another common feature with the proverbial wisdom literature. Consequently, it is of Elohim he speaks, not Yahweh. It is *'ādām*, 'humankind', whom he is observing, not *'îš*, or any one man or particular race. There are also frequent comments about business: domestic and foreign trade and investments, money, partnerships, socio-economic classes, politics, obituaries, sexuality, nightlife and other everyday subjects of any culture that direct us to think past the primarily 'religious' messages of the vast majority of the rest of the OT. This open discussion of the realities of busy everyday life common to all societies is more cosmopolitan in nature. See for instance Dahood's description of the commercial nature of Ecclesiastes' vocabulary (1952: 221). This explains Ecclesiastes' use of a few 'foreign' words (Aramaic and Persian) that have infiltrated the vernacular of the day, but are filtered out of the formal, literary and religiously guarded locution of the scribal Hebrew of the OT.

7.3. Poetic or proverbial

There are at least five main poetic sections of Ecclesiastes: 1:4–11; 2:4–8; 3:1–8; 7:1–17; 12:2–7. These are either Hebrew poetry of the artistic sort, or proverbs using poetic structures. I have already mentioned that there are few waw consecutives in the book, and this is due not only to the philosophical nature (versus any historical method), but to the substantive poetry sections as well. The poetic books have favoured single words, such as the key word *'āmāl* (labour) in Ecclesiastes, which appears much more often in the wisdom and psalmic literature (84%; Foresti 1980: 420). I have also found that they have favoured word clusters like *hebel/rûaḥ/ṣēl*, indicating that the poetic books have their own linguistic culture. Very specifically, *hebel*, when pronounced normally, requires the exhalation of breath. In this sense it is onomatopoeic, or imitative of its meaning (Bertram 1952: 30; Seybold 1978: 355). Ecclesiastes also uses alliteration many times; for example, 1:2, 14, 17; 2:1, 11, 17, 21, 23, 26; 3:19; 4:4, 6, 16; 6:9; 12:8.

7.4. Oratorical

Probably the least often identified but the most obvious characteristic of the genre of Ecclesiastes is that it is a *speech*! However, the book is largely treated and annotated by commentators as if it were a literary work rather than a transcription. This single category alone explains the vernacular nature of the language rather than the typical formal and literary language of the rest of the OT. It also by definition makes the presentation immediately vulnerable to the editing of oral tradition and thus a challenge to dating the text. A speech raises the question of who is present and how the content should be understood because of a targeted live audience rather than an unseen reader. It raises the question of the coherence of the speech, and whether it was condensed, thus compromising any conventional structure that has so far eluded scholars. So the important matters of commentary 'introduction' are at issue, from language and dating, to style and structure.

7.5. Autobiographical

Equally obvious is that the book has a significant autobiographical element, primarily in the first two chapters. This is consistent with the prophets' authenticating their subsequent message of revelation by describing in the first literary section the setting in which they were inspired. Here in Ecclesiastes, the speaker authenticates his subsequent message of reflection with an autobiographical introduction as well. Attempts to align Ecclesiastes with 'fictional' autobiographies of the surrounding cultures overemphasize any extra-biblical parallels, underestimating the biblical models (Isaksson 1987: 39–68; Longman 1998: 17–20).

7.6. Vernacular

The Hebrew throughout the OT is a literary language that was not spoken in everyday Israel. In other words, it is a linguistic style of the scribes that would have sounded 'stuffy' to the ordinary Israelite, very distinct from the familiar vernacular language they would have used with one another in normal circumstances. A formal Greek language style, with which the vernacular koine dialect of the NT contrasts, was of course used in classical literature. In the OT times this is reversed. The vernacular Hebrew is suppressed in the OT by the highly stylized literary dialect of the religious establishment. However, remnants of this vernacular language are thought to be discovered in various places in the OT. When the relatively few grammatical and lexical components of this colloquial language are collected from the OT books, one sees that the following (all found in Ecclesiastes) form a high proportion of them (Fredericks 1988: 36–46):

- anticipatory pronominal suffix
- discordant subject and predicate
- missing definite art.
- unassimilated art.
- subject and predicate couched in prepositional phrases
- conjunctive waw verbal forms
- infinitive absolute with waw
- absence of the hoph.
- third masculine plural pronoun for the f.
- *'ănî* as first person singular pronoun
- *'et* with pronouns
- *'et* with the nominative
- *zôh* as f. singular demonstrative pronoun
- *šĕ* as relative pronoun
- contractions

These colloquialisms found within the eclectic genre of Ecclesiastes (philosophical, proverbial, poetic, cosmopolitan and oratorical) explain why the language of this speech is unique and impervious to oversimplified comparisons with the standard Hebrew, early or late, of the Bible or the Mishnah. Arguing for a date in the Persian period, Seow concludes that the typical, easy ascription of Ecclesiastes to being late Biblical Hebrew is too simplistic (1996: 666): 'The language of the book, however, does not reflect the standard literary Hebrew of the post-exilic period. Rather, it is the literary deposit of a vernacular, specifically the everyday language of the Persian period...' It is this vernacular nature as well as the poetic or philosophical use of language in Qoheleth's speech that invite the biblical translation of *hebel* to be 'temporary' rather than 'vanity', which is found in the more formal literary Hebrew in the history of Israel's religion. That Ecclesiastes represents the colloquial language of Israel has been suggested by many; for example, Lowth (1770: 491), Jastrow (1919: 205–208), Barucq (1968: 12), G. R. Driver (1970: 232–239), Elyoenai (1977: 11–21), Piotti (1977: 56), Isaksson (1987: 195–196) and Wise (1990: 250–251).

8. LANGUAGE

The combined impact of these six genre traits above is greater than simply the sum of them. Though some commentators may consider one or the other, rarely are two of them (and never more than two) given aggregate weight in evaluating the linguistic issues in determining the nature of Ecclesiastes' language and date. These characteristics of Ecclesiastes' genre make the book nearly incomparable with the rest of the OT and render any analyses of the language that do not consider them to be merely simplistic academic exercises. Eaton (1983: 19) concludes:

> The difficulty is that the linguistic data show that Ecclesiastes does not fit into any known section of the history of the Hebrew Language.... the language of Ecclesiastes does not at present provide an adequate resource for dating.... Certainly no other document possesses precisely the same characteristics, and no reliable date can be given this way. The language of Ecclesiastes is probably of interest more in dialectology than chronology.

Ironically, one of the leading commentators on Ecclesiastes dismisses one linguistic scholar's analysis because it concluded that the book is written in an unparalleled form of Hebrew, while that same commentator himself is attracted to a fringe theory that believes the book is so unparalleled that it was actually not even written originally in Hebrew, but in Aramaic (Fox 1989: 155)! Confusion like this abounds on the subject of the language's uniqueness. Useful surveys of the history of linguistic research of Ecclesiastes can be found in studies by Fredericks (1988: 11–23), Schoors (1992: 1–16), Bianchi (1993) and Seow (1997: 11–21).

8.1. Three 'influence' theories

Three theories of the nature of Ecclesiastes' language that have had spasmodic support through the last half-century are (1) an Aramaic translation theory, (2) a Canaanite-Phoenician influence theory and (3) the belief that there is a north Israelite dialect behind the peculiarity of the language. That the original text of the book was written in Aramaic and then translated into the Hebrew was introduced by Burkitt (1922) and debated hotly between its proponents, Zimmerman (1945, 1949, 1973, 1975) and Ginsburg (1950, 1952), and its main critic, Gordis (1946, 1949, 1952). The suggested improvements in interpretation provided by this theory generally amounted to no more than the exegetical preferences of the proponents rather than being better linguistic solutions in themselves.

8.1.1. Canaanite-Phoenician influence

Though Dahood's Canaanite-Phoenician influence theory (e.g. 1952, 1958, 1962, 1965, 1972) has found some followers, Gordis (1968) successfully demonstrated the equally Hebraic nature of the evidence proposed by Dahood. Gordis argued that the relatively slight linguistic distance between the Canaanites and Phoenicians would of course bring their cognate grammatical and lexical features and their commonalities to our attention when studying the Hebrew of any biblical book.

Related to the suggested influence of the northern cultures of Ugarit and Phoenicia is the theory that there is a substantive influence of a north Israelite dialect on Ecclesiastes. Such a dialect has been assumed for over a century by scholars, though no one had attempted to formulate a description of this alleged dialect until Rendsburg (1990, 1992). This dialectical theory is significantly challenged by the difficulty to identify north Israelite texts and books in the OT in the first place. Even if texts could be shown to be north Israelite, the presence of any so-called northern grammatical-lexical traits have proven to be much more exceptional than pervasive. In other words, the alleged north Israelite features are inconsistently present, and not present as a distinctive group in any of the supposed north Israelite books or passages. Besides, these north Israelite traits have been previously identified as vernacular elements in Biblical Hebrew instead, thus making the theory of a geographical dialect unnecessary. It has been proposed that what appears to be a north Israelite dialect is instead really a northern scribal tolerance for the vernacular that is not found in the more conservative southern scribal traditions. Such a proposal would explain how colloquialisms surfaced in the transmission of certain biblical texts (Fredericks 1988: 32–43; 1996).

8.1.2. Mishnaic Hebrew

Most twentieth-century commentary on Ecclesiastes presumed that an overwhelming number of lexical and grammatical features of its language were either from the late period of the OT's writing or from the intertestamental period, reflecting the Hebrew of the Mishnaic literature. Detailed analyses, however, by Isaksson (1987: 197) and Fredericks (1988), have shown clearly that the Hebrew of Ecclesiastes is that of the biblical times and, consequently, subsequent studies have been slower to assert its affinity with the Mishnaic language. Though Lohfink (2003: 4) still holds strongly to the Mishnaic Hebrew theory, and Schoors (1992: 222) holds only to some influence, Seow (1997: 11, 20) apparently rejects it.

8.1.3. Late Biblical Hebrew

Though identifying Ecclesiastes' language to be as late as the Hebrew of the Mishnah is a fading perspective, that the language is from the later phase of Biblical Hebrew is still the dominant view despite the considerable evidence to the contrary. Ironically, two recent proponents of this view, Seow (1997: 20–21) and Schoors (1992: 221–224), express affinity with the very theories of Ecclesiastes' language that have discounted their own supposed evidences of later Biblical Hebrew influence. Both Fredericks's proposal that Ecclesiastes is essentially a speech in the more colloquial vein and the less likely north Israelite dialect proposal are entertained by Seow and Schoors as having some validity, but by doing so, their lists of late Biblical Hebrew traits are drastically reduced to a number that is in the end far less considerable. But by so doing they present alternative interpretations to most of the specific evidences in their own lists of grammatical or lexical features indicating lateness. Yet loyalty to the late Biblical Hebrew theory persists nonetheless.

Take for instance Schoors's analysis of the grammar of Ecclesiastes, which concludes that over thirty features are typical of late Biblical Hebrew. He readily admits some features are less supportive than others and that some are indications of colloquial or regional dialects. He also admits that there are some traits that reflect the philosophical nature of the language. If one subtracts further those features listed as late Biblical Hebrew that in fact occur in early Biblical Hebrew as well, at best, there are a few traits that may lead one to conclude that the language of Ecclesiastes is more in transition from early Biblical Hebrew to late Biblical Hebrew than from late Biblical Hebrew to the Hebrew of the Mishnah. In a substantive linguistic category, the verbal system, Schoors believes the structures are largely similar to early Hebrew. Furthermore, Isaksson (1987: 196) concludes that of the six distinctive linguistic features of late Biblical Hebrew crystallized by Naveh and Greenfield (1984: 199–121), only one is traceable in Ecclesiastes. The other five are very different from the language of Ecclesiastes.

There is a long list of words found in early books only once or twice and not again until the clearly late books of the OT. A list of such words starting only with aleph and gimel is given in Fredericks 1988: 195–196. Gordis (1960: 400) explains, 'That one phrase occurs in an early Biblical text, and the other in a late, is purely a matter of chance, which is to be expected since only a part of ancient Hebrew literature has reached us in the Bible.'

The number of alleged Aramaisms in the book is often inflated by the inclusion of words like those ending with the abstract forms *–ût* and *–ôn*. These are clearly words expected in a philosophical work like Ecclesiastes that emphasizes the conceptual evaluation of life. Also it is common knowledge that Aramaisms in general entered the Hebrew language even before the time of Solomon. The question is whether these Aramaisms (if they are indeed Aramaisms rather than Hebrew words that show up in later Aramaic texts) are definitely of a later dialect. Certainly, four words or phrases appear only in the later Aramaic (*zĕmān, kĕ'eḥad, tāqap, ḥûṣ min*). However, in his standard book on Aramaisms in the Bible, Wagner describes 151 in early Biblical Hebrew alone (1966: 149–150). The mere four in Ecclesiastes is then not unexpected, especially given its unique nature as we have seen above. Other noted scholars of the Hebrew language, like Hurvitz (1968: 240) and Polzin (1976: 10), discount for dating purposes the importance of Aramaisms in a text. Most recently, Hurvitz (2007: 34) can only conclude that any words that may be considered late may determine the date of Ecclesiastes' composition 'or its committing to writing' – an important qualification that leaves room for a 'modernization' of the oral tradition of an earlier speech.

There are two Persian loanwords in Ecclesiastes: *pardēs* and *pitgām*. Their occurrences appear to many commentators as an example of a later setting for the book. Again, however, Hebrew linguists for over a century have argued against Persian words necessarily being a late indication for a text's setting (Delitzsch 1975: 84; S. R. Driver 1913: 449; Dornseiff 1959: 200; Longman 1998: 13). Israel's far-reaching trade in the pre-exilic era would surely have brought the country's leaders and traders to a knowledge and absorption of some Persian words. The later books of Chronicles, Ezra, Nehemiah, Daniel and Esther have 26 Persian words used 109 times, though Ecclesiastes has only these two words used just once each (Fredericks 1988: 242–245).

Alleged Greek phrases and words in Ecclesiastes are even more unfounded, since all instances sighted have adequate biblical precedent or natural Hebrew meanings and have no need for explanations based on Greek (Fredericks 1988: 246–249; Seow 1997: 16). It is primarily a presupposition of a Greek *philosophical* influence on Ecclesiastes that has caused some to identify native Hebrew words and phrases to be Grecisms.

9. TEXT

Though the language of Qoheleth is one of the most debated in the Hebrew Bible, its textual history is one of the least controversial. Most see little corruption of the text, and Gordis concludes that what we read is basically 'in the form in which it left its author's hand' (1968: 138). The Kethibh–Qere variants are minimal with but one making any substantive difference (see 'Notes' at 11:6).

10. STRUCTURE

It is the goal of every commentator to retain and reveal any and all strains of linear thought in a text. When it comes to Ecclesiastes, this is apparently impossible. A systemic, cumulative progression in thought which is sustained to a climactic end is not found in the speech. Since the structure is so elusive, commentators have done their best to bind similar material together, stretching literary units to absorb as many verses as possible. An elaborate structure is suggested by Wright in a series of articles (1968, 1980, 1981, 1983) and by Rousseau (1981). Others find only numerous contiguous topics with little connection; for example, Galling (1969), Crenshaw (1987), Longman (1998) and Brown (2000).

Whatever unity there may be is maintained primarily by four rhetorical, poetic determinants:

1. Poems about cyclicity and transience: 1:2–11; 3:1–8; 12:1–8.
2. Refrains of Enjoyment: 2:24–26; 3:12–13, 22; 5:18–19; 8:15; 9:7–9; 11:9–10.
3. Recurrent, formulaic *hebel* conclusions: 1:2, 14; 2:1, 11, 15, 17, 19, 21, 23, 26; 3:19; 4:4, 7–8, 16; 5:10; 6:2, 4, 9, 11–12; 7:6, 15; 8:10, 14; 9:9; 11:8, 10; 12:8.
4. Proverbs that contribute a conventional wisdom structure to a reflective speech.

Perhaps future rhetorical analyses will eventually connect all the dots in this speech and a more seamless structure will be revealed. Short of that, my hypothesis is that, rather than a linear progression that would oppose Qoheleth's significant theme of cyclicity, the medium of recycling forms and concepts is in part the message of his speech. Ogden's many articles and Kamano's work (2002) are very good starts on the sojourn to find larger rhetorical units. The reader will also meet many additional proposals in this commentary along these lines.

I suggest the following 'units', which are more or less clear, depending on the unit and its context. These divisions will be supported by detailed explanations under the 'Form and structure' sections:

Ascription	1:1
Cycles in nature and experience	1:2–11
The search for wisdom	1:12 – 2:3
Autobiography leads to catharsis	2:4–26
Human action and providence	3:1–22
Wise living in relationships	4:1 – 5:9
Qualified advantages of labour	5:10 – 6:9
Death's implication for the wise	6:10 – 7:22
A search for Lady Wisdom	7:23 – 8:1
Realistic wisdom in the royal court	8:2–15
Disappointments and ironies	8:16 – 10:1
Career management in the court	10:2–20
Life's storms	11:1 – 12:8
Epilogue	12:9–14

TEXT AND COMMENTARY

ECCLESIASTES 1:1

Translation

¹The teachings of Qoheleth, son of David, king in Jerusalem.

Notes on the text

I translate *dibrē* as 'teachings', since the genre of a work determines the nature of these 'words'. The content that follows this introductory *dibrē* at the beginning of prophetic books is more sermonic, whereas Ecclesiastes is more didactic.

'Qoheleth' is the literal transliteration of the Hebr., and as the nominal abstract in the form of the f. sg. participle. It is a title describing a position within an assembly, but not with any inherent religious meaning. It appears to serve as a name since it is anarthrous in five of its six occurrences. In 7:27, 'Qoheleth' is anarthrous only because of an errant word division, and 12:9 has the art., denoting a position and precluding it from actually being a name. It is used again in 1:2, 12 and 12:8, 10.

That 'king in Jerusalem' refers to Solomon, not David, is clear from 1:12 and 2:9.

Form and structure

The phrase 'words of [name]' introduce other OT books. For example, 'The words of Nehemiah, son of Hacaliah', 'The words of Jeremiah, the son of Hilkiah' and 'The words of Amos'. Ecclesiastes starts out this way as well but most closely parallels the introduction to another edited document attributed to Solomon, Prov. 1:1, 'The proverbs of Solomon, the son of David, king of Israel.'

This introductory verse is part of the framing of this speech that introduces the person Qoheleth and introduces his philosophical conclusion (1:2), and then reverses that order at the end by repeating the philosophical conclusion (12:8), followed by fuller comments about Qoheleth (12:9–11). The editor, who opens the speech here in 1:1 and closes the speech in 12:9–14, reminds us who this teacher is midway through these teachings in 7:27.

Comment

The implied setting for this speech is an assembly where the audience is expecting the one who assembled them to speak himself. The *qāhāl* (assembly) has been called together by the qoheleth, 'assembler', 'convener', and we are about to study the oral teachings of this convener. Lit. the 'words of Qoheleth' in this case are to be interpreted as the 'teachings of the Convener'. To call him 'the Teacher' is too narrow and does not give a true description of his official role, though, in fact, the Convener in this setting is indeed teaching. Solomon, a Convener in the OT, lit. 'assembled' (*qāhal*) people for the ceremonial temple consecration (1 Kgs 8:1; 2 Chr. 5:2). He attracted many others to hear his teachings, including the Queen of Sheba and foreign dignitaries (1 Kgs 4:34; 10:1). Perhaps it was one of these visits that inspired a writer to author the speech we are about to investigate, since the philosophical and cosmopolitan nature of this speech would have been fitting for those settings. Of course, the setting may be a domestic training assembly for court officials as well. From the little evidence we have we cannot know for sure.

As in Proverbs' pattern, this ascription's inclusion of Qoheleth being a king is affirmation that what is to be addressed is spoken of not only from the perspective of authority, but from royal experience. The speech will frequently speak about kings from the vantage point that would best be observed and commented upon by a king himself.

Explanation

Few who ascend to the highest level of government, whether king, prime minister, despot or president, also aspire to observe, analyse and address publicly the most profound philosophical and theological questions. Though most of these highest leaders are presumably well read, there is apparently something incongruous about possessing the greatest authority a society will allow and publishing one's thoughts on the deepest questions of life. There have been very few philosopher-kings like Solomon or Marcus Aurelius. We would be better off as a race if there were those who desired to be profound thinkers and citizens of both the terrestrial and celestial kingdoms. This was Qoheleth's goal: to enlighten his assembly about the importance of wisdom, including the nature of being (impermanence), God (eternal and just), humanity (imperfect yet responsible), ethics (What is the good?), truth (revealed and discovered), the value of very hard work and the tragedies of oppression.

One should study Ecclesiastes with the goal of becoming a 'ruler' who employs biblical wisdom – a ruler whose realm is one's own brief life and its needy and passing surroundings. Though the perspective of Qoheleth is that of a king, he is aware that all, kings and labourers, struggle with a fallen world and the embedded curses in the daily routines common to all humanity. Managing these routines makes us all sovereigns in our own right.

ECCLESIASTES 1:2–11

Translation

²'Breath of breaths,' said Qoheleth, 'Breath of breaths. Everything is
  temporary!'
³What is the advantage to the one who labours laboriously under the sun?
⁴A generation goes, a generation comes,
  yet the earth remains for ever.
⁵So the sun rises,
  then the sun comes panting to its place,
  rising there again.
⁶Going to the south and turning to the north,
  turning, turning, goes the wind,
  and upon its turns the wind returns.
⁷All the rivers go to the sea,
  yet the sea is not full;
  to a place where rivers go,
  there they go again.
⁸Everything is wearying beyond what one could say.
  Eyes are not satisfied by what they see,
  and ears are not full of hearing.
⁹What has been, it will be,
  and what has been done is what will be done,
  so there is nothing new under the sun.

¹⁰It is said, 'See this? It's new!'
  Already it has existed for ages before us.
¹¹There is no memory of those who were earlier,
  nor of those to come will there be any memory by their successors.

Notes on the text

2. Here for *hăbēl hăbālîm*, 'breath of breaths' is the lit. translation. The superlative is phrased in Hebr. by a root in the nominal const. form followed by the same root's pl. abs. form; for example, 'the sky of skies (the highest skies) cannot contain you' (1 Kgs 8:27); and 'Song of songs (the best of songs)' (Song 1:1); and in the NT we are told in Hebraic superlative phrasing that Christ is the 'King of kings and Lord of lords' (1 Tim. 6:15). The reduced segholate in this *hebel* const. phrase is paralleled by other similar vowel reductions in Biblical Hebr. and therefore is not evidence for any later Aram. influence (Fredericks 1988: 122).

I translate *hebel* lit. as 'breath' until its fifth occurrence in the verse, when I translate it as 'temporary'. As discussed at length in the 'Introduction', the metaphorical is far more frequent than the literal use in the OT, and exclusively so in Ecclesiastes.

3. 'advantage': *yitrôn* simply means 'remainder', without commercial implications like 'profit' as some propose. It is an example of abstract nouns with *-ôn* and *-ût* endings in Ecclesiastes, which some consider Aramaisms. These endings, however, are found naturally in Biblical Hebr., with higher proportions in literature such as Proverbs and Ecclesiastes due to its more abstract, philosophical content (Fredericks 1988: 136–138). For a survey of interpretation of this word, see Ingram 2006: 130–149.

'the one': *'ādām* occurs 49 times, whereas *'îš* only 10. As Schoors clearly shows, this preference is due to the universalistic nature of Qoheleth's speech (1998b: 17). I translate it simply as the generic 'one', since that is its intent, and an appropriate option does not exist in Hebr.

'labours laboriously' (*'ămālô šĕya'ămōl*): *'āmāl* and its derivatives occur disproportionately in the wisdom literature and Psalms, occurring in these books 63 of 75 of its biblical instances, and around 35 times in Ecclesiastes alone (Foresti 1980: 420). Its contexts are often fraught with the emotional pain of grief, affliction, violence and so on (Seow 1997: 104). As in 1:2, Qoheleth repeats the root as a poetic device, using the cognate accusative phrase 'labour which he labours' to emphasize the grievous toil that cursed humanity has been doomed to exert since the Fall.

'under the sun': *taḥat haššāmeš* is not a Grecism as many suggest, since it is used universally in other cultures during the earlier OT times (Murphy 1992: 6). This phrase is introduced as a favourite qualifier for Qoheleth, and is used 29 times in this speech. Its parallel phrase 'under the skies [heavens]' is used an additional 3 times (1:13; 2:3; 3:1).

4. 'generation': some feel that *dôr* means 'around', thus poetic in itself, and refers to the natural cycles, not human generations (Ogden 1986: 91–92; Whybray 1988: 105–112). However, human generations are probably meant, since people are the focus in 1:2, and the poem ends by mentioning prior and later people. Furthermore, it is the usual meaning when paired with 'for ever' (Exod. 3:15; Lev. 6:18; Pss 33:11; 146:10), and Qoheleth emphasizes generations again (2:12, 18; 4:15).

'the earth': Fox proposes *hā'āreṣ* does not refer to the physical earth, but to 'humanity' (1999: 166). Ps. 104:5, however, is a strong parallel; there the earth stands for ever as well and is the stage for natural phenomena, as it is here in 1:4–7.

5. Some suspect the well-attested waw consecutive *wĕzāraḥ* (rises) to have been metathesized because all the surrounding verb forms are participles. This unnecessarily imposes the interpreters' personal expectations on to the text.

Similarly, *bā'* (comes) parallels the 'coming' generations in 1:4.

7. The contracted relative pronoun *še-* (translated 'where' here) is used 68 times in Ecclesiastes, while the usual Biblical Hebr. form *'ăšer* appears 89 times. Lamentations, Jonah and some Psalms use both forms as well (Fredericks 1988: 103). Often cited as an indication of a late date for Ecclesiastes, it shows rather the vernacular nature of the language (see 'Language' in the 'Introduction'). Qoheleth uses the colloquial contraction frequently to ease his delivery of life's deepest truths.

8. *haddĕbārîm* probably means 'things, matters', though the temptation is strong to translate as 'word' to complement 'eyes' and 'ears'. Here three grammatically parallel clauses denote human limitations and wearying attempts to experience reality exhaustively: negative particle, imperfect, agent, infinitive.

Whether *yĕgē'îm* (wearying) is adjectival, describing the passive result (weary), or more actively participial (wearying), is ambiguous. Nevertheless, it echoes the toiling labour of 1:3.

9. 'what, that which': *mah-še-* has been listed as an allegedly late form; however, its components and parallels are typical Biblical Hebr. (Fredericks 1988: 104–105).

10. 'already' (*kĕbār*): used in Mishnaic Hebr., but many early Biblical Hebr. texts contain words used only in that biblical book and Mishnaic Hebr. (Fredericks 1988: 228).

'for ever': *'ōlāmîm* as a pl. subject with a sg. verb, grammatically speaking, is 'the commonest of all colloquialisms' according to G. R. Driver (1970: 234). The frequent occurrence of *hāyāh* ('has been'; 1:9; 48 times) and *'ōlām* ('ever'; 7 times) in Ecclesiastes shows the philosophical nature of the speech in its very vocabulary, the former dealing with 'being' (Schoors 1998b: 21) and the latter with indefinite time and its implications.

11. *ri'šōnîm, 'aḥărōnîm*: does 'earlier' and 'later' refer to things in general, people or ages (which have all been suggested)? Since the former means 'people' in Deut. 19:14 and Job 18:20, and since it refers to future people in Eccl. 4:16, and, since these nouns are m. ('things' would prefer f.), the reference is probably for 'people'.

Form and structure

The significant theme of 'transience' in 1:2, in its mere seven Hebr. words, is full of poetic nuances. First, is the superlative form mentioned above. Secondly, the word *hebel* is onomatopoeic, sounding in its pronunciation like the meaning of the word. One must aspirate twice with the initial he-sound, then again with the soft bet, pronounced as '-vel'. So the speaker illustrates what the nature of a breath is simply by saying the word!

Thirdly, just as breaths follow themselves in the breathing process, in our verse *hebel* repeats itself five times. This models the pattern of cyclic breathing of life, which will be illustrated by the cyclic patterns of nature in vv. 4–11 and the cyclic patterns in human existence observed throughout the book. Each breath is only one stage in the continuous cycle of breathing. It is in this cyclic regularity of life, its deeds and consequences, where the proverbial principles of wisdom are derived.

Fourthly, the repetition not only models breathing, but also accentuates the theme by simply reviewing it for mnemonic purposes. This then provides the opportunity for the fifth poetic device, a highly alliterated sentence: *hăbēl hăbālîm ... hăbēl hăbālîm, hakkōl hābel* (1:2). This penchant for an alliterated pronouncement that all is temporary is repeated in 1:14, 2:1, 11, 17 and 3:19. We will be introduced to another frequent alliterated expression for temporariness, *rě'ût rûaḥ* (whim of the wind) in 1:14.

And sixthly, at the end of the speech the sentence is repeated, yet in a slightly abbreviated form (12:8). Clearly, these twin phrases are meant to be the alpha and omega of the speech, the poetic, alliterated, thematic introduction and conclusion. Everything in between these nearly identical sentences in the book is meant to elaborate on their fundamental, sweeping truth that *everything is temporary*. There can be no missing this theme of Qoheleth: all the stops have been pulled to declare it.

This verse stands alone as a unit, like its twin in 12:8. It expresses the overarching reality that forces the following question. And it is this question that introduces the prologue to the entire speech in vv. 3–11. In turn, 3–11 illustrates these recurring breaths of life through the recurring natural events on the surface of the earth.

There have been two introductory elements in Ecclesiastes so far: the author (1:1) and the key observation concerning transience (1:2). Now, v. 3 is the first response to the overwhelming truth about temporariness introduced in v. 2, posing a rhetorical question that will be the focus of Qoheleth's attention.

Structure:

1:3 = question about advantage to wearying human labour
1:4–7 = nature's own wearying labour
  1:4 = temporary changes, but enduring base of the *earth*
  1:5 = temporary changes, but enduring, cyclic consistency
    of *sun*
  1:6 = temporary changes, but enduring, cyclic consistency
    of *wind*
  1:7 = temporary changes, but enduring, cyclic consistency
    of *rivers*
1:8 = accentuates the wearying labour of 1:3
1:9–11 = temporary changes, but enduring cyclic consistency
  of 'innovations'

To illustrate the importance of the rhetorical question posed in v. 3, a series of examples are given in vv. 4–11 to compare the circularity of labouring generations with the cyclic flow of natural phenomena and the pre-existence of human 'innovations'. Many have seen the motifs of circularity and cyclicity as extending throughout Ecclesiastes in both its contents and its form; see for instance Carasik (2003). The rolling participles and high density of repeated words in this section are linguistic techniques to match the message of constant change through repetition. This is a pericope of participial phrases expressing the constant flow of generations, winds, sunrises and rivers through a relentless pounding of repeated words and their derivatives: *hebel* (5 times) 1:2; labour (twice) 1:3; generation (twice) 1:4; come (twice) 1:4–5; rise (twice) 1:5; the sun (twice) 1:5; place (twice) 1:5, 7; go (5 times) 1:6–8; turn (4 times) 1:6; wind (twice) 1:6; return (twice) 1:6–7; sea (twice) 1:7; rivers (twice) 1:7; not full (twice) 1:7–8; do (twice) 1:9; be (7 times) 1:9–11; whatever (twice) 1:9; new (twice) 1:9–10.

Comment

2. Since this theme is essentially a repetition of the one word, *hebel*, in various forms, and since the meaning of that word has been discussed at length in the 'Introduction', suffice it to say that the utter brevity of 'everything' is the meaning of this verse. It is the foundational premise for the speech's ultimate conclusion: 'Since everything is temporary, be wise, be diligent and be appreciative while you can.' We should not miss the literal emphasis of this verse that *everything* is as temporary as a breath. Of course, the 'everything' of this verse means less than *absolutely* everything, which would include God himself and his deeds. Yet it means more than simply the human labour mentioned in the next verse. Qoheleth never

questions the eternality of God: he is the source of the infinite (3:11), and whatever he does lasts for ever (3:14). Even within the next couple of verses Qoheleth tells us that the earth stands for ever, one of the God-created backdrops of passing human existence.

The reader will find this interpretation at odds with the many different Bible translations and the views of most other commentators. However, words like 'vanity, futile, meaningless, absurd, foul, false' are inconsistent with the explicit content of Ecclesiastes, or are foreign to the OT's meanings for *hebel* (breath). But when the book is studied methodically by considering *hebel* to mean 'temporary', the reader will discover a book that speaks clearly to the effects of the Fall. So one should not presume that this introductory motif is a cry of despair. Since we will find many instances in this speech where the brevity of something is actually preferred, we should defer judgment on any emotionally overwhelming impact of this motif and wait for the speech to unfold. However, even as 'temporary', this is at least a statement of fact that contrasts with one's intuitive appreciation of the infinite (3:11). On the other hand, brevity is the fact that serves as a consolation at times in Ecclesiastes as well.

3. The full force of the Fall and God's curse on simple work to become toilsome labour is felt by this rhetorical question. The *cause* of the grief and frustrating work is given in Gen. 3:17–19:

> Cursed is the ground because of you,
>   in grief you will eat from it . . .
> By the sweat of your face
>   you will eat food
> until you return to the ground.

But is there is any advantage in working with, or even against, that curse? Qoheleth dares ask the question that reason demands, 'Since everything is temporary, are there any advantages to my gruelling labour under the sweltering sun?' This question does not challenge the value of simple human 'activity'; instead, it groans over the strenuous, arduous grind of daily work and effort. So the topic of concern in Ecclesiastes is not the meaning of life or an assessment of the human condition as a whole (contra Fox 1998: 225). This speech is sharply focused, a reaction and answer to the particular question of slavish toil. It also intentionally stings those who are so lazy as to conjure a question whether one should even get out of bed. 'Why should I even get up and work so hard?' In other words, it is a question of character and morality, comparable to many passages in both Ecclesiastes and Proverbs dealing with diligence (cf. Prov. 20:13; 22:13; 26:13–14).

Eventually, the question is answered positively in many passages, proving that *yitrôn* (advantage) and *ṭôb* (good) can be obtained in one's life when it is lived wisely and diligently. For example 2:13, 7:11–12 and

10:10 speak of the advantages to wise conduct, and 3:13, 3:22 and 5:18 encourage taking advantage of the joy found in labour itself! (See 'Introduction', pp. 38–40.) Throughout his discourse, Qoheleth explains that there is great value to much of life, including wisdom and law, God's gifts and joy. Interpretations of Ecclesiastes based on *hebel* meaning 'meaningless' or 'vain' would naturally see this to be a rhetorical question, with its presumed answer being, 'There is no advantage to labouring laboriously. How could there be if everything is futile?' But this is not the 'Thesis' of Ecclesiastes, which presumes a negative answer (Fox 1999: 165); rather, it is the key question whose positive answer will be determined in Qoheleth's complete discussion of human existence and efforts, currently standing with no presumed answer until Qoheleth's speech is fully heard.

The significance of the qualifying phrase 'under the sun' is that Qoheleth considers to be temporary those things not found in heaven with God (5:2), and perhaps, as Seow (1997: 105) suggests, not found in the netherworld below, since neither is brightened by the sun. Furthermore, Qoheleth introduces the sun in this verse as a recurrent motif in Ecclesiastes that will describe both reality's curses and blessings. Though the sun intensifies the punishment of toil, it is also something only the living are blessed to see (7:11; 11:7). So the phrase 'under the sun' is synonymous with 'while under the sun' or 'while alive'. In this way, the *place* of humanity insinuates the *temporal span* of humanity; place means time (5:18; 6:5, 12; 8:15; 9:9–10; 11:7). Since God is above the sun, in the heavens (5:2), Qoheleth speaks of one's spirit returning to be with God, over the sun, after toiling under the sun (12:7).

4–7. Qoheleth defines deftly all the dimensions 'under the sun'. The swirlings of the wind are charted to be north and south explicitly, and the course of the sun to be east and west implicitly, providing the length and width of earth's 'plane'. Furthermore, the vertical dimension is defined starting with the highest realm of the sun (1:5), then descending to the middle domain of the wind (1:6) and finally further down to the river plains (1:7). Qoheleth sets these time and space parameters of reality after the fleeting nature of generations and the ageless tenure of the earth are described in 1:4.

What goes on under the sun, then, is the subject of 1:4–11. Qoheleth's summary is that whatever is happening now has happened and will continue indefinitely. Clearly, the temporariness of all generations is emphasized here compared with the relatively eternal earth, which hosts these human and natural cycles (Loader 1986: 20; Murphy 1992: 7; Garrett 1993: 284). Qoheleth introduces our 'coming and going' here, but it is always on his mind, speaking of it specifically in 5:16[15] and 6:4. And, one's successors are spoken of often (2:12, 18–19, 21; 3:2; 4:8, 13; 6:3). In fact, it is poetic in itself that here he mentions first the 'going', then the 'coming', since for all who hear Qoheleth their arrival or birth is not the issue, but their termination or death is, and what is done productively before death. He uses 'going' to mean death again and again to alarm those who are sluggish to become diligent and wise (3:20; 6:6; 9:10; 12:5; cf. Ps. 39:14; Job 10:21; 2 Sam. 12:23).

Generations, as well as the sun, wind and rivers, come and go, as do the 'new' things that are really only repetitions of the old. All things run their circuits with great regularity and seasonal temporariness. However, as a series of temporary repetitions, they form a permanence of change – permanent in total, temporary in part. Farmer summarizes this section, 'All the processes of creation on earth are transitory or fleeting' (1991: 153). Yet there is an underestimated, undergirding stability to the ever-changing surface of human experience. The earth remains for ever, even the changes never cease upon it. Whybray is correct, then (1989: 40): 'Nothing in this passage suggests that there is anything *futile* about the behaviour of the elements. On the contrary, Qoheleth sees their intense activity as both predictable and positive, contributing to the stability of the earth (v. 4*b*).'

In fact, David translates the natural revelation of the sun's cycles into the verbal revelation expressing God's glory and craftsmanship:

> He has set a tent for the sun [in the skies].
> It is like a bridegroom coming out of his bedroom
>   rejoicing like the virile, ready to run his course.
> It goes from one end of the skies, following its circuit to the
>   other end.
> Surely nothing is hid from its heat.
>
> (Ps. 19:4b–6)

It is *because* the earth remains that I translate, 'So the sun rises ... rising there again'. All three elements – sun, wind and rivers – are described as circuit riders that return to their point of origin. Along their circuits, the sun pants, the wind swirls and the rivers somehow simply return to the sea. Consistent with the sun and wind, the rivers return, again, to their source. Though this implies the evaporation and precipitation process (Job 36:27–28), it is the only way rivers can return or do anything 'again'.

In 12:2, we will hear of yet another natural cycle – the clouds 'return' as well, after the rain. That is not a bad thing, nor is the sea's absorptive nature, which keeps it in check, so that it does not overwhelm its shores.

Regardless of the consistency achieved by these temporary, repetitious cycles, they are still wearying! Life is challenging in an arduous way: the laborious labour (1:3), the panting, puffing sun (1:5), the ever-turning wind (1:6), unfilled seas (1:7) and life's wearying experiences (1:8) – all emphatically suggest the lead question 'What's the advantage?' The sun only completes its cycle after puffing and panting, reminding us of the breathing process in 1:2 and the exhausting work of the labourer in 1:3 (see Isa. 42:14, where *šā'ap* implies distress). Some see a contrast in this passage to the royal persona of the sun in Ps. 19:5–7. But even there the sun is said to arise and run a race, surely panting when finished. Even the wind exerts itself by winding its way on its many epicycles, nearly writhing to its starting point.

8–11. The three grammatically parallel clauses about speaking, seeing and hearing express the wearying frustrations of experiencing reality. All things are wearying because human and natural events exhaust the power of language to explain them; yet, like the sea, neither the eyes nor the ears are ever fully satisfied by seeing or hearing them. However, this is in sharp contrast to the joy we are supposed to be experiencing. Qoheleth recommends joy and satisfaction in life throughout his speech, but in this introductory section raises a question of how that is possible when wearisome labour produces only temporary benefits. His concerns are carried over into 1:13, 18, where this frustration that comes from wise observations can be full of serious grief and sorrow.

Structurally, 1:9–11 are explanations of v. 8. Specifically, vv. 9–10 explain why v. 8 is true: the eyes and ears are dissatisfied because there is nothing new for them to experience. There are only a limited number of sensations to maximize their stimulation. Then v. 11 explains why anyone would even suggest anything is new: we have such short memories of what was done before that it just appears we are seeing or hearing something new!

What the wind and rivers do on the permanent earth is cyclical and temporary, and what humans do from passing generation to generation on the permanent earth is the same (cf. 2:12; 6:10). This reiteration is by definition a series of transient events, however identical or similar they may be to one another. However, this is more than mere naturalism playing itself out. We hear in 3:15 that cyclicity is God's design in both his creation and in its maintenance through natural and human events. God's plan is to ensure cyclicity. But just because there is nothing new, does not mean we can foretell the future fatalistically. Qoheleth's historiography does not propound a circular history, nor is it deterministic. Though God has ordered the earth's phenomena to be recurring in general, and though the parts in themselves are not new, his sovereign, mysterious acts, along with our timing and combination of wise and foolish actions still make life unpredictable.

Since all human activity and its achievements are only temporary, there is a natural tendency to hope they will be remembered, thus become 'eternal' at least in human memory. However, we will be reminded again and again by Qoheleth that we certainly cannot count on being remembered to sustain our accomplishments. In fact, as emphasized in this introductory section, the opposite occurs – human attentiveness is hopelessly weak and ultimately momentary, leading to foolish announcements that something new has been accomplished.

Not only are our acts forgotten, but someone else can be given credit for *their* 'innovation' of what was actually ours. It would be superficial, however, to see these and other references in Ecclesiastes to 'remembered' and 'forgotten' as matters of mere recollection of facts. OT theology is indebted to the rich meaning of being 'remembered' as being given attention and care by God:

> Who is man that you remember him,
>   the son of man that you care for him?

> (Ps. 8:4)

Qoheleth's frequent comments about being remembered or forgotten allude to the relative care one generation has for the preceding generations, of which recollection is simply a *symptom* of the problem.

We conclude in 1:8–11, then, where we started in 1:2–3: What advantage is there after all our wearying toil under the sun? If there is not even any respect for our hard work, why labour laboriously? Cf. 2:16. And finally, 1:11 reminds us of the waves of succeeding generations mentioned in 1:4, who, as we now know, do not value new things, much less invent them.

Explanation

Since the theme of 'transience' is expressed by the repetition of the one word *hebel* in various forms, and since the meaning of that word has been discussed at length in the 'Introduction', suffice it to say that the utter brevity of 'everything' is the meaning of v. 2 in this introductory section. It is the foundational premise for the speech's ultimate conclusion: 'Since everything is temporary, be wise, be diligent and be appreciative while you can.'

There is an illogical leap taken that presumes that the transitory must by nature be useless – since God is the ultimate Good and is eternal, anything temporal must be meaningless. Thus the jump from translating 'breath' as 'temporary' to equating it immediately with 'vanity'. But this type of thinking is the basis for the heresy of ancient gnosticism, where the transient physical creation, including the human body, is dismissed as inherently bad. Actually, transience was built into the world at creation, even when it was declared to be 'good'. Furthermore, 3:1–8 explains that there are temporary seasons for all wise activities. Granted, some actions are mentioned there that are only necessary because of the Fall, but there are also those that are done in the daily, natural pursuit of stewardship even in the new heaven and earth.

Qoheleth considers four categories of reality to be temporary, which are referred to often throughout the speech: life itself, human efforts and their results, pleasure and tragedies. A more specific list of what he considers to be momentary is given on page 30 of the 'Introduction'.

We certainly more than sympathize with the question 'What is in it for me?', for we have all literally asked the question ourselves. Why should we work so hard? What is the return? What is the point? The question is earthy, frequent and ordinary. It is not ethereal, strange or philosophical. The question is natural because the curse was not. We were created for labour but not *laborious* labour, according to Genesis. If toil accompanied by sweat and grief was how our work was reprogrammed by a just and disciplining God, it is understandable, in fact quite perceptive, to ask, 'If we are members of passing hordes through history, if nothing we do can be said to be profoundly and truly innovative, if there is no credit given for creativity, if we cannot perpetually stimulate the senses, if we or our achievements are not long remembered, why labour so arduously? Why sacrifice ourselves so willingly and generously to the effects of the Fall?' Qoheleth does not answer these questions immediately, preferring to incite us to the same level of frustration he experienced.

Being 'under the sun' is what brings the sweat, and the questions the sweat inspires express obvious grief and frustration. But the sun becomes an example itself of the cycles it oversees. God, having created the sun and other natural elements, sets them on a cyclic course because he prefers 'what has been pursued before' (3:15). This cosmology, in its stable circuits, testifies to God's consistency through his natural world, its times and seasons. But these phenomena also prove that it is his consistency that makes wisdom, including its aphorisms, true. God's faithfulness is more certain than the earth's existence. He is faithful *to himself* through the righteous judgment of the curse, and *to us* in his cosmic and ethically predictable arrangement of natural and moral law. If people are irremedially annoyed by this, that is their folly. However, remediation is presented through Qoheleth's speech and his answers to questions that preoccupy us all at times.

History is linear and eventually moving towards perfection under Christ, yet follows the same plot through the ages, only with different people as the characters. But, even though the image of the winding natural circuits portrays that there is nothing new under the sun, that is far from conveying that they are monotonous or meaningless. Billions of earth's human inhabitants have come and gone, and those fortunate to live a reasonable length of time have performed thousands of acts. Yet if for a large proportion of these people there was no understanding of the meaning and advantages to their gruelling labour, Qoheleth considers them impoverished souls regardless of the amount of their wealth.

Every culture has its ways to continue stimulating the eyes, ears, taste buds and tactile senses. Yet there is always a search for more. But the progressively more and more diverse ways to stimulate ourselves through technology, wealth and removed taboos has not satisfied, and will not satisfy a soul created for more than the sensual. The senses are never satisfied; they are only exhausted without achieving absolute fulfilment. We are incapable of creating anything utterly new because we have finite limitations shared with others who think similarly.

It is the responsibility of the church and its believers to depend on the faithfulness of God seen in his natural and special revelations – to find the cultural connections that pave the way to a mutual understanding of God's ways and words between the redeemed and the unredeemed. The consistencies in God's character and actions give the church an enormous resource with which to interact with the common grace found in every culture without compromising the special grace that has come through Christ and his Word. The unsatisfied, searching peoples of the world are hungering for a holistic satisfaction of senses and soul, and need the perspective of the church which understands the regularity of nature and human generations to be from the God who alone should be worshipped rather than his created order or past generations.

ECCLESIASTES 1:12 – 2:3

Translation

[12–13]I, Qoheleth, have been king over Israel in Jerusalem and I have devoted myself to search and explore with wisdom everything done under the skies. It is a tragic affliction God has given to afflict the sons of men. [14]I have observed all the activity done under the sun, and really, it is all temporary and like the whim of the wind. [15]What has been twisted cannot be straightened, and what is lacking cannot be counted.

[16]I said to myself, 'Really, I have amassed and increased wisdom beyond all my predecessors in Jerusalem because my heart has examined wisdom and knowledge thoroughly.'

[17]Because I devoted myself to know wisdom and knowledge, madness and folly, I know this also is like the whim of the wind. [18]Surely, in much wisdom there is much sorrow, and increasing knowledge increases grief.

[2:1]I said to myself, 'Go ahead, and let me test you with pleasure, so enjoy what is good.' But really it was also temporary. [2]I said, 'Laughter is madness, but joy – what does this accomplish?'

[3]I explored with my heart how to drag my flesh along with wine while my heart guided me along with wisdom in order to grasp folly until I might see what is good for the sons of men to do under the skies the few days of their lives.

Notes on the text

12. 'I': because *'ănî* is used exclusively rather than *'ānōkî* in Ecclesiastes (29 times), this trait has been linked to a theory of the book's late language and origin since other later books have the same preference. However, *'ănî* is the preferred form in Biblical Hebr. when adjacent to the verb (S. R. Driver 1882: 222–224), which it is 26 times. Also the shorter form was the colloquial preference long before it became a literary preference (Harris 1939: 74), which fits the vernacular fabric of Qoheleth's speech.

'have been king': the perfect aspect here has confused some in the past, but the stative use of the perfect has long been recognized (Isaksson 1987: 76–77; GKC 106g [a]).

13. Qoheleth loves verbal intensification through contiguous synonyms, cognate accusatives and alliteration. Here *lidrôš* and *lātûr* are contiguous alliterated synonyms. Yet some commentators imagine a distinction in meaning, 'to search broadly and explore deeply' respectively; for example, Crenshaw 1987: 72, 145. Conversely, others think these verbs mean 'to search deeply and explore broadly', respectively (Eaton 1983: 62). However, the words are probably interchangeable (Longman 1998: 79). The same words accompany each other again in 7:25.

'under the skies': *taḥat haššāmāyîm* is a poetic equivalent to 'under the sun', revealing Qoheleth's creative freedom to denote the terrestrial.

'affliction ... afflict': *'inyan* and its cognate verb *'ānāh* carry this Biblical Hebr. meaning (Zimmerli 1962: 151, 168; Lauha 1978: 38, 45–46) and continue the wearying, struggling motif from 1:3–11. Those disposed to a late date, for example Bea (1950: 12), Wagner (1966: 92) and A. Schellenberg 2007: 144, prefer 'occupation ... occupy'.

14. *wehinnēh hakkōl hebel* (and, really, it is all temporary) and *rĕ'ût rûaḥ* (whim of the wind) confirm Qoheleth's penchant for poetic devices like alliteration.

'whim of the wind': *rĕ'ût* in this verse and *ra'yôn* in 1:17 are simply different morphologies from the root *rā'āh*, which can mean either 'to shepherd', 'to associate with' or 'to desire'. Most commentators correctly prefer the latter, yet almost invariably misinterpret the grammar (see 'Introduction', p. 53).

rā'āh (observe) is a rich word used variously by Qoheleth: 'to see, to observe or examine, to reflect, to enjoy' (Schoors 1998b: 26–33; see also Van Hecke 2007). It is used over 20 times as well to express Qoheleth's conclusions.

15. 'straightened': *tāqan* is sometimes listed as an Aram.; for example, Wagner 1966: 120. However, the Aram. dialects in which the word is found were susceptible to Hebraic influence instead; for example, Jewish and Christian-Palestinian Aram. and Syr. Loretz sees as possible an indigenous Hebr. alternative to *tākan* (1964: 25).

'lacking': *ḥesrôn* reaches as far back to Ug. (Gordon 1965: 403) as it does forward to Mishnaic Hebr. (Kid 32b). Its abstract ending is conveniently used for assonance with *litqôn* (straightened) in this verse's chiastic structure.

16. 'I said to myself': here and in 19 other phrases in Ecclesiastes, *'ănî* (I) is found immediately after the already conjugated verb: 2:1, 11–15, 18, 20, 24; 3:17–18; 4:1, 4, 7; 5:17; 7:25; 8:15; 9:16 (with the third person m. sg. pronoun in 9:15). This 'posterior pronoun' construction clarifies the exact 'tense' in which Qoheleth is speaking to be the simple past or 'preterite' (Fredericks 1988: 63–82). The form is found rarely in Biblical Hebr.; for example, 2 Sam. 17:15, Song 5:5–6, Dan. 10:7 and 12:5, where the simple past is probably intended as well. Others have thought it emphasizes the subject, as it does in 1:12 where, however, there is an anterior pronoun (GKC 35b, 135a), or to emphasize a thought about to be expressed (Isaksson 1987: 163–171), or a sign of the colloquial language (J. Macdonald 1975: 162–166). This approach to the syntax does not preclude the simple past to be expressed without the posterior pronoun, as is typical.

'I have amassed and gathered wisdom': *gādal* and *yāsap*, like *dāraš* and *tûr* in 1:13, are simply summative synonyms and no fine distinctions are probably intended.

17. 'Since I devoted myself': this is the first of only three waw consecutive imperfects in Ecclesiastes (4:1, 7), another reason for some to see the book as an example of later Hebr., when the consecutive verbs are more sparse. However, Ecclesiastes has no need for this phraseology, since his speech is not primarily historical narrative and since the consecutive forms would hardly have been used in the vernacular. The waw consecutive perfect occurs 16 times. See Fredericks 1988: 62–65; Isaksson 1987: 194–197.

'wisdom and knowledge': though these words are almost always parallel in Ecclesiastes, the MT here does not recognize the phrasing as clearly as the LXX, Syr, Tg and Vg. Four nouns, then, are governed by one infinitive, *lāda'at*. Furthermore, the precedent was set for the nominal interpretation of *da'at* by the last two words in the just previous verse, a precedent eventually solidified, since *da'at* occurs only if *hokmāh* escorts it (1:16–18; 2:21, 26; 7:12; 9:10; 12:9).

'madness and folly': like wisdom or knowledge, amass or gather, and search or explore, this duet is another example of near, if not actual, synonyms. If there is a difference, the former is more incoherent, the latter more disobedient.

2:2. 'what does this': Ecclesiastes' vernacular prefers shorter words than longer. As in the case of *'ănî*, *zōh* is preferred exclusively over its longer, predominantly literary, Hebr. equivalent *zō't* (2:24; 5:15, 18; 7:23; 9:13). For other possible contractions in Qoheleth's vernacular, see Fredericks 1988: 40–41.

3. 'until': the same unique *'ad 'ăšer* (*še-*) is found in Song 1:12; 2:7, 17; 3:4–5; 4:6; 8:4. Also found in the ancient song in Judg. 5:7.

'few days': *mispar* means a limited number as opposed to an indefinite amount, speaking of the transience of the days of life.

Form and structure

Not only does 1:12 – 2:3 form its own triparallel structure, but its three sections serve as introductions to the sections within the larger unit, 2:4–26. So I will comment on them as a distinct unit. These prolepses, or introductory summaries, have as their literary function to cover briefly topics about to be discussed in greater length.

1. Qoheleth's resolve is to investigate all activity, including his own unprecedented achievements, by distinguishing wisdom from folly: 1:13, 16–17; 2:3 → 2:4–14.
2. Furthermore, he is compelled to share his agony in the process: 1:13, 18 → 2:15–21.
3. Finally, he questions and discovers the value of labour, wisdom and joy: 2:1–2 → 2:22–26.

One can see Qoheleth's parallel units and their similar flow in thought in the table below. Each section moves from his firm resolve to investigate, to his conclusion of brevity, to a further cryptic, proverbial explanation. Inclusios bracket the unit in 1:12–13 and 2:3.

	1:12–15	1:16–18	2:1–2	2:3
Resolve to examine the works of humanity	I, Qoheleth, have been king over Israel in Jerusalem and have devoted myself to search and explore with wisdom everything done under the heavens. It is a tragic affliction God has given to afflict the sons of men. 14. I have observed all the activity done under the sun, and really,	I said to myself, 'Really, I have amassed and increased wisdom beyond all my predecessors in Jerusalem, since my heart has examined wisdom and knowledge thoroughly.' Because I devoted myself to know wisdom and knowledge, madness and folly,	I said to myself, 'Go ahead, and let me test you with pleasure, so enjoy what is good.'	I explored with my heart how to drag my flesh along with wine while my heart guided me along with wisdom in order to grasp folly until I might see what is good for the sons of men to do under the heavens the few days of their lives.
Conclusion about brevity	it is all temporary and like the whim of the wind.	I know this also is like the whim of the wind.	But really, it was also temporary.	
Cryptic further comment	What has been twisted cannot be straight, and what is lacking cannot be counted.	Surely, in much wisdom there is much sorrow, and increasing knowledge increases grief.	I said, 'Laughter is madness, but pleasure – what does this accomplish?'	

In the larger scheme, 1:12 – 2:3 serves as an introduction to himself, his heart for wisdom and his reasons for severe concern for the human condition. His wisdom leads him to the understanding that everything is temporary, which leads to a full-blown inner conflict to the point of utter despair, comparable to a Job: 'So I hate life . . . all is temporary and like the whim of the wind' (2:17). But for Qoheleth, eventually there is consolation and resolution in 2:24–26. In that sense, there is a psalmic structure in 1:12 – 2:26 – starting out as a lament, yet ending positively – blaming God at the outset (1:13–18) but praising him at last (2:24–26).

Of course, all of this is the extension of Qoheleth's opening question 'What is the advantage in all one's laborious labour under the sun?' Labour is not only excruciating nor simply frustrating or wearying (1:5, 8) – now we know that it is full of sorrow and grief as well. Yet this is not where the wise, including Qoheleth, can dwell. Though they frequent these profound places of anxious agitation, their home is in God's comforting care.

Comment

12–13. V. 12 leaves no alternative to Qoheleth's being identified as Solomon. David and Solomon were the only two kings to rule Israel from Jerusalem, since the rest of the Davidic kings ruled only the southern populace in 'Judah'.

One is impressed with the tenacity of Qoheleth's search, which is expressed with increasing intensity at the start of nearly every sentence in this section. He devoted himself to search and explore everything with wisdom. He observed all human activity. He amassed unprecedented wisdom by examining wisdom and folly thoroughly. He not only devoted himself to understanding wisdom, but madness and folly as well. He tested himself with pleasure and explored with body and soul, persisting until he knew categorically what is best for humanity to pursue during our brief lives. He has an explicit hope that there will be an answer to his question about the advantage to gruelling labour, while exerting all his own gruelling labour to discover it! He does nothing less than 'give' (*nātan*) himself to this punishing task that God 'gives' (*nātan*) to humanity in general. In this sense, he is more obedient than the rest of humanity who remain unwilling to complete God's assignment of life assessment.

It is clear as well that Qoheleth's observations are limited to human actions. It is 'what is done' under the sun (*naʿăśāh*; 1:13), 'the deeds which are done' (*maʿăśeh naʿăśāh*; 1:14). It is to find out what is good for the sons of men 'to do' (*ʿāśāh*; 2:3) that is the focus of Qoheleth's quest for determining what are wise and foolish deeds, and what are the advantages to them. This means that we are investigating human activity, not the metaphysical heights of human meaning (Fox 1999: 133) or the breadth of everything that ever happened, though observations of nature and

God's dealings are indeed made by Qoheleth along the way. Identified as Solomon, he is the archetypal assessor of life accomplishments because Solomon's were so numerous and diverse. His achievements in architecture, diplomacy, agriculture and other commerce, as well as the arts and sciences, are clearly delineated in the histories and paralleled in the passage 2:4–9.

Furthermore, he does not give only his brain to this endeavour; he also gives his 'heart' (*lēb*) and 'flesh' (*bāśār*). In Hebr., the 'heart' is not merely an organ or part of the person; it is all of that person's total consciousness – not solely intellectual reason, but experiential insight that has been gained through the avenues and alleys of emotional, sensual, physical and spiritual experience. The heart, then, is a synecdoche for the whole of a person (see Koosed 2006: 46–52 for a study of the word in Ecclesiastes).

The historic significance of Qoheleth's royal autobiographical comments is his unconventional, prophetic frankness about human ambitions – they amount to nothing more than pretentious efforts to 'be great'. He is a king, but one who has experienced all it means to be one of the most powerful and successful ever. Qoheleth's break from royal autobiographies is profound in that his conclusions are realistic and humble rather than arrogant. In 1:12 – 2:26, he deconstructs the royal haughtiness and opulence of his contemporary as well as preceding peers. His own conformity to the paradigm for a royal lifestyle confirmed for him that even that level of accomplishment was only temporary. He was wise but humbled by the process: an element of true wisdom.

Qoheleth introduces Elohim in this speech as a giving God. He prefers always to refer to God as the universal Creator, thus always Elohim, rather than Israel's own covenant God, Yahweh. Elohim, was a name for God not only in Israel but in her neighbouring ANE nations; and in a speech devoted to drawing conclusions about life for all humanity it would be the preference over a uniquely Israelite name based on a divine covenant intended exclusively for them; that is, Yahweh (Jehovah). Comparable to Paul's cross-cultural strategy to reference the 'unknown god' at Mars Hill, Qoheleth's apologetic goal is to speak universally, without the ethnocentrism that would close the ears and hearts of his international audiences. This is not to say that Elohim is not personal and caring, though admittedly what God allots to humanity includes misery. Still, we will hear he is the 'giver' (*nātan*) of wisdom, knowledge and pleasure (2:26), the sense of the eternal (3:11), enjoyable work and its fruit (3:13), the very days of life (5:17), one's riches (5:18) and our spirit (12:7).

God is directly responsible for this tragic affliction of experiencing and honestly assessing and reacting to this fallen world. Within a couple of verses Qoheleth will describe part of this affliction as the inability to change the twisted realities of this world (1:15). It is not simply 'the way things are'. It is not just an unfortunate inevitability, but is a severe scourge given intentionally by God as part of the Edenic curse, causing sorrow and grief (1:18; cf. Farmer 1991: 155–156). The affliction is foreshadowed in part in 1:8, where frustration and disillusionment accompany seeing, hearing and speaking of the cyclicity and temporality of human activity. It is not merely an inconvenience, but a tragic affliction comparable to other woes for which Qoheleth uses the same phrase; that is, being utterly alone with no one to enjoy one's riches (4:8) or when all one's wealth is suddenly wrenched away (5:14). All that will follow in this speech which, in a shallow moment, one could dismiss as simply negative thinking or the disillusionment of an old cynic, is instead the only appropriate response to a world under the curse.

14–15. Having observed human activity under the sun, Qoheleth introduces his most thematic pronouncement: all is temporary and like the whim of the wind. This conclusion is one reason why exploring human activity is such an affliction. One would like to think that there is an eternal value to human activity as there is to God's (3:14). However, such impertinence, though unrealistic even in humanity's pre-Fall condition, ends in disappointment for those hoping for an eternal return from their post-Fall exertions of exhausting effort.

Seven times this phrase *rĕ'ût rûaḥ* surfaces in Eccl. 1:14, 2:1, 17, 26, 4:4, 16 and 6:9. Its equivalent, *ra'yôn rûaḥ*, occurs in 1:17. Translated by many as 'desiring' or 'chasing the wind', or some similar connotation of futility, some assess the noun sequence of const.–abs. to be the objective genitive. However, this syntax is as easily the subjective, possessive genitive, as some commentators render the phrase. *rĕ'ût*'s cognate, *ra'yôn* (will, desire), is used exactly in this way in 2:22 (desire of the heart). Here I translate *rĕ'ût rûaḥ* accordingly as 'the whim of the wind', connoting the unpredictable wind's desire, which changes incessantly. Whether there are seasonal winds that bring cold and rain from the north-west, or torrid, dry winds from the south-east, or the daily breezes from the west or east (Seow 1997: 108), or the swirls of unstable air, or the all too stable windless days, the wind's direction is whimlike, unpredictable and only temporarily one-directional. Qoheleth had mentioned this exact phenomenon just seven verses earlier (1:6).

To reinforce his pronouncement of the transitory nature of human effort, Qoheleth composes (or quotes) a proverb that echoes chiastically the previous metaphors of breath and wind. The wind's path is crooked and twists from one direction to the other: it just cannot be straight! Equally, the days or years *not* assigned to a life, event or activity cannot be counted: they do not exist! Trying to straighten the wind or add missing years does not help. Later, in 7:13, we find the same terminology about God's twisting things and the futility of any attempts to undo it: 'Consider the work of God, for who can straighten what he has twisted?' It is God's sovereign actions, not capricious chance, nor an impersonal determinism of the laws of nature, as Pinker (2008: 400–403) suggests, that provide irreversible challenges to life. The proverb, then, speaks to the futility of trying to change the fleeting nature of reality, not, as some interpret it, that

Qoheleth is frustrated in trying to make sense of an unintelligible world (e.g. Brown 2000: 30).

16–18. It was suggested over a century ago that the resumptive pronoun, for example *dibbartî 'ănî* (I said), is used by Qoheleth 'to mark the stages in the author's meditations' (S. R. Driver 1892: 202). Though no grammatical reason was given then, it has been argued that in Ecclesiastes' unique style this syntax distinguishes the simple past from other tenses covered by Hebrew's broad 'perfect' aspect (Fredericks 1988: 63–82). Here, for instance, Qoheleth is isolating his statement to a particular time in the past: 'I said to myself'. He is not expressing a general impression he has held for a long time. We will find this syntax especially frequent when he recounts his cathartic episode of utter despair in 2:11–26. Usually the pronoun is merely deemed redundant (e.g. Lys 1977: 143).

Qoheleth's reputed wisdom was obtained by his thorough examination of knowledge (mentioned five times 1:16–18 alone) as well as its opposites, madness and folly. It was not due to an innate intelligence quotient, nor even to a pure endowment by God, as in Solomon's case (1 Kgs 3:7–12). It was the result of Qoheleth's subjecting himself to the agony of his own relentless search for wisdom. Qoheleth confirms here the promise of God to Solomon (1 Kgs 3:12) and the annals of Solomon's deeds from his unprecedented wisdom (1 Kgs 10:23). Qoheleth's assessment does not specify that he was greater in wisdom than just those who were kings before him, but included any predecessor in Jerusalem, such as elders, wise men, prophets and so on. He was undoubtedly more conscious of his predecessors, whether kings or not, than subsequent students of the Bible are, so his statement is not to be applied simply to David, but to others such as Adoni-zedek (Josh. 10:3).

The full thematic pronouncement in 1:14 is split into half; 'whim of the wind' is applied here in 1:17, the other in the third parallel section, 2:1. Qoheleth leaves no doubt that he is aware that the momentary value of human activity referred to in 1:14 includes his own pursuits even if *they* are directed towards wisdom – 'this also (*gam*) is like the whim of the wind'. Proverbs presents wisdom as a path to happiness (2:10; 3:13–18) and Qoheleth will too, eventually (2:24–26). His proverb here in 1:18, however, sees it as a path to grief *as well*. Given his testimony of 'increasing (*yāsap*) wisdom' in 1:16, the assumption here is that the same phrasing and this proverb are original to Qoheleth.

Sorrow and grief are in store for those brave enough to glance, if only briefly, yet wisely, at the horrendous events of human history. The very question guiding Qoheleth's speech (Why labour so strenuously?) implies the anxiety of a stressed human race. The wearying, unsatisfying observation of reality (1:8) and futile attempts to add value to what is only temporary (1:14, 17) are just the beginning to Qoheleth's litany of disturbing truths discovered by one's increasing wisdom. We hear the words of Hab. 1:3 in the background:

Why do you make me look at sin
  and force me to observe troubles?
Destruction and violence are before my eyes –
  strife and contention appear.

Inadequate assessments of the history of biblical wisdom, including Ecclesiastes, see the writer's comments to be outside the realm of traditional wisdom. Characterizations of Proverbs as one-dimensional wisdom that disallows any negative consequences to the wise or innocent are only caricatures of traditional wisdom. This is comparable to the foolishness of a Bildad and Zophar. Proverbs's wisdom includes many complaints such as:

The poor's farm may produce abundant food,
  but injustice destroys it.

                                                              (13:23)

Furthermore, most proverbs have a negative side, which should challenge all of those reflecting on the Proverbs. The cries of the innocent victims of the proverbial wicked fool are heard by the sensitive readers of the Proverbs and Ecclesiastes alike. Consequently, insipid distinctions between Proverbs and Ecclesiastes and Job make only for theologies-of-convenience of the OT. Qoheleth's style is to expand on the moral polarity found within many proverbs, expressing both joy and despair, even in the same sentence (3:4, 8). They not only coexist, but are interdependent, mediated through wisdom. For Qoheleth, it is the morbid reality of foolishness and its consequences, and of death and its finality, that accentuates the joy and fullness of a life lived wisely (3:20–22; 7:2–4).

2:1–2. The first three verses of ch. 2 should be associated with the previous verses more than those following, since they have the same rhetorical structure. Also the simple past, or preterite phrasing, appears again indicating that this 'test' was a singular event rather than a continued mode of examination. This eliminates 2:1 as an introduction to 2:4–9 as part of a 'royal experiment'. Qoheleth's accomplishments described in those verses obviously spanned years, if not decades.

We will hear very positive recommendations of 'joy' (śimḥā) throughout Qoheleth's speech as an 'advantage' (2:10, 26; 3:12, 22; 5:18; 11:8–10). His synonymous recommendation is to 'experience the good' (rā'āh ṭôb; 2:24; 3:13, 22; 5:17; 6:6; see 'Introduction', pp. 38–39, on the theme of 'pleasure and joy'). But early here in 2:1–3, he includes even joy in the ephemeral realm. It 'also' (gam) is temporary.

There is a distinct demarcation between laughter and pleasure in Qoheleth's mind. As in Proverbs, shallow laughter is foolish, while pleasure is a blessing (7:3–6; 10:16–17, 19; cf. Prov. 10:23; 14:13; 26:19; 29:9). This distinction, however, is lost on many, who assume that the automatic answer to all of Qoheleth's rhetorical questions is in the negative. For instance, Crenshaw (1987: 77) recognizes the relative and limited value of true joy compared to laughter, but jumps to the conclusion that Qoheleth implies there is no ultimate value to joy. However, when listening to Ecclesiastes, one needs to be patient and let Qoheleth answer only when he is ready to grant his listeners any resolution to the tension his rhetorical questions create. 'What does it do (*'āśāh*)?' is the equivalent of 'What advantage (*yitrôn*) is there?' As first-time listeners in Qoheleth's assembly, we are still awaiting an answer to both!

3. This inclusio verse paired with 1:13 echoes the same goals and strategies with five common features: (1) to explore, (2) with wisdom, (3) the deeds, (4) of the sons of men, (5) 'under the skies' (*taḥat haššāmāyîm*). It should be noted that the phrase 'under the skies' is a rare alternative to 'under the sun' in Ecclesiastes, occurring only in these inclusios and 3:1. Qoheleth's designed use of the phrase is for this particular structural purpose. So 2:3 closes this subunit, which serves as the 'executive summary' for the next twenty-three verses.

What exactly Qoheleth did to his flesh with wine draws one to a most obscure point in Ecclesiastes. The fundamental biblical meaning for *māšak* is 'to pull' or 'lead'. This is nearly synonymous with *nāhag* (to lead), which is what his heart was doing as well. The parallel phrasing is assisted by the instrumental beth with both wine and wisdom. Wine tows the groggy body along, while wisdom leads the lightened heart to wisdom. This parallels the phrasing that follows – Qoheleth is grasping folly through wine until he finds the advantages he is looking for through wisdom. It also parallels the findings in the previous verse where frolicking laughter is subordinated to what is, so far, ambivalent pleasure:

2:2   Laughter vs. Joy
2:3a   Wine vs. Wisdom
2:3b   Folly vs. Good

One need only fast-forward to 7:2–4 and 10:16–19 to hear more of Qoheleth's opinion on these divergent scenarios.

There are two further indications of Qoheleth's pervasive awareness of temporary aspects of life. Only grasping folly 'suggests the fleeting nature of sensual pleasure' (Crenshaw 1987: 78). Plus the phrase 'few days' speaks bluntly to our momentary life (see also 5:17; 6:12). Even without the qualification of fewness, to measure life in mere 'days' effectively accents our brevity.

Explanation

Qoheleth dares to delve into the realities of this world, which most, whether atheist, theist, pantheist or Christian, purposely avoid in order to protect their comfort zones. Of course, it is not true for those who have the least time simply to contemplate the brunt of realism. Those who live sorely afflicted lives of abuse, hunger, flight from war and physical exposure have very little to consider but survival alone. The rest of us somehow anaesthetize ourselves from the overwhelming onslaught of the Fall's implications rather than feel the inevitable sorrow and grief that belong to those who follow the call to wisdom. We just do not want to know. We can elevate the relatively minor 'afflictions' we experience to a comparable level of those who are the worst afflicted people on the globe. Qoheleth's standard of wisdom, however, does not allow for this self-insulating naïveté. He is firmly within the camp of biblical revelation that portrays the world in its desperate, horrendous condition of folly and exploitation, and does not expect to be the only one to go on this journey – he says the quest is an affliction for all the sons of men. Yes, there is rest eventually, and comfort; but that should come from God, not man-made blankets beneath which to cower.

His general conclusion to his search is made in reference to the introductory question raised in 1:3 about the value of hard work; and by looking at the activities of all, whether king or labourer, he concludes that those activities and their outcomes are temporary – like the whim of the wind. This conclusion is neither reactionary nor revolutionary, since often the OT explicitly emphasizes the transitory nature of the person and actions. It is, of course, an implicit message of every biblical account that cannot speak to any condition or circumstance as more than ephemeral. The NT, then, cannot say anything different even if it does have a clearer view of eternal life than the OT. Under these skies and sun everything is temporary. Christ's own life among us was especially temporary, most of his apostles suffered early deaths, but their lives had critical value beyond the immediate results of their living days.

Christian realism also submits to the sometimes impenetrable synergy of God's and our sovereignty. There are situations we cannot change, though many we are obliged to change. Those non-negotiable circumstances God has twisted and turned, and those elements of life permanently missing, are his opaque design hiding the beauty of all that he does (3:11). Our prayers can consist of demands on God, presuming that his duty is to keep some 'promise' we have selectively imposed. But since our hope is in *him*, it cannot be in our errant expectations of him.

Yet again, one cannot expect to be wise unless one intentionally investigates the world and imposes on it the standards, priorities and solutions of a Christian view of the world that matches God's. Qoheleth amassed wisdom as a blessing and gift from God (2:26; cf. 1 Kgs 3:12), but it was supplemented with his specific intense search for wisdom as well as lifelong observations and responsible conclusions. Unfortunately, OT wisdom literature is marginalized in preaching and teaching, and primarily so because it *does* raise the complicated questions of human wisdom and how it interacts with that of God. Proverbs is simpler perhaps, but it too can open challenging discussions of God's care and troubling permission of disaster and trauma, just as Job and Ecclesiastes do. A pulpit shepherd, however, will not only study and thereby fathom the biblical principles of wisdom, but will, like Qoheleth, teach the people by presenting 'satisfying words ... words of truth' (12:10).

Rather than pleasure being an end in itself, Qoheleth uses it as a test to determine what is really valuable. Though he will show us the blessing of joy and pleasure throughout his speech, it will be evident that they are what are left after a process of elimination. That does not demean pleasure as a last resort; in fact, it justifies it as God's primary blessing from one's arduous labour. It is what we *want* to hear but would not presume to be true apart from God's provision. Others tell us, and hopefully we trust that success, popularity, power, sex, lavish food and money are nothing compared to the pleasure and peace with God and others enjoyed in moments of constructive work and sensible consumption.

Engaging our national and global culture will require the church to preach more than simply the means of salvation, which is unfortunately narrowly defined as justification. The fullest extent of sanctification is to throw ourselves into a search for wisdom that will make us first-responders to others' call for answers to life's threats and disappointments. This was the passion of Qoheleth, not only to separate and categorize folly and wisdom, not only to feel the burden of wisdom and its lucid awareness of the tragedies for humanity, but to console and direct the weary and confused towards God's sovereignty.

ECCLESIASTES 2:4-26

Translation

[4]I made the most of my activity. I built houses for myself. I planted vineyards for myself. [5]I made gardens and forests for myself, and I planted in them trees of every fruit. [6]I made for myself watering ponds to irrigate the sprouting groves. [7]I bought for myself male and female servants and owned their children they bore in my house. I also possessed more livestock, both herds and flocks, than all my predecessors in Jerusalem. [8]I collected for myself silver and gold, and unique treasures of kings and the provinces. I assembled for myself men and women singers and the delights of the sons of men, abundant breasts. [9]So, I became greater and increased beyond everyone before me in Jerusalem; especially my wisdom supported me.

[10]Now, I did not hold back anything my eyes desired, nor did I restrain my heart from any pleasure, for my heart enjoyed all my labour, and this was my reward from all of my labour.

[11]But, I turned to all of my hands' activities and my laborious labour, and really, it was temporary and like the whim of the wind, so there was no lasting advantage

under the sun. [12]So I turned to examine wisdom and madness and folly: Surely, what will the man succeeding the king do? That which has already been done! [13]But I saw that there is an advantage of wisdom over folly, as there is an advantage of the light over the darkness. [14]The wise, his eyes are in his head, but the fool walks in darkness. Yet I knew the same thing happens to both.

[15-16]Now I said to myself, 'As it happens to the fool, it happens to me too. So why was I too wise?' So I said to myself that this also was temporary since there is no age-long memory of the wise along with the fool because both will already have been forgotten in the coming days. How the wise dies along with the fool! [17]So I hated life because all the activities done under the sun grieved me, for everything is temporary and like the whim of the wind.

[18]I also hated all of my labour that I laboured under the sun, since I must leave it to my successor. [19]Who knows whether it will be a wise person or a fool, yet he will control all my estate for which I have been wise and laboured under the sun. This also is temporary. [20]So I allowed my heart to despair over all my labours that I laboured under the sun. [21]For there is one who labours successfully with wisdom and knowledge, but gives his reward to one who did not labour with him. This is also temporary and a great tragedy!

[22-23]Surely, what is there for a man in all his labour and heart's desire for which he labours under the sun, since grief and sorrow are his affliction all his days? Even at night his heart has no rest. Also this is temporary. [24-25]Nothing is better for one than to eat and drink and for his soul to enjoy the good in his labour. I saw that this was also from the hand of God, for who can eat and be glad without him? [26]For he gives wisdom and knowledge and joy to the one who is good before him. But to the sinner he gives the affliction to gather and heap up to give to the one who is good before God. This also is temporary and like the whim of the wind.

Notes on the text

5. 'forests': *pardēs* refers to Artaxerxes' own forest in Neh. 2:8, from which beams and lumber were commissioned to help rebuild Jerusalem. This Pers. loanword is found elsewhere only in Nehemiah and Song 4:13. This is an expected cosmopolitan word given Solomon's many political and commercial contacts with that part of the world. See Fredericks 1988: 242–245 for a fuller discussion.

6. *mēhem* ('from them', untranslated) does not agree in gender with its f. antecedent, *bĕrēkôt* (ponds). GKC 135o, after citing other biblical examples, attributes the weakening of gender agreements to the surfacing of the colloquial dialect. In all five cases in Ecclesiastes where one would expect the f. pronoun, Qoheleth uses the m. (2:6, 10; 10:9; 11:8; 12:1).

7. *hāyāh* (owned): since this sg. verb does not agree in number with its pl. subject *bĕnē*, a colloquialism is suspected; see 'Notes' at 1:10 concerning this grammatical feature.

'livestock': *miqnē* is apparently the const. state, but the abs. and const. vocalizations of III-Weak nouns is inconsistent in Ecclesiastes (GKC 93rr). If the word is in the abs., it stands as the most general word for 'livestock' (BDB 889a) including cows, sheep, horses, goats, asses and camels. *bāqār* and *zō'n* follow as subcategories: herds and flocks, large and small livestock.

8. 'abundant breasts': *šiddāh wĕšiddôt* is both an etymological and grammatical challenge. *šad* means 'breast' (here appropriately with a f. ending), and the syntax of a sg. form followed by its dual or pl. form is a pre-exilic Hebr. sequence denoting the appropriate multiple ('a woman or two', Judg. 5:30), or here in Ecclesiastes, an indefinite but impressive plurality. See Fredericks 1988: 138–139.

On 'province', see 'Notes' at 5:8.

11. 'I turned': here and in v. 12, Qoheleth uses the posterior pronoun to accentuate the single point in time when he concluded that there was no lasting advantage to his labour. See 'Notes' at 1:16. This construction is found frequently throughout the second chapter, indicating observations and conclusions made at a single past point in his life.

12. 'wisdom and madness and folly': this noun, waw–noun, waw–noun conjunctive clause is the early Hebr. syntax as opposed to late Biblical Hebrew's noun, noun, waw–noun (Kropat 1909: 62).

'What will the man [do]': one of the most perplexing syntaxes in Ecclesiastes, and no solution offered is convincing. It seems most natural to assume an elliptical syntax implying 'to do' in anticipation of the cognate accusative 'that which already has been done', consistent with Qoheleth's penchant for such constructions (see Smelik's 1998 article for a more thorough discussion of the alternatives).

14. 'the same thing happens to both': *miqreh* is a neutral term, nowhere in the OT amounting to the more philosophically loaded terms 'fate' or 'chance'. The word is an example of the early nature of Qoheleth's Hebr., found only here, in 3:19 and 9:2–3, and in 1 Sam. 6:9, 20:26 and Ruth 2:3. Machinist's 1995 article has the fullest analysis.

'both': *hakkôl* often refers to just the two things in view, in this case the polar opposites, again in 2:16, 3:19–20, 7:18 and 9:1–2.

15. 'I said', 'I was too wise': the resumptive or posterior first person sg. pronoun occurs twice here and once again in vv. 18 and 20, reflecting there was a single point in the *past* when Qoheleth drew these conclusions, not throughout his life.

'to me too': *gam-'ănî* either means emphatically 'even me', sounding arrogant, or, more humbly, 'also me'.

17. The use of *'al* as a synonym for *'al* for the directional preposition (to me) is mistakenly cited as a late grammatical trait by many, like Lauha (1978: 8, 205). Though this flexibility is also seen in Aram., Sperber lists numerous examples of the interchangeability of these two prepositions throughout Biblical Hebr. (1966: 288, 633–634; cf. BDB 757c).

18. 'my labour': we have seen both the nominal and verbal derivatives of the root '*āmal* as early as 1:3. There is an advanced, metonymous meaning to the nominal lexeme which denotes the resulting fruit of that labour, surfacing in 2:22, 3:13 and 9:9 as well (Seow 1997: 136).

'my successor (after me)': seven times attention is given to reality 'after' a person's brief life ends, emphasizing the ephemeral nature of human life: 2:12, 18; 3:22; 6:12; 7:14; 9:3; 10:14.

19. 'will control': *šālaṭ* is often cited as evidence of the lateness of Ecclesiastes' language (Whitley 1978: 27; Wagner 1966: 113–114). Again, however, this is unconvincing, since the root occurs as early as Gen. 42:6, and is widely attested in Akk., Arab. and perhaps Ug. (Gibson 1978: 158b), in addition to Hebr. and Aram. (Fredericks 1988: 239–240).

21. The anticipatory pronominal suffix found here (he gives it [i.e.] his reward), in 4:10 (woe to him [i.e.] the one) and in 4:12 (he overpowers him [i.e.] the one) is considered by some as colloquial (Segal 1980: 85; G. R. Driver 1970: 236), adding to the unique vernacular quality of the grammar and vocabulary of Qoheleth's speech.

'great tragedy' (*rā'āh rabbāh*): more alliteration again, along with the usually alliterated *hebel*. Qoheleth uses *rā'āh* in Ecclesiastes as 'evil or wicked' (7:15; 8:11; 10:5), but more often as some grievous tragedy in general (1:13; 2:17, 21; 5:13, 16; 6:1; 7:14; 8:6; 9:12; 11:2, 10; 12:1).

'successfully': or 'advantageously'. *kišrôn* is synonymous with *yitrôn*, as most would attest; for example, Hertzberg 1963: 131; Lauha 1978: 110.

22. 'is': *hōweh* as a participial cognate to the usual consonantal root *hāyāh* is cited by some as an indicator of a later language. But as Barton (1908: 95) and Gordis (1968: 224) note, this morphology of the root is used as early as the ancient poetry of Gen. 27:29; it is also found in Isa. 16:4.

'his heart's desires': *ra'yôn libbô* is the same subjective, possessive genitive construction used by its cognate *rĕ'ût* in conjunction with *rûaḥ* in 1:14, 17. It is synonymous with the heart's desires mentioned in 2:10, where 'desire' and 'pleasure' are used.

24. 'Nothing is better than': possibly due to haplography, a comparative prepositional beth has been omitted in the MT, inconsistent with the other 'better than' statements (3:12, 22; 8:15) and with the Syr, Tg, Vg and some LXX MSS.

'his soul': *nepeš* is a component of the 'heart' (*lēb*) in Ecclesiastes. Whereas the latter denotes the entire inner being, *nepeš* identifies nothing more than the desires or drives (4:8; 6:2–3, 7, 9; 7:28 [to search]).

'I saw': leaving his focused analytical and emotional account of his inquiry behind, this is Qoheleth's last 'aorist' form until 3:16.

25. 'be glad': *ḥûš* has various suggested meanings, since the Hebr. denotation 'hasten' hardly fits the context (BDB 301b). It is probably from an Akk. root meaning 'rejoice', as some have argued (Ginsberg 1946: 26; Dahood 1958: 307–308; Lauha 1978: 58). Standard discussions of the term are Ellermeier 1963a: 197–217 and de Waard 1979: 509–529.

'without him': *ḥûṣ min* as a preposition is unique to Ecclesiastes in Biblical Hebr. Its closest parallel is Aram. (S. R. Driver 1913: 474; Wagner 1966: 37).

mimmennû should be read here with the LXX and certain Hebr. MSS. The context suggests strongly that God is the object of the prepositional phrase. Yod and waw are written only slightly differently, making a scribal error probable here. Raising these grammatical and lexical uncertainties to the level of intentional literary 'ambiguities' is gratuitous; for example, Byargeon 1998: 367–372.

Form and structure

We saw within the first proleptic emphasis of 1:12 – 2:3 Qoheleth's purpose to investigate all activity by distinguishing wisdom from 'madness and folly': 1:13, 16–17; 2:3. So in 2:4–14 he begins an investigation recounting two aspects of his own achievements. First, in 2:4–9 he reports his accomplishments and the pleasure he received from his labours. Contrary to many who see this section as an experiment in pure pleasure, the content clearly emphasizes diligent work that *earned* pleasure. Secondly, in 2:10–14 he analyses these wise achievements in the light of their temporality. His elation voiced in 2:10 is balanced by the realism of 2:11–14, which in turn will deteriorate into his momentary funk of 2:15–23. In a second proleptic emphasis in 1:13, 18, he shares his agony experienced in the process. Using the same words, 'grief' and 'sorrow' (1:18), Qoheleth elaborates on this agony in 2:15–23, expressing angry hatred for life and its labours because of their temporality caused by various frustrating limitations (2:23). In the third prolepsis, 2:1–2, he questions and sets out to determine whether there is anything good that comes from one's labours all one's days. It is precisely this question Qoheleth asks in 2:22–23, and then answers immediately in the affirmative in 2:24–26.

There is a lengthening of the syntactical units as 2:4–8 develops. Though not purely so, the subject matter of magnifying and increasing wise accomplishments is appropriately expressed through phrases that gradually build and increase in length (see the table below).

Translation	Hebrew Syllables	Acquisitions: Direct Objects
I maximized my activity, 4a	6	1
I built houses for myself, 4b	6	1
I planted vineyards for myself, 4c	7	1
I made gardens and forests for myself, 5a	10	2
I planted trees of every fruit in them, 5b	10	1

Translation	Hebrew Syllables	Acquisitions: Direct Objects
I made for myself watering ponds to irrigate the sprouting groves, 6	21	1
I bought for myself male and female servants and their children they bore in my house, 7a	17	3
I also possessed more livestock, both herds and flocks, than all my predecessors in Jerusalem, 7b	24	3
I collected for myself silver and gold, and unique treasures of kings and the provinces, 8a	21	3
I assembled for myself men and women singers and the delights of the sons of men, ample breasts, 8b	24	3

There does appear to be a function of the recurrent *hebel* theme at the end of small units like 2:18–19, 2:20–21, 2:22–23 and 2:24–26. Their role, however, is not quite as distinctive as some make them (Wright 1980: 50; Murphy 1992: 21) and appear to be more suggestive of emotional outbursts than syllogistic conclusions.

There is also a linguistic key to the theme of this section in that no fewer than twenty-five times Qoheleth uses forms of *'āmāl* (labour) and *'āśāh* (do) to link his observations and conclusions to the thematic question 'What is the advantage to one's labours?'

Comment

4–9. Qoheleth maximized, literally, his *activities*, not his pleasures. Though he repeatedly indicates his work was for himself (*lî*), accentuating who benefits, he does not imply that pleasure was the primary goal. Even in 2:10, where he emphasizes his joy, we will hear it is to be found in his labours, not in mirth. In 1 Kgs 9:19, Solomon is described as one who builds extensively according to his 'desire' (*ḥāšaq*), the same word for his incentive to build the temple (1 Kgs 9:1). There the description of Solomon is one with passionate motivation. It is unsurprising, then, that here in Ecclesiastes, consecutive verses describe Qoheleth's interest in the benefits of joy (2:3), followed immediately by his highly motivated building projects (2:4) that refer to the fuller description in 1 Kgs 9.

In some translations, these 'building projects' may sound like quaint efforts to ease one's life. In reality, however, they are understated, somewhat generic descriptions of vast building projects that occupied much of Qoheleth's career. 'House', though usually referring to a home or family, can be a generic term for many types of buildings. This single word in 2:4 is a synecdoche for Solomon's enormous building projects, including many entire cities containing residential, commercial and military properties; for example, Tadmor, cities in the Hamath region, Gezer, Beth-horon, Baalath (2 Chr. 8:1–6; 1 Kgs 9:15–19). Likewise, the agricultural prowess Qoheleth speaks of in 2:4–6 is not primarily recreational. Rather, he designed and managed huge wine, fruit and timber industries (1 Chr. 27:26–28). The 'parks' or forests of kings were not aesthetic escapes; they were large productive plots used for lumber, whose seedlings required constant irrigation (Neh. 2:8)! These are the 'pools', or better 'ponds', being discussed, comparable to the Siloam canal.

His ordered gardens may have been relaxing, but even then they were a visual metaphor in the ancient world for the control a king had over his entire kingdom (Brown 2000: 32). Furthermore, with terminology reminiscent of the Garden of Eden, Qoheleth describes his achievements as those of one who took seriously God's primary commission of earth's management (Gen. 1:26–28). As Verheij notes (1991: 114), common words to both the Eden account and Ecclesiastes 2:4–6 include 'plant' (*nāṭaʿ*), 'garden' (*gan*), 'trees of all fruits' (*ʿēṣ kol-perî*), 'to water' (*šāqāh*), 'to sprout' (*ṣāmaḥ*), 'to do or make' (*ʿāśāh*). Just as the Edenic passage is the first manifestation of human sovereignty over an earthly domain, Solomon's activities are a description of an aggressive management of an economic and political enterprise. Another Solomonic tradition, 1 Kgs 4:33, echoes the Genesis account of humanity's primary commission where, in addition to being extolled specifically for his botanical knowledge, it is said, 'he spoke of trees, of cattle, of fowl, of creepers and fish', all in Hebr. terminology met in Gen. 1:26, 29. Furthermore, Eden, as a garden, was not a place for idle pleasure; it was a place of work and responsibility, even before the Fall. Of course, gardens are a setting for his favourite song, Song of Songs, where his vineyards are also mentioned prominently (Song 1:14; 8:11).

Qoheleth bought servants who, of course, were fruitful and multiplied, bearing him servants-from-birth (Exod. 21:2–11). There were of course those too who were conquered and became additional servants or slaves (1 Kgs 9:20–22). He inherited his father's livestock, which included cattle, camels, asses, sheep and goats (1 Chr. 27:29–31), and his imported horses numbered in the thousands (2 Chr. 9:25–27; 1 Kgs 4:22–23). Gold and silver, from tribute and commercial trade, came into Israel by the ton (1 Kgs 10:14–21; 2 Chr. 9:27). These treasures were not always in bullion and ingots – Qoheleth accumulated unique treasures of kings and 'the provinces'. These included apes, peacocks, ivory, fabric, jewels, spices, weapons and even more horses (1 Kgs 10:22–25)! These provinces were possibly the counties of the Israelite state described in 1 Kgs 4:7–19. However, coupled with and following after 'kings', these areas probably refer to Israel's non-chartered possessions, outside the tribal territories. See A. R. Millard (1981) for a discussion of Solomon's accumulated wealth, especially gold.

'Delights' (*taʿănûgôt*) refers in the OT to various types of pleasures: Prov. 19:10, luxury; Song 7:6, physical beauty; Mic. 1:16, children; 2:9, houses. Its verbal root has objects including God, material blessings, maternal breasts (Provan 2001: 72). What exactly Qoheleth identifies as the 'delights of the sons of men' is difficult to determine. There are three biblical passages where 'delight' and 'breasts' appear together in the same context: here in Ecclesiastes, in another Solomonic book, Song 7:6 and in Isa. 66:11 (verb). Though there is nothing inherently sexual in the term *ta'ănûg*, the consonantal similarity here in Ecclesiastes to 'breast [and] breasts' (*šad*) in the immediate vicinity of *ta'ănûg*, makes my translation etymologically and grammatically probable, thus referring to Solomon's extensive harem (1 Kgs 11:3). *šad* is ironically a m. noun elsewhere, but here in Ecclesiastes it is f. On the other hand, if Qoheleth uses 'sons of men' generically for 'humanity', this sexual rendering would be less convincing. When Qoheleth wanted to speak of the male gender, he was likely to use *'îš*, the usual word for 'man' (e.g. in 7:28).

Qoheleth revives here the comparison in the first prolepsis (1:16) between his predecessors' achievements and his own, using *gādal* and *yāsap* in concert. 'I became greater and increased...' Through all of his efforts and achievements, it was 'especially' (*'ap*) Qoheleth's wisdom that stood by him, supporting him in some general way that he does not explain in detail here (though we do know from the rest of this speech and the other Solomonic traditions). It was only six verses earlier that he described having to drag his body along while his mind was guided by wisdom. However, the clear pre-eminence of wisdom, highlighted by this emphatic particle, will be picked up within the next few verses (2:12–14).

10–11. This, then, is an affirmative answer to the rhetorical question of 2:3, 'Pleasure – what does this accomplish?' Qoheleth's experience leads him to conclude, 'my heart enjoyed all my labour since this was my reward from all of my labour'. *ḥeleq* refers to a restricted and assigned share or portion, which many render as 'reward', since the word has an overall positive connotation in 2:21, 3:22, 5:18–19, 9:9 and 11:2. Later, he confirms this conclusion twice using the same *śimḥāh*, *ḥeleq* and *'āmēl* terminology and phrasing: 'There is nothing better for a man than to enjoy (*śimḥāh*) his labour (*'āmēl*), for that is his reward (*ḥeleq*)' (3:22); 'accept his reward (*ḥeleq*) and enjoy (*śimḥāh*) his labour (*'āmēl*)' (5:19). In other places, this reward of enjoying one's labour is not spoken of as a *ḥeleq* but more definitively as a gift from God: 2:24–25; 3:13.

But do Qoheleth's wise accomplishments provide the answer to the overarching question in Ecclesiastes: 'Is there any advantage to all of this hard work?' If there is an affirmative answer to 2:3 and pleasure, is it also an answer to 1:3 regarding any advantages to labour? Receiving one's reward, or even one's lot, cannot be seen logically as anything but an advantage over not receiving one. But Qoheleth in the very next verse says there is *no* advantage. But then, again, only two verses later he affirms emphatically there *is* an advantage! Here is where virtually all commentators believe he is either just plainly contradicting himself in 2:10–14, or they resort to qualifying what he means by 'no *yitrôn*'. For instance, assuming his *reward* to be real, does not mean he concludes there is any *lasting* advantage (Longman 1998: 94; Brown 2000: 34). In the light of Qoheleth's affirming there was a reward to his labours (2:10), and that there is an advantage to wise actions over folly (2:13–14), we conclude that Qoheleth speaks only of passing advantages, since all human experience, including joy and God's blessings, are only temporary – a conclusion he reaches in 2:26 as well. Farmer (1991: 153, 157) explains this accurately:

> Qohelet will argue that none of the good things we work so hard to acquire are permanent or enduring. This is not to say that work or things which are gained through work are without value. They are like a breath, which is precious to the one who breathes it. But also like a breath, they cannot be grasped and kept. . . . The value hard work has is the pleasure one feels in doing it (v.10), but no amount of work can produce material benefits that can be grasped and permanently gained 'under the sun'.

12–14. Qoheleth set out to understand wisdom, madness and folly back in the introductory sections in 1:17 and 2:2–3. Now, since he comes to the disappointing conclusion that his wise accomplishments are only temporary, he returns to the subject to see if there is any real advantage to wisdom by again comparing it to folly and madness. More specifically, he asks what the person who comes after him can do differently, since he himself has already done it all. In asking this question he universalizes his own experience – and that of everyone else. It is not Qoheleth's achievements alone that are temporary, for all the works of humanity will fall into eventual ruin and decay. In 1:9–11, Qoheleth emphasized that there is nothing new to be done under the sun (cf. 6:10), and, besides, all is forgotten anyway. Here he applies those principles in an introductory way, while his attention 'turns' (*pānāh*) from his predecessors (1:16; 2:7, 9) to his successors (2:18–21).

Though wisdom's advantages are only temporary, still, for Qoheleth, they are real. The advantages to wisdom have been the implicit and explicit assumption to this point, though their temporariness has now proven disenchanting. Most commentators rush to admit the 'relative' worth of wisdom, yet Qoheleth speaks unequivocally about its *absolute* value over folly; for example, Brown 2000: 34; Hubbard 1991: 85. Rather than wisdom simply being relatively better than folly, Qoheleth asserts their differences are like night and day. Later, in 10:2, he says they are as opposite as right and left. Though it has taken well into the second chapter for us finally to hear clearly what we expected to hear at the outset, it will be a major theme throughout the rest of the speech as well; for example, the advantage to knowledge is that wisdom gives life to its possessors (7:12); the advantage of wisdom is success (10:10).

See the 'Introduction' for a list of wisdom's advantages and success as seen by Qoheleth.

He unsurprisingly then aligns himself with standard proverbial wisdom, where the traditional pre-eminence of wisdom is not only in concept but in the structure of the statements as well: wisdom is spoken of first, then folly is contrasted (2:13–14):

> But I saw that there is an advantage for wisdom over folly as
> there is an advantage of the light over the darkness.
>
> (Eccl. 2:13; cf. John 12:35)

> The way of the righteous is like the light of the dawn . . .
> The way of the wicked is like the darkness . . .
>
> (Prov. 4:18–19)

> The wise, his eyes are in his head,
> but the fool walks in darkness.
>
> (Eccl. 2:14)

> The sensible see evil . . . the simple just continue and are
> punished.
>
> (Prov. 22:3)

> Walking with the wise will make one wise,
> but the friend of fools will be destroyed.
>
> (Prov. 13:20)

Gordis theorizes that since Qoheleth does contain such traditional wisdom throughout, he must be merely quoting the traditions in order to dispute them (1968: 103–108). This is based on the faulty assumption that if Qoheleth believes everything is futile, somehow his orthodox statements must be neutralized. This theory, however, is unnecessary if Qoheleth is saying that everything is temporary. Besides, there are no explicit or syntactical indicators that these statements should be in any way discounted. In fact, it is the conventional truth within these verses that serves to intensify the disappointments to follow; that is, the advantages were so rewarding that their transience is emotionally devastating.

Does Qoheleth have an answer to his programmatic question 'What is the advantage in all one's laborious labour under the sun?' Yes, it appears he does: the advantage to one's labours is that they provide the joy that comes from wise achievements. However, the joy and the achievements are only temporary. He is about to show how short that joy can be as he spurts a disgruntled spirit without restraint. Yet again, even that disenchantment gives way to an appreciative spirit in 2:24–26! Everything is temporary.

15–17. There is the common assumption that Qoheleth is referring in vv. 14–16 to death as the common reality to 'both' (*kōl*) the wise and the fool. This is very possible given his similar expression in 3:19, but there he names explicitly the commonality to be death. For him, however, what is worse than death is being *forgotten*, the exact inevitability he most immediately and literally specifies in 2:16. He does not speak of death until the end of that verse, and not again until 3:2. The same logic and suspended identity of the *miqreh* (happening) is used in 9:2–5, where the same result occurs to the wise and to fools; that is, since they both die – they are forgotten. There the most immediate and explicit identity appears to be inevitable death, but the fact of death is possibly only the means to the worst of common happenings: not being 'remembered'. So I render the *hebel* clause in v. 15 as a synonymous phrase introducing one's short-lived legacy, 'not … age-long'.

Nevertheless, the desperation of Qoheleth, expressed so strongly in v. 17, is apparently for three distinct reasons: being forgotten, death and the compromising, if not destruction, of the fruit of his wisdom (18–21). But rather than three separate tragedies, they are essentially all one. First, 'forgotten' means more than merely not being recollected; it means to be intentionally marginalized out of existence. Relationally speaking, 'remember' in the OT often means much more than merely 'bring to mind'; rather, it refers to *intentionally* dealing with the object with a concentrated sense of responsibility (Pss 63:6; 119:55; Lam. 3:19–20). It is the same for being forgotten, since it often means to be consciously neglected. Fortunately, the deceased wicked are forgotten and despised (8:10); but unfortunately, Joseph was 'forgotten' by the official even while alive (Gen. 40:23; also Judg. 3:7; Ps. 10:12)!

If the common result referred to here in 2:14 is one's legacy being at least neglected, if not obscured by design, then the apparent second reason for the temporariness of his wisdom's fruits, the post-mortem disrespect for that legacy, is simultaneously identified. If a fool destroys his legacy, there will be no memory. Thus one can be remembered in history as kings and some wise persons are, but none of their wise deeds may ever come to light once their successor suppresses them or neglects to maintain their 'memory'. Though we remember persons like Solomon and innumerable others in a purely cognizant way, it is impossible to respect adequately their every work of commendable accomplishment (much less if the person is poor and despised; 9:15). Qoheleth thereby expands on his parallel to 1:9–11 about innovations and one's eventual obscurity by giving the reasons for his generalizations voiced there.

Consequently, it is the legacy itself that is judged to be 'temporary' (*hebel*) in 2:15. That it is 'indeed temporary' or 'also temporary' is hard to determine, since *gam* and its context allows both. I prefer 'also', since Qoheleth seems to want to enumerate fleeting aspects of life rather than merely to emphasize them.

The fact that all die 'together' (taking '*im* as 'with') then becomes less the main horror, and more simply the means to the larger tragedy of contemptuous obscurity; after all, Qoheleth in the next phrase hates life itself! So death itself, ironically, can be overemphasized here, since not only do all die (3:2, 19–22; 6:6; 8:8; 9:3), but there are ambivalences about death in 3:2 and 7:1: it can actually be the *preferred* state! For Qoheleth, there are other things worse than death in addition to being forgotten; for instance, oppression (4:1–3) and an ensnaring woman (7:26). See the discussion of death in the 'Introduction'.

There is the view that, because of the common result to fools as well as the wise, 'traditional' OT wisdom has been discounted if not contradicted by Qoheleth; for example, Crenshaw 1987: 84. However, there is no claim in the wisdom literature that one's legacy will be *eternal* ('*ōlam*), or even long-lasting, though it might be blessed to some extent (Prov. 10:7). In fact, the wisdom literature is silent on the subject. In this sense, Qoheleth is consistent with the established wisdom that Solomon was foundational in developing. Ps. 49:10–12 agrees:

> One sees that the wise die just like the fool and the brute perish,
> leaving their wealth behind them....
> they may call their estates by their own name,
>   but one's legacy does not live on.

Furthermore, it is critical to understanding Qoheleth's despair that he is *asking* why he was 'excessively' (*yōtēr*) wise. It is an overstatement to attribute his disenchantment to be about wisdom per se, *since* it is its excessive amount that brings him to such despair. He has already spoken of the virtues of wisdom with superlative language. That he is about to explain his deep disappointment about great wisdom is expected, since he has already introduced his great sorrow and grief, which back in 1:18 come from increased wisdom and ample knowledge. Too much wisdom and righteousness brings too much sorrow. Later, in 7:16, Qoheleth will repeat his phrasing about his bitter experience, 'Do not be excessively wise; why debilitate yourself?'

V. 17, then, is his emotional conclusion to his logical premises of 2:15–16.

Understandably, Qoheleth hates life for its accompanying grief and brevity. But why are his feelings so strong? The first reason is psychological: as in all frustrations or disappointments, his expectations are momentarily unrealistic – as if any true benefit from wisdom would have an *eternal* duration or any truly *permanent* fruit. The second reason is theological: it would hardly have been a divine curse if he were passive about the Fall, or loved its impact. That Qoheleth hates life, and the gruelling nature of work on a cursed earth, was nothing less than the very design of God's judgment in the first place. God himself would have failed if Qoheleth's reaction to the realities of a temporary and tragic life was less than extreme hatred! Job too hated life – for a while at least (Job 3:3–20; 10:8–19; 14:1–2). It is as if one thought traditional wisdom were insipid in its conclusions when contrasting Qoheleth's realistic conclusions about life. Besides, Qoheleth's world view is balanced, since within just a few verses his brief catharsis is equally matched by divine consolations in 2:24–26.

The temporary and uncharacteristic nature of this outburst is noted by commentators such as Ogden 1987: 48 and Fox 1999: 187. That this is momentary is indicated in v. 20 by Qoheleth's use of the pi., of *yā'ēš*, which indicates that he *allowed* his heart to descend to these depths, letting loose his emotions (Eaton 1983: 71; see GKC 52g for this permissive sense of the pi.). This implies he *knew* better and that his wisdom would guide him eventually again, as it did in 2:3, 9. Of course, we do see this soon in 2:24–26.

18–21. He not only hates life but also the labours and fruit associated with life, since he will lose them to some successor. And this ultimate loss is not all that torments Qoheleth. More anguishing still is the question of to *whom* his estate will be left. It may be a fool, but even if it were someone wise to some extent (2:12), he might not have invested anything personally in Qoheleth's acquisition. The latter situation is more than irksome, since he highlights the importance of working partnerships over solitariness in 4:8–12. He implies here in 2:19 that if his estate could be left to someone with whom he partnered to build it, that would be acceptable. When one has little invested personally, one tends to take foolish risks. The poet of Ps. 39:6, like Qoheleth, speaks simultaneously of the brevity of life and possessions, and the anonymity of the succeeding possessor of one's estate: 'Surely, they are in turmoil temporarily (*hebel*); one heaps up, but does not know who will gather.'

Qoheleth describes in v. 19 what can actually happen, since it will happen to him personally. 'There is one', begins an observation that is not universal, only occurring often, at most. That it is not too often, however, is sure given the extraordinarily responsible way in which these people carry on their business: they work wisely, with knowledge, and are successful! Herein we have an excellent definition of wisdom in this short phrase – wisdom is the successful use of knowledge! Qoheleth says similarly in 10:10, 'The advantage of wisdom is success.' Nonetheless, his reward is given to another. The person may not necessarily be a royal or familial successor; the possibilities are left open simply for someone, somehow (cf. 5:14; 6:2). Giving one's reward to another is found in 2:26 in the moral reverse, from the fool to the wise. There it is divine justice; here it is a great moral tragedy. Here lies the coherent meaning of *hebel* as 'temporary', rather than 'meaningless' or 'vanity'; it is hardly 'meaningless' if there is this much hardship and heartache.

Whether one identifies Qoheleth with Solomon historically, or as a fictional device, it is natural to muse whether Solomon's son Rehoboam is intimated in this passage, the one who miserably – within a short time –

managed to split the glorious kingdom into two warring nations (1 Kgs 11:41 – 12:24). If a fictional device, then, since 'Solomon' is describing his personal experience and feelings, it would be impossible for any ghost-writer to be oblivious to this glaring historical tragedy. If truly Solomonic, then depending on Qoheleth's age, he may see the potential problems with Rehoboam.

22–23. The climax of Qoheleth's investigation, which he began in 1:12, is now reached. The third subject, introduced in 2:1–2 is picked up here in his resolution to the trials of 2:14–21. Here, wholly encapsulated in one intellectually and emotionally weary question, he reviews for us his entire speech so far. It is the identical question we heard initially in 1:3, which was based on the same premise of the temporality of everything human of 1:2, only now it is laden with the same 'afflicting' (*'inyān*) 'grief' (*mak'ōb*) and 'sorrow' (*ka'as*) to which Qoheleth introduced us and brought us to share with him vicariously (1:13, 18; 2:17–18). Finally, he has shown us why he made such drastic, unsettling statements at the beginning of his speech. Harking back to the question of toiling labours (1:3), to the panting sun (1:5), to the wearying nature of everything (1:8), to the affliction of wisdom (1:13), to the grief and sorrow of knowledge (1:18), to the madness of laughter (2:2), to dragging the body (2:3), to the hatred of life and work (2:17–18), to the heart's despair (2:20), one has reason to ask whether there are any advantages in life.

These two verses form only one question, v. 23 giving three human conditions as further reasons for asking the first part of the question in v. 22: affliction, restlessness and transitoriness. The focus narrows to the single concern of the shalom of the 'heart' (*lēb*; vv. 22–23) or 'soul' (*nepeš*; v. 24). Since the heart's desires drive one's labours (2:10, 22), even to the point of restlessness at night (v. 23), what should it take to satisfy them so that one sees an advantage from laborious efforts? This is a question Qoheleth has already answered positively in 2:10, and will do again in vv. 24–26, and repeatedly throughout his speech. Consequently, it is not a rhetorical question presuming a negative answer, contrary to those commentators who are forced to such a conclusion because of their mis-interpretation of the word *hebel*. For them, if everything is meaningless, vain or absurd, there can be no positive answer to Qoheleth's thematic question; for example, Murphy 1992: 26; Longman 1998: 105. On the other hand, even though everything is temporary, there is still significant meaning in the moments.

What is it that Qoheleth considers temporary in v. 23? Is it that whatever answer there is to his question, it too will be only temporary? Or is it, as Farmer explains (1991: 158), the very state of despair to which Qoheleth has given himself is fleeting because the consolations that follow are more than adequate?

24–26. For all of Qoheleth's emotion, he does not ever deny the underlying facts he recounts in vv. 15–23. However, now he no longer 'allows himself to despair' but finds immediate consolation in God's grace. Some see as lackluster his pronouncement that 'Nothing is better'; for example, Crenshaw 1987: 88; Longman 1998: 107. However, it is actually Qoheleth's form of the superlative – it does not get any better than this! Rather than saying it is 'good', Qoheleth says it is 'the best', thereby giving in these three verses the definitive answer to his programmatic question 'What advantage is there to one in all his laborious labour under the sun?' There are various ways Qoheleth answers this positively. The whole *tôb* complex contributes through phrases such as *'ēn tôb min* (2:24; 3:12, 22; 8:15). Also *rā'āh tôb* ('to see [as] good', or 'enjoy'; 2:1; 3:13; 6:6). Schoors (1998b: 33) explains, 'In connection with Qohelet's quest for abiding profit, the word [*tôb*] has the connotation of "beneficial, efficacious, of lasting value . . . "' For a survey of the interpretations of *tôb*, see Ingram 2006: 169–249. Furthermore, by using the very word in question, 'advantage' (*yitrôn*), we have seen Qoheleth's preference for the value of wisdom (2:13–14; 7:12; 10:10).

For the first of several times, Qoheleth recommends the basic, simple pleasures of life as one's advantage in toil. He counsels the inquisitive who dare to ask the difficult questions, the ones who think long and deeply about this fallen world and the implications of the curse of the earth and humanity; these he counsels to enjoy the simple gifts available to most, regardless of their estate. Eating, drinking and enjoying the very labour that drives one to question life's advantages are found explicitly *to be* the 'advantage' here and in 3:12–13, 22, 5:17–18, 8:15 and 9:7. Hubbard provides a concise parallel analysis of these synonymous passages, concluding that 'in various forms this conclusion is the heart of the book, the key to its purpose and positive message' (1991: 92–93). In similar passages, the pleasures of life are commended as well (9:8–10; 10:17; 11:7, 9–10). Admittedly, there is a stark difference between the exotic advantages in 2:4–10 and these simple benefits of life (cf. Phil. 4:11–13). Yet regardless of the material value, 'there is nothing better' implies that the benefits at the end of the day, or at the end of one's life, are equal: equally temporary but equally satisfying.

> How blessed are all those who fear the LORD,
>   who walk in his ways.
> In eating of the fruit of your hands,
>   you will be happy, and it will be well with you.
>   (Ps. 128:1–2)

By recommending 'eating and drinking', Qoheleth is not endorsing vain indulgence but a wholesome enjoyment of the 'good life', in OT phraseology (Smend 1977). Actually, he strongly criticizes revelry in 2:3, 7:2–4 and 10:16, thereby aligning himself with Isaiah and Paul who alike scorn the indulgent cynicism of simply 'eating meat and drinking wine, for tomorrow we die' (Isa. 22:13; 1 Cor. 15:32). Common grace allows a Sophocles to conclude, 'There is no happiness where there is no wisdom' (Antigone: Exodos).

That these are normative encouragements is also clear because in addition to the gifts of eating, drinking and getting enjoyment in one's labour, are God's further blessings of wisdom, knowledge and the acquisition of others' assets. V. 25 asks who can eat and enjoy life without God? (Cf. Ps. 107:8–9; Matt. 6:33; 1 Cor. 4:7; 10:30–31; 1 Tim. 4:4–5.) This question is a pivot within these three verses, looking at the previous verse and turning to the subsequent verse for the same answer. God gives the food and joy in v. 24, and the joy again in v. 26. Thus the consecutive *kî* statements. That wisdom is a divine gift was Solomon's own experience (1 Kgs 3:9–12), as well as that of the craftsmen Bezalel and Oholiab (Exod. 31:1–6). It is a gift of the Spirit to certain persons especially (1 Cor. 12:8) but also to anyone who genuinely requests it (Jas 1:5).

Furthermore, in his justice God takes from the sinning fool and gives to those he is pleased with. This is an obvious principle consistent with traditional wisdom writings and biblical theology as a whole, and consequently presents problems to commentators who cannot absorb it into their understanding of Qoheleth's speech. For instance:

> the sinner's estate passes to the godly.
>
> > (Prov. 13:22b)

> The one increasing wealth from usury or excess interest
> > gathers it for one who cares for the poor.
> >
> > > (Prov. 28:8)

> Though one heaps money as if it were dust and clothing like
> > mud,
> > the righteous will wear the clothes and the innocent will
> > > divide the money.
> > >
> > > > (Job 27:16–17)

Christ uses the same principle in his parable of the servants and how they invested their money, the poorest performers losing their assets to the better (Matt. 24:45–47; 25:26–29; Luke 19:11–27). In the long run, the meek will inherit the earth from the oppressors, who were only enjoying it by lease (Matt. 5:5). We have in these verses, then, an orthodox position on the sovereignty, justice and shepherding care of God who provides for those who are 'good in his sight'.

Apart from the numerous moral passages that speak positively of wisdom and diligence specifically, Qoheleth uses the typical terminology for the 'sinner', the 'righteous', for those who 'fear God' and those who do not. He also affirms the imminent and eventual judgments of God. So his moral world and its consequences are the same as that of the OT and NT. Who is 'good before God' in this passage, then, is not hard to ascertain. In 3:12, Qoheleth says that in addition to joy, there is nothing better than to 'do good (*'āśāh ṭôb*) as long as they live'. This exact Hebr. phrase for righteousness appears in Pss 14:1 and 34:14, and is repeated by Qoheleth in 7:20 when he contrasts moral conduct (see below at 3:12 for a fuller discussion). Later, in 5:1, the opposite phrase, 'do evil (*'āśāh rā'*)', is used as a warning (also 8:11), and to fear God is preferred (5:7; also 7:18; 8:12–13). The one who is 'good before God', the same description of the righteous one of 2:26, is contrasted with the 'sinner (*ḥôṭē'*)' who succumbs to the adulterer in 7:26. The 'sinner', then, is mentioned here in 2:26 and is sighted in 5:5, 7:20 and 9:18 as well. Finally, though the same thing happens to them all, it is perfectly clear in 9:2 that Qoheleth is working with traditional definitions of the righteous, the wicked, the good, the ceremonially clean and unclean, the pious as well as the delinquent sacrificer, the sinner, the one who vows and the one who does not. Additionally, the justice of God is explained in orthodox terms and unsurprising pericopes. In this passage, the sinner experiences affliction and the loss of his estate, and in 3:16–17, 8:10–13 and 11:9, God's judgment is explained in conventional terms. As Crenshaw (1987: 141) puts it, 'Qohelet was no iconoclast in matters dealing with ethical conduct.'

It becomes problematic, of course, for those commentators who hear Qoheleth to say that all is meaningless, vain or absurd, to comment on these typical OT descriptors of morality and its consequences. They are driven to alternative meanings and interpretations for otherwise straight-forward Hebr. terminology. Guesses are made about the meaning of 'sinner', such as 'lucky' and 'unlucky', 'fortunate, unfortunate', 'offender' (Ginsberg 1955: 139; Hertzberg 1963: 94–95; Fox 1999: 189). But Whybray's response is more reasonable (1989: 64; also Eaton 1983: 132), noting it is more than tenuous to prefer a handful of morally neutral uses in the OT for *ḥôṭē'* when nearly six hundred cases of the word and its cognates have the incontrovertible meaning of 'sin, sinner', especially when the other uses in Ecclesiastes itself clearly mean 'sinner'. Of course, there is the oft-used mechanism of not attributing the point to Qoheleth but to an unknown correcting commentator who is supposedly setting things right; for example, Barton 1908: 84.

Qoheleth concludes this section in a way that he concludes two others, 3:19–22 and 6:8–9, by bringing into congruence three themes: 'transience', 'advantage or reward' and 'enjoyment'. The message is unmistakable and repeated in part or fully many times: though only temporary, our advantage or reward in life is to enjoy what God provides. In the case of our passage at hand, even though the righteous may receive that which the sinner owns only momentarily, the enjoyment of it by the righteous is just as temporary.

The next section of Qoheleth's speech appears to begin rather abruptly, but in fact supports this section as an apologetic for why *everything* is temporary under the sun.

Explanation

Qoheleth's main objective in his speech is to instruct his audience in the realism of kingdom living, which, like that of the poets of Pss 39 and 73, includes recounting his successes and exposing his emotional and experiential lows. It is a familiar OT pattern, whether it is David, Job, Habakkuk or many others, that the genuine, unmasked feelings of the jubilant or distraught are heard by the Almighty equally. Accomplishments are not discounted out of feigned humility, nor are catharses muffled out of shame. However, while sitting in twenty-first-century passive pietism, when we hear either of these autobiographical poles of perspective, we become uncomfortable. Recounting personal success or distress is frequently muzzled by a systemic theological stoicism. Qoheleth, on the other hand, describes his experiences with the greatest candour. If we can bear listening to him for the first few moments, any initial objection will be reversed to undeniable assent. His genuineness, if heard in its entirety, attracts the attentive minds and hearts of the honest.

Qoheleth is not shy about sharing what he has thoroughly enjoyed in his life. While taking us on a short journey through his assessments of life and the value of hard, exhausting work, he stops to survey *his own* efforts. But his explanation is couched within an awareness of the primary commission God gave to humanity in Eden. Elsewhere, Solomon is heralded for his compliance with our original purpose to subdue and maintain the creation as vice-sovereigns (1 Kgs 4:32–33). Solomon enjoyed his labour. Elsewhere in Solomonic history he is said to be passionate particularly about his building projects. Qoheleth loved to create, build, manage, lead and succeed; no wonder that the realization of someone else becoming the 'subduer' or 'governor' (*šalîṭ*) of his efforts hurt him the most. Enjoying our work is a *command* in Ecclesiastes, and enjoying its fruit is the inevitable blessing. Going to work with 'Monday morning blues' and 'thank goodness it's Friday' are symptoms of disobedience to this command. Not only are we to 'work six days', but God promises that we can enjoy that work as well. If it is not a delight to go to work, we must have the wrong job. If one is on a perpetual search for job satisfaction, one may need to consider alternate fields of vocation.

The advantage of wisdom over folly could not be expressed any more strongly by Qoheleth nor any more consistently with Proverbs and Job. It will become more and more evident through his speech that the truths of traditional wisdom cultivate the fruits of our labour, the advisable principles for success and enjoyment. An unfortunate tendency of the church has been its nearly sole emphasis on justification and subsequent episodic piety. Yet the Bible provides an inexhaustible source of wisdom, proverbs, sayings and maxims, all of which offer profound, practical truths for moment-by-moment application to our lives as vice-sovereigns. These wisdom tenets are from the infinite genius of the Godhead, given to humanity from a source that pre-existed the creation, referred to as Lady Wisdom in Prov. 8:22–36. They are included in the 'light' that the Word's life brought to all his creation (John 1:4–5; 3:19). They are comparable to the wisdom of Christ, which also excels folly as light does darkness; fools who do not love his light, stumble along in spiritual darkness (John 1:6–7). Wisdom found in a reverent relationship with God is a goal as well as a gift. We obtain it by obedience to the point of being 'good before God', then our wisdom is enhanced by divinely generated and communicated spiritual insight. In the midst of many instructions for being wise, James, the NT wisdom writer, says that wisdom is also something to be requested as a gift from God, 'If you lack wisdom, ask him and he will give it generously!' (Jas 1:5). There is a circular, upward spiral to joy and shalom.

Consequently, Qoheleth does answer his initial question about whether there is any advantage to hard work. In a word, the answer is 'joy'. But it is the profoundest joy that comes from the simplest of experiences: food, drink and rewarding work. The joy does not proceed from these gifts themselves but from the Giver, who thinks enough of us to remind us of his grace and justice. The joy is in the receiving, not in any self-generated affluence. The joy is within the shepherding care of the Sovereign, not in the vegetables and wine themselves. In fact, if they become the focus, we dishonour God, 'for who can eat and be glad *without Him*?' Christ's instructional prayer simply asks for 'our daily bread'. Furthermore, Paul's instructions to Timothy remind us of our place as stewards of God's generosity and echo Qoheleth's humility, 'Since everything created by God is good, we should not reject it, but receive it with thankfulness' (1 Tim. 4:4).

A portion of Christ's Sermon on the Mount is especially interesting at this point. He tells us in Luke 12:22–31 that we are not to give in to Qoheleth's despair, nor to be anxious about life. Instead, we are to look at the birds who are fed by the Lord and who, in God's providential care, are adorned as Qoheleth implies he was adorned (2:4–9). The Lord addresses the brevity of life and says stress over our estate does not lengthen our lives, so we are to seek God's kingdom. This directly follows a passage, however, that also has Qoheleth-like features. Christ's parable of the rich fool in Luke 12:13–21 is probably a commentary on Ecclesiastes. Having received fruit from his labour, a rich man tells his heart he should tear down his barns to build larger ones to store his increased harvest. He says he will eat, drink and enjoy those fruits, and cease from the labour that produced them. God rebukes the fool for not taking the temporary nature of his life seriously, and tells him that someone else that very night will receive the fruit for which he has worked. The parable's point is that one should keep enjoying kingdom *work* for God rather than idling life away. The fool's attitude is precisely the opposite of that which Qoheleth encourages. Having received fruit from his labour, Qoheleth tells his heart to eat, drink and *rejoice in his labour*, not to cease from it. He takes his temporariness seriously, even bemoaning the fact that someone else will receive it whenever he dies. The conclusion: keep enjoying your labour and acknowledge its fruits as a gift from God.

For Qoheleth, the superiority of wisdom is clear, though its possession brings increased anguish and pain. His goal is to bring us to continual awareness of the temporality of life, the brevity of wisdom's benefits, and the tragic circumstances and outcomes of life that wisdom exposes. Qoheleth drags us through the realities of human anxiety and disappointment, which are genuine feelings and expected reactions from those who glory in God's perfection and future reclamation of a fallen world. His objective is to convince his listeners that they have not lived a profound life unless they have experienced its trials and tribulations as well as its blessings. Like the foolish city-saviour of the parable in 9:13-16, Qoheleth explains his despair of not only being forgotten by the next generation but being despised as well, regardless of his wisdom. As he does in the litany of unjust results of 9:11, Qoheleth laments the inappropriate handling of his accomplishments after he dies. He does not shelter us from the truth about wisdom here in this passage or throughout his speech.

Though even death may be accepted as inevitable and even preferable, depending on one's circumstances, there are those who wish to create a legacy that will live past their death into the ages. Any combination of personal vanity and a genuine desire to achieve great things even if for no less than the kingdom leads only to disillusionment. As we grow in wisdom and eventually discover that there are but a few years left to serve the kingdom, we finally conclude, humbly, that whatever our achievements, they will have less impact on our successors or society than our idealistic visions had expected. History notes and respects the efforts of an infinitesimally small fraction of the earth's inhabitants, and the intensities of even these legacies are evanescent, fading with every passing year. Anyone who sees their eternal significance referred to in their journals and diaries or autobiographies has not sat at the feet of Qoheleth. Any artist, ruler, entrepreneur, hero, scientist or theologian who aspires to be read about in a 'Who's Who' should understand that their innovations, awards, writings, or whatever feats that are honoured now, will be assessed in the new earth much more modestly compared to the pomp with which they were first celebrated.

We cannot be judgmental, looking down at Qoheleth's confessions of despair. Those who consider themselves righteous but have never hated life have not taken God's sovereign justice, including the curse, seriously. How vapid a world view it would be if any wisdom culture, in any age of any society, did not hate the human condition experienced by both the wearied individual and by beleaguered humanity as a whole. How insensitive to reality or intentionally oblivious to a distressed world can we be if, in our crystal cathedrals, we smile and count *our* blessings only publicly? And perhaps worse, how dishonest can we continue to be when asked how things are going and we respond invariably, 'Fine'? We have been brainwashed by the heresy of 'fineness' when even as believers we live lives punctuated by 'cursedness'. Are we perpetually moribund, then? No, nor are we to be perpetually giddy with delight. Qoheleth prescribes a wisdom that is balanced.

ECCLESIASTES 3:1–22

Translation

¹There is a definite time for everything,
   a suitable time for every choice under the skies.
²A time for birthing, but a time for dying;
   A time for planting, but a time for plucking the planted;
³A time for killing, but a time for healing;
   A time for demolishing, but a time for building;
⁴A time for weeping, but a time for laughing;
   A time of mourning, but a time of dancing;
⁵A time for discarding stones, but a time for collecting stones;
   A time for embracing, but a time for shunning embracing;
⁶A time for seeking, but a time for destroying;
   A time for keeping, but a time for discarding;
⁷A time for tearing, but a time for sewing;
   A time for being silent, but a time for speaking;
⁸A time for loving, but a time for hating;
   A time for battling, but a time for peace.

⁹What advantage has the worker in all his labour? ¹⁰I have seen the affliction God has given to afflict the sons of men.
   ¹¹He has made everything beautiful in its time. He has also given them the sense of eternity in their hearts so that humanity will not understand the deeds God does from beginning to end. ¹²I know, then, there is nothing better for them than to be happy and to do good in their life. ¹³Surely, everyone should eat, drink and enjoy one's labour; it is God's gift.
   ¹⁴I know that everything God does will remain for eternity; nothing can be added on, and from it nothing can be taken, for God works so that they will revere him. ¹⁵Whatever is already has been, and whatever is to be already has been because God seeks what has been pursued before.

[16]Furthermore, I have observed under the sun that in a place of justice there is wickedness instead, and in a place of fairness there is wickedness instead. [17]I said to myself, 'God will judge the righteous and the wicked, for there is a time for every choice and for every deed there.'

[18-19]I said to myself concerning the sons of men, 'God severely tests them to show them that they are themselves but an animal,' since it happens to the sons of men and to the animal alike, the same for both – as one dies, so dies the other because there is one breath to both. So there is not an advantage to humanity over the beast, for both are temporary. [20]Both go to one place. Both are from the dust, and both return to the dust. [21]Who knows the breath of the sons of men, when it ascends above; and the breath of the beast, when it descends towards the earth?

[22]So I have observed that nothing is better than that one enjoys his activity, for it is his reward, since who will reveal to him what will succeed him?

Notes on the text

1. 'definite time ... suitable time': zĕmān as well as 'ēt denote singular, temporary moments of time, and as synonyms are the polar opposites to 'ôlām (eternity). Nothing in the terms denotes a cosmic or theological determinism, though they do suggest the 'occasions' when an action is timely. Wilch's 1969 volume on 'ēt is the most thorough study of the word; see also Rudman 2001: 40–48. zĕmān is considered an indication of a late date for Ecclesiastes, since its other cases are all post-exilic. However, the word dates back to 1800 BC in Akk., and is used in an Amarna letter, so very possibly it entered Hebr. long before the exile.

'choice': predominantly in the OT ḥēpeṣ reflects a positive emotional state, thus 'pleasure, delight'. There are instances where, more neutrally, the *pursuit* of a desire, a 'preference, choice', is meant; for example, Judg. 13:23; Job 31:16; Isa. 44:28; 46:10; 48:14. Both meanings appear in Ecclesiastes: probably 'pleasure' is meant in 5:4 and 12:1, 10. However, where the context is hardly positive, the more basic meaning of a preference or choice, whether causing pleasure or not, is the obvious intent. Thus, here in 3:1 and 3:17, 'choice' is preferred, since killing, weeping, mourning, hate, war and injustice could hardly be a delight (also 5:8; 8:3, 6; 12:1). Mundane renderings which do not express the intentionality of this root, such as 'matter, event, affair', are preferred by those holding to a late Biblical Hebr. theory; for example, Staples 1965: 110–112; Whitley 1978: 30.

2. 'for birthing, but a time for dying': Seow is correct in seeing these forms as gerunds with the prepositional lamed, parallel to the nominal forms and lamed in v. 1 (1997: 160). Translating the conjunctive waw as 'but' expresses these opposites more emphatically; see Lys 1973: 300–301.

5. 'shunning embracing': the pi. of the second occurrence of *ḥābaq* emphasizes the fleeting suitability of embracing because the intensive form implies an indefinite and inappropriate length.

6. 'for destroying': in Ecclesiastes and the rest of the OT (BDB 2a) the pi. of *'ābad* means 'destroy' (7:7 and 9:18). Expecting Qoheleth to choose expressions that intuitively are more 'opposite' leads most commentators to ignore the natural force of the pi. and to translate, 'give up as lost'.

9. 'worker': this restatement of the programmatic question introduced in 1:3, and reiterated in 2:22, includes *'āśāh* (work), a more general term that includes the more rigorous labour (*'āmēl*).

11. 'beautiful': *yāpeh* means 'beautiful, fair' elsewhere in the OT. Again, a preference for a more neutral, non-emotive meaning is preferred by commentators believing the book to be negative and late, such as 'fitting, appropriate'.

'the sense of eternity': in this passage, which is preoccupied with time, *'ôlām* can mean nothing other than its usual OT meaning, 'eternity, indefinite duration', as it does in every other Ecclesiastes instance: 1:4, 10, 2:16, 3:14 and 9:6 (thus Jenni 1953: 24–27; Zimmerli 1962: 168, 172; Lys 1977: 346). Nonetheless, lexical creativity surfaces among translators when rendering this otherwise very common and usually uncomplicated word: 'world' (drawing anachronistically from the Mishnah: Gordis 1968: 231; cf. Isaksson 1987: 176–189); 'ignorance' (Whitley 1978: 32); 'toil' (requiring textual emendation and based on a loose parallel with 8:17; Fox 1999: 211). These alternatives distract one from the word's normal meaning used again only three verses later (3:14), and they detract from the main point of this chapter about time. See Ellermeier's extensive excursus on the word, 1967: 302–322.

'end': *sôp* is thought by some to be a late word (even an Aram.; Wagner 1966: 87) simply because it occurs in 2 Chr. 20:16 and Joel 2:20 (Hertzberg 1963: 28; Polzin 1976: 146). Rather than late, the word is an example of frequent nominalizing of infinitives of indigenous roots (cf. Amos 3:15; GKC 84ac).

12. 'for them': the incongruence between this pl. form and the sg. pronominal suffix on *běḥayyāw* (in his life) is not rare in Ecclesiastes and is evidence of the vernacular.

'do good': *'āśāh ṭôb*. To sustain an amoral rendering here, some commentators prefer to determine this phrase's meaning from a different Hebr. phrase, *rā'āh ṭôb* ('fare well'; Galling 1934: 362; Loretz 1964: 48; Murphy 1992: 30). Yet its natural and identical meaning, 'do good', encourages righteous behaviour elsewhere in Ecclesiastes itself and other biblical authors. Even if the phrase was amoral, 2 Sam. 12:18 provides a biblical precedent rather than Gr. alternatives, which some have suggested (Whitley 1978: 34; Braun 1973: 53–54).

14. 'everyone will revere him': lit. 'they will fear before him'. However, the reference is to the 'everyone' mentioned in v. 13.

15. 'what has been pursued before': *rādap* predominantly means 'to pursue', particularly with aggressive force. Thus the two other niphals of this root in the OT do refer to those pursued by enemies (Lam. 5:5) or impersonal terrors (Job 30:15). So the 'persecuted' may be meant, per Garrett 1993: 301. However, in a few poetic and wisdom texts, the verb also denotes general pursuits of bribes, righteousness, peace, the good; for example, Isa. 1:23; Hos. 6:3; Prov. 21:21; Job 38:21. The passive, then, would be those objects of pursuit, and in Qoheleth's phrasing, what has already been pursued. The missing art. with *nirdāp* is another example of its erratic use in the vernacular.

17. The resumptive first person pronoun following the already con-jugated perfect is Qoheleth's indication of the simple past, and occurs in 3:16–18 three times. This passage moves from a general observation in 3:16 expressed without the resumptive *'ănî* to these simple past instances when he, at one point, 'said' these conclusions to himself.

'there [at God's judgment]': given the two emphatic forms, *šāmmāh* in v. 16, which refer to oppressive human judgment, here the shorter *šām* suffices as a reference to the place of *God's* judgment, where justice prevails. See Whitley (1978: 34–35) for a survey of alternatives for this obscure end to this sentence.

18. 'God severely tests them to show them that they are themselves but an animal': two emphatic forms are combined with an obscure verb, resulting in a tentative translation. *lěbārām* (tests them) probably begins with an emphatic lamed prefix to the perfect of *bārar* (to purify, test) with the pl. suffix. Then the pl. pronoun *hēmmāh* (themselves), echoing the last two syllables of the previous word, *běhēmāh* (animal), accentuates that it is humanity itself whom God tests with a humiliating common experience with subhuman life – death.

19. 'since it happens to the sons of men and to the animal alike, the same for both': this initial clause is verbless and is translated here more naturally.

'both': though *hakkōl* usually means 'all', where the context is dealing with only a pair, 'both' is most natural.

21. 'breath': though *rûaḥ* can mean 'spirit', it would not be used in this sense in reference to the animals.

'when it ascends above ... when it descends': the question that interests commentators the most is whether the initial *hē'* on each infinitive is the definite art. or interrogative *hē'*. MT treats them as the former, but LXX, Vg and Pesh., the latter. With *mî yôdēa'* initiating the verse, it is a question one way or the other. The real question is what is implied by the elliptical phrasing for which all commentators improvise and translate along the lines of 'whether' the breath ascends. There is no articulated object of knowledge as in 6:12 and 8:1, nor conditional particles (2:19) to determine definitively the nature of the question. So translating 'who knows when' these events take place is equally viable. It fits both the conviction about

God's timing of terminal breaths referred to in 3:2 and God's prerogatives in 3:11, and is consistent with 12:7 and its declaration that the human breath does indeed ascend.

Form and structure

Qoheleth's first poem included a litany of nature's temporary but continuous cycles (1:4–7). He went on in that section to use those natural metaphors for explaining the temporary but continuous cycles of human activity as well. That section started with God's providential actions and transitioned to human activity. In 3:1–22, the reverse rhetorical sequence carries Qoheleth's thoughts about human activity into a discussion of God's providence. He also uses opposite syntactical schemes: where in ch. 1 he uses rolling participles, in our new section he starts with staccato infinitival phrases. To use Qoheleth's favourite metaphor, 3:1–8 *breathes* rhythmically with metrical inhaling and exhaling. A time for this, a time for that (a cadence of polarity and opposition); inhale, exhale; inhale, exhale. The poem's very structure breathes decisions in and out of reality, since they and their times are measured events with only temporary appropriateness. As Haupt (1905: 12, 34) translates:

> All lasts but a while
> and transient is everything under the sky.
> Transient are births and deaths,
> transient planting, uprooting [etc.].

The cyclical seasonal forces of nature of 1:3–7 are now imitated by seasons of wise human efforts.

Qoheleth begins his poem of ch. 1 with the programmatic question 'What advantage is there to one's labour?' In this section, he reverses the order, ending this poem with the same question. To further define what these labours are, we have his autobiographical listing of accomplishments in 2:1–8 as well as these seven pairs of opposite choices in 3:2–8, with common choices in both: 'building' (*bānāh*; 2:4; 3:3), 'collecting' (*kānas*; 2:8; 3:5), 'birth' (*yālad*; 2:7; 3:2), 'planting' (*nāṭaʿ*; 2:4–5; 3:2) and 'laughing' (*śāḥaq*; 2:2; 3:4). Consequently, we would expect again some closure to the question, as we found in ch. 2. If everything is temporary, what is the advantage of labouring so hard?

3:1–8 starts bluntly, perhaps indicating a splice in the speech, though there are at least four conceptual links with 2:16–26: death, temporariness, wisdom and joy. Dying and its terminal effect on others' care for our achievements are put in perspective; dying, like everything else, has its time in the cosmic order. All human choices are only temporary, and a fuller listing is provided here. What are the wise choices made by those who are 'good before God'? How does joy fit into the tragic human condition?

The *metaphorical* function of the pairings in 3:2–8 is often missed by commentators who strive to identify with great exactness a tight and unduly definite meaning for each. However, the fourteen polar choices are intentionally nebulous and by design encourage multiple applications. So trying to determine the specific scenario Qoheleth had in mind for each of these pairings is actually counterproductive. Furthermore, many commentators misidentify the polar opposites as merisms – poles at either end of a continuum of related activity. This is a misnomer, since apart from birthing and dying (3:2a), the rest of the pairings do not have any inherent continua of activity – one either does something or its opposite. In most pairs, nothing in between is conceivable. Also it appears quite subjective to apply any systematic progression in thought or sustained logical grouping of these phrases for all seven verses. However, perhaps oddly enough, the components of every other verse seem related, whereas the remaining verses appear more random. That is, the two lines in vv. 2, 4, 6 and 8 are clearly analogous, whereas the two lines in 3, 5 and 7 are not.

There is no reason to assume that any of these pairings contain anything inherently evil, morally negative or unwise. This dichotomizing does not hold up, for instance, in speaking or remaining silent, nor does it hold in the case of collecting or throwing stones. Yet it is the *timing*, not the *nature*, of these acts that determines whether any are to be judged moral, negative, positive or evil. This weakens any case for an elaborate rhetorical structure based on chiasms allegedly juxtaposing 'pleasant' and 'unpleasant' activities; for example, Loader (1986: 33–35). Logically speaking, chiastic structures can be overrated when there are only as few as four components involved, since it is a fifty-fifty chance the components will be chiastic – otherwise they can only be parallel!

Following the poem is a brief theology of divine and human work; briefly put, we are to trust the sovereign God who gives enjoyment to those who work righteously and wisely. Since it is true that our labour is an affliction, as God intended it to be from the Fall, are there any consolations one can expect from an understanding God? In fact, this whole passage serves as a series of consolations to the strenuous toil and painful decisions one must make in life. Nonetheless, God does much more than simply control these seasons; he supplements human activity with his own decisive acts. Qoheleth realistically affirms our responsibility to make hard choices while armed with only finite understanding and afflicted souls and bodies, and that, in part, is how God works so that we are forced to trust and respect his sovereignty. 3:9–22, then, presents Qoheleth's theology of God's sovereignty and human responsibility, broaching this most perplexing of theological matters. He also tackles the most challenging questions for the believer's faith, including injustice, crushing labour and death.

This section of the speech consoles the listener by delineating the overwhelming power and actions that should elicit trust in the God of the OT. In an orthodox way, Qoheleth balances the non-negotiable power and prerogatives of God with his grace that sustains those who still live under the sentence of the Fall (see the table below).

	Consolation	*Sovereignty*
3:10		God afflicts humanity with labour
3:11	God has made everything beautiful in its time God has set eternity in the heart	God makes everything beautiful in its time God has set eternity in the heart All God's ways are not known
3:12–13	Humanity must rejoice, do good Also eat, drink and enjoy labour	God's gift is to enjoy life
3:14		God's deeds are for ever God's deeds are immutable
3:15		God ensures that the past is repeated
3:17	God will bring eventual justice to all	God will bring eventual justice to all
3:18–21		God humbles humanity as mortal creatures
3:22	Humanity must be happy in life	

For more extended discussions of this section's form, see Galling 1961: 1–12; Eissfeldt 1970: 69–74; Lys 1973: 299–316; Whybray 1991: 469–483; Blenkinsopp 1995: 55–64; Jarick (2000); Rudman 2001: 4–48, 83–94.

Comment

1–8. Qoheleth now embarks on the journey that requires delicate navigation between the reefs of divine sovereignty and human responsibility. Aware that time can be measured as both brief and a seeming eternity, he carefully affirms the need for apt decisions during the temporary moments of life, the *'ēt*s and *zĕmān*s, yet admits their absorption into the eternal (3:11) decisions of God. These opportune moments and suitable seasons are fleeting, and their brevity emphasizes Qoheleth's theme of 'the transitoriness of everything'. Lohfink (1987: 237) notes this thrust in 3:1–8: 'how effusively Qoheleth describes humanity's ever new and constantly vanishing moments!' Brown (2000: 41) agrees: 'Permanence is not part of the chronological equation'.

'ēt occurs in Ecclesiastes 40 times, 29 times in 3:1–8 alone. The word can refer to God's predetermined times, as in 3:17 concerning his judgment

times. However, *'ēt* can also refer to those decisions for which the person is held accountable as a vice-sovereign over God's world, and which are calculated by human experience and wisdom. Nehemiah does exactly this after contemplating the best response to Artaxerxes (Neh. 2:6): he gave the *'ēt*, the opportune time for his leave of absence. This is the same meaning as when Qoheleth prescribes, 'a wise heart knows the suitable time (*'ēt*) and discernment, for there is a suitable time and discernment for every choice' (8:5–6). And later he announces, 'Blessed are you ... whose princes eat at the suitable time, for strength, and not drunkenness.'

Within 3:2–8 lie examples of these decisions that must be made by those who are good in God's eyes, using the wisdom God gives them but realizing that the end of one matter is always the beginning of that which will have another end. It is not only the wisdom literature that maintains that there is a meaningful obligation to choose righteousness or the way of wisdom; it is a presupposition of the whole OT's covenantal relationship between the individual, community and God. There is the humble voice in Prov. 16:9, 'One's heart plans his way, *and* (not necessarily 'but') the LORD directs his steps,' as far as human calculations and planning go. Yet that voice does not contradict the call in the rest of Proverbs, Ecclesiastes or any other OT book to wise, diligent behaviour on the part of those who wish to be good in God's eyes, and who have been entrusted with the management of themselves and their spheres of influence. The synergy of Prov. 21:31 is the middle ground that affirms both:

> The horse is prepared for the day of battle,
>   and [not necessarily 'but'] the victory is the LORD's.

This is far from a fatalism based on divine determinism as interpreted by Hubbard (1991: 100–101) or Rudman (2001: 47–48).

It is thought that, since these examples of activity are begun by the experiences of birth and death, the whole poem describes God's determination of the times. This is partially because of an errant identification of the gerundial infinitive *lāledet*, which does not mean the intransitive 'to be born' but the act of 'birthing'. Krüger (2004: 75) argues this, noting that the rest of the verbs are active in this poem. Since the timing of birthing and dying is not necessarily involuntary, nor always determined randomly outside human choices, even these are included in a list of human activity. Furthermore, as in the case of all of this poem's pairings, the brevity of the syntax, with few qualifiers, encourages the widest application. So calculating ovulation to determine the eventual time of birth, and factoring the relatively constant gestation period per species, could lead to wise timing decisions for animal breeders, as well as persons tempted by illicit sex having to live with its potential 'birthing' results. Seow (1997: 160) finds here a grammatical parallel with the birthing ibex in Job 39:1. Because of the reference to *wild* beasts there, knowledge of the time for birthing is impossible. Still it shows the gerundial form of this root applied universally to animals as well as humans.

In respect to dying, Qoheleth says later that death is not something the individual can always control (8:8), but is something that can be hastened by unwise or immoral choices (7:17; also 10:8–11). Even the next seven words – the time to choose to kill – implies there is a time for dying, as there is a time for war in 3:8. Seow also comments correctly that these are not necessarily patterns that always occur in the experience of the same individual. In other words, this is not a statement about how *each* person's birthing and dying is timed, but how *any* birthing and dying is timed for creatures in general. In OT life, there are appropriate times and seasons for ending life: capital punishment or war, or killing animals that are diseased, nutritious or sacrificial (3:3). The challenge for the wise is to decide when life should be continued through healing efforts to sustain it or when life should be terminated for legitimate reasons.

The agricultural parallel to birthing and dying also affirms the beginning and end of everything: planting and plucking. The meaning of *'āqar* is uncertain given it has only one other biblical instance in another poetic passage (Zeph. 2:4), but though the root may not mean 'harvest', it could refer to uprooting tubers, plucking grains or picking fruit from trees, or other constructive ends to what has been planted (2:5). 11:4–6 likewise assumes that there is a responsible time for farming processes like sowing and reaping, and that hard work increases the probability of success. Proper timing in agriculture is exactly the point of Prov. 20:4:

> The lazy does not plow in season,
>   so he has nothing at harvest.

Demolishing can be a positive first step to rebuilding again or for leaving space for another use (3:3). As in the case of tearing and sewing (3:7), it could be an issue of stewardship of resources. There is nothing inherently negative in the first action of breaking things down. It could be the destruction of idols and cultic sanctuaries or the walls of enemy cities (cf. Jer. 1:10). The tearing can be for subsequent constructive uses, from lowly patches to downsizing for children's clothing. In this sense, Qoheleth is not offering precise antonyms to emphasize negative or positive events; rather, he is saying that different decisions are appropriate at different times. For instance, it would be particularly simplistic in Ecclesiastes to consider weeping and mourning (3:4) as exclusively negative when he speaks in 7:2–4 of their superior moral nature to certain times of laughing and (presumably) dancing. There are times when laughter is offensive to Qoheleth (2:2; 7:6) and when sorrow is commendable (4:1–2; cf. Mark 2:18–20; Jas 4:9). However, most interpretations reverse this preference when dealing with 3:4 because of the supposition that Qoheleth is posing opposite *value* to each of the poles. Certainly, the application of these activities, then, is situational, there being proper and good times for weeping, laughing, mourning and dancing.

Throwing and collecting stones (3:5) are specific cases of throwing or keeping anything, which is exactly the point in the next verse. Again, these are not inherently good or bad – it all depends on the brief moment and how best to manage that moment and its contents. Nevertheless, more than any other pairing, the throwing and collecting of stones have received the most attention by commentators. Reference is often made to the practice of throwing stones on one's field to render the field unusable by a conquering enemy (2 Kgs 3:19, 25; Isa. 5:2), perhaps the same ones collected previously to clear the field for planting and to build the stone fences. The reader is referred to virtually any other commentary to read infatuations that throwing stones may insinuate insemination. The reference here to casting stones is intentionally vague, since stones can be used as weapons slung or dropped from city walls; as symbols of a childhood pastime; for building cities and their walls; as assets to be invested with an expectation of returns (11:1). Ultimately, it is not the stones that are central; rather, the act of collecting or distributing *anything* is the point. Later, we hear about the wisdom needed when collecting heavy stones by quarrying (10:9).

The embraces of 3:5 are of any type, including social protocols of greeting and parting or the most intimate expressions of fondness. The pairing is unique in using the same root (*ḥābaq*) for both poles, the second pole negating the first: 'A time for embracing, but a time for shunning non-stop embracing.'

'Seeking' is a theme of Qoheleth's, not only here in 3:6 but when discussing his pursuit of wisdom (1:13; 2:3; 7:25, 28–29; 8:17; 12:10). But again, this seeking is of any sort. When Qoheleth uses the pi. of *'ābad* elsewhere (7:7 and 9:18), he means 'destroy', so unless there is a reason to insist on antonyms, the meaning is probably the same here. Again, even destruction need not be negative as we saw in 3:3. In a sense, destroying is the opposite of seeking, since the latter expresses the desire to possess, the former, to prefer the possession's end.

Timely speech is important to Qoheleth (7:10, 22; 8:4; 10:20; 9:17), just as it is in the rest of the wisdom literature. By far the plurality of maxims in Proverbs is related to wise speech (see Fredericks 1993: 58). And rather than silence being the negative pole in this pairing, for Qoheleth it is a positive virtue, especially while in the temple (5:1–2). Far from being negative in Israelite wisdom, silence is a virtue of the highest order; for example, in Proverbs:

The one holding his tongue is wise.

(10:19)

An understanding man holds his tongue.

(11:12)

A trustworthy man keeps a secret.

(11:13)

A wise man keeps his knowledge to himself.

(12:23)

How good is a timely ('*ēt*) word!

(15:23)

Even a fool is considered wise when silent.

(17:28)

However, as the psalmist reflects on how his mourning turned into dancing, like Qoheleth, he recounts how his silence was turned into thankful songs of praise (Ps. 30:11–12).

Inconsistent with passive pietism, statements such as 3:8 prescribing hatred can disturb those not adequately impressed either with the legitimacy of the emotion or the serious threat of evil and its Author. Even God hates the boastful sinner and those addicted to violence (Pss 5:5; 11:5). Inconsistent with pious pacifism, statements like Qoheleth's that prescribe just wars can disturb those who believe them unbiblical. War in the OT is an instrument of God's judgment, and in the NT the final war signals the long awaited return of our glorious, heroic Lord and Saviour.

9–11. Since the Fall in Eden, God has intensified the severity of our labour as an act of judgment, so 3:9 asks about the 'worker' who 'labours'. Working, according to Genesis, is good, but frustrating labour is due to the curse. He revives the question here in 3:9 that was just asked in 2:22, and answers it similarly – whether there is an advantage to labour is answered positively by describing the sovereign, divine gifts of joy and wisdom (3:12–13). But before he answers the question directly, he mentions another unpleasant fact. The God-given affliction experienced in seeking wisdom (1:13) is again an issue here; however, this time the affliction is the frustration of being endowed with an inkling of the eternal but being unable to fathom the works of God from beginning to end.

Since this 'poem of the times' emphasizes the decisions of life, which indeed often are unpleasant, Qoheleth now provides a theodicy. He blends further stark realities about the human condition with reassurances that God is firmly in control and that divine acts are unchangeable but generous, not fully understood but purposeful.

That God has made everything beautiful in its own time is the greatest statement of divine providence in the whole of Scripture. It is the theorem from which the believer's hope is derived that all things work together for good for those who love God (Rom. 8:28). It is a statement far beyond pragmatism that directs one to the glory of an artistic cosmic manager, the creating and sustaining God. Furthermore, it is his 'timing' ('*ēt*) and its perfection that are highlighted in 3:11 and 3:17, and that set the standard for our aptly decided daily activities. Following 3:1–8 and its emphasis on the role of the individual as vice-sovereign over creation's time and resources, is 3:10–22, which speaks of God's own sovereign administration of his creation. We are to find the right season for our efforts, just as God does. God has instilled an awareness of what eternity is (3:11), and this is a reason for humanity's moral culpability, according to Paul: 'Since the creation of the world God's invisible attributes, eternal power and divine nature have been clearly seen, understood by what has been made, so that they are without excuse' (Rom. 1:20).

This awareness of the eternal, which drives us to honour God and to submit to his will, also afflicts us with a narrow window. We can see clearly but not necessarily widely. The breadth of God's acts from beginning to end is not wholly viewable, since he is eternal as well as omnipresent (cf. Isa. 40:28; 55:8). It is not only time that precludes exhaustive knowledge but also space. However, again, Qoheleth is not saying that we know nothing about anything or that we cannot know God's plans. Both views are extreme positions Paul flatly denies and Qoheleth contradicts throughout his speech. In this passage alone he 'knows' what God has afflicted humanity with (3:10); he knows that God does everything beautifully (3:11); he knows that God gives gifts (3:13); he knows that God will eventually judge the wicked (3:17). Even our affliction of limited knowledge is a beautiful blessing, since who really would want to know *all* the exact future acts of God, especially in our personal lives? Paul reflects this figuratively, 'Now we see in a mirror dimly ... but then I will know completely, as I am now completely known!' (1 Cor. 13:12).

12–13. Qoheleth now gives in vv. 12–13 the answer to the programmatic question whether there is any advantage to hard labour. He looks back to 3:9, 2:22 and 1:3, but also looks forward to 3:19, 22 where he admits there is one sense in which humanity has no advantage over animals; that is, death. Rejoicing, eating and drinking and enjoying work are the same answers to the same question posed before. Yet there is an additional positive answer to what is good for humanity to pursue, and that is moral uprightness. Of course, this is not really new, since it is implied in 2:26, where it is said that God gives even greater joy to those who are good in his sight. This moral caveat to enjoyment is found later too in 11:10, where youth are encouraged to enjoy life but to remember that God will bring them to judgment for all their actions. The same phrase *'āśāh ṭôb* (do good) is the uncontested meaning in 7:20, and of course the moral translation is normal to other biblical references; for example, Gen. 29:26; Ps. 37:3, 27. The antonymous grammatical and lexical phrase 'do evil' is used freely by Qoheleth (4:3; 5:1; 8:11–12). Only a rigid stripping of all conventional wisdom from Ecclesiastes would lead to eliminating this otherwise clear injunction to righteousness.

14–15. Central to this chapter's theological excursus is the foundational, traditional wisdom precept that to fear God is to be wise. In this one subject alone Qoheleth places his speech in the mainstream of biblical wisdom, emphasizing it again in 5:1–7 and 8:12–13. The reasons to revere God are given here as well: humanity should fear God because of the natural revelation that shows his mighty, eternal works, because of the absoluteness and consistency of his providence and because of his ultimate, fair judgment. Commentators have read into this passage a different meaning to 'fear', one more along the lines of 'terror' because they see this standard wisdom concept to be twisted by Qoheleth to portray a God whose cruel intention is to frighten humanity into submission (Crenshaw 1987: 100; Longman 1998: 124). Of course, this is quite contrary to the giving God of the previous two verses and the just God of 3:17.

In what way exactly does God work so that humanity will fear him? Qoheleth answers this in six ways. First, we have just heard that God has afflicted humanity with only some knowledge of his ways (3:10–11). Secondly, his eternal power and discretion are reasons to honour him. Some of his eternal acts are played out on this earth, which is in itself an example of an act of his that 'remains for ever' (1:4). Eaton (1983: 81) highlights this attribute with the following short summary.

> His actions endure *for* ever.... The 'eternity' in man's heart [3:11] must be connected with the 'eternity' of v. 14. 'Eternity' was important in Israel's heritage.... an eternal covenant had been inaugurated (Gn. 9:16).... An eternal priesthood (Ex. 40:15) and an eternal kingdom (2 Sa. 7:13) were bestowed by a God eternally merciful (Ps. 111:5).

Now, his deeds are both beautiful and eternal – the exact opposite of humanity whose deeds are soiled and temporary. Surely the emphasis on the eternality of God's works implies the transience of ours.

A third reason to fear God is the absoluteness of his providence (3:14). Though humanity is encouraged to accomplish wisely many timely acts in 3:1–8, trying to dislodge God's plans and acts is not among them. Add immutable to 'beautiful' and 'eternal' as descriptors of God's sovereign actions. This is yet another consolation for those who rest in God and respect God's administration of his kingdom. Later, Qoheleth is more explicit in this consolation:

> Consider the work of God; indeed, who is able to straighten
> what he has bent?
> In the day of prosperity be happy, but in the day of adversity
> consider that God has made them both.

(7:13–14a)

Earlier, he observed in 1:15, 'What has been twisted cannot be straight, and what is lacking cannot be counted.' Discreet resignation to life's non-negotiables is a perfect prescription for sanity.

Fourthly, the consistent manner of his providence is a reason for revering God (3:15). In language very reminiscent of 1:9, Qoheleth reviews for us the cyclicity of human action. But here he goes on to give the reason. God seeks and assures the repetitiveness of human and divine activity, because he prefers it that way; he prefers what has been pursued before. He seeks his own self-consistency and trustworthiness, and expects human compliance with the same moral principles found in the conscience and in both the testaments. The fifth and sixth reasons to respect God are because of his justice (3:17) and his imposition of the curse of death (3:19).

16–17. In vv. 16 and 17, Qoheleth presents another disappointment; yet again, it is another consolation as well. The injustices are quite undefined in this verse, and cannot be relegated exclusively to the physical courts. More generally speaking, injustice can lie in the structures of the community where the leaders are responsible for fairness way before it becomes a formally legal issue in the courts. This too is included in Qoheleth's lament.

However, he is a realist: he knows injustices occur even within his own cities' gates where judges sat to adjudicate, though Solomon personally warned these judges, 'You do not judge for man, but for the LORD who is with you in the matter of judgment ... Fear the LORD; be careful what you do, for the LORD our God will have no part in unrighteousness, partiality, or taking bribes' (2 Chr. 19:6–7).

Earlier he had prayed at the temple's dedication ceremony, 'Hear from heaven and act and judge your servants, punishing the wicked ... and justifying the righteous' (2 Chr. 6:23).

He hopes for justice to prevail and encourages his listeners that it will prevail (5:8). But he also explains the dire implications of slow and ineffective justice (8:11). The prophets, like Qoheleth, decried injustice in the city courts:

> [Woe to those] who justify the wicked for a bribe,
>   and take away the rights of the righteous!
>   (Isa. 5:22–23; also 29:21)

> I know your sins ... you who oppress the righteous, accepting
>   bribes,
>   turning away the poor in the gates.
>   (Amos 5:12)

> The prince and the judge ask for a bribe.
>   (Mic. 7:3)

It is certainly 'under the sun' where these injustices occur, surely not above it from where Qoheleth expects fairness and righteous judgment. It is there (*šām*) where justice is found, since everything God does is beautiful in its timeliness:

> God will judge the world righteously,
> He will render equal justice for all people.
>
> (Ps. 9:8)

> When I choose an appointed time (*mô'ēd*), I judge with equity.
> (Ps. 75:2)

> God stands in his assembly;
>   he judges among the rulers.
> Do not rob the poor because of his poverty, or crush the
>   afflicted in the gate,
>   since the LORD will plead their case, and rob the soul of the
>   robber.
>
> (Prov. 22:22–23; also 17:15, 26; 18:5;
>   24:11–12, 23–25, 28–29; 29:7)

Consequently, the courtroom injustices of 3:16 are only temporary and will be righted by God's eventual just judgments. It is unclear whether God's judgment will be within the person's lifetime, through natural, legal or other means of retribution. The point is, it will be in *God's* time. Qoheleth speaks unequivocally and with the same orthodoxy of the prophets and psalmists when he asserts here that justice will come to both the righteous and the wicked (a point worth repeating as far as the editor was concerned [12:14]). Of course, those who cannot conceive of Qoheleth being orthodox in any way typically discount his theology here, suggesting it may even be a later addition by a correcting editor; for example, Crenshaw 1987: 102. Even while he construes Qoheleth to deem everything absurd, Fox (1999: 229) admits, 'Qohelet never abandons moral and religious principles or repudiates the principle of divine justice.'

18–21. God proves to humanity through the recurring curse of death that we are animals, finite mammals who are also merely God's creations: equally subject to his will; equally dust; equally distant from his infinite transcendence. We even share the same 'breath of life in our nostrils' (Gen. 2:7; 7:22). God's intention for death ever since the Fall was for the dust, whether of human or beast, to become dust again (Gen. 3:19; Job 10:9; 34:14–15; Pss 104:29; 146:4). Furthermore, the Fall brought humans and animals even closer in identity, since humanity became less reflective of God's image and more beastly in its lusts and conduct. Qoheleth has already referred to the equalizing function of death for the fool and the wise (2:16). Now, in v. 19, he humbles all of humanity to the appropriate level of the beast, agreeing with the psalmists who object to the arrogant distancing of ourselves from the beast, when, in fact, we are morally despicable as well as temporary:

> For he sees wise men die, the foolish and senseless perish
>   alike....
> But man in its 'honour' will not endure; he is like the beasts that
>   perish.
>
> (Ps. 49:10, 12)

> You are gods, you all are sons of the Most High.
> Nonetheless you will die like men.
>
> (Ps. 89:6-7)

Why does he test humanity so? So that we will respect him as the Creator and Judge.

If the *rûaḥ* of v. 19 is the same for both human and animal, then this alone precludes any reading of the word to mean more than 'breath'. Though *rûaḥ* can mean 'spirit' in Hebr., in this context it can mean only what is common to all animal life: breath. Consequently, this is not a passage dealing positively or negatively with an afterlife, since it is not discussing the immortality of the soul or spirit. Presumably, Qoheleth uses *rûaḥ* here for 'breath' to distinguish it from the more common governing metaphor *hebel*, which he also uses in this verse to summarize the common attribute of humanity and the animal kingdom. If any passage attests to *hebel*'s meaning to be 'temporary' in Ecclesiastes, this one does, since the whole point of the comparison is to show that both beast and people are temporary, as Whybray (1989: 79) and Krüger (2004: 93) argue. Respectively, they conclude, 'the meaning of *hebel* would probably be "fleeting," "ephemeral," or "transient"; and, "*hebel* here ... means "ephemeral, transitory" rather than "worthless"'.

From the sole perspective of breathing and dying, since the Fall, humans truly do not have an advantage over animals. The error most commentators make at this point, however, is to overextend Qoheleth's conclusion to all comparisons of humans and animals when he is not speaking of human equality to animals in every regard. Because there is the advantage of joy for the wise over the fool, Qoheleth will soon affirm again the advantage of joy that comes from hard work (3:22). It is the certainty of death and the brevity of life that lead Qoheleth to a familiar and positive conclusion soon in 3:22. So to cite this passage to support an interpretation of Ecclesiastes where Qoheleth is saying there are no advantages to hard toil would distort the text. Qoheleth is about to conclude this unit of 3:1–22 as he did in 2:24–26 by (as mentioned above) bringing into congruence three themes: 'transience', 'advantage or reward' and 'enjoyment'. Though we may be as transient as the beasts, our advantage and reward in life is to enjoy our work and its fruits. In fact, the noun *môtar* (advantage) is used only in the Solomonic corpus, here and in Proverbs. In all three cases, he commends gruelling toil and diligence – two themes within Ecclesiastes:

In all strenuous labour there is advantage (*môtār*).

(Prov. 14:23)

The plans of the diligent surely bring an advantage (*môtār*).

(Prov. 21:5)

There is a challenge given to the wise in v. 21, though it is syntactically obscure as to what the real question is. In this unit discussing the timing of God, the elliptical phrasing suggests that what we are challenged to know is exactly when the individual's breath will ascend above, and when the beast's breath will descend. The assumption is not *whether* there is any return of the breath, nor which *direction* people's breath will go, since this is known in 12:7 ('the breath will return to God who gave it'). If it is not 'whether' or 'where', then 'when' is the logical preference. Since God's timing is beautiful, when breath is expired and ascends is God's prerogative. Like Qoheleth's statements on birthing and dying (3:1; 8:8), it is at God's discretion, and it is unpredictable when one precisely will breathe his or her last (3:11). Finally, humanity's returning to dust generation after generation further exemplifies the cyclical nature of God's preference to resurrect the past (1:9; 3:15).

22. Qoheleth's conviction that there are definite advantages to hard, toiling work has been mentioned enough times by now that he abbreviates that thematic description of those advantages simply to enjoying one's deeds without mentioning explicitly eating, drinking, working and being righteous. Though one's advantages do not include a life without death, they do include the rewards from one's diligence.

Since the previous verses have been shown not to discuss an afterlife, the question 'Who will reveal to him what will succeed him?' reverts to Qoheleth's cathartic conclusions of 2:18–21. One cannot know whether one's accomplishments will be respected and built upon, or whether they will be despised and destroyed. So enjoy those activities now, because it is impossible to know what the succeeding events will be under the sun after one dies like the beast.

Explanation

We are offered in this passage Qoheleth's (if not the entire Bible's) most succinct 'essay' on the central theme of all the Scriptures: *the sovereign God's shepherding of his vice-sovereign humanity*. Without precisely answering the sovereignty or free-will questions, he assembles the frame within which God and humanity weave the fabric of life and its divine and human responsibilities. Here Qoheleth confronts us squarely with the free-will versus determinism tension that has always perplexed the finite human mind, and he is no more a mechanical determinist than any other biblical writer who broaches the subject. Granted, God determines in a non-negotiable way many human activities. However, there are decisions he leaves to us and fits into his eternal plan.

The warp of time and its role in God's providence has left perplexing questions, perhaps temporarily, perhaps eternally. Yet after all of his afflicted study of the world and all its matters, Qoheleth is able to utter the words of ultimate, comprehensive faith – God has made everything *beautiful* in its own time! This is the greatest statement of divine providence in the whole of Scripture. It is the theorem from which the believer's hope is derived that all things work together for good for those who love God (Rom. 8:28). It is a statement far beyond describing God as a divine pragmatist, a distant, cosmic manager who at best manipulates energy and matter to assert his prerogatives within his unlimited power. Instead, it glorifies God as an artistic designer, who enjoys a proactive and interactive relationship with his creation, particularly with those he expects to reflect the same attributes – human beings.

Though we are finite, God has blessed humanity with an etching of the eternal on our soul, an imprint that guides our thinking towards our infinite God and his innumerable, incomprehensible ways. Without this capacity, we would be even more equivalent to the beasts that obey out of instinct rather than awe. On the other hand, with this eternal intuition we must be satisfied to know that God distributes his grace in palatable and unpalatable ways, and with only selective disclosure of his works and reasoning (other than that he prefers the patterns of the past). In other words, we are 'blessed' to know too much that it hurts (1:13) and too little (3:11) because we must trust.

Nevertheless, though we are limited in many designed ways, Qoheleth emphasizes human responsibility by placing it at the fore of this passage. Just as God does everything beautiful in his timing, we are expected to do everything in its time as far as we are empowered to do so. We were created in God's image, we are to be mature as he is mature (Matt. 5:48), and we are to reflect his nature in the timing of our activities. In these 'Beatitudes of Solomon', we hear the call to compose our works according to the rhythm of life's staccatos, whole notes and rests. Between the absolute statutes for the believing community and the utter freedom of rest and recreation lies the moment-by-moment decisions that impact the success and shalom of ourselves and those for whom we are accountable. Christian sanctification syncopates diligence with patience, restraint with spontaneity, persistence with realism, justice with mercy, even love and hate. Biblical principles abound to assist the believer in these frequent decisions that make up every day. Our 'Edenic gardens' in which we toil each day are to be subdued and managed by our timely *decisions*, not ruled by circumstances said to 'overwhelm' us, or by others who invade our sovereign realms.

So what if we do strive to be wise, diligent and productive, what is the advantage? Qoheleth's thematic question of 1:3 reappears here, not after a negative passage about work, but after one of the highest callings to wisdom and success. The question persists, and will for the rest of the speech if not only implicitly. Though the answer to this question has already been given clearly in 2:10–14 and 24–26, Qoheleth recycles the question to go even deeper theologically. Again, we are encouraged to enjoy life by our eating, drinking, working and righteous pursuits, since this is our advantage in our hard work! This is not a call to hedonism, however defined, but the implicit message of Eden – work and enjoy the fruit of your garden, or resist and work much harder for the same reward. Nonetheless, the same reward is offered before and after the Fall, even after Adam misplaced his reverence. Because of the simplicity of the answer, we miss it. Instead, we add our own afflicting standards of what an 'advantage' should entail. We improvise a better answer to the question, such as our hard work should earn us God's grace, should grant us fuller understanding of God's mysterious ways, make us more popular and reputable, enamour our children, defeat our enemies, canonize us! We should be perfectly healthy, very wealthy and have few or no trials. But these are not Qoheleth's answers: he experienced great affliction even in seeking wisdom without chasing evasive, improbable fantasies.

All things do work beautifully for those who fear God, and he helps us to revere him in various ways. We respond to him in awe and worship because his ways are beyond our understanding, yet his grace is felt intimately. His infinite might is only hinted at by the expanse, power, diversity and grandeur of the cosmos. His plans are impregnable, eternal purposes that remain uncompromised since an unknown past. He is faithful and predictable to an extent that we can trust him without his being reduced to a manageable entity. His moral law can be seen commonly enough in all cultures, even in sorely pagan societies so that adequate order still reigns in the midst of human defiance. His justice will prevail and the systems of injustice will be dismantled even if not replaced with perfect theocracies. And finally, according to Qoheleth, we fear God because we are so clearly unlike him, as creatures closer to beasts; only we have the capacity to love and fear the Creator. We fear and love God not because he is safe, but because, as C. S. Lewis describes his divine lion, Aslan, God is *good*.

It is understandable that when God's perfect sovereignty is mentioned, especially his beautifying providence, that the issue of injustice should crop up as an explicit challenge. Qoheleth anticipated this and discusses the subject specifically. Injustice, simply put, is an immoral act from which others feel the consequences. Since we live perpetually in relationship, injustice is the most frequent sin. Of course, the severity of the injustice varies in the widest ways. The continuum goes from imperceptible injustices to rape and other forms of torture and genocide. How are these woven into a beautiful fabric? We are told in this passage that we cannot know the ways of God from beginning to end. We can wink at this consolation with condescension and arrogance, or we can accept it as truth, even if we feel disarmed to defend God's justice. Furthermore, the pain and oppression in this fallen world should not be muted by Christians in order to feel more comfortable with their God. There is no acceptable posture other than sunken sorrow for the excruciated. There is no other appropriate response than helping those within our reach. But again, in the vein of synergy with God, we must trust that his justice will come in his own time. Very often we see it, but other times we do not, though it has in fact occurred. The rest of the cases we leave in the trustworthy hands of the Almighty.

We must not get carried away with our status before God. Because we are in his image, because we have souls, because Christ died for us, because God desires us to reign with him for ever, does not make us closer to God's essence than to the essence of animals. We are far superior to the beast, but are equidistant as the beast from God's infiniteness. God proves to us through the recurring curse of death that we are animals, finite mammals that are merely God's creations: equally subject to his will; equally dust; equally distant from his infinite transcendence. He works all things according to his sovereign will, whether it is the falling sparrow or the reigning king (Eph. 1:11; Matt. 10:29; Prov. 21:1). Our DNA is very similar to that of other mammals – we even share the same 'breath of life in our nostrils' (Gen. 2:7; 7:22). Furthermore, the fall brought humans and animals even closer in identity, since humanity became less reflective of God's image and more beastly in its lusts and conduct. God's intention for death ever since the Fall was for the dust, whether of human or beast, to become dust again (Gen. 3:19; Job 10:9; 34:14–15; Pss 104:29; 146:4). But, though there is no advantage over the beast in respect to death, Qoheleth wants to assure us that there is still a definite advantage for humanity *in life*.

Qoheleth will have told us often by the time he is done that we are to make the most of the here and now, the most of our work, the most of our wisdom and joy. It is not that he does not have a perspective on the afterlife; it is that he does not want his people to be distracted by it. We do not know what Qoheleth specifically believed about life after death, and do not need to know when accepting his message of managing life and its advantages. Though the immortality of the soul helps complete a comprehensive theology, it is unnecessary to give deep meaning to the 'now' of our existence. Eternal life is a *further* blessing; it is not the main blessing for those who are already walking with God and enjoying his presence and gifts. So Qoheleth's charge is to be happy in this life without worrying about what happens on earth after we die. We cannot know what will follow our death, so make it count now! Guessing at what the future holds for survivors of our death at the expense of *all* current, God-given enjoyment is unwise. In fact it is irreverent! Self-flagellation, sanctimonious sacrifice or any form of unnecessary deprivation is unimpressive to God. Rather, accepting his gifts are the sign of respect and appreciation.

God is sovereign and expects us to act wisely as his vice-sovereigns in this world even though we do not have exhaustive knowledge, immediate justice or divine status. Our advantage to performing our duties is an enjoyable life regardless of the imperfections of ourselves and our surroundings.

ECCLESIASTES 4:1 – 5:9

Translation

[1]So I again considered all forms of oppression under the sun. Oh, see the tears of the oppressed, yet there is no comforter for them! Though power comes from their oppressors' hand, for them, there is no comforter. [2]Those who were already dead I considered more fortunate than those who were still alive. [3]But better than both is the one who has not yet existed, who has not seen the evil deeds that have been done under the sun. [4]So I have seen that every labour and every advantage from one's actions are surely someone else's envy. This also is temporary and like the whim of the wind.

[5]The fool who folds his hands eats his own flesh. [6]Better a palm full of rest than two hands full of toil and a whim of the wind. [7]So I again considered brevity under the sun. [8]There is the one who is without a beneficiary, not even a son or brother, and there is no end to all his toil, even his eyes are not satisfied with wealth. 'But for whom am I toiling and depriving my soul from pleasure?' This is also temporary, and it is a tragic affliction.

[9]Two are better than one because there is a good reward for their toil. [10]For if one falls, the other one can lift up his companion. But too bad for him, the one who falls, but there is not another to lift him up. [11]Also if two lie down together, they are warm – but how will only one be warm? [12]And if someone overpowers him who is alone, two will stand against him. And a cord of three strands is not torn quickly.

[13]Better a common yet wise young man, than an old yet foolish king who does not know enough to be warned. [14]For he comes out of prison to reign, though in his kingdom he was born poor. [15]I have observed all the living and their ways under the sun – they side with the next young man who stands in his place. [16]There is no end to all the people, all those whom he led, yes, surely his followers were not pleased with him. Indeed, even this is temporary and like the whim of the wind.

[5:1[4:17]]Watch your footsteps when you go to the house of God, and go near to listen rather than to offer a sacrifice of fools who do not know they are doing evil. [2[1]]Your mouth should not be quick, nor your heart hasty to speak a word before

God, for God is in heaven, and you are on the earth. So let your words be few. [3][2]Surely fantasies come from many afflictions, just as many words do from the voice of the fool. [4–5][3–4]When you make a vow to God, do not hesitate to pay it, for there is no pleasure in fools. So pay your vow. It is better not to vow than vowing but not paying. [6][5]Do not let your mouth cause your whole body to sin, and do not tell the messenger that it was a mistake. Why should God be angry at the sound of your voice and destroy your hands' work? [7][6]Indeed, in the middle of many fantasies and brevities, and many words, truly fear God!

[8][7]If you see oppression of the poor and justice and righteousness stolen away in the province, do not be terrified by the matter, since each official oversees another official and there are other officials over them. [9][8]Furthermore, there is an advantage to a land – a king devoted to a cultivated field.

Notes on the text

1. 'again considered': lit. 'returned and considered', using the very rare waw consecutive imperfect in Ecclesiastes – only in 1:7 and 4:1, 7. Qoheleth uses the waw consecutive perfect more frequently, yet still not often because of the combination of the speeches' philosophical and vernacular nature.

The posterior, resumptive *'ănî* (I) would be expected here and in 4:4, 7, since he 'returned' at one point in the past to analyse something closely again (see discussion on p. 78 about the simple past).

'all forms of oppression': Qoheleth did not see *all* the oppression, only all *kinds* of it.

2. 'I considered more fortunate': *šābaḥ* is difficult to translate, since it means to 'elevate in esteem', which would usually imply merit, something the dead are obviously unable to achieve. Here the irregular posterior *'ănî* (I) follows the equally irregular use of the infinitive abs. as a finite verb. The pronoun, even in this combination, restricts the tense to the simple past. Rubenstein (1952: 362–367) suggests that this syntax, which recurs in 8:9 and 9:11, is a sign of the vernacular, since its simpler form continues the predication more efficiently than any formal conjugation.

'ădenāh, 'still' here, *'ăden* in 4:3 (both from *'ad* and *ḥēnnāh*, BDB 725b) and *'illû* in 6:6 are all vernacular contractions comparable to the more colloquial English contractions such as 'I'd' for 'I would' and 'he'll' for 'he will'.

4. 'every labour and every advantage from one's actions are surely the envy of someone else': the exact meaning of this phrase is evasive, since it is unclear who the envious one is. Is it the one who has been successful because of his own jealousy, or is his success the envy of others? I propose the latter because it fits the context of 4:1–3 better and it is more consistent with Ecclesiastes to see toil's advantages as good.

8. 'beneficiary': lit. 'a second', but implies someone close enough to be a current recipient or eventual heir.

10. 'too bad': archaic, 'woe'. '*î* occurs elsewhere only in Mishnaic Hebr., and is thus considered late (Di Fonzo 1967: 192; Whitley 1978: 43). There are many cases of a biblical word occurring once or twice in early Biblical Hebr. but only again as late as Mishnaic Hebr. For instance, another interjection, *hē'*, appears only in Gen. 47:23, Ezek. 16:43 and in Mishnaic Hebr.

The anticipatory pronominal suffix *ô*, which refers to the one referred to in the next word, is a colloquialism appearing here, 'for *him*, the one', and again in 4:12, 'overpowers *him* who is alone'.

13. 'young man': *yeled* could be upwards in age to the over-forty crowd of Rehoboam's sorry advisors (Eaton 1983: 95).

'common': *miskēn* does not necessarily mean 'poor' in the ANE, per Seow (1997: 185), though we learn later that the young man was indeed 'poor' (*rāš*, 4:14). The word itself is an Akk. loanword rather than an Aram. (Whitley 1978: 44).

15. 'the next young man': who exactly is this *haššēnî* (the second)? Is he the first successor to the first king as in 4:13–14, or a second successor, thus the third king mentioned? This question is discussed at length in most commentaries but virtually all conclude, probably correctly, that there is a succession of three rather than only two kings in this passage.

16. 'all those whom he led, yes, surely his followers': these people are those whom the king stood 'before' (*lipnêhem*) and who 'followed' (*hā'aḥărônîm*) this king as their leader in a political and spatial sense, rather temporally preceding or postdating in time; for example, Delitzsch 1975: 280.

'whim': *rĕ'ût*'s less common synonym *ra'yôn* is used here in this *hebel* formula; however, the formula is still alliterated.

5:1. 'who do not know they are doing evil': the phrase is elliptical and has been translated as above or in a way that portrays the fool as not knowing *how* to do evil. The latter option is impossible, for that is why they are fools: they certainly know how. They know it is wrong to offer shallow worship; it is just that they are too foolish to recognize that what they are doing is folly! Thus the warning later (v. 6) that to plead ignorance or to claim to having simply made a mistake will fall on deaf ears.

2. 'be quick': *bāhal* (hasty) is considered by many to be a late Aram. (Murphy 1992: 46), even though as a ni. it appears in Prov. 28:22 and Zeph. 1:18. An argument is made that there is a drift from 'terrify' to 'hasten' in Aram., and, since *bāhal* has these meanings in Hebr. as well, there must have been Aram. influence. However, G. R. Driver (1931b: 253) and Palache (1959: 12–13) show that 'fear' and 'hasten' are simultaneous meanings for two other roots that are indisputably native Hebr.: *ḥûš* (Driver) and *ḥēpeṣ* (Palache). Vanderkam (1977: 245–250) sees *bāhal* to mean 'speak passionately' and from a root common to Akk., Arab. and Eth.

4. 'pleasure': see 'Notes' at 3:1 for the two meanings for *ḥēpeṣ* in Ecclesiastes.

6. 'messenger': *mal'āk* simply means 'messenger', but the challenge is determining what official this actually is. Is it an angel responsible for the temple or its altar (Ginsberg 1950: 30; Rofé 2003: 369–370)? Is it the priest himself, drawing upon a rough parallel with Mal. 2:7 (Lys 1977: 59; Seow 1997: 196)? I prefer the option of a vow collector who is lit. a 'messenger' (Scott 1965: 226; Gordis 1968: 249) rather than to inject what would be any surprising angelic participation into routine temple business. The use in Malachi is unique, paralleling a priestly messenger with a prophetic, if not the messianic, messenger (Mal. 3:1–7). See Salters (1978: 97–100) for a survey of the various views.

7. 'in the middle of many fantasies and brevities, and many words': Gordis (1968: 249–250) makes easy what for most others has been a genuine challenge. Taking the prepositional beth as 'in [spite of]', he paraphrases the earlier caution in 5:1–3 to revere God in heaven while frenetically pursuing 'religion' on earth.

8. 'province': *mĕdînāh* has been cited errantly as a late Aram., since it is a common root found in Ug., Arab. as well as Hebr. It occurs as early as 1 Kgs 20:14–15, 17, 19.

Form and structure

This unit, 4:1 – 5:9, continues on from Qoheleth's brief comments about unjust relationships in 3:16–17, by the initial phrasing 'again I considered'. Though he will touch on the issue of meaningful labour, his thrust in this section is to go deeper into relationships, both human and divine. When 4:1 – 5:9 is contrasted with the previous, highly theological, discussion of time and its role in human and divine wisdom (3:1–22) and with the following, focused treatment of wealth and joy (5:10 – 6:9), the profound role of relationships surfaces as an adhesive for the six components: 4:1–4 (oppression), 4:5–8 (isolation), 4:9–12 (cooperation), 4:13–16 (substitution), 5:1–7 (veneration) and 5:8–9 (administration). The 'solitary man' scenario in 4:5–8 does provide a contrast to the 'partners' of the following section, 4:9–12. In turn, these 'partners' balance out the oppressive potentialities of the mismatched envious oppressors in 4:1–4. These contrasting relationships form a loosely connected sequence. The hierarchical checks and balances of 5:8–9 resume the themes of 'unjust relationships' from 3:16–17 and 4:1–2. The cultic admonitions in 5:1–7 are different in tone, yet the stark one-to-one relationship of the sovereign, heavenly God with the impulsive, disingenuous fool indeed frames the ultimate relationship. Such a juxtaposing of human–human relationships with the individual–God relationship is certainly the basis for the structure of the decalogue and Christ's executive summary of the law and the prophets: 'You must love the Lord your God with all your heart, all your soul and all your mind. This is the first and primary commandment.

A second is like it; you must love your neighbour as yourself' (Matt. 22:37–39).

There are a few rhetorical aids in 4:5–8, where, because wealth has been shown to be so fleeting (4:4), Qoheleth renews the formulaic assertions of toil's temporary value. After the thematic refrain 'temporary and like the whim of the wind' in 4:4, he repeats the latter phrase, 'whim of the wind', in 4:6, and the former part, 'temporary', in the introduction and conclusion to his dispiriting vignette in 4:7 and 4:8. This weaving of various renditions of the theme of 'temporality' through these three verses leaves the clear impression that labour has no lasting value. Also in 4:6, we have the second in a litany of 'better than' statements in Ecclesiastes that affirm there are advantages in life – some things are better than others! Additionally, what appear to be contradictory proverbs in 4:5 and 4:6 force one to think wisely, not mechanically, and the wise should be able to handle the implied riddle (Prov. 1:5–6). The classic example of this type of pairing of proverbs is where one is instructed both to answer a fool, but *not* to answer the fool (Prov. 26:4–5).

For clarity, all verse references in ch. 5 are numbered according to the English translation rather than the Hebr. text. The Hebr. verses are one verse earlier. Thus one will find the Hebr. verse 5:2 to be referenced as 5:3 in this commentary.

Comment

1. Qoheleth now, 'again', broaches the subject of oppression for which five verses earlier he gave a consolation (3:16–17). He spoke of injustice there, but concluded that God's justice would eventually prevail. Yet it is not a glib consolation he offers there or here. Some commentators read this as a comment about socio-economic oppression only, a severe reduction of its scope. Oppression can come from all quadrants of life and is rampant at many levels in any given society: the womb, one's family, religious leaders, lenders, any unsecured road or alley, the workplace, the courts, possibly one's own local or higher government, or from foreign invasion, domination and confiscation of people and property. OT law, wisdom and prophetic discourse flow with efforts to pre-empt or express indignant grief over the unavoidable, overwhelming, abusive power from evil hands. Job's self-defence lists the ways by which he avoided being an oppressor himself (Job 29:7–20; 31:14–32; cf. Deut. 15:7). It should be remembered, however, that, as in Job's own situation, oppressive circumstances can be God-initiated or at least permitted for his purposes. Israel's regular cycles of tribal and national oppression and salvation are chronicled from Judges to Kings. Both internally and externally imposed, these times of severe discipline and deliverance present a story of the nation's obedience and disobedience, yet God's faithfulness persists.

Oppression by humanity, however, is the evil extreme of implementing the primary commission to subdue the earth (Gen. 1:28). Subduing the earth is to be done by the divine example and instructions for administering daily affairs at all levels and in all contexts. Brute, self-seeking abuse is contrary to the generosity of a giving God and to the principles for developing and ensuring a peaceful, loving community. Furthermore, common grace, not to speak of Israelite ethics, required the defence of the oppressed. That oppression is morally wrong is clearly implicit, and a reason for sympathy:

> Those oppressing the poor are insulting their Creator.
> (Prov. 14:31)

> Speak up for those unable to speak, defend the perishing,
> Speak up and judge fairly, decide in favour of the poor and
>   needy.
> (Prov. 31:8–9; also 28:15–16)

We already have a hope in the midst of hopelessness, provided by the previous section and the trust expressed there that God does everything beautifully in his time (3:11) and his perfect justice is the final word (3:17; see also 5:9).

So distressed is Qoheleth over there being no comfort for the oppressed that for emphasis he repeats it twice, lest anyone too smugly dismisses the tragedy. Actually, there may have been efforts to be comforting, perhaps as useless as those of Job's counsellors (Job 16:2), but perhaps with words of incomparable wisdom; still, there was no one who could successfully comfort these victims. Qoheleth is not a fatalist – he can report only from an impotent distance about the oppressed who have no comfort in sight. Brutal monarchic dictatorships surrounded him, and perhaps their representatives were present during this speech! Solomon, whose wisdom was sought after by even oppressive nations, expects that the righteous king will do as follows:

> For he will deliver the needy when he cries for help,
>   the afflicted also and him who has no helper.
> He will have compassion on the poor and needy,
>   and the lives of the needy he will save.
> He will rescue their life from oppression and violence;
>   and their blood will be precious in his sight.
> So may he live; and may the gold of Sheba be given to him.
> (Ps. 72:12–14 NASB)

Some of those convinced that Qoheleth is at best a cynic complain about his apparent inaction and that he does not offer a prescription for the cure; of course, neither do these commentators (4:1). Apart from the complaint ignoring the previous verses in ch. 3, it is true that 'fixing' is not always the goal of reviewing reality. Often the review is simply to alert the morally comatose, not to offer the easy answer in a sound bite; for instance:

> The poor plead for mercy,
>   but the rich answer with insults.
>
> (Prov. 18:23 NLT)

Besides, this is not the part of Qoheleth's speech where he offers many solutions. Later, he will become more of a problem solver.

2–3. That Qoheleth is not an impassive onlooker is shown by the extreme to which he goes to find comfort for the oppressed. Speaking specifically of suffering and being traumatized, death – according to Qoheleth – is better than life, although it is far from an appealing alternative. This will become less of a shocking response from Qoheleth, since he repeats it later in 6:3–5 and in 7:1, 26. Temporality is not always a curse: it can be one's deliverance. Paul echoes the same sentiment: 'I do not know which to choose ... having the desire to depart and be with Christ, for that is very much better' (Phil. 1:22–23; also Isa. 57:1–2). Though Qoheleth is not pitching the benefits of an afterlife, release from this life is nonetheless preferred. Where oppression reigns, those who have already died at least avoid current and additional mistreatment. The adverbs used in 4:2–3 are nearly the most important words in their sentences. They reflect grammatically the theological emphasis of 3:2 – that there is a timeliness to birth and death. Qoheleth is relieved for those 'already' (*kĕbār*) dead, who have escaped their oppression as opposed to those 'still' (*ʿădenāh*) alive (4:2). He is hoping other births which have not 'yet' (*ʿăden*) been, can be postponed until it is safe again (4:3). Qoheleth, by a circuitous route, actually affirms life by bemoaning only its timing. Suicide, abortion, infanticide or euthanasia are not options here. Qoheleth is not saying that it would have been better if these pitiful victims had *never* existed (per Seow 1997: 177–178), just that some would be better off dead rather than having to live under the current oppressors. This sentiment is more moderate than that of Job and Jeremiah, who, in understandably cathartic moments, appear to wish they had *never* been born at all (Job 3:3–20; Jer. 20:14–18).

4. This verse affirms that there is an advantage to one's labours. Unfortunately, the work and its fruit are envied by others. This, then, is not a negative comment about toil and success themselves; rather, it is Qoheleth's observation that the advantages from toil are envied by others to a point of possible tragic oppression and confiscation of the fruit of one's labours (cf. Exod. 20:17). Jealousy can be a positive description of a protective posture of God for his people, or a husband for his wife;

otherwise, in the OT it is a damaging attitude that can lead to rage and violence (Prov. 6:34). Again, Proverbs speaks similarly to Qoheleth:

> There is plenty of food for the poor in his field,
>> but it is swept away by a lack of justice.
>
> (Prov. 13:23; cf. 23:10)

So rather than this verse noting a capitalistic, competitive incentive principle, as many suggest, it describes the reason for much of the oppression referred to in 4:1. These advantages and successes have only a breathlike duration for the original owner as well as for the oppressor; thus they are temporary and like the whim of the wind:

> Don't tire yourself for wealth; stop considering that!
> Will not your eyes dart to see it, and – it is gone?
> For riches grow wings and fly away to the sky like an eagle.
>
> (Prov. 23:4–5)

Consequently, Qoheleth goes on in 4:5–8 to recommend moderation.

5–6. These two verses abruptly introduce a scenario of imbalanced living and effort. In a riddle format, Qoheleth juxtaposes two proverbial truths to which one would initially respond with some consternation. First, an indolent fool is described who is not industrious enough even to oppress others – there is not enough motivation even to be envious of others. He folds rather than uses his hands for any productive work, the hands being depicted as cooperative, intimate partners in laziness. The sluggard does not even try to succeed, and of course is impoverished.

> A little sleep, a little slumber, a little folding of the hands when
>> lying down –
> Then poverty will come like a thief, neediness like a shielded
>> robber.
>
> (Prov. 6:10–11; also 12:11; 24:33–34)

The 'eating sluggard' is a proverbial theme, graphically portrayed as a fool too lazy even to bring food up to his mouth from the dish (Prov. 19:24; 26:15; also 19:15; 20:13)! Isa. 49:26 describes self-cannibalism as God's judgment against Israel's oppressors. It is a biological fact that without food the body will 'eat' its own body mass to the point of emaciation. By implication, diligence is recommended in 4:5, as it is in 9:10 and 10:18, but here it is qualified both in this moderating proverb and in the scenario to follow. Diligence is not the thrust of this passage, since if no time is set aside for enjoyment one cannot enjoy labour's even temporary rewards, regardless of one's hard work. A whim of the wind can rapidly make it disappear.

However, quiet rest is good too, especially when balanced with toil. But this rest is very different from the fool's idleness in that it is earned, not simply presumed. Qoheleth affirms the deserved rest of the labourer: 'The sleep of the worker is sweet, whether he eats a little or a lot' (5:12). This is the rest of the evening or sabbath (Exod. 23:12), not sleeping late into the morning. It is the proper proportion, using one hand each for rest and work. Whereas 4:5 says the hands are only full of themselves, 4:6 speaks against hands that are only full of labour. This healthy alternation of work and rest is consistent with Christ's encouraging words that his yoke is easy (Matt. 11:30), it is fine to take breaks (Mark 6:31) and his charge not to be anxious for food and drink (Matt. 6:31). He says that God will give these basic needs, just as Qoheleth says frequently (2:24–25; 3:12–13). But as Paul demands, the lazy who do not work should not be fed; instead, they should be encouraged to work quietly and eat their own bread (2 Thess. 3:10–12).

7–8. A person who does not understand this balance of rest and work is the subject of these next verses. Here is a solitary man toiling for wealth but not taking the time to enjoy it before it is gone like a breath. The scenario is introduced as an example of transience and concluded so; the brief term of labour – and its possible enjoyment – is expressed in the first and last phrases. However, this example of the fleeting nature of wealth is especially a tragic affliction because this person's problem is self-imposed. He voices a rendition of our programmatic question about the advantage of hard toil, 'For whom do I labour?' His quest for an advantage is voiced relationally: What benefit is there, since there is no heir, either younger brother or son? So he is not a miser who is unfair or ungenerous; he simply has no family for whom the fruit of his labour can be a gift of himself and his devotion. Unfortunately, even in this he does not grasp that the advantages are for *him* to enjoy as well. Rather than availing himself of labour's advantages (*yitrôn*), he afflicts himself with the opposite, the disadvantages of 'self-deprivation' (*ḥāsēr*). Thus the restfulness of 4:6, and the advantages referred to in Qoheleth's refrains of joy are not experienced, because this solitary soul is not accepting God's gifts. He has two handfuls of toil rather than one of rest and one of enjoyment. Tragic!

9–12. These verses introduce a relief to the negative relational scenarios started in 4:1 about oppressive competition and concluded so far in 4:8 about lonesome toil. Qoheleth sets the solitary man in 4:8 – pitifully alone, without family or heir – in diametric opposition to the advantages of human companionship and cooperation.

In this section we hear again Qoheleth's emphasis on success, which reaffirms that he is far beyond his fleeting emotional outbursts against all wise work in 2:18–20. He understands the importance of enjoying work and life, and here describes some of those benefits in the context of fruitful relationships. 'Two are better than one' because there is a good, not a meaningless, reward (*śākār*) for their labour (*'āmal*)! *śākār* (wage, reward) is synonymous with *ḥēleq* (reward), and joins the cache of words Qoheleth uses to speak of the advantages to work in answer to his initial question in 1:3, 'What profit . . . ?' If everything were futile, there would be no basis on which to say anything was better than another.

The advantages to partnership are found not only in the economic profits from joint efforts but also in availing deliverance from any 'fall' – physical or metaphorical. Such partnerships bring comfort and warmth, protection and victory. Some commentators see the common strain to these advantages to be the benefits of travelling together. Such a search for a unifying motif is commendable but probably too restrictive for Qoheleth's purposes. As in 3:1–8, the short linguistic strokes are not intended to paint detailed landscapes but to suggest scenes into which the listener places applicable persons and objects. For instance, lying together for warmth was a good idea for travellers through the cold desert nights, but is also applicable for a frail king who needs another body for warmth to survive (1 Kgs 1:1–4) and appropriate for shepherds, spouses and watchmen (while off their shift!). These benefits, then, are metaphorical as well as generic – not merely a familiar story or specific circumstances intended to limit the imagination of Qoheleth's audience.

It is a form of speech found in wisdom literature to incrementalize the truths offered by adding another number to the saying. So, for instance, in Prov. 30:15–17, 21–23, 29–31, a numeric proverbial technique is to move from two to three to four examples, or simply from three to four. Here in Ecclesiastes, we move from two partners to the better advantage of three partners, something already expressed in the Gilgamesh epic where such a human alliance is compared with a three-stranded rope as well (see Shaffer 1969: 159–160; also de Savignac 1978 for a fuller discussion of parallels between Ecclesiastes and Gilgamesh).

13–16. Qoheleth has moved within ch. 4 from speaking about relationships of oppression to isolation to cooperation, and now to substitution. Whether one sees this passage chronicling a succession of either two or three kings, the relationship of losing one's position to another is nonetheless a main point. Qoheleth's commentary on the succession of kings reaffirms his interest in 2:18–21 in the inevitable passing of one's kingdom or estate to another, and how fleeting one's impact can be. The situation is reversed in these verses, however, since Qoheleth's wise reign was very possibly going to be followed by that of a fool. Here a foolish king is replaced by a wise young man. The Hebr. of this passage has various ambiguous phrases, and for a very efficient yet thorough survey of this passage's many challenges to interpretation, see Wright 1997: 142–154.

The supremacy of wisdom that Qoheleth stresses in 2:13–14, and that has been substantiated pervasively, is accentuated here by asserting that wisdom, even with poverty, is better than folly with the prerogatives of royalty. Though we are not told precisely why this young man was in prison, he nonetheless is from humble origins: he is born poor and is an ex-convict. Incarceration in those days was not in lifelong penitentiaries for hardened criminals; such individuals would have been executed. Often, those in prison were there as political enemies or debtors. Either reason would be applicable in this context, either as a threat to the current foolish king, or because of some indebtedness as a poor person. The king's status, however, is slightly more known: he was simply unteachable. There is no reason to excuse his behaviour because of senility or some other affliction. Like Solomon, he could have lost his wisdom through the debility of age or pomposity. Qoheleth echoes conventional wisdom:

> It is better to listen to the rebuke from the wise
>   than to listen to fools sing.
>
> (Eccl. 7:5)

> Words from the wise heard quietly
>   are better than a shouting ruler around fools.
>
> (Eccl. 9:17)

> A fool is impressed with his own decisions,
>   but the wise listen to advice.
>
> (Prov. 12:15)

> Those who take advice are wise.
>
> (Prov. 13:10)

> Those listening to instruction will prosper,
> and those trusting the LORD will prosper.
>   (Prov. 16:20; also 15:22; 19:20; 28:16)

Godly wisdom is available to all who are teachable, whether they are young or old, princes or paupers. Surely Solomon's father, the sheepherder David who rose above King Saul, is an example of this. Elihu is another (Job 32:4–11). How or why this wise, young man became the king of the land in which he was born poor is not told. It is unimportant to the account, as are a number of details in this intentionally underdeveloped story. In all of its vagueness, this vignette simply sketches a frequent political scenario. Qoheleth is interested in general principles while describing his world view, so any direct, obvious historical allusions would compromise that. Though it would have been hard perhaps for the Israelites present in the audience not to think of David or Joseph (e.g. Ogden 1980: 315), no one biblical story fits all the parts, and that would have been just as glaring as any similarities. David was apparently not in prison, and Joseph never became Pharaoh. Consequently, no Israelite figures, whether in early or late biblical history, specifically qualify.

We noted in ch. 2 that Qoheleth was more horrified of being 'forgotten' or marginalized than of death itself. Qoheleth's fictional king here is marginalized for his foolishness and understandably replaced by a wiser leader. Nevertheless, even this young leader's popularity and ability to manage is temporary. The new king's subjects – whose loyalty to their new king is not necessarily based on their leader's wisdom – will inevitably prove fickle; he will find himself like the poor wise man who saved a city in 9:16, completely forgotten. Those innumerable followers he leads will become disenchanted with him, and eventually even this wise king is replaced by another and presumably forgotten as well. This is not only implied but said explicitly; surely his popularity is temporary and like the capriciousness of wind. The whims of the masses and the reign of the wise are as momentary as the direction of the wind; so Gordis 1968: 244 and Fox 1999: 224. This section of Ecclesiastes, 4:13–16, has received more attention than many others, and good articles to reference are Ogden 1980, Wright 1997 and Weisman 1999.

5:1–3. Qoheleth now treats the human–divine relationship after three sections dealing with human relationships. It should be clear by now, in studying Ecclesiastes, that Qoheleth's comments about wisdom are consistent with the poetic books – especially Proverbs – and with the histories and prophets as well. This temple passage we are about to discuss is consistent as well with the theology and cult of ancient Israel. It is possible to view Qoheleth as less than an orthodox theologian and sage only if one subscribes to an errant understanding of *hebel* as 'vain, futile, meaningless, absurd'. This one pervasive mistake in translating a critical word in Ecclesiastes has displaced an otherwise natural reading of a Hebr. realist's sensible, though edgy, orthodox world view.

Qoheleth's tone to this point has been reflective and suggestive rather than imperative. But now, when he addresses the issue of worship, he takes on a stern and direct demeanour. After 5:1–7, he does not return to quite this level of strict tone, though he does begin a directive style again in ch. 7. Some, to various degrees of specificity, have seen clear structures in 5:1–7. Spangenberg (1998) gives the best historical survey of structural approaches to this section in addition to offering a specific parsing of the phrases into a parallelism, building on Lohfink's analysis (2003: 76). These readings reach a bit far, but are right to assume there is at least a simple parallel in 5:1–3 and 5:4–7: cultic action (sacrifice) and listening, not speaking (5:1–2), is followed by a cryptic 'dream aphorism'. This is paralleled by the cultic action of speaking (vowing, 5:4–6) followed by another cryptic 'dream aphorism' (5:7).

The picture here is of an impetuous fool running into the temple with a burning desire for some fantasy for which he wants to strike a deal with God through sacrificing and vowing. Though it is commendable to come to the temple to make sacrifices and to take vows, the temple is also a place to listen to the reading of the Law and the teaching of the priests; it is not a place to be rash and unthinking, to rattle off some dreamy fantasy. The gladness with which one responds to an invitation to go to the 'house of the LORD' humbly reflects the wise heart to come (Pss 5:7; 95:6; 122:1; Mic. 4:2; Heb. 12:28). Jas 1:26 says, 'If one thinks one is religious without bridling the tongue, he deceives himself and his religion is useless.' Though this evil or irreverence may not match that of the wicked who come and go from the temple in 8:10, we will find that this fool's tendency merely to talk but not walk in obedience may end in God's destructive judgment (5:6). One is reminded of David's point 'LORD, who may dwell in your sanctuary ... those who speak truth in their hearts' (Ps. 15:1–2). The inferiority of inappropriate, disingenuous sacrifices compared to other acts of obedience is a common theme in the OT: 1 Sam. 15:22; Prov. 15:8; 21:3, 27; Isa. 1:12–17; Hos. 6:6; Amos 5:21–24; Mic. 6:6–8. Hypocrisy of this sort was the most frequent target of Christ's rebuke of the NT religious establishment. Furthermore, the 'walk' of the wise and fools often literally refers to their feet and is a 'wisdom' theme: see Prov. 1:15–16; 4:26–27; 19:2; Job 31:5; Ps. 119:101.

In the previous section, it was the inability of the old king to listen that aided his demise as the wise youth ascended. In 3:7, the virtue of silence was noted. Qoheleth concludes later in 10:14 with nearly identical language to 5:3 here, 'The fool multiplies words'. Proverbs again supports Qoheleth:

> When there are many words, sin is not absent.
>
> (Prov. 10:19)

> See one who speaks hastily? There is more hope for a fool than
>   for him.
>
> (Prov. 29:20)

And James agrees (Jas 1:19), 'Be quick to hear, slow to speak'. Consequently, it is especially true that restraint in one's speech would be advisable while in a place established for veneration and learning. God is not a peer with whom to blabber and chatter. Ps. 46:10 is blunter: 'Shut up; know that I am God!' Christ instructs his disciples before modelling a very short prayer: 'When you pray, do not be like the hypocrites who love to pray standing in the synagogues. ... While praying, do not use senseless repetitions like the Gentiles who think they will be heard better if they say a lot' (Matt. 6:5, 7).

Qoheleth warns his listeners that God is to be revered as the God of heaven, reminding us of his powerful description in 3:10–18 of God's sovereignty and divine prerogatives, and of psalmic reminders:

> Who is like the LORD our God whose throne is on high?
>
> (Ps. 113:5)

> Our God is in heaven; he does whatever he wants.
>
> (Ps. 115:3)

This first half of these parallel units ends in a comment about the dreams or fantasies that come from affliction. The meaning of this phrase has always eluded consensus. However, a good case is made for the metaphor to be synonymous with Qoheleth's thematic, momentary 'breath' (*hebel*) by Seow (1997: 200), referencing Job 20:8:

> He flies away as a dream, so they can't find him;
>   just like a vision in the night he vanishes.

These dreams are remembered often only when one is anxious, afflicted and sleeping lightly. Another possibility is that these dreams are delusions of success that the fool can only talk about and never pull off. So he comes to the temple to make a deal for a miracle through vows and sacrifices. The passage remains challenging. However, though there are lexical similarities between these verses and Jacob's dream at Bethel, that Qoheleth is intentionally subverting orthodox reverence in worship contorts a clear-meaning passage (contra Fidler 2006: 7–21).

4–7. In this second half of the parallel injunctions, the cultic topic changes from sacrifices to vows. Vv. 4–5 are nearly a direct quote from Deut. 23:21–23, thus completely orthodox and consistent with ceremonial law (also Ps. 50:14). Vows were voluntary until made, when they became an obligation with great penalty for ignoring them. Since they were unnecessary, Qoheleth and Deuteronomy suggest cautious wisdom, not overcommitting, and no 'mistakes' (*šĕgāgāh*). Lev. 4:22–27 and Num. 15:24–29 make sacrificial provisions for sins that are unintentional and claimed to be *šĕgāgāh*. Qoheleth's perspective is that a plea bargain is not allowed in this case. Because of this stringency, a translation of 5:1 that implies the fool is so foolish that he does not know he is even doing evil is probably wrong. See 'Notes' above at 5:1. Presumably the messenger to whom one should not even try offering a lame excuse is one of the priests' agents sent into the provinces to collect what was vowed.

The penalty for flippant vowing is ominous, to say the least (Josh. 9:18–20). Qoheleth repeats his concerns about fools speaking to their own destruction in 10:12–13. There it is the fool who destroys himself with his words, but this process could include bringing God's direct destructive judgment upon the sinner's work and estate as mentioned here. Perhaps these fruits of the sinful labourer are given to the righteous who do come to listen and obey (2:26). Thus these reckless words have only transient (*hebel*) value. In the midst of all the frenetic haste to sacrifice, vow this and that and be 'religious', we are relieved to hear that we are simply to revere God instead. There are no grounds to doubt that Solomon has reverence for God as the foundation for this lecture and for wisdom and righteousness in general. Paul also instructs those considering the sacrament of communion not to be hasty and risk personal harm (1 Cor. 11:27–30).

8–9. Qoheleth's sorrow for the oppressed expressed in 4:1–4 is not the result of his being shocked by their ill treatment, for he is intensely aware of such cruelty. These verses localize the oppression of 4:1 and the injustice and unrighteousness of 3:16 within the realm of a righteous king. Even in kingdoms such as Solomon's realm, there are cases of injustice. However, he waits until the end of his comments about relationships to describe this more frequent reality of administration in a fallen world where these environments are indeed correctable. The checks and balances in an administrative hierarchy where officials are held accountable by a fair king should be a consolation during temporary injustices. One should not be surprised or unduly terrified by instances of abuse of power in the land, since an effective, wise king will profit his land by cultivating his bureaucracy and controlling how his administrators conduct their affairs. The whole land profits when the king has a 'cultivated field'. Metaphorically speaking, by tending his personnel, removing the weeds and softening the soil, the proverbial agri-king protects his land and its people. Notice the agricultural metaphors in Proverbs:

> A wise king winnows the wicked,
> driving the threshing wheel over them.
>
> (20:26)

> A king who sits on the judgment throne,
> winnows all evil with his eyes.
>
> (20:8)

See also 14:35, 16:12, 20:28, 25:5, 28:2–3 and 29:4, 12. This may be one way by which God administers justice eventually in his time (3:17), and one hopes it is a temporary crisis that a wise king will correct. Here is an 'advantage' (*yitrôn*) to the hard work of the king's duties in administration. Though 'labour' (*'āmāl*) is not used literally, garden toil is intimated (Gen. 3); thus this is a positive answer to our thematic question whether there is any advantage to hard work, including people management (1:3).

Explanation

Personal relationships are the greatest blessing and greatest challenge for living wisely. People demand perpetual attention and return more frequent frustrations than any other source. They also bring the love and assistance that make each day bearable, if not fully pleasant. In this passage, Qoheleth covers many relationships (including 'no relationship') and, primarily, their difficult challenges.

The biblical theology of both the OT and NT honours the poor and oppressed and rebukes the believing community's denigration, at least, if not exploitation, of its weakest members. The position of the wisdom literature is that God has created both the rich and poor, the powerful and the weak, and he will vindicate them even if he does not always immediately deliver them (Prov. 22:2; 29:13). However, though each individual must answer for himself, there are times when standing in gaping horror is all that the individual can do, as he observes the genocides of the Third Reich, Bosnia and Rwanda, the ideological purges of the Inquisition, Stalin, Khmer Rouge and Darfur, and the torture squads of child pornographers and Islamic terrorists. Oppression comes in many different forms; for example, psychological, sexual and physical abuse by a spouse, parent or stranger; physical oppression of the unborn, child labourers, women sex slaves; sociological oppression by a despot or an ethnic majority; spiritual oppression by a primitive, cultic witchdoctor or by a church that excuses excessive 'authority' of its preachers, elders, husbands and fathers with twisted theologies of male 'superiority'. Truly, for the persecuted or sorely oppressed, not to have been born yet is a blessing – a future birth has a better chance of seeing a subsequently satisfying life.

The church has a very spotty record when it comes to defending the weak and poor. There have been great eras, including when early Christians saved discarded girl and other unwanted babies, the medieval church was a refuge for the sick and needy, Wilberforce initiated critical social reforms in England, and missionary orphanages, hospitals and enormous relief organizations were established. However, portions of the conservative pole have a politics of economic 'natural selection', while portions of the liberal pole honour an adult's 'choice' over the life of a helpless unborn child. We hear self-pitying sermons agonizing over persecution of believers' rights in the United States while Christian indifference encourages real, rapacious and deadly persecution of believers around the world, daily! The church must do better.

There is another oppressive condition – labouring through life without relatives or partners. We hear both sides of the coin from Qoheleth. We hear of the tragedy of isolation (4:7–8), and the benefits and consolations of partnering (4:9–12), painfully juxtaposed to accentuate by contrast the plight of the lonely. They get up in the dark, work until dark, go to dinner in the dark, rest in the dark and, regardless of their wealth, cannot satisfy their desire to work with or for someone who matters. On the other hand, what a fulfilling life it can be when there are those with whom we can work, go through trials, comfort and protect each other and synergize our strengths to be more successful and profitable in our life's objectives. One hopes the isolated man can find a partner equally isolated with whom the benefits of companionship can be enjoyed. Whether the companion is a spouse, a business partner, a fellow 'enthusiast' of any sort, the benefits are more than the sum of the output of each individually. However, the strongest relationships are formed under adversity, under profound common experiences that can change lives and impact kingdom work. This is not a passage encouraging simply golf or crafts friendships.

The opposite of companionship is witting or unwitting competitive relationships where one wins and the other loses. The competition itself is not bad, since diligence and wisdom should, of course, 'win out' over foolishness. However, bullying and oppression under the pretence of healthy competition is a ruse that vigilant believers will not only avoid, but will identify and discourage in the 'works done under the sun'. The ultimate competition at Armageddon is the model for aggressive attempts to defeat the enemy's nihilistic strategies to deconstruct God's providential economy of grace and justice. Though Christ's disarming of Peter in Gethsemane continues to be the military strategy for the church until Armageddon, every legal and ethical stratagem is employed to compete against evil folly. So young, rising leaders who replace ineffective leaders who are arrogant about their irrelevant messages and strategies, are a refreshing sight and relief for any organization. Yet in our era, an infatuation with political and media celebrities has taken over large portions of the news media, reducing public awareness to tabloid addiction. Qoheleth speaks to such shallow, fleeting and fickle attention given to leaders, even to deserving ones, regardless of their age.

Being old does not imply being wise, neither does wealth or social position. Yet structures abound which imbue leadership with unquestionable power, and which discourage or crush wisdom coming from any level. This can be at every institutional and societal level. Fortunately, there are leaders in government, the workplace and the church who are there because of their wisdom, having displaced entrenched, unteachable authorities. Sometimes their youth or humble backgrounds, or both, are despised, making the task more difficult. Elihu had to ask that his youth would not disqualify a hearing of his wisdom. Luther as well as other saints, through their wisdom, directed the church from far below its highest echelons. Denominations, the local church, its pastors and leaders need to be teachable as well. Wisdom abounds in its lay members: businessmen, artists and professionals from all works of life can bring deep, practical, spiritual insights into the church from the milieus in which they live and have a daily impact. The priesthood of believers cannot be simply a moniker where the 'professional clergy' are thought not only to have the keys to the church, but to have sole access to some imagined mysterious principles of spiritual living, leadership and church management. The pastor's role is to be a teachable servant who seeks guidance from those around, above and 'below' in order to best meet others' needs.

The individual's relationship with God is described in this passage within the sanctuary motif. Though the setting is specific, the principles are universal, since they represent an expected, perpetual posture of reverence before God. Whether we rush carelessly into the sanctuary or into any responsibility with a presumption that we know what is best and the Lord must bless it in any event, is foolishness. The vibrant relationship of listening to God and responding to his revelation is a living principle of sanctification for Qoheleth. Whoever is to be listened to and whatever they say is left open in this passage, but wisdom and truth should be pursued as if they will certainly be revealed by God through whatever means he wishes: 'But if any lack wisdom, ask of God who gives to everybody generously ... but ask in faith without doubting' (Jas 1:5–6). The assumption is that when one comes with a sacrifice, God is looking further for a relationship where he confers the blessing of wisdom on the worshipper, not where the worshipper attempts to bless the Lord with relatively vacuous words. Even vows, if with any pretensions of 'being serious', are best left unsaid. We cannot feign devotion with preposterous promises to God. Devotion is proven by teachableness and humility while pursuing the Lord's will, not our own fantastic innovations.

God's response to foolishness is more than annoyance – it can be punitive or redemptive anger, and potentially destructive in large proportions. Our relationship with God is not a hobby. It is not a tepid investment with moderate gains or losses. Recreational religiosity, lukewarm commitment and simple sipping of the deep spiritual substance of our privileged relationship with him can lead to a violent reaction from God (Rev. 3:16).

Finally, in an organization where the leader is trusted for his or her fairness, for professional prowess and for accountability policies and procedures integrated throughout the organizational chart, people should not be alarmed by exceptional injustices. The 'system' should work; so frantic alarm and mass hysteria over injustice is unnecessary. It is a fallen world where self-seeking souls can be mistakenly hired or promoted. Whether it is government, business or ministry, sinful people will affect the organization. So accept resignedly some inevitable and hopefully infrequent abuse of power. To echo Qoheleth in another context, 'You know you are guilty of the same thing yourself' (7:22). It is natural to feel that injustices towards us are more egregious than to anyone else. However, placing our experiences in the wider picture of all human experience should be a consolation if we are within a watchful and shepherding context.

ECCLESIASTES 5:10 – 6:9

Translation

[10–11]Money does not satisfy whoever loves it; whoever loves many possessions – no increase. This also is temporary, since when prosperity increases so do those who eat it. So what advantage is it to its possessors except for their eyes to view it?

[12]Sweet is sleep to the common worker whether he has eaten a little or a lot. But the many possessions of the rich do not allow them to sleep. [13]There is a sickening tragedy I have seen under the sun – wealth hoarded to the owner's own severe detriment. [14]For that wealth perished in a tragic hardship, so when bearing his son, there was nothing in his hand. [15]As he came from his mother's womb, he returns just as naked, taking nothing from his labours that had come into his hand. [16-17]This also is a sickening tragedy: in every way he came, he goes. So what advantage is there for the one who labours for the wind, who eats in darkness all his days, and in deep sorrow, even in his anxiety and grief?

[18]Look at what I saw: it is good and beautiful to eat and to drink and to enjoy one's labour which one labours under the sun the few days of one's life that God gives, since it is one's reward. [19]Really, everyone to whom God gives riches and wealth and has empowered him to eat from them and take his reward, happy in his labour – this is God's gift! [20]So he will not dwell on the days of his life for long because God answers through the joy in his heart.

[6:1-2]There is a tragedy I have seen under the sun, and it is overwhelming for humanity: a man to whom God gives riches, wealth and honour so that he lacks nothing he desires for himself, but God does not empower him to eat from them because a stranger eats from them. This is temporary and a sickening evil.

[3]If a man fathers a hundred children and lives many years – because there are so many days in his years – but his soul is not satisfied with goodness, or he has no gravesite, I say the miscarriage is better off. [4]For he comes in brevity and leaves in darkness; in darkness even his name is covered. [5]He does not even see or experience the sun. There is more rest for him than for the other. [6]Even if the father lived two thousand years but did not enjoy any goodness, do not both go to the same place?

[7]All one's labour is for his mouth, but even the appetite is not satisfied. [8]Really, what advantage does the wise have over the fool? What is there for the afflicted who know how to walk wisely before the living? [9]The view of the eyes is better than the roving of the soul. This too is temporary and like the whim of the wind.

Notes on the text

10. 'no increase': the second phrase is verbless, but rather than assume *śābaʿ* should be imported to this phrase, as most translations assume, the terse syntax should be allowed to speak for itself.

11. 'what advantage': *kišrôn* is synonymous with *yitrôn*, as most would attest; for example, Hertzberg 1963: 131; Lauha 1978: 110.

'its owners': lit. 'masters' (*bĕʿāleyāh*). The discord in number between this pl. form and the pronominal suffix in 'his eyes' may imply a pl. of majesty (GKC 124i).

'to view it': a few understand this to mean the burden of 'oversight'; for example, Zimmerli 1962: 192. But the simpler meaning, to view, is preferred by most; for example, Lys 1977: 18; Lohfink 2003: 78.

12. 'common worker': the word for the blue-collar worker, *'ōbēd*, is used here.

'not give him rest nor sleep': the hiph. participle of *nûaḥ* means 'give rest'. Some render this as a late rabbinic meaning, 'permit', but even this meaning is found in Biblical Hebr. in Judg. 16:26 and Ps. 105:14.

14. 'hardship': some commentators specify the loss to be business-related and ascribe fault on the owner for taking too much risk; for example, Scott 1965: 229–230; Galling 1969: 102–103. However, the classical biblical meaning of *'inyān* is less speculative and allows for any number of causes for the loss in addition to formal business dealings (Zimmerli 1962: 193–194; Hertzberg 1963: 131) and some of these reasons are of course mentioned in this section.

16. 'in every way': *kol-'ummat* is considered by some to be an Aram. only in the way the word is hyphenated, though its Hebr. origin is not denied; for example, Lauha 1978: 107. Isaksson suggests it is a Hebr. colloquialism (1987: 195).

'labouring for wind': *larûaḥ* is unique in syntax compared to its highly formulaic and usual pairing with *hebel*. Still, the temporary presence of the wind, in its coming and going, is the metaphor for the coming and going of this tragic person who does not benefit from his labour.

17. 'who eats in darkness all his days, and in deep sorrow, even in his anxiety and grief': a sequence of words introduced by waws concludes this verse and is a challenge for translation. Possibly the best explanation is Whitley's (1978: 55), which finds biblical precedent for distributing the beth of the first phrase to these other three circumstances of this poor soul.

18. 'beautiful': for *yāpeh*, see 'Notes' at 3:11.

19. 'empowers': for *šālaṭ*, see 'Notes' at 2:19.

20. 'answers': *'ānāh* here means 'answer', not 'occupy', as some presume along with a late date for Ecclesiastes. As in 5:13 above, a late Hebr. nuance to the word is unnecessary. Often the circular argument is given that this use is comparable to the late meanings found in 1:13 and 3:10. However, we have seen in those verses that a classical meaning, 'afflict', is preferable there too. For arguments for 'answer', see Delitzsch 1975: 303–304, Gordis 1968: 256 and Lohfink 2003: 84–85.

6:2. 'honour': this word completes a Solomonic triad found in 2 Chr. 1:11–12 as well: riches, wealth and honour. The idea that *kābôd* does not mean 'honour' but instead 'abundance' (Salters 1979: 283–284; Seow 1997: 210) is jarring given this *exact* biblical phrasing elsewhere. That one cannot 'eat honour' is obvious. But it is equally obvious that if there are two of three things that can be eaten from, namely wealth and riches, a sensible listener will easily make the distinction, especially when heard in the vernacular.

3. 'no gravesite': Seow (1997: 211) believes this phrase refers to a reserved burial *place* as it does in Deut. 34:6. This is preferable to the abstraction of burials in general.

5. 'for he comes in brevity': since the miscarriage is spoken of as a person, we translate 'he'.

'sun': no art. with 'sun' is consistent with the colloquial nature of Qoheleth's language.

'experience': *yāda'* here has the fullest meaning of 'to know'; that is, to experience. The miscarriage not only does not see the sun; it cannot feel its warmth.

6. 'even if': *'illû* is a contraction meaning 'if'. Since it occurs elsewhere only in Esth. 7:4 and post-biblical Hebr., some assume it is a later biblical word. However, Esther is not indicative of late Biblical Hebr. (Polzin 1976: 2) and contractions are more prevalent in a vernacular dialect with which Ecclesiastes already has many parallels.

9. 'view of the eyes': *rā'āh* can mean 'enjoyment', but, since this conclusion is parallel to the benefits of viewing referred to in 5:11, the rhetorical structure recommends a comparable rendering. For a fuller discussion, see Ellermeier 1963b: 1–20.

Form and structure

The Masoretes were correct in seeing 6:9 as the conclusion to the first half of Ecclesiastes. As a distinct section bound together rhetorically, it ends a series of developed and distinct sections (1:3–11; 1:12 – 2:3; 2:4–26; 3:1–22; 4:1 – 5:9), but is followed by a litany of more loosely connected and less developed sections until the concluding section of the speech in 11:1 – 12:8. Appropriately, 6:9 marks the last instance of the compound description 'This is temporary and a whim of the wind' conclusion, though *hebel* is used alone to conclude some observations in the second half of the speech. Furthermore, the joy refrain is expressed in the most thorough way so far and is the cumulative summary for Qoheleth's answer to the 'what advantage' question that drives his speech. It may not be going too far to say that this section is a summary to all that precedes it. Certainly it weaves the previous major themes of 'death', 'possessions', 'temporality', 'tragedy', 'God's sovereignty', 'the advantages to effort' (asked and answered three times) and 'the limited, but real, joys of life'.

This section of Ecclesiastes is one of the most intricately developed pericopes in the entire OT. There is an introduction (5:10–12) that sets three subjects before us (comparable to the role that 1:13 – 2:3 played in introducing 2:4–26) that will be developed twice in the two parallel units found in 5:13–20 and 6:1–9. Furthermore, this same section is also structured chiastically. My comments below will primarily follow the parallel structure, however, and the reader is referred to the detailed rhetorical analysis in Fredericks 1989: 17–35, which shows the coextensive chiastic and parallel structures in 5:10 – 6:9.

The flow of thought in these parallel units moves from a description of those who have property, to the temporary nature of the property, to the familiar question of 'what then is the advantage', to the answer of contentment and joy. The section serves, then, as more than merely a topical introduction but as a structural foreshadow of how the following material is constructed. Using the same roots in most cases and obvious synonyms in the others, the movement in all these verses is from the possession of wealth (they who love it and its increase) to its transience by different causes (*hebel*) to the question of what then is the advantage of one's labour, to a qualified positive recommendation to enjoy the present situation, whatever it might be; the latter being nothing less than the repeated thematic recommendation of Qoheleth elsewhere; for example, 2:24–25; 3:12–13, 22; 8:15; 9:7, 9; 11:9. So it is a section made up of three units that parallel the whole flow of Qoheleth's thought about joy and wisdom being the answer for those disillusioned about brevity in life. Indeed, these are themes found throughout Ecclesiastes; thus this unit is not unique in its content. But the separation of 5:10 – 6:9 from the immediate surrounding material is clear, since these issues are distinctly combined at the outset of the unit and continued through its length (see the table below).

	5:10–12	*5:13–20*	*6:1–9*
The wealthy	Money does not satisfy whoever loves it; whoever loves many possessions – no increase.	wealth hoarded to the owner's own severe detriment	a man to whom God gives riches, wealth and honour so that he lacks nothing he desires
Temporary property	This also is temporary, since when prosperity increases, so do those who eat it.	wealth perished in a tragic hardship	God does not empower him to eat from them because a stranger eats from them. This is temporary
What advantage?	So what advantage is it to its possessors?	So what advantage is there for the one who labours for the wind?	Really, what advantage does the wise have over the fool?
Contentment and joy	. . . eyes to view it – sweet is sleep to the common worker	it is good and beautiful to eat and to drink and to enjoy (see good) his labour	The view of the eyes is better than the roving of the soul

There is then a parallel development in these two halves of 5:10 – 6:9. Starting with tales of woe for the once rich, then emphasizing the inevitable journey into and out of life, these passages both press the question about one's advantage that begins the entire book.

However, there is yet another parallel schema found in this same section (see the chart below).

5:10–12		Introduction
13a	I.	There is an evil
b		A. Riches possessed
14a		B. Riches lost
14b	II.	Begetting
14c		A. Having nothing
15–16a		B. Coming and going
16b	III.	What advantage from toil?
17		A. No satisfaction
18–20		B. Contentment
6:1	I.	There is an evil
2a		A. Riches possessed
b		B. Riches lost
3a	II.	Begetting
b		A. Having nothing
4–5		B. Coming and going
8a	III.	What advantage from toil?
7b		A. No satisfaction
9		B. Contentment

It should be clear from the dual patterning of 5:10 – 6:9 along chiastic and parallel lines that it is an indivisible unit and should be well considered before any more broad schemata are proposed for the whole book of Qoheleth. For instance, Wright's (1968) schema includes this unit in a quite large section, 4:17 (Hebr.) – 6:9, and this passage could be absorbed conceivably in both its chiastic and parallel structures. Consistent with Wright's thesis, the extended *hebel*-clause in 6:9, which includes *rĕ'ût rûaḥ*, is certainly climactic, as concluded earlier in this study. Yet whether it closes as large a section as that beginning at 4:17 (Hebr.) is doubtful. Even Wright's comments on 4:17 (Hebr.) – 5:6 lack any clear connection with 'toil' or 'loss', the very themes supposedly basic to 4:17 (Hebr.) – 6:9 and that bear on 5:9 – 6:9. Loader's analysis of this passage with its view towards polarity is quite instructive in seeing how Qoheleth constructs his argument in detail along consecutive contrastive ideas (1979: 81–87; 1986: 62–70). Polarity is, of course, an effective pedagogical technique in which Qoheleth excels throughout and which Loader tracks nearly exhaustively. On the other hand, the structures of Qoheleth that divide 5:9–19 (Hebr.) from 6:1–9 (e.g. Rousseau 1981: 213–214) or terminate the unit prematurely (e.g. Laurent 2002, 5:9 – 6:6) are disturbed by our rhetorical or structural conclusions.

Comment

10–12. These three verses introduce the whole section by announcing how inadequately money and abundance can satisfy, especially if one is infatuated with money and its probably elusive increase. It is important that it is the 'lover' of wealth who will not find any satisfaction, however, since in this very section it is said that material prosperity can make one glad (5:19–20; 6:2). The second phrase in v. 10 goes beyond saying there is no satisfaction by stating tersely that neither is there any *sustainable, lasting* 'increase' (see 'Comment' at 2:11). 5:10 – 6:9 emphasizes many reasons why any 'increase' or advantages are merely fleeting and ultimately unsatisfying, including the facts that consumers multiply (5:11), awful events occur (5:14), God transfers one's wealth to another (6:2) or one consumes them oneself (6:7). And who specifically are these consumers of one's wealth? Presumably they come from all directions: employees or servants, one's children, one's wives, the poor, the tax collectors and so on. Proverbs warns about an increase in friends as well, or are they real 'friends'?

> The rich have many friends.
>
> (Prov. 14:20)

> Wealth increases many friends.
>
> (Prov. 19:4)

> Everyone is the friend of a gift giver.
>
> (Prov. 19:6)

Since possessions are only temporary, an important question in Qoheleth surfaces here, as it often does, 'What is the advantage in life?' (1:3; 2:11, 13; 3:19; 5:16; 6:8, 11; 7:11; 10:10–11). In this case, what is the advantage to the owner of increasing goods while they are being consumed by others? Qoheleth believes that what you can do is sit by and view the prosperity being gnawed away. This modest reward should not be underestimated, however. To hold one's possessions will be frustrating; simply amassing them will not satisfy. But seeing one's possessions serving those who consume them can make a neutral statement about consumption into an affirmation that there is value to money and property when others benefit as well. Looking at 4:8 is especially helpful, since there the eye is not satisfied with wealth because there is no dependant or other person to enjoy it too. Qoheleth speaks of unsatisfied eyes (1:8; 4:8; cf. Prov. 27:20) as well as satisfied eyes (2:10; 5:11; 6:9; 11:9).

But Qoheleth does not stop at the sight of one's property being enjoyed by others. He further answers the question of what advantages there are to one's labour by commending the peaceful, relaxed sleep of the common labourer. Since the virtue of hard work and moderate wealth is the formula for a peaceful but productive life, the common worker can sleep under any circumstances and be more satisfied than the wealthy (Prov. 30:8–9). Christ says, 'Do not worry about your life, what you will eat or drink; or about your body, what you will wear. . . . Who of you can add a single hour to your life by worrying?' (Matt. 6:25, 27; also 1 Tim. 6:6–9, 17). And Heb. 13:5 concurs: 'Keep your lives free from the love of money and be content with what you have.' The unsettled mind about the rate of income and its distribution as well as the unsated drive to strive for what is only temporary, leave the person too disturbed to sleep. The dignity and wisdom of the common man is extolled in 4:13 and 9:15 as well, contrary to those who might cast Qoheleth as an elitist; for example, Crenshaw 1987: 129. The realism of Prov. 17:1 is refreshing: 'Better a crust of bread with peace and quiet than a house full of feasting and strife.'

13–14a. Much like that certain case of a man in 4:7–8, these verses speak about a specific scenario, not of general truths applied to everyone. Both men amass wealth but find themselves in opposite circumstances. In that case, a man had no son to pass his riches on to. Here a man has no riches to pass to his son. This is a sickening tragedy because the hoarding of material things was the beginning of this person's problems. His materialistic priorities so distanced him from the realities of life that it was inevitable he would end his days in depression (5:17). Proverbs is aware of this tragedy:

> The wealth of the rich is their fortified city,
> They imagine the high walls are secure.
>
> (18:11; cf. Prov. 10:15)

However, these assets are not secure and are lost in an unspecified way. God's sovereignty is the cause for such a loss in 6:2, but in these verses, the emphasis is on the culpability of those whose great love is money. Farmer (1991: 153) aptly compares this short-term, self-centred heart to the hoarding of manna by the Israelites. Rather than depending on the Giver, it is human nature to depend only on what is given. As Christ instructs his followers, 'Do not store up treasures on earth, where they are eaten by moths, destroyed by rust and stolen by thieves. . . . Wherever your treasure is, there are the desires of your heart. . . . You cannot serve both God and money' (Matt. 6:19, 21, 24).

14b–17. Now, this destitute father has a son with nothing to support either of them, nothing to satisfy either's needs. Contrary to 5:11, where we find that when wealth *increases*, so do its consumers, v. 14 reveals a particularly vicious malady when consumption increases just at the time when wealth *decreases*. I take vv. 15–17 as referring to the man who lost his hoarded wealth rather than to his new son. It appears that this is a near-parable with one main character. The new son illustrates the essential poverty of arriving naked into the world and having nothing; he is not the focus of this scenario (contra Gordis 1968: 253).

Qoheleth emphasizes his pervasive theme on 'the temporality of life' by the 'coming and going' phraseology (1:4, generations; 3:20, humans and beasts), and here his voice is added to that of the wise and poets who remind especially the rich of the obvious – one takes nothing more out of one's brief life than what one brings into it:

> Naked I came from my mother's womb,
>   and naked I will leave.
>
> (Job 1:21)

> [The rich] will take nothing with him when he dies,
>   his splendour will not go down with him.
>
> (Ps. 49:17)

> We brought nothing into the world, and we cannot take anything out of it. (1 Tim. 6:7)

Qoheleth acknowledges death as one pole of our life's continuum, often pairing our origin and destiny to frame life's transience (3:2, 20; 5:15–16; 7:1; 12:7).

What, then, is the advantage to this person's labour? Well, because of his poor priorities, the usual positive response of joy and contentment is not given in vv. 13–17. Since riches are so easily lost, those who have loved and laboured for nothing else than riches have no advantage – they have laboured for the wind. The coming and going of the whimsical wind, its temporary presence, pictures the coming and going of the person. Not only have such individuals laboured for what is only transitory; the 'additional' (*gam*) sickening tragedy introduced in v. 16 is literally that – psychological and physical sickness! This wretched soul lives all the rest of his days in darkness, in great suffering and bitterness. This is the same darkness in which all fools walk according to 2:13–14. This person is spoken of in 1 Tim. 6:10, 'For loving money is the root of all sorts of evil. Some who are eager for money, have wandered from the faith and pierced themselves with many sorrows.' Similar circumstances plague another father in 6:3. Even if that father had a hundred children, if he is not satisfied throughout an exaggerated long life, he is worse off than a stillborn who is allowed to come and go in darkness.

18–20. The three subsections of 5:10–20 move from considering the frustrations of wealth in 5:10–12, to the expanded and more intense tragedies of 5:13–17, to this section, where the utter contrast is considered – a blessed life for anyone God favours (2:26). Another scenario is begun in these verses where the few people to whom God grants riches are allowed to retain them and enjoy them for life. It is possible, therefore, whether a common man (5:12, 18) or a rich man (5:19–20), to enjoy life as God blesses it. Whereas in 5:13, 17 we met a sickening evil Qoheleth had witnessed – riches that backfire – here we meet the 'beautiful' (*yāpeh*) and 'good' (*ṭôb*) life, where eating now is not in darkness and bitterness but in joy. Where there was no advantage to the hoarding man who has lost his wealth, now there is a definite advantage for those who enjoy the simple pleasures God gives. In this 'advantage refrain' in 5:18, we have Qoheleth's fullest expression of the temporary but real advantages to laborious toil, using all the significant lexical components found in the previous and later summaries: he has 'seen' (*rā'āh*) to be 'good' (*ṭôb*) and 'beautiful' (*yāpeh*) in one's 'labour' (*'āmāl*), the 'eating' (*'ākal*), 'drinking' (*šātāh*) 'under the sun' (*taḥat-haššemmeš*) during the 'few' (*mispar*) 'days' (*yĕmê*) God 'gives' (*nātan*) as a 'reward' (*ḥeleq*).

Even if the days are few, if they and their contents are the gift of God, how could they be meaningless or absurd, as most commentators would interpret Ecclesiastes? Qoheleth could not be any more explicit in affirming that there are definite advantages to hard work, especially when God adds his blessings. This is God's 'answer' to the trying, exhausting days of the labourer. He blesses those he chooses with gifts that keep their mind on the present when they can be productive rather than in the past when they can do nothing.

6:1–9. In this case, the sovereignty of God is seen in his choice to allow or not to allow one to enjoy one's gift of great wealth, but the unfortunate division of chapters here divorces these two parallel and contrasting expressions of that sovereign will.

1–2. Here, in 6:1–6, we have yet another 'unfortunate man' parable like those in 4:7–8 and 5:14–17. Though the exact problem in 5:14 cannot be specified, the net result is the same: both scenarios end as a sickening tragedy (5:13; 6:2). If any description of these tragedies is given, it could hardly be 'meaningless'. Instead, it is one further example of the transitory nature of the fruits of one's labours. Furthermore, in these first two verses there is a parallel sequence to 5:18–19 where the man was allowed to eat from his reward, but here the once-blessed man cannot eat from it, since a stranger is given that privilege. The reason for this bitter loss referred to in 6:2 is that God has transferred wealth to someone else. No explanation is given for how or why God keeps some from enjoying the wealth he gave them. Nothing is said, for instance, about whether or not the person deserved to be stripped of his riches and honour, as in 2:26. But whoever now enjoys these blessings is not even family or friend!

This scenario in 6:2 is rich in allusion both to an individual's personal prosperity and to that of Israel. It is Qoheleth's own God-given 'riches, wealth and glory' to which 2 Chr. 1:11–12 refers: 'I will give you riches, wealth and honour like none of the kings before you' (cf. 1 Kgs 3:13). This gifting from God is also not to be discounted by Israel: 'You say to yourself, "My power and the strength of my hand gave me this wealth." But remember the LORD your God, since he is the one who gives you the power to get wealth' (Deut. 8:17–18). And the loss of any God-given wealth is solidly a part of Job's theology: 'The LORD gave, and the LORD took away; blessed be the name of the LORD' (Job 1:21; cf. 1 Sam. 2:7).

God also reserves the right to give Israel's prosperity to an alien nation: 'The fruit of your land and all your labours will be eaten by strangers, and you will have nothing but cruel oppression all of your days.'

3–6. Whether or not these verses refer to the same man as the one introduced in the scenario of 6:1–2, the clear reading is that 6:3–6 is a generalization as well. And comparable to the once-rich man of 5:13–17, the point is that regardless of the number of offspring, one or one hundred, children certainly do not mitigate a disconsolate life. What is usually seen as one of the greatest blessings, one's own offspring, might only add to the dilemma of the impoverished. The person of 5:14 who has nothing in his hand, then, is in the same fix as this person here in 6:3–6 whose soul is not satisfied while alive or even at his burial. Though one may be blessed with many children and a long life, if there is no contentment, it would have been better if one had never lived that life. It would have been better for that person not to extend his few months in the womb to a life after birth, a life that would bring the darkness of sorrow, anxiety, sickness and grief – like that described in 5:17. This is an even more traumatic comparison than what we heard in 4:3, since there it was life *deferred* that was preferable. Here it is the opposite preference – definite, premature death. This preference is not unique in the OT, or in any culture for that matter. Job uses the same metaphors of darkness, light and rest:

> Perish the day I was born....
> Let that day be darkened.... neither let the light shine upon it.
> May darkness and shadows claim it again!
> Why did I not perish at birth, die while proceeding from the
>   womb?
> I would be lying in peace, asleep and at rest....
> Like infants who never see light.
> (Job 3:3–5, 11, 13, 16)

Jeremiah felt similarly:

> Curse the day I was born...
> cursed be the man who informed my father ... 'A son is born to
>   you'....
> For he did not kill me in the womb,
> with my mother as my grave.
> (Jer. 20:14–15, 17)

Another ancient sage, Ahiqar, represents all other cultures, those during the time of Qoheleth, before and since: 'My son, better is death than life to the man who has no rest' (Thomas 1961: 273).

We find that the one who laboured for wind (5:16) suffers in darkness comparable to that into which the stillborn descends (5:17). The description of the destiny of the stillborn, here in 6:4, is expressed in three consecutive prepositional phrases, similar to 5:17. Also the 'coming and going' of the stillborn is referenced with the exact terminology of 5:15, though of course the difference is in the duration between the coming and going. However, this contrast of their lifespans, in fact, serves to accentuate the similarity of their situation. The peace of the unborn, though they lived only briefly, would *exceed* the longer life of the man immeasurably, even if the longer life was two thousand years. At first in 6:3, the lifespan is just 'many years' – in 6:6, it is extended to fictitious lengths to make the point. It is true that the miscarriage does not see the sun, yet neither does he experience the tragedies in life; he has more 'rest' than the man who has many children yet cannot provide good things for himself or them. In that rest, the miscarriage is more like the easy-sleeping common labourer of 5:12 than the opulent rich or the now bankrupt, pitiful fictional father (see Isa. 57:1–2 for the pleasant 'rest' of the dead). Clearly, then, a temporary life is not in itself so bad, since the quality of life matters. However, this is not licence for any person to usurp the divine prerogative in respect to the unborn.

Socially acceptable standards for honour such as virility and old age amount to nothing if life is not full of the satisfaction wise labour can bring to a life that God so blesses. This includes being able to fund at least a burial site. Those who cannot afford to reserve a place to be buried (see 'Notes' above at 6:3) have more in common with the miscarriage than one might at first think. Like these miscarried ones, they are disposed of in a nameless, ignominious place. In this sense they even go to the same place, literally (Crenshaw 1987: 126), and they do go to the same place, generally speaking – Sheol, the grave (cf. 3:20; 9:10). Similarly, Jeremiah is told not to have children, since their non-existence would be better than suffering, dying and having their body disposed of like manure on the ground as their burial plot (Jer. 16:2–4).

7–9. Qoheleth returns to the point that started this section (5:10): people seem never to be satisfied. There it was with silver; here it is with anything! He also returns to the thematic question of his speech: since the fruit of one's labour has a limited effect on the unquenchable desires of the soul (6:7), what is the advantage to the wise, even if they are poor? The predominant concern of 5:10 – 6:9, satisfaction from the fruit of one's labour, is addressed at the earliest and latest positions in the unit while moving from concern with the wealthy (5:10–11) to observing *everyone's* situation in 6:6–9: the labourer, the wise and the poor.

Negatively speaking, the answer in 5:17 implies that there is no satisfaction, since the man there lost his wealth. The man has toiled for the wind and has nothing now to show for his labour. He does *eat*, but in darkness with a body and soul that are in terrible, unsatisfactory condition. In 6:7, we hear that toil can lead only to the advantage of *eating*, since the soul's desires are never satisfied. In both of these sections there may be bare sustenance, but the whole person is afflicted (5:17) or at least frustrated

(6:7), since he is never fulfilled. So in that sense we are back to the topic of 5:10 again – the insatiable materialistic soul.

Positively speaking, the enjoyment is real, though it may not reach the ecstatic, sensationalistic euphoria that many might foolishly expect. Together in parallel 6:7 and 6:9 speak of the gratification that can come from the fruit of one's labour for both the mouth and the eyes but not fully for the endless desires of the soul, especially as it meanders in perpetual search of satisfaction. Yet there are modest advantages: eating and viewing one's blessings. Qoheleth encourages enjoyment even in the context of the challenges, tragedies and burdens of life.

The question, then, whether there is a benefit to a life lived wisely is asked directly, and the answer is 'Yes', as long as one enjoys and is content with what the Lord has provided through one's wise labours. The pre-eminence of wisdom over folly is Qoheleth's explicit conviction, for example in 2:13–14, as well as a counterpoint to all the other themes within his speech. Now it is asked as well, what advantage is there for the afflicted? There is something to what they know that completes the parallel with the wise over the fool. Perhaps it is close to James's sentiments, 'Has not God chosen this world's poor to be rich in their faith?' (Jas 2:5). Exactly what it is they know is difficult to determine from this metaphorical language; but we infer this is the wisdom mentioned in the previous and parallel phrase. Here the walking, or 'going', is a metaphor for living as it is in 2:14, so even the poor are able to walk wisely and to obtain the advantages of wisdom, unlike the soul's carnal, roving pursuit of unattainable fulfilment:

> The one working his land will be satisfied with food;
>> but the one pursuing fantasies lacks discernment.
>>>> (Prov. 12:11)

The last words heard in 5:10 – 6:9 again are *gam-zeh hebel* (this too is temporary), only now in its more full and climactic form concluded by *rĕʿût rûaḥ* (whim of the wind), as in 1:14; 2:11, 17, 26; 4:4. Though the enjoyment of one's possessions with the mouth and eyes is better than the wandering soul, one should not count on it indefinitely, for such privileges are usually fleeting – they are best enjoyed now (similarly, see Garfinkel 2007: 62). The fuller statement of transience in 6:9, which includes 'the whim of the wind', marks the end of this section, indeed the end of the first half of Qoheleth's speech.

Explanation

This section is the most sustained section on wealth, money and enjoyment in the entire canon, and is undoubtedly the focal point and object of Paul's commentary on the subject in 1 Tim. 6. Qoheleth balances the assets and deficits surrounding money and wealth: it is a gift for some (5:18; 6:2); it can be protection (7:11–12); the deserving sometimes do not have it (9:11); it is unfulfilling for some (4:8; 5:10–12); it is a heartbreaking loss for others (5:14; 6:2), and to an extent it is an affliction to everyone (10:19). Along with the negative value of wealth there is an equal appreciation for the positive theme of 'enjoyment' by all those who are able or, better, enabled by God's will to benefit from it.

The wealthy are prime candidates for disappointment, especially if they are prone to love their money (1 Tim. 6:10; Heb. 13:5; Luke 12:15). Not only is it impossible to 'take it with you' in an eschatological sense (Job 1:21; Jas 1:11), but even on this side of eternity one may not have it long! Money travels fast – out of one's pocket – for a number of reasons. Unexpected large bills, disasters in the financial markets and in one's career, litigation, fraud, burglary and other hardships are possible with no certain financial recovery in sight. Whatever the apparent reason 'under the sun' might be, it is God's discretion to give and to take away, and the believer will need to trust while holding on to much or little (Prov. 10:22). As with nearly every responsibility before God, there is a trusting and a trying mode. It is unwise for one to try independently to amass wealth by roving about (6:9) and hoarding (5:13) everything around at the expense of others. Instead of moral compromises to supplement what God has provided, or will provide, one is expected to trust him for his perfect amount of blessing, while labouring honestly and fairly to gain a reward.

This is the message of Ecclesiastes: everything in life is temporary, so we need to be vigilant, though not anxious, about the uncertain future as God moulds and unfolds it. But those who love money will wither into depression when their beloved wealth leaves them for another. Since they will have laboured for wind, the once-wealthy will now sleep with only depression, disease and darkness. Such despondency can create a desire for death itself. Job's preference for never having been born, since his life was divested of satisfaction and contentment, is reflected by Qoheleth as well.

On the other hand, the commoner can sleep deeply and be quite satisfied with the modest pleasures that should be adequate for anyone's contentment. These simple sources of enjoyment are more easily renewed, though they are deemed inferior by those addicted to a possibly non-renewable 'higher standard of living'. But, whether one is blessed with minimal or optimal wealth, the advantage to one's labour is the wonderful ('beautiful'; *yāpeh*) condition of contentment with God's rewards and the labour that sets the table with food and drink which at least sustains, if not indulges, one's small span of life.

The church is responsible for teaching the right balance of wealth, contentment and stewardship from the pulpit. But the church must also model that balance through how well it uses its resources. It should exercise financial stewardship over its buildings, staff, salaries and programming expenses. What is true for the individual believer is also true for the collection of believers called 'the church'. The church is populated significantly by the impoverished in undeveloped or underdeveloped nations (not to speak of the deplorable condition of those to whom the deprived minister!). While the church can count millions within its family who are the very poor whom our Lord prefers to call his own, it is critical for its leaders to serve them most effectively without favouring those with gold rings and fine clothes. What could satisfy the soul of the affluent church more than filling the destitute church with its untold resources, the vast wealth that God has put in its hands?

ECCLESIASTES 6:10 – 7:22

Translation

[10]Whatever is, already has been identified and its nature is known – a man indeed is unable to prevail against whatever is stronger than himself. [11]Since there are many things that increase impermanence, what advantage is there for a man? [12]Who knows what is good in life for a man the few days of his brief life, for he spends them as a shadow. For, who can tell him what will be after him under the sun? [7:1]A good name is better than precious burial ointments, but the day of death is better than the day of his birth. [2]Better to go to a funeral home than to a party house, since it is everybody's destination and the living take it to heart.

> [3]Sorrow is better than laughter,
> for in a tragic face is a heart matured.
> [4]A wise heart is at a funeral home,
> but a foolish heart is at a house of pleasure.
> [5]Better to hear rebuke from the wise
> than for a man to hear a song of fools.
> [6]Really, as the crackling thorns under a pot,
> is the fool's laughter.
> Also this is temporary.
> [7]Surely extortion makes a fool of a wise person,
> and a bribe destroys one's heart.
> [8]Better is the end of a matter than its beginning;
> and the patient spirit is better than the proud spirit.
> [9]Do not rush your spirit to be angry,
> for anger rests in the gut of fools.
> [10]Do not say, 'What was it about the previous days that was better than
> these?', since asking this does not come from wisdom.
> [11]Wisdom is good with an inheritance,
> so there is an advantage for those who see the sun.
> [12]For wisdom is a shadow – money is a shadow;
> yet the advantage to knowledge is that wisdom gives life to its masters.

[13]Consider the work of God – for who can make straight what he has
    bent? [14]In the pleasant days, be pleased; but in a tragic day
    consider – surely God has made the one as well as the other in
    order that man will not discover anything after him.
[15]I have seen both in my fleeting days:
    there is a righteous man who dies in his righteousness,
    but there is a wicked man who lives on in his wickedness.
[16]Do not be excessively righteous and do not make yourself too wise –
    why overwhelm yourself?
[17]Do not be excessively wicked and do not be foolish – why die when it is
    not your time?

[18]It is good that you seize the one as well as the other; do not let your hand let go
of these, for whoever fears God comes through with both. [19]Wisdom is strong for
the wise, more than any ten rulers in the city. [20]But there is not a righteous man on
earth who does good and does not sin. [21–22]Also do not concentrate on every word
spoken, or else you will take seriously your subordinate cursing you, for your heart
knows many times you too have cursed others.

Notes on the text

10. 'has been identified and its nature is known': lit. 'its name has been
called and it is known what it is'. We take 'naming' to be *recognizing*
something for what it is rather than a deterministic reading by other
interpreters. The m. pronoun *hû'* serves as the verbal copulae, as in 3:15; cf.
1:9–10. So what something 'is' refers to its nature as well as its existence.
    'a man indeed': *'ādām* is the subject of the next phrase rather than an
object of what 'is known'. The implication is that one of the recurring
realities is the subordination of the individual under overpowering circumstances. Many others disregard the Masoretic division of the verse to make
sense of its syntax; for example, Gordis 1968: 262–263; Murphy 1992: 57.
The waw introducing *lō'-yûkal* is translated as an asseverative; Whitley
gives several examples of OT parallels (1978: 61).
    'prevail against': *dîn* usually means 'to judge'; however, it ranges
semantically into the practical act of judgment 'disputing, governing',
preparing us for the prevailing 'entity' described two words later by
tāqap.
    'whatever is stronger': whatever is stronger need not be a personal entity.
Prevailing forces could be divine forces or other people (4:12), but there are
other forces that a person cannot control or vanquish that should not be
precluded here; see for example 8:8.
    11. 'matters': *dābār* can mean 'word' or, more generally, 'matter, things';
the same choice was presented in 1:8. Qoheleth has described many *things*
or *matters* that intensify the transience of everything, including death – the

focus of 7:1–4. Up to this point, an argument for the meaning 'words' is based on a narrower understanding of the previous verse as a reference only to *verbal* contentions; for example, Longman 1998: 177. However, a guess is hazarded here that a double entendre is intended where 'words' are meant as well as 'matters', since in the following verse four words or phrases denoting transience are stacked.

'what advantage is there for a man?': this key phrase for Qoheleth is often obscured here by some translations. However, it serves here, as it does in the other instances, as the critical thematic question he addresses throughout the speech (1:3; 3:9; 5:11, 16).

12. 'few days': for *mispar*, see 'Notes' at 2:3.

'he spends them': Whitley (1978: 61) is an example of those who see a Grecism here; but see Ruth 2:19 for *'āsāh* as 'spending time', per Gordis 1968: 264.

7:1. An English translation does not do justice to this chiastic alliteration of 'good', 'oil' and 'name': *ṭôb šēm miššemen ṭôb*.

'his birth': the pronoun is considered by most to be indefinite, 'one's birth', because the chapter division is presumed meaningful. However, the pronoun references the man in 6:12 who cannot tell the future, making at least this stich of the verse original to Qoheleth, not a recited aphorism.

2. 'party house': *mišteh* refers to feasting in general, not to any specific ceremony or celebration.

3. 'heart matured': given that this saying is between statements commending righteous melancholy over levity or even joy, and, since *kî* introduces a logical consequence, it appears that an improvement of the whole 'inner person' (*lēb*) is described here as 'being made better' (*yîṭab lēb*), thus wiser and more mature (see Rudman 1998: 465–468).

5. 'a song of fools': in forcing too stringent a parallel with 'rebuke', some define the very general word 'song' as 'praise'. With Whybray (1989: 115), I see no need for this limitation. Instead, the general form fits the unity of this section, referring to the full repertoire of festive, whimsical or even crass songs of foolish revellers.

6. The repetition of sibilants in this verse is onomatopoeic (*hassîrîm taḥat hassîr kēn śeḥōq hakkesîl*), making the sounds of the hissing and sizzling of a thorny stem on fire under a cooking pot.

7. 'Surely': here *kî* serves as an emphatic particle, though those believing this verse is connected to the previous one see it as causative.

'extortion ... bribe': *'ōšeq* and *mattānāh* can mean respectively 'oppression' and 'gift', but pull each other mutually towards these negative financial meanings while holding polar positions in the proverb's word order. The discordant m. predicate *wî'abbēd* with the f. *mattānāh* is a hint of the vernacular.

'makes a fool': this po. form of *hālal* has the same meaning as in Isa. 44:25.

8. 'a matter': *dābār* again refers to a more general 'thing', as in 1:8; 6:11. See discussions there.

9. For the meaning and dating of the pi. of *bāhal*, see 'Notes' at 5:2.

'rush your spirit': prepositional beth used before the object *rûaḥ* is also read in Prov. 16:32.

11. 'with': in this context *'im* is not used as a simile but as a comparative preposition.

12. 'wisdom is a shadow – money is a shadow': the terse parallelism initiating this verse is like that of 3:2–8. The parallel prepositional beths play a definitional role – wisdom is a shadow. Historically, they have been changed to kaphs or even deleted, while the beth of equation has been grammatically acceptable in Hebr. (beth *essentia*; GKC 119i). Regardless of these linguistic changes, even as a beth *essentia* the phrasing is metaphorical.

13. 'In the pleasant days, be pleased': 'pleasant' and 'pleased', as derivatives of the same root, reflect the repetition of derivatives of *ṭôb*.

For *tāqan* as an Aram., see 'Notes' at 1:15.

14. 'surely': emphatic *gam*.

'in order that': *'al-dibrat še-* is similar phrasing to Aram. *'al-dibrath dî*. So Ecclesiastes is thought to reflect a later linguistic era. However, the Aram. parallels are found in texts that could equally have been Hebraized. The phrase is probably a Hebr. calque (Fredericks 1988: 234–235).

15. 'both': here again *kōl* refers to two things, thus 'both', avoiding the unnecessary exaggeration that Qoheleth has seen absolutely everything! He has seen the two tragic ironies that follow.

16. 'do not make yourself too wise': the hith. of *ḥākam* denotes more than simply 'to be wise'. Instead, the stem's thrust would be to *cause* oneself to be wise, reflexively – something the epilogist warns against as well (12:12; cf. 1:13, 18).

'overwhelm yourself': another hith. expresses 'to astound or appall' oneself to ruin (BDB 1031). It does not mean 'to kill oneself'.

19. 'is strong for': scanning commentaries shows that commentators are perplexed about rendering this intransitive verb *'āzaz*, even though it can be so translated; for example, BDB 738.

'any ten': the rulers are indefinite and probably refer to a round number of rulers, however many in the city there may be.

'rulers': see 'Notes' at 2:19 concerning the lateness of this root.

20. 'But': the adversative use of *kî* is rare but attested in Hebr.; see for example Murphy 1992: 69.

21. 'do not concentrate': lit. 'do not take to your heart'.

'take seriously': *šāma'* (to hear) often implies more than merely sensing sound. It connotes listening intently, with great attention.

'or else': *'ăšer lō'* is equivalent to 'lest, or else' (GKC 165b).

'subordinate': though 'servant' is a literal meaning, it can reflect service in general by anybody, thus a subordinate or subject of any description.

Form and structure

According to the Masoretes and the rhetorical structure discussed in 5:10 – 6:9, Qoheleth now introduces this second half of his speech. He does so in the same way he opened his entire speech in 1:2–3, thereby reviewing the thematic question with identical phraseology and sequence of thought as he did at the beginning. Since those opening verses, when he declared everything under the sun to be temporary (1:2), he has highlighted many things that intensify the transitory nature of life and its fleeting activities. So he asks again, since life is characterized by temporariness (1:2; 6:10, 12), 'What is the advantage for humanity' (1:3; 6:11), followed by his synonymous phrasing of that question, 'What is good for humanity?' (6:12).

There should be little doubt, then, of what is still on his mind and how he wants to investigate it even further. Reaching back to the sentiments in 5:1–7, here in 6:10–11 Qoheleth reminds us to keep our words few when it comes to speaking of the almighty God and future plans, lest we expose our finitude too embarrassingly. With the backdrop set for the utter sovereignty of God, Qoheleth then restates in 6:11–12 his thematic pronouncement (temporariness) and consequently asks his thematic question (Any advantage? Any good?).

However, this second half of the speech generally lacks the larger, more thorough discussions of the first half (except for 6:10 – 7:18 and 11:1 – 12:8). The structure of Ecclesiastes begins looking more like that of Proverbs in its almost random grouping of subjects that might run a few verses of similar thought, then change spasmodically to a totally unrelated verse or group of verses addressing a different topic. So it appears that 7:23 – 10:20 is a looser composition of wisdom sayings, vignettes, short discussions, general observations and/or conclusions.

This section, 6:10 – 7:22, then goes on to discuss the implications of death for the living. Qoheleth's speech begins with the passing of generations (1:4), ends with the passing of the individual (12:7) and is bisected by verses on the matter here in 6:10 – 7:22. Having asked what we know about what follows our death (6:12), he encourages us about our reputation (7:1). Then, in 7:2–4, Qoheleth explains that the death of others should remind us of our own fragile existence and the necessity of living wisely, knowing that our own funerals are imminent. He then begins describing profound perspectives that encourage living wisely in 7:7–22. First, in 7:5–6 he prefaces his remarks by presenting us with contrasting voices at a funeral. While the wise are speaking and giving counsel, the noise and clamour of drunken song and grating laughter can be heard in the background.

There are important connections with verses about money (7:11–12 and 7:7) and patience (7:13 and 7:8), and there is a vague connection about righteousness with the following section of various sayings in

7:19–22 (7:15–16 and 7:20). Qoheleth structures much of this section in poetic parallelism consistent with conventional proverbial wisdom. Vv. 11 and 12 are in parallel, as are 16 and 17. V. 15 contains a parallel within itself.

Being the pragmatist he is, Qoheleth affirms the advantages of money, but the superiority of wisdom (7:11–12); the enjoyment of the good days but the sovereignty of God even in the tragic days (7:13–14); resigning oneself to certain apparent injustices, so learning to pace oneself in reverence of God (7:15–18); the advantages to righteousness but the pitfalls of overextending oneself (7:15–17); the need for moderation and the moral obligation to God to be sensible (7:18). Throughout these realistic assertions, some of which are shocking to the shallow, Qoheleth's main concern is what contributes to a lengthier life. Of course, he acknowledges God's prerogative to trump any sequence of wise actions or any number of years of righteous living (7:14b, 15), but the tension between human responsibility and divine rule is implicit in this pericope, as it is in any profound discussion of morality, its consequences and God's ultimate sovereignty.

Comment

10–12. The frugality of the fifteen Hebr. words in v. 10 has somehow produced a proliferation of large, historic, dramatic and theological interpretations that span the garden of Genesis to the ash heap of Job. A tradition of interpretation has developed that names God, Adam and Job as players in this verse. However, consistent with Qoheleth's style in this speech, historic allusions are counterproductive, since he is speaking of cross-cultural truths in universal terms, not recounting Jewish history. Consequently, Adam is not referred to by the word '*ādām*, nor is Job's dispute with God implied as an example of an individual's 'argument' (*dîn*) with God, and God is not necessarily the one who does the naming nor the prevailing, since Qoheleth is not too shy to mention God, if he is indeed referring to him. For an overreading along these lines, see Garrett 1993: 317–318.

The point of this verse, as it blends into the next, is that human frailty and vulnerability to anything stronger can render anyone a fleeting spirit on a seemingly endless time line. Since there is nothing new under the sun, human transience, like everything else, is a recurrent event and unfortunately an inevitable experience. That the nature of things has already been identified and classified through the common experiences of every passing culture and generation has already been spoken to in Qoheleth's opening observation in 1:9–10.

What exactly, then, is it that is too strong and against which one cannot prevail? It could be anything that is so strong as to accelerate our already fleeting demise or cause death itself: God, war, king (8:4), thief, murderer, disease and so on. The Hebr. does not denote anybody or anything specific. Humans are transient, and, as in the past, all will succumb. Later, Qoheleth reminds us that no man has power over death, there is no discharge in war, the battle is not necessarily to the strong, and tragedy can ambush anyone (8:8; 9:11–12). 'No one escapes the power of the grave!' (Ps. 89:48).

Following the exact logic of his opening remarks in 1:2–3, Qoheleth jousts in 6:11: If every aspect throughout our experiences is marked by transience, then, again, what *is* the advantage for anybody? Since man is unable to prevail against those things that determine life and its experiences to be only momentary, what is man's advantage? He opens the second half of his speech, then, with the same thematic observation – temporariness – and the same understandable question: 'What advantage is there?'

What magnifies life's brevity, including the events experienced in that life is the many *dĕbārîm*. This ambiguous word usually demands that the interpreter translate as 'matters, events, things' or as the 'words' that express them. Given his penchant for alliteration, wordplays and artful rhetorical structures, we hypothesize that he means both. Whether he actually intends both meanings does not deflect the thrust of his point. Yet if he does intend a double entendre, a chiasm results where synonymous renderings of the thematic question 'What advantage, what is good?' is bracketed by statements about temporariness:

6:11   A   Since there are many things (and words) that magnify
           impermanence,
       B   what advantage is there for a man?
6:12   B^{I} Who knows what is good in life for a man, in the
       A^{I} few days
           brief life
           as a shadow...
           after him under the sun?

In the 'Introduction' (p. 28) we observed the constellation of words in the OT and in Ecclesiastes that cluster at times in different combinations to express impermanence in life. Here in 6:12, we have four key lexical 'magnifiers' of the transience of experiences in life and of life itself: few days, brief life, shadow and 'after him'. It is precisely the mounting of these ideas that is intended, so Longman's argument that *hebel* could not mean 'transitory' here without being 'awkwardly redundant' misses the point that each of these phrases is not identical but cumulative (1998: 178). For instance, that life is transitory is accentuated by the fact that it is measured in days, not months or years. Furthermore, shadows are temporary, since the sun and clouds pass overhead for only portions of the day (1:5; 12:2; cf. 8:13). The imagery of the sun and shadows is extended by Qoheleth as he concludes 6:12 with his well-loved phrase 'under the sun'. This sun

and these shadows return later in 7:11–12. Job and David use the idiom
as well:

> Our days on earth are as fleeting as a shadow.
>
> (Job 8:9; also 14:2)

> My life passes quickly, like the evening shadows.
>
> (Ps. 102:11; also 144:4)

> I fade like a shadow at dusk.
>
> (Ps. 109:23)

> Our days on earth are as a passing shadow, gone quickly with
>   no trace.
>
> (1 Chr. 29:15)

Qoheleth asks in 6:12 whether anybody knows what is good – whether
there is an advantage and what it would be. For some, this second
rhetorical question of this section automatically assumes a negative
answer, namely, that no one knows (Crenshaw 1986: 274–288). Though
that may have been the case in 2:19, it is not the case in 3:21 and 8:1
anymore than it is here. Who knows? The implied answer is that the *wise*
know what is good for a person in life. A foolish answer would be 'No one
knows,' but those listening closely to Qoheleth's speech would have been
able to answer his question immediately based on what they had heard in
the first six chapters. Furthermore, the very next verses answer the
'advantage' question with what is lit. 'good' (*tôb*; 7:1–3, 5, 8, 11, 14,
18). Not only could they have answered, 'Our days can best be spent by
wise living and enjoying our work and God's gifts' (2:13–14, 24; 3:22;
5:18), but within only a few more verses they would have been able to give
many more examples of what is good and an advantage in life.

One's inability to tell the future, particularly those events relevant to
one's life, has already been an issue for Qoheleth – one of which, for a
moment at least in 2:18–19, he lost total perspective. Assuming one's
transience, he asks a third rhetorical question: whether any advantage can
come after one's death, even though it obviously cannot be experienced.
This leads directly into what could be an advantage in this case, though we
know even this cannot last indefinitely.

7:1. As is often the unfortunate case, a chapter break has been imposed
on the otherwise smooth flow of thought between 6:10–11 and these
beginning verses of ch. 7. This artificial division obscures answers to the
critical, thematic questions that have just been asked about the advantages
for the living and what is good for them *now*. The previous verses also set
the context for these answers in 7:1–6 by emphasizing the temporariness
of the individual and raising the question of who can tell him what will

happen 'after him' (6:12), a euphemism for 'his death' (7:1b). Far from those questions being merely rhetorical, they are answered directly here by Qoheleth who cites examples of what is 'good' for one while alive and what advantage there can be after one's death. These answers are not intended to address thoroughly the thematic questions; rather, they focus on death for the moment. Views held that here in ch. 7 Qoheleth is reciting traditional wisdom only to modify or even contradict it (e.g. Lohfink 2003: 90–91; Murphy 1992: 62–63) are unnecessary when one understands that his profound, unvarnished realism is consistent with biblical wisdom. Crenshaw aptly summarizes this whole section: 'By pondering the implications of life's brevity and death's inevitability, we may acquire insight or even real wisdom' (1987: 134).

Prov. 22:1, a close parallel, contributes to a long list of literary connections in the *Corpus Salomonicum* (see 'Introduction' pp. 33–36):

> Choose a good reputation over great wealth.
> Better than silver and gold is being well esteemed.

'Great wealth' (and its ironic results) was the theme of the section just prior to this (5:10 – 6:9). Here, rather than precious metals, precious oils are in mind, especially, since they were common in funeral settings such as we are about to discuss in the next three verses. Ten verses earlier, even a burial plot was in question, much less the attending ointments for a respectable ceremony. Though we cannot be certain which purpose for oil is meant, here its comparative function subordinates its role as a *means* to respectability to the *respect itself*. Qoheleth was anointed with oil when crowned. Oils were used medicinally to postpone death. Negatively, however, one's reputation can be ruined by the way one earns enough money to afford the exorbitant luxury of costly perfumes, so it is better to be known for one's wisdom and righteousness than for one's riches (Prov. 28:6; cf. 'Comment' at Eccl. 5:12–13). Qoheleth is aware that a reputation depends on the miserably short memories of those after us (1:11; 2:16). Yet however long and wide one's esteem may reach is a better advantage than the mere material manifestations of respectability.

For multiple reasons, according to Qoheleth, one's non-existence can mean relief. It can even occur at a beautiful moment (3:11), so the sentiment that it is preferable to life should not be shocking and surely is not cynical. Cynicism about death is better voiced by fools who are afraid of it than by those who are wise enough to embrace it. Death is literally preferable according to 4:1–3 and 6:3–6. Job and Jeremiah's personal circumstances are the same as those of the holy, elderly saints in our own personal lives who often express their desire for the Lord not to tarry in bringing them to himself. In Paul's more explicit eschatology death is preferable (Phil. 1:23). But even if one were to presume, contrary to its cultural and religious neighbours, that Israel did not have a well-developed view of an afterlife, some would still look forward to the peace death brings – especially those whose ordinary lives have been marked by agony and misery. This is not to say on the other hand, that death is an occasion for great joy, nor that, generally speaking, a live dog is not better than a dead lion (9:4). The advantages to life which Qoheleth repeatedly summarizes make a life worth living until the proper season, even in a tragically fallen world.

2–4. This sequence of three verses contains two parallel thoughts, 7:2 and 7:4, split by a proverb which is itself commented on more fully in 7:5 and 7:6:

> 7:2 Funeral home is better than a house of pleasure
> 7:3 Sad face covers a maturing heart
> 7:4 Funeral home is better than a house of pleasure

The OT prophets Jeremiah and Isaiah use Qoheleth's same antithesis of mourning and revelry. Jeremiah tells his listeners not to frequent the funerals of those whose reputations are not good, who were unfaithful and should be forgotten (16:5). He then goes on to discourage going to their parties as well, since the emptiness of such merriment will be only temporary (16:8–9). On the other hand, Isaiah tells the Israelites to wear clothes of sober mourning rather than to dance, play and feast, and then rationalizes their irresponsible, frivolous merrymaking with the fatalism of fools: 'Eat, drink and be merry for tomorrow we die!' (22:12–13). It is this perverse, twisted logic that Qoheleth and Christ speak against (Luke 12:16–21). Later, in this speech, Qoheleth condemns disgusting partying (10:16; cf. Luke 6:25). For him, the wise understand the difference between enjoying God's gifts of food and drink and the abuse of those gifts by chasing them alone: 'eat at the appropriate time for strength' (10:17). So this longer passage in 7:2–6 is a commentary on Qoheleth's shorter conclusion in 2:1–2: Go ahead, and let me test you with pleasure, so enjoy what is good. But really it was also temporary. I said, 'Laughter is madness'.

However, just prior to 2:1–2 is Qoheleth's inextricable bond of wisdom and sorrow: 'Surely, in much wisdom there is much sorrow, and increasing knowledge increases grief' (1:18). Furthermore, we are told in 3:4 that the wise will be able to determine the time for mourning and weeping. So we expect Qoheleth to restate the same truth ironically here in 7:3 – under a sad face is a maturing heart. We read *yîṭab lēb* to refer to improving the heart, making the heart better, since we were just told that the wise take death 'to heart'. Though the phrase could mean to make the heart joyful, one might find this conclusion out of place and to recommend going straight to the parties! The point is not to eradicate sorrow but to appreciate it for the wiser perspective it brings.

The precise ways in which one's heart becomes wiser are enumerated in 7:5–18. At first there are three literary hooks – reputation, rest and responsibility. A significant benefit in attending a funeral is that it will make one wiser at least about one's own death, including what will be one's remaining reputation (7:1a). One's reputation is a common focus at funerals and is expressed through formal eulogies or informal conversations and reminiscences. The sobriety at the house of mourning is accompanied by a poetic quietness that reflects the rest, peace and quiet of the deceased (7:1b; 6:5). Just as important is what is learned from the wise who are in attendance at the funeral (7:5). It would be appropriate to hear Qoheleth's later words at a funeral as a challenge to wiser, responsible living; for instance: 'All that your hand finds to do, do it with all your strength, for there is no doing, planning, knowledge or wisdom in Sheol where you are about to go' (9:10). It is at a funeral where it would be fitting to hear the words of Moses as well:

> Teach us to number our days,
>   so that we will grow in wisdom.
>
> (Ps. 90:12)

5–6. The superiority of wisdom itself (2:13–14) and the virtue of teachableness expressed pervasively through Proverbs are all presumed in 7:5a. We have already heard about the hazard of ignoring wise instruction in reference even to kings (4:13). The wise words of instruction, advice and counsel that are heard in a quiet surrounding (9:17) serve as the utter contrast to the deafening roar of the raucous party behaviour described here:

> He who listens to a life-giving rebuke will be at home with the
>   wise.
>
> (Prov. 15:31)

> A rebuke impresses a discerning man,
>   more than a fool's hundred lashes.
>
> (Prov. 17:10)

> Listen to advice and instruction,
>   and in the end you will be wise.
>
> (Prov. 19:20; also 19:25)

> Like an earring of gold, or ornament of finer gold,
>   is a wise man's rebuke to a listening ear.
>
> (Prov. 25:12)

These references to the song and laughter of fools connect these two verses with the previous ones. Jeremiah prophesies, 'Do not attend their feasts and parties. . . . I will end the happy singing and laughter' (16:8–9).

Apparently these are foolish songs of fools comparable to the crass limericks of pubescent boys. Amos 6:5–6 paints the picture:

> You sing trivial songs to the harp.... You drink wine by the
>   bowlful
> and perfume yourselves with fragrant lotions.

Again, Proverbs is explicit:

> Do not associate with those who drink too much wine
>   or gorge themselves with meat,
> for drunks and gluttons become poor...
>
> (23:20–21)

The laughter of the fools at these parties is as short-lived as the thin dried thorns in a fire. Nothing could be cooked over such a useless fire, and nothing can be gained from the fools' shallow laughter (Pss 58:9; 118:12).

So to what specifically is this *hebel* clause at the end of 7:6 referring? Is it a statement about the transience of humanity that makes these funerals even necessary, thus covering the whole section of (6:10 – 7:6)? Perhaps, but I take it as a statement limited to v. 6 alone, comparable to Qoheleth's conclusion to the value of pleasure and laughter in 2:1–2.

7. I surmise that the wise is not the victim here but instead is the one guilty of extortion. Even the wise can sin (7:20) and stoop to intimidating another person physically, emotionally, legally or even ecclesiastically. This could include requesting or implying that a bribe be made by another to receive a favourable action, as well as offering a bribe oneself to derail someone else from justice. But the result is a shattered heart of the wise person whose conscience is still not calloused enough to remain unaffected by the abuse of any leverage. The extent of this destruction of heart may be temporary or permanent depending on the maturity of the wise person or how often any extortion is practised. It is expected that the wise be magnanimous, not predatory, and these illegal means to obtain what one does not deserve are tempting at least and demoralizing to the wise who should know better. These abuses are not necessarily political in nature, contrary to those who so specify (e.g. Garrett 1993: 319–320), but are common behaviour of those seared in conscience and inebriated with authority. The Law, Prophets and Writings all denounce extortion and bribery and warn of its debilitating results:

> [He] who refuses to gain from extortion and whose hand does
>   not accept bribes...
> is the man who will dwell on high.
>
> (Isa. 33:15–16)

> Greed brings trouble to one's family,
>   but those who hate bribes will live.
>
> (Prov. 15:27; cf. Eccl. 7:12)

> Do not take a bribe, for a bribe obscures one's sight and twists the word of the righteous. (Exod. 23:8)

8–9. In phrasing reminiscent of 7:1, we again find here in v. 8 that an end can be far better than its beginning. These two 'better than' phrases interpret each other and imply that if one patiently waits until the end of certain matters, withholding judgment, one's patience will prove wiser than jumping to self-centred conclusions at the start. Thus the verse supports the earlier contention that there is a season for everything (3:1–2), including a time to react and a time to wait, and is the principle behind waiting patiently for the proper time politically (8:2–7; 10:4) and financially (11:1), and waiting for justice to prevail (8:12–13). The phrasing also uses dimensional figures of speech which traverse horizontal time (8a) and describe spirit as extending in 'length' (*'erek*) as well as ascending in 'height' (*gĕbah*); as Longman interprets 8b, 'Better long patience than soaring pride' (1998: 187).

James affirms wisdom's importance for patient persistence during trials (1:2–5, 19); patience is a fruit of the Spirit (Gal. 5:22; 1 Cor. 13:4). David demonstrates this generous patient spirit rather than royal arrogance during Shimei's disrespectful ranting and raving against him. David's hope is that he be rewarded by God for his humility during this distressing time (2 Sam. 16:11–13). Proverbs hates arrogance as well, using identical words:

> Pride goes before destruction,
>   and arrogance (*gōbah rûaḥ*) before a fall.
> Better humility (*šĕpal-rûaḥ*) with the afflicted,
>   rather than to share plunder with the proud.
> (Prov. 16:18–19; cf. 16:5)

The 'patience' and 'anger' themes in vv. 8 and 9 are also connected in Psalms and Proverbs:

> Cease from anger; leave rage alone;
>   do not fret yourself; it only leads to evil.
>
> (Ps. 37:8)

> Better length (*'erek*) [before] anger than the warrior,
>   and the ruler of one's own spirit than conquering a city.
> (Prov. 16:32)

So Qoheleth's views are traditional regarding the undermining effect of inappropriate anger, even admitting that his own angry catharsis about life was short-sighted (2:17–26). Later, he warns against defensiveness and anger, noting that we ourselves are often the source of such emotions. We may become angry and defensive as a result of our own actions towards others or because our emotions lie too shallow in our hearts and surface too quickly. Or they are expressed too often, so have taken deep root in the heart (Heb. 12:15). Such a view fully endorses the many proverbs that speak against anger; for example, 14:29; 29:11. Excuses for righteous indignation and frustration may appear to abound: 'things were better back then, before the funeral' (7:10); 'Why did God bend life so tragically?' (7:13); 'Why can I not know what will happen after I die?' (7:14); 'Why do some righteous die early and some deviants live longer?' (7:15).

10. One reason the complaint voiced here in 7:10 is not wise is that it is shortsighted and impatient. However, there are at least three other reasons why Qoheleth warns against being too quick to prefer the 'olden days'. First, it is not wise to ask this question, because it means one is not as aware of the past as one should be. Really, the past is not considerably different from the present because everything is repeated anyway – there is nothing new under the sun (1:9; 2:16; 3:15; 6:10). Secondly, the 'present carries a morally binding force all its own. Wisdom informs the living of these days, not the reliving of the "former days"' (Brown 2000: 77). Any escapism from the present to the past will distract the wise from being preoccupied with their present responsibilities. Finally, this refusal to live the present life God has set before us keeps us from enjoying the blessings God has provided. When we enjoy God's blessings *now*, we will not be tempted to long for the past (5:20). Consequently, this is not a challenge to conventional wisdom, since conventional wisdom learns from the past but does not necessarily prefer it.

11–12. Contrary to a morbid bitterness about how things used to be (7:10), Qoheleth prescribes enjoying a post-funeral (7:2–4) inheritance! Inherited assets enjoyed in wisdom are an advantage for those who survive the deceased and still see the sun. 'In the pleasant days, be pleased!' (7:14a). Seeing the sun is more than just a synonymous phrase for 'under the sun' or to be alive. In 11:7, seeing the light of the sun connotes delight and enjoyment. Particularly the youth who survive the elderly are expected to delight in seeing the sun (12:2).

Money and property are not in themselves bad; in fact, by them, one enjoys the fruits of one's wise labour. Wisdom and money are compatible benefits to their possessor, and their parallel value is expressed in parallel verses:

11a Wisdom ... inheritance (asset)	12a Wisdom ... money (asset)
11b advantage	12b advantage
11c living	12c living masters

So Qoheleth reaffirms that there are advantages in life, answering positively again the thematic question found in 1:3 and its frequent rephrasing 'What

advantage is there…' *yitrôn* (advantage) and *ṭôb* (good) are used synonymously again in 7:11, namely seeing the 'good' of something is to see
its 'advantage'.

While these two verses show a partnership between wisdom and money,
they also at least imply, if not assert, three distinctions: better to have both
wisdom and assets than only assets (5:10); better to have both wisdom and
assets than simply wisdom (9:16); yet, it is better to have wisdom than
assets. Though both wisdom and assets are powerful tools, wisdom alone
may save one from an 'early' death:

> Long days of life are in [wisdom's] right hand,
> in her left are wealth and honour.
>
> (Prov. 3:16; also 9:11–12)

However:

> Wealth does not profit in a furious day,
> but righteousness delivers from death.
>
> (Prov. 11:4; also 3:13–18)

Solomon was not rewarded with wisdom because he chose wealth; rather,
he received wealth merely as an accoutrement to the wisdom he preferred
(1 Kgs 3:11–12).

An example of exactly why there is an advantage to wisdom and
money is explained in v. 12: both are a protecting 'shadow' (*ṣēl*; Gen.
19:8; Judg. 9:15; Lam. 4:20). The shadow is a metaphor Qoheleth has
used previously in this section to ascribe brevity to life (6:12). It is a
member of the constellation of metaphors he uses to describe the
transitoriness of life and its events. Elsewhere he has attributed brevity
to wisdom (6:8–9) and money (5:10–14), so shades of temporariness
are felt in this verse, even though the main point is the positive pro-
tectiveness of a shadow. Though temporary shelters, wisdom and money
are shelters nonetheless. Money buys bodyguards, armies and city
walls. It buys better quality food and better care from professionals who
require payment. Qoheleth often alludes to how wisdom protects one
from harm. We are about to hear the wisdom of balance in life (7:16–17);
we will hear of protecting oneself from an ensnaring woman (7:26),
a king's wrath (8:2–6; 10:4, 20) and a besieging enemy (9:16, 18).
Cautions about protecting oneself through carefulness with tools and
snakes come later in 10:8–11. The Solomonic tradition is behind this
wisdom:

> The one listening to [wisdom] will dwell safely,
> and be relieved from the fear of tragedy.
>
> (Prov. 1:33; also 4:6; 8:35–36)

Seow (1997: 249) and Brown (2000: 78) argue fallaciously that, since Qoheleth considers wisdom and money to be similar in their protective-ness, Qoheleth considers their overall value to be equivalent. This is an impossible deduction from the context, where Qoheleth explicitly affirms the superiority of wisdom. He then continues with the argument through-out his speech that confirms the benefits of wisdom in lengthening life. Similes are comparisons, not equations.

13–15. The positive assessments of wisdom and assets in 7:11–12 now give way to the counterweight of 7:13–15. There is a brief recollection of the previous verses in 14a where one is encouraged to enjoy the pleasant days. Enjoying those days, however, will be interrupted by adversities that are measured and proportioned according to God's sovereign management of his creation. Paul shares his personal experience, and James and Peter also inspire the faithful to meet adversity with inner balance:

> I have learned to be content in whatever circumstances I am. . . . I have learned the secret of being filled and going hungry, of having abundance and suffering need. (Phil. 4:11–12)

> Consider it all joy . . . whenever you encounter trials. (Jas 1:2)

> So be glad . . . even if it is necessary to endure trials for a while. (1 Pet. 1:6)

These three verses (13–15) address the reality of adversity encountered by the wise; they acknowledge God's irreversible, sovereign acts, and counsel a willing acceptance of them. Such acceptance should be a source of confidence for those undergoing adversity; they should accept such trials rather than try uselessly to counter or avoid them. 'Who can make straight what God has bent?' What is 'bent' includes tragic days (v. 14), which in turn can include early deaths of the righteous (v. 15). The inevitability of God's actions are responded to by the unfaithful with frustration, but those who trust him respond with contentment and righteous resignation. Isa. 45:7 relays God's claim to be the creator of both the world and its circumstances (cf. Prov. 16:4):

> [I am] the One who forms the light and creates the dark,
>   causing peace and creating tragedy.

Qoheleth's concise statements of God's absolute sovereignty found here in 7:13 as well as in 1:15 and 3:14 are meant to build confidence and define boundaries within which one can act wisely. On the other hand, God, in his sovereign acts, reminds us that we cannot always rely on the laws of probability and being wise in our own eyes. In this sense one cannot know what will follow one's transient life – what will happen after one dies.

The transience of life referred to in the last phrase of v. 14 is now continued in Qoheleth's summary of ironic justice in v. 15. Seow (1997: 252) and Krüger (2004: 139) are examples of those who believe Qoheleth to use *hebel* in this verse in the sense of 'transient' or 'fleeting'. Qoheleth has seen much in his brief life, including the following two things: some righteous die young and some wicked live long. This is a way God has bent life for some, and it can be a challenge to understand; the 'tragic days' God has made may include death even for the young and wise, making their life too temporary in our human judgment, especially when there are those who live longer in spite of their sin. To say that this statement contradicts 'conventional wisdom' is to trivialize OT wisdom as unrealistic and naive. The OT's theology, and wisdom literature in particular, could hardly be caricatured to be of the belief that there were no exceptions to the general truth that God's blessing is upon the righteous and his curse upon the wicked. Abel, Jonathan and Naboth are examples of many who died too early, and shedding innocent blood was an abuse of power that the prophets spoke against continually. Pss 37 and 73 reflect honest struggling with these bent aspects of God's administration. The faithful may die young in various tragic ways: being murdered, dying in accidents, succumbing to terminal illnesses, dying in prison, being tortured, oppressed and martyred for the faith. This realism sets up the next two verses, which respond with the need for a balanced life. But Isaiah has a larger view of things, a view that can see the beauty of even the righteous dying early:

> The righteous perish, but no one takes it to heart.
> Gracious people are taken away, but no one understands,
>   for the righteous are removed from the evil to come.
> Those who walk uprightly peacefully enter and rest in their
>   'beds'.
>
> (57:1–2)

This is the LORD's consolation to Josiah: he would die, but mercifully not see the evil to follow (2 Kgs 22:18–20).

16–18. Distinct from the previous three, these three verses speak of the other side of the coin – we need to be wise in our endeavours when God's sovereign choices are not known or understood. Living within one's boundaries and limitations is an act of reverence for God. Vv. 16 and 17 in their opposing, yet still harmonizing, pitch render a dissonance like that of the riddle of Prov. 26:4–5:

> Do not answer a fool according to his folly . . .
> Answer a fool according to his folly . . .

The parallel structure of vv. 16 and 17 describes pragmatically the threats of excesses, as the wisdom literature often does, but it does so at the risk of appearing tolerant of sloppiness in one's sanctification and of nonchalance about one's sinfulness. In fact, however, not being overly righteous or overly wise is in itself, ironically, being wise. Less probably, the reason for this instruction is that it is a reason for the short life of the righteous referred to in v. 15 (Delitzsch 1975: 324). More probable is that one should not deceive oneself in thinking that a long life can be assured, thus avoiding the truth of v. 15, by extending oneself beyond one's means. Overdoing righteousness is trying too much with too little time, too little talent, with too little support or any other necessary resources. Since nothing can change what God has bent, being overly righteous will not guarantee that one will live longer; one will simply end up overwhelmed. Moderation allows priorities to surface so that the finite limits of the person can be considered and balanced in wisdom. Wisdom can give life (7:12), but its excess can ruin it.

It is hardly necessary to comment here on the clear biblical message that wickedness curbs life by endangering the fool each day. Though some wicked may live a longer life, God's more frequent prerogative is to speed their demise:

> Men of bloodshed and lies will not live half of their days.
>
> (Ps. 55:23b)

> [The wicked] were snatched away before their time.
>
> (Job 22:16)

However, it is the command not to be *overly* wicked that causes some concern. The truth is that everyone has an amount of evil within them. In this sense an instruction simply not to be evil would be an understatement. Yet wickedness is especially hazardous when a tolerance for it in one's life has been developed, so do not rush death. So to say that Qoheleth prescribes any intentional wickedness is a misreading. It is aptly put by Fox (1999: 262), 'to condemn "much" is not to approve of a little'. Qoheleth's presuppositions are consistent, then, with traditional biblical theology: be righteous; be wise; do not be wicked; do not be foolish. John reflects the NT teaching, 'God's children do not *practise* sinning' (1 John 5:18).

Realizing the jolting impact of these two verses, Qoheleth immediately introduces God as the one who expects this balance, not Qoheleth alone. Though what is said in 7:16 might be surprising, one is obligated to make positive sense of it because true wisdom and respect for God's instructions will hold it as a parallel truth to what is more easily understood in 7:17. The 'golden mean' interpretation of 16–18 that claims Gr. influence on Qoheleth (e.g. Schwienhorst-Schönberger 1998: 181–203) is unnecessary for two reasons. First, as Strange (1969: 127) argues, Qoheleth's prescription is not that one should be equally moderate in one's intentional pursuit of wickedness and folly, righteousness and wisdom. Instead, his prescription is to restrain oneself from an errant pursuit of their extremes. Secondly, a Semitic source clearly provides a more probable parallel than Gr. The Proverbs of Ahiqar has a passage recommending steering between extremes (see Choi 2002: 371–372). For helpful monographs on 7:15–18, see Strange 1969; Whybray 1978: 191–203; Brindle 1985: 243–257; Schwienhorst-Schönberger 1998: 181–203; Lux 1992: 267–278; Choi 2002: 358–374; Shnider and Zalcman 2003: 435–439.

19. Qoheleth has just told his audience that if they fear God they will firmly grasp both principles of restraint in vv. 16 and 17 so that their hand does not weaken to the point of letting go of them. Now, he encourages them in their tenacity by assessing the strength of such wisdom to be stronger than that of any ten rulers in a city. The proverb, then, is not intrusive or misplaced as some think; for example, Fox 1999: 256. Rather, it is linked to the very words of the hand-strength of the previous verse. This saying also has a supporting parable that speaks about wisdom's ability to save the city whose rulers were impotent (9:14–15). 2 Sam. 20:15–22 tells of a wise woman's salvation of her city.

20. Qoheleth confirms his orthodoxy by restating in Solomonic terms the fact that everyone sins and no one is able to claim perfection: 'there is not a righteous man on earth who does good and does not sin'. This is a foundational biblical doctrine:

Who can say ... I am pure from sin?

(Prov. 20:9)

for there is no man who does not sin. (1 Kgs 8:46)

For all have sinned ... (Rom. 3:23)

Qoheleth's observation about universal sinfulness looks forward as an encouragement not to take the offences of others so seriously (7:21–22), and looks back at those who might be trying to contradict its truth by overextending themselves (7:16). If one were to strive to be perfect, overly righteous and wise, Qoheleth puts the hope to rest. The verse also confirms in parallel phrasing that his other statements about righteousness or sinfulness are not the equivocations of a cynic but undeniable directives to 'do good' ('āśāh ṭôb; 3:12), and not to 'do evil' ('āśāh rā'; 5:1). He will reference the Fall and its moral implications yet again by concluding in the following section that though God made humanity moral, it sought out many man-made moral options (7:29).

21–22. 'Moral realism' is one of Qoheleth's subthemes in this section. In continuing his caution against overextending oneself in the pursuit of righteousness (7:16), he affirms that self-restraint is a reverent position to hold (7:18; cf. Gal. 5:23), maintains that the truly humble confession of anyone is a frank admission of imperfection (7:20), and says that if one were to judge subordinates for their curses, one would be guilty of hypocrisy and arrogance. After all, one may hear their subordinates' disrespectful comments, but one's own maligning of others has happened *many* times. Though Qoheleth does not speak of forgiveness of the subordinate specifically, he does underline the basic sinfulness of all, including those in authority. The issue is not one's response to subordinates; it is one's self-estimation in the situation. 'You hypocrite! Take the log out of your eye first' (Matt. 7:2, 5; also Rom. 2:1). Shalom is less disturbed when one realizes that the seriousness of the subordinate's comments is as negligible as the seriousness of one's own cursing of others. Taking it too seriously could lead to public humiliation: 'The wise hide their dishonour' (Prov. 12:16).

Explanation

It is impossible to prevail against death and the circumstances that usher it into the forefront of our minds. However, never underestimate the human ability to live in denial about death. Brushing it briefly in youth, ignoring it in the frenetic routine of adulthood, medicating against it in old age and fighting it while in hospital, the *certainty* of death is kept at arm's length for as long as possible. Oh, and by all means, avoid the soul who dwells on it too often or too long, if at all. Of course, there is a healthy emphasis on *life* in our thinking, since it is God's precious gift to see the sun daily and it is the only time we can accomplish something of an advantage (9:10). Still, there is a tremendous advantage in keeping an ear to death and what can be learned from it. It is the great mentor for diligence, sobriety, love, generosity, reverence and humility. Death forces the most profound questions to be asked, but mercilessly mocks those who sleep through its lessons. But, leveraging its absolute certainty to our advantage is one of Qoheleth's subthemes. This section of the speech, then, does not consist of thoughts that depress; thinking appropriately about death leads one to see the severity of God's curse on sin, but also convinces one of the need to enjoy one's life wisely, since there is much to accomplish before we pass on and experience the ultimate rest from life's turbulence.

Qoheleth does not refrain from meddling in our habit of death-denial. He even goes as far as to deal with our social lives. If given a chance to go to a funeral, go! Even more helpful, if the choice is between that and golfing, the preferred choice is plain. Rather than continuing a seamless pursuit of life and its privileges, allow the interruption of a funeral to enrich your life and, ironically, enhance life's blessings. The funeral and party events may not actually be scheduled at the same time, and the choice may not be about the identical hour. The message is that where one's heart and mind are at any time might indicate the seriousness with which one approaches the brevity of life.

There is more to be learned at a funeral than one would think, given the few words that can or should be spoken. The setting and occasion alone are more eloquent than the eulogies that often obscure the real issue. The fleeting life is literally portrayed in the album of photos from birth to the days before the death. The ages of the attendees are the visible parentheses within which our own life is placed. The misplaced laughter and shallow comments clutter the space around the coffin that pleads for attention as the destination of all who are looking elsewhere around the room.

At the funeral, the reputation of the deceased will often be couched in terms of character. It will hardly be about the assets that were accumulated, only about how they might have been distributed. The reputation of the deceased – the only thing that remains for examination – may be magnified at the burial ceremony even though in whispered conversations mourners talk of the shallowness of respectability. Others, in their self-delusion, will continue to convince the pretentious of the importance of wealth and the dignity of leaving behind a sound financial portfolio. Words of wisdom should be sought at the funeral rather than reaffirmations of trivial, superficial pursuits or mindless chatter and laughter that mutes the resounding finality of death.

While Qoheleth is speaking about finality, he reflects on the end of things in general. Just as the day of one's death may be better than birth, the end of any matter may be better than its beginning. So patience is recommended, since it allows the person to watch God's sovereign care as well as to watch for the appropriate time to act most effectively. Since there is a suitable time and choice for everything (3:1; 8:5–6), hasty decisions and reactions to current circumstances will lead to counter-productive conclusions. Pride and hungering for accolades about one's 'decisiveness' may in the end be the undoing of a project or career! Expressing anger, or worse, being overpowered by it, is caused by flinching at the fleeting moment's challenge rather than taking the long view and discerning the probable outcomes given time and God's hidden yet compassionate methods. Job's friends are a perfect example of such tunnel vision. God himself is slow to anger (Ps. 145:8). Though anger in itself is not sin, when it is comfortable to visit frequently or even dwell in a person's spirit and habits, it becomes the resident enemy that eats away at wisdom and vitality.

Such a short-sighted approach to daily challenges can be seen even when a person waxes philosophical about the larger flow of life. The impatient soul jumps to the conclusion that these times are worse than the good old days – the greener days on the other side of the present tense. Access to global news twenty-four hours a day can give us the false impression that there are new tragedies occurring, unlike any that were known in the past. But human nature has not changed, nor the abuse of power in all its hideous forms. For the individual, Qoheleth does tell us of the time when the aged realize they no longer have the same pleasure they enjoyed while young (12:1), but there is no implied bitterness in that resignation. To complain bitterly about the present because one thinks the past more pleasant shows that it is the fool who is oblivious to the past. Nothing has changed, since all that has happened in the past is happening now. Besides, our responsibilities are in the present regardless of our selective memory about the past. Furthermore, God's generosity allows for joy even for those who may have to become more skilled at finding it among the tragedies and pains that often accumulate in our lives. Our wisdom should become progressively more adept at finding the perfection in God's present plan.

Though the love of money is the root of all sorts of evil, and though Qoheleth is intent to put wealth in its place in 5:10 – 6:9, he acknowledges the advantage to money, especially when bound with wisdom. An inheritance is good if it is not squandered or risked, since money protects from the onslaughts of drought, illness, litigation or abandonment. Clearly, those without money can suffer more than those with it. But wealth is a false security when not coupled with wisdom (Ps. 73:10–20). The debilitating impact of wealth on the soul may not be a public spectacle, but the wise see the dangers and are able to balance God's gifts through proper stewardship of material blessings.

Even Nebuchadnezzar could attest to God's immutable will – no one can deflect his will nor should even question its power (Dan. 4:34–35). Another king-figure, Qoheleth, instructs the rest of us, who have not nearly the authority, that wisdom accepts God's providence whether it is apparently negative or positive. But rather than passively or blindly living during times of local, national or global distress, the wise will observe such distress and conclude in each instance that God is sovereign, responding in reverence rather than fatalistic apathy. An obvious case of God's perplexing ways is when he allows what appear to be flagrant injustices, such as the death of the righteous, when death should have taken the wicked instead. Here again, Qoheleth refutes the foolish, untimely application of elementary wisdom principles used by Job's counselling friends to much more complicated circumstances. Martyrs for Christ, those who personify the most blatant of contradictions to our finite expectations of a caring God, become the seeds of the church whose justice will finally come (Rev. 6:9–11).

We are met with yet another comment from Qoheleth that jars our pat theologies. He cautions the believer from being too righteous or wise. Far from being a call to moral mediocrity, this is a *pastoral* caution. How many Christian families have suffered because of the overextension of one or both parents in the 'life of the church'? Qoheleth's advice does not question the motives or accuse the overly zealous of self-righteousness. However, he does warn them about an imbalance that exhausts the believer with an overwhelming 'to do' list of righteous and wise activities. There are those who are so excessive in their good and wise activity that they never rest. They can appear very holy, but in their zeal or in their working outside their strengths, they are only destroying themselves physically and emotionally. The epilogist warns similarly, 'beware of a lot of bookwork – it is endless – and much study tires the flesh'. Additionally, keeping the sabbath is at play here, as well as taking time to enjoy the fruits of one's labours and God's gifts of joy and pleasure.

Wisdom literature chooses the tongue as its most frequent target for moral instructions. Reminding us of our own imperfections, Qoheleth advises composure when maligned by others, even subordinates! 'Forgive our sins as we forgive those who sin against us' (Matt. 6:12). No children of God are more maligned than the pastor and his family. The exposure to cries of 'hypocrisy' is so much greater from the parishioners' daily safe-zones that escape the view of others in the pew. God bless those who serve us as spiritual leaders with patience and hopefully with impervious ears to our unfair expectations and comments.

ECCLESIASTES 7:23 – 8:1

Translation

[23]All of these matters I have tested with wisdom. I said, 'I want to be wise.' But it was far from me. [24]Whatever has been is far and very deep; who can find it? [25]I set especially my heart to know and to explore and seek wisdom and an explanation, and to know the evil of folly and the foolishness of madness.

[26]Then I found more bitter than death the woman whose heart is snares and nets, and her hands are chains. A good person before God will escape from her, but the sinner will be taken by her. [27]Qoheleth says, Look, this is what I have found by adding up matters to find an explanation. [28]Something my soul still seeks, but I have not found: I have found one man out of a thousand, but a woman among all those I have not found.

[29]Consider what I have found: that God has made man upright and they have sought many explanations. [8:1]Who is like the wise man, and who knows the interpretation of a matter? The wisdom of a man gives light to his face and makes its stiffness to relax.

Notes on the text

23. 'these matters': zeh (this) is nebulous and probably refers to everything in the speech so far.

'I want to be wise': the cohortative intensifies Qoheleth's resolve.

24. 'very deep': the duplication of an adjective like ʿāmōq amounts to intensification (GKC 133k), but not to the level of a superlative (contra Seow 1997: 260; see also GKC 133l).

25. To indicate the simple past clearly, and placing this exploration for wisdom in the definite past, Qoheleth again uses the first person pronoun after the perfect, as in 1:16 and some eighteen other times; see 'Notes' at 1:16.

'especially my heart': the waw before *lēb* is perplexing, but is emphatic (GKC 154a.n1b). The need for this emphasis is that he had also set his *flesh* to explore for wisdom in the parallel, introductory section (2:3), which did not lead to positive results.

'explanation': *ḥešbôn* surfaces in 7:25, 27, 29 and 9:10. Its only biblical precedent is in the later book 2 Chr. 26:15, by when it has taken on a much more specific meaning of 'invention'.

'the evil of folly – and the foolishness of madness': peculiar Hebr. construction which we read as the const.–abs. syntax. Though no art. is found on the second noun in each pairing, the art. is used loosely in Qoheleth and further indicates a more casual grammar of his vernacular.

27. The words are separated incorrectly in MT, and should read *'āmar haqqohelet* (said [the] Qoheleth), with the art., confirming this is a *title* Qoheleth holds. The term is used as m. in 1:2 and 12:8.

28. To 'find a woman' in Prov. 18:22 is the only other case in the OT where *māṣā'* and *'iššāh* are paired.

'those': refers to the women whose heart is snares in 7:26.

8:1. 'interpretation': occurs in verbal and nominal forms in reference to dreams in Gen. 40:5 – 41:15, but there in an Aram. form, where here we have the Hebr. spelling.

The unassimilated art. in the preposition–substantive form is evidence of the vernacular. It is a peculiarity to Ecclesiastes in its frequency (1:7; 6:10; 10:3).

Form and structure

Though 6:10 marks the Masoretic punctuation 'centre' of this speech (see 'Form and Structure' on 6:10 – 7:22), this section marks another 'centre'. Where 6:10 – 7:22 revived the 'temporary' and 'advantage' motif of 1:2–3, this section, 7:23 – 8:1, revives the 'search' motif of 1:12 – 2:3. At least nine linguistic parallels are found between both sections (see the table below). There is also a subtle parallel in the pursuit of foolish pleasure (2:1–3) and the ensnaring sexual pleasures alluded to in 7:26.

There is another reason to elevate this to a 'central' point in the speech: an ancient Hebr. listener as well as any modern student of the wisdom literature cannot appreciate this passage and not hear Prov. 1 – 9 in the background. Qoheleth uses this allusion to accentuate his renewed wisdom search. The youth of Prov. 1 – 9 is to seek out Lady Wisdom and avoid Slut Folly.

The division of sections in Ecclesiastes is one of the many intriguing challenges in commenting on the book. Only three possible views of this

	1:12 – 2:3		7:23–29	
Explicitly Qoheleth	1:12	Qoheleth	7:27	Qoheleth
Wisdom as a tool	1:13, 16	by wisdom	7:23	by wisdom
Universal scope	1:13	all that has been done	7:23	All this
Commitment	1:13, 17	I gave my heart to [seek]	7:25	I turned my heart to [know]
Seek and explore	1:13; 2:3	to search and to explore	7:25, 28–29	to explore and to seek
Frustration	1:13	it is a tragic affliction	7:23	it was far and deep
Wisdom and madness	1:16–18; 2:2–3	wisdom, knowledge, madness, foolishness	7:25	wisdom, knowledge, madness, foolishness
Deliberation	1:16; 2:1	I said to myself	7:23	I said, 'I . . .'
Testing	2:1	I will test	7:23	I tested

section's terminus can be conceived, but all three views are advocated and each by many commentators. Either the section ends after 7:29 (e.g. Beentjes 1998: 303–315; Jones 2006: 211–228), after 8:1 (e.g. Baltzer 1987: 127–132) or after 8:1a (e.g. Eaton 1983: 117–118; Loader 1986: 94–97; Fontaine 1998: 143–145). Does 8:1 swing backwards to 7:23–29, or forwards to 8:2–15? However, the verse speaks of wisdom and its nature as broadly as the preceding verses, not as narrowly as the following verses about political wisdom, specifically. I conclude that the section ends with this question: in the light of the stark realities presented in the previous verses, who will prove themselves wise in interpreting any of life's riddles? It almost asks for a raising of courageous hands. Furthermore, comparable to the relieving conclusions of 2:24–26 that followed tortuous observations there, and similarly in the Psalms frequently (e.g. 73), the bitter taste of foolishness (7:26) is relieved by the soothing enlightenment of wisdom (8:1b). Of course, those who believe the rhetorical question 'Who is like the wise man . . . ?' must imply the negative 'No one' presumably would be compelled to divide the verse to distance the contradicting notion that wisdom is possible and enjoyable at that!

Many monographs have taken a special interest in this section: Fox and Porten 1978: 26–38; Lohfink 1979: 259–287; Baltzer 1987: 127–132; Rudman 1997: 411–427; Long 1998: 101–109; Fontaine 1998: 137–168; Christianson 1998: 109–136; Pahk 1998: 373–383.

Comment

23–25. This section begins with Qoheleth's summary of his speech so far. In language nearly identical to that of his introduction to this speech, he reviews his lifelong desire to be wise, and to be able to distinguish wisdom from sinful foolishness. 'All of these matters' refer to all that Qoheleth has presented in 2:4 – 7:22. Consequently, as we are now accustomed to expect from Qoheleth, we are simultaneously looking for a profound conclusion as well as realistic limitations on that conclusion. Since his search for wisdom is 'with wisdom', we know Qoheleth presupposes a foundational wisdom with which to pursue even greater knowledge and explanations of what is under the sun. Though this passage surely wrestles with the remoteness and depth of true, ultimate and perhaps exhaustive wisdom, the passage itself, as well as all that precedes and follows it, clearly speaks of the possibility of wisdom, not its impossibility. The results are just as successful subsequent to this reintroduction of his search for wisdom as they were after his first such introduction in 1:13 – 2:3.

Qoheleth himself raises the anxiety of ever finding wisdom by admitting that it is remote and very deep. But the Hebr. simply says that it was far away and very deeply submerged, not necessarily that it was inaccessible. Vv. 23 and 25 claim it took a journey of exploration, observation, seeking and reasoning to discern the difference between wisdom, evil, foolishness and just plain madness. Qoheleth knows what is fundamentally right and wrong, what he is searching for are the principles of more advanced discernment. From the immediate context we know his search did indeed work, but only after strenuous effort at reaching it. His rhetorical questions in 7:24 and 8:1 are motivating challenges to the wise, not sighs of cynical fatalism. The question 7:24 asks is who will find wisdom; that of 8:1 asks who can interpret or explain it. Those who rise to the occasion will experience Qoheleth's conclusion where he revels in the light and relief of wisdom. This is not to deny that there is a wisdom inaccessible to man regardless of the extent of his wisdom. This is spoken of later in 8:17 along lines with which Agur and Job agree (Prov. 30:1–4; Job 28:12–23). In those passages it is God's plans and actions that are beyond comprehension. We have already heard Qoheleth speak in these terms (3:14; 7:13–14).

26. According to this section, in Qoheleth's search for discernment between wisdom, folly and madness, he was able to explain five principles: (1) foolishness is like being snared by the seductress; (2) truly wise men are extremely rare; (3) no wise women are found among seductresses; (4) humanity continually seeks the explanation of things; (5) wisdom can be relieving.

The first of these conclusions we find here in 7:26: wisdom can be found after a far and deep search, but not by entangling oneself with the foolishness that ensnares like an adulteress. The main question about this verse is whether Qoheleth is simply using the subject of an ensnaring woman as an example of the foolishness he sought to pinpoint, or, on a higher level, is he assuming that his audience presumes he is not speaking of such a mundane example but is referring more profoundly to the proverbial Adulteress? In Prov. 1 – 9, Solomon describes wisdom and folly at length through the double-meanings of personifying Lady Wisdom and

Slut Folly. The latter is a seductive adulteress who overpowers the simpleton. She is one from whom to flee (Prov. 5:7–8), otherwise, speaking both literally and metaphorically, she traps him by her foolishness, leading him to death. Ironically again, for Qoheleth, death is not the worst thing that can happen: the taste of such a woman is so bitter that death is preferred! These passages in Proverbs mix the warnings against literal fornication with warnings against fooling around with metaphorical Folly. That Eccl. 7:26 uses this same didactic method is observed by several scholars; for example, Farmer 1991: 179; Brown 2000: 83–84; Krüger 2004: 146–147.

Identical or similar motifs of seizure, catching, bitterness, death, snaring and trapping are paralleled in Proverbs:

> For the adulteress's lips drip honey...
> but eventually she is bitter as wormwood,
>   sharp as a two-edged sword.
> Her feet are death bound.
>
> (5:3–5a)

> Do not let your heart desire her beauty,
>   nor let her eyelids catch you.
>
> (6:25)

> So she seizes him, kisses him...
> he follows her as a deer into a trap...
> as a bird hastens to the snare....
> Her house is the way to the grave.
>
> (7:13, 22–23, 27)

On the other hand, Qoheleth is just as impressed with the positive relationship with a loving wife as he is in his Proverbs, so the stark contrast between love and lust is equivalent in both books:

> Enjoy life with a woman whom you love. (Eccl. 9:9)

> Rejoice in the wife of your youth...
>   why be stimulated by an adulteress, my son?
>
> (Prov. 5:18, 20)

> The one finding a wife finds goodness.
>
> (Prov. 18:22; also 19:14)

Some commentators insist 'the woman' in 7:26 is an abstraction for 'all women', meaning that for Qoheleth the entire gender is worse than death; for example, Longman 1998: 204; Fox 1999: 269. Others identify her according to her qualifying description, the particular woman who is ensnaring. Furthermore, some who see 7:28 as affirming that no women are wise jump in their logic to claim that 7:26 affirms that all women are unwise and ensnaring. But centring comments on gender wars and accusations of misogyny only trivializes the profound nature of Qoheleth's observation and rich allusion to the 'wisdom' theme of the Wisdom and Folly in Prov. 1 – 9. It also contradicts his encouragement to enjoy and love one's wife for all of one's brief life (9:9).

The righteous and wise soul will avoid the traps and nets of Folly, but the weak sinner will fall prey to her entrapments. The 'good person' and the 'sinner' are contrasted again here, as they were in 2:26. Attempts to circumvent the plain sense of these terms and render them in an amoral sense are unnecessary and actually contradict Qoheleth's high consciousness of sin only six verses earlier (7:20; see 'Comment' at 2:24–26 and 3:12–13). Rudman represents those who believe that in this phrasing there is an implicit determinism by which no one could be held morally blameworthy (Rudman 2001: 107; also Loader 1986: 92; Krüger 2004: 88). Rather than a natural reading where it is the responsibility of the person to please God (5:1–7; 7:18), in Rudman's interpretation, the person good in God's sight is merely the one whom God has forced to be such. By this reasoning any purpose in teaching wisdom is precluded, since one is not free to be, or not to be, wise.

27–28. These two verses, 7:27–28, are particularly interesting for several reasons. First, 7:27 is the only identification of Qoheleth as the speaker apart from 1:2 and 12:8. It is a climactic point of some sort, and probably indicates a more profound moment of reflection. However, perhaps his title 'the assembler' is used merely as a pun, since he is assembling one observation to another to find an explanation of wisdom's difference from folly (cf. 12:11).

What Qoheleth is about to reveal about his findings is that there is something he has *not* found. He begins these two verses with this ironic twist. Secondly, he says he *still* is seeking something, and so far has found only one man in a thousand who qualifies for it. Exactly for what that one man qualifies, we are not told. Thirdly, we are not told whether it is one man out of a thousand 'men' or simply out of a thousand people in general. So far, then, interpreters are dealt two ellipses that challenge solving this riddle. Fourthly, what is it that differentiates the one man who qualified for something from 'those' (*'ēlleh*) women who never qualify? Who is the one who can solve this type of riddle, asks 8:1. It is in the pl. demonstrative pronoun, *'ēlleh* (those), where the riddle begins to unfold. But to whom does the pronoun refer? This too is indefinite – a fifth complication. Does it refer to the thousand? The thousand what? Thousand men? Of course not: one would not find a woman among a thousand men. A thousand people generally speaking? Surely one would find hundreds of women there, not zero. So where have women been most recently observed? In 7:26! These are the women to whom we are referred; it is these fornicators among whom Qoheleth could not find any women of the nature Qoheleth is seeking. But what is that nature? What can one find very rarely in men yet never in loose women? We are driven to the answer: 'Wisdom'. The solution to this riddle with five complications is that no wise woman will be found among these unsavoury ones, and one will find very few who are truly wise even among the rest of the people: 'I have found one wise man out of a thousand, but I have not found a single wise woman among all those seductresses.' There are those who plead for the 'plain sense' of this passage to be admitted, namely that Qoheleth is a misogynist. We cannot read this passage plainly; it is anything but plain! Furthermore, any interpretation of this passage from within the predominantly male school of commentators that hints at the inferiority of women's wisdom does so with Lady Wisdom herself chuckling demeaningly at the very thought. Of all people, Qoheleth would have known that.

29, 8:1. 7:29 is a perfect example of where theological eisegesis can usurp the simple meaning of the words. Qoheleth begins his fourth 'finding' with phrasing that places us back in Gen. 3, where humanity was created morally upright but fell to its spiritual and physical death (again Qoheleth shows much more than an amoral sensibility). Consequently, the pl. form of ḥešbôn is considered by many to have a different meaning here in v. 29 from the singular uses in this very section where it has meant 'explanation' (7:25, 27). But, consistent with the term's use in Ecclesiastes throughout, Qoheleth acknowledges that God created humanity upright and now commends humanity for constantly seeking 'explanations'. Human ingenuity is praised in Job 28:1–11, though rightfully deflated when compared with the deepest of wisdom that only God has (28:12–28).

This praise for seeking explanations is followed immediately in 8:1 by an encouragement to pursue the wisdom that guides such explanations. We know it is a word of encouragement, since, according to 8:1b, wisdom is not only possible; it is relieving! The reader has just been challenged by a complicated riddle in 7:27–28, and now the clarion is given to solve it. That is the meaning of pēšer (interpretation): to interpret the obscure. In Gen. 40:5 – 41:15, it is the obscure nature of dreams that requires Joseph's interpretations. Here it is the obscurity of a riddle that requires the skill and wisdom for deciphering. The prize for such skill is a changed psyche, from a firm, braced face to a face of peace and composure. Anxiety, anger, sorrow and frustration can create a hardened facial expression, but the enjoyment of life and wisdom will bring it relief. This happens in Qoheleth's own experience in 2:23–26. There he was agitated to the point of hating life and despairing of all fruits from his labour. But wisdom prevailed and his realism appreciated the rejuvenation of wisdom as well as God's other gifts.

Explanation

In pursuing devotional time, the pious can have many wonderful goals in order to become more spiritually active. Availing ourselves of the means of God's grace, which comes through Bible study, meditation and prayer, is a requirement for a mature walk through the day's activities and responsibilities. The intimacy of time spent alone with our Lord and Saviour, our heavenly Father and the Holy Spirit binds our spiritual composition with that of the infinite, all-powerful, all-wise and loving God. It is our time to affirm our fear and reverence for him and his unfathomable decisions. It is just one of many times during the day that we praise him for his being and thank him for his minute-to-minute provisions. It is a time of humility before him as a sinner who even if sometimes righteous is nonetheless finite and frail.

Many other reasons move us towards him, but one reason surely must be that we are earnestly searching for the practical wisdom that comes from a developed view of the world as God sees it. Preaching, teaching, participating in small groups, reading biblically based books are all fine, but there is something about Qoheleth's approach that is even more profound and effective: his search is original to himself; he takes the time to draw conclusions from experience while revering God. Rather than a Christian's life being filled only with the understanding of others, the discipline of private personal reflection on personal, local, national and global realities is the most effective way to develop a perspective on life that is unique to our relationship with the Lord and the calling he has given us in his kingdom. We lack the skill of customizing God's wisdom for our individual lives, so substitute the experiences and decisions of strangers for ours. Such exploring is strenuous work; it brings one very far and deep, and brings a level of world awareness that is at first daunting, intimidating, demanding and thus unwelcomed – every reason to avoid the search and simply buy someone else's spiritual journey off a retail shelf. It is our nature to look for explanations; it is against our nature to look for them in our own study of both the Scripture and our personal relationship and experiences with its Author.

Foolishness is not a condition – it is a practice! The fool is foolish because he consistently and purposely subjects himself to circumstances. He follows his nose, not bothering to look for pitfalls, traps and snares. He prefers this life of abject passivity where he is always acted upon rather than acting on. In this, the fool is fully wicked. He is neither a pitiful subnormal intelligence nor innocent in his decision to be indecisive. These people are easy prey for those who would take advantage of them. Dark forces, human and demonic, see them as servile means to their ends. One's predators may be a woman or a man – their prey can be either or both. The abuse may be sexual, but more often is not; it is just that OT wisdom literature uses the sexual motif as one of its symbols for this co-dependency in folly and sin. Qoheleth denigrates the seductress here but prizes a healthy and rewarding marriage in 9:9. Yet sexual purity is scoffed at in our society; infidelity is frowned upon only *publicly*. Seductions by phone, Internet, video, print or cable television are destroying marriages and families without a spouse even leaving the house. Lusty carousing and fornication can be done in the privacy of one's own home.

Ecclesiastes has a reputation for austerity, if not outright pessimism or cynicism. This is, of course, due to a misreading of the book and its key word, *hebel*. There is a clear side of Qoheleth that is relaxed and joyful. It may simply be hard to warm up to him with all of his depth and perhaps unapproachably superior wisdom. He is, however, concerned about his listeners. The epilogist tells us he sought a 'satisfying' word for his hearers. His encouragement to his student is that wisdom 'gives light to his face and makes its stiffness to relax'. What a wonderful description of what he is trying to do in this speech. His pastoral advice to his audience is for them to enjoy life, its fruits, its people, the sun. After all of his ominous observations and conclusions, he gives us a chance to relax and smile.

ECCLESIASTES 8:2-15

Translation

²Keep the word of the king especially because of an oath to God. ³Do not be hasty to walk away from him. Do not persist in damaging comments, because he does whatever he chooses to do. ⁴There is power in any word of the king, so who will say to him, 'What are you doing?' ⁵⁻⁶ᵃWhoever keeps a command will experience nothing evil, since a wise heart knows a suitable time and judgment – yes, for every choice there is a suitable time and judgment.

⁶ᵇ⁻⁷Really, humanity's misery is heavy, since no one knows what will happen, since no one can announce what anything will be. ⁸No one has authority to restrain the wind with the wind, nor is there authority over the day of death, nor exemption during war, nor will wickedness deliver its masters.

⁹I have seen and personally considered all of this that has been done under the sun – a time when one man rules harmfully over another. ¹⁰But in such cases I have seen the wicked buried, even the ones entering and leaving from a holy place, and they are forgotten in the city where they did these things. Also this is temporary.

¹¹When a sentence against evil conduct is not executed swiftly, then the heart of the sons of men is full of intent to do evil. ¹²Though a sinner does a hundred evil things and lives longer, still I know that it will be well for those who fear God, who fear him publicly. ¹³But it will not be well for the wicked, and he will not lengthen his days as a shadow, since he does not fear God.

¹⁴There are temporary experiences on the earth, namely there are righteous people who experience things as if they were wicked, and there are evil people who experience things as if they were righteous. I say that this too is temporary. ¹⁵So I

commended happiness, since there is nothing better under the sun for man than to eat and to drink and to be happy, for it accompanies him in his labour during the days of his life which God has given him under the sun.

Notes on the text

2. The initial pronoun, '*ănî*, has no verb and is probably a textual error. Rather than guess at a verb, I do not translate the pronoun.

'especially because': the waw that introduces '*al dibrat* is emphatic; see 'Notes' at 7:25.

'oath to God': both objective or subjective genitives are possible here, but I prefer the objective, comparable to Shimei's oath made simultaneously to the Lord and to Solomon in 1 Kgs 2:43.

3. 'Do not be hasty': *bāhal* in the ni. means 'to be terrified' or 'to be hasty' (for the latter, see Prov. 28:22).

'persist in damaging comments': Waldman (1979: 407–408) and some commentaries argue this phrase is specifically about conspiracy and rebellion, seeing *dābār* to refer ambiguously to a 'matter, affair'. However, an explanatory repetition of the word at the end of v. 4 suggests a verbal understanding; that is, it is the 'word' spoken that is inapt at least, if not wrong or mischievous: 'What are you doing?'

'chooses to do': for *ḥepeṣ* as 'choice', see 'Notes' at 3:1.

4. 'power': *šiltôn* is a typical abstract form of an early Biblical Hebr. root. See discussion of its alleged lateness at 'Notes' at 2:19.

5. 'suitable time': for '*ēt*, see 'Notes' at 3:1.

6. 'choice': for *ḥepeṣ*, see above, v. 3.

7. 'no one knows': the subject here is the generic '*ādām* (humanity).

8. 'wind': *rûaḥ* here may mean 'wind' (Zimmerli 1962: 216), 'life-spirit' (Crenshaw 1987: 152; Hubbard 1991: 183–184) or 'anger' (Irwin 1945: 130; see BDB 925a). Wind is a critical symbol in this speech, particularly its unpredictability (1:6; 11:5; cf. Prov. 30:4), though death (the absence of life-spirit) is explicit in the following stich. I prefer 'wind', though its thrust is intentionally or unintentionally vague.

'during war': lit. 'in war', thus different from legal discharge *before* a war, as in Deut. 20:5–8.

'wickedness': this natural reading is preferred over unwarranted textual changes required by a preference by some for 'riches' ('*ošer*; Galling 1969: 110; Whitley 1978: 73).

9. The infinitive abs. used as a finite verb, *nātôn* ('applied'; also 9:11), is an example of what some consider to be late linguistic features in Ecclesiastes (GKC 113z). However, numerous instances of this in early Biblical Hebr. speak clearly against such generalizations (Hammershaimb 1963: 90). It is also found in the seventh-century Yavneh-Yam letter (Gibson 1971, 1: 29; Isserlin 1972: 200).

'harmfully': similar phrasing is found in 5:13, 'to his *own* hurt', since there was no possible object than the subject. However, here, 'another' person is the natural and closest referent of the pronominal suffix *lō*.

10. 'But in such cases': a composite form of three particles: adversative waw, prepositional *bēt* and *kēn* (thus). This verse is one of the most grammatically challenging in Ecclesiastes. I stay close to the received text, since a sensible translation can be derived from it. For the complexities of the text, see for example Serrano 1954.

'a holy place': the universal nature of Qoheleth's observations perhaps intentionally leaves the exact identity of this vague.

'they did these things': *kēn-'āśû* is clumsy in English, 'they did thusly', so I translate it as an objective phrase.

11. 'sentence': *pitgām* is one of only two Pers. words in Ecclesiastes. The universal purview of Qoheleth especially would allow foreign *political* words to surface. On Pers. words in Ecclesiastes, see 'Notes' at 2:5.

12. 'a hundred evil things': as in 6:3, Qoheleth refers elliptically to 'one hundred'. There 'children' were presumed to be numbered. Here 'evil' is explicitly numbered, but in the const.; *mě'at* has no abs. This ellipsis is probably vernacular.

'lives longer': lit. 'lengthens him', another elliptical phrase similar to the syntax in 7:15.

14. 'temporary experiences': lit. 'breath that is done', but as Longman explains (1998: 230), the syntax is difficult with only the substantive *hebel* with *yēš*, so an expanded phrase is necessary.

'experience things as if': lit. 'it happens to them like . . .', an ambiguous phrase that eludes a smooth translation.

Form and structure

Especially in historical narrative, one finds discrete units separated by the specific times recounted. Prophetic speeches are marked by 'Thus says . . .', and Job and Psalms have the speakers clearly marked. Song of Songs and Ecclesiastes on the other hand are disjointed to a great extent. Between two sections introduced by reflective statements (7:23; 8:16) is this section that bursts upon us with a command to loyalty and righteousness under royal administration. The previous section dealt with wisdom in the abstract, and the next section after this one will deal with wickedness in the abstract. In a sense, this section, especially given how it closes in 8:15, is an example of how the countenance of the anxious can be turned to that of the satisfaction of the wise, as 8:1 summarized the previous section.

The first verses of this section deal with the very concrete pressures on the one who reports to the king or at least his senior management. Even during very difficult times, wisdom will lead to loyalty to the king for theological, legal and very pragmatic reasons (vv. 2–6). These thoughts are followed by a supporting philosophy of realism, so characteristic of Qoheleth, which generalizes about uncertainties and limitations that require one to take as few political risks as necessary (vv. 7–8). A wicked, inept and abusive leader may cause a wise person to consider rebelling or defecting if evil is not checked (vv. 9–11). Granted, poor leadership will let evil run rampant; nonetheless, consolation is provided for those who obey and honour God publicly (vv. 12–13). Qoheleth concludes this section by emphasizing again the temporariness of rampant wickedness and the mitigating advantages for the wise who toil in labour – the simple joys of life, including eating and drinking (vv. 14–15). His persistent themes of 'brevity' and 'joy' throughout his speech recur here in this section, with the temporariness of political tragedies specifically being emphasized in vv. 10, 13 and 14. A linear progression is as follows:

2–4	Be careful to be loyal to the king, regardless of the wisdom of his actions.
5a	Your wisdom will protect you from the king and possibly poor decisions.
5b–6a	Wisdom helps one to know suitable times for actions and judgments.
6b–8	Human limitations are a burden, but wickedness will not protect one.
9	For example, oppressive overseers harm others.
10	But such wicked people will rule, and then be buried and forgotten.
11	If such wicked people are not punished, evil will accelerate.
12	Sinners appear to sustain themselves.
12	But it will go well for the righteous.
13	Besides, the wicked will not really prolong their days.
14	Realistically, there are injustices we will encounter.
15	But enjoy your life nonetheless during the days God gives you.

Comment

2–6a. Qoheleth starts this section of his speech from the perspective of a king (1:12; 2:8–9) who draws the listener into the intrigue of court and national politics by describing the challenges to working in government and to ruling justly. He begins in these verses with instructions about personal survival in the royal system, progresses to a discussion of justice in general (vv. 12–14) and closes with his thematic consolation of shalom (v. 15). The target of this speech, as I mentioned in the 'Introduction', is the vast administrative personnel in his government, and this becomes clearer the further into the speech we go. We hear echoes in Paul and Peter who express the same encouragements for subordinates to submit to their authorities and to do so as pleasing God, rather than merely humans (Rom. 13:1–2; Eph. 6:5–8; Col. 3:22–23; 1 Pet. 2:13–14, 17).

Obeying the king held a double responsibility: to the king, and to God through an oath made to God. We have seen the importance of keeping vows made to God in 5:2–6. There one is warned to pay any vows in a timely way, not prattle with excuses, or one will be treated as a fool, and God will destroy one's accomplishments. A more deadly result, at Solomon's own hand, came from Shimei's breaking of his oath to God to submit to Solomon's commands (1 Kgs 2:41–43; also Exod. 22:11; Josh. 9:18–20). Using identical terminology, Solomon states elsewhere that the one who 'keeps a commandment, keeps his soul' (Prov. 19:16). Later, the Proverbs advise, 'fear the LORD and the king ... who knows what disaster may come from them both?' (24:21–22).

Parallels have been found between these sentiments of Qoheleth and those of Ahiqar (e.g. Jones 2006: 219–223), though parallel principles would apply in many ancient monarchies' structure. There are significant differences too, however: for instance, Qoheleth does not have the softer laudatory tone for the king's utterances as Ahiqar does (Qoheleth nowhere describes the king's command as 'soothing' or 'gentle'); nor does he liken the king to God, especially in terms of the king having any 'functional divinity' (obedience to the king depends on the higher divine authority to which one swears). However, the severity of the king's command is expressed as strongly by Qoheleth, though that is not peculiar simply to Ahiqar and Qoheleth, and is implicit, if not explicit, in any monarchic polity.

Though walking away from the king (perhaps without being dismissed?) is clearly discouraged, there is a predominant cadre of words referring to speech in 8:2–5 that presses the phrase *dābār rā‘* of 8:3 towards bad speech or 'damaging comments' rather than towards acts of rebellion or resignation (see Waldman 1979: 407–408 and Garrett 1987: 169). Mouth (v. 2), oath (v. 2), word (v. 4), say (v. 4), command (v. 5) provide a context dealing with speaking rather than acts of dissent. Probably what Qoheleth has in mind is a subordinate digging himself a deeper and deeper hole while attempting to exempt himself from a king's definitive, non-negotiable command. A chiasm, then, is possibly intended in these verses:

A   Keep the word of the king...
   B   do not persist in damaging comments,
      C   because he does whatever he chooses to do.
      C¹   There is power in any word of the king, so
   B¹   who will say to him, 'What are you doing?'
A¹   Whoever keeps a command...

The reasoning behind this counsel to comply is the same as that given previously by Qoheleth – there is a suitable time (*‘ēt*) for every decision, including a time to speak and a time to remain silent (3:7). Perhaps there will be another, more appropriate, time, or another way to challenge discreetly the king's command; but if the time is not right, the wise will know. The emphasis on timing in 8:5–6 builds on the theme of 'wise timing' in 3:1–8, and is repeated when the timing in dispensing of justice is the topic Qoheleth addresses in v. 11. Jones (2006: 223–224) believes 'judgment' in vv. 5 and 6 means God's judgment, as it does in 3:16–17. However, both humanity and God are able to 'time' their judgments wisely: God judges the wicked and the righteous in a judicial sense, and people may or may not make wise judgments in a more general calculating sense of the word 'judgment'. The latter is precisely the point of 8:2–6b and 8:11. Human 'judgment' in these verses refers to the discernment necessary to make wise decisions suitable for challenging times (cf. Judg. 13:12), whereas 3:16–17 is speaking in divine juridical terms.

Subordinates might underestimate the resolve in a king's commands, since they do not know what goes into the king's decisions. The derisive question 'What are you doing?' is made to all levels of human and divine rank, but the fool reveals increasingly his folly as the rank he addresses rises. The question becomes more disrespectful when it is asked of those who know more about what they are doing and when they wisely refuse to reveal all the reasons. Job says he *knows* better than to ask this of God (Job 9:12; cf. Isa. 45:9); nonetheless, and understandably, he cannot refrain from doing so repeatedly. This expectation of humility and loyalty in respect to the king is resumed in 10:4 and 10:20. In 10:4, one's words are to be spoken from humble poise; in 10:20, one's words are to be kept to oneself. In Prov. 20:2, the wrong words spoken to the king can be fatal, and Prov. 25:3 describes the thoughts of a king to be often indeterminable.

6b–8. Though there are expectations that one act appropriately at the appropriate time within the royal court (8:5), there are obvious finite limits to one's knowing even present realities exhaustively, let alone knowing the future (8:7). Ogden (1979: 349) explains, 'though [wisdom] may know the "times," wisdom does not know the future'. This is part of the misery of being human, which Qoheleth has mentioned already (1:13, 18; 2:17, 23). However, this is not to preclude *some* knowledge of the future based on patterns of the past (1:9) or because of God's promises (8:12). In reviewing Qoheleth's statements about life and its contents, they are to be understood in the normal discourse of everyday expressions, not as technical declarations of unexceptional apodictic formulas comparable to the style of systematic theologies or mathematical dissertations. However, Qoheleth does know something about the future; for example, 8:12 affirms that there will be justice for the wicked and for the righteous. He may not know much about the future, but the balancing counsel is that one can know what is wisdom, for now.

We are told exactly why life can be emotionally oppressive and physically threatening in 8:8. These 'inevitabilities' illustrate, however, both the reasons and the consolations for obeying a superior. Admittedly, since one cannot know all the implications of their actions, life's limitations certainly do leave everyone vulnerable – including being vulnerable to a king's poor or at least debatable decisions. Similar reminders of frustrating human limitations are found later in 9:11–12. No one knows when trouble will come their way, so they should rely on the imperfect but structurally more secure governmental institutions rather than going it alone. No one can restrain the unpredictable whims of the wind (or king), nor can they control the day of unavoidable fatality whether in war or not (3:8). So avoiding futile efforts to reverse the course of the irreversible should at least not increase the misery of human life but instead provide a reason for wise resignation. Although wickedness is pervasive (8:14), it will not ultimately prevail for those addicted to it (8:12–13). Again, Qoheleth continues to speak about sinful wickedness in the context of orthodox OT theology and wisdom. Those who practise wickedness, whether kings or not, will not find their ultimate deliverance from it, since, according to 8:13, wickedness does not prolong life. Instead, it is the number of days God grants that determines one's brief length of life (8:15).

9–10. In the midst of this discussion of administrating wisely as a subordinate and as a king, Qoheleth assures his audience that his reflections have been thorough; these are not impromptu thoughts spoken haphazardly. So 'all of this' refers to his initial comments about the subordinate's responsibilities, and also refers to the following comments about social, judicial and eschatological conclusions about justice. In a sense, v. 9b serves as the title for this section on wise administration: 'A time when one man rules tragically over another'. It explains the reason for all the topics discussed in 8:2–15. Unjust leadership puts wise subordinates in tough positions of servile compliance (vv. 2–5), believes itself invincible (v. 8), winks at cultic hypocrisy (v. 10), allows the proliferation of evil (v. 11) and strains any faith in justice (vv. 12–14). We know Qoheleth is concerned about intentional injustice from his commiserations for the oppressed in 4:1–3 and 5:8. We will also find in 10:16–18 that he is distressed by the royal leaders whose indulgent and thus negligent administration impacts an entire nation negatively.

A consolation comes in 8:10, however. In such cases of injustice, even when any public holiness is feigned by these oppressive or lax leaders, they will be buried like everyone else; their life will be temporary as will any memory or any respect for their deeds. Those residents of the city whom these leaders oppressed, and who witnessed their leaders' hypocrisy in local cultic observances, will fortunately be able to forget the leaders and their foolish leading. As we saw in 2:16–17, however, being forgotten is more than falling victim to the memory lapses of others; it is to be marginalized, despised in every regard. Therefore, v. 10 provides an example of what happens to the social bully in 8:9, proving that the masters of wickedness will not be delivered by evil (8:8d). Again, this proves that all is temporary, fortunately even the wicked themselves.

Without minimizing the complexities of the morphological, lexical, grammatical, syntactical and textual issues discussed at length in commentaries and a few articles, I translate v. 10 as straightforward and as consistently with the MT as possible.

11–13. An implication of poor leadership is the behavioural latitude given to the wicked who will victimize the weak and those who abide by the laws of the land. We will be told in 9:3 that human nature is evil; actually, it is so foolish it would be better described as 'insane'. It would not take too much judicial slackness to allow a community or nation to be morally and socially devastated. If the will of leadership is weak, or worse, is itself corrupt, injustice and social decay will of course abound. Long durations between violations and any subsequent legal action give perpetrators more opportunity to harm the societal fabric of civility and safety.

> So the law is numbed and justice never prevails,
>> since the wicked surround the righteous
>> so judgment comes out perverted.
>>> (Hab. 1:4; also Judg. 2:19; 17:6)

Deferred punishment also encourages those who otherwise would be deterred from wrongdoing by a system of fair but swift punishment. We heard similar perspectives on the failure of justice systems back in 3:16, with a resolution in the next verse. Also 5:8 admits to the fact of injustices but prescribes a king who exercises staff discipline, cultivating the leadership for fairer management of the people. We will hear again in 10:5–7 about disturbing inverted justice, and the indolent leaders of 10:16–18 also strike us as those under whom justice would hardly be given a chance, and whose land is rampant with crime, corruption and abuse. Like Eccl. 5:8–9, Prov. 25:5 portrays the opposite scenario:

> Remove the wicked from the king's presence,
>> and his throne will be secured by righteousness.

Vv. 12 and 13 present two challenges central to the interpretation of Qoheleth's speech. First, for those who interpret Ecclesiastes to be predominantly an argument of despair regardless of any pronounced virtues of wisdom and righteousness, this passage (as well as numerous previous passages) presents something of a contradiction. The commendation found here is perfectly consistent with what is defined as the beginning of wisdom elsewhere in the wisdom literature, namely the fear of God. It also condemns wickedness and the self-delusion of its masters. Secondly, regardless of one's understanding of Ecclesiastes as a whole, there appears to be a prima facie contradiction within the two verses on whether the wicked can or cannot prolong their days through their wickedness. For those who believe this sage often contradicts himself, there is less of a problem. Yet these verses clearly concur with OT ethics from which many commentators claim Qoheleth has disengaged.

The key questions for v. 12 are who the sinner is Qoheleth is discussing and what the sinner is prolonging. The immediate context tends to identify the sinner with the criminal of v. 11 whose life continues unabated because his sentence is delayed – if he is charged at all. Common sins or evil deeds of an ordinary person that amount to only 'a hundred' would not classify that person as anyone other than a saint. So these 'sins', if they are an egregious number, must be very serious, presumably of the 'judicial sentencing' (*pitgām*) rank. If it is his number of days that are lengthened because of the absence of swift sentencing and its execution, an extended life is only an illusion. V. 15 will tell us again what Qoheleth has said before: the days of one's life are determined and dispensed by God alone. So the burial of the wicked in v. 10 and the exoneration of the one who fears God mark the perspective about justice which Qoheleth relies on and with which he encourages his audience. Besides, Qoheleth *knows* that it will be well for the pious – it is not merely a probability from his observations or a wishful reflection. He ended his most desperate reflections with this certainty in 2:26. Proverbs and the psalmists all agree with Qoheleth:

> The fear of the LORD extends one's days,
> > but the wicked's years will be shortened.
> > > > (Prov. 10:27; cf. 16:4; 24:19–20)

> When the wicked sprout up as the grass, and sinners flourish –
> > they are to be destroyed for ever.
> > > > (Ps. 92:7; also 1:5–6; 37:1–2, 35–36; 58:10–11)

Isa. 57:1–2 extends the logic by arguing that the righteous who die are saved from the evil to come – an act of mercy by God (see 2 Kgs 22:18–20).

The life of the wicked may be lengthened if their execution is delayed (vv. 11–12), but at the end of the day they will not even be as long as an elongated shadow before dusk (v. 13). Some contend that 'shadow' (*ṣēl*) has the same meaning here as it does in its other occurrences in Ecclesiastes; that is, the wicked are as fleeting as a shadow (Ogden 1987: 138; Krüger 2004: 161). The brevity of the wicked's impact is a relief, a consolation that accompanies the frustrating truth of 8:14.

14. The apparent 'success' of the wicked is a recurrent theme in all of the OT and cannot be relegated to any specific time in human history, much less that of a single nation like Israel. Granted, Qoheleth is more talkative about inverted justice in this one speech (3:16; 4:1; 7:15; 9:11, 18; 10:1), but it is not a view of reality that he holds in distinction to the rest of the

OT. The righteous, innocent poor are main players in the Proverbs, often the victims of the wicked. So these injustices are no more absurd or meaningless to Qoheleth than to the established wisdom and prophetic culture of the OT. Injustices are to be expected in a fallen world where Cain murders Abel, Joseph is imprisoned for rebuffing the seduction by his master's wife, and innocent, loyal Uriah is murdered by his own king. An implicit deed–consequence expectation is the backdrop of Qoheleth's theology. It is the exceptions that disturb him. He is not alone, however. The wise, the poets and the prophets cannot ignore what at times stares them in the face. While surveying the obvious exceptions of a foundational sense of justice based on common grace and that maintains at least a modicum of order in a nation, they question God's justice in unison:

> Why do the wicked still live,
>   living on and becoming powerful?
>
> (Job 21:7)

> I saw the success of the wicked...
>   they are not in trouble like others.
>
> (Ps. 73:3, 5)

> Why has the wicked's way prospered?
> Why are the treacherous at ease?
>
> (Jer. 12:1)

> Why do you look favourably on the treacherous?
> Why are you silent when the wicked swallow those who are
>   more righteous?
>
> (Hab 1:13)

This verse is more general than the similar inversion of justice in 7:15, which speaks of death. Here Qoheleth does not tell us the source of the unfair experience, the type of the experience nor whether it is fatal. What he does emphasize, though, by introducing and concluding this verse with the same pronouncement, is that fortunately these cases of injustice are still only momentary and do not upset God's ultimate plans for justice (cf. 2:26; 3:16–17; 8:10, 12–13). Farmer (1991: 182) explains the coherence of Qoheleth's thoughts here: 'Qoheleth first denies that retribution takes place "under the sun" and then affirms that this is a "breath," a temporary state of affairs.' After all, the wicked are eventually buried (8:10), criminals are generally sentenced (8:11) and the moral fabric of a society is usually mended to at least a bearable degree. The situation is temporary because of his conclusion in vv. 12–13.

15. Now Qoheleth concludes with his familiar encouragement. In spite of the tragic implications of the Edenic Fall that the righteous and innocent witness and experience personally, they are to enjoy the simple yet fulfilling benefits of wise and persistent toil. This is a shalom consolation, but it is also a commendable way of life on its own merits, even before the Fall. Finding happiness in our responsible daily work is the intent of the Hebr. here rather than interpretations that render this refrain in shallow and frivolous terms, like 'having fun' (NLT). Whybray notices a gradual crescendo in the string of shalom consolations found in 2:24, 3:12–13, 22, 5:18–20, 8:15, 9:7–9, 11:7–10 (1982: 87–98), and this rendition is no less a recommendation of holistic joy than the earlier ones. Furthermore, this particular expression makes labour the beneficiary of the other joys of eating and drinking, which accompany and perhaps relieve a bit of toil's harshness. In the previous refrains, labour is simply an attending joy with no closer *causal* relationship.

This unit has been unflinching in voicing concerns about the threatening circumstances of life, and human limitations in understanding them, much less changing or avoiding them. Yet it also includes many implicit and explicit consolations:

5	Wisdom can deliver from tragedy.
8	The wicked will not be delivered by their wickedness.
10	The wicked are buried and forgotten.
12–13	Justice will come to the wicked.
	It will be well for those fearing God.
14	Injustice is temporary.
15	Enjoy life, for God ultimately determines the days.

The phrase 'days of his life which God has given him' is also familiar phrasing by Qoheleth (5:18) and is a direct summation of 8:8, 10, 12–13 in its identification of God's sovereignty as the ultimate authority over the wind, death, justice, the righteous and the wicked. Humans have no authority over death, and the wicked's days are numbered regardless of any apparent extension by unexecuted sentences (8:11).

Explanation

A large part of submitting to the sovereignty of God is the responsibility to submit to that of mere mortals. If submission to the will of a perfectly loving God is a challenge for us, suffering directly or indirectly under an inept leader can tempt us to think that it is unbearable. Plus, given our tendency to elevate what is tolerable to the nearly intolerable just by an attitude of ingratitude, even the best of organizational situations can annoy one to the point of disloyalty. Qoheleth cautions against insubordination, as does the NT, repeatedly. Since there are no perfect leaders, and, since they are in their positions by God's permission, and, since God is aware of our being pinched between authority and freedom, there is no alternative other than at least to ride out the waves of indiscretion and possibly even disaster. Besides, disloyalty presumes the authority is unteachable. Our role may be to muster the courage at the right time and in the right way to solve the crisis with the authority rather than defect or retract into sulking. And, of course, there is always the distinct possibility that the problem is not with the leader but with us.

Short of sinning, the subordinate should not despise any direction from a superior as incidental or optional. If the demands are doable and ethical, one has an obligation before God to comply. The Bible is full of examples of very capable people having to submit to unbelieving authorities and being very successful because of their wisdom: Jacob, David, Joseph, Daniel, Esther, even Christ. Submission to human power was a daily routine even for these great people.

Of course, it is wisdom that Qoheleth assumes will protect one from poor decisions at the top. There is a season even for being captive to the wrong directions, policies and strategies. Though human limitations are a burden, wisdom helps one to know suitable times for actions and judgments and does not advise sinning to deliver one from apparently unjust circumstances. Wisdom is patient and understanding of the larger picture. Wicked people will rule, but will eventually be buried and forgotten. The question is, can we wait that long? We may not have a choice if we are talking about national or world leaders. We may have to wait even longer for order to be restored if the legal system is too lenient or inefficient.

These are words for those who are in authority as well. There are those who serve an organization under our direction, and they are the ones who are listening to the words above because they find themselves working under our own defective leadership at times. We are guilty of poor decisions, abuse of authority, slight or great, and we should honour the patience and dignity of those who suffer while we bungle our power by not applying wisdom thoroughly enough in the family, company, government, church, ministry, school or university.

Trusting God for justice in his world can be a difficult task. On the grand scheme, we see child-trafficking, genocide, political and familial torture, abortion, extortion, terrorism and slavery. Where is God? If he is all-powerful, where is his might to make things right? If he is love, when will the horrors end? On a more personal level, when will my life as a believer be at least as smooth and easy as it is for the wicked around me? More pointedly, when will justice make my life even more free and peaceful than theirs? It appears that sinners not only survive but thrive, and for a longer lifespan than believers! For the most part, the vast majority of such complaints are petty and come from ingratitude for what we do have in Christ, excusing our selfish insulation and inactivity on behalf of those who really are in the terrifying situations. However, there are moments in our own lives and the lives of our brothers and sisters that are almost unbearable. In the intensity of those moments God is faithful to provide his Comforter to those who are sensitive to the Holy Spirit's presence; what else could be offered that could substitute for those intimate moments between the trusting and the Trusted? And short of death, when the ultimate and perfect healing comes, the trials, though severe, are only temporary even if they seem endless.

Furthermore, there is a rampant entitlement mentality in the church. There is the presumption based on arrogance and greed that preaches and teaches that God owes us a trouble-free life under the sun – because he has allegedly promised it. Regardless of the examples of Job, Jeremiah, Christ and Paul, not to speak of the countless martyrs through the millennia, the church has teachers within it that blind their sheep to the realities of both Scripture and the devout Christians who suffer not for their sin or that of their parents, but for the glory of God. This insidious preaching prefers the tactics of the Accuser – fabricating a case against the faithful before their Lord – over God's sanctifying method of testing the Christian through trials and suffering. It trivializes the serious repercussions of the cosmic rebellion that united forces below and above the sun, and prematurely confers absolute exemption from the curse to the truly 'mature', who fall for the offer.

Still, given all the disappointments, tragedy and heartbreak for the believer, Qoheleth assures the listener that the sinner is unable to add anything to his lifespan, and, all be told, the one who fears God and is not ashamed of such fear will find that his or her experience in God's kingdom will go well – not perfectly, but *well*. Not disease-free, but well enough. Not well off, but well enough. What does 'well enough' mean? What is the advantage for the one who fears God? Eat, drink and be happy in Christ. We want so badly to hear Qoheleth at least *mention* eternal life. It would seem such a better answer. But really it would not be better because it would not provide the incentive for the believer to see and appreciate God's blessings *now*.

ECCLESIASTES 8:16 – 10:1

Translation

[16–17a]As I devoted myself to know wisdom and to see the affliction that is inflicted on the earth, even though sleep is not seen in one's eyes day or night, still, I observed that one is unable to understand all God's work, the work which is done under the sun. [17b]Even though one labours in searching, one will not understand it all. And even if the wise say they know, they cannot understand it all. [9:1a]Indeed, I devoted myself to all of this so to explain it, because the righteous and the wise and their actions are in God's hands.

[1b]Furthermore, no one knows when either love or hatred will come – both are ahead. [2]Both occur to everyone the same: for the righteous and for the wicked, for the good and for the clean and for the unclean, for those sacrificing and for those not sacrificing; as for the good as for the sinner, the one who swears an oath as the one who fears an oath. [3]This is a tragedy in all that is done under the sun; indeed, there is the same event to both, since even the heart of the sons of man is full of evil, and madness is in their heart in their lives. Afterwards – to the dead!

[4]So there is confidence for whoever is joined to all of the living; clearly, a living dog is better than a dead lion. [5]For the living know they will die, but the dead know nothing, nor is there any reward for them, since their memory is forgotten. [6]Even the love, hatred and jealousy towards them will have perished already, and there will no longer be a portion for them from all that is done under the sun.

[7]Go, eat your food with pleasure, and drink your wine with joy in your heart, since God has already approved your works. [8]Always wear white garments and do not let oil be lacking on your head. [9]Enjoy life with a woman whom you love all the days of your brief life which he has given to you under the sun – all of your brief days – for it is your portion in life and in your labours which you labour under the sun. [10]All that your hand finds to do, do it with all your strength, for there is no doing, planning, knowledge or wisdom in Sheol where you are about to go.

[11]I again considered under the sun that the chase is not to the swift, nor the battle to the strong, nor even food for the wise, nor even riches to the discerning, nor even favour to the knowledgeable, for timely episodes happen to everyone. [12]Certainly, no one knows one's time. As fish seized in a treacherous net, and as birds seized in a snare, the sons of man are trapped like them at a tragic time when it suddenly falls on them.

[13–14]Even this I have observed as wisdom under the sun, and it impressed me – There was a city with only a few men in it and a great king came and surrounded it and built large siege works against it. [15]Now, he found a wise common man there who saved the city by his wisdom; yet no one remembered that specific common man.

[16]So I said, Wisdom is better than strength,
   but the wisdom of a common man is despised,
   and his words, they are not heeded.
[17]The words of the wise are heard when quiet,
   more than a ruler's shouting among fools.
[18]Wisdom is better than weapons of war,
   but one sinner destroys a lot of good.
[10:1]Dead flies cause a perfumer's oil to produce a stinking smell,
   a little folly is respected more than wisdom and honour.

Notes on the text

16. 'still, I observed': though it is only a waw with the perfect, the flow of thought suggests 'still'.

'affliction inflicted': lit. 'affliction done'. See 'Notes' at 1:13. The afflictions referred to are the apparent injustices of 8:14 and those discussed in the rest of this unit. It also hints at the affliction given by God when one gives the heart to understand wisdom.

'one's eyes': the third person pronominal suffix refers to *hā'ādām* near the beginning of v. 17.

17. 'even though': this phrase is expressed by *gam kî* in v. 16, here, by *bĕšel 'ăšer*. Qimron and Strugnell (1985: 405) conclude that since it appears in only the late Aram. texts it is improbable that there is any Aram. influence on Ecclesiastes here. It also appears in Jon. 1:7, 12.

'understand it all': lit. 'find it'. Most commentators see Qoheleth's concern to be the *thoroughness* in depth and/or breadth of discovery, since he affirms elsewhere that he has found out at least certain things.

9:1. 'actions': *'ăbādêhem* is considered an Aram. on the basis of its vocalization; for example, Wagner 1966: 122. However, this vocalization is found with other roots in earlier Biblical Hebr.; for example, Zeph. 1:4; Judg. 6:2; 8:26; 1 Sam. 23:14, 19. Also there is no contrasting Biblical Hebr. precedent for the const. state for comparison (see Fredericks 1988: 233–234).

'both are ahead': in Qoheleth's frequent use of polarity, 'both' is more literal; see also 2:14, 16, 3:19–20, 7:18 and 9:2. In the Hebr., the discordant suffix 'them' with the sg. 'man' is possibly a colloquialism.

2. 'both occur to everyone the same': since the first *kōl* refers again only to the two inanimate subjects in 9:1, love and hate, it is translated 'both' here in 9:2. Though the word is used twice in the same phrase here, the Hebr. listener naturally hears 'everyone' in the second case, since it refers to people. It is unnecessary to emend *hakōl* to *hebel* as does LXX, Vg and Fox 1999: 291.

'for the good': some delete the phrase, thinking Qoheleth constrains himself to pairings in this verse rather than freely adding this third element in the clause; for example, Longman 1998: 225. This positive attribute ('good'; *ṭôb*) disturbs the symmetry here; a negative attribute disturbs the symmetry in 9:6 (jealousy; *qin'ā*).

4. 'confidence': the root denotes trust and security, rather than simply hoping; compare the only other instance of *biṭṭāhôn* in 2 Kgs 18:19//Isa. 36:4.

'clearly, a living dog': this prepositional lamed is the emphatic lamed. See for example Whitley 1978: 80.

5. 'reward': see 4:9 where *śākār* meant 'reward'.

6. 'the love, hatred and jealousy towards them': the suffixes on these attitudes are translated here as objective, not subjective.

As in 1:10, *'ôlām* ([no] longer) and *kĕbār* (already) denote together something less than 'infinity (for ever)'. Here it emphasizes the whole balance of time 'under the sun'.

'jealousy': the same word, *qin'ā*, is used similarly in 4:4, where powerful bullies target enviously the weak or poor.

9. 'a woman': not 'the' woman.

10. 'explanations': see 'Notes' at 7:25.

11. 'chase is not to the swift': there is no precedent for *mērôṣ* in Biblical Hebr., so it is dubious that it means an athletic event. However, 'swift' has military contexts in the OT (Seow 1997: 307).

'timely events': hendiadys of *'ēt* (appropriate time) and *pega'* (event). The ubiquitous translation of *pega'* as 'chance' is without lexical support. The word simply means 'an occurrence, a happening', and carries no concept of luck or randomness.

15. 'he found': the subject of the qal perfect is unclear, leading some to assume it is the hostile king who somehow found the commoner in the city while besieging the city from outside (Fox 1999: 299). Others render the qal to be a rare case of the passive qal; for example, Crenshaw 1987: 166.

'that specific common man': three definite articles of specificity, plus *'et*, denotes a high level of focus here. For *miskēn* as 'commoner', see 'Notes' at 4:13.

'and he saved the city': *millat-hû'* is Qoheleth's verbal form for the preterite, by adding the pronoun to the conjugated verb. See 'Notes' at 1:16. The disappointing proverb in 9:16 is thought to be a commentary on the failure of the commoner to be heard – a reason for many to conclude that *millat* denotes only the potential of deliverance (Crenshaw 1987: 166–167). However, this would require an unprecedented definition of *zākar* in the last phrase (Fox 1999: 299).

16. 'I said': because the commoner *did* deliver the city, Qoheleth reports his immediate reaction at that time. Appropriately, he speaks in the simple past again. See above at 9:15.

18. 'war': *qĕrāb* is considered an Aram. If so, pre-exilic instances are found in 2 Sam. 17:11 and Ps. 144:1.

10:1. 'dead flies': the const. state 'flies of death' is a problem. Either we emend the text to create a verbal clause (Seow 1997: 311), use parallel biblical references and translate irrelevantly 'deadly flies' (LXX), or we accept this as acceptable phrasing for 'dead flies' (Longman 1998: 238).

Form and structure

Following a section that exhorted court employees to loyalty and right-eousness under a royal administration, is this section, which warns of the disappointments and ironies of life in general. Though life's disappointments and ironies are an integral thread throughout Qoheleth's speech, this unit, 8:16 – 10:1, appears to be a specific commentary on the subject, and particularly on the subject's most recent discussion in 8:14–15. In this new section, his disappointments are more concentrated and his observations more descriptive, while, at the same time, his shalom consolations are described more broadly and specifically as well.

The difficulty of determining the parameters of this unit is shown by the numerous ways commentators place 9:1 in a rhetorical context: 8:2 – 9:10 (Eaton); 8:9 – 9:10 (Lys); 8:10 – 9:12 (Hubbard); 8:16 – 9:6 (Lohfink); 8:16 – 9:10 (Galling; Fox); 8:16 – 9:12 (Zimmerli); 9:1–10 (Whybray; Hertzberg; Brown); 9:1–12 (Murphy; Krüger). However, we see 8:16–17 starting a new unit in a similar fashion to 1:13 and 7:23, with repetitions of *universal scope, personal commitment*, a desire to *seek and explore* with a goal of giving an *explanation* (see the table below). However, in these two verses, Qoheleth is concerned first with what God does. Then, in 9:1, he begins again to look specifically at human activity.

	1:13 – 2:3		7:23–29		8:16 – 9:1	
Universal scope	1:13	all that has been done	7:23	All this	8:16; 9:1	The affliction(s) ... work of God ... works of wise
Personal commitment	1:13, 17	I devoted myself to [seek]	7:25	I turned my heart to [know]	8:16	I devoted myself to know
Explanation			7:25, 27, 29	to [know or find] an explanation	9:1	to explain it
Seek and explore	1:13; 2:3	to search and to explore	7:25, 28–29	to explore and to seek	8:17	labours in searching
Frustration	1:13	it is a tragic affliction	7:23	it was far and deep	8:16	sleep is not seen in one's eyes day or night ... labours in searching.

Though the righteous and wise are in God's sovereign care, they cannot depend on exhaustive knowledge, obtained by thorough discovery, to foretell whether it is embracing love or impending hatred that they will soon meet (9:1). This is the agnosticism of future events that Qoheleth continues to lament. But the insult that is added to this injury is that both the wicked and the righteous will experience love and hatred in their lives (9:2–3). Since death is another leveller that treats the righteous as the wicked, the devout as the pagan, one should enjoy one's brief life (9:7–9) and aggressively pursue one's activities because of the brevity of life (9:10). The ironic equal treatment that the wicked and righteous are said to receive back in 8:14 and 9:1–2 are commented on with even more detailed examples of the ironies of life (9:11–12). All that he can say is that the 'timely episodes and circumstances' are at the root. Qoheleth does not hazard foolish guesses at the reasons; he simply faults finite knowledge for failing to forewarn the faithful. He then shares a parable as an example of when wealth and favour do not follow understanding and discernment (9:13–15). Despising the wise commoner (9:15) is a commentary on the lack of favour for the wise (9:11), which is a commentary on the disrespect for the wise (9:1), which is a commentary on the righteous experiencing things as if they were wicked (8:14). Both the commoner and the king are surprised by the outcome. The king does not conquer the city (the battle was not to the strong – 9:11); the wise commoner was not honoured. Qoheleth concludes with proverbs that speak alternately to the failures and successes of wisdom and the persistent strength of folly even in the company of wisdom (9:16 – 10:1). He does not speak of any pervasive dominance of folly but nonetheless acknowledges its horrible frequency.

Comment

16 – 9:1a. The parallels between this introduction to a new section and two other similar introductions (1:12–17; 7:23–25) are charted above. The scope has been all-inclusive in the three sections, but on reading them one finds the distinction between divine and human actions is fairly clear. Human actions are referenced in 1:13–14, 7:25, 26 and 9:1, divine actions, in 1:13, 7:29 and 8:17. In these two verses, the works *of God* are in view. God's ways are not known exhaustively, though of course they are known partially. Certainly, we know about some of God's works. While we can know God's works in past and present, we cannot understand them all the time, and even when we understand them, we do not fully understand. Qoheleth hardly argues anywhere that we can know *nothing* about God and what God does! Even in 3:11, Qoheleth reveals what God does and goes on to explain why: 'He has made everything beautiful in its time. He has also given them eternity in their hearts so that humanity will not understand the deeds God does from beginning to end.' It is the sense of 'knowing' pertaining to 'understanding' that Qoheleth explains here as well (see 'Comment' at 3:9–11, where the translation is 'understand' rather than 'finding out'). And in 7:29, he knows that God made humanity upright, even though he says that knowledge of the past is 'far and very deep' (7:23–24). His point here in 8:17 clearly means again that one cannot apprehend and comprehend everything that God does in its totality, from beginning to end (Prov. 16:9, 33; 19:21; 30:1–4; Job 28:12–23; Rom. 9:16). In this sense, Paul (who certainly does not shy away from asserting many things about God, his deeds and their meaning) asserts in reverence:

> Oh, the deep riches of God's wisdom and knowledge!
>   How unsearchable are his decisions,
>   and unfathomable his ways!
>
> (Rom. 11:33)

We can know, but not always or completely understand.

The frustration Qoheleth has from his searches appears in his conclusions equally, though he expresses them somewhat differently, as the

comparison in the table above shows. In these two verses, Qoheleth alludes
to both of the categories of affliction he has mentioned before in his speech:
the affliction of an arduous pursuit of knowledge that demands 'labouring', sleepless nights and days, as well as humanity's afflictions that he will
discuss more thoroughly in 9:1 – 10:1. In 8:16–17a, he alludes to no sleep
with still no complete understanding; this is paralleled perfectly by his
comment about laborious searches with no complete understanding being
obtained. The affliction of an inability to sleep has been a concern for
Qoheleth before (2:23; 5:12). His sentiment is voiced similarly by the
epilogist: 'excessive devotion is wearying to the body' (12:12). 'Seeing
sleep' is of course an ironic phrase because if one's eyes are open they
cannot see that they are closed for sleep.

The righteous, the wise – these are the people he focuses on in 2:26 and
8:14; and it is their *actions* that define their righteousness and wisdom, not
only their knowledge. Faith without works is dead. Here the righteous
and the wise are identified with each other, if not synonymously, at least
inextricably. Furthermore, Qoheleth's focus on human action again
informs us about the other side of the synergy between divine sovereignty
and human responsibility. We found Qoheleth's interest in 8:16–17 to be
in God's work; now, the remainder of this section, to 10:1, is about human
action and its implications. The truth that the wise and their actions are in
God's hands does not imply a determinism that obviates human freedom
or responsibility. However, it does speak to God's ultimate oversight,
and possible intervention, either in the course of human history or in
individual human actions. The righteous and their works are in God's
hands, and it is his caring hands to which 2:24–26 alludes. It is exactly this
theologically heavy but compact phrase 'the righteous and the wise and
their actions are in God's hands' that balances the rest of this section. It is
the overarching truth in the midst of all the uncertainty and irony of human
limitations.

1b–3. Interpretations offered by some who portray Qoheleth as a
pessimist or cynic identify the source of love or hate to be God himself.
However, 'love' and 'hate' reappear and are accompanied in 9:6 by the
very human characteristic of 'jealousy', and their appearances in these two
verses serve as inclusios framing 9:1–6. The addition of jealousy to love
and hate in 9:6 recommends the interpretation that these are human acts
mentioned in 9:1, not divine acts. Though God's covenantal preference for
his people is sometimes described as jealousy, such an allusion is unlikely in
the midst of a passage lamenting the same future for those keeping and
those *not* keeping the covenant stipulations. Qoheleth has mentioned
before that 'humanity's misery is heavy, since no one knows what will
happen' (8:6b, 7). This is his point here too in that no one knows what he
or she will receive from others: love or hate? That was part of the affliction
of 8:16–17 too. Whether the wise will encounter loving or evil and envious
actions is unknown. Whether it is the malicious deeds of the powerful, as in

8:9, or the unexplained injustices that come to the righteous in 8:14, or those about to be noticed in 9:11–12, one just does not know.

V. 2 explains partially why the tragic inverted justices of 8:14 occur. Simply put, it is because the same occurrences happen to everyone. Loving actions are shared by all, but so are acts of hate and jealousy. He does not go so far as to say they occur equally, as extensively, as frequently or identically to both the righteous and the wicked, only that love and hate do come eventually to both. So he is not saying there is no moral order; he is saying that order is not immediately apparent nor always experienced. Furthermore, the common experience for the righteous and the sinner referred to here is not that they die. I discussed a similar misconception by commentators at 2:15–16a, where the common experience is to be marginalized and forgotten, not to die. Death does not come up until the very end of the next verse. The most immediate context here concerns love and hate from others. Ceremonial purity, faithful sacrificing and reverent commitments sealed by oaths do not disqualify one from being touched tragically by hate, spite or even violence while living between the utopias of pristine Eden and the redeemed new earth.

One should expect hatred, since ugly behaviour comes to all, because historically the heart of humanity has been full of evil, since the Garden Fall:

> every intent and thought of humanity's heart was only evil all the time. (Gen. 6:5)

> for the inclination of a person's heart is evil from youth ... (Gen. 8:21)

There is no room for sanctimony here, however, since even the righteous and wise know they have maligned others (7:20–22). The curse subjects us not only to the thorns of the ground but also to the diabolical deeds of our fellow humans, and the latter are only exacerbated by poor justice systems (5:8–9; 8:11). Qoheleth now for the first time broaches the subject of death, and phrases it just as death ends life – precipitously: 'Afterwards – to the dead.' This includes everybody.

4–6. What 'confidence' do the living have in a world full of uncertainty and limitations? Their confidence is that there *is* a profit (9:5) and portion (9:6); in other words, that there is an 'advantage to one's labours' (1:3). It is not a future reward. It is the portion one should experience *now*, while alive and able to appreciate such a reward. There is no better symbol of 'confidence' than the lion, 'the king of the forest'. But even its confidence is useless when dead; the skittish gutter dog has more confidence. The dog at least trusts he will have enough to eat; the dead have no reason to expect anything. See Brown 2000: 92 for excellent comments on this animal motif.

Within a few verses, 9:10 will recommend strong efforts in life for this same simple reason – there are no efforts from the grave. Qoheleth has given exceptions to this rule: when oppression is severe (4:1–3) and when there is no confidence that one can experience the basic advantages and joy to life (6:3–6; also 7:1). However, Qoheleth's rule of thumb is, 'The light is sweet, and it is good for the eyes to enjoy the sun' (11:7).

That the memory of those behind us is forgotten is no surprise, Qoheleth tells us this often (1:11; 2:14–16; 4:13–16). However, the worst fate is to be forgotten, in the OT sense of being disrespected (see 'Comment' at 2:15–17).

Reviewing the obvious prepares for a definitive answer now to Qoheleth's thematic question 'What advantage is there to one's laborious labours?' (1:3). Explicit in 9:5 ('profit'; śākār) and 9:6 ('portion'; ḥēleq) is the confidence that for the living there *are* advantages, the ones frequently summarized in Qoheleth's shalom refrains (2:24–26; 3:12–13, 22; 5:18–19; 8:15; also 11:8–10). These advantages are described in 9:7–10, advantages that can be pursued and enjoyed only while alive (9:7–10).

Love and hatred are resumed from 9:1 here in 9:6, forming rhetorical brackets for this subsection. It is somewhat unclear in the Hebr. whose love, hate and jealousy has perished, but we understand it to mean that the deceased are no longer available as objects of others' memory, love and hateful jealousy. Though in 9:1 the wise and righteous were uncertain of whether it was love or hatred that was ahead of them, now they have no such anxieties.

7–9. In the previous section, 8:14–15 served as conclusions – there are injustices to the righteous, but enjoy life anyway. These same verses serve as prolepses to fuller presentations of the same sequence of reasoning, 9:1–3 (8:14) and 9:7–10 (8:15). Though the wise and righteous attract hatred, and though they die like the wicked fool, they are still to enjoy life. Six specific enjoyments are now recommended: food, wine, presentable clothing, perfumes, one's spouse and one's work. This rendition of the shalom refrain is unique in intensity in two ways. First, these are refreshing elaborations of what was becoming very formulaic. These recommendations are interesting in their detail and enhancements of the previous refrains. Secondly, Qoheleth has turned from mere comparative statements to imperatives in order to express what Brown describes as the 'moral urgency' of pursuing enjoyment (2000: n. 93).

There are obvious parallels between these verses and ANE wisdom from both the Mes. Epic of Gilgamesh and the Egypt. Heretical Harper Songs:

> Of each day make thou a feast of rejoicing,
> Day and night dance thou and play!
> Let thy garments be sparkling fresh,
> Thy head be washed; bathe thou in water.
> Pay heed to the little one that holds onto thy hand

Let thy spouse delight in thy bosom!...
Put myrrh upon thy head and clothing of fine linen upon thee.

(Gilgamesh: *ANET* 467)

Pour myrrh on your head, dress in white linen, anoint your head
    with genuine oil that belongs to a god,
increase your beauty ... follow your heart in the fellowship
    with your beautiful one.

(Antef: Fischer 2002: 108, 111)

There is some hesitation to see these texts as influences on Qoheleth (e.g. Whybray 1989: 145; Krüger 2004: 174), but OT wisdom can certainly borrow and then redeem its neighbours' wisdom gleaned through common grace. This is what the epilogist will praise Qoheleth for in 12:9.

Qoheleth begins this section of consolations in v. 7 as he does in all the others, with a charge to eat food and drink, even wine, with pleasure and joy within one's heart. Happy eating is a basic advantage for the wise regardless of the amount or quality of the cuisine (Prov. 16:8; 17:1; Luke 2:46). As in Ps. 104:14–15, wine is a gift of God for cheering the heart. Qoheleth is not recommending wine to induce a drunken stupor, since that is hardly joyous. He is not an antinomian anymore than he is an ascetic. Additionally, maximum enjoyment comes only when one knows one is at peace with God, though it is unclear what God has already approved, exactly. Is it the acts of the righteous and wise that lead them to a point of enjoying God's gifts deservedly, or is it the very enjoyment of those gifts that has been approved? I interpret this approval to be of the life and actions of the righteous. After all, they are the ones who are the subject of most of 9:1–10, and it is consistent with the reasoning of 2:24–26 and other passages. God clearly gives the gifts of enjoyment to those who are 'good in his sight' (2:26), who 'do good in one's life' (3:12) and are 'good ... before God' (7:26). It explains why younger listeners are told in 11:8–10 to pursue their dreams while keeping in mind God's possible *disapproval* if they stray outside righteous parameters.

Any attempt to spiritualize or to find deep metaphors in Qoheleth's plain language of encouragement to wear white and to oil one's head should be ignored. The primary meaning is to relax in white clothing because it is cooler, and to moisten the scalp and hair with sweet oil. The thrust here is that one should enjoy a clean, refreshing, presentable attire and appearance.

The syntax here in v. 9 demands one to enjoy life with 'a' woman, rather than 'the' woman, counselling discretion in one's choice before marriage, not after. Implicit here is a caution to enjoy life with a woman chosen from love rather than one whom circumstances or other pressures demand, such as a premarital conception or economic gain. However, once this woman has been identified to be a truly loved spouse, we should then recognize this woman to be the woman of Gen. 2:23, Prov. 5:15–19, 18:22 and Prov. 31, not the degenerate Qoheleth described in 7:26. We notice two more nuances to Qoheleth's instruction about a man's relationship with his wife. It is clearly one's *life* that is to be enjoyed with the spouse, not just the woman herself as an object of his enjoyment. She is to be a partner in life's happiness, one without whom life cannot be full. Furthermore, that one woman ('a woman') is to be a partner and helper *all* of one's days. The expectation is that this partnership is to be lifelong, not an episode or an experiment; it is to be dissolved only when death itself parts them.

A critical juncture of six of Qoheleth's thematic words and phrases is found in this focus on a spouse: temporary, toil, portion or advantage, enjoyment, God-given and under the sun. All of these are Qoheleth's key words to ask and answer his programmatic question introduced in 1:3, 'What is the advantage in all one's laborious labour under the sun?' – including even the emphatic cognate accusative 'laborious labour'. The advantage or *portion* to one's *labours under the sun* is to *enjoy* one's spouse in the *fleeting* days he (*God*) *has given*. The 'portion', Qoheleth's synonym for 'advantage', includes all of the six specific enjoyments in 9:7–10. They are the portion which the dead cannot enjoy in 9:5–6. The preposition is not incidental in the phrase 'it is your portion in life', since these previous verses and the following verse emphasize death, when enjoyments like 9:8–9 will no longer be possible. The unit of measuring time is also important; these units are fleeting (*hebel*) *days*, not even fleeting years that constitute our 'brief (*hebel*) life'. This cumulative effect drives even some of those who understand Qoheleth to be a pessimist to interpret these cases of *hebel* as 'temporary'; for example, Gordis 1968: 337; Crenshaw 1987: 158; Seow 1999: 302; Krüger 2004: 166.

10. Qoheleth's speech is at its core a theology of work – a theology of God's primary commission to humanity to subdue the earth according to wise principles. Toil is never far from Qoheleth's other consolations, since he views work as a blessing, especially when the specific work is determined by the labourer himself ('whatever your hand finds to do'). Qoheleth's view of work is that it is meaningful as a God-given source of emotional and material enjoyment. There is an innate human need to subdue the earth, as husband and wife working together (Gen. 1:27–28; 2:20). Though toil is the irritant that has moved Qoheleth to ask 'What advantage is there . . .' he realizes that the sweating, draining and all-consuming affliction of work, even after the Fall, can still be satisfying. He lauds hard work in 2:4–9, 4:5, 10:18 and 11:4–6. In fact, this one verse, 9:10, foreshadows the entire concluding unit of his speech, 11:1 – 12:8.

Being told to apply one's efforts 'with all one's might' is a poor joke if Qoheleth believes everything is vanity, meaningless or absurdity; it reduces Qoheleth to be an insensitive driver of senseless human activity.

Diligence is a hard sell if the one ordering it says it is the same as nothing. Qoheleth is certainly straightforward about there being no opportunity to work or plan wisely in Sheol, but he is hardly saying here that one's labours are just as *useless* now as they are *non-existent* in death. Rather, he encourages hard work in life because life is temporary.

One's preferred work will include wisdom and explanations, but as Ps. 146:4 (also Isa. 38:18–19) explains:

> Man's spirit leaves; he returns to the earth;
>   that day, his thoughts perish.

'Returning to the earth' is in Qoheleth's phrasing too in 3:21 and 12:7, and is synonymous with 'dust to dust', going to one's grave, death. Sheol is as shadowy an OT concept as it is a place. Qoheleth does not advance in any way a doctrine of the afterlife. Though every culture around the Israelites believed in it, it is unimportant to his point. Qoheleth's point of view is from being under the sun, not above or beyond it in an afterlife.

The rest of this unit observes in an alternating manner both the disappointments and successes of wisdom in life. Through this rhythmic commentary, Qoheleth illustrates the uncertainties of 9:11–12 and provides some explanation of why life is so unpredictable:

Disappointment	9:11–12
Success	9:13–15a
Disappointment	9:15b
Success	9:16a
Disappointment	9:16b
Success	9:17–18a
Disappointment	9:18b – 10:1

11–12. Five ironies are listed in 9:11. The first two are military examples and the other three deal with wisdom generally, setting the stage for the military and wisdom motifs in 9:13–18. Also each of the latter three ironies is introduced by the accentuating 'even', emphasizing the greater tragedy of these ironies associated with wisdom. One thinks of Asahel, the swiftest of men, who died a soldier's death by Abner's spear (2 Sam. 2:18–23). Though swift, he lost. These ironies are the exceptions in life, mentioned to show human inability to predict or presume future events. Qoheleth does not claim them as the rule. In fact, ironies are not necessarily tragic; they could be fair and just. After all, the commoner does deliver the city (9:15). Compare the following biblical view of the ironic:

> The horse is prepared for the battle day,
>   and victory is the LORD's.
>
>   (Prov. 21:31; also 1 Sam. 17:47)

> The mightiest will not save his soul,
>   the archer will not stand his ground,
>   the swift of foot will not escape
>   nor will the horseman save his soul.
>
>   (Amos 2:14–16)

It is not Qoheleth's point to find the ultimate cause of these ironies, since that still would not explain the reasons anyway. The point is that they demonstrate unpredictability. So he concludes in the most general way, 'timely episodes happen to everyone'. This important word for Qoheleth's world view, 'appropriate time (*'ēt*)', is used three times in these two verses. The appropriate timing of events was highlighted in 3:1–8 and 8:5–6, and was deemed 'beautiful' in 3:11. Consequently, Qoheleth is consistent with biblical views of God's sovereignty, since his speech has no theology of 'chance'. It is quite the opposite. Interestingly enough, the only other place in Biblical Hebr. where *pega'* is used is in the *Corpus Salomonicum* (1 Kgs 5:4).

These 'timely episodes' are exemplified dramatically by again reducing humans to the level of animals (3:18–20). Like naive fish and birds, we are told in 9:12 that one does not know 'one's time'. The right time for many of one's actions can be known (3:1–8), but not the timing of the ironies. 'One's time' does not refer only to death, though it does refer to some tragedy as inescapable and precipitous as a hunter's trap. 'One's time' only refers to death in 7:17 because 'death' literally appears in the phrase – here it is much more general.

13–15. Why is this commoner's wisdom so impressive for Qoheleth? It is impressive because the contrast between wisdom and brute power is so stark! What exactly the commoner's wisdom consisted of is not described, being less important than the general principle that wisdom's strength *can be* impregnable. The overwhelming odds are underscored with several explicit terms: the city was *small*, *sparsely* populated and included a *commoner*. On the other hand, outside the walls was a king who was *great*, who had *great* weapons, both facts that imply many troops. The drama's setting is drawn as polarized as possible. Since Qoheleth 'saw' this and it impressed him, the story probably originated in historical observation and presumably occurred at other times in his part of the world. Also the preterite verbal form is used of the commoner's deliverance of the city (see 'Notes' at 9:15). Israelite history recounts a wise woman cutting a deal with Joab, who was mounting siege works against her city's walls (2 Sam. 20:15–22). She is within the city and Joab is outside it, yet they negotiate directly with each other with the wall between them. She has Sheba's head cut off and it is thrown over the wall. Here, in 9:15, the king somehow 'finds' the wise commoner who delivers the city in an unknown way. Perhaps the king's spies found him in the city or the king inquired verbally from outside the walls, like Joab did. See Weisman (1999) for a fuller discussion.

This story is couched within a series of alternating statements that are encouraging or disappointing about wisdom. The encouraging success of the commoner (9:13–15a) is followed by the disappointment that he was not remembered or respected by those around or after him (9:15b). The man proved the superiority of wisdom over strength, rulers and weapons (9:16a, 17–18a; cf. 4:13; 7:19) but also proved that often the common person is not respected, simply because of his position in the social structure. The wise are forgotten regardless of who they are! Qoheleth has made that clear before (2:16; 4:16; 9:5). At least this common man is remembered by Qoheleth, if by no one else, as an example of how love or hate meets the wise (9:1, 6) and of when there can be no 'favour to the knowledgeable' (9:11).

16 – 10:1. Wisdom's superiority to strength has been spelled out by Qoheleth before. One of the advantages is wisdom's *protection* even to the point of saving lives (7:12)! The commoner's deliverance of the city demonstrates that succinctly. Furthermore, by defeating a king wielding elaborate weaponry and siege works, the commoner demonstrates that wisdom is stronger than weapons as well (9:18). Even when soft-spoken, wisdom is stronger than the emotional shouts of a distressed or frantic ruler, especially if that ruler is among other fools (cf. 7:5; Prov. 19:25). Wisdom from Proverbs and Psalms agrees:

> A wise person is strong,
>   and a knowledgeable man strengthens power further,
> for wise counsel will prepare you for war.
>   (Prov. 24:5–6; also 20:18; 21:22; Ps. 33:16–17)

> Whoever is slow to get angry is better than the mighty,
>   and whoever controls his emotions is better than one
>   capturing a city.
>   (Prov. 16:32)

As true as the foregoing comments are about wisdom, Qoheleth is transparent enough to tell us what wisdom is designed to tell us – there are timely episodes for everyone (9:11)! One can be ignored, despised, even hated, just for not being an aristocrat. Even enormous success does not guarantee respect. This should sound familiar:

> A prophet does not lack honour except in his home town, among relatives, even his own immediate family. (Mark 6:4)

> The poor is hated even by his neighbour,
>   but many love the rich.
>   (Prov. 14:20; also 19:7)

Though the commoner proves that one wise person can destroy a lot of might, it is also true, unfortunately, that one sinner can destroy a lot of good. This is what triggered Qoheleth's catharsis in 2:18–21. Who would steward the extraordinary achievements he left behind? Very possibly an inept, foolish, even wicked, 'successor'. Sin and foolishness can outweigh the good because of what they can undo in such a short time. Something as good, valuable and beautiful as the fragrance of perfume can be turned to rot by tiny meddlesome flies. Paul prefers to use the image of a little leaven, which affects the entire loaf, to lament the impact of one fornicating sinner on an entire body of believers (1 Cor. 5:6).

Explanation

God's ways are known only partially. For one reason, if he were to reveal them all to us, our limited minds would be full and we still would know only a part of his ways. But we would not want to know all his ways. They would be frightening, not only in the number of his ways, but in their complexity, their tolerance for evil, their way-too-distant resolution to what in our minds are pressing issues. We do not want to know all God's future ways; we simply could not handle it. Problems known in advance, but concerning which we are helpless, consume all our precious attention now. It is not God's judgment that we know, only some of his ways; it is his blessing.

Nonetheless, wisdom should be what we search for the hardest – all other benefits worth pursuing will follow. But Qoheleth is kind to warn us that searching for wisdom is hard work, just as implementing it is. It requires consistent study of the whole Bible, not just our favourite books or verses. Unflinching analysis of what the Scripture says as we read and study it is our responsibility, not somebody else's. We cannot merely delegate that analysis to an interpreting elite. The Bible was written to normal people with normal intelligence, not to a panel of brilliant experts who alone can decipher the secret code of allegory and types. The search entails painful application of its findings, disturbing our comfortable habits and preferences. It also requires perpetual vigilance to sustain our wise actions and the fruit it produces.

The wisdom of the Christian will lead to the conclusion that it is indeed great to be alive, in spite of the alternative (death) being even better for us as individuals. Our confidence and trust is that this life can be rewarding and satisfying for as many days as God gives us. Regardless of the challenges of life, we instinctively prefer living to dying, even with eternal shalom ahead of us. Qoheleth emphasizes the joy of living rather than pointing to any refuge in death because there are advantages to a life of wisdom and righteousness. We can be satisfied that God is satisfied with our activities, including our enjoyment of food and wine, comforts of leisurely clothes and refreshing fragrances and the pleasures of a secure marriage with a lifelong spouse who is a contributing, equal partner. Apart from these things and the appreciation and enjoyment of the labour that makes these pleasures possible, Qoheleth implies there is little else for which one could ask. Oh, it would be nice to have some music and dancing too (2:8; 3:4).

At the end of the day, Ecclesiastes is a lecture on the theology of work, not on the meaning of life. The question Qoheleth poses at the start and throughout his speech is whether there is any advantage to one's hard work. Why bother to work hard if there are no advantages? He has answered the question in the affirmative many times through the shalom refrains and again in the less formulaic comments on those aspects of life that might prompt the same, nagging 'Is it really worth all the hard work when life is so full of disappointments?' Again, Qoheleth leaves no room for a self-pity that distracts from the pleasures that come from productive work. Besides, mastering one's environment by exerting wisdom and strength and creatively producing a positive result for oneself and others is a divine-like act comparable to God's acts of creation, providence and service. This is a pervasive teaching in both canons: 'Whatever you do, do your work from the soul, for the Lord' (Col. 3:23); '[do] not fall behind in diligence' (Rom. 12:11). Besides estate planning, our ability to assist others can be done only while alive; there is no management of daily affairs from the remote site called Sheol.

Believers will encounter both love and hate from others. We will not always know in advance from where either will come. Of course, we all expect to be loved, given the virtues we see in ourselves. But the hate, where does that come from? Well, apart from the rare situations when one may actually deserve it, the human heart is full of evil and jealousy. If one is successful and blessed, of course hatred and envy will come at least from those who are not, and maybe even from those who are as well. Christians especially should expect the ire of those who are threatened by biblical truth that condemns their lifestyles, choices and perceived autonomy from absolute truth. We will be ridiculed by those with seared consciences who do not understand the value of purity, peace and civility. It has always been that way; nothing has changed. All that can change is the perspective of the wise who understand and cope with such hatred and animosity.

Equal to or worse than being hated is being neglected when credits are being handed out for achievements. Only the fool expects always to be congratulated for doing something noticeably good. And sometimes the fool does get the credit while the one who deserves the credit goes unnoticed and unappreciated. Life is fraught with misplaced honour (10:6–7); we may even have been the recipients of unmerited commendations. But we remember more of the opposite times. The choice is to harbour the offence until it festers bitterly, or to accept it with a sense of humour and the perspective of 8:1, 'The wisdom of a man gives light to his face and makes its stiffness to relax.' What God causes or allows in his unpredictable sovereignty is eventually fair. Mature Christians are confident of their eventual exoneration, knowing it will be well for those who fear God.

Then there are those awful circumstances that come from no fault of anyone. They are tragic and often terminal. No one knows when that diagnosis will come, when that natural disaster will strike, when death will assert its right to steal the soul. These overpowering events can be received with humility and gratitude only if wisdom has blessed the person so far. The rest of the excruciating journey may be brief, with light to follow, or it may lead to an eternal dead end.

Until death, we continue using our modest resources for greater good, with the encouragement that God enjoys using the wisdom of the weak to embarrass the folly of the strong. This inversion of power is an example of God's sense of humour. He delights in deflating the arrogant, in humiliating the proud. That is part of their being disciplined or even judged. God loves the humble, simple and weak, and despises the conceited, sophisticated and brutal. He loves the crèche, carpenters and the cross, but topples thrones, kings and armies. He prefers his people to break bones with soft words (Prov. 25:15), to conquer the unbeliever through gentleness (1 Pet. 3:1), to combat an attack with a turned cheek (Matt. 5:39). And, as we have heard from Qoheleth a couple times, God expects the wisdom of the subordinate to compensate for the error of the superior authority.

Unfortunately, less is greater than more in terms of the negative as well. Less wisdom, unrighteousness and foolishness can carry more weight than wisdom and goodness. It does not take much to spoil the beauty and moral order around us. Of course, God knew that from the beginning, when he watched the simple act of eating fruit lead to the devastating results of the curse and the subsequent horrors of human history.

ECCLESIASTES 10:2-20

Translation

[2]A wise person's heart goes to his right, but the heart of the fool goes to his left. [3]So even while the fool continues walking on his way, his heart errs, saying to everyone he is a fool.

[4]If the temper of the ruler rises against you, don't leave, because composure soothes great offences. [5-6]There is a tragic situation I have seen under the sun, a real mistake coming from the ruler: foolishness is elevated to great heights, while the rich sit in the lowest place. [7]I have seen servants astride horses and princes walking as servants on foot.

[8]Whoever digs a pit may fall into it, and whoever breaks through a wall may be bitten by a snake. [9]Whoever quarries stones may be hurt by them, but whoever splits trees may benefit from them. [10]If the axe is blunt, and one does not sharpen its edge, then one has to exert more strength. So the advantage of wisdom is success.

[11]If the unenchanted serpent bites, then there is no advantage for the enchanting master of the tongue.

[12]The words of the mouth of the wise are favourable, but the fool's lips consume him. [13]The beginning of his mouth's comments is foolish and the end of them is insanely evil. [14]Yet the fool multiplies words. No one knows what will be, so who will tell him what will be after him? [15]The labour of fools so wearies them that they do not even know to go to a city.

[16]Woe to the nation whose king is young and naive, and your princes feast in the morning. [17]Blessings to the nation whose king is a son of nobility and your princes eat at an appropriate time for strength, not for drunken indulgence. [18]By laziness the rafters sag, and because of slack hands the house leaks. [19]Food is prepared for laughter, and wine makes life merry, and money afflicts everyone.

[20]Also in your wise knowledge, do not curse the king, and in your inner rooms do not curse the rich person, for a bird from the sky will carry the voice and the master of flight will reveal a matter.

Notes on the text

2. 'goes to his right ... goes to his left': lit. 'to the right ... to the left'. These verbless clauses demand an interpretative translation, and, since the next verse speaks of 'walking', I translate accordingly.

3. 'even while the fool continues walking': Qoheleth's use of contractions hints at his speaking in the vernacular. In this case three words or particles are contracted, *kĕšehssākāl*. The participle (*hōlēk*) denotes the persistent foolish walk.

4. 'temper': lit. *rûaḥ* (spirit). Comparable phrasing is found in Judg. 8:3, where 'anger' (*rûaḥ*) is healed.

'composure': this word, typically used for physical well-being, can also be used for emotional health (BDB 951; Fredericks 1988: 201–203).

5. 'a real mistake': with other commentators, the prefixed kaph is translated as emphatic (GKC 118x).

6. 'foolishness is elevated to great heights': The ni. indicates that foolishness was placed on high, identifying the fact as the ruler's error. That *rabbîm* (great) is anarthrous troubles some commentators to the point of emendation. However, Qoheleth's erratic use of the art. is characteristic and colloquial.

7. 'on foot': lit. 'on the ground'.

8. *gûmmāṣ* (pit) is considered by some to be a late Aram.; for example, Wagner 1966: 39–40. However, the earliest occurrence in Aram. is in Jewish Aram., making the direction of borrowing uncertain. Furthermore, the antiquity of the word is shown by Akk. and Ug. cognates.

9. 'may benefit from them': *sākan* means 'to be a benefit' – here, in the reflexive ni., 'benefit oneself'. Said by some to be a late word, but Ug. uses the same root (Lipinski 1973: 193; Kottsieper 1986: 220–221). This phrase, though found in perfect syntactical parallel with the previous three statements, is antithetical in describing the *benefit* from the trade, rather than the *danger*.

10. 'axe': *barzel* means 'iron, a generic tool'. But an axe is probably meant in this context, as in Deut. 19:5.

'So the advantage of wisdom is success': the syntax is unusual, but nearly all who do not import a post-biblical meaning here render the phrase similarly. In addition to commentaries, see Frendo (1981).

11. 'the [enchanting] master of the tongue': lit. 'the master of the tongue'. This imagery is used because Qoheleth's purpose is to introduce the rest of the anatomy of a foolish mouth and lips in vv. 12–13.

12. 'are favourable': to whom favour goes from the words of the wise is unclear – to the wise himself or to others? I leave the thought as ambiguous as the text does.

15. The verse has two grammatical inconsistencies: the m. *'ămal* and its f. sg. verb; the pl. 'fools' and the suffixed sg. pronoun that refers to them.

'do not [even] know to go to a city': the exact meaning is unclear, but I verbalize what is perhaps an implied emphasis on the simplicity of the task of 'going to town'.

16. 'young and naive': lit. 'is a child'. This is metaphorical for describing immature, unwise leadership. See 'Comment' below.

'feast': lit. 'eat', but the connotation is eating an irresponsible amount at an inappropriate time.

18. The dual form of sloth, *'ăṣaltayîm*, probably anticipates the two hands in the next phrase in the verse.

19. Translation is challenging here. The sentence contains 'laughter', something for which Qoheleth has not been a great protagonist (2:2; 7:3, 6), though there is a time for it (3:4). 'Enjoy' has no negative stigma so far; in fact, it is a major theme. 'Money' is a subject on which Qoheleth is ambivalent (7:11–12; 5:10–14). The three additional components (waw, *'ānāh* and *kōl*) have significantly different meanings for each: the waw before *kesep* is of course very elastic; *'ānāh* can mean 'afflict' or 'answer' in Biblical Hebr., and *kōl* can mean 'all things', 'both' or 'everyone'.

20. 'Also, in your wise knowledge': *maddā'ăkā* is based on *yāda'*, 'knowledge'. But in biblical parlance, this knowledge is often experiential, thus used frequently in conjunction with wisdom, even in Ecclesiastes (1:16; 9:10; and frequently in Proverbs).

'the master of flight': lit. 'owner of wings'.

'a matter': *dābār* probably means 'matter' rather than 'word'.

Form and structure

Whereas the previous unit (8:16 – 10:1) primarily laments very specific disappointments and ironies in life, this new unit (10:2–20) speaks with

more resolve and constructive instruction on how to manage life regardless of those uncertainties. A rhetorical turn from descriptions of the effect
of the fool on others (9:18; 10:1) to its effect upon himself is marked by
10:2–7, the opening to this unit. The subsequent unit (11:1 – 12:8) sums
up Qoheleth's message with more general ideas about wise diligence
during one's fleeting life. There seems to be an erratic sequence of
proverbial observation, wisdom imagery and imperative instruction in this
unit that could distract the listener from the total impression Qoheleth
wishes to make. All of this material converges on the topic of career
management for court officials – the audience of Qoheleth's speech.

General observations about the fool's careless speech and actions, and
instructions about how the wise should avoid such folly, are supplemented
with imagery and metaphor. The stupidity of the fool (10:2–3, 14–15) sets
the fool opposite the wise in typical proverbial polarity. The dangers of
careless labour (vv. 8–11) are more than instructions for common
labourers who pursue these skills or trades (pit digger, renovator, quarry
worker, charmer); they are images for the court staff who should not be
careless in their conduct before an unwise king (vv. 4–7). The image of the
inept 'lord of the tongue' (v. 11), in turn, introduces to us those fools who
are unable to control their tongue (vv. 12–14). Direct instruction of a
prophetic sort clearly divides responsible leaders from derelict leaders who
feast and drink with endless monetary resources (vv. 16–19), and this is
emphasized through the proverbial metaphor of a deteriorating building
(v. 18). Fidelity to the establishment is encouraged by referring to the bird,
which reveals all sedition (v. 20). One might prefer a tighter structure, but
Qoheleth is as reluctant to provide it here, as he is fastidious in providing it
elsewhere (1:12 – 2:26; 5:10 – 6:9; 11:1 – 12:8). A bit more structure is
offered by 10:2–4 and 10:20, which serve as brackets, both passages
emphasizing loyalty to the king and rulers.

Comment

2–3. These two verses mark a structural shift, now discussing the effect of the
fool on himself. The perfect proverbial parallelism and polarity of wisdom
and folly on which much of Proverbs is based is followed in 10:2. Then the
'synthetic' proverbial model is found in 10:3 (compare with the structure of
Prov. 21:16). These two proverbs converge to show the fourfold stupidity of
the fool: (1) he chooses the wrong way (*derek*) in the first place, (2) then, while
he continues his foolish direction, (3) he errs again, (4) broadcasting his
foolishness to all those around him.

The moral antithesis of folly and wisdom, expressed here by 'left' and
'right', is typical in the wisdom literature. The imagery of the two opposite
directions of the 'heart' of the wise and fools was delineated in 7:4 to be
towards the funeral home or the party house, respectively. The utter

polarity of folly and wisdom was expressed even earlier in this speech as well as in 2:14, where the fool walks not 'to the left', but in 'darkness'. As in Jon. 4:11, those who do not fear God cannot even tell right from left; that is, right from wrong. In Ps. 16:8, the supporting Lord is to the right, comparable to the supporting role of wisdom for Qoheleth (2:9). The right side is considered the 'appropriate side' in most cultures. Jacob's right hand was the blessing hand (Gen. 48:17–18), and it is to the left that the wicked will be sent at the judgment (Matt. 25:41).

A frequent image in Proverbs is that of one's heart giving thought to the direction (*derek*) one will go:

The wisdom of the prudent discerns his way (*derek*).
(Prov. 14:8; 21:29)

The prudent discerns his steps.
(Prov. 14:15)

The man wandering from the way (*derek*) of understanding
will rest in the assembly of the dead.
(Prov. 21:16; also 28:26)

The fool's failure to discern the appropriate direction will define
him publicly.
Fools' hearts announce their folly.
(Prov. 12:23b; also 13:16)

The obvious confusion and waywardness of the fool is addressed again in 10:15, where he cannot even get to his destination.

4. Common features between this verse, its possible elaboration in its following verses, and the king-subordinate passage in 8:2–6 send the imagination in many directions. This section is an example of wise responses to a sovereign leader's commands referred to in 8:2–6. The setting and scenario of the two passages are similar: a ruler addresses a subordinate in a private or public setting; there is a moment, at least, when an authority speaks, probably with questionable wisdom; yet, the subordinate's wisdom requires poise and keeping his stance. The difference here is that the ruler has become angry and is possibly *rebuking* the subordinate rather than simply issuing a command. The ambiguity of the phrasing does not specify who is responsible for the 'great offences'. We understand this phrasing to indicate that the subject soothes himself about the *ruler's* offences by seeing them in the context of how the real world works: the subject responds wisely with patience and with an understanding of life (Prov. 12:16–17). In 8:2–6, the proper response was the same: be patient and understand the importance of timing. Qoheleth has noted in 8:1 that 'The wisdom of a man gives light to his face and makes its stiffness to relax.' Additional reasons for this

interpretation are found in the immediate castigation of a foolish decision from the authority in 10:5–6. This is probably the offence of 10:4. Also this unfair, foolish inversion in personnel management reflects the ironies of 9:11, only twelve verses earlier. And, even more recent than that, in 9:17, we heard about the ineffectiveness of a ruler's shouting compared to quiet wisdom. Anger itself is rebuked by Qoheleth in 7:9 (cf. Prov. 14:29–30). Peter understands how the world works as well: 'Servants, respectfully submit to your masters, not only to those who are good and reasonable, but even to those who are harsh. For it is commendable for a man, in conscience before God, to bear up under sorrow when unjustly suffering' (1 Pet. 2:18–19; cf. 1:6).

5–7. The 'mistake' (šĕgāgāh) for which the ruler is responsible and that the subject must accept graciously is probably a directive that put inept people in responsible positions – the same thoughtless, culpable sort of mistake that the fool gives as his useless defence to the temple official (5:6). Qoheleth is deeply troubled by the unjust and destructive delegation of authority to those incapable of using it wisely. These tragic reversals in administrative structure are lamented in the summary of ironies in 9:11 and throughout this speech (2:18–19; 3:16; 7:15; 8:14). This abhorrence of unsuitable people in power is consistent with OT sociology; actually, the scenario is a sign of the Lord's profound judgment against his people (Isa. 3:4–5). Despicable Haman's experience is a most graphic depiction of this injustice, where King Ahasuerus promoted the fool who expected to ride a horse with pomp (Esth. 3:1; 6:7–11). Proverbs defines the appropriate social order:

The fool is the servant to the wise.

(11:29b)

It is not appropriate for a fool to live luxuriously,
    nor indeed for a slave to rule princes.

(19:10; also 26:1)

Horses were affordable for only kings, rulers, princes and others who were wealthy. For those who could not afford horses, donkeys were an option, though the masses usually walked. Certainly, the image raises questions about 'elitism' in the ANE world, a social concept Qoheleth seems to endorse. It is not a 'liberation message' by any means. Yet it does speak of an orderly society which works according to the OT social order where slaves are slaves for a reason; there are, inevitably, princes who have jurisdiction within a monarchy; the rich may have a legitimate claim to the fruit of their labours and to be in high places. Some specific reasons why such inversions are destructive are given in 10:16–17, where again it is affirmed that nobility should administer the realm (see 'Comment' there).

8–11. Just as the deteriorating building of 10:18 comments on the slackness of the inept ruler in 10:16, and just as the uncontrolled snake of

10:11 introduces the hazards of not mastering one's tongue, this passage comments on the care needed when dealing with any dangerous activity, including confronting an angry king. Of course, there is an independent value to each of these illustrative comments (vv. 8–11, 18), each carrying its own wisdom and implied instruction. Wisdom or safety precautions are needed by every professional, including hole diggers, construction workers, quarrymen, even snake charmers and government officials. To describe the import of these verses simply as uncertainties or anomalies of life would be missing the point of this whole unit. These images convey a moral responsibility to be careful and vigilant if one wishes to take advantage of wisdom and be successful. In this sense, these images are double entendre notes. They serve a rhetorical purpose as very practical examples, nearly parables, of how to stand before the king, comparable to Christ's parable in Matt. 7:24 about building on rock rather than sand. The point of Prov. 27:12 is identical:

> The wise foresees danger and prepares;
>> but the simple keep going and pay for it.

Pits were dug for various reasons in the ANE: trapping animals, providing water, storing food and burying the dead. The mindless could find themselves stepping into the hole they themselves had dug. Similar phrasing in Prov. 26:27 (also Pss 7:14–16; 35:7–8; 57:6–7) suggests that this 'digging a pit' may be in order to snare others, and one's falling in is suitable retribution – a point quite different from the assumption that one should be careful in dangerous circumstances. On the other hand, as Lauha (1978: 187) explains, the Hebr. word for 'pit' (*gûmmāṣ*) is unique in Biblical Hebr. because Qoheleth needed it here, specifically, as a synonym to distance 'pit' from its retributive meaning in the proverbial and poetic literature where other roots are used.

Structures ranging from rubble stone hedges, to clay-brick houses, to fortified city walls had inevitable crevices that were home to numerous species of animals, including the irritable snake (10:8). Amos 5:19 describes the danger of snake bites that could occur simply by leaning against the clay walls of a house. The snake emerges again in v. 11 as an occupational hazard if not charmed by its owner. Perhaps the charmer himself is bitten before he starts the charming, in which case he should probably cease while he has the chance. The observation of the biting damage of the serpent is a rhetorical hinge that contributes to the list of dangerous activities as well as introducing the biting, ungracious tongue of the fool (10:12). David describes the viperous effects of the wicked tongue in this same way:

> From the womb the wicked wander about telling lies.
> Their venom is like the venom of a snake,
>> like a cobra which stops its ears,

So that it does not listen to the voice of charmers,
　the skillful enchanters.

(Ps. 58:3b–5; cf. Matt. 12:34)

Dire results come to those who are ill-prepared for their hazardous
responsibilities. Their careless or untimely performance of their basic duties
can be worse than simply unprofitable; without careful preparation disaster
will follow. For every choice there is a suitable time and judgment. Qoheleth
has already told his audience that wisdom serves as protection (7:12; 9:18),
and these observations are further examples.

Literally, according to normal Biblical Hebr., the pronouncement about
splitting trees (10:9) would be rendered, 'whoever splits trees may benefit
from them'. Yet this disturbs what one might prefer to be a series of four
grammatically parallel statements, all referring to danger. However, since
the very next sentence speaks of the benefit of sharpening a cutting tool,
and the image portrays the advantages of wisdom (10:10), we tolerate, in
fact we *enjoy*, the subtle break with the previous sayings while transition-
ing to the conclusion to the matter.

In three Hebr. words, admittedly expressed in what appears to be
awkward syntax, Qoheleth summarizes the entire message of his speech!
'So the advantage of wisdom is success.' The thematic question introduced
in 1:3 and referenced throughout the speech, 'What is the advantage in all
one's laborious labour under the sun?' is answered again in the most
economical phrasing.

12–14. The phrase 'master of the tongue', which concludes v. 11, initiates
words associated with the mouth in vv. 12–14 to express the fool's most
frequent sin – speaking. Tongue (v. 11), mouth (vv. 12–13) and words (vv.
12–14) are proverbial images found in Proverbs repeatedly; for example:

The lips of the righteous are nourishment to many.

(10:21)

The lips of the wise preserve them.

(14:3)

The tongue that heals is a tree of life.

(15:4)

Pleasant words are like a honeycomb.

(16:24)

Particularly related to our unit and to 10:4 and the ruler:

Whoever has grace (*ḥēn*) on his lips has the king as a friend.

(Prov. 22:11; cf. Ps. 45:2)

Self-consumption is certainly a result of foolishness; Qoheleth uses the idea in 4:5 about the lazy. But the effects of foolish words are more than 'eating one's *words*'; the effects can be terminal, devouring one's own self. Destruction from words may come by foolish promises, getting caught as a false witness, making the wrong people angry, etc. (Prov. 10:21; 17:20; 18:6–7; 19:5, 9; Jas 3:6). Furthermore, such actions are not only harmful to oneself; they are insanely evil, even *criminal* at times.

Qoheleth obviously believes in restraint; his ellipses are frequent, his thoughts expressed tersely as proverbs or quips. He believes there are times to keep quiet (3:7), times to listen (5:1–7; 7:5; 9:17). However, the fool chatters on and on about nothing, while the wise will neither waste the time nor suffer the consequences from foolish *planning*. 'Even the fool is deemed wise when he keeps silent' (Prov. 17:28). Only fools talk about what is going to happen in the future, since no one can know the future (3:22; 6:12; 8:7). James talks about the folly of predicting the future given our transitory, fleeting lives (4:13–16; also 1:26). In fact, he also uses the example of 'going to the city'! Though probably this is not an allusion to Ecclesiastes 10:15, the resemblance is helpful.

But what exactly is the 'labour' that so wearies the fool that he cannot make his way? I take it to refer to the only labour the fool knows and accomplishes – talking. That is why he is a fool – he only talks, endlessly. His talking is extremely wearying, since he multiplies his words from the start of the day until its end; it is an all-consuming activity. The extent of his weariness reminds us of the sluggard who is too weary or too lazy even to eat (Prov. 19:24; 26:15). Here Qoheleth measures the fool by the fool's not even knowing to go to the city. I have translated the Hebr. quite lit. 'they do not even know to go to a city', since it is ambiguous whether it is how he goes, when he goes, why he goes or where he goes that identifies him as a fool (see 10:2–3). However, by itself, the phrase sounds as if the fool does not even know enough *that* he should go to the city. During times of war or famine – or if one were guilty of manslaughter (Num. 35:6–28), going to the right city could well have been life saving.

16–17. Here it becomes most evident that the audience for Qoheleth's speech is primarily an assembly of government workers from Israel, and perhaps other countries as well (1 Kgs 4:34; 10:1). The whole unit, as the speech comes to a close, is a direct address to those who may find themselves closer to one of the two political and administrative poles defined in these two verses. How should one rule when power and wealth invite less accountability? In a prophetic voice, Qoheleth's answer is the same as Isaiah's:

> Woe to those rising in the morning, pursuing hard liquor,
>   who stay late in the evening until wine inflames them.
> They have harps and lyres at their banquets,
>   the tambourine, flute and wine.
>   (Isa. 5:11–12; also 28:7–8; 47:8; Prov. 23:19–21)

The Hebr. uses the word *na'ar*, which can have the meaning 'servant' or 'youth'. The *Corpus Salomonicum* records that Solomon saw himself as a 'child' (*na'ar*), because he was unwise, *immature* in wisdom (1 Kgs 3:7) – exactly the meaning here in 10:15. Prov. 1:4 also connects the root with naïveté. In fact, it is God's *judgment* when 'youth' (*na'ar*) and 'babes' rule (Isa. 3:4–5, 12). Granted, there may be exceptions when even a 'youth' (*na'ar*) may be wiser than an unteachable king (Eccl. 4:13–16); but the common attribute of both youth and servants is their unprofessional administration of the weighty duties of governing. Prov. 30:21–22 recounts two situations that the earth cannot bear: a servant who becomes king and a fool who does not lack 'food' (*leḥem*). Both of these unbearable conditions are present under an inept king.

On the other hand, there are those lands whose leaders are disciplined by training and experience, who eat at the appropriate 'time' (*'ēt*) for strength to be even greater leaders. They are the ones who receive Qoheleth's instructions in 7:2–4, 6 with understanding and consent. They are the sons of nobility, educated individuals who have been brought up knowing how to administer, as opposed to thugs and barbarians who have usurped power or have been appointed by a king as foolish as that in 10:4–7! It is the pragmatics of administration that Qoheleth speaks to here, not a sociological theorem of equality (see Van Leeuwen 1986: 603–604). The latter he has spoken to already in 4:13. This is not elitism; it is simply the result of a well-functioning society. Qoheleth has attempted to console those troubled by dysfunctional leadership (5:8–9), and it sounds as though he whole-heartedly endorses the 'Sayings of Lemuel', which command the king to keep sober in order to protect the oppressed (Prov. 31:4–5).

18–19. Moving from 'prophet' to sage, Qoheleth uses the proverbial style of synonymous parallelism, drawing on the rich wisdom tradition on the subjects of diligence and sloth to brace these political principles in vv. 16–17. Delays in repairing the flat ANE roofs led not only to the rafters drooping but eventually to the roof leaking, ruining the contents of the home or business. Here the royal 'house' and its resident political administration are warned that self-indulgent sluggards will only procrastinate the routine decisions necessary for the daily administration of a government. This indolence is the opposite of the urgency of the biblical work ethic that Qoheleth mandated in 9:10 (see Prov. 10:4; 18:9; 20:4; 28:2).

V. 19 is one of Ecclesiastes' challenging texts. It follows a positive and two negative statements about industriousness. When over half the words in a sentence are ambiguous in their denotation or connotation, humble exegesis is in order (see 'Notes' above). Both the most positive and negative translations and interpretations offered by commentators can make sense. I prefer the admittedly subtle translation above that is similar to the more straightforward description in Isa. 5. I have already commented above about the parallel attitudes regarding carousing in Isa. 5:11–12 and the verses in this unit. Further, in that same chapter, we read:

> Woe to the heroes of wine drinking,
>   and the champions of hard liquor;
> Who justify the wicked for a bribe,
>   and steal the innocence of the righteous from them.
>
> (Isa. 5:22–23)

Given Qoheleth's comments against feasting in 7:2–4, 6, and warnings about bribery in 7:7, I prefer a rendition of 10:19 that closes the loop on food, wine and money in the same negative way Isaiah does (see also Prov. 29:4). Though we might translate the comments about food and wine relatively neutrally, when it comes to money coupled with the root that most frequently means 'afflict' in Ecclesiastes, *'ānāh*, the verse turns the last moment to a rebuke of the abuse of food, wine and money. Qoheleth has earlier extolled food and wine as gifts from God and approved by him for pleasure and comfort (9:7). However, in the case of these poor leaders, money, though not bad in itself, will be used by the powerful for themselves while the populace suffers (see 4:1–3; cf. Ps. 73:12). If Qoheleth is *quoting* two proverbs in 10:18–19, it might explain the dissonance in the same vocabulary used by him in this speech and in that of the traditions.

20. Again, we hear an appeal to loyalty, as in 8:2–6 and 10:4. The apparent detached position of this verse in the structure of 10:2–10 does not remove it from relevance to the unit. On the contrary, it acts as the final bracket to the beginning one in 10:2–4, where care is advised when dealing with the king, *anywhere*: in his presence or far away from his presence in one's inner reasoning, or in bed (cf. Ps. 36:4; 2 Kgs 6:12)! The patience Qoheleth exhorts from those who hear others curse them (7:21–22) is not a strong point of every leader. It is often a mystery how someone knows what someone else has said. So this preposterous explanation is given playfully.

Explanation

For an age and culture that would prefer not to distinguish too absolutely the 'left' from the 'right', the right from the wrong, biblical truth is an impediment to the unbridled freedom that individuals, society and the enemy's world wish to claim. Whether it is the total world's population that is ambling about like fools without following the Light of the World, or a society that has plucked its roots from the fertile, productive ground of the Word, or the individual who refuses to apply the revealed wisdom in both canons, the result is the same: humiliating self-destruction. However, praise be to God, this world continues to reflect the order of the Creator (by Christ's upholding power, Heb. 1:3), societies must establish a minimal basis for order (if for no other reason than to sustain its leaders) and individuals must comply with the common grace of their conscience (even if reluctantly). But, still, Lord, come quickly!

The instruction in this chapter centres on the workplace, where a substantial number of adults spend many of their waking hours, and where folly, then, is displayed on a regular basis. Pleasant working conditions with civil people are a wonderful blessing, whether they are at work, in the church or civic organizations. But working with some people can call for an extra measure of patience and wisdom. That is especially true if one's *supervisor* is not exactly one with the understanding and discernment of a Qoheleth. Anger from anyone is disconcerting, but especially if it might jeopardize one's livelihood. It is especially devastating if the anger is misplaced, and by one who may be disposed to errant decisions and rants. One of the most troubling and destructive practices of management can be the way in which human resources are handled, including hiring, compensation and promotions. The truly skilled and knowledgeable personnel are not always hired or rewarded appropriately (9:11). Favouritism, nepotism, lust and extortion can place reckless fools in positions that are way over their heads, to the understandable irritation of those passed over and to the serious detriment of the organization. Prov. 26:10 is graphic in describing poor hiring 'Like an archer wounding everyone is the one hiring a fool or passer-by.' Compensation can also be unfair, discriminating against those whom, as a class or as an individual, management purposely or blindly marginalizes.

What is the solution? Well, perhaps the wise cannot change the decisions or practices of others, but they can certainly understand them and cope with them through patience and careful reactions based on an understanding of human nature and organizational politics. Precautions against disrespect have already been given (8:2–6), consistent with Paul's teaching (see 'Comment' at 8:2–6a). Even things said 'in confidentiality' or 'between us and the doorpost' will probably make its way to the person, leader or not. Eavesdropping, gossip, slips of the tongue, body language and other subtle means of communication will betray the disloyal. Regardless of whether the Christian can change the workplace culture or environment or not, one should tend to business and be excellent at what one does – that is a person's success. The damage that might come to a subordinate from careless work (vv. 8–11) is not limited to the labourers whose jobs entail physically demanding and dangerous duties. Less physically hazardous work has its own dangers if done carelessly: micro-management from above, reprimands, notices, demotions or even termination. On the other hand, 'Do you see a skilled workman? He will stand before kings, not obscure people' (Prov. 22:29). The consistent application of wisdom will bring success in any environment, including the marketplace.

We may have trouble at times with our managers, but how do we manage our own tongue? No single topic of moral responsibility in the wisdom literature is mentioned more frequently than our speaking. Those who are righteous control the tongue; fools are unable or willing to do so. In the wisdom literature, a metric instrument for gauging folly is the *number* of words one speaks (an ominous thought for preachers, professors and commentators). James calls the tongue a boasting, inflammatory, defiling, restless, cursing, bitter and poisonous organ (Jas 3:5–11). Indeed, who could tame *that*? This is precisely why Proverbs and Ecclesiastes dwell on it, and it is precisely the problem with Job's nemeses: Zophar, Bildad and Eliphaz. The mouth not only shoots out its bitter venom to afflict others; it swallows that venom to the fool's own destruction, eating away at his soul, infecting his heart and making his next words even more vicious. Christ says that even sophisticated, honoured people like religious leaders can be guilty of this (Matt. 12:34).

And then there are those expense accounts for leaders. The appetites of these individuals can be voracious for doing so little physical labour. Their palates seem unquenchable with food and drink, and at all hours of the day and night. What would we do without 'happy hour' anyway? Seriously, it is not only the squandering of an organization's money and resources that is at stake, but the mental, emotional and physical condition in which to make decisions on behalf of others. An ethically debilitating habit of meeting the exaggerated needs of the flesh will affect the whole performance of the leader. How blessed is the organization whose leaders are satisfied with the basics and are healthy examples of restraint and stewardship.

Will the local church take responsibility for addressing in all specificity the issues that most of its members struggle with during the work week? Christians have such a wonderful opportunity to transform their culture and society through the daily, routine activities of the marketplace. It is a frontier of sanctification that ought to be explored and developed by churches and seminaries. Instead, they have intentionally left the marketplace to parachurch organizations, even though Scripture is replete in its teaching on the subject. What a wonderful impact would be made for the kingdom if our spiritual leaders were intensely attuned to the marketplace and took God's interest and instructions about it into the Sunday morning pulpit and midweek prayer meeting!

ECCLESIASTES 11:1 – 12:8

Translation

[1]Forward your food over the water's surface, for you may find it after several days. [2]Divide a portion to seven, even eight, since you do not know what tragedy will occur on land.

[3]When the clouds are full of rain they empty it on the land. And whether a tree falls to the south or the north, any place the tree falls, there it is. [4]The one who observes the wind may not sow, and the one who watches the clouds may not reap.

⁵Just as you do not know what is the way of the wind – as the way of limbs in the womb of the pregnant – so you do not know the work of God who does both. ⁶In the morning sow your seed, and until the evening do not relax your hand, since you do not know which effort will succeed or whether both of them alike will be good.

⁷So, sweet is the light, since it is pleasurable for the eyes to see the sun. ⁸Certainly, if one lives many years, one should be pleased in all of them, but one should consider the dark days, since there will be many. All that comes is temporary.

⁹Enjoy your youth, young man, and let your heart be pleased with your young days. And go in your heart's direction and with your eyes' desires. Yet know that God will bring you to account for these things. ¹⁰So avoid grief in your heart and direct tragedy away from your body, since youth and darkness are temporary.

12:1So consider your Creator in your young days –
  before tragic days come and years draw near when you will say, 'I have
      no pleasure in them!';
²before the sun, the light, the moon and the stars are darkened, and
      clouds
  return after the rain; ³in the day when –
  the watchmen of the house tremble,
  and men of valour cower;
  the grinders are ceasing, since they are so few,
  and those looking through windows darken,
⁴and the doors in the street are being shut
  while the sound of grinding diminishes;
  though one wakes to the sound of the bird
  the voice of these daughters of song is lowered;
⁵even from the very heights they fear the terrors along the road;
  disgusting is the almond tree,
  the grasshopper drags itself along,
  broken is the caperberry bush;
  surely one goes to one's eternal home
  while mourners wander in the street;
⁶before the silver cord is removed,
  and the golden bowl is smashed,
  the jar is broken at the spring,
  and the wheel is crushed in the cistern.
⁷Then the dust returns to the earth from which it came,
  and the breath returns to God who gave it.
⁸Breath of breaths, everything is temporary! – says Qoheleth.

Notes on the text

3. 'there it is': the verb's root form is *hāwā'* rather than *hāwāh*, an exchange of consonants found in early and late Hebr., contra Schoors 1992: 42–43.

5. 'what is the way of the wind': *derek* can mean 'direction', but here, probably 'way, manner, habit'.

'limbs': *'eṣem* is an elastic term with meanings ranging from 'bones' to 'whole person' to 'substance' to 'emotions' to 'limbs' (BDB 782).

'not know the way' is implied in the second comparative statement as well. We find parallel comparisons introduced by kaph without a conjunctive waw as in Deut. 1:17 and Song 1:5 (cf. Ps. 58:10, using *kĕmô-*).

'pregnant': could be any pregnant creature, including a human.

'does both': *hakkōl* here means 'both'.

6. 'until the evening': the prepositional *bēt* of '*in* the morning' is not repeated here with 'the evening' (as it is with 'night' in 2:23). The prepositional lamed strongly suggests '*to* the evening' (cf. Gen. 49:27; Job 4:20; see also Lys 1977: 28; Hertzberg 1963: 200).

7. 'So, sweet is the light': the waw conjoins logically the previous verse on the work *day* in the light to the phases of one's work *life*; for example, Lohfink 2003: 133–134. It is not an emphatic introduction to a new section; for example, Longman 1998: 259.

9. 'bring you to account': lit. 'judgment', but not necessarily an extreme form of condemnation.

10. 'avoid grief in your heart and direct tragedy away from your body': lit. 'let grief lack from your heart and cause tragedy to pass away from your body'.

'darkness': this is the most literal and viable translation, the root *šāḥar* meaning 'be black'. The blackness or darkness is presumed by many to be the hair colour of youth, but there is nothing said here about hair as there is, explicitly, in Lev. 13:31, 37.

12:1. 'your Creator': *bôrĕ'êkā* is the pl. of 'majesty'; for example, Krüger 2004: 190.

3. 'men of valour cower': the hith. of *'āwat* speaks of a voluntary folding of the body rather than time and old age overtaking a body with crookedness.

4. 'in the street': this phrase is used here and in v. 5. The word *šûq*, and more impressively this prepositional phrase, recurs only in the Solomonic tradition (Prov. 7:8; Song 3:2).

5. 'disgusting is the almond tree': I translate as a hiph. and according to the K *wĕyan'ēṣ*, though admittedly this is one of the most challenging phrases in Ecclesiastes.

'drags itself along': lit. 'carries itself'. The hith. of *sābal* is unique in Biblical Hebr. but reflects the struggling grasshopper here (similarly, Gordis 1968: 345).

tāpar is the hiph. in MT, but I read the hoph. with the LXX and other MSS, as well as some commentators; for example, Murphy 1992: 112.

6. 'silver cord is removed': to maintain a consistent theme of literal brokenness in all four phrases dealing with cord, bowl, jar and wheel, the Q *yērāteq* is preferred by most, raising still other challenges; for example,

Schoors 1992: 39–40. However, mere aesthetic preferences are inadequate to trump the K *yērāḥēq*.

'in the cistern': for *'el* as burying 'in', see Gen. 23:19, 25:9 and 49:29.

7. 'breath': for this sense of *rûaḥ*, see 'Notes' at 3:21. The subsequent and concluding verse of the speech highlights its synonym *hebel*.

8. 'breath of breaths, all is temporary': see 'Notes' at 1:2.

Form and structure

This unit concludes Qoheleth's speech in two rhetorical ways. First, the passing of generations (1:4) certainly foreshadows a theme of 'death' in the speech, but, more specifically, sets up the precise mid-section (6:12 – 7:4), and this concluding unit on the effect of death not only on the deceased but also on those who survive him or her. Secondly, this final unit is the third poem on transience and cyclicity after 1:4–11 and 3:1–8. This poem serves as a bracket (inclusio) for Qoheleth's entire speech, since it matches the poetic introduction in 1:3–11. That poem, as well, emphasized the motions of nature – the sun, wind and water (rivers) return time after time. In this final poem, it is the clouds that return, predictably. Then the final bracketing statement 'Breath of breaths, everything is temporary!' not only serves as the general conclusion to all of Ecclesiastes, but is also the conclusion to this unit in particular. Of course, this was Qoheleth's design – to conclude with a unit that logically and poetically demonstrated the transitory nature of each human life and its contents, and for 12:8 to be the simultaneous conclusion to both his poem and his speech. It is clearly not the conclusion of the epilogist, so it belongs in this unit rather than in the epilogue. This unit 11:1 – 12:8, then, is a summary of Qoheleth's call to joy and wise labour before death takes the opportunity away.

As with nearly every unit in Ecclesiastes, there is no unanimity on the boundaries of these verses either. There are those who hold 11:1 – 12:8 together; for example, Barton 1908: 179–196; Eaton 1983: 139–151, 'the whole section highlights the nature of commitment to Israelite theism'. However, most separate this span of verses into at least two separate units around 11:7, 8 or 9 as well as variously including 12:8 in the unit, most notably, Ogden 1983: 1984 (see the survey of views in Fredericks 1991: 95–96).

There is a structural unity within these concluding verses that appropriately brings the pervasive themes of 'wisdom', 'diligence', 'enjoyment' and 'God's sovereignty' under the overarching theme of 'transience'. At least seven rhetorical features show the cohesiveness of this unit:

1. There is a pervasive vocabulary of nature: water (11:1); land (11:2–3; 12:7); clouds, rain, trees (11:3; 12:2, 5); wind (11:4–5); fauna (11:5; 12:4–5); light and sun (11:7; 12:2); moon and stars (12:2); dust (12:7); 'breath' (*hebel* and *rûaḥ*, 11:8, 10, 12:7–8).

2. This *implies* a creation theology, which is also explicit – a creating, sovereign God over nature and life (11:5, 9; 12:1, 7). It is his sovereign will over the natural order, but more significantly over human destiny, that lies behind human experience. He allows us, therefore, to become successful through the acquisition of wisdom; we can experience enjoyment within moral limits, and can live fulfilled, but temporary, lives as dust.
3. Grain-agriculture bridges from 11:4, 6 to 12:3–4: postponing or stopping one's work because of meteorological observations of stormy winds and rain – reasons to reconsider sowing, reaping and milling (11:4; 12:3–4).
4. Trees are ruined in 11:3 and 12:6.
5. Uncertainties that characterize 11:1–6 are the necessary backdrop to the ominous certainties of 11:9 – 12:8.
6. The dusk of life (11:8 – 12:7) is foreshadowed by the dusk of day (11:6).
7. The initial waw in 11:7 retains its most natural function as a conjunction rather than marking a new section unit.

The rhetorical device of proleptic parallel structure is initiated in 11:8, where the commands to 'enjoy' and 'remember' are expanded into their own commentaries in 11:9–10 and 12:1–6, respectively. This was first seen by Witzenrath (1979). However, there is also an overlain chiastic pattern that extends this parallel bonding back to 11:3. Just such a simultaneous use of parallelism and chiasm was also found in 5:10 – 6:9. At the core of this chiasm is a reminder of the sovereign, adjudicating God who qualifies the moral limits to the enjoyment he allows, and even encourages and expects:

11:3	A	clouds and rain			
7		B	light and sun		
8			C	consider dark days	
				D	all that comes is breath
9					E enjoy your youth
					F know that God will judge
10					E' enjoy your youth
				D'	youth is breath
12:1			C'	consider God before dark days	
2		B'	sun and light		
	A'	clouds and rain			

This impact of the rain on other elements of nature affects the length of the subsequent literary sections. In 11:3–6, the rain affects the trees, sowing and reaping, delaying the resumption of the chiasm until v. 7. Likewise, the rain in 12:2 continues the chiasm's thrust through the rest of the unit by its impact on the agrarian environment and community (12:3–7).

As Qoheleth has repeated often before, this final unit also notes what cannot be determined or controlled: misfortunes (11:2); where a tree may fall (11:3); the wind's whim (11:5); a fetus's *in utero* movements (11:5); God's activity (11:5); which efforts will succeed (11:6). However, as before, Qoheleth notes that there are wise preparations for future uncertainties: to distribute one's property (11:1); to diversify one's distribution (11:2); to consider the weather wisely (11:4); to work a full day (11:6); to enjoy life now (11:7–10); to consider God's sovereignty (11:9; 12:1, 7).

Parallelism is found at least three times in 11:1–9 alone. First, vv. 1 and 2 are parallel in syntax and thought. Secondly, vv. 3 and 5 present the inevitable or unpredictable nature of the world, and vv. 4 and 6 prescribe what would be wise responses. Thirdly, vv. 9 and 10 are parallel in their encouragements to youth to enjoy life and contain sober caveats following each encouragement.

The poetic ambiguity of 12:3–7 has, of course, spawned numerous interpretations. However, the most popular interpretation is that it is a description of the emotional and physical deterioration of the aged. By this interpretation, the 'grinders' in 12:3 represent the aged's teeth, and interpreters identify variously the 'watchmen' as ailing knees, ribs, legs, arms or hands. Or better, perhaps, according to other commentators, the 'men of valour' are the arms, or rather, are they the thighs? After these many centuries, no wonder the poem is still open to many different perspectives on the anatomical interpretation alone. In addition to the commentaries, see the following for contributions to the discussion on this poem: Buzy (1932), Leahy (1952), Loretz (1964), Sawyer (1975), Witzenrath (1979), Gilbert (1981), Ogden (1984), Youngblood (1986: 397–410), Fredericks (1991), Beal (1998: 290–304), Kruger (1998) and Dulin (2001).

Adequate attention should be given to the more literal, meteorological understanding, where the pervasive motif is the storm itself that affects the entire community. The destruction from the storm that looms for the community and its natural surroundings in 12:3–6 is, then, a metaphor for the destruction of the aged's body, his physical vessel as described in 12:7. The comparison made is that the response of those who witness the demise of an individual's life is like their response to a threatening and catastrophic storm. In Leahy's words, Qoheleth 'uses the imagery of a thunderstorm with the object of setting forth the fear, melancholy and desolation which grip a household upon which death has cast its shadow' (1952: 300). When the 'storm' has passed, it leaves a shattered body to be buried – dust to dust (12:7). This meteorological interpretation, which I follow below, revives the neglected but more literal interpretation of Umbreit (1818), Ginsburg (1861), Leahy (1952) and Loretz (1964). Perhaps Qoheleth was so poetically gifted as to construct anatomical and meteorological imagery simultaneously, but I am not convinced the anatomical interpretation adequately follows the previous 'storm' theme that sets up this poetic unit.

Comment

1–2. These two verses are parallel proverbs in grammar, syntax and thought; an imperative is given that one should distribute one's property elsewhere for reasons concerning the future. The most general meaning common to both is that of wise stewardship of one's possessions to avoid disaster. The debate whether these verses refer to business *or* compassion misses the singular impact of the general truth. Such an either/or specificity was not Qoheleth's intent any more than it was in 3:2, 5, 7 to limit the application of the principles of wise timing simply to seeds, stones or cloth. Some suggest that these verses advise taking reasonable risks in foreign trade and diversifying one's investments to protect against an unforeseen tragedy (Gordis 1968: 329–330; Longman 1998: 255–256; contra Fredericks 1991: 99). However, this maritime investment interpretation is weak as a sole application of these proverbs, since, evidently, there may not be any *certain* return on the investment – one might find merely the principal again, if that. Many others prefer to interpret the diversified distribution to those in need as a merciful act. Often, however, the rationale in this interpretation is that there is the ulterior motive of getting something in return in the event that one finds oneself in need. Yet if presented with an either/or decision, the merciful interpretation is more sensible because of ANE parallels, including Prov. 19:17; for example, Brown 2000: 101; Krüger 2004: 192. On the other hand, the generality of these proverbs allows for a business and compassion application. It also allows for protecting one's possessions by placing them somewhere safer. If hordes (people or insects) are coming to ravage the land, there is no better place for one's possessions than to be afloat.

Qoheleth's numerical technique of intensification is common in the OT where a progression from x to x + 1 (e.g. '*seven*, even eight') is not to be understood literally (see Prov. 30:18; Amos 2:4). It is interesting that Israelite law required that one distribute a portion of one's assets to the poor for at least *seven* years, if necessary (Deut. 15:7–11; cf. Prov. 28:27; Matt. 5:7; Eccl. 2:26). Hoarding one's wealth is a foolish thing, according to Qoheleth (5:13–14). Offering 'bread' or 'food' (basic elements of joy) to others who are in need makes sense, given Qoheleth's theme of 'joy'. One might see the results of the merciful distribution of their possessions in the lives of the poor. Again, it is interesting that Joseph's wisdom directed the storage of food for *seven* years prior to the impending tragic famine on the land (Gen. 41:34–36; cf. Job 5:19–20).

3, 5. Qoheleth's intense interest in natural theology, which started in 1:4–7, continues here in vv. 3–6 by his observations of clouds, rain, land, trees, wind, *in utero* life and seeds. These self-evident truths in vv. 3 and 5 state what is certain under God's sovereignty (3:11, 14; 7:13–14; 8:16–17) and what limits any wise planning for the future. Such planning will always entail an element of risk, as warned in 11:1–2, since natural events are beyond our control. The storm caused by the clouds and rain is strong enough to fell a tree, and this chain of events confirms the fact of unchangeable events at the hand of God. This storm motif is elaborated much more extensively later in 12:3–6.

One cannot know the 'way of the wind' because its manner is unpredictable and impermanent. Using north and south coordinates in 1:6, Qoheleth assures us of its varying cycles, and in 8:8 he notes its intransigence. But of its more specific 'whims' no one knows, as Christ himself affirms: 'The wind blows where it wishes and though you hear its sound you do not know from where it comes or where it is going' (John 3:8). Nor are the 'kicking' movements of the fetus's limbs in the womb predictable. Qoheleth's conclusion by analogy, then, is that God's other activities are unpredictable as well.

4, 6. The list of uncertainties in 11:2–5 is the context of vv. 4 and 6 and their encouragements towards wise decisions that at the end of the day might produce favourable results. Since God's providence is not always predictable, wisdom demands that one be vigilant and proactive when a *day* is young (vv. 4, 6) and when a *person* is young (vv. 8–10). The wise will watch the wind and clouds to determine when to sow and harvest, since excessive wind will blow away seed that has been sown and a soaking rain will rot grain that is cut and left on the ground. After all, Qoheleth believes there is a time for planting and harvesting (3:2b), as did James, 'the farmer waits patiently for the valuable fruit of the land until it gets the early and late rains' (5:7). Most commentators see v. 4 as an indictment of the lazy fool who gazes idly into the skies, but such an interpretation, where Qoheleth recommends sowing and reaping *regardless* of the weather, is hardly consistent with his wisdom of *timely* activity. There is a time for everything. The emphasis here is on *knowing* in respect to the wind; there is no certainty, but there are wise, timely estimates.

Since God's ways are unpredictable, one should be busy all day storing up the fruits of one's labour for sustenance during unexpected shortages; 'The one tilling the land will have plenty of food' (Prov. 12:11; 28:19). Qoheleth has just concluded the previous unit with words about diligence (10:17–18), but in this unit he places diligence within a natural theology that understands the uncertainties of life: 'Do not brag about tomorrow, since you do not know what a day brings' (Prov. 27:1). So one must work hard both in the morning and in the afternoon until evening, since at least one of the shifts should prove productive, if not both! We learned in 9:10 that whatever one does must be done with full strength and resolve, because the Sheol-grave certainly will not allow any activity, and that warning foreshadows much of this final unit of Qoheleth's speech.

Vv. 4 and 6 are examples of wisdom literature's juxtaposing opposite instructions as a riddle to be pondered and solved. Here in 11:4, not sowing is encouraged, but then again in 11:6, sowing is strongly encouraged. Qoheleth implies in 11:4 that it is wise to observe the wind's strength and its potential to blow recently sown seeds away and to observe the clouds to determine whether or not it is the best time to reap. On the other hand, weather permitting, 11:6 demands sowing seed. Timing is everything in applying wisdom. These two instructions, then, are of course true; the difference is in the applicability of each to the individual and to his or her circumstances. Similarly, Prov. 26:4–5, speaking to a fool is first discouraged, then encouraged.

The day of sowing is both literal and metaphorical for the 'day' of one's working life, before the dark (evening) days of old age. Thus v. 6 is proleptic to 11:8 specifically, and through the remainder of the unit.

7–8. Because the day of labour can be productive, particularly when one is young enough to work and enjoy the fruits of one's labour, seeing the light of the sun is an inspiration. This observation and conclusion to 11:6 is the thrust of the initial waw in v. 7. So rather than clouds and rain, rather than the dark evening, the sunlight is not just good but 'sweet' (*mātôq*), a word used usually for honey in the OT. This is in complete contrast to the depressing darkness of 5:17 for the one who has lost everything *before* death – for the one who has no fruit from his labour. It is also an opposite experience to that theorized by Qoheleth earlier in 6:3–5. There it is said with nearly identical phrasing that if one 'lives many years' (*šānîm rabbôt yiḥyeh*) yet is not pleased with life, it is better that the sun *not* be seen. So if you are enjoying life, enjoy the sunlight now while you can, because more challenging and dark days loom ahead when you near the evening of life. 'Right now, it is great to be alive' is the backdrop for the next two verses, which instruct the young to rejoice and pursue judiciously the pleasant aspects of life.

Qoheleth's thematic refrain about transience is repeated here as both an incentive and a consolation; *all* that comes is *hebel*, a fleeting breath. This is an obvious reason for delighting in the light when young: it will not last. But it is also a consolation, since the dark days will not last either: *everything* coming is temporary, including youth and old age. This same point of the transience of youth and old age is paralleled in the concluding words of v. 10. In reference to these instances of *hebel*, Kamano (2002: 242) believes them to 'support this message, providing a characteristic of human life: ephemerality. Since life is ephemeral, humanity should make the best of this reality.'

9a, 10a. Just as vv. 1 and 2 are parallel, and vv. 3, 5 and 4, 6 are, vv. 9a, 10a parallel 9b, 10b. The first parts of each verse encourage youth towards enjoying life and avoiding grief, a positive and negative approach in instructing how to achieve the pleasant life advised in vv. 7 and 8. This advice in 9a and 10a is then followed by ominous notes to mitigate any irresponsibility one might think was allowed by the encouragements.

This is the last of the seven enjoyment refrains Qoheleth has woven throughout his speech (2:24–26; 3:12–13, 22; 5:18–20; 8:15; 9:7–9). This is a more qualified refrain, however, buffered by the realities of God's judicial sovereignty and the utter brevity of each stage of life. Qoheleth's thought here is identical to that in 2:10–11, and these similar statements are inclusios between which are the more extended Refrains of Enjoyment. There he said that satisfying his *eye's* desires and *heart's* pleasures was his reward for his wise labour (2:4–9). Yet his realism forced him to admit that his reward had no lasting advantage. What he concluded earlier in his life he now teaches to the young. What he concluded at the beginning he now mentions again at the end – enjoy the fruits of your labour now, since this advantage will not last (see Watson 1989 for a survey of the eye–heart word pair). 'Enjoy' and 'be pleased' in 11:9 find near opposites in 11:10, 'grief' and 'tragic evil'. The latter conditions are to be avoided in the first place, not extracted after the fact. The sense is not that grief should be removed, nor that tragic evils should be eliminated, but that their presence should be wisely pre-empted, avoiding both emotional and 'physical' (*bāśār*) stresses. The grief of increasing knowledge and wisdom will inevitably come (1:18).

Out of context, Qoheleth's words sound contradictory to Num. 15:39, where Moses instructs the people *not* to follow their own hearts and eyes. However, there the desires were clearly unlawful; that is, theologically adulterous. Here the presumption is that those not-yet-old are not always wayward, but that they are often responsible. As in 2:10–11, the pleasure follows productive work. Without sinning, one's eyes and heart can lead them to drink wine (9:7), enjoy food (2:25), be sensual (9:9), seek the sun (11:7), enjoy a rest (4:6), clean up (9:8), pursue dancing, embracing, peace, laughter and love (3:4–5, 8), appreciate money (7:11–12), take pleasure in gardens and music (2:5, 8). But excesses and untimely pursuits, even of these actions, are what Qoheleth warns the young in his audience about and for which they are judged accountable (4:4; 5:10; 7:2, 4, 26; 10:16, 18). Qoheleth's audience probably included officials of every adult age, young and old. The 'youth' he is talking about is not pre-adulthood or adolescence; rather, it is the time of life when one is not considered 'old'.

9b. The youth in Qoheleth's audience have a fresh memory of 10:16–19, a passage that warns against excesses in pursuing pleasure. And the certainty of God's judgment has wound its way through this speech, including here and in the editor's final verse of the book (2:26; 3:17; 5:6; 8:12–13; 12:14). So Qoheleth needs only to mention tersely the implications of foolishness. There is no need to envision the Judgment Day here any more than in the other passages in Ecclesiastes, since, in the OT, God's retribution comes by various means. To his own in-history destruction of people or their possessions he adds a person's own self-inflicted consequences to wickedness and foolishness, as well as harm from others or even a redistribution of one's wealth to others (2:26; 6:1–2; cf. Ps. 81:11–12). The caveats in 9b and 10b refer in parallel to 12:1 and 12:2–8 respectively, where the judicial sovereignty of God is echoed in 'Consider your Creator', and the brevity of youth and old age are painfully poeticized in the subsequent verses.

10b. Again, Qoheleth uses parallelism to tighten his argument. That youth and dark days are both temporary is repeated from 11:7. The point is that *all* that comes is temporary, even the dark days that can trouble the enjoyment of youth. This is simultaneously a discouragement about youth and an encouragement about the relief of death. There is a time for birthing (while young), and a time for death (3:2). Death can be better than life (7:1). Grief, sorrow, affliction and weariness are fortunately only temporary (2:23). See 'Notes' above that 'dark' refers to the days of old age rather than the hair of the young, though many commentators will inconsistently claim that *hebel* means 'fleeting' here but not two verses earlier in 11:8; for example, Brown 2000: 104–107; Crenshaw 1987: 181. Krüger translates more reasonably as 'fleeting' in both instances (2004: 190).

12:1–2. These two verses expand the thoughts of 11:8–10, where it is said that God is to be remembered as the judge of youth's passions. Here Qoheleth names God the 'Creator', the maker of everything (3:11, 14; 7:13–14, 29; 11:5), and again God is to be 'considered' for his sovereignty. The length of a person's life is at the creative discretion of God, who gives life in the first place (12:7; 5:17; 8:15; 9:9). This theology of creation and retribution is the reason for 'fearing God' (3:14; 5:6; 7:18; 8:12–13). But God the Creator is also the 'giver' of all good things (2:24, 26; 5:18). Also the same 'younger days' are continued from 11:9, when one's response to God's creation, including the sunlight, should be one's delight. In 12:1, that delight of youth is repeated as a temporary opportunity before days and years of pain and suffering move in like a storm. The warning of darkness that accompanies the storm in 12:2 has already been given in 11:8, 10.

Qoheleth's instruction to respect God and to enjoy his gifts while possible is sustained in this pericope by the thrice repeated 'before' (12:1–2, 6), which emphasizes the brevity of pleasure and the finality of death – before time runs out. The clouds of 11:3–4 return with a vengeance in 12:2–7. In the earlier passage, the wind lays a tree out; now it not only demolishes trees but the human body as well (12:6). The clouds return 'after the rain', a disappointing and terse note on the recurrent curse of old age. One would hope the *sun* might be what returns, but only more challenges and trials move in instead. Indeed, the inverse is better – it is better to see the light and the sun (11:7) after the clouds more frequently during one's youth.

3–5a. The storm motif now rises to its apex, having only been foreshadowed in 11:3. The decrepit anatomical interpretation of these verses, where the people, flora and fauna all refer to physical deterioration, does little justice to the explicit storm motif introduced in 12:2. Rather, 12:2–7 compares the trauma of the dying and dead to the impact of an approaching and destructive storm. The opening phrase 'in the day when' refers to the time when the clouds and rain return (12:2). The return of another storm is met with tremendous fear and precaution. The watchmen and even the men of valour cringe at the intensity of the coming storm, perhaps because of the snapping, pounding thunder. This 'storm' has no respect for position or might, just as death is no respecter of persons.

The women who grind the grain are chased into their homes by the storm. Gradually, milling comes to a halt, since most have already gone inside. They have shut their doors and windows and are sullenly watching the impending disaster. These lines of the poem are chiastic, whereas those about the men in v. 3 are parallel. Incidentally, activity 'in the street' is unique to the *Corpus Salomonicum*. It is the scene for fear and mourning here in our passage but also for wayward youth (Prov. 7:8) and a frantic, frustrated lover (Song 3:2).

The birds whose sounds may have been heard in the morning are now intimidated into quietness by the coming tempest. The usually energetic, uplifting chirps of the birds are not heard due to the ominous, threatening sounds of the storm that fill the air. After all, their very perch may see the same devastating impact of the rainstorm that felled the tree of 11:3. Either in flight or from their high perches, they fear the tempest and the terrors it will bring 'along the road'. Those terrors are eventually realized. Because of the storm there is a horrid, disgusting sight of what was once the beautiful almond tree and caperberry bush. Now they are torn and dismembered. The once flying grasshopper is now humbled to a sluggish crawl. The almond tree, grasshopper and caperberry bush are all battered by lashing winds and pounding rain. These are the tragic results the birds observe from their heights.

5b–7. The first and last phrases in 5b–7 are the most intriguing theologically, and what is between them is challenging but aesthetically effective. This section of the poem finally melds the death and storm comparison. That the passage is referring to impending death is finally made explicit in the climactic exit and return of the breath to God, leaving behind grief-stricken survivors. The imagery of an ended life is brutal and final: life is removed, smashed, broken and crushed! The storm that brings death in its wake has stupefied the people and birds in the community of the dying. At the end of the storm, a burial of the deceased brings mourners who wander in the street, still stunned.

By this third instance of the preposition 'before', one is reminded of the main point and command from 12:1 – to respect God while one is still young. The series of this prepositional construction (12:1–2 and here) lengthens this one poetic sentence now to six verses. Some commentators, understandably, try to reconstruct a single cistern scene in v. 6, which is created by these four parallel images. But, as in the case of the anatomical puzzle they try to reconstruct in vv. 3–5a, the various attempts to make the words fit stumble over one another. For instance, the silver cord and bowl are thought by some to refer to parts of a suspended oil lamp whose light may represent the spirit that ascends to God. The common earthen jar may represent the physical body, which, being made of earth will return broken to the earth. However, the inarguable interpretation is that the four images individually or collectively picture the death of the physical body. My translation is intended to be as literal as possible to allow for the reader's own reconstruction. Yet if one were forced to combine these four images, perhaps a bowl which is strung on a cord, and a pitcher which is lowered by a pulley, all in their vulnerability to the tremendous storm, crash into the well (the burial pit), the grave (Sheol), into the dust, ruined or broken.

Now, where is this eternal home (v. 5b) and to where does the *rûaḥ* (spirit or breath?) return (v. 7b)? Are they the same place or not? Is the eternal home where the buried body is, or to where the spirit ascends with God? The 'eternal' home probably refers to what we just saw pictured in the immediate context: the pit, the grave, the home for the body. 'Eternal home' in the Ahiram and other ANE inscriptions means the tomb (Seow 1997: 364; Fox 1999: 328; cf. Job 30:23), and given Qoheleth's cosmopolitan genre, this common understanding would be the first to be heard. After all, the whole point of Qoheleth's poem is not to offer a future consolation to death. Rather, in looking at life 'under the sun', his instruction is to live fully, *now*! This is not a denial of an afterlife; it is simply not an explicit affirmation of it. The question will remain about Qoheleth's specific view of an afterlife, since it would have been a distraction from his message to focus on that side of death. Provan (2001: 93–94), in reference to this passage, gives a good, brief summary of biblical passages about the dead – where the body and soul go. But, what about the *rûaḥ*? Is its return to its Creator not at least an allusion to a resurrection? Probably not. The *rûaḥ* here, in this context, is the life-breath common to beasts and humans that Qoheleth discussed in 3:18–21. However, whereas 3:21 poses a troubling question about *when* the breath rises, here it is affirmed *where* to and to *whom* it rises. It actually returns to God, who created it. The *rûaḥ* is not the 'spirit' or 'soul' here any more than it was in ch. 3.

8. That the breath *returns* to God and dust *returns* to dust is an application of one of Qoheleth's recurrent themes: cyclicity. Cycles are a 'godly' interest according to 3:15; he prefers what has been pursued before. Generations and nature reflect this (1:4–7), as does human activity (1:9–10). Life is made up of the cycles of opposite activities performed at the right (or wrong) times (3:1–8). Loyalty cycles through to whoever is in power (4:13–16). The clouds return after the rain (12:2). Now, Qoheleth recycles his thematic conclusion about life from 1:2, 'Breath of breaths, everything is temporary!' Qoheleth ends his speech as he started. A second rhetorical device is Qoheleth's artistic *ending* of his speech using the *ending* of one's life as the motif. A third device is the immediate sequence of *rûaḥ* (life-breath) and *hebel* (breath) only six words later. Human breath is the metre not only of one's life but of the duration of all that is done under the sun.

That a youth should consider the Creator before death is hardly a message that can be concluded with a summary that everything is 'meaningless'. Whatever level of confusion any commentator would claim for Qoheleth, he is either the ultimate fool for so completely negating his message as his final thought, or his conclusion truly is, 'Everything is temporary.' The temporariness of life and its deeds is clearly Qoheleth's conclusion, not only for 11:1 – 12:7, but for his entire speech and its several conclusions.

Having the rest of his speech behind us now, it is clear that enjoying one's brief life, conducting oneself wisely and working hard are Qoheleth's strong constructive and meaningful convictions, not simply suggestions in the light of a meaningless or absurd existence. Life and its events may be merely momentary experiences, but are critically important to us and to God.

Explanation

The conclusion to Ecclesiastes is the same as to that of life: death. Likewise, in this passage he anticipates that ending with calls to diligence and enjoyment – the prerequisites to a life well lived before death. Diligence in distributing one's possessions to better places is one application of wisdom to our labour and its fruit. Stewardship of God's gifts includes securing and investing them where they can continue to improve through their own growth and where they can improve the life of others. We invest our assets to add more to their value, spinning off interest and dividends, all in obedience to Christ (Matt. 25:14–30). Those increased assets continue to grow and can be distributed to help others along the way or at the end of a season. Our investments in the kingdom should be diversified and placed in capable, proven hands that in turn invest those gifts in the lives of others. Good business practices make for good kingdom practices, since the latter is always the ultimate goal. The uncertainties in life are added incentives to invest in diversified ways. It is best to put our assets someplace where tragedy cannot find them, if not in a financial portfolio, perhaps overseas in a Christ-centred clinic or in a micro-enterprise effort.

Life's uncertainties are also an incentive for diligent planning and working during the workday. That 'workday' is also a metaphor for the time in our life when we are able to work – when the sun is shining in the morning and afternoon, and when it shines on our youth. However, the unknown cannot be allowed to petrify us by confusion or complacency, nor can we allow the knowledge of life's expected, inevitable events to become an excuse for fatalism. Qoheleth's advice is to look for the suitable time for all activities but never to slack off from productive work when circumstances are not conducive to any one activity. One can enjoy the sweet sun and light of day at the same time as using the back rather than lying on it. There will be no enjoyment of the sun if there are no advantages in life. The sun is only the monotonous reminder of a life lived in the darkness and despondency of the idle.

Opportunities for success are fleeting – the hours go fast during the day and youth speeds into old age. So enjoy life *wisely* while young! Before the dark years come, follow the worthwhile desires of your eyes and heart while there is time. Prepare your path, avoiding debilitating circumstances. Be proactive in steering away from danger. These are thoughts of the wisdom literature not expressed in typical teachings on sanctification or the 'deeper life'. There is a paternalistic withholding of such effusive encouragements to enjoy life. Comparable to neutralizing the blatant praise of sexual relations in Song of Songs, teachings on pursuing one's desires are rarely heard. We instead obsess on *finding* 'the will of God for my life', presuming he is purposely evasive. We write and read volumes about strategies that only obliterate the most natural indication of that will – the heartfelt desires, motivations and visions that come from within through the Spirit. Rest assured, the conscience of the righteous will perform its role in guarding against any licence by following God's leading in our lives, a wonderful freedom, indeed!

This 'judgment' Qoheleth speaks of is not always deferred to the Judgment Day. There are many ways that God judges, and fortunately that judgment comes to us on a regular basis, since God disciplines those he loves (Prov. 3:12; Heb. 12:5–6). God's judgment comes by our own self-inflicted wounds from irresponsible decisions. It comes directly through the painful conviction of sin from the indwelling Spirit or from the two-edged Sword. Judgment can come through 'injustice' from others, or from the fair wardens of justice. God is also the Creator who should be remembered in one's youth. Following the desires of one's heart may be so enjoyable that it becomes a distraction, keeping us from a constant focus on the Judge and Creator.

God creates the rain, clouds and the storms that can devastate human efforts and much of nature too. He has also created the frail body that will eventually be crushed by time and by life's storms. The trauma of death, like a ravaging storm, reaches everyone – not only the deceased, but also all who watch the devastation take its toll. No comfort or consolation we can bring to anyone's deathbed is greater than, or more spiritual than that shown by Christ as he wept at the tomb of Lazarus. The one who knew the hope of the resurrection better than any other still grieved the loss of a friend. Unfortunate attempts to defer or even suppress one's own grief because of the better state in which the deceased now lives are totally unnatural, and inadvertently thumbs one's nose at the Creator's design to show the gravity of sin since the Fall.

There have been times before in Qoheleth's speech when we wanted him to affirm everlasting life; he may annoy some again here by not resorting to that encouragement. Perhaps it was not mentioned before in order to emphasize the consolations God provides in this life. Here it is obvious that given the theme of this speech, 'Everything under the sun is temporary', the whole point would be missed if the subject were changed at this stage to a counterpoint. It would have been counterproductive to allow the audience to catapult their thoughts out of this present world for which they are accountable into a future that has no such accountabilities.

The church must caution itself about fostering an other-wordly mentality among its people who have been called to make this world work as well as possible. To deny eternal life would be a travesty against God's people and his revelation. To encourage them with their immortality is a pastoral obligation. However, it is also an obligation to review the moral necessity repeatedly to apply the principles of biblical wisdom to every crevice of our life *now*, while we can, during this fleeting life.

ECCLESIASTES 12:9–14

Translation

[9]Now, because Qoheleth was wise, in addition, he taught the people knowledge continually and listened intently, and he studied; he adapted many proverbs. [10]Qoheleth searched to find satisfying words; so what has been written straightforwardly are words of truth.

[11]The words of the wise are like goads and the masters of these collections are like firmly set nails. They are given by one Shepherd.

[12]But in addition to these, my son, beware of a lot of bookwork – it is endless – and much study tires the flesh.

[13–14]Let us hear the end of the matter, everything! Fear God and keep his commandments. Surely, this includes everyone. Surely, God will bring every action to judgment beyond all secrecy, whether good or evil.

Notes on the text

9. 'Now ... in addition, he': the opening waw indicates the beginning of a new section rather than a continuation of the preceding verse. Here and in 12:12, *yōtēr* means 'that which is extra or additional'. Here what is additional is Qoheleth's extensive activities beyond being simply wise.

'because Qoheleth': the relative *še* indicates causality (with Seow 1997: 385), thus the reason for Qoheleth's subsequent list of wise activities.

'listened intently': four piels explain Qoheleth's achievements as a wise man: *limmad* (teach), *'izzēn* (listen intently), *ḥiqqēr* ([re]search, study), *tiqqēn* (arrange). The presence of the surrounding pi. stems may be the reason for *'āzan* (listen) being drawn into its only occasion as a pi. in the OT.

'adapted': for *tāqan*, see 'Notes' at 1:15. Here it means 'to arrange in a literary sense'.

10. 'satisfying words': see 'Notes' at 3:1 on Qoheleth's homonymous use of *ḥēpeṣ*. I translate the phrase to express the epistemological effect on the listener – they are delightful because they are true.

'so what has been written': the prefixed waw is resultative and the qal passive participle *kātûb* is quite natural. The commentaries wrestle unnecessarily with emendations, most frequently changing it to an infinitive abs.; for example, Longman 1998: 275; Fox 1999: 352.

'straightforward words of truth': the noun *yōšer* means 'straightness' and is used here adverbially.

11. 'masters of collections': *'ăsuppôt* probably refers to wisdom collections rather than assemblies of people. The latter is an interpretation imported from the Talmud, where it refers to the Sanhedrin. There is no context here for any such assemblies, whereas the words of the wise referred to in the previous phrase are by definition a collection.

'firmly set nails': lit. 'planted nails' and refers to the stable, solid state of the expert masters of the wisdom collections.

'Shepherd': the word is capitalized to indicate the divine Shepherd (Pss 23:1; 80:1; Isa. 40:11), along with many commentators.

12. 'beware of excessive bookwork': with Shields (2000: 123–126), we read *hizzāhēr* as the beginning of a new clause but translate the infinitive clause as a substantive. To 'do books' does not imply the writing or publication of books, as most commentators interpret and translate. Such a translation misses the very general meaning of *'āsāh*. The 'use' of books is probably in view here, per Loretz 1964: 159; Scott 1965: 256; de Boer 1977: 87–88. Furthermore, the phrase is parallel syntactically and conceptually with the subsequent comment on 'much studying'.

13. 'Let us hear': with the Vg and Whybray (1989: 173) we read the qal cohortative here rather than the ni.

Form and structure

In this final section of Ecclesiastes, a new teaching authority makes his own closing remarks about the commendatory work of Qoheleth as well as the importance of wisdom and righteousness in general. We heard this person's voice only faintly in 1:1, 7:27 and 12:8, but now his voice is centre stage, and we find ourselves tuning our ear to *his* authority on certain matters. This new instructor puts Qoheleth's entire speech within a pedagogical framework, certainly to highlight the content of Qoheleth's wisdom but also to comment on the means by which Qoheleth became a wise man and the responsibilities that come with that status. Qoheleth is lifted up as the model of the wise man whom only the extremely dedicated wisdom student should aspire to become.

There is no consensus on what type of wisdom learning environment existed in Israel or whether it was formal or informal. We have the familial terminology in the wisdom literature for the wisdom student, 'my son', but an institutional definition of a wisdom school or even guild is not found in the OT. Yet it appears that we are within that 'environment' here in the epilogue. And there is the same question about the setting of this epilogue as with Qoheleth's speech itself: is it *live, oral* direct discourse or is it *written* as direct discourse? Was there ever an initial, oral delivery? Nonetheless, whether Qoheleth's words are first recited by oral tradition or read from a manuscript, they are revered by this teacher for their content and then qualified constructively with an orthodox call to fear God, to obey his commandments and to remember God's judicial finality and thoroughness. In this way, Qoheleth is an admired 'guest lecturer' who, in the eyes of this new instructor, has great wisdom and whose speech should be drawn into the mainstream of Israelite wisdom discourse.

Ogden (1987: 208) sees two sections to this epilogue, vv. 9–11 and 12–14. This seems clear enough in that *wěyōtēr* begins each section in the Hebr. text, and where vv. 9–11 speak of the wisdom community, including Qoheleth in the third person, vv. 12–14 are first or second person imperatives, addressed to the individual or to us all. I would add that vv. 9–11 close with the wisdom-directing God, and the judging God closes vv. 12–14, the epilogue and the book itself.

A flow of thought in the epilogue precludes any multiple epilogist or other theories that see it as a sequence of add-on comments.

9a	Praises Qoheleth's teaching and listening.
9b	Describes his studying and editing.
10	Reviews that editing process and the resulting truth of the final product.
11a	Identifies uses for the collections, for correction and stability.
11b	Explains why the collections are effective: they are divinely directed.
12	Warns the faint-hearted from aspiring to be one of these wise men, because of the rigour.
13–14	Encourages all to commit at least to the basics of righteousness, even if not to becoming a wise man.

Some see one, two, even three, separate components due to separate epilogists or because of a topical disconnect. For instance, Crenshaw (1987: 189–190) sees the first three verses as comments by a devoted student that needed to be mitigated by a second epilogist. This epilogist sets the record straight by reciting Hebrew orthodoxy in distinction to what Crenshaw believes to be Qoheleth's refutation of traditional wisdom.

Comment

9-10. Even though Qoheleth as a realist has driven the theme of the 'utter transience' of all of which humanity is a part, he is *still* considered to be a wise man. Either by self-attestation (1:13; 2:9, 15, 19; 7:23, 27–29) or here, by the epilogist, Qoheleth is presented to be wise in his conclusions. If he quotes conventional wisdom only to deconstruct it, or if he is in revolt to the act–consequence framework of conventional OT wisdom, then how is it that the epilogist places Qoheleth among the sages to be honoured? The epilogist would himself be in revolt regardless of his endorsement of fundamental Judaism (v. 14), or another epilogist would need to be posited in order to correct them both. This is a standing question for those who insist that Qoheleth's message is that everything is meaningless or absurd. However, once Qoheleth is heard correctly to say that everything under the sun is temporary, not meaningless, the wisdom of Qoheleth's epilogist is exonerated.

In fact, Qoheleth is placed on a pedestal as the model wise man in his teaching, study and writing. The first three verses, or first half of this final unit in Ecclesiastes, are about wisdom sayings: teaching them, studying and then adapting them, writing them acceptably as words of truth, acknowledging their stabilizing strength as divine directives and discouraging any tepid commitment to becoming their master – all with Qoheleth as either the centre, or at least an example of the wisdom function.

Qoheleth was successful as a wise man, not only because of his knowledge but because of his application of that knowledge for the benefit of the people. He was a listener as well as a teacher. It is unclear whether his listening is to the people he teaches or to those who taught him, or both. Nonetheless, he is the wise listener as well as the wise instructor, not the one who answers before listening (Prov. 18:13). Qoheleth also 'listened' to reality around him, seeking and inquiring incessantly (1:13, 16–17; 2:1, 3, 11–12; 4:1, 7; 7:23, 25, 28; 8:16; 9:1, 11, 13). He was a student of life, but for the purpose of drawing not only philosophical but extremely practical conclusions about how to live it. It is implied that his teaching the people wisdom was a continuous passion, perhaps even a profession.

Qoheleth was a student of wisdom literature as well, both domestic and foreign. This commentary has reviewed similarities in thought from Aram., Egypt. and Bab. literature, and possibly these are included as sayings he contextualized within the Israelite faith and culture. Here we hear that he was a 'collector' and 'arranger' of proverbs – something we see some wise person doing in the book of Proverbs and here in Ecclesiastes. We understand by this that Qoheleth adapted, maybe even corrected, wise sayings deficient in some way either in their aesthetics or content. These 'proverbs' consist not only of two- to three-line aphorisms; the word *māšal* (proverb) refers in the OT to longer statements as well, including riddles, allegories and parables (see Eaton 1983: 153).

Pleasing or satisfying words for Qoheleth are not the comfortable words of light recreational reading. They are not the ear-tickling words that placate the soul superficially or soothe the conscience artificially (2 Tim. 4:3). Instead, the delightful aspects of these words are in their expression of the truth about life and God. These elements are aesthetically, rhetorically, philosophically and theologically satisfying. They bring intellectual, emotional and spiritual delight in their arrangements, adaptations and impact on the people. We have seen Qoheleth's interest in satisfying the rhetorical palate through the elaborate use of poetry, metaphor, alliteration, parables, refrains, chiasms, parallelism and prolepses. Satisfying words are enjoyed too when Qoheleth uses them to express the reliability of conventional wisdom, including the assurances of the present joy that can come from wise, diligent toil or the promise of eventual justice in God's perfect timing.

In this wisdom vocation, in all his listening, teaching, arranging and writing in pleasing ways, it was always Qoheleth's objective to speak and write the truth. That truth is spoken in direct, straightforward ways in his speech. He listened to and was discipled by Lady Wisdom:

> I will speak about noble things;
>   and when my lips open they will say what is right,
> and my mouth will speak truth.
>
> (Prov. 8:6–7)

11. The focus of the wise is introduced as it is elsewhere in the wisdom literature as 'words of the wise' (Prov. 1:6; 22:17; 24:23; 30:10. 'Words of the wise' is also found as a phrase within certain proverbs themselves (Prov. 12:18; 13:14; 14:3; 15:2, 7; 16:23). Sometimes these collections contain painful prodding or lessons, particularly for those too often like the simple-minded youth of Prov. 1 – 9. Qoheleth's words, even in this speech, pricked his audience with goadlike words to instruct and motivate them towards more responsible living under the sun. This image is especially vivid, since examples of ANE sharp cattle goads included those fitted with a metal point at the end of a wooden shaft, or nails driven through a shaft's end to protrude from the other side.

Perhaps a populist interpretation would allow anyone to be a 'master' (*ba'al*) of these collections of wise sayings. However, having just heard the extraordinary efforts by Qoheleth in respect to these words of the wise, his immediate example probably defines who a master would be and the extent of one's life investment to become one. Such an investment of one's life would lay such an intellectual, moral and spiritual foundation that the wise man could be described as a firmly set nail – taking hold tightly, deeply and strongly. What specifically are these collections that are mastered? That would depend on the dating of Ecclesiastes and Proverbs, since the latter is our clearest biblical example of a collection of wise sayings. However, certainly there were extra-biblical databases of wise sayings that would have been classified as authoritative, including Solomon's (Prov. 1:1), those transcribed by Hezekiah's men (Prov. 25:1), Agur (Prov. 30:1) and King Lemuel (Prov. 31:1). Extra-biblical collections mentioned in the OT attest to the use of literary references that may or may not have enjoyed revelatory status; for example, the Book of Jashar (Josh. 10:13; 2 Sam. 1:18).

The expression that these collections are 'given by one shepherd' tilts an interpretation towards God being that shepherd. First, the collections of wise words themselves are the most obvious object of the phrase rather than the goads and nails, which God, of course, does not give. Secondly, God is the giving God in several Qoheleth pronouncements; for example, 1:13; 2:26; 3:10–11; 5:18–19. Though this is not Qoheleth speaking here, the epilogist's theology is consistent with Qoheleth's. Thirdly, that there is only one shepherd is accentuated by *'ehād* (one shepherd) rather than simply an indefinite 'a shepherd'. This definitive phrasing seems to require a singular identification. Fourthly, that God is indeed a 'shepherd' is an OT theme (Gen. 49:24; Pss 23:1; 80:1; 95:7; Isa. 40:11). Finally, this concluding statement of this first half of the epilogue about *God-given* wisdom sayings finds its parallel in the concluding thoughts in 12:14 about fearing God and keeping the *God-given* commandments. Prov. 2:5–6 also juxtaposes the fear of God with God as the source of wisdom, with Wisdom's commandments in the background in 2:1:

> Then you will understand the fear of the LORD...
> For the LORD gives wisdom.

God's presence is clear and dramatic in this unit already, so it is not strained to see him referenced in v. 11 by the biblical ascription of 'Shepherd'. Many understand the shepherd to be God: Gordis 1968: 354; Eaton 1983: 154; Loader 1986: 134; Ogden 1987: 210; Whybray 1989: 172.

12. The wisdom student is now goaded in v. 12 with a warning about aspiring to be one of the wise men described so far in the epilogue. Though to what 'these' refers is ambiguous, I presume it refers to the collections of wisdom sayings mentioned. Otherwise, if it means very generally 'in addition to these things', while being followed by no less than the imperative, it becomes a vestigial clause, since there is nothing previous to this thought for which the student could be responsible: it is reduced to a phrase like 'Well, anyway...'

A moderate approach to the study of wisdom is recommended here, not a total abstinence from it. Unless one wishes to pursue the rigours of not only studying arduously in becoming wise, but also teaching incessantly and publishing wisdom, as Qoheleth did (vv. 9–10), and unless one has a passion for reading all that claims to be wisdom, to study, analyse and reformat it, one should be satisfied with just reading 'the collections'. To become a master of them, as the epilogist explains the process, is not for the casual reader. The epilogist discourages the faint-hearted and lazy from aspiring to being one of these wise individuals. It is a warning, not a prohibition. It is then perhaps even an indirect challenge to those who, even after this warning, still aspire to be counted among the wise men. Qoheleth himself groaned about the gruelling task of wisdom studies:

> As I devoted myself to know wisdom and to see the affliction that is inflicted on the earth, even though sleep is not seen in one's eyes day or night, still, I observed that one is unable to understand all God's work, the work which is done under the sun. (8:17)

13–14. God's role as judge continues to the end of Ecclesiastes – in fact, it concludes the entire book. The conclusion to the matter is that the appropriate human response is reverent obedience. Those who hear Qoheleth ascribing meaninglessness and futility to everything, by definition, are forced to read this epilogue as a correction to his pessimism. For them, there might be a connection between the injunction here to fear God and in Qoheleth's speech (3:14; 5:7; 7:18; 8:12–13), but there is a perceived disconnect between his speech and the 'commandments' of God. The assumption is that Qoheleth could hardly affirm the commandments if he could not even affirm traditional wisdom. In fact, however, these two verses bind wisdom and the fear of God and his commandments together in the same way Qoheleth does in 5:1–7 (also 8:2). If the epilogue is seen as a corrective to Qoheleth's theology, then that passage has to be seen as corrective as well. For that matter, 9:2 and its moral polarity between keeping the commandments and not doing so would need to be excluded. This is probably the most we can expect, since wisdom literature in general speaks relatively little of the Law anyway, preferring to highlight the informal relationships between people rather than the legal ones.

But, really, God's commandments include all instruction given by the one Shepherd, including those that come through the wisdom collections. Like the commandments that the Good Shepherd expects those who love him to keep (John 14:15), the term 'commandments' refers to more than 'the Law' – believers, whether they have lived before or after Christ, are held responsible for many other commandments.

Fearing God is a foundational dogma of the entire OT, including Ecclesiastes and the other wisdom literature. Fearing God, which includes following his commands, is the beginning of wisdom (Prov. 9:10; Job 28:28; Ps. 111:10). Reading Qoheleth's speech leaves one to conclude that there is little distance on this basic doctrine between him and orthodoxy. Frequently as well we hear of the sinners, the ones who do evil; these are undoubtedly those who live apart from God's commands, not those who simply 'make mistakes', as we have heard some commentators suggest earlier in this commentary. What standards would Qoheleth have had in mind, regardless of the cultural milieu, if not the commandments in general, since he acknowledges them and even uses them in his instruction? No definitive statement about divine judgment could ever be made without reference to inspired moral standards.

Finally, the epilogist encourages obedience to God, since everything we do will be judged. This is either the implication or direct message of several verses in Ecclesiastes (2:26; 3:17; 5:6; 6:2; 8:13; 9:7; 11:9). As in 11:9, this is not necessarily during a final judgment. Judgment surely comes before then in many ways, and for everyone. But the thoroughness that the epilogist has in mind, which includes everything everybody has done, perhaps implies such an event. Paul echoes the epilogist in his expectations of an all-encompassing judgment, even of believers! 'We must all stand before the judgment seat of Christ so that each of us will receive what we deserve for the good or evil we have done while in the body' (2 Cor. 5:10).

Before Paul, Christ had reaffirmed Qoheleth's words: 'You must give an account on the day of judgment for every idle word spoken' (Matt. 12:36).

Explanation

All mature believers are teachers in some setting, though the thoroughness of their own understanding will be proportionate to the age and number of sheep they are called to shepherd. Whether friend, parent, ruling or teaching official in a church, theologian or commentator (yikes!), there should be a progressively increasing expectation that the instructor emulate Qoheleth in all his study and mastery of wisdom. Instructional shepherding requires an unrelenting search for truth, that which is found in the Word as well as that discovered through a fair analysis of God's creation. It also includes understanding how those outside the church think, whether their ideas are consistent with Scripture, and how far these ideas have been affected by common grace or by intentional or inadvertent lies about God's world and his administration of it. To follow Qoheleth's example, though, requires that one move beyond simply speaking in abstract terms. The proverbial literature and Ecclesiastes are hardly exercises in philosophical rumination: their sole goal is to drive the people to diligent and righteous obedience. They are not drawn-out teachings that numb the average and immature mind, leaving the mind and ears too exhausted to take the first step to practical work in the kingdom.

The objective for teaching is to convey 'satisfying words'. But, since such satisfaction is found in many different ways, the wise teacher will arrange words that nourish the soul with what it needs for the time. Suitable teaching includes the right combinations of encouragement, conviction, admonition, questions, wholeness, depth and breadth, to name just a few. However, the wise counsellor does more than satisfy through messages that entertain, are humorous or mesmerize with incessant storytelling (though, of course, there is a place for modern parables). To amuse, affirm or awe his listeners is not the starting assumption in Qoheleth's teaching. He has no interest in people leaving completely impressed with his knowledge but holding little effective light to shed on their path in the marketplace the next day.

People will hear the truth from someone they trust, even if pricked along the way. They are certainly prepared to hear a message like that of Qoheleth, a message that encourages joy, promises eventual justice for the righteous and confirms the security of God's plans. But they also need to hear that there are many unanswerable questions, that sin must be avoided, death is inevitable and there is only a temporary value to labour.

To be this type of teacher in large circles of maturing Christians takes commitment to do all that Qoheleth did. This is no place for one who wishes to make only a modest attempt at a teaching ministry at the expense of the poor sheep who deserve more. Preparation and delivery of edifying teaching is 'laborious labour', as Qoheleth alliterates in 1:3, but the advantages to self and Kingdom are profound. There is more to study than the *Reader's Digest* version of the Bible – the 'New Testament and Psalms'.

The end and summary, not only to Ecclesiastes, not only to the wisdom literature, but to all of revealed instruction, is to fear God by obeying him. This is not 'changing the subject'; it *is* the subject of Ecclesiastes. If Qoheleth says anything, it is that one should fear the sovereignty of God and apply the Shepherd's revealed principles of wisdom and righteousness (3:12). 'Fearing' God is often diluted simply to mean 'respect' and 'reverence', but this challenges common sense: it is a total lack of emotional apprehension of the One Spirit who is infinite in presence, power and knowledge. All literal calls to 'fear' God cannot be reduced merely to granting him the common courtesy of 'respect'! Our cultural church has succeeded in making God so soft and servile that fearing him is almost an insulting request. But:

> Let us cleanse ourselves ... perfecting holiness by fearing God.
> (2 Cor. 7:1)

> Work out your salvation with fear and trembling. (Phil. 2:12)

Judgment Day is an event that the church has nearly implied to be a no-show opportunity for believers washed in the Saviour's blood. However, there will be many surprised souls when their acquittal comes only after a public reading of the list of offences against God and humanity. This public reading must be done if God's deserved glory is to be magnified for his mercy in forgiving so horrendous a list of sins. An acquittal comes only after charges have been made. God's very glory and honour, his perfect expectations and perfect love, require that the fullest extent of our sin be realized by all in order to appreciate but a fraction of his grace. The reach of God's judgment goes beyond any secrecy through which one would hope to veil one's sin. There may be several reasons for the hiddenness of sin. We have heard about the weak human memory from Qoheleth; we have also heard of our very limited knowledge. Nonetheless, the sobering alarm is that whatever sin one designed to be in secret will not escape notice:

> You have put our iniquities in front of you,
>   our secrets in the light of your presence.
>
> (Ps. 90:8)

Blessed be the God and Father of our Lord Jesus Christ, the Father of mercies and God of all comfort; who comforts us in all our affliction so that we may be able to comfort those who are in any affliction with the comfort with which we ourselves are comforted by God. (2 Cor. 1:3–4 NASB)

BIBLIOGRAPHY

CITED COMMENTARIES ON ECCLESIASTES

Barton, G. A. (1908), *A Critical and Exegetical Commentary on the Book of Ecclesiastes*, Edinburgh: T. & T. Clark.

Barucq, A. (1968), *Ecclésiaste – Qohéleth: Traduction et commentaire*, Paris: Beauchesne.

Bea, A. (1950), *Liber Ecclesiastae qui ab Hebraeis appellatur Qohelet nova e textu primigenio interpretatio latina cum notis criticis et exegeticis*, Rome: Pontifical Biblical Institute.

Brown, W. P. (2000), *Ecclesiastes*, Louisville: Westminster John Knox.

Crenshaw, J. L. (1987), *Ecclesiastes: A Commentary*, Philadelphia: Westminster.

Delitzsch, F. (1975), *Proverbs, Ecclesiastes, Song of Solomon*, Eerdmans: Grand Rapids.

Di Fonzo, L. (1967), *Ecclesiaste*, Turin: Marietti.

Eaton, M. A. (1983), *Ecclesiastes*, Downers Grove: IVP.

Ellermeier, F. (1967), *Qohelet*, Herzberg: Erwin Jungfer.

Farmer, K. A. (1991), *Who Knows What Is Good? A Commentary on Proverbs and Ecclesiastes*, Grand Rapids: Eerdmans.

Fox, M. V. (1999), *A Time to Tear Down and a Time to Build Up*, Grand Rapids: Eerdmans.

Galling, K. (1969), *Der Prediger*, in E. Würthwein, K. Galling and O. Plöger (eds.), *Die Fünf Megilloth*, 2nd ed., Tübingen: Mohr, 73–125.

Garrett, D. A. (1993), *Proverbs, Ecclesiastes, Song of Songs*, Nashville: Broadman.

Ginsburg, C. (1861), *Coheleth, or the Book of Ecclesiastes*, New York: KTAV.

Gordis, R. (1968), *Koheleth – The Man and His World*, New York: Schocken.

Haupt, P. (1905), *The Book of Ecclesiastes: A New Metrical Translation with an Introduction and Explanatory Notes*, Baltimore: Johns Hopkins University Press.

Hertzberg, H. W. (1963), *Der Prediger*, Gütersloh: G. Mohn.

Hubbard, D. A. (1991), *Ecclesiastes, Song of Solomon*, Dallas: Word.

Jastrow, M. (1919), *A Gentle Cynic*, Philadelphia: Lippincott.

Kidner, D. (1976), *A Time to Mourn, and a Time to Dance*, Downers Grove: IVP.

Krüger, T. (2004), *Qoheleth: A Commentary*, Minneapolis: Fortress.

Lauha, A. (1978), *Kohelet*, Neukirchen-Vluyn: Neukirchener.

Levy, L. (1912), *Das Buch Qoheleth*, Leipzig: Hinrichs.

Loader, J. A. (1986), *Ecclesiastes*, Grand Rapids: Eerdmans.

Lohfink, N. (1980), *Kohelet*, Stuttgart: Echter.
——— (2003), *Qoheleth*, Minneapolis: Fortress.
Longman III, T. (1998), *The Book of Ecclesiastes*, NICOT, Grand Rapids: Eerdmans.
Lys, D. (1977), *L'Ecclésiaste ou Que vaut la vie? Traduction, Introduction générale, Commentair de 1,1à 4,3*, Paris: Letouzey et Ané.
Michel, D. (1988), *Qohelet*, Darmstadt: Wissenschaftliche Buchgesellschaft.
Murphy, R. E. (1992), *Ecclesiastes*, Dallas: Word.
Ogden, G. S. (1987), *Qoheleth*, Sheffield: JSOT Press.
Provan, I. W. (ed.) (2001), *Ecclesiastes, Song of Solomon: From Biblical Text to Contemporary Life*, Grand Rapids: Zondervan.
Schwienhorst-Schönberger, L. (2004), *Kohelet*, Freiburg: Herder.
Scott, R. B. Y. (1965), *Proverbs; Ecclesiastes*, Garden City: Doubleday.
Seow, C. (1997), *Ecclesiastes*, New York: Doubleday.
Siegfried, C. G. (1898), *Prediger und Hoheslied*, Göttingen: Vandenhoek & Ruprecht.
Whybray, R. N. (1989), *Ecclesiastes*, Grand Rapids: Eerdmans.
Zimmerli, W. (1962), *Das Buch des Predigers Salomo*, Göttingen: Vandenhoek & Ruprecht.

OTHER WORKS

Anderson, W. H. U. (1997), *Qoheleth and Its Pessimistic Theology: Hermeneutical Struggles in Wisdom Literature*, Lewiston: Mellen.
Azize, J. (2000), 'Considering the Book of Qohelet Afresh', *ANES* 37:183–214.
——— (2003), 'The Genre of Qohelet', *Davar Logos* 2:123–138.
Baltzer, K. (1987), 'Women and War in Qohelet 7:23–8.1a', *HTB* 80:127–132.
Bartholomew, C. G. (1998), *Reading Ecclesiastes: Old Testament Exegesis and Hermeneutical Theory*, Rome: Pontifical Biblical Institute.
——— (1999), 'Qoheleth in the Canon?! Current Trends in the Interpretation of Ecclesiastes', *Them* 23:4–20.
Beal, T. K. (1998), 'C(ha)osmopolis: Qohelet's Last Words', in T. Linafelt and T. K. Beal (eds.), *God in the Fray: A Tribute to Walter Brueggemann*, Minneapolis: Fortress, 290–304.
Beentjes, P. (1998), ' "Who Is Like the Wise?": Some Notes on Qoheleth 8,1–15', in Schoors 1998a: 303–315.
Berlejung, A., and P. Van Hecke (eds.) (2007), *The Language of Qohelet in Its Context: Essays in Honour of Prof. A. Schoors*, Leuven: Peeters.
Bertram, G. (1952), 'Hebräischer und griechischer Qohelet: Ein Beitrag zur Theologie der hellenistischen Bibel', *ZAW* 64:26–49.
Bianchi, F. (1993), 'The Language of Qohelet: A Bibliographic Survey', *ZAW* 105:210–223.
Blenkinsopp, J. (1995), 'Ecclesiastes 3:1–15: Another Interpretation', *JSOT* 66:55–64.

Boer, P. A. H. de (1977), 'A Note on Ecclesiastes 12:12a', in R. H. Fischer (ed.),
    *A Tribute to Arthur Vööbus: Studies in Early Christian Literature and Its
    Environment, Primarily in the Syrian East*, Chicago: Lutheran School of
    Theology, 85–88.
Bolin, T. (2005), 'Rivalry and Resignation: Girard and Qoheleth on the Divine–
    Human Relationship', *Bib* 85:245–259.
Braun, R. (1973), *Kohelet und die frühhellenistische Popularphilosophie*, Berlin:
    de Gruyter.
Brindle, W. A. (1985), 'Righteousness and Wickedness in Ecclesiastes 7.15–18',
    AUSS 23:243–257.
Burkitt, F. C. (1922), 'Is Ecclesiastes a Translation?', *JTS* 23:22–28.
Buzy, D. (1932), 'Le portrait de la vieillesse (Ecclésiaste. XII, 1–7)', *RB*
    41:329–340.
Byargeon, R. W. (1998), 'The Significance of Ambiguity in Ecclesiastes 2,24–26',
    in Schoors 1998a: 367–372.
Carasik, M. (2003), 'Qohelet's Twists and Turns', *JSOT* 28:192–209.
Choi, J. H. (2002), 'The Doctrine of the Golden Mean in Qoh 7,15–18: A
    Universal Human Pursuit', *Bib* 83:358–374.
Christianson, E. S. (1998), 'Qoheleth the "Old Boy" and Qoheleth the "New
    Man": Misogynism, the Womb and a Paradox in Ecclesiastes', in
    A. Brenner and C. R. Fontaine (eds.), *Wisdom and Psalms: The Feminist
    Companion to the Bible*, Sheffield: Sheffield Academic Press, 109–136.
——— (2007), *Ecclesiastes through the Centuries*, Oxford: Blackwell.
Crenshaw, J. L. (1986), 'The Expression *mî yôdēa* in the Hebrew Bible', *VT*
    36:274–288.
Crüsemann, F. (1979), 'Die unveranderbare Welt: Überlegungen zur "Krisis der
    Weisheit" beim Prediger (Kohelet)', in W. Schottroff and W. Stegemann
    (eds.), *Der Gott der kleine Leute*, Munich: Kaiser, 80–104.
Dahood, M. (1952), 'Canaanite–Phoenician Influence in Qoheleth', *Bib*
    33:30–52, 191–221.
——— (1958), 'Qoheleth and Recent Discoveries', *Bib* 39:302–318.
——— (1962), 'Qoheleth and Northwest Semitic Philology', *Bib* 43:349–365.
——— (1965), 'Canaanite Words in Qoheleth 10:20', *Bib* 46:210–212.
——— (1972), 'Northwest Semitic Philology and Three Biblical Texts', *JNSL*
    2:17–22.
Delsman, W. C. (2000), *Die Datierung des Buches Qoheleth. Eine
    sprachwissenschaftliche Analyse*, Nijmwegen: Nijmwegen University.
Dornseiff, F. (1959), *Antike und alter Orient*, Leipzig: Koehler & Amelang.
Dor-Shav, E. (2008), 'Ecclesiastes, Fleeting and Timeless: Part I', *JBQ*
    36:211–221.
Driver, G. R. (1931a), 'Studies in the Vocabulary of the Old Testament I', *JTS*
    32:38–47.
(1931b), 'Studies in the Vocabulary of the Old Testament II', *JTS* 32:250–257.
——— (1970), 'Colloquialisms in the Old Testament', in D. Cohen (ed.),
    Melanges M. Cohen, The Hague: Mouton, 232–239.

Driver, S. R. (1882), 'On Some Alleged Linguistic Affinities of the Elohist',
    Journal of Philology 11:201–236.
——— (1892), *A Treatise on the Use of the Tenses in Hebrew*, Oxford:
    Clarendon.
——— (1913), *An Introduction to the Literature of the Old Testament*,
    Edinburgh: T. & T. Clark.
Dulin, R. Z. (2001), '"How Sweet Is the Light": Qoheleth's Age-Centered
    Teachings', *Int* 55:260–270.
Eissfeldt, D. (1970), 'Alles Ding währt seine Zeit: Qoh 3.1–14', in A. Kuschke
    and E. Kutsch (eds.), *Archäologie und Altes Testament: Festschrift für
    Kurt Galling*, Tübingen: Mohr, 69–74.
Ellermeier, F. (1963a), 'Das Verbum *ḥûš* in Koh 2:25', *ZAW* 75:197–217.
——— (1963b), 'Die Entmachung der Weisheit in Denken Qohelets: Zu Text
    und Auslegung von Qoh. 6:7–9', *ZTK* 60:1–20.
Elyoenai, M. (1977), מחקרים בקהלת ובמשלי, Jerusalem: Kiryat Sefer.
Ewolde, J. (1997), *Developments in Hebrew Vocabulary between Bible and
    Mishnah*, in T. Muraoka and J. Ewolde (eds.), *The Hebrew of the Dead
    Sea Scrolls and Ben Sira*, Leiden, Brill, 17–55.
Faulkner, R. O. (1956), 'The Man who Was Tired of Life', *JEA* 42:21–40.
Fidler, R. (2006), 'Qoheleth in "The House of God": Text and Intertext in Qoh
    4:17 – 5:6 (Eng. 5:1–7)', *HS* 47:7–21.
Fischer, S. (2002), 'Qohelet and "Heretic" Harpers' Songs', *JSOT* 98:105–121.
Fontaine, C. R. (1998), '"Many Devices" (Qoheleth 7:23 – 8:1): Qoheleth,
    Misogyny and the Malleus Maleficarum', in A. Brenner and C. R.
    Fontaine (eds.), *Wisdom and Psalms: The Feminist Companion to the
    Bible*, Sheffield: Sheffield Academic Press, 137–168.
Foresti, F. (1980), '*amal* in Koheleth: "Toil" or "Profit" ', *ETL* 31:415–430.
Fox, M. V. (1977), 'Frame-Narrative and Composition in the Book of Qoheleth',
    HUCA 48:83–106.
——— (1986), 'The Meaning of *Hebel* for Qoheleth', *JBL* 105:409–427.
——— (1989), *Qohelet and His Contradictions*, Sheffield: Almond.
——— (1998), 'The Inner Structure of Qoheleth's Thought', in Schoors 1998a:
    225–238.
Fox, M. V., and B. Porten (1978), 'Unsought Discoveries: Qohelet 7:23–8.1a',
    HS 19:26–38.
Fredericks, D. C. (1988), *Qoheleth's Language: Re-evaluating Its Nature and
    Date*, Lewiston: Mellen.
——— (1989), 'Chiasm and Parallel Structure in Qoheleth 5.9–6.9', *JBL*
    108:17–35.
——— (1991), 'Life's Storms and Structural Unity in Qoheleth 11.1–12.8', *JSOT*
    52:95–114.
——— (1993), *Coping with Transience: Ecclesiastes on Brevity in Life*, Sheffield:
    JSOT.
——— (1996), 'A North Israelite Dialect in the Hebrew Bible? Questions of
    Methodology', *HS* 37:7–20.

—— (1998), 'Diglossia, Revelation, and Ezekiel's Inaugural Rite', *JETS* 41:189–200.

Frendo, A. (1981), 'The "Broken Construct Chain" in Qoh 10:10b', *Bib* 62:544–545.

Frydrych, T. (2002), *Living Under the Sun: Examination of Proverbs and Qoheleth*, Leiden: Brill.

Galling, K. (1934), 'Stand und Aufgabe der Kohelet-Forschung', *ThR* 6:355–373.

—— (1961), 'Das Rätsel der Zeit im Urteil Kohelets (Koh 3, 1–15)', *ZTK* 58:1–12.

Garfinkel, S. (2007), 'Qoheleth: The Philosopher Means Business', in K. F. Kravitz and D. M. Sharon (eds.), *Bringing the Hidden to Light: The Process of Interpretation: Studies in Honor of Stephen A. Geller*, Winona Lake: Eisenbrauns, 51–62.

Garrett, D. A. (1987), 'Qohelet on the Use and Abuse of Political Power', *TJ* 8:159–177.

Gianto, A. (1992), 'The Theme of Enjoyment in Qohelet', *Bib* 73:528–532.

Gibson, J. C. L. (1971), *Textbook of Syrian Semitic Inscriptions*, vol. 1, Oxford: Clarendon.

—— (1978), *Canaanite Myths and Legends*, Edinburgh: T. & T. Clark.

Gilbert, M. (1981), 'La description de la vieillesse en Qohelet XII.7, est elle allégorique?', VTSup 32, Leiden: Brill, 96–109.

Ginsberg, H. L. (1946), *The Legend of King Keret*, New Haven: Yale University Press.

—— (1950), *Studies in Koheleth*, New York: Jewish Theological Seminary of America.

—— (1952), 'Supplementary Studies in Koheleth', *Proceedings of the American Academy of Jewish Research* 21:35–52.

—— (1955), 'The Structure and Contents of the Book of Koheleth', VTSup 3, Leiden: Brill, 138–149.

Good, E. M. (1981), *Irony in the Old Testament*, Sheffield: Almond.

Gordis, R. (1946), 'The Original Language of Qoheleth', *JQR* 37:67–84.

—— (1949), 'The Translation Theory of Qoheleth Re-Examined', *JQR* 40:103–116.

—— (1952), 'Koheleth – Hebrew or Aramaic?', *JBL* 71:93–109.

—— (1954), *The Song of Songs: A Study, Modern Translation and Commentary*, New York: Jewish Theological Seminary of America.

—— (1955), 'Was Koheleth a Phoenician?', *JBL* 74:103–114.

—— (1960), 'Qoheleth and Qumran: A Study of Style', *Bib* 41:395–410.

—— (1965), *Ugaritic Textbook*, Rome: Pontifical Biblical Institute.

Gordon, C. (1965), *Ugaritic Textbook*, Rome: Pontifical Biblical Institute.

Hammershaimb, E. (1963), *On the So-Called Infinitivus Absolutus in Hebrew*, in D. W. Thomas and W. D. McHardy (eds.), *Semitic Studies Presented to G. R. Driver*, Oxford: Clarendon, 85–94.

Harris, Z. S. (1939), *Development of the Canaanite Dialects*, New Haven: American Oriental Society.

Hengel, M. (1974), *Judaism and Hellenism*, London: SCM.
Holm-Nielsen, S. (1974), 'On the Interpretation of Qoheleth in Early Christianity', *VT* 24:168–177.
Hurvitz, A. (1968), 'The Chronological Significance of "Aramaisms" in Biblical Hebrew', *IEJ* 18:234–240.
—— (2007), 'The Language of Qoheleth and Its Historical Setting within Biblical Hebrew', in Berlejung and Van Hecke 2007: 23–34.
Ingram, D. (2006), *Ambiguity in Ecclesiastes*, New York: T. & T. Clark.
Iovino, P. (2001), ' "Omnia vanitas". Da Qohelet a Paolo', in G. Bellia and A. Passaro (eds.), *Il Libro del Qohelet: Tradizione, Redazione, Teologia*, Milan: Paoline, 337–356.
Irwin, W. A. (1945), 'Ecclesiastes 8:2–9', *JNES* 4:130–131.
Isaksson, B. (1987), *Studies in the Language of Qoheleth*, Uppsala: Almqvist & Wiksell.
Isserlin, B. S. J. (1972), 'Epigraphically Attested Judean Hebrew, and the Question of "Upper Class" (official) and "Popular" Speech Variants in Judea during the 8th–6th Centuries B.C.', *AJBA* 2:197–203.
Janzen, J. G. (2008), 'Qohelet on Life "Under the Sun" ', *CBQ* 70:465–483.
Jarick, J. (2000), 'The Hebrew Book of Changes', *JSOT* 90:79–99.
Jenni, E. (1953), 'Das Wort *'olam* im Alten Testament', *ZAW* 65:1–35.
Johnston, D. (1880), *The Authorship of Ecclesiastes*, London: Macmillan.
Johnston, R. K. (1976), 'Confessions of a Workaholic: A Reappraisal of Qoheleth', *CBQ* 38:14–28.
Jones, S. C. (2006), 'Qohelet's Courtly Wisdom: Ecclesiastes 8:1–9', *CBQ* 68:211–228.
Kamano, N. (2002), *Cosmology and Character: Qoheleth's Pedagogy from a Rhetorical-Critical Perspective*, Berlin: de Gruyter.
Klopfenstein, M. A. (1972), 'Die Skepsis des Qohelet', *TZ* 28:97–109.
Koh, Y. V. (2006), *Royal Autobiography in the Book of Qoheleth*, Berlin: de Gruyter.
Koosed, J. L. (2006), *(Per)mutations of Qohelet: Reading the Body in the Book*, New York: T. & T. Clark.
Kottsieper, I. (1986), 'Die Bedeutung der Wz. *šb* und *skn* in Koh 10,9: Ein Beitrag zum hebr. Lexikon', *UF* 18:213–222.
Kropat, A. (1909), *Die Syntax des Autors der Chronik*, Giessen: Töpelmann.
Kruger, H. A. J. (1998), 'Old Age Frailty vs. Cosmic Deterioration: A Few Remarks on the Interpretation of Qohelet 11,7 – 12,8', in Schoors 1998a: 399–411.
Lambert, W. G. (1975), *Babylonian Wisdom Literature*, Oxford: Clarendon.
Lauha, A. (1955), 'Die Krise des religiösen Glaubens bei Kohelet', VTSup 3, Leiden: Brill, 183–191.
Laurent, F. (2002), *Les biens pour rien en Qohélet 5.9–6.6 ou la traversée d'un contraste*, Berlin: de Gruyter.
Lavoie, J. J. (2006), '*habel habalim hakol habel*: Historie de l'interprétation d'une formule celebre et enjeux culturels', *Science et Esprit* 53:219–249.

Leahy, M. (1952), 'The Meaning of Ecclesiastes 12:1–5', *ITQ* 19:297–300.

Lipinski, E. (1973), '*Skn* et *Sgn* dans le sémitique occident du nord', *UF* 5:191–207.

Loader, J. A. (1979), *Polar Structures in the Book of Qohelet*, Berlin: de Gruyter.

Lohfink, N. (1979), 'War Kohelet ein Frauenfeind? Ein Versuch die Logik und den Gegenstand von Koh 7,23–8,1a herauszufinden', in M. Gilbert (ed.), *La sagesse de l'Ancien Testament*, Gembloux: Duculot, 259–287, 417–420.

——— (1987), 'The Present and Eternity: Time in Qoheleth', *TD* 34:236–240.

Long, V. P. (1998), 'One Man among a Thousand, but Not a Woman among Them All: A Note on the use of *māsā'* in Ecclesiastes vii 28', in K. D. Schunk and M. Augustin (eds.), '*Lasset und Brücken bauen...*', *Collected Communications to XVth Congress of the International Organization for the Study of the Old Testament, Cambridge 1995*, Frankfurt am Main: Lang, 101–109.

Longman III, T. (1991), *Fictional Akkadian Autobiography*, Winona Lake: Eisenbrauns.

Loretz, O. (1964), *Qoheleth und der Alte Orient: Untersuchungen zu Stil und theologischer Thematik des Buches Qohelet*, Freiburg: Herder.

Lowth, R. (1770), *De sacra poesi Hebraeorum praelectiones*, Göttingen.

Lux, R. (1992), 'Der "Lebenskompromiss" – ein Wesenszug im Denken Kohelets? Zur Auslegung von Koh 7, 15–18', in J. Hausmann and H. J. Zobel (eds.), *Alttestamentlicher Glaube und Biblische Theologie: FS. Horst Dietrich Preuss*, Stuttgart: Kohlhammer, 267–278.

Lys, D. (1973), 'Par le temps qui court (Eccl 3.1–8)', *ETR* 48:299–316.

Macdonald, D. B. (1936), *The Hebrew Philosophical Genius: A Vindication*, Princeton: Princeton University Press.

Macdonald, J. (1975), 'Some Distinctive Characteristics of Israelite Spoken Hebrew', *BO* 33:162–175.

Machinist, P. (1995), 'Fate, *miqreh* and Reason: Some Reflections on Qohelet and Biblical Thought', in Z. Zevit (ed.), *Solving Riddles and Untying Knots*, Winona Lake: Eisenbrauns, 159–175.

Maussion, M. (2005), 'Qohélet vi 1–2: "Dieu ne permet pas..."', *VT* 55:501–510.

Meek, T. J. (1960), 'Translating the Bible', *JBL* 79:328–535.

Millard, A. R. (1981), 'Solomon in All His Glory', *VoxEv* 12:5–18.

Miller, D. B. (2000), 'What the Preacher Forgot: The Rhetoric of Ecclesiastes', *CBQ* 62:215–235.

——— (2002), *Symbol and Rhetoric in Ecclesiastes: The Place of Hebel in Qohelet's Work*, Atlanta: SBL.

Murphy, R. E. (1981), 'Qohelet's "Quarrel" with the Fathers', in D. Y. Hadidian (ed.), *From Faith to Faith*, Pittsburg: Pickwick, 235–245.

Naveh, J., and J. C. Greenfield (1984), 'Hebrew and Aramaic in the Persian Period', in *Cambridge History of Judaism*, Cambridge: Cambridge University Press, 1:115–119.

Ogden, G. S. (1979), 'Qoheleth's Use of the "Nothing Is Better Form"', *JBL* 98:339–350.
—— (1980), 'Historical Allusion in Qoheleth 4:13?', *VT* 30:309–315.
—— (1983), 'Qoheleth XI 1–6', *VT* 33:222–230.
—— (1984), 'Qoheleth XI 7–XII 8: Qoheleth's Summons to Enjoyment and Reflection', *VT* 34:27–38.
—— (1986), 'The Interpretation of *dôr* in Ecclesiastes 1.4', *JSOT* 34:91–92.
Pahk, J. Y. S. (1998), 'The Significance of *ašer* in Qoh 7,26: "More Bitter than Death Is the Woman, *if* she Is a Snare"', in Schoors 1998a: 181–203.
Palache, J. L. (1959), *Semantic Notes on the Hebrew Lexicon*, Leiden: Brill.
Peisker, C. H. (1962), *Hebräische Wortkunde*, Göttingen: Vandenhoeck & Ruprecht.
Perdue, L. G. (1994), *Wisdom and Creation: The Theology of Wisdom Literature*, Nashville: Abingdon.
Pinçon, B. (2008), *L'énigma du bonheur: Étude sur le sujet du bien dans le livre de Qohélet*, Leiden: Brill.
Pinker, A. (2008), 'The Principle of Irreversibility in Kohelet 1,15 and 7,13', *ZAW* 120:387–403.
Piotto, F. (1977), 'Osservazioni su alcuni usi linguistici dell'Ecclesiaste', *BeO* 19:49–56.
—— (2004), 'La descrizione degli elementi naturali in Qo 1,4–7. Problemi esegetici e linguistici', *BeO* 46:207–248.
Polzin, R. (1976), *Late Biblical Hebrew*, Missoula: Scholars Press.
Qimron, E., and J. Strugnell (1985), 'An Unpublished Halakhic Letter from Qumran', in J. Amitai (ed.), *Biblical Archaeology Today: Proceedings of the International Congress on Biblical Archaeology*, Jerusalem: Israel Exploration Society, 400–407.
Rad, G. von (1961), *Genesis*, Philadelphia: Westminster.
—— (1962), *Old Testament Theology*, New York: Harper & Row.
—— (1972), *Wisdom in Israel*, Nashville: Abingdon.
Ranston, H. (1925), *Ecclesiastes and the Early Greek Wisdom Literature*, London: Epworth.
Rendsburg, G. (1990), *Linguistic Evidence for the Northern Origin of Selected Psalms*, Atlanta: Scholars Press.
—— (1992), 'The Galilean Background of Mishnaic Hebrew', in L. I. Levine (ed.), *The Galilee in Late Antiquity*, New York: Jewish Theological Seminary of America, 225–240.
Rofé, A. (2003), 'The Wisdom Formula "Do not Say . . . " and the Angel in Qohelet 5.5', in C. Exum, H. G. M. Williamson and D. J. A. Clines (eds.), *Reading from Right to Left: Essays on the Hebrew Bible in Honour of David J. A. Clines*, London: Sheffield Academic Press, 364–376.
Rose, M. (1999), *Rien de nouveau: Nouvelles approches du livre de Qohélet*, Fribourg: Editions Universitaires.
Rousseau, F. (1981), 'Structure de Qohelet i 4–11 et plan du livre', *VT* 31:200–217.

Rubenstein, A. (1952), 'A Finite Verb Continued by an Infinitive Absolute in Biblical Hebrew', *VT* 2:361–367.

Rudman, D. (1997), 'Woman as Divine Agent in Ecclesiastes', *JBL* 116:411–427.

——— (1998), 'The Anatomy of the Wise Man: Wisdom, Sorrow and Joy in the Book of Ecclesiastes', in Schoors 1998a: 465–472.

——— (2001), *Determinism in the Book of Ecclesiastes*, Sheffield: Sheffield Academic Press.

——— (2007), 'The Use of לבה as an Indicator of Chaos in Ecclesiastes', in Berlejung and Van Hecke 2007: 121–141.

Salters, R. B. (1978), 'Notes on the History of Interpretation of Qoheleth 5,5', *ZAW* 90:95–101.

——— (1979), 'Notes on the Interpretation of Qoh 6,2', *ZAW* 91:282–289.

Savignac, J. de (1978), 'La sagesse du Qôhéléth et l'épopée de Gilgamesh', *VT* 28:318–323.

Sawyer, J. F. A. (1975), 'The Ruined House in Ecclesiastes 12: A Reconstruction of the Original Parable', *JBL* 94:519–531.

Schellenberg, A. (2007), 'Qohelet's Use of the Word ענין: Some Observations on Qoh 1,13; 2,23.26; 3,10 and 8,16', in Berlejung and Van Hecke 2007: 143–155.

Schoors, A. (1992), *The Preacher Sought to Find Pleasing Words: A Study of the Language of Ecclesiastes*, Leuven: Peeters.

——— (1998b), 'Words Typical of Qohelet', in Schoors 1998a: 17–39.

——— (2003), 'Theodicy in Qohelet', in A. Laato and J. C. De Moor (eds.), *Theodicy in the World of the Bible*, Leiden: Brill, 375–409.

——— (ed.) (1998a), *Qohelet in the Context of Wisdom*, Leuven: Peeters.

Schultz, R. (2005), 'A Sense of Timing: A Neglected Aspect of Qoheleth's Wisdom', in R. L. Troxel, K. G. Friebel and D. R. Magary (eds.), *Seeking Out the Wisdom of the Ancients*, Winona Lake: Eisenbrauns, 257–267.

Schwienhorst-Schönberger, L. (1994), *'Nicht im Menschen gründet das Glück' (Koh 2,24): Kohelet im Spannungsfeld jüdischer Weisheit und hellenistischer Philosophie*, Freiburg: Herder.

——— (1998), 'Via media: Koh 7,15–18 und die griechisch-hellenistische Philosophie', in Schoors 1998a: 181–203.

Scott, R. B. Y. (1971), *The Way of Wisdom in the Old Testament*, New York: Macmillan.

Segal, M. H. (1980), *A Grammar of Mishnaic Hebrew*, Oxford: Clarendon.

Seow, C. (1996), 'Linguistic Evidence and the Dating of Qohelet', *JBL* 115:643–666.

——— (1999), 'Qohelet's Eschatological Poem', *JBL* 118:209–234.

Serrano, J. (1954), 'I Saw the Wicked Buried (Eccl 8,10)', *CBQ* 16:168–170.

Seybold, D. (1978), '*hebel*', in *TDOT* 3:313–320.

Shaffer, A. (1969), 'New Information on the Origin of the "Three-fold Cord" (Hebrew)', *ErIsr* 9:159–160.

Shank, C. H. (1974), 'Qoheleth's World and Life View', *WTJ* 37:57–73.

Shields, M. A. (2000), 'Re-examining the Warning of Eccl. xii 12', *VT* 50:123–127.

—— (2006), *The End of Wisdom: A Reappraisal of the Historical and Canonical Function of Ecclesiastes*, Winona Lake: Eisenbrauns.

Shnider, S., and L. Zalcman (2003), 'The Righteous Sage: Pleonasm or Oxymoron? (Kohelet 7,16–18)', *ZAW* 115:435–439.

Smelik, K. A. D. (1998), 'A Re-Interpretation of Ecclesiastes 2,12b', in Schoors 1998a: 385–389.

Smend, R. (1977), 'Essen und Trinken – Ein Stück Weltlichkeit des Alten Testaments', in H. Donner, R. Hanhart and R. Smend (eds.), *Beiträge zur alttestamentliche Theologie*, Göttingen: Vandenhoeck & Ruprecht.

Sneed, M. (2003), 'A Note on Qoh 8,12b–13', *Bib* 84:412–416.

Spangenberg, I. J. J. (1998), 'A Century of Wrestling with Qohelet: The Research History of the Book Illustrated with a discussion of Qoh 4,17 – 5,6', in Schoors 1998a: 61–91.

Sperber, A. (1966), *A Historical Grammar of Biblical Hebrew*, Leiden: Brill.

Staples, W. E. (1943), 'The "Vanity" of Ecclesiastes', *JNES* 2:95–104.

—— (1955), 'Vanity of Vanities', *CJT* 1:141–156.

—— (1965), 'The Meaning of *hepes* in Ecclesiastes', *JNES* 24:110–112.

Strange, M. (1969), *The Question of Moderation in Eccl 7:15–18*, Washington, D. C.: Catholic University of America Studies in Sacred Theology.

Thomas, D. W. (1961), *Documents from Old Testament Times*, New York: Harper & Row.

Umbreit, F. W. C. (1818), *Koheleths des weissen Königs Seelenkampf*, Gotha: Becker'schen Buchhandlung.

Vanderkam, J. (1977), 'BHL in Psalm 2:5 and its Etymology', *CBQ* 39:245–250.

Van Hecke, P. (2007), 'The Verbs ראה and שמע in the Book of Qohelet: A Cognitive-Semantic Perspective', in Berlejung and Van Hecke 2007: 203–220.

Van Leeuwen, R. (1986), 'Proverbs 30:21–23 and the Biblical World Upside Down', *JBL* 105:599–610.

Verheij, A. (1991), 'Paradise Retried: On Qohelet 2:4–6', *JSOT* 50:113–115.

Waard, J. de (1979), 'The Translator and Textual Criticism (with Particular Reference to Eccl 2,25)', *Bib* 60:509–529.

Wagner, M. (1966), *Die lexikalischen und grammatikalischen Aramaismen im alttestamentliche Hebräisch*, Berlin: Töpelmann.

Waldman, N. (1979), 'The *dābār rā* of Eccl 8:3', *JBL* 98:407–408.

Watson, W. G. E. (1989), 'The Unnoticed Word Pair "Eye(s)"//"Heart" ', *ZAW* 101:398–408.

Webb, B. G. (2000), *Five Festal Garments*, Downers Grove: IVP.

Weisman, Z. (1999), 'Elements of Political Satire in Koheleth 4,13–16; 9,13–16', *ZAW* 111:547–560.

Weissflog, K. (2006), 'Worum geht es in Kohelet 8,10?', *BN* 131:39–45.

Whitley, C. F. (1978), *Koheleth: His Language and Thought*, Berlin: de Gruyter.

Whybray, R. N. (1978), 'Qoheleth the Immoralist? (Qoh. 7.16–17)', in J. G. Gammie (ed.), *Israelite Wisdom: Theological and Literary Essays in Honor of S. Terrien*, Missoula: Scholars Press, 191–220.

—— (1982), 'Qoheleth, Preacher of Joy', *JSOT* 23:87–98.

—— (1988), 'Ecclesiastes 1.5–7 and the Wonders of Nature', *JSOT* 41:105–112.

—— (1991), ' "A Time to Be Born and a Time to Die," Some Observations on Ecclesiastes 3:2–8', in M. Mori, H. Ogawa and M. Yoshikawa (eds.), *Near Eastern Studies: Dedicated to H. I. H. Prince Takahito Mikasa*, Wiesbaden: Harrassowitz, 469–483.

—— (1998), 'Qoheleth as a Theologian', in Schoors 1998a: 239–265.

Wilch, J. R. (1969), *Time and Event: An Exegetical Study of the Use of 'et in the Old Testament*, Leiden: Brill.

Willmes, B. (2000), *Menschliches Schicksal und ironische Weisheitskritik im Koheletbuch: Kohelets Ironie und die Grenzen der Exegese*, Neukirchen-Vluyn: Neukirchener.

Wise, M. O. (1990), 'A Calque from Aramaic in Qoheleth 6:12; 7:12; and 8:13', *JBL* 109:249–257.

Witzenrath, H. (1979), ' "Süss ist das Licht . . . ": Eine literaturwissenschaftliche Untersuchung zu Koh 11, 7 – 12, 7', St. Ottilien: Eos.

Wright, A. G. (1968), 'The Riddle of the Sphinx: The Structure of the Book of Qoheleth', *CBQ* 30:313–334.

—— (1980), 'The Riddle of the Sphinx Revisited: Numerical Patterns in the Book of Qoheleth', *CBQ* 42:38–51.

—— (1981), ' "For Everything There Is a Season": The Structure and Meaning of the Fourteen Opposites (Ecclesiastes 3,2–8)', in M. Carrez, J. Doré and P. Grelot (eds.), *De la Tôra au Messie: Mélanges Henri Cazelles*, Paris: Desclée, 321–328.

—— (1983), 'Additional Numerical Patterns in Qoheleth', *CBQ* 45:32–43.

—— (1997), 'The Poor but Wise Youth and the Old but Foolish King (Qoh 4:13–16)', *CBQ* 29:142–154.

Young, I. (1993), *Diversity in Pre-Exilic Hebrew*, Tübingen: Mohr.

Youngblood, R. F. (1986), 'Qoheleth's "Dark House" (Eccl. 12:5)', *JETS* 29:397–410.

Zimmerman, F. (1945), 'The Aramaic Provenance of Qoheleth', *JQR* 36:17–45.

—— (1949), 'The Question of Hebrew in Qoheleth', *JQR* 40:79–102.

—— (1973), *The Inner World of Qoheleth*, New York: KTAV.

—— (1975), *Biblical Books Translated from the Aramaic*, New York: KTAV.

Zuck, R. B. (ed.) (1994), *Reflecting with Solomon*, Grand Rapids: Baker.

THE SONG OF SONGS

To Carol, with whom I have learned,
and am learning, to love.

'Come now, my darling, my fair one.'
(Song 2:10)

'Many waters are not able to extinguish love,
And rivers cannot overflow it.'
(Song 8:7a)

AUTHOR'S PREFACE

Of all of the books in the Bible, the Song of Songs is the most poetic, the most beautiful and the most mysterious. Scholars vary widely on nearly every part of its interpretation, and expositors ponder its rightful place in theology and its relevant application to life. Virtually every verse presents challenges in text, philology, image, grammar or structure. Consequently, the Song has on the one hand inspired a vast body of commentary, but on the other hand has prompted many readers to abandon the effort to comprehend its meaning. In fact, at the same time that the scholarly literature on the Song has multiplied, the book has been virtually ignored in the preaching and teaching of the churches.

In this present commentary on the Song of Songs, I endeavour to interpret the ancient song cycle in terms of its literary genre as Hebrew poetry. In addition to attending carefully to its textual history, philology and grammar, I have examined as well its literary features, such as similes, metaphors, repetitions, contrasts, sound plays and structural devices. Throughout my exposition, I have sought to remain sensitive to the emotions the poet desires to reproduce in the reader.

One feature I have employed requires a word of explanation. Throughout the commentary, I have used the names Solomon and Shulammith to refer to the two major figures in the Song. By using the name of Solomon, I am not assuming that the writer of the Song was King Solomon, but only that Solomon is the literary persona used by the poet. Detailed discussion regarding the authorship of the book is presented in the introductory section of the commentary. I am also aware that the reference to the female character in Song 6:13 is probably a gentilic term, 'the Shulammite', rather than a personal name. I have chosen, however, to call her Shulammith in order to maintain a vivid sense of an individual person. To my thinking, the intense personal relationship between the two characters that is developed in the Song of Songs justifies taking this admitted minor literary licence in making reference to both of them by means of personal names, rather than using colourless labels such as lover and beloved, male and female, or man and woman.

The production of a book is not the accomplishment of an individual person alone. I am grateful to the series editors of the Apollos Old Testament Commentary, David Baker and Gordon Wenham, and to Philip Duce, Theological Books Editor at IVP, for their kind invitation to me to write this volume, and also for their support and assistance throughout the whole process of research, writing and editing. My copy editor, Eldo Barkhuizen, has done meticulous work in preparing the manuscript for publication. I have appreciated both his attention to detail and his affirming spirit. For the past twenty-five years I have taught the Song of Songs to classes at Linworth Baptist Church and Cedarville University, and the encouraging responses and penetrating questions of my students have prompted me to scrutinize the book more deeply. It would have been impossible for me to complete this project apart from a sabbatical leave granted by Cedarville University. I am particularly thankful to Duane Wood, Jack Riggs and Chris Miller for making that year of intensive research possible. During my time of study at Tyndale House in Cambridge, England, Bruce Winter was the consummate host, and the research fellows, visiting scholars and postgraduate students were a source of continual encouragement.

Words cannot express my profound appreciation to my children – Jonathan, Christiana (and Bill) and Joel (and Sharon) – who have been unwavering in their support for me and their interest in my research in the Song of Songs. My prayer is that they all will come to experience the quality of intimacy portrayed in the Song. My deepest gratitude goes to my wife, Carol, whose love for the Lord, for beauty, for literature, for life and for me are truly extraordinary. Throughout every hour of this long project she above all has been in my thoughts, and with all my heart I dedicate this work to her.

Daniel J. Estes

INTRODUCTION

1. CANONICITY

Among the early Jewish scholars, there is only scant evidence of any significant dispute regarding the canonical status of the Song of Songs, and indeed Rabbi Akiba exclaimed in the Mishnah that 'the world itself was not worth the day on which this book was given to Israel' (*Yadaim* 3.5). Aquila, Symmachus and Theodotian all included the Song in their collections, and by the time of the Babylonian Talmud (sixth century AD) the consensus of the rabbis was that the book was indeed part of the Hebrew Scriptures. It became one of the five festival scrolls read by Jews on the major holy days each year, with the Song of Songs read on the eighth day of Passover.

Because the Song was included in the Jewish canon, Christians adopted it as part of the OT. Bishop Melito of Sardis listed the Song of Songs in his collection of biblical texts in the late second century AD. None of the Church Fathers argued that the Song was of doubtful status.

There were, however, two questions raised that have been linked with the issue of the canonicity of the Song of Songs. First, the early rabbis discussed whether the books of Esther, Ecclesiastes and Song of Songs would defile the hands, and many of the rabbis concluded that the books would not have that effect. Although this has often been construed as a debate about canonical status, it is better to see it as a question of ritual uncleanness. The three books in question are distinctive in that they do not

269

contain the name of Yahweh. As Broyde (1995: 73) concludes, 'A close review of defiling of the hands reveals that it is linked at least partially to the presence of God's name in the text. These three scrolls were thus treated – according to those who deny that they defiled the hands – like short verses in the Bible that lacked God's ultimate name.'

The second question was prompted by the erotic content of the Song. In the fifth century AD, Theodore of Mopsuestia argued that the Song should be excluded from the canon of Scripture because it spoke explicitly of human erotic love (G. L. Carr 1982: 495). His position was condemned by the Council of Constantinople, which excommunicated him posthumously. In the sixteenth century, Sebastian Castellio raised similar objections to what he considered the lasciviousness of the Song, and for this reason was forced out of Geneva by John Calvin (Baildam 1999: 140). Within the Jewish community, there is indirect testimony from Rabbi Akiba that some people were treating the Song as erotic lyrics to be sung at banquets, and it is evident that the Song was typically interpreted allegorically as the love of Yahweh for Israel, but there does not seem to be any direct evidence rejecting its inclusion in the canon based on its erotic content.

It has often been claimed that the canonicity of the Song is due to its connection with the figure of Solomon. Just as Moses was viewed as the lawgiver and David the psalmist of Israel, so Solomon was the biblical epitome of wisdom (1 Kgs 3:12). The superscription in Song 1:1, 'The most excellent song which is of Solomon', according to this view, secured the Song's authority through its association with Solomon (Saebø 1996: 270). In that case, then, the Song could be viewed as wisdom literature, perhaps expanding on the theme of human erotic love found in Prov. 5:15–19 (cf. Murphy 1973: 422).

Because the Song has frequently been read as an allegory, many interpreters presume that its allegorical interpretation caused it to be included in the canon of Scripture. For example, Marsman (2003: 80) contends:

> The allegorical rabbinic exegesis has always maintained that the real protagonists of the Song of Songs are not Solomon and his wives, but God, as the groom, and Israel as the bride. The Targum to the Song of Songs exemplifies this type of exegesis most exuberantly. It is doubtful whether the Song would ever have been included in the canon were it not for this allegorical interpretation.

Fox (1985: 252) speculates that the Song began as secular lyrics, but their use in religious celebrations eventually prompted the religious leaders to legitimize them by reinterpreting them allegorically. This claim, however, is rejected by Barton (2005: 2), who argues persuasively, 'On the contrary, allegorical reading in ancient times was practiced precisely on books that had a high status.' He concludes, then, that allegory is not the *cause* of canonicity, but it is the *consequence* of canonicity. Moreover, D. M. Carr (1998b: 175–176) demonstrates from the early rabbinic writings that the allegorical approach did not supplant midrash in Jewish interpretation until the seventh century AD.

What is undeniable is that among both Jewish and Christian scholars there was an early and nearly unanimous acceptance of the Song of Songs as belonging in the biblical canon.

2. DATE

Interpreters have a wide variety of opinions regarding the date of the composition of the Song of Songs. The three major viewpoints are the time of Solomon in the tenth century BC, the time of Hezekiah in the late eighth century BC and the post-exilic period.

White (1978: 17) observes the numerous parallels in language and themes between the Song of Songs and the ancient Egyptian love songs from the New Kingdom period from 1550 to 1080 BC (cf. Foster 1974; Lichtheim 1976: 181–193). Goitein (1993: 63–65) argues from these parallels that the Song was composed during the reign of Solomon, who had diplomatic and marital connections with Egypt. On the other hand, Leick (1994: 68–69) points to the similarities between the Song and the Sumerian bridal songs from much earlier times (third–second millennia BC), which could possibly indicate that the Song followed a more general ancient literary pattern rather than being borrowed directly from the Egyptian texts (cf. G. L. Carr 1982: 495–496; Loprieno 2005: 108).

Additional support for the tenth-century date has been suggested by the localities cited in the Song. The geographical features mentioned include many sites located in the northern kingdom of Israel during the divided monarchy period, and this 'would be perceived as natural if the book were composed during the era when the borders of the Israelite kingdom were maximally extended' (Goitein 1993: 63) under the rule of Solomon. In addition, the wealth and tranquility of the age portrayed in the Song matches well the biblical depiction of the reign of Solomon, and the luxury items it cites fit well with Solomon's extensive mercantile activities (Rabin 1979: 216; cf. 1 Kgs 10:22–25); although Malena (2007: 182–183) argues from parallels in Ezek. 27 for a later, exilic date. Furthermore, G. L. Carr (1984: 18) suggests that several verbal parallels to the Ugaritic literature, as well as some archaic grammatical and linguistic forms, sustain a date around the time of Solomon.

The early Jewish tradition from the Babylonian Talmud suggests that the Song could have been written during the time of Hezekiah. At that time, the northern kingdom had already been taken captive by Assyria, which would allow for the references to the geographical features in that part of the land. In addition, the Assyrian policy of resettling captives from various countries brought an influx of refugees to Israel (2 Kgs 17:24–33), which could explain why the Song contains many traces of Aramaic, the international language of the ANE.

This was also a time when trade flourished between Israel and Arabia, facilitated for the most part by Aramean merchants (Brenner 1983: 79). Nissinen (1998: 624) argues that the closest Mesopotamian parallel to the Song of Songs is found in the Love Lyrics of Nabû and Tašmetu, which derive from the seventh century BC, the same time as when Assyria extended its political and cultural hegemony over Israel and Judah.

The predominant view among recent scholars is that the Song was composed during the post-exilic period, while the land of Israel was under Persian or Hellenistic rule. The vocabulary and grammar of the text appears to have several features that point to a post-exilic date. For example, the Song employs a high percentage of plene spellings, numerous Aramaisms, an apparent Persian term, a purported Greek word, and forms that are comparable to Mishnaic Hebrew. From this evidence, Dobbs-Allsopp (2005b: 71) concludes that the Song is written in late Biblical Hebrew during the time of the Persian, or Achaemenid, rule over Israel (539–323 BC).

This assessment, however, has its critics. Goitein (1993: 62) argues from the Babylonian Talmud Ḥullin 137b that Mishnaic Hebrew is not a late stage of Hebrew, but rather a local dialect of Hebrew that ran concurrently with the language of the Torah (cf. also Garrett 2004: 17). Young (1993: 161–162) argues reasonably that the apparent Persian loanword *pardēs* in 4:13 does not require a post-exilic date, but it could well have been an ancient term that entered several languages, including Hebrew, at an early time, and that 'appiryôn in 3:9 is not a Greek term, but instead is derived better from Sanskrit. Moreover, M. H. Segal (1962: 484) notes that as poetry the Song probably had a long history of oral transmission before it was reduced to writing, so that the late features of its language may be indicative of the date of its written form rather than its time of original composition.

In conclusion, the date of the Song is inextricably linked with several other questions, including its transmission history, the relationship between Israelite literature and texts in other ANE cultures, the authorship of the book and its unity. No one has yet made a convincing definitive argument for the date for the Song. The references to Solomon can be explained either as indicators of authorship or as part of the literary colouring of the Song. The mention in 6:4 of Tirzah, the early capital of the northern kingdom, is not necessarily conclusive evidence for an early date (Murphy 1990: 4; contra Garrett 2004: 20, 228). If the Song is an anthology or a song cycle, then it would be quite possible that the individual lyrics could have been composed over an extended period of time (Hubbard 1991: 257). Or, the unified Song could have originated early, perhaps even in the time of Solomon, and then been edited several times in the succeeding centuries, which would explain its unusual linguistic features (Fox 1985: 190). In view of this conflicting and incomplete evidence, it would be judicious to be cautious in claiming a definite date for the composition of the Song of Songs.

3. AUTHORSHIP

If the superscription in 1:1 were taken as a statement of the authorship of the book, then it would specify Solomon as the author, and the date would thereby be established in the tenth century BC. The Hebrew preposition *lĕ* plus a noun often does indicate authorship, but that is not its only or necessary meaning. It could in fact mean 'dedicated to', 'in the style of' or 'referring to', among other possibilities. This grammatical ambiguity has prompted interpreters to make a variety of observations about the plausible author of the Song.

In recent years, several scholars have argued from the data of the Song that its author in part (Murphy 1990: 70) or wholly (Goitein 1988; 1993; LaCocque 1992: 139–140) was a woman. Lavoie (2000: 76–77) notes that the woman character in the Song speaks almost twice as long as the man, and that she has both the first and the last word. Because the lyrics often reflect vividly the feelings of Shulammith, especially in 1:2–6, 3:1–4, 5:1–7, 10–16, Brenner (1985: 56) proposes that female authorship is a distinct possibility, although she also grants that 'there is no reason why a male author should not be able to recreate an authentic representation of female emotions through his psychological and poetic insights'. Several biblical oral texts were composed by women, including Gen. 21:16–17, 25:22, 29:35, 30:24, Exod. 15:21, Judg. 5:1–31, Ruth 1:8–9, 4:14, 1 Sam. 1:10, 12–15, 2:1–10, 1 Kgs 10:9 and Prov. 31, although Clines (2005: 99) rightly points out that there is no definitive evidence for female literacy in ancient Israel. Throughout the ANE, both poetry and prose were often composed and performed by women (Lavoie 2000: 80–81), and that possibility should be considered for the Song of Songs. At very least, the author manifests a remarkably insightful understanding of the feelings, desires and sensibilities of women.

The reference to Solomon in the superscription indicates that from an early date in its transmission the Song was connected in some way to him. The subject of human love is an integral element of wisdom teaching (cf. Prov. 5:15–19), and because Solomon is presented as the paradigmatic figure of wisdom in 1 Kgs 3:12, 4:29–34[5:9–14] it is unsurprising that his name would be connected with lyrics that extol love as God intended it to function (Childs 1979: 574; Saebø 1996: 270). It may then be, as Sparks (2005: 142) suggests, that 'Song of Songs is a wisdom text that took up and combined various love songs and then framed them to teach young Jewish women propriety in matters of love and sexuality'. In this view, the reference to Solomon is a link with the biblical wisdom tradition (Gledhill 1994: 22).

The traditional view, and the view still held by some scholars today (R. M. Davidson 2007: 561–569), is that the superscription is a genuine attribution of authorship to Solomon, which would mean that the text originated in the tenth century BC. Within the OT, authorship formulas are used to link Solomon with much of Proverbs, Ecclesiastes, Song of Songs and Pss 72 and 127. In addition, the late apocryphal book of Wisdom of Solomon is attributed to him, although it was definitely composed in post-exilic times. Within the Song of Songs, Solomon is mentioned seven times (1:1, 5; 3:7, 9, 11; 8:11–12), and the king is referred to more generally in 1:4, 12 and 7:5[6]. The Song seems to reflect a prosperous and peaceful setting, which would fit well with the glorious reign of Solomon, and it is evident that the writer is familiar with the opulence of the royal court. Tournay (1980: 8–9) notes several links between the Song and ancient Egyptian poetry and art, which could be explained by the commercial interactions between Solomon and Egypt (1 Kgs 10:28–29), as well as by Solomon's marriage to the daughter of Pharaoh (1 Kgs 7:8). Furthermore, in the Canticles Rabbah the deduction of Rabbi Jonathan was that the Song was the literary achievement of Solomon's youth, and that later in life he wrote Proverbs and Ecclesiastes (Dell 2005: 11).

Because of the grammatical ambiguity of *lĕ* in the superscription in 1:1, the author of the Song cannot be proven conclusively. In addition, it remains to be examined whether the Song was composed as a unity by a single individual, or if different hands wrote numerous lyrics that were brought together into an anthology by an editor. Although it is undeniable that the predominant point of view in the Song is feminine, that fact does not necessarily confine its authorship to a woman. The key to literary excellence is the ability to communicate convincingly through the characters in the composed text, and to do that writers must often reflect viewpoints of a gender, ethnicity, class, culture or economic status different from their own. In the case of the Song, the insightful portrayal of Shulammith is an indicator of superb literary artistry, but it does not necessarily indicate that the author was a woman.

The numerous explicit and implicit links between Song of Songs and the wisdom literature detailed by Dell (2005: 8–26) give strong support to the legitimacy of reading the Song as a wisdom text. The sapiential character of the book would in itself explain the references to Solomon without the necessity of taking Solomon as the actual author of the Song.

Another relevant factor that needs to be considered is the literary genre of the Song. If the Song were written as an imaginative poetic lyric rather than as a realistic autobiographical narrative, then the characters of Solomon and Shulammith could be regarded as idealizations of love. It could well be that their two names, both drawn from the *šlm* root that speaks of perfection or completion, indicate that the Song of Songs is intended to be read as an extended proverb (*māšāl*) of ideal intimacy instead of as the historical record of the relationship of two specific individuals.

4. INTERPRETATIONAL APPROACHES

The Song of Songs has prompted a wide variety of interpretations by both Jewish and Christian scholars. Alexander (1996: 14) provides a useful bibliography of surveys of the history of the interpretation of the Song. Succinct but substantive surveys of the various interpretative options can be found in Rowley (1965: 195–245), White (1978: 20–28), Murphy (1990: 11–41) and Garrett (2004: 59–91). In his massive commentary on the Song of Songs, Pope (1977: 89–229) presents an extensive history of the divergent understandings of the book. More recently, Pelletier (1989) and de Ena (2004) have compiled detailed analyses of the history of interpretation. In reflecting upon the longstanding interpretative challenge posed by the Song, Brettler (2006: 185) observes well:

> The statement that best encapsulates the problems of the Song of Songs is the simile attributed to Sa'adiya Gaon, the head of the Babylonian Jewish community in the tenth century: 'It is like a lock whose key is lost or a diamond too expensive to purchase.' ... Its magnificence is well recognized, yet it refuses to be unlocked (though many have claimed to have found its missing key).

4.1. Non-literal approaches

The history of the interpretation of Song of Songs has been heavily marked by non-literal interpretations, and in particular allegorical renderings of the meaning of the text. Allegorical interpretation seems to have originated in the Greek culture, as Theogenes allegorized the stories of Homer in order to go beyond their literal referents (Louth 1994: 242–243). The reinterpretation of the traditional Greek myths and legends in terms of philosophical concepts arose at least in part because of the problematic nature of the ancient stories, in that they were often violent, immoral or apparently devoid of positive ethical values (Menn 2000: 425–426).

Platonic philosophy and later Neoplatonism, both of which held to a dualism between the spirit and the material, were impetuses for allegorical interpretation in early Jewish and early Christian commentary. Harman (1978: 67) observes, 'If a dualism is maintained between body and spirit, with the body the lower element and the less spiritual, then it is easy to see how this would affect biblical interpretation in general and specifically the interpretation of a book such as this.' Origen, the most prominent early allegorist of Song of Songs, was influenced significantly by ascetic and Gnostic tendencies that viewed the material world as evil (Tanner 1997a: 27–28).

Allegory exploits the openness of imagery, which makes it amenable to reinterpretation (Kirsten Nielsen 1998: 182). By this means, it endeavours to develop culturally relevant messages from classic texts that originally said something else (Menn 2000: 426). Early Jewish and Christian interpreters found the sexual descriptions of the Song embarrassingly graphic, so they reinterpreted the language to make the book speak of a variety of other theological themes. This avoidance of the erotic language of the book continued to dominate the interpretation of the Song until recent times.

The earliest Jewish writings are nearly completely silent about the Song of Songs, with no indisputable references to it in the apocryphal literature, Wisdom of Solomon, Philo or Josephus, and only slight allusions to it in 4 Ezra (Stone 2007: 226–233) and Sirach (Lyke 2007: 59–60). In the Mishnah, Ta'anith 4.8 cites Song 3:11 in the context of a song of friends and lovers.

The Jewish midrashic literature contains three major works on the Song of Songs, Canticles Rabbah, Aggadat Shir Hashirim and Midrash Shir Hashirim. In these interpretative texts, the rabbis took individual verses from the Song and related them to a wide variety of situations (D. M. Carr 1998b: 175–176). As Kates (2006: 213) notes:

> The Song of Songs allowed the rabbis to read the history of Israel as a love story, to read the Torah as a dialogue of love between God and human beings. They enlisted the passionate energy, the sensual specificity and richness, and the erotic power of the Song's language into their quest to articulate their deepest and most intimate knowledge of relationship.

These selective biblical intertextual comments laid the interpretative groundwork for allegory, but full-blown allegory in the Jewish tradition came only several centuries after Origen popularized it among Christian interpreters.

The Aramaic Tg of the seventh or eighth century AD contained the first extended Jewish historical allegory of the Song, and it may have been written to counter triumphalist Christian readings (Dove 2000: 136–137). In contrast to the earlier midrashim, which consisted of eclectic anthologies of comments, in the Tg 'Israel's historical narrative emerges as the overarching structure for understanding the entire book of the Song of Songs from beginning to end' (Menn 2000: 424), that is, from the exodus from Egypt to the coming of Messiah. This systematic correlation of the text of the Song with the history of Israel became the archetype of historical allegory of the Song (Alexander 1996: 23).

Throughout the medieval period, the allegorical approach of the Aramaic Tg was followed by many subsequent Jewish commentators, including Saadia (tenth century), Rashi (eleventh century) and Ibn Ezra (twelfth century). In addition, the allegorical linkage of the Song with the exodus caused it to be read as the festal scroll for the eighth day of Passover. Furthermore, the book also was interpreted in mystical terms of the relationship between the Divine Shekinah and the individual soul in the thirteenth century Zohar (Green 2006: 214–227), and Maimonides developed from the Song an extended metaphor of the love of the individual pious soul for God (Blumenthal 1995: 83). His student Gersonides in the fourteenth century approached the Song as a philosophical allegory on the subject of epistemology.

Within the Christian community, Hippolytus (c. 170–236) and Origen (185–254) wrote continuous allegorical commentaries on the Song of Songs, thus beginning a long tradition of Christian non-literal interpretation of the book. D. M. Carr (1998b: 177) observes:

> Hippolytus and Origen are decisively different from their Jewish predecessors and contemporaries in one important respect: whereas datable Jewish interpretations tended to approach the Song atomistically and pluralistically, both Hippolytus and Origen inaugurated a tradition of attempting to master the Song through a continuous commentary form, in which a single allegorical approach or set of approaches was pursued verse by verse across a stretch of chapters.

It was not until the Aramaic Tg that the Jewish interpreters adopted this form of extended commentary.

Origen wrote two major works on the Song from somewhat different approaches (Nichols 2007: 237–262). His ten volumes of commentary (only four volumes of which are extant today) provide a mystical interpretation focusing on the love between Christ and the individual soul. His homilies are allegorical interpretations that focus on the relationship between Christ and the church. His approaches became two of the major lines of interpretation of the Song in the medieval period. What was especially significant was that Origen was 'the first patristic author positively to exclude any interpretation of the text that is not of a spiritual character' (King 2005: 38). His towering influence meant that among Christian scholars literal interpretation of the Song was for the most part abandoned for nearly fifteen hundred years.

Gregory of Nyssa (c. 334 to c. 394) viewed the Song as tracing the course of the soul as it progresses towards perfection. According to Gregory, 'the faculty of desire is placed in the soul to create a longing for God. The Song of Songs uses erotic images to excite this desire and train it to long for union with God who is beyond the grasp of all image and concept' (Laird

2002: 517–518). The Song, then, points to a union between the soul and God that is a continual quest that can never be totally satisfied (Louth 1994: 251).

Augustine (354–430) insisted that the love between Christ and the church is the literal meaning of the Song, and not an added allegorical understanding. M. W. Elliott (2000) provides a thorough study of Augustine's position and other Christological interpretations of the Song in the late patristic commentaries from 381 to 451.

In the medieval period, there are more Latin MSS of the Song than of any other biblical book, and more sermons on the Song than on all other books except Psalms and John (D. M. Carr 1998a: 413). Matter (1990) presents an extensive introduction to the medieval development of the subgenre of Song of Songs commentary, and Turner (1995) discusses usefully twelve medieval commentaries on the Song of Songs, ranging from Gregory the Great (590) to John of the Cross (1578). What is evident is that the medieval commentaries directed the erotic force of the Song towards spiritual objects (D. M. Carr 1998b: 177).

Three major lines of non-literal interpretation of the Song dominated the medieval writings. Ecclesiological readings, such as the commentary by the Armenian Gregory of Narek (c. 945–1003) and the *Glossa ordinaria* (early twelfth century) considered the Song as an allegory of the love between Christ and the church. The twelfth-century commentator Honorius Augustodunensis developed an unusual eschatological approach by which the Song foretells the conversion of the Jews to Christianity in the last days (Matter 2006: 242). Giles of Rome took a similar salvation-history approach to the Song, a position Dante adopted in his *Divine Comedy* (Pertile 2006: 268–269). Nicholas of Lyra (1270–1349) was a particularly prominent figure, because his *Postilla litteralis* was reprinted forty times, thus heavily influencing biblical interpretation in the late medieval period. Nicholas followed the earlier lead of Aponius (Pope 1988: 315–316) as he extended Rashi's exegesis of chapters 1–6 of the Song as an allegorical history of Israel by reading chapters 7–8 as the history of the church (Dove 2000: 135–136). In his view, the Song of Songs traces the relationship between God and his people, both Israel and the church.

A second line of interpretation began in the twelfth century in the writing of Rupert of Deutz (d. 1129) and others (Linardou 2004: 85). This Mariological approach saw the Song describing the love between Christ and the Virgin Mary.

The view found most frequently in the late medieval period is the mystical interpretation, in which the Song traces the spiritual progress of the individual soul, thus turning 'the eroticism of the Song toward a broader eros directed at God' (D. M. Carr 1998a: 425). In the twelfth and thirteenth centuries, this position was represented in the writings of Mechthild of Magdeburg, Hadewijch of Brabant and in particular in

Bernard of Clairvaux (1090–1153), who wrote eighty-six sermons on the initial portion of the Song. Murphy (1981: 514) observes:

> In the sermons Bernard demonstrates a wide-ranging knowledge of the Bible and of the human affection of love. He is not the technical exegete, nor does he rely on the allegorical method (which of course is not absent from the sermons). He ranges far and wide across the relationship of the individual person to God. In short, he is a mystic, and he writes for those who would use the Song for the purpose of knowing and loving God.

Later, in the sixteenth century, Teresa of Avila (1515–82) and John of the Cross (1542–91) used the Song to speak of the mystery of the union between the individual soul and the divine. In her *Meditations on the Canticle*, Teresa presents a basic text for her own spiritual progress (Götz 2004: 9).

Among Protestant interpreters in the Reformation period, even Luther and Calvin, who typically employed a literal hermeneutic, treated the Song as an allegory (Kiecker 2001: 126). Cocceius developed an extreme form of historical allegory in which he traced in the Song the history of the church up to the triumph of Protestantism over the papacy (Rowley 1965: 210).

The non-literal approach has dominated the study of the Song of Songs until relatively recent times, and is still held by some today, although with some different emphases. For example, Davis (1998) considers the Song, probably penned in the post-exilic period, as a highly imaginative evocation of the intense mutual love between God and Israel, and also the land of Israel. Hamilton (2006) argues that the Song was written in order to nourish hope in the messianic King who will overcome the curse and lead his people back to the Garden of Eden.

It is undeniable that the Bible contains some genuine allegories in Isa. 5:1–7, Ezek. 16 and 23, and Gal. 4:21–31, but they are marked as allegories by the biblical writers (Brettler 2006: 186). Within the OT, numerous passages refer to the love between Yahweh and Israel in the language of marriage, including Isa. 54:5–7, Ezek. 16:8 and Hos. 2:19–20. In the NT, similar imagery is used to speak of the love between Christ and the church in 2 Cor. 11:2, Eph. 5:22–33, Rev. 19:7–9 and 21:2, 9–10. Thus both the genre of allegory and the use of the marital image for the relationship between God and his people are attested in the biblical text.

It is important to distinguish between 'allegory' and 'allegorizing', the latter meaning to treat as an allegory a text that was intended to convey a literal meaning. As Munro (1995: 13) notes, the allegorical interpretations of the Song tend to read it through the lens of the prophetic metaphor of Israel as the unfaithful wife of Yahweh. What such interpretations teach may not necessarily be bad theology. In fact, 'such interpretations represent sublime truth that is legitimately taught elsewhere in the

Scriptures, but it has been imported by the interpreter into the Song of Songs' (Estes 2005: 398). Through allegorization, interpreters have used the imagery of the Song to articulate their own theological beliefs. Rather than starting from the intention of the text, they have read into it their own preconceptions. The sheer volume of such theological accretions to the text has typically obscured or rejected the literal meaning.

When a text is allegorized, there is no objective standard by which the accuracy of the interpretation can be measured. As Tanner (1997a: 30) observes, even though the allegorical method has dominated the interpretation of the Song, 'it suffers most from the novelty of suggestion and lack of consensus of meaning. The fanciful interpretations lack objectivity as well as any means of validation. This approach leads to numerous, differing interpretations that are limited only by the ingenuity of the commentators who write them (Garrett 2004: 74). Moreover, it fails to explain the detailed language of the text, in particular, the items cited in the songs of description. Terrien (1985: 35) reasons cogently:

> the imagery of the Song includes so many concrete allusions to the anatomy and physiology of the sexes and to the delights of erotic love, with precise references to the senses of touch, smell, taste, sight, and hearing, that the original poet could hardly have accumulated these motifs for a 'spiritual purpose'.

4.2. Typological approaches

The typological approach follows the pattern of allegory in developing spiritual parallels, but it seeks to maintain objective controls by retaining the literal sense as well (Parsons 1999: 402). Following the example of typico-prophetic messianic psalms, such as Ps. 22, typology affirms the historical setting of the text, but then shifts the focus of interpretation to a fulfilment in Christ. It is thus rooted in a theology of history 'according to which earlier events not merely match later events in formal outline, but are prophetic anticipations of them; they are in a certain way causative of the events which they anticipate' (Turner 1995: 107–108). Typology, then, claims that a double meaning was intended by the author, and it looks for links between the OT account and the NT event or teaching that it foreshadows (G. L. Carr 1984: 24).

The Bible does indeed use the language of human love and marriage to speak of the relationship between Yahweh and Israel in the OT (Lyke 1999: 211–212) and between Christ and the church in the NT. Wendland (1995: 48) justifies a fuller typological sense of the Song by arguing that 'the very superfluity and saturation of figuration would intimate that there is something more to the message, that is, over and above the celebration of a man's and a woman's love'. According to this view, the Song of Songs speaks of a human love, but in addition to that it is intended to serve as a pointer to the greater theological significance of the relationship between God and his people.

The text of the Song, however, gives no signal that it is intended to be read as a type, and the NT does not draw this connection, as it does with the typical messianic psalms, despite the strenuous effort by Mitchell (2003: 29–66) to adduce parallels between the Song and the NT texts. Even though typology claims an intended double meaning, in practice the spiritual dimension of Christ's love tends to drown out the literal message of human love (Parsons 1999: 402). Furthermore, typology invites the same kind of subjectivism that is the bane of allegorical interpretation.

4.3. Dramatic approaches

The dramatic approach to the Song of Songs was anticipated early in the Christian era, for the LXX MSS Sinaiticus and Alexandrinus, as well as some of the Old Latin MSS, supplied marginal notes in which they assigned verses in the Song to different characters (Clark 2005: 279). Hippolytus and Origen used these designations in developing their literal sense of a marriage song written by Solomon in the form of a drama.

It was not until the nineteenth century, however, that the dramatic view emerged as a challenger to the hegemony of non-literal approaches that had dominated the interpretation of the Song of Songs for well over 1,500 years. Delitzsch, in his 1875 commentary, presented the Song as a pastoral drama tracing the love of two characters. Although his view was adopted by many, and in recent times has been revived by Goulder (1986), a more popular approach was proposed by Ewald. Building from the earlier suggestion by Ibn Ezra, Ewald argued for a three-character drama, a love triangle featuring a young woman who is pursued by King Solomon, but despite all of his enticements he cannot win her love, and she chooses to remain true to her shepherd lover. This approach was popularized by S. R. Driver, who influenced many to accept it by including it in his introduction to the OT, which was long the standard in the field. In recent times, this understanding of the Song has been adopted in various forms by Mazor (1990), Cainion (2000), Hill and Walton (2000), Kaiser (2000), Provan (2001) and Stoop-van Paridon (2005).

Although the dramatic approach to the Song must be commended for its attention to the literal reading of the text, it does present some significant interpretative difficulties. As Brenner (1989: 71) has observed, there are no dramatic instructions in the Song, so the plot and the characters must be read into the text, thus introducing extensive subjective considerations. In addition, there is little evidence for dramatic literature among the Semitic peoples in general, and in particular among the Hebrews the genre is unknown (Bakon 1994: 218). Sendrey (1969: 463–464) argues reasonably:

one has to consider the all-round lack of historical evidence with regard to the existence of dramatic plays in Ancient Israel. As in the life of other ancient peoples, plays of this order would have constituted such important events in Israel's existence that they could not possibly have been passed in silence by biblical and post-biblical chroniclers. Josephus and Philo too make no mention whatever of Jewish theatrical performances.

The various dramatic interpretations of the Song vary considerably, which raises the suspicion that they may emerge more from the reader's speculation than from the text's meaning. Also, many of the dramatic renderings read as romantic stories that sound peculiarly modern. A major difficulty for the three-person drama is that it requires that the male speeches be divided between the king and the shepherd lover, a process that leaves the shepherd with very little to say. Even more problematic is that in some places Shulammith has to be construed as speaking *about* her shepherd lover when she is actually pictured as speaking *to* Solomon, which puts her in a rather awkward position (Garrett 1993: 359). Furthermore, in 1:12–14 the references to king and beloved seem to be speaking of the same person, and as V. Sasson (1989: 410) notes, in the Psalms, king and shepherd are both used as metaphors to refer to Yahweh, not to two distinct individuals. An additional difficulty is that the three-person approach necessarily makes Solomon a villain who tries to seduce Shulammith, which would conflict with his status as the exemplar of wisdom in biblical thought and later Jewish and Christian theology.

In view of these factors, it seems best to conclude with Dell (2005: 13) that 'the consensus of opinion seems to be that to read drama into the piece is actually to force it unnaturally into a shape that it doesn't naturally have'.

4.4. Cultic approaches

As ANE literary texts began to surface in the late nineteenth century and the early twentieth century, a number of poems with apparent similarities to the Song of Songs prompted several scholars to propose cultic approaches to the biblical text. In 1906, Erbt suggested that the Song was a collection of Canaanite poems describing the love of the sun god Tammuz and the moon goddess Ishtar. Meek (1922: 1–14) developed the cultic interpretation of the Song by appealing to biblical references to the Tammuz cult in Ezek. 8:14 and Zech. 12:11. This type of fertility cult was common throughout the ANE world, as evidenced by the Sumerian Dumuzi and Inanna (cf. Sefati 1998 for the definitive critical edition of the Dumuzi–Inanna songs), the Akkadian Tammuz and Ishtar, and the Canaanite Baal and Astarte/Anat. Kramer (1969: 89–90) argued that the Israelites adopted this cult from its neighbours:

As has been noted repeatedly by biblical scholars, traces of this fertility cult are found in a number of books in the Bible, and though the prophets condemned it severely, it was never fully eradicated. In fact, the prophets themselves did not hesitate to draw some of their symbolism from the cult, and the frequent descriptions in the prophetic writings of the relations between Jahweh and Israel as that of husband and wife indicate the existence of a Sacred Marriage between Jahweh and the goddess Astarte, the Canaanite counterpart of the Mesopotamian Ishtar-Inanna.

The closest literary parallel to the Song of Songs is no doubt the Assyrian love lyrics of Nabû and Tašmetu. As Nissinen (1998: 597) observes:

> Even a cursory reading shows the structural, metaphorical and literary affinity between the Love Lyrics of Nabû and Tašmetu and the Song of Songs. The overall structures of both texts have two significant features in common: the dialogical structure and the poetic form. Moreover, individual passages of both texts are analogous to a high degree, for instance those employing the *wasf* type of body description, the garden imagery, and the topos of the nocturnal yearning of the woman.

Throughout the ancient world, this kind of fertility ritual functioned as sympathetic magic that attempted to induce the gods to release their blessing upon the land (Rowley 1965: 224).

In evaluating the cultic approaches to the Song of Songs, it must be recognized that the literary parallels between the Song and the ANE cultic texts are rather general, and can be explained by the fact that all of the texts are speaking about love. Love lyrics throughout the world and in every epoch draw upon many common themes and motifs, so it should be unsurprising that the language of the Song is similar in some respects to the fertility texts. In addition, erotic language can be used to speak of both human love and divine love. Nissinen (1998: 626) observes:

> The love and eroticism of divine and human beings could be described and celebrated with the very same words, similar language of love could be used for the praise of gods as well as for pure entertainment; it could be interpreted in concrete or metaphorical terms. This was probably because love was understood as a divine attribute, and human love was expressed under divine patronage.

Whitesell (1995: 94–98) concludes that a close examination of the texts demonstrates that the Song actually subverts and rejects allusions to the

Dumuzi–Inanna myth. Similarly, Kirsten Nielsen (1998: 152) has pointed out that the characteristic motif of mourning in the ancient fertility rites is absent from the Song. From a broader theological perspective, pagan fertility rites were antithetical to Israel's exclusive allegiance to Yahweh, as the contest between Elijah and the prophets of Baal in 1 Kgs 18:20–40 pictures so emphatically. The notion of sacred marriage, therefore, would probably not have been remotely acceptable within the faithful Israel community (White 1978: 24). In view of this evidence, it is implausible that a song cycle extolling fertility rites would have been included as part of the biblical canon in ancient Israel.

4.5. Literal approaches

Although non-literal approaches dominated the interpretation of the Song of Songs throughout the ancient and medieval periods, there are some early references to a literal reading of the text. In the Mishnah, *Ta'anit* 4.8 cites Song 3:11 in the context of a song of lovers. Early Jewish commentary did not deny the literal meaning of the Song, but it constructed an allegorical meaning over it (Phipps 1988: 9), as was imitated later by the dual interpretation by Ibn Ezra (Murphy 1990: 31–32). Against those who discount these ancient literal readings, Sendrey (1969: 465) responds:

> The contemporaries of those who compiled the Canticles certainly understood better the basic character of the poems than did the later generations, whose minds were biased by its manifold allegorical and moralizing interpretations. The early readers of the Song of Songs have indeed taken the love poems in their literal meaning, and young men used to sing them as erotic ditties in wine houses. This attitude, naturally, constituted a 'sacrilege' in view of the canonicity of the book, a fact that aroused the raging ire of Rabbi Akiva (c. 132 C.E.), as we learn from the rabbinical literature.

Within the Christian community, Theodore of Mopsuestia (c. 360–429), in reading literally the erotic language of the Song, came to the position that the book should be excluded from the canon of Scripture because it was simply secular poetry in which Solomon extolled the daughter of Pharaoh. For this teaching he was declared a heretic by the second Council of Constantinople in 553. In 1544, Castellio came to much the same conclusion as Theodore, as he considered the Song immoral and unworthy of the canon, and consequently Calvin evicted him from Geneva.

Throughout the sixteenth to eighteenth centuries, there was an increasing emphasis on the literal meaning of the Song, although the literal sense was usually accompanied by additional meanings beyond the plain sense of the text (Corney 1998: 512). A significant step in the emergence of the literal approach as a major interpretative position came in 1693, when Bossuet 'developing an earlier, minor strand of tradition, suggested that the Song was nothing more than a celebration of the seven-day nuptials of Solomon and Pharaoh's daughter' (Alexander 1998: 19). This understanding of the Song was followed by Lowth, Percy and other leading scholars in the eighteenth century. In particular, Herder in 1778 described the Song as a collection of songs celebrating the joys of human erotic love (cf. the excellent monograph on Herder's work by Baildam 1999).

In the nineteenth century, Ginsburg (1857) built his influential dramatic interpretation upon a literal understanding of the Song. In 1873, Wetzstein drew specific parallels between the Song and the Syrian marriage customs he had observed, including a seven-day marriage celebration (cf. similar wedding celebrations in Gen. 29:27 and Judg. 14:12, 17) and descriptive catalogues of parts of the male or female body (*wasfs*).

The popularity of the literal approach continued to grow throughout the twentieth century, despite the notable exception of the allegorical treatment by Joüon. In the past generation, scholarly literature on the Song has predominantly taken the literal perspective, although other positions have also been proposed. Most of the major exegetical commentaries since 1990 view the Song as speaking of human love. Ayo (1997: 19) summarizes the situation: 'In twentieth-century criticism the reading of the Song of Songs as secular love poetry is widely accepted by biblical scholars as the primary place to begin even though further levels of meaning can be added to the literal reading of the text.'

Probably the key factor leading to the adoption of the literal approach is the evident linkage between the Song of Songs and the secular love poetry in the ANE. Fox, in an influential 1985 monograph on the Song of Songs and the ancient Egyptian love songs, argued from their extensive similarities that the Song is concerned with secular, sexual love. Nissinen (1998: 624) observes that love poetry was common throughout the ANE world, and that the parallels to the Song in theme, imagery and description are striking. Building upon Fox's study, Sparks (2005: 127–143) enlarges the discussion by presenting a summary and analysis of the parallels between the Song and the love poetry of ancient Mesopotamia, Egypt and Ugarit.

Within the OT, the Song of Songs is the only major example of love poetry, but there are several references (Jer. 33:10–11; Ps. 45) that suggest that songs were performed at wedding feasts. In addition, Kaiser (2000: 111), in discussing Prov. 5:15–23, observes that 'the metaphors used are so similar in some key places in Song of Songs that the presumption for similar concepts must be the first line of interpretive thought'.

Several objections have been raised against the literal approach of interpreting the Song of Songs. Barton (2005: 5–6) claims that there is no evidence that any ancient serious interpreter read the Song literally. The extant evidence, however, reveals that though the literal approach was indeed a minor voice until modern times, it is attested and implied in some of the ancient literature. Davis (1998: 540) is surprised that the Song has no happy ending, but it just stops in an open-ended way. In response, the theme of the Song is the continuing progress of intimacy, which is not a goal to achieve, but a star to guide and inspire the lovers. Thus the final lingering chord in 8:14 is a particularly appropriate way to end the Song. Finally, Patmore (2006: 243) objects that the themes that Fox finds shared by the Song and the Egyptian love literature are commonplaces found in the love texts of many cultures. His point is true in part, and that is what gives a sense of universality to the Song, but Murphy (1990: 46) rightly details the many specific features that justify the validity of Fox's conclusion:

> Like the biblical Song, the Egyptian poetry vividly portrays commonplaces of human sexual attraction and affection: intoxication with the beauty and charms of one's beloved, yearning for the lover's presence, love-sickness, the overcoming of natural and social obstacles to be together, the joys of physical intimacy, and the like. Moreover, the Egyptian and biblical works breathe a common atmosphere of sensual pleasures: seeing, hearing, touching, smelling, tasting. And the environments of love they depict similarly abound with perfumes, spices, fruits and flowers, trees and gardens.

In conclusion, there seems to be compelling justification to read the Song of Songs literally as a song of human erotic love. There may well be additional theological significance that can legitimately be drawn from the Song, but its primary meaning is centred in what it communicates about intimacy between a man and a woman.

5. LITERATURE

In contrast to law, which defines the divine stipulations for humans, narrative, which traces the history of God's people, or prophecy, which calls God's people back to his covenant requirements, the Song of Songs is poetry. In fact, the Song is the most thoroughly poetic book in the Bible, as it endeavours to recreate in the reader the experience of intimacy that permeates the book. More specifically, the Song is lyric poetry, rather than dramatic or narrative poetry, because it directs the attention inwards to feelings instead of outwards towards a plot (Linafelt 2005: 251).

In its quality, the Song of Songs is excellent poetry, and the poet's exquisite craftsmanship is seen in the text's rare vocabulary, striking metaphors and phonological features (Falk 1990: 106; Kirsten Nielsen 1998: 181). Hunt (1996: 70) observes well:

> Poetic richness ... can be partially dependent on compressed
> sensory images: the more senses involved in images, the greater
> the memorability of sensory experience to create a poetic land-
> scape. The imagery of *Canticum* is of the highest density of
> compressed sensory images, particularly used for evoking
> sensuality.

Poetry is notoriously difficult to interpret, and many biblical scholars
find themselves much more adept in working with prose. Part of the
problem in reading the Song of Songs can be traced to the priorities in
biblical scholarship over the past two centuries. Meyers (1987: 210)
explains:

> The critical tools honed and sharpened in the analysis of the
> pentateuchal, prophetic, and historiographic literature of the Bible
> have been inadequate to deal with a biblical book that differs in
> essential ways from the rest of the scriptural corpus. The poems,
> after all, are fundamentally secular in their celebration of human
> love. Biblical scholarship oriented towards religious meaning and
> development, not surprisingly, has been disadvantaged in its
> approach to literature that extols emotion derived from human
> response to another human rather than to God.

Poetry is also highly compact and compressed, for the poet exploits the
full range of lexical and phonological possibilities in creating a richness of
meaning (Fokkelman 2001: 151). The interpretation of the Song, then,
requires imagination and poetic sensitivity. The reader must enter imaginatively into the literary world constructed by the poet. Only those who are
willing to suspend their disbelief to enter into the ideational world of the
Song will be able to be sensitive to the emotions inherent within it.

A great poem will express excellent content through exquisite form. The
artistry of form, however, is not merely an ornament to draw attention to
itself, but is designed to enhance the communication of the poet's intricate
message (Wendland 1995: 46). Instead of using realistic description, the
Song employs a wide range of poetic images calculated to evoke the sensory
and emotional responses of the reader. In addition, numerous rhetorical
strategies are employed in order to draw the reader into the emotions of the
characters. For example, in 2:8 'behold' (*hinnēh*) suggests breathless and
immediate reporting of a scene, and in 2:8–9 a series of participles present
the action as occurring vividly. Throughout the Song, imperatives and
vocatives give the illusion of immediacy (Exum 1999a: 50–51). The poet
also uses many wordplays, both alliterations of consonants and assonances
of vowels, to suggest subtle nuances of meaning. The four extended songs of
descriptions use series of lyrical images 'to create in hearers an emotion
similar to the poet's own' (Grossberg 1989: 64).

Although the Song of Songs as a book of lyric love poetry is unique in the Bible, it bears significant similarities to poetry in various ANE cultures. Watson (1995: 254) presents a succinct bibliography of recent studies of the love lyrics from Sumer, Egypt, Assyria, Babylon and Ugarit. White (1978) and Fox (1985) have demonstrated numerous parallels between the Song and the Egyptian love lyrics of the New Kingdom period. Nissinen (1998), however, argues against Fox and suggests that the closest structural, metaphorical and literary parallels to the Song are found in the seventh-century BC Assyrian love lyrics. Although there are indeed many similarities between the Song and the love lyrics of other ANE cultures, some of these are the kinds of factors common to love poetry throughout history, and not necessarily indicative of direct dependence. In addition, the substantial differences should also be noted, for the Song without directly speaking of Yahweh situates its view of intimacy within the world view that permeates the OT. It is probably best to conclude that the poet of the Song of Songs was generally aware of love poetry in the larger ancient milieu, and that this knowledge no doubt influenced the language and images of the Song, but that the poet was not directly dependent upon any one particular document.

One of the most striking poetic features of the Song is its use of sensory images. These images are drawn from a variety of contexts, but in particular the realms of nature, architecture and horticulture (Walsh 1999: 130–131). All of the senses are employed, including sight, hearing, smell, touch and taste. For example, in 2:10–13 the language of springtime is evoked, as love is awakening Solomon and Shulammith to the joy and vividness of life. Just as nature is poised for new life at the onset of springtime, so this is the ideal time for the love of the couple to begin to blossom.

Some of the images sound strange to the modern ear because they belong to a culture and time considerably different from the present. For instance, describing a woman's hair as a flock of goats winding down Mount Gilead would hardly be considered a compliment today! In order to understand and appreciate the poet's use of the image, the reader needs to enter into the poet's world. This can often be done by reflecting upon other biblical uses of the image, the use of the image in comparable ANE love poetry, and by careful consideration of historical, geographical and horticultural data that illumine the language the poet employs. One also needs to be aware that many of the images in the Song are complex, in that they evoke multiple senses simultaneously (Grossberg 1989: 61). Landy (1987: 309) observes well:

> An image in the Song always evokes a combination of sensory qualities, which are selected according to their relevance in context, and of associations of ideas, deriving from common experience and literary tradition. Thereby it fulfills two functions – communicating the emotions of the lovers and reflecting upon their meaning and value.

The erotic subject matter of the Song could easily be debased into pornography in the hands of a less capable poet, but the Song ennobles its sublime theme by its poetic artistry. In the wedding-night scene in 4:12 – 5:1, while describing the couple's sexual foreplay, the poet's language is candid but not crude. The indirect images of a sealed spring and a locked garden that is at last entered are the poet's means of describing their first sexual intercourse. As Solomon and Shulammith approach that sublime moment, the language becomes more poetic and allusive, and yet the attentive reader is able to discern what the poet does not say explicitly. Four times in the Song (5:1; 6:13; 7:9[10]; 8:14) sexual intercourse is clearly implied rather than described in explicit terms, as though the focus of the camera shifts away from the action and the reader is left to imagine what the poem does not reveal directly. Ayo (1997: 19) accurately assesses the artistry of the Song:

> The Song presents very erotic poetry, although it is never lascivious. The erotic quality of the love depicted is always reverent and respectful of the dignity of the beloved. It never descends to the objectification of the body characteristic of pornography. Though the Song is sensual, it is never prurient. The imagery never depicts sexual intimacy without the veil of indirection, circumlocution, or allusion. Although it is straight-forward and unabashed in its celebration of the human body, the Song remains modest and persistent in its awareness that to reveal less is to reveal more. Sexuality thrives not only on open disclosure but also on further hidden mysteries.

6. UNITY

In considering how the whole Song fits together, scholars have come to a wide diversity of positions regarding the coherence of its collection of lyrics. Hwang (2003: 97) observes:

> Some believe that the Song has an 'overarching macrostructure' and they have divided the Song into five to nine poems. Others argue that there is no substantial connection between the micro-structural units, and they usually divide the Song into a large number of poems, and the collection of these semantically unrelated poems is called an anthology.

Gordis (1974) argues that the Song is an anthology of works written over five centuries of Israel's history. Falk (1990) finds thirty-one pieces that are unified only by the literary conventions of ancient Hebrew poetry. Kirsten Nielsen (1998: 182) contends that the man and the woman are not a specific couple, but rather represent any man and woman in love. One of the most extreme positions is that of Landsberger (1954: 215–216), who takes an atomistic approach that divides the Song into many very short fragments of unrelated love poems that speak of different people and situations. Similarly, Krinetzki (1981) finds fifty-two lyrics, which he divides into six groups.

There does, however, seem to be significant evidence pointing to some kind of unity in the Song. The primary reference of 'song of songs' in 1:1 is probably an evaluation of its superlative quality, but, as R. M. Davidson (2003: 44) and Garrett (2004: 26) suggest, it may well also secondarily indicate that the text is a unified Song consisting of several individual lyrics, that is, a song cycle. The content of the Song also implies that it is a unity. The Song is marked by a pattern of dialogue that draws its lyrics together (Murphy 1977: 488). In addition, the basic character portrayal is consistent throughout the Song to such an extent that 'even commentators who see the Song as an anthology tend to read it as though its attitude toward love is uniform and the protagonists are the same two people throughout' (Exum 2000: 29). Furthermore, a common world of imagery permeates the lyrics of the Song (Murphy 1990: 3). The Song abounds with repeated expressions that function as literary connections between the individual poems, and thus reflect the appearance of deliberate design, so that Rowley (1965: 222) concludes, 'The repetitions that occur leave the impression of a single hand, and there is a greater unity of theme and of style than would be expected in a collection of poems from several hands, and from widely separated ages.' The closing section of the Song in 8:5–14 features the final appearances of the prominent characters and themes of the book, and by this means brings a sense of closure to the song cycle. These factors when viewed together suggest that the Song of Songs is a more unified text than are the biblical anthologies contained in Psalms and Proverbs or the classical Greek and Latin anthologies (Garrett 2004: 30).

But what kind of unity is it that draws together the Song? The dramatic approach argues for narrative unity with an explicit linear storyline. It has already been demonstrated, however, in the discussion of the dramatic interpretational approach, that the Song does not present a complete narrative development. Although there may well be a faint narrative line that can be traced throughout the Song, D. M. Carr (1998a: 421) is accurate when he contends that 'there is no clear plot or logical sequence. All attempts to find a linear drama in the Song have failed to gain consensus.'

The data in the Song can better be explained in terms of the literary unity of an impressionistic song cycle. The frequent refrains, parallel scenes and inclusios suggest a degree of conscious literary organization and unity. There also seems to be a loose temporal progression from youth to old age, with a parallel progression of maturity in intimacy between Solomon and Shulammith that functions as a literary plot for the Song (cf. Exum 1999a:

60). The related songs in the cycle only suggest the overall storyline, but do not fill in the details as a true narrative would. The Song, instead, is an impressionistic song cycle that celebrates intimacy as it progresses from early attraction into maturity. Ayo (1997: 17) insightfully likens the Song to a quilt or a picture album that presents its message in an indirect and impressionistic manner:

> The Song of Songs presents a quilt of many colors and of a rich texture, a variegated mosaic made of many-splendored fabrics. Here is an intimate family album of courtship days made up of many candid photos arranged to allow the viewer to see the picture quickly. Here is no well-wrought novel from beginning to end, but rather a collection of epistles and episodes, moments of lovetalk and snapshots beyond description, a love story line as old as woman and man and as fresh as the ineffable yearning for divine love that wells up within the human breast today as yesterday. The Song of Songs is thus a patterned quilt with pieces of poetry that are pieces of the life of a woman and a man in love.

7. STRUCTURE

Because the issues of unity and structure are intertwined, it is not surprising that scholars have taken many different positions on the structure of the Song of Songs. Mariaselvam (1988: 45) presents a chart of twenty-one published positions of the structure of the Song, ranging from five to fifty-two units in the book. It is evident that one's interpretation of the Song begins with a view of its organizing structure. The four major alternatives are (1) an atomistic approach, in which there is no intended structure; (2) a chiastic or recurrent pattern of structure; (3) a linear or narrative structure; or (4) an impressionistic or poetic structure. Underlying all of these positions is the methodological question of how structural units are determined. In a recent study, Roberts (2007) has analysed the wide variety of Hebrew textual features that combine to signal the opening, closure and cohesion of lyrical units, thus pointing the way towards a more objective consideration of the structure of the Song.

The *atomistic* approach is championed by Landsberger (1954) and Falk (1990). Both of these scholars view the Song as containing a high number of unrelated lyrics that have been brought together into an anthology. In this view, there is no intentional organizing structure to the book.

Numerous recent interpreters have proposed *chiastic* structures for the Song. The chiastic approach finds intricate patterning across the whole book, particularly of the ABCBA kind. Some key proponents of this form of structure in the Song are Shea (1980), Webster (1982), G. L. Carr (1984), Dorsey (1999), R. M. Davidson (2003), Garrett (2004) and Exum

(2005c). This approach does indeed yield many interesting observations that can enhance appreciation of the literary artistry of the Song. It is troubling, however, that there are many significant variations among the competing chiastic proposals. If the organizing structure of the Song were indeed chiastic, then it seems as though its details should be able to be replicated with greater consensus by independent analyses. Hwang (2003: 104–105) goes to the heart of the issue:

> A number of scholars have made attempts to find the chiastic structure in the Song, but they have failed to generate wide acceptance. The key problem is that the sizes and numbers of both the micro-structural and the macro-structural units vary significantly. Their disagreement over the sizes and numbers of various units arouses suspicion among scholars that some form of subtle manipulation of the evidence is necessary to make their patterns work.

Viewing the structure of the Song in a linear fashion leads to the attempt to find an explicit narrative that is the backbone of the book. This approach is developed in greatest detail by the various dramatic interpretations of the Song. Wendland (1995: 35–46) presents a detailed literary-structural analysis in which he sees the book progressing towards two peaks, in the garden scene in 4:16 – 5:1 and in the statement on the supreme value of love in 8:5–7.

Although an implicit temporal and thematic development can be traced in the Song, the linear approach seems to require a degree of precision that exceeds the actual data of the text. Thus it seems better to structure the Song in an impressionistic or poetic way. The thematic centre of the Song is found in 4:16 – 5:1, where Solomon enters Shulammith's garden for the first time. The first half of the Song builds towards this moment when the couple first experience sexual intimacy on their wedding night. The second half of the book reveals how their intimacy continues to grow and deepen as the couple explore the joys and challenges of drawing closer together within the bounds of their marriage relationship. The refrains with subtle but significant variations in 2:16, 6:3 and 7:10[11] provide textual support for the progress in their sense of mutuality, which is a primary factor in intimacy. The final two verses, with open-ended invitation to the continued enjoyment of love, form a fitting climax to a song cycle that traces the progress of intimacy. In an impressionistic manner, the Song traces the awakening of intimacy leading up to marriage in 1:1 – 3:11, the celebration of intimacy on the wedding night in 4:1 – 5:1 and the maturing of intimacy within marriage in 5:2 – 8:14. Rather than presenting a detailed, explicit plot line, the Song uses a collage or kaleidoscope of scenes that suggests a story (cf. Wagner 2007: 548) in a fashion analogous to the impressionistic paintings of Monet and the impressionistic music of Debussy.

8. THEME

Apart from the superlative use of the divine name in 8:6, there is no explicit reference to God in the Song of Songs, although R. M. Davidson (2005) has argued plausibly for several implicit references to God. Nevertheless, the Song speaks of a key theme in God's overall plan for humans, because when the Song is read literally, it links sexuality and spirituality in a profound way. As D. M. Carr (1998b: 413) observes, the message of this ancient song cycle addresses a major need in the contemporary world:

> Today, however, the Song of Songs has at best a peripheral place in our culture. This is unfortunate not only because it means that we have lost touch with a vital element of our heritage, but also because the Song, properly understood, can help us to overcome the separation between sex and spirituality that is a hallmark of our society, can help us to learn what it means to be a whole person in the world.

By this means, the Song counters the longstanding and false dichotomy between the physical and the spiritual that has often been a major influence upon Christian doctrine and practice. Garrett (2004: 102) observes insightfully, 'The Song achieves something that medieval Christian culture could not fathom and that modern and postmodern culture cannot artfully attain: a man and a woman who maintain passionate desire for each other in the context of conventional morality.'

The association with Solomon in 1:1 suggests that the Song may be rooted in the Hebrew wisdom tradition (Sparks 2008: 284), of which Solomon was regarded as the prototype. In fact, its connection with Solomon encourages the interpreter to read it 'in the light of the wisdom traditions and their reflections about how God made the world and what is good for humanity' (Kirsten Nielsen 1998: 181). After a careful analysis of Song of Songs and Proverbs, Dell (2005: 20) concludes that there are indeed extensive connections between the two books, and Sadgrove (1979: 248) extends the parallels to include the other wisdom texts as well. For example, when Wisdom speaks in Sir. 24.13–17, it clearly echoes the language of the Song of Songs (Lyke 2007: 59–60).

In specific terms, the Song of Songs employs many of the same images as in Prov. 5:15–19. As Grossberg (1994) has noted, Prov. 1 – 9 presents two contrasting pictures of sexuality, but its major focus is on warning against the strange woman and her enticements leading away from wisdom and life. The positive encouragement in Prov. 5:15–19 to enjoy fully one's wife, and in particular the sexual delights that may be found in her, is developed in much greater detail in the Song of Songs. The Song, then, in effect serves as a commentary on the wisdom instruction in Prov. 5:15–19, as in both texts the wisdom teacher extols the delight that can be found in emotional and sexual intimacy within the marriage relationship.

It is possible that the final words in Song 5:1, 'Eat, O friends, drink and become intoxicated, O lovers!', are an invitation by God encouraging Solomon and Shulammith to enjoy fully the sexual feast that they have just sampled for the first time. This echoes the divine command to the first human couple in Gen. 1:27–28 to be fruitful and multiply in a world that was described as very good (Gen. 1:31). In this light, the Song 'celebrates the human capacity to love as ordered by the creator' (White 1978: 134).

The biblical texts speak of many aspects of love, but the Song of Songs is distinctive in its extensive, although not exclusive, attention to the erotic aspects of love within the marriage relationship. The language of sexuality is often used in a figurative way in prophetic denunciations of idolatry and political alliances (Ezek. 16; 23), as well as literally to condemn immoral behaviour (Deut. 22:13–29). Only rarely does the Bible speak of erotic love in a positive light, as it does in Prov. 5:15–19. In the Song of Songs, however, the key theme is that erotic intimacy within marriage is God's good and sacred gift to be enjoyed, nurtured and protected. In God's design, sexual delight is a profound part of the richness of the marriage relationship.

By focusing upon erotic love within the marriage relationship, the Song presents a stark contrast to the debased moral standards that prevailed in the ANE world. In addition, the Song also was countercultural in that it viewed marriage not as an economic contract or merely for the purpose of procreation, but primarily as the rightful context for the sexual pleasure and fulfilment of the couple. As Terrien (1985: 48) observes, 'The poet of the Song of Songs is not embarrassed by the pleasure of the two lovers. There is no shame, no sin of the flesh as such, and carnal love is celebrated in terms of wonderment beyond the limitation of natural phenomena.' The wedding-night scene in 4:8 – 5:1 is replete with delight in sexual foreplay leading into intercourse, and the metaphor of eating and drinking that concludes this tender episode reflects 'the nourishment, delight and satisfaction desired from and found in each other' (Payne 1996: 329).

Although the Song of Songs clearly speaks about sexuality, its overarching theme is intimacy and its development within a loving relationship. Intimacy speaks of the drawing together of two people into a closeness that entails emotional, psychological and physical dimensions (R. M. Davidson 2007: 601–602). Thus the Song begins with a note of yearning by Shulammith for Solomon (1:2), and then throughout the song cycle 'there is a dynamic movement of longing that becomes a structural principle in the poem as it moves forward incrementally from one stage of yearning to the next' (Fisch 1988: 86).

The first three chapters of the Song are dominated by the language of desire. Many scholars have presumed from the statements in passages such as 1:4, 13, 17, 2:4–6, 17 and 3:4 that Solomon and Shulammith are involved in lovemaking and sexual activity from the beginning of the Song. The language in chapters 1–3, though it certainly expresses their intense longing for sexual intimacy, does not require the consummation of their sexual relationship prior to their wedding night. In fact, if the Song were to celebrate premarital sexual activity, it would fly in the face of the rest of the OT, in which such behaviour is proscribed. Schwab (2002: 132) observes rightly, 'The attitude of the Hebrews towards virginity and marriage would prejudice a reader of the Song of Songs to see in it a celebration of wedded bliss, not of premarital sex. . . . The loss of virginity outside of marriage is not something that the Hebrews would have celebrated.' At times when Shulammith's desires are especially highly aroused, so that she longs to be embraced and fondled by her lover, her emotions are checked in 2:7 and 3:5 by the caution 'Do not incite or excite love until it is pleased.' It is also noteworthy that in 3:3 and 5:7 the watchmen patrolled the city in part to prevent and punish illicit sexual behaviour, because in ancient Israel 'free and unrestricted sexuality was taboo' (Fokkelman 2001: 190). No doubt there were incidents of premarital sexual activity in ancient Israel (cf. 2 Sam. 13:1–14), but it was considered illicit and disgraceful (cf. Deut. 22:13–29). In view of the broader OT evidence, White (1978: 27) is on firm ground in concluding that 'the Song must be interpreted in light of the Israelite social ethic and cannot, therefore, be understood as a tract justifying pre-marital sexual intercourse'.

If the structure of the Song of Songs is viewed as an impressionistic unity with general temporal development, then several textual details support the virginity of Shulammith on her wedding night. None of these points in itself is conclusive, but when taken together the data builds a strong probable cause for her virginity up until 4:16 – 5:1. The first of four songs of descriptions in the Song occurs in 4:1–5, which follows immediately the procession of Shulammith in 3:6–10 and the invitation in 3:11 to view Solomon on the day of his wedding. The language in this *waṣf* is much more explicit and erotic than anything that Solomon has said up to this point in the Song, but it is echoed in the subsequent songs of description in the second half of the song cycle.

The references to Shulammith's veil (*ṣammâ*) in 4:1, 3 are debated, but this rare term could well denote her wedding attire. As van der Toorn (1995: 332) states, the wedding veil functioned as 'a symbol of chastity to be lifted at the consummation of the marriage'. It is also interesting to note that the term for 'bride' (*kallâ*) is used only in 4:8–12 and 5:1, which could suggest that Shulammith and Solomon have by this time been married (although like 'sister', it could rather be used in a figurative sense).

In 2:17, Shulammith expresses her desire that Solomon fondle her breasts all night until the daybreak, but the text does not record any positive response by Solomon to her invitation. By contrast, in 4:6, Solomon echoes her previous words and then expresses his resolve to do what she requested from him:

Until the day breathes and the shadows flee,
I will eagerly go to the mountain of myrrh and the hill of
frankincense.

After the record of Solomon's proposal of marriage to Shulammith in 2:10–13, he pictures her in 2:14 as a dove in the concealed places in the cliffs. This language of hiddenness and inaccessibility is echoed in 4:8, when he calls her to come with him from the remote region of Lebanon and from the dens of lions and the mountains of leopards. Coming after the song of description in 4:1–5 and before their lovemaking in 4:12 – 5:1, Solomon's language may well reflect his sensitivity to Shulammith's fears as she enters into the new experience of sexual intimacy.

As they prepare to make love, Solomon in 4:12 describes Shulammith as a locked garden and a sealed spring. When this language is compared with Prov. 5:15–19, there is a strong likelihood that it is intended to refer to her chastity on their wedding night. It is only in 4:16 that Shulammith calls on the north wind and the south wind to awaken and blow on her garden, because now (contra the contexts in 2:7 and 3:5) it is the right time for love to be excited. Shulammith also invites Solomon to come into her garden that has up to this time been locked against all intruders, and then in response to her invitation Solomon exclaims in 5:1, 'I am coming into my garden, O my sister, O bride'.

A final interpretative indicator of Shulammith's virginity on her wedding night may be implied in 8:10. If the metaphors of a door and a wall in 8:9 refer respectively to the prospects of Shulammith's sexual accessibility or sexual inaccessibility, then her exclamation that she was a wall when her breasts became towers would indicate that when she reached the age of sexual maturity she was still sexually pure. It was at that time that she found šālôm, that is, genuine intimacy, in Solomon.

The Song of Songs is not a modern romantic movie that builds towards the moment of sexual intercourse, nor is it a fairy tale in which the characters overcome obstacles until they get married and live happily after. Rather than focusing upon sex or marriage, the major theme of the Song is the maturing of intimacy in its full sense, not just in its sexual aspects, that leads into the commitment of marriage and then continues to grow within the marriage relationship. The second half of the Song reveals how Solomon and Shulammith overcome challenges to the continued growth of their intimacy after their wedding, and how as a result they are able to achieve deeper maturity in their love.

Chapters 5 and 6 form an extended scene in which their intimacy is threatened by indifference (5:3), but then rekindled by appreciation and gratitude (5:16). When the couple are reconciled, their progress in intimacy is marked by increased spontaneity and confidence in lovemaking, because they have grown in their sexual and psychological unity (7:9[10]). The threefold refrain with subtle but significant variations in 2:16, 6:3 and

7:10[11]) is a textual clue that their growing sense of mutuality is replacing their previous self-interest.

In the final chapter of the Song, Shulammith expresses in 8:10 what is in reality a microcosm of the book: she was a wall (her virginity before marriage), her breasts became towers (she came to the point of sexual maturity) and then she found šālôm (intimacy with Solomon). By this means, Shulammith discloses the sense of wholeness and completeness that she has found in an intimate marital relationship blessed by God. The lingering chord with which the Song ends in 8:14 suggests that the delight in intimacy that Solomon and Shulammith have found continues to become richer and deeper over a lifetime.

Although the Song of Songs seems in many ways to breathe the air of paradise, it is also realistic about the threats to the achievement of genuine intimacy. Solomon and Shulammith have to contend with strong desires and drives for sexual union before it is the right time (2:7; 3:5). As Exum (1998: 245–246) expresses well, 'Desire in the Song of Songs seems to be always already anticipating its satisfaction, the poetry continually capturing a moment of tension, of arousal on the brink of fulfillment.' In 2:15, Shulammith discloses her fear of the little foxes that are devastating the vineyards, that is, young men who are eager to violate young woman as they arrive at the time of sexual maturity. In 3:7–8, Solomon provides an armed guard to protect his bride from an unspecified danger in the nighttime. Shulammith's insensitive response to Solomon in 5:3 reveals how indifference and selfishness can dull love and derail intimacy. Throughout the Song, then, intimacy must contend with both internal and external factors that conspire against it.

In tracing the growth in intimacy between Solomon and Shulammith, the Song of Songs presents in literary picture what it teaches by principle in 8:6–7 about the nature of love. This wisdom saying near the end of the song cycle is the only directly didactic statement in the Song (Exum 2005b: 79), but actually the Song indirectly teaches much about what love is and what love can accomplish.

Both Solomon and Shulammith speak of the exclusivity of love, the intense loyalty that is directed towards one person alone. Webb (1990: 97–98) observes:

> Read as the single poem that it is, the Song is not about love in an abstract sense. Nor is it about a whole series of casual love encounters. It is about love between two people who are deeply committed to each other. It is this context of commitment which saves their love from being exploitative and enables it to surmount difficulties and move on to mature consummation.

To Solomon, Shulammith is unique (6:9). She, in turn, discloses that she has reserved for him all of her sexual pleasures (7:13[14]). The exclusive commitment of their love for one another expressed by the figure of a seal of ownership in 8:6 coheres with the wisdom admonition in Prov. 5:15–17 (NIV):

> Drink water from your own cistern,
>   running water from your own well.
> Should your springs overflow in the streets,
>   your streams of water in the public squares?
> Let them be yours alone,
>   never to be shared with strangers.

Love in the Song of Songs is especially marked by mutuality. In contrast to Proverbs, in which masculine perspectives predominate, the Song has an intense focus on the woman's perspective, with the majority of lines spoken by her. As Goitein (1993: 59) observes, in the Song the reader encounters 'a new relationship between the two sexes, a relationship of equality and amicable mutuality'. The first four scenes in the Song deal in parallel fashion with the two lovers, and then they are pictured in animated conversation with one another in 1:15 – 2:3. In 5:12, Shulammith draws upon Solomon's earlier compliments of her as she describes him, thereby implying a sense of reciprocity and mutuality between them. In the love-making scene in 7:8–10[9–11], their intimacy produces joyful mutuality as Shulammith breaks into Solomon's words and completes his thought. It is also significant that the root šlm is used eighteen times in the Song, most prominently in 8:10, when Shulammith exclaims that she has found šālôm in Solomon. Payne (1996: 331) assesses well the mutuality of love expressed in the Song:

> The relationship between the man and the woman then is one where each participates, equally and mutually, as a man or as a woman, towards the other. There is initiative and response by both of the lovers to each other. No note of priority or sub-ordination intrudes, except as each is subordinate to the other in love. Yet there is no blurring of their maleness and femaleness: to do that would be to render this vibrant song bland.

The Song, then, in its focus on the mutuality of love pictures the original divine intention that man and wife should become one flesh (Gen. 2:24).

Shulammith's words about Solomon in 7:10[11] may well point to a broader intertextual significance of the nature of love. When she says, 'I am my beloved's, and his desire is for me', she uses the term těšûqâ, for 'desire', found elsewhere only in Gen. 3:16 and 4:7. Lavoie (2000: 79) reasons:

> By electing to use this rare word, this verse in the Song is really redirecting the Genesis text and completely transforming it. The

curse of Gen 3:16 is changed into a blessing. Desire is a joy, not a judgment. The love relationship is no longer unilateral but reciprocal. Moreover, it is no longer the woman who yearns for the man, as in the patriarchal text of Gen 3:16, but the man for the woman.

The Song demonstrates that love as God designed it, to be exclusive and mutual, could in part turn back the damaging effects of the human fall into sin.

In the broader canonical perspective, the Song of Songs can also be viewed as a pointer to the inestimable quality of love that God has for his people. It is not unusual for metaphors to point in two directions simultaneously. For example, when God is called a father, the human experience of fatherhood enables the reader to understand aspects of God's relationship with his spiritual children. At the same time, however, one can learn much about how to be a human father by considering and imitating how God functions towards his people. In an analogous way, when Hos. 2 (cf. also Isa. 62:5; Jer. 2:2; Ezek. 16:8) uses the metaphor of marriage to communicate Yahweh's pain because of Israel's unfaithfulness, the prophet uses familiar human experience to elucidate what Israel has done and the deep hurt it has brought to Yahweh. Yahweh's persistent love in spite of Israel's adultery prompts him to draw her back to him in bonds of love and reconciliation. The metaphor uses the human experience of a gracious response to marital unfaithfulness to explain how Yahweh continues to love Israel in spite of its idolatry. In Hos. 3, Yahweh calls his prophet to reach out to Gomer with the same kind of love Yahweh has demonstrated towards Israel. Although Hosea does not draw out the point explicitly, it would be legitimate for a person whose husband or wife has been unfaithful to appropriate the metaphor of Yahweh's persistent love as a pattern for seeking reconciliation with a spouse who has violated the marital bond. In the NT, Paul in Eph. 5:22–33 clearly employs the relationship between Christ and the church as the example for marital love. Thus he charges wives to submit to their husbands as the church submits to Christ, and he commands husbands to love their wives as Christ loved the church. The human experience of marriage, then, enables Christians to understand how Christ loves them and how they are to submit to him. On the other hand, Christ's relationship to his church gives Christians a pattern to govern their relationships within marriage. The marriage image is also used in Rev. 19:6–8 when Christians are united with Christ at the marriage supper of the Lamb. In serving as a pointer to divine love, the Song of Songs is not read as an allegory, nor is it viewed typologically, but instead the Song in addition to its literal meaning also yields legitimate theological and ethical significance that illustrates truths taught explicitly elsewhere in the biblical texts.

9. PURPOSE

Why was the Song of Songs included in the biblical corpus? As has been discussed above, this song cycle was probably not intended to be construed as an allegory of divine love, although it has most often been read in that manner throughout its interpretative history. Neither is it a drama or narrative tracing the actual experience of a specific couple. The extravagant descriptions, rather, seem to point in the direction of an idealization of love, and the frequent use of the *šlm* root, in the names of the main characters (Solomon and Shulammith) who find *šālôm* (8:10), may well provide lexical support for this understanding of the Song.

As its primary purpose, the Song of Songs is written to celebrate erotic love within the bounds of marriage as God's good gift. The Song, however, is not intended just to extol love, because the numerous links to the wisdom literature suggests an additional didactic purpose as the Song endeavours to teach about the nature of intimacy. As Webb (2000: 24) states, 'It is meant to lead us, via its presentation of the love of this man and this woman, to reflection on the nature of love itself.' Furthermore, implicitly the Song calls its readers to accept the teaching of the Song so that their values and behaviours may be transformed. By this means, the Song of Songs supplements the other wisdom texts as it calls its readers to seek the kind of intimacy Yahweh has designed for the blessing of his people.

TEXT AND COMMENTARY

SONG OF SONGS 1:1

Translation

¹The most excellent song which is of Solomon.

Notes on the text

1:1. The phrase *šîr haššîrîm* follows a typical Hebr. pattern for the superlative (Waltke 14.5d), as in the comparable expressions 'holy of holies' in Exod. 26:33 and 'vanity of vanities' in Eccl. 1:2.

The *lĕ* preposition introducing *šĕlōmōh* can be reasonably construed in several ways, including 'dedicated to', 'in the style of' and 'referring to'. The frequent use of the parallel *lĕdāwîd* in the titles of psalms suggests that *lĕ* could well be read as an indication of authorship (Murphy 1990: 119), but that cannot be demonstrated certainly, so the ambiguous 'of' is used in this translation.

Goitein (1993: 65) suggests that *'ăšer* (which) should be vocalized as *'āšîr* with the sense 'I will sing', comparable to Ps. 59:16, in which case it would be a song dedicated to Solomon, but there is little reason to justify emending the vowels of the MT reading.

Form, structure and setting

The sound play in this introductory verse, with its repeated *š* sounds, signals the poetic character of the book. The superlative construction *šîr haššîrîm* indicates that it is a song of literary excellence, and the sg. form *šîr* may also hint at the nature of the book as a cycle comprising several songs related to a central theme, rather than as an anthology of disconnected love songs (Exum 2005c: 91).

Comment

1. The term *šîr* is often, but not exclusively, used for lyric songs and especially for love songs (cf. Isa. 5:1 and Ezek. 33:32). It could well refer to a wedding song, for music was typically employed in wedding celebrations (Jer. 7:34; 16:9; 25:10; 33:11; cf. Murphy, *ABD* 6:151). If the reference to Solomon is taken as an indicator of authorship, that would suggest the setting for the book, but the meaning of the *lĕ* preposition is ambiguous, so one should be cautious in drawing conclusions regarding the authorship of the Song from this grammatical construction. Detailed discussion of the question of the authorship of the book is given in the introduction.

Explanation

This *šîr* is a song of great celebration. The contents of the book indicate that it is intended to celebrate human love within the parameters of God's design. The songs that comprise this excellent cycle are not a random collection of unrelated lyrics, and they do not form a tightly written dramatic poem, but are an impressionistic song cycle celebrating intimacy as it progresses from first attraction into maturity. Whether or not Solomon was the writer or compiler of this song cycle, his name at least suggests some sort of linkage between the book and the wisdom tradition, because Solomon was regarded as the paradigmatic figure of Hebrew wisdom (cf. 1 Kgs 4:29–34[5:9–14]), just as Moses was connected with the law and David with the Psalms. The Song can usefully be regarded as a commentary on the wisdom instruction in Prov. 5:15–19, where the young man is urged to find delight exclusively in emotional and sexual intimacy with his wife, because within the OT 'it is only within the marital context that sexual love is condoned' (Dell 2005: 17). Hess (2005: 39) reasons well:

> This association with Solomon provides an anchor for the Song in the biblical wisdom tradition and relates to this material in the canon. No longer separated from the Bible as a collection of love

songs, the book takes on a unified significance that cannot be reduced to secular humanism. Nor can its imagery within the context of physical love be ignored and give way to purely allegorical interpretation. The connection to Solomon places the book within a historical wisdom tradition of literature recognized by the church as possessing divine inspiration.

This Song, then, is more than secular love poetry, for the reference to Solomon, the traditional patron of Hebrew wisdom, places it within the sphere of Yahweh's perspective on human love.

SONG OF SONGS 1:2–4

Translation

SHULAMMITH

> ²May he kiss me with the kisses of his mouth!
> Because your love is more pleasurable than wine,
> ³Your oils are good in scent,
> Your name is like refined oil,
> Therefore the maidens love you.
> ⁴Draw me after you, let us run!
> The king has brought me into his chambers.
> Let us rejoice and be glad in you,
> Let us extol your love more than wine.
> Rightly do they love you.

Notes on the text

1:2. 'May he kiss me': Bloch and Bloch (1995: 137) note that *yiššāqēnî* evokes the Hebr. verb *šāqâ* (to cause to drink [wine]). In addition, as Mariaselvam (1988: 64) observes, the sound effect of kissing is simulated by the pronunciation of *yiššāqēnî minněšîqôt pîhû*.

'Your love': the pl. *dōdeykā* is rendered 'your breasts' in LXX and Vg, perhaps in confusion with the Hebr. word *dadayim*. The pl. form *dōdîm* in the Song of Songs (cf. also Prov. 7:18; Ezek. 16:8; 23:17) typically refers to sexual lovemaking (Bloch 2006: 155), which here in 1:2 is played out in her imagination.

The shift from third person to second person is also found in 4:2 and 6:6, as in other biblical poetical references such as Amos 4:1 and Mic. 7:19, and also in the Phoen. and Ug. literature (G. L. Carr 1984: 72). However, Perry (2005: 529–533) argues well that the first line of v. 2 is Shulammith's exclamation of desire for Solomon. She then states three reasons in 1:2b – 1:3b that justify why the maidens agree with her positive assessment of Solomon in 1:3c.

3. His 'name' (*šēm*) is a sound play with 'oil' (*šemen*), as also in Eccl. 7:1.

tûraq is textually suspect, and *BHS* suggests the reading *tamrûq* (cosmetic treatment), as in Esth. 2:3, 9, 12 (*BHQ* 56). The renderings of LXX, Aquila and Vg presuppose *mûrāq*: 'poured-out oil'. This would be oil of the highest quality. Both Hebr. terms are derived from the root *ryq*, a sound play with *rêaḥ*.

4. The use of three cohortatives (*nārûṣâ*, *nāgîlâ* and *nazkîrâ*) suggests the language of her desire, not the description of actual facts. The lines 'Let us rejoice and be glad in you, / let us extol your love more than wine' have typically been regarded as the words of the maidens to whom Shulammith has referred in 1:3. S. M. Paul (1995: 596), however, makes a strong case for reading the plurals in this verse as plurals of ecstasy, similar to the usage in several Sum. and Akk. love lyrics. By this means, Shulammith 'in her fit of ecstasy, is referring solely to the sexual joys she alone will experience with her mate'.

mêšār is an accusative of manner that is here used adverbially (Joüon 126d) in the sense of 'rightly', rather than in a moral sense as 'righteousness', as in LXX.

Form, structure and setting

This initial lyric in the Song is unified by six repeated terms. The words of Shulammith's soliloquies (1:2a; 1:4b), in which she discloses her inner thoughts about Solomon, contrast in form with the direct addresses in which she articulates what she says, or would like to say, to Solomon. Fox (1983: 200–201) notes a similar use of the literary device of enallage in the Egypt. love songs, as he comments on this passage in the Song:

> The sudden shifts of person convey shifts of perspective. The girl moves back and forth between the first person pl., where she includes the other girls in her appreciation of her lover's beauties, and the third person pl., where she dances verbally out of the group in order to add a certain objectivity to her statement about the public estimation of his loveworthiness.

Shulammith's words of desire in 1:4a build in intensity from 'draw me after you' to 'let us run' to 'the king has brought me into his chambers'.

Comment

2. Rather than constructing a realistic narrative setting, the song cycle begins imaginatively *in medias res*. In soliloquy, Shulammith expresses her initial positive impressions of Solomon and her incipient desire for him. By longing for the kisses of his mouth, she indicates that she is not thinking of a ceremonial greeting, but for a physical expression of genuine affection. As 8:1 suggests, this kind of public display by a man and a woman who were not blood relatives was not socially acceptable in that culture. Even in this first scene of the Song, Shulammith admits that the prospect of his love has an intoxicating effect on her, because it brings to her greater pleasure than what wine would produce (cf. Ps. 4:7; Eccl. 9:7). Keel (1994: 44) insists that *dōdîm* refers here to foreplay and sexual intercourse, but he fails to consider the possibility that this is the poetic language of imagination, not realistic description. At this initial point in the Song, Shulammith expresses her desire for intimacy (v. 2) and her desire for companionship with Solomon (v. 4).

3. *ălāmôt* refers to the young women of the court, elsewhere called the daughters of Jerusalem, who do not rise to the status of queens or concubines (6:8). Shulammith is not the only woman who is attracted to Solomon; the other women of the court also find him desirable. The name refers to a person's character and reputation (cf. 1 Sam. 25:25). If she is thinking of Solomon, a second level of reference may also be involved, because his name is derived from the verb *šālēm* (to be perfect, complete). Although Shulammith is aware of Solomon's wealth, status and refinement, she is most impressed by his name, or reputation. His good character, verified by the same perception by the young woman of the court, is his salient feature that causes her to find him attractive. She appreciates him both aesthetically and ethically. He is a man in whom she finds pleasure, and for whom she has respect.

4. Using the language of desire, Shulammith longs for Solomon to draw her after him as he singles her out. Up to this time, she has observed him from a distance, and she likes what she has seen, but now she wants to get to know him better. She wants them to run together, using for the first time the kind of figurative language that will predominate in the Song. Throughout the song cycle, their love is pictured as being cultivated in the freedom and spontaneity of a rustic setting, not within the confines of urban, court life. In her imagination, she pictures the king bringing her to a private place, although it must be noted that 'his chambers' (*hădārāyw*) do not necessarily refer to his bedroom (cf. Bloch and Bloch 1995: 139), as many have supposed. Even if Solomon's bedroom is envisioned (cf. the use of the term in 3:4), it could well be used in a proleptic sense that signals to the reader where this relationship will eventually go rather than describing what is actually taking place at the time of Shulammith's speech (Garrett 2004: 127).

Explanation

2–4. The Song of Songs is written as poetry, which employs the vivid language of imagination rather than realistic description. From the inception of the Song, the dominant f. perspective is set forth (Lavoie 2000: 77), as Shulammith expresses her longing for intimacy with Solomon as an inner monologue that expresses her private thoughts and wishful longings (Arbel 2000: 93). Only rarely does the Bible present love from the viewpoint of a woman (cf. Michal's love for David in 1 Sam. 18:20, 26). In the Song of Songs, Shulammith's emotions and thoughts receive primary attention, and the inner thoughts of Solomon are developed to a much lesser extent by the poet. True intimacy begins with desire for a person whom one values as attractive and worthy.

SONG OF SONGS 1:5–8

Translation

SHULAMMITH

> [5]I am black but beautiful, O daughters of Jerusalem,
>   Like the tents of Kedar, like the curtains of Solomon.
> [6]Do not look at me because I am sunburnt, because the sun has
>   scorched me.
>   My mother's sons were angry with me,
>   They placed me as the keeper of the vineyards.
>   My own vineyard I have not kept.
> [7]Make known to me, whom my soul loves, where you will graze,
>   Where you will cause [your flock] to lie down at noon.
>   Otherwise I will be as one who picks lice beside the flocks of your
>   companions.

SOLOMON

> [8]If you yourself do not know, O most beautiful among women,
>   Go out along the footprints of the flock,
>   And graze your kids by the dwellings of the shepherds.

Notes on the text

1:5. In the expression 'black but beautiful' the waw should probably be taken in an antithetical sense, as also in 5:2 (Joüon 172a; cf. Ogden 1996: 444–445).

Kedar refers to a Bedouin tribe, but its root *qdr*, meaning 'to be dark', also reinforces Shulammith's description of herself as black and sunburnt.

6. Exum (1981: 416–419) argues that *'al tir'ûnî* should be read as an asseverative, with the sense 'indeed, look at me', but this use of *'al* is very rare in biblical Hebr. It is better to view this expression as parallel to 2:1, as Shulammith regards her appearance as inferior to that of her peers.

Bergant (2001: 14–15) notes that the repeated sibilant sounds in this verse 'suggest the sizzling sound of something cooking. The heat of the sun has actually cooked her skin.' 'My own vineyard' (*šĕllî*) emphasizes that her body was under her control, in contrast to the literal vineyard where her brothers exercised their authority (Waltke 16.4d).

7. The Hebr. term *kĕ'ōtĕyâ* has been rendered in various ways: 'as a veiled woman' (perhaps a reference to a prostitute, as in Gen. 38:14–16, or possibly for mourning or as a disguise), 'as one who strays' (RSV, JPS, which follow Symmachus in transposing the consonants of the verbal root to *tā'â*), 'as one who is wandering around' (Stoop-van Paridon 2005: 65), and 'as one who picks lice' (NEB). Emerton (1993: 138–139) argues persuasively for the last of these alternatives (cf. Driver 1974: 159–160).

Waltke 18.3c notes that the clause beginning with *lāmâ* introduces an indirect question that functions rhetorically to introduce an undesirable alternative.

8. 'O most beautiful among women' is a comparative superlative formed by the definite adjective *yāpâ* followed by the group *nāšîm* (women) prefixed by the *bĕ* preposition (Waltke 14.5c).

Form, structure and setting

The second lyric in the Song is marked by numerous contrasts that reflect Shulammith's sense of insecurity. As she speaks to the daughters of Jerusalem in 1:5–6, either in direct address or within her own mind in soliloquy, she describes herself as 'black but beautiful'. Unlike the women of the court, her skin has been scorched by the sun as she laboured in the vineyards, but she has not been able to keep her own vineyard (her body) lovely according to the accepted standards of the day. In contrast to her ambivalent self-assessment, Solomon addresses her as 'most beautiful among woman' (1:8). In 1:5–6 Shulammith uses the language of the vineyard (*nṭr* and *kerem*) to speak of her painful past, but in 1:7 employs the language of pasturing as she looks to a hopeful future, a motif that Solomon picks up in his response to her in 1:8.

The general description 'black but beautiful' in 1:5 is expanded in particular detail in the rest of the lyric. In 1:6, Shulammith describes the process by which her skin became blackish as she was compelled by her brothers to keep the vineyard. In 1:8, Solomon echoes her term *nā'wâ* from 1:5 as he extols her 'loveliness' (*yāpâ*) as exceeding that of all the women.

This brief lyric is a microcosm of the entire song cycle, which traces Shulammith's increasing confidence as she flourishes under Solomon's affirming love.

Comment

5. As Shulammith describes herself as black but beautiful, she is painfully aware that her appearance does not measure up to the conventional definition of f. beauty in her ancient culture (Hostetter 1996: 36). Her skin, which has been burnt by labour outdoors (cf. the parallel use of the verbal form in Job 30:30; Lam. 4:8), identifies her as from the working class, rather than from the aristocracy (against V. Sasson 1989: 407, who contends unconvincingly that she is the daughter of Pharaoh). Compared with the other young women of the court, the daughters of Jerusalem who have enjoyed ease and luxury (cf. Isa. 3:16–26), Shulammith feels out-classed and unworthy of Solomon's attention. Bloch and Bloch (1995: 140) observe, 'Sunburned skin is associated with a lower social status, a fair complexion being the mark of those who could afford not to work outdoors. In ancient Egypt. and Gr. art, the women are shown as having lighter skin than the men, probably because the women worked indoors.' As she looks at herself, she sees herself as dark as the black woollen tents used by the Bedouin tribe of Kedar. Nevertheless, she also recognizes that she is 'beautiful' (*nā'wâ*), using a term that implies her desirability (cf. 2:14; 4:3; 6:4). In her beauty, she is like the curtains of Solomon, perhaps a reference to the lovely veils of the temple that were dyed in blue, purple and crimson (2 Chr. 3:14).

6. The term *šĕḥarḥōrĕt* (sunburnt) is used only here in the OT, and is probably a stylistic variant of *šĕḥōrâ* ('black'; 1:5; cf. Brenner 1982: 121), referring to her complexion that has been scorched by the intense Middle Eastern sun (cf. Pss 91:6; 121:6; 2 Kgs 4:18–20; Jon. 4:8). Shulammith does not want to be evaluated only in terms of her physical appearance, of which she is deeply embarrassed, but she wants others to look past the surface to discern her true inner beauty (Falk 1990: 168). The reason for the brothers' harsh treatment of Shulammith is left unstated, but in her mind it was unjustified, a sentiment that seems to be supported by the commendable way in which the rest of the Song speaks of her. Keel (1994: 49) notes that the job of watching over the vineyard 'was normally for men (8:11–12; Isa. 27:2–3), who were thought more fit than young women to drive away thieves, wild boars (Ps. 80:13[14]), and foxes (cf. Cant. 2:15)'. In this verse, 'vineyard' is used in two senses, first of the literal vineyard in which Shulammith was compelled to labour, and then as a literary figure for her physical body. In a similar way, the image of a garden refers to Shulammith's body in 4:12 – 5:1. Vineyards were luxury assets in the ancient world (cf. Eccl. 2:4), and were often leased to tenants who worked them (cf. Song 8:11).

7. The phrase 'whom my soul loves', used also in 3:1, 4, describes Shulammith as 'thirsty for life, full of yearning' (Keel 1994: 52). She speaks in the language of shepherding, which throughout history has been a conventional feature of love poetry, and an image that becomes one of the prominent motifs in the Song of Songs. Shulammith wants to know where Solomon will take the customary noon siesta out of the intense heat of the sun while his flock grazes (cf. Ps. 23:2). She suspected that he would then be available for a private rendezvous, but she would have to know where she could find him, so that she would not have to while away her time in an unfruitful search for her beloved.

8. Solomon replies to her request with gentle words that accept and affirm her. Rather than just giving her the information for which she has asked, he first addresses her as 'O most beautiful among women', an expression that must have touched her heart (contra her self-deprecating words in 1:5–6). He then adopts her language of shepherding as he encourages her to bring her young goats along the path of his flock. She will find him by the dwellings of the shepherds. Although in 1:7 she hesitated to take the risk of seeking Solomon, his words of direction indicate that she will indeed find there the one whom her soul loves.

Explanation

5. Although Shulammith describes herself as black in v. 5, her explanation in v. 6 makes it clear that this is not a racial indicator (Fox 1985: 101), but is rather a reflection of her lower social class. In the ancient world, as in the contemporary world, prejudice could be rooted in a variety of factors. Shulammith's initial insecurity arises from viewing her appearance in the light of social conventions, rather than considering fully the internal beauty of her humble and unpretentious character. Among other things, the Song traces the growth in her confidence as she is transformed by the power of love.

6. Shulammith's father is noticeably absent in the Song, while her mother and brothers are mentioned several times each. Although her brothers are represented as having noble intentions in protecting her virginity (8:8–9), they seem to have been insensitive to her feelings here in 1:6. In addition, she appeals to the court women not to look contemptuously on her appearance. Although the Song speaks of ideal intimacy, it is set against the painful backdrop of family stress and social disdain.

7–8. At this early stage in their relationship, Shulammith has an emerging love for Solomon that she wants to nurture. Uncertain of herself and fearful of ridicule by others, Shulammith is not prepared to take great risks. She, therefore, asks how she can connect privately and constructively with him without attracting undue attention or ridicule. Solomon's reply to her affirms her in the area in which she feels least confident. She perceives herself as inferior to the privileged women of the court, but Solomon uses a superlative to indicate that he sees her as the most beautiful among women. Later in the Song, the daughters of Jerusalem adopt this language in 5:9 and 6:1 as they speak to Shulammith. Solomon also focuses on the interests they share in common, their pasturing of small livestock, as he endeavours to draw her closer to him despite the significant distance between their backgrounds. This common ground serves to provide the connection needed by the couple in their fledgling relationship.

SONG OF SONGS 1:9–11

Translation

SOLOMON

> [9]To my mare among the chariots of Pharaoh
> I compare you, my darling.
> [10]Your cheeks are beautiful with circlets,
> Your neck with strings of beads.

CHORUS

> [11]We will make for you circlets of gold with points of silver.

Notes on the text

1:9. Pope (1970: 58–59) concludes that the *î* ending of *lĕsusātî* 'has nothing to do with the possessive suffix, but is, as many commentators have recognized, the survival of the old genitive case ending'. However, the pronoun suffix on *ra'yātî* (my darling) supports the parallel reading 'my mare' for *lĕsusātî*.

10. Horsnell, *NIDOTTE* 2:268, suggests that the term *ḥărûzîm* may be related to the Arab. *haraz* (a necklace of shells or pearls).

Form, structure and setting

This song opens with a startling image in which Solomon compares Shulammith's effect upon him to that of a mare among stallions. He then speaks in terms of literal description as he praises her cheeks and neck accented by her modest jewellery. This prompts the women of the court to offer to embellish her with gold and silver jewellery that is more appropriate to her excellent beauty and value.

Comment

9. The poetic image 'my mare among the chariots of Pharaoh' has prompted several different renderings. Some commentators link v. 9 with the following descriptions in vv. 10–11, concluding that Shulammith's jewellery is compared to the fine ornamentation on Egypt. royal chariot horses (Murphy 1990: 134; Goulder 1986: 17). Barrick, *TDOT* 13:489, suggests that it refers to her physical perfection. Pope (1970: 59) cites an epigraphical reference narrating how a mare was used to bring the stallions in the Egypt. chariotry of Thutmose III to confusion, thus reducing them to weakness. In view of this parallel, the image then could speak of Shulammith's powerful sexual allure to men who see her (cf. Hubbard 1991: 282; contra Garrett 2004: 144–145). She has captivated Solomon in a way the other woman have not.

ra'yātî is Solomon's customary affectionate term for Shulammith. He uses this term nine times in the Song, almost always in the first half of the book, and she uses the parallel term *rē'î* for Solomon in 5:16. The expression can mean 'companion, friend', or, as with the NIV, 'darling'. Solomon typically uses *ra'yātî* in contexts that praise her beauty. G. L. Carr (1984: 82) notes, 'The central meaning of the verbal root is to guard, care for, or tend, with an emphasis on the delight and pleasure which attends that responsibility.'

10. It may be that the image of the decorated chariot horses of Pharaoh in v. 9 prompts Solomon to describe Shulammith's beauty as accented by her jewellery (Alter 1985: 194). Picking up her self-description in 1:5 as 'beautiful' (*nā'wâ*), Solomon states that her cheeks are 'beautiful' (*nā'wâ*) with circlets and her neck with strings of beads.

11. The change from first person sg. in v. 9 to first person pl. in v. 11 is regarded by Goulder (1986: 17) as a pl. of majesty referring to Solomon, but it could better be rendered as referring to the chorus of court women, as in 1:3c. They hear Solomon's praise of Shulammith's circlets and strings of beads, and resolve to adorn her in a way more suitable to her attractiveness and worth. In place of her modest ornaments, they will make for her circlets of gold with points of silver. Konkel, *NIDOTTE* 3:151–152, explains the difficulties in determining the precise referent, but the general sense is clear, that they intend to upgrade her accessories to include precious and valuable items in keeping with her worth.

Explanation

9–10. Using a striking image that sounds strange to present readers, but was apparently comprehended by his ancient audience, Solomon compares Shulammith to a mare among the chariots of Pharaoh. He has previously lauded her as the most beautiful among women, and now tells her that he finds her powerfully alluring. In praising her, Solomon describes the beauty of her skin, which she earlier deprecated as black (1:5) and scorched by the sun (1:6). He speaks what she needs to hear as he affirms her where she feels most inferior. Understanding her feelings as she compares herself unfavourably to the other women of the court, Solomon speaks to her heart as he nurtures their love by his praise for her. In gracious tones, he addresses her fears and needs, demonstrating sensitivity prompted by love.

11. By taking the initiative to adorn Shulammith with luxury items, the court women play an important role in the development of her relationship with Solomon and in her own personal development. Throughout the Song, and in particular in ch. 8, the maturing relationship between Solomon and Shulammith is situated within a loving and protective community. Intimacy, then, draws from the larger social context and builds back into it. As the NT teaches frequently, love should be the distinguishing mark of God's people (John 13:34–35), and love is nurtured best in community (1 Thess. 3:12; 1 John 3:16–18).

SONG OF SONGS 1:12–14

Translation

SHULAMMITH

> [12]While the king was at his table
>   My nard gave its scent.
> [13]My beloved is to me a sachet of myrrh
>   That lies between my breasts.
> [14]My beloved is to me a cluster of henna
>   In the vineyards of Engedi.

Notes on the text

1:12. *mēsab* refers to a circular banquet table, not to a couch for sleeping (cf. Garcia-López, *TDOT* 10:128).

'Nard' (*nērd*), a costly ointment from the Himalayan region of Nepal, occurs in the OT elsewhere only in the wedding-night scene in 4:13–14, but that does not mean it refers specifically to sexual activity whenever it is used, any more than kissing, which usually accompanies sexual activity, would always demand physical intercourse (contra Keel 1994: 63).

13. The term *ṣĕrôr* describes a small sachet made of cloth strips in which money or precious objects were placed for safekeeping, and at times was used for a protective amulet (Snaith 1993: 23; Keel 1994: 65).

'Myrrh' (*mōr*) refers to a fragrant resin found in Arabia, and used in both solid and liquid form (Hausmann, *TDOT* 8:557). The term is used extensively in the Song of Songs. For an extensive description of myrrh and frankincense in the ancient world, see van Beek 1960: 70–95.

14. 'Henna' (*kōper*) is a yellow blossom often used as a perfume (cf. 4:13). The similar term *kĕpārîm* in 7:11[12] may also refer to henna bushes, rather than to villages, as it is often translated. It is probable that in the royal gardens of Engedi the highest quality plants were grown (G. L. Carr. 1984: 85).

Form, structure and setting

All of this short song is in the voice of Shulammith. She begins in 1:12 with a literal statement, in which she recalls that her nard was a scent that reached out to the king while he was dining in public at his table, apparently with his male guests. In 1:13–14, Shulammith uses two metaphors to indicate the effect that Solomon's love has on her in her private space. He is like a sachet of myrrh that lies between her breasts when they are separated at night, and he is like a cluster of henna in the vineyards of the oasis of Engedi that bring delight in a wilderness place. Similar progressions from literal to figurative language are also evident in 1:6 and 8:11–12.

Comment

12. The juxtaposition of statements about the king in 1:12 and the beloved in 1:13–14 seem best to speak of the same person, rather than to two rivals for Shulammith's love, as held by the three-person dramatic approach to the Song. As Solomon is dining, probably at this time in history only with his male guests, Shulammith still has a pleasurable effect upon him. In contrast to the visual images Solomon uses in 1:9–10, Shulammith here employs images of scent to communicate the affection she has for her beloved. The fragrance of her nard, an ointment used both to moisten dry skin and to mask bodily odour caused by the hot ANE climate, can be detected by him from a distance. Just as she responded positively to the scent of his oils in 1:3, so now she describes how the scent of her perfume endeavours to evoke a similar response in him. Although nard refers literally to the pleasurable aromatic scent, it also serves as an image of the pleasure she herself desires to bring to him.

13. The literal scent of Shulammith's nard in 1:12 prompts her image of Solomon's love as myrrh in 1:13. Using poetic language that reflects her heart, rather than a prose description of a literal reality, she describes the effect his love has on her. In the public context of a banquet, her nard brought pleasure to Solomon at a distance (1:12), and in a similar way she portrays how his love is like a sachet of myrrh that continues to bring feelings of joy and delight to her as she sleeps through the night. Although perfumes were indeed used in connection with lovemaking in

4:14 and in Prov. 7:17, here they may rather be part of her imaginative anticipation.

Many commentators have read sexual activity into this image of a sachet of myrrh that lies between her breasts. If, however, the Song follows an impressionistic but sequential progression, and Shulammith is depicted as a locked garden and a sealed spring on their wedding night (4:12), then the image in 1:13 should not be rendered as premarital sexual union. The language in chs. 1–3 certainly expresses intense longing for sexual intimacy, but it does not demand the consummation of their sexual relationship prior to their marriage. Premarital intercourse is consistently proscribed throughout the OT (cf. Deut. 22:23–29), so it is unlikely that it would be affirmed here, even though sexual longing is clearly in evidence very early in the Song.

14. It seems evident that Shulammith here employs the language of imagination, for she compares Solomon to a cluster of henna in the vineyards of Engedi. By evoking the lush oasis west of the Dead Sea, which was the site of the royal spice and fruit gardens (Keel 1994: 67), she suggests the nourishing, life-giving effect that Solomon has on her life. This metaphorical reference may well be determinative for regarding *lîn* in 1:13 in a figurative sense as well.

Explanation

12–14. Song of Songs employs all of the senses as it explores and describes the progress of intimacy. In 1:10 Solomon used images of sight, but in 1:12–14 Shulammith speaks in the language of smell. By using images of scent, Shulammith relates the lingering effects of pleasure that can reach out from a distance. True intimacy longs to be with the one loved, but it entails more than physical contact. Even when they cannot be physically present with one another, lovers can find joy and refreshment in their thoughts and in their feelings for each other. In an analogous way, 1 Pet. 1:8 declares that Christians who do not see Jesus Christ at the present time while on their earthly pilgrimage can still rejoice with inexpressible joy.

The image of Solomon as a sachet of myrrh represents the continuing enjoyment that love brings to those who have fallen under its delightful spell. Shulammith finds that even when she sleeps alone she holds close to her heart the precious and protective treasure of his love. Even when the lovers are out of one another's sight, they are not out of each other's hearts. In a similar way, Solomon's love for Shulammith refreshes her spirit in the same way as the Engedi oasis brings life to the barren wilderness. Even at a distance, the delight of love lingers.

SONG OF SONGS 1:15 – 2:3

Translation

SOLOMON

> ¹⁵Behold, you are beautiful, my darling!
>   Behold, you are beautiful.
>   Your eyes are doves.

SHULAMMITH

> ¹⁶Behold, you are beautiful, my beloved, how exceedingly pleasant!
>   Yes, our couch is lush foliage.

SOLOMON

> ¹⁷The beams of our houses are cedars;
>   Our rafters are junipers.

SHULAMMITH

> ^{2:1}I am a crocus in Sharon, a lotus in the valleys.

SOLOMON

> ²Like a lotus among the briers,
>   So is my darling among the maidens.

SHULAMMITH

> ³Like an apricot tree among the trees in the forest,
>   So is my beloved among the young men.
>   I sit delightedly in his shade,
>   And his fruit is sweet to my palate.

Notes on the text

1:15. 'Behold' (*hinnāk*), echoed in 1:16 by Shulammith's *hinněkā*, signals a strong and excited exclamation. This construction is repeated in 4:1. Exum (2005c: 112) observes that by using this term the poet creates 'the illusion of immediacy by bringing what the lovers see immediately before our eyes'.

16. Meier, *NIDOTTE* 3:122, notes that *nā'îm* speaks of an object's intrinsic agreeableness or pleasantness.

ra'ănān is typically used in the OT to describe trees (Abegg, *NIDOTTE* 3:1153; Mommer, *TDOT* 13:558), so here it is best rendered as 'lush foliage' rather than as a spot of lush grass (Bloch and Bloch 1995: 147); cf. the LXX reading *syskios* (thickly shaded).

17. 'Our houses' (*bāttênû*) is pl. This could be a poetic pl. of indetermination (Joüon 136j), but it may be that the rustic image of houses speaks of the wide range of their relationship. They are not confined by one geographical location, but all of creation is available to their love (cf. G. L. Carr 1984: 87).

The pl. pronouns could be a continuation of Shulammith's speech, for she is the speaker in 1:16 and 2:1. However, the alternating speech pattern that pervades 1:15 – 2:3 could more likely suggest that Solomon is here speaking for the two of them.

Although the precise identification of *běrôt* is debated by botanists, Zohary, *IDB* 2:293, may well be correct in concluding that it refers to a species of juniper that was highly valued for its durability, just as cedar was.

2:1. BHS proposes without evidence changing 'I' to 'you' to make this verse the words of Solomon describing Shulammith, but this reading disregards the extant textual data as well as the conversational structure of 1:15 – 2:3.

šôšannâ may well be an Egypt. loanword that should be translated as 'lotus' (Štrba 2004; Suderman 2005; Schmoldt, *TDOT* 14:553), but it could perhaps be regarded here as a general category of springtime flowers rather than a particular species (Zohary, *IDB* 2:295).

2. *ḥôaḥ* refers to a thorny, noxious weed (Younger, *NIDOTTE* 2:44), which has no beauty, pleasant scent or edible fruit.

3. *tappûaḥ* has been rendered as 'apple' or 'citron', but it may possibly best refer to the apricot tree (Zohary, *IDB* 2:286; Jacob and Jacob, *ABD* 2:806–807; Borowski 1987: 129–130), because the apple has only recently been introduced to Palestine, and the citron has an acidic taste (G. L. Carr 1984: 89; Bloch and Bloch 1995: 149). Exact identification is difficult, because the Song of Songs frequently cites exotic fruits and spices not native to Israel.

ḥimmadtî and *yāšabtî* are perfects that could refer to completed action, or, more likely, be rendered as statives expressing a state or condition (Williams 1976: 29).

Form, structure and setting

This song is characterized by alternating speeches by Solomon and Shulammith, and 'the joyous repartee of their words signals the growing intimacy in their relationship' (Estes 2005: 409). The changing voices are explicit in 1:15–16 and 2:2–3, and they are implicit but plausible in 1:17 – 2:1. The speakers trade direct compliments in 1:15 and 16 as they express how they regard one another as beautiful. In 1:17, Solomon builds upon the poetic image used by Shulammith in 1:16. In 2:1–3, both characters use comparative language, with Solomon in 2:2 turning Shulammith's tepid self-description in 2:1 into a strong affirmation of her excellence compared to the young women, and then Shulammith echoing his words of 2:2 in her praise of him in comparison to the young men in 2:3. Throughout the lyric there is a chain of cause–effect constructions that builds inexorably to the climax of their mutual affirmation in 2:2–3. Their verbal repartee in this lyric is preceded and followed by extended soliloquies by Shulammith in 1:12–14 and 2:4–7.

Comment

1:15. 'Beautiful' (*yāpâ*) picks up from 1:8 the theme of Shulammith's beauty. Solomon is continuing to affirm her in the area where she needs to be reassured. The metaphor 'your eyes are doves' has been interpreted in several ways: as a comparison to the oval shape of her eyes (Bloch and Bloch 1995: 147), as a poetic convention borrowed from Egypt. art (Snaith 1993: 25) or to their shining irridescence (G. L. Carr 1984: 86). Keel (1994: 71) may well be closest to the mark when he cites parallels in Song 4:9, 6:5 and Isa. 3:16 to support the rendering 'enchanting' or 'seductive'. Stendebach, *TDOT* 11:39, suggests that this metaphor should be translated 'your glances are messengers of love', viewing the dove in its biblical use as a conveyor of messages (cf. Gen. 8:8–12). In the OT, eyes often reflect a person's inner disposition, as in Prov. 6:17, 22:9 and Job 22:27. Extensive examples are cited in *DBI* 256.

16. This verse is an echo and expansion of 1:15, as Shulammith expresses excitement and delight which match that of Solomon. Both of them express 'an objective affirmation of the worth and value of the other, an enthusiasm for what is good and beautiful in the other' (Payne 1996: 333). In the Song, Shulammith often uses the rustic imagery with which she is familiar, and which also is a staple of love poetry throughout history. Goulder (1986: 18) literalizes the figure by asserting without evidence that 'a royal bed would be kept fresh by being strewn daily with new-cut foliage and rushes'. In view of the perfumes and spices elsewhere used for that purpose (cf. Prov. 7:17), it seems better to regard Shulammith's description of their couch as a figurative expression indicating that the whole world is the domain of their love.

17. The first person pl. pronouns make the identification of the speaker of this verse ambiguous. Either Shulammith is continuing in unbroken speech from 1:16 through 2:1, or else she and Solomon alternate their speeches throughout the section. Both cedar and juniper were used in the construction of the temple (1 Kgs 6:15), because they provided the highest quality building materials. In this context, however, in which numerous plants are mentioned in 2:1–3, it is more probable that the trees themselves rather than their wood as lumber are in view. Instead of being confined within the walls of a physical structure even as grand as the greatest of Solomon's buildings, the love the couple enjoy can be circumscribed only by the totality of nature. V. Sasson (1989: 410) suggests:

> In nature the royal couple's love is divested of the trappings of the palace which can only act as a barrier to their expression of love for each other. In nature their love finds its true and innocent self. To put it slightly differently – and perhaps more accurately – the poet realizes that, although love can flourish within the confines of the palace, it is in nature that it can find its ultimate fulfilment or its ultimate destiny. Nature is love's palace.

2:1. Continuing to use the language of her rural background, Shulammith compares herself to a *ḥăbaṣṣelet*, probably a bulb flower such as a crocus or a daffodil, and more generally to the springtime flowers represented by *šôšannâ*. Bloch and Bloch (1995: 148) argue that parallels to prophetic statements in Isa. 35:1–2 and Hos. 14:6–8 make 2:1 'an expression of a young woman's proud awareness of her blossoming beauty'. In the immediate context, however, Solomon's reply to her in 2:2 uses a corrective comparison to the briers to describe her true beauty among the young woman in contrast to her modest and self-effacing description of herself. This verse, then, has much the same spirit as 1:5, where Shulammith says, 'I am black but beautiful'. It seems best to read 2:1 as Shulammith regarding herself as a common blossom, pretty indeed but nothing special, although she does hint that she is aware that her beauty may well develop in the future. Snaith (1993: 27) catches her sense: 'Certainly the poet is not describing a rare flower of outstanding beauty here. The girl feels she is only one among many; she is just one crocus among the thousands which carpet the ground in the spring.'

2. Solomon picks up her modest self-description as a flower in the valleys and turns it into a compliment by explicit comparison. Although she may feel ordinary in her appearance, he says that her beauty exceeds that of the other young woman. Compared with Shulammith, the maidens who cause her to feel deficient are just undesirable briers (cf. Gen. 3:18, where closely related terms are used to describe the cursed earth that will produce thorns and thistles). As Keel (1994: 80) notes, 'Thorns are a symbol of misery (2 Kgs. 14:9) and curse (Hos. 9:6), of a bleak and deadly world (Isa. 34:11–15)...'

3. Shulammith imitates Solomon's compliment of her by contrasting him to the young men. The other men are dangerous, like the inhospitable forest that was the haunt of wild animals in ancient Israel (cf. Mulder, *TDOT* 6:215), but Solomon is like a life-enhancing fruit tree (Keel 1994: 82). She unpacks the connotations of her image, noting that Solomon like an apricot tree provides both shade and fruit for her. Shade is often used in the OT as an image for protection from danger, and here it speaks of safety out of the blazing hot sun. As fruit, Solomon brings delight to her life. Ginsburg (1970: 141–142) notes well:

> The comparison between the delight which she had in the company of her beloved, and the agreeable enjoyment which a shady tree affords, will especially be appreciated by those who have travelled in the East, and had the opportunity of exchanging, in the heat of the day, their close tents for an airy and fragrant bower.

Bloch and Bloch (1995: 150) and others read this as an erotic reference, but the poetic image does not require that sense. Against this rendering, it may be noted that Shulammith says that she sits, not lies, in his shade, a physical position that does not as easily suggest sexual activity.

Explanation

1:15. As a loving relationship progresses, a couple should become more comfortable in expressing their feelings to one another. In this lyric, Solomon and Shulammith for the first time are depicted in animated conversation *to* each other, rather than making individual statements *about* each other. Although in 1:8 Solomon does reply to Shulammith's question in the previous verse, in this passage their language is much more spontaneous. In 1:15, he discloses that he finds her beautiful and enchanting, as her radiant eyes mirror the love in her heart.

16–17. This song employs the language of longing and desire. By use of figurative language the couple signal to each other their growing delight. Shulammith imagines in 1:16 their couch in the lush world of nature. Her language of desire, echoed by Solomon in 1:17, in contrast to 4:16 – 5:1 in which Solomon enters her previously locked garden, does not require sexual intimacy at this point in their relationship. That will come at a later and better time.

2:1–2. The metaphorical language of nature continues into 2:1–3 as the couple continue to speak to one another. In Shulammith's estimation, she considers herself as only a common wildflower, reiterating her modest self-descriptions from ch. 1. Solomon senses and answers her real, but unstated, concerns. By complimenting Shulammith on her superiority to the other maidens, Solomon focuses on ministering to the needs of her heart, rather than on what he can receive from her. His considerate concern for her feelings evidences his thoughtfulness for her, a mark of growing love.

3. It is evident that Shulammith finds in Solomon's love the rest and refreshment that eluded her in her own family. When this song is compared with Shulammith's words in 1:5–6, several contrasts emerge. In place of the scorching sun that she endured, now she enjoys the refreshing shade that Solomon provides her. The harsh treatment by her brothers has been replaced by Solomon's tender care. Instead of having to toil in the vineyard, Shulammith is now free to taste the fruit. Solomon's love is beginning to transform her life and alleviate her pain. The prophet Hosea uses similar language in Hos. 14:4–8[5–9] to foretell how Yahweh's love will bring renewed blessing and fruitfulness to Israel after the nation returns to him. Bergant (1998: 39) remarks perceptively:

> As we give ourselves to another and accept the gift of that other in return, we become both trusting and trustworthy. The vulnerability that may have formerly frightened us can, in the embrace of mutual respect, be converted into unguarded and unpretentious openness. Love creates new communities of acceptance and respect.

SONG OF SONGS 2:4–7

Translation

SHULAMMITH

⁴He has brought me into the house of wine,
  And his look upon me is in love.
⁵Sustain me by raisin cakes, support me by apricots,
  Because I am faint with love.
⁶O may his left hand be under my head;
  And O may his right hand embrace me.
⁷I adjure you, O daughters of Jerusalem,
  By the gazelles or by the does in the field,
  Do not incite or excite love until it is pleased.

Notes on the text

2:4. Gordis (1969: 203–204) argues from the Akk. parallel *dagâlu* that the Hebr. term *degel* can mean an 'object looked upon with astonishment or admiration', so he renders the line as 'his look upon me was in love'. The sense of this metaphor is that Solomon's public response towards Shulammith openly communciates his love for her.

5. 'Raisin cakes' (*'ăšîšôt*) is used only five times in the OT for a clump of raisins pressed into a solid mass (Driver 1950: 144). In Isa. 16:7, Jer. 7:18 and Hos. 3:1, the term is used in contexts of pagan fertility worship, but that is not the case in 2 Sam. 6:19 and 1 Chr. 16:3, where it refers to a stimulating food given to others (Snaith 1993: 31). The connection with apricots in this verse suggests that *'ăšîšôt* is used as a symbol for love, not as a cultic reference (Murphy 1990: 132–133).

The pl. verbal forms in this verse seem to indicate that Shulammith is speaking to the court women rather than to Solomon. In 5:8, when Shulammith again states that she is faint with love, she specifically addresses the daughters of Jerusalem.

6. The verbal form of 'embrace' (*tĕḥabbĕqēnî*) in the second line is a jussive with an optative sense expressing a strong desire. Although no verb is used in the first line, the same optative sense is implied.

7. The oath formula implies swearing by Yahweh, because swearing by other gods was tantamount to idolatry (Schneider, *TDNT* 5:459; Pope, *IDB* 3:576). This construction represents a strong statement, in this case prohibiting the arousal of sexual passion.

The expression 'by the gazelles or by the does in the field' is taken by Keel (1994: 92) to refer to the easily frightened animals that were connected with the goddess of love. Gordis (1974: 28) argues plausibly that the language is a close imitation of the names 'the God of hosts' and 'God Almighty', and he demonstrates that traces of this background can be construed in the LXX and the Midrash. Several recent commentators, including Fox (1985: 110), Murphy (1990: 137), Snaith (1993: 33–34), Grossberg (2005: 231) and R. M. Davidson (2007: 622–623), have accepted this approach to the understanding of the oath. LaCocque (1998: 63–64) reasons, 'No one in the Israelite audience of the poem could have missed such transparent allusions. The formulation could not be construed as a slip of the tongue or a mere poetic substitute for the customary religious content of an oath; besides, the occasion was neither casual nor perfunctory.'

The prohibition uses wordplay, as the hiph. of *'ûr* (incite) is intensified to the pol. form of the same verb, meaning 'to excite'.

Form, structure and setting

This short soliloquy by Shulammith takes its place after the repartee of the couple in 1:15 – 2:3 and before Shulammith's description of the approach and proposal by Solomon in 2:8–14. The subject of 'love' (*'ahăbâ*) dominates this passage, being used in vv. 4, 5 and 7. Shulammith is faint with love (2:5), but it is not yet the time for love to be satisfied (2:7). Her expressed desire for intimacy (2:6) causes her to realize her vulnerability to sexual temptation, so she calls upon the court girls not to excite her passion (2:7). The sound play in the adjuration in 2:7 imitates the language of an oath in the divine name while employing the dialect of rustic love poetry. The original readers of the Song would probably have caught the double reference in the play on words.

Comment

4. As used frequently in Num. 2 and elsewhere, *degel* is a pole used for identifying a tribal space. Thus its main purpose is for communication. In Song 2:4, Solomon 'has displayed his love for all to see' (Martens, *NIDOTTE* 1:919). G. L. Carr (1984: 91), following Pope, argues that the final line should be read 'his intention was to make love'. Goulder (1986: 19) goes even further, speculating that Shulammith can sense the strength of Solomon's sexual feelings by feeling this standard (a euphemism for his aroused penis) pressing against her. It is true that in the Song *'ahăbâ* often has the sense of lovemaking, but its specific meaning must be determined from its use in the context. If Shulammith urges in 2:7 that *'ahăbâ* not be aroused until the proper time, then the use of the term in 2:4 should not be pressed into a description of sexual intimacy. At most, it could speak of her heightened sexual desire, but this desire remains under control at this time.

5. Solomon's attention is having a powerful effect on Shulammith, and in her excitement she begins to feel 'intense longing that feeds on love and leaves one languid and in need of the sustenance that only love can bring' (Exum 2005b: 87). Using images familiar in ancient love poetry, Shulammith calls for emotional sustenance under the figure of raisin cakes and apricots. Fruits such as these were often used in the rituals of fertility cults, practices condemned in no uncertain terms by the OT prophets, but that use was derived from a more general and legitimate use in the ancient world.

6. The verb *ḥābaq* here, as in Prov. 5:20, refers to sexual touching. Snaith (1993: 32) agrees with the NIV that 'the verse should be taken as a factual description of the position of the two lovers'. He goes on, however, to grant that this could be her position in a dream, which would coincide with reading it as a wish rather than as a statement of fact. In her imagination, Shulammith envisions Solomon fondling her sexually (cf. Sefati 1997: 541 for the similar desire expressed by Inanna in a Sum. love song). Her words in 2:6, then, explain her self-description in 2:5 as faint with love. As her love for Solomon grows, she has to contend with powerful sexual desires and drives that could easily overwhelm her better judgment and moral virtue.

7. The text of this verse is repeated exactly in 3:5 and with slight variations in 8:4. The speaker is ambiguous. Many scholars, including Ginsburg (1970: 143), G. L. Carr (1984: 93) and Goulder (1986: 20), consider it a continuation of Shulammith's speech in 2:4–6, and that may well be the case, although it is also possible to construe it as the voice of Solomon. Shulammith recognizes that the feelings of her desire for Solomon which she has expressed are so strong that she could easily slip into immoral behaviour. She calls on the daughters of Jerusalem to be careful not subject her love to external influences that would arouse it prematurely (Botterweck, *TDOT* 5:96; Schwab 2002: 49). There will be a proper time for longing to be aroused into sexual intimacy (cf. 4:6), but it is not yet that time.

Explanation

4. In 1:12, Shulammith and Solomon were separated in a public setting, and yet their affection for one another reached across the room. In 2:4, Solomon's love for her is conspicuous in the banquet hall, so that it is apparent to all. As their relationship develops, both of them are investing in it, for in 2:4 Solomon demonstrates his love for her, and in 2:5 Shulammith confesses that she is faint with love. Unlike many ancient marriages, which were fundamentally financial transactions between the two families, the relationship in the Song of Songs centres on true love, which deeply engages the emotions of the couple. Genuine love includes more than just feelings, but also not less, for love involves the total person, including the emotions. In similar language, Hos. 11:8 expresses Yahweh's heart for Israel as all his compassions are kindled for the nation.

5. Even though Shulammith uses the language of food to express her need for sustenance, the faintness that love produces cannot be cured by food, but only by intimacy. The emotional intensity of love that causes the lover to feel faint leads one to lean upon the one who is loved. This is part of the transformation from individualism to mutuality that is prompted by love.

6. Glickman (1976: 43–44) makes a useful distinction between harmful repression that denies feelings and appropriate suppression that brings dangerous impulses under control. It is perfectly understandable and proper that people in love would have sexual longings, but such passions must be kept in check until they can be fulfilled with the right person and at the right time. As the Song will proceed to demonstrate, the right person for sexual intimacy is one's spouse, and the right time is after the commitment of marriage. Ayo (1997: 251) observes perceptively, 'Sex is an easy intimacy, on a superficial level at least, and early preoccupation with its intense fascination will crowd out exploration of those gentle and tentative sharings of heart and soul that create bonds among good friends as well as mature lovers.'

7. In a developing romantic relationship, the increasing intensity of emotions needs to be kept under control. Just because sexual desire is strong, that does not make sexual activity right. *DBI* 938 notes well:

> For all the changing customs of weddings through the centuries, the emotions surrounding them are universal. The emotional intoxication of the lovers in the Song of Songs is that of any

couple in love, even though the literary expression of those feelings is partly rooted in ancient love poetry. One of the realistic touches of the Song of Songs is the anticipation of the couple as they think about the upcoming wedding day.

Both Song 2:11–13 and 8:8–11 indicate the importance of the right and proper time in a relationship. Love, therefore, must not be forced into sexual intimacy until it is the right time, for love must be allowed to take its natural course. Real love does not need artificial or premature stimulation. Because unwholesome peer pressure can combine with personal desires to produce moral failure, it is important that friends take seriously their responsibility to encourage others to retain their purity in the face of the powerful temptations to enjoy sexual pleasure before marriage. As Song of Songs demonstrates well, the tension between innocence and intimacy can be resolved in a God-honouring way only within the marital relationship.

SONG OF SONGS 2:8–14

Translation

SHULAMMITH

⁸I hear my beloved!
Behold, he is coming,
Leaping over the mountains,
Bounding over the hills.
⁹My beloved is like a gazelle or a young stag;
Behold, he is standing behind our wall,
Gazing at the windows, peering through the lattices.
¹⁰My beloved responded by saying to me,
'Come now, my darling, my fair one.
¹¹'For behold, the winter has passed by,
The rain has passed away, it is gone.
¹²'The blossoms have appeared in the land,
The time of singing has arrived,
And the voice of the turtledove has been heard in our land.
¹³'The fig tree has ripened its early figs,
And the vines of Semadar have given a scent.
Come now, my darling, my fair one.
¹⁴'O my dove, in the concealed places in the cliffs, in the steep hiding
   places,
Show me fully your appearance, let me hear your voice,
For your voice is pleasant and your appearance is beautiful.'

Notes on the text

2:8. 'Voice' (*qôl*) has a wide semantic range. It could refer to the sound of Solomon's speech, or to the sound of his approach, but it could also be used in a figurative way to speak of his approach to Shulammith from a distance. Joüon 162e states that *qôl* followed by a genitive is often used as an exclamation, 'I hear my beloved!'

'Behold' (*hinnēh*) suggests breathless, immediate, on-the-scene reporting (Longman 2001: 119). This sense is reinforced by the participles that indicate action taking place at the time when she reports it, thus focusing the attention of the reader on the action in progress (Exum 2005b: 81).

9. Waltke 7.4.3a regards the pl. *'ayyālîm* as 'a kind of generalization whereby a whole species of animal is designated by a plural form', and renders the expression 'a young stag'.

'*Our* wall' probably refers to Shulammith's family home, or specifically, as in 3:4 and 8:2, the home of her mother. This was a place of safety and security for her (Keel 1994: 96).

10. Stendebach, *TDOT* 11:218, notes that the combination of *'ānâ* and *'āmar* suggests a stereotyped dialogue formula, and should be translated 'he responded by saying', implying a quick lively response.

The reflexive pronoun *lāk*, used with the imperatives *qûmî* and *lĕkî*, emphasizes Shulammith's personal, conscious response to Solomon (cf. Waltke 11.2.10d).

The invitation *qûmî* could be used in its primary physical sense 'arise', as in 5:5, but more probably is used here and in v. 13 as an auxiliary verb, as in Gen. 27:19 and Ps. 95:1 (Bloch and Bloch 1995: 154).

11. *sĕtāw* is a loanword from Aram., and occurs only here in the OT. G. L. Carr (1984: 97) observes that the Tg on Gen. 8:22 uses it as a comment on *hōrep* to refer to the winter.

12. Two verbal roots *zmr* are attested in the OT, one meaning 'to prune' and the other 'to sing'. Goulder (1986: 23; contra Lemaire 1975: 26) argues that the parallel references in v. 12 are to non-human activities, so it may be better to render *zāmîr* as the singing of the birds rather than as the human activity of pruning the vines. Although the LXX and Symmachus clearly refer to pruning in their translations (cf. Snaith 1993: 38, who links the verse with the Gezer calendar that places the second pruning of the vines in June), pruning was generally done early in the spring (Shea 1993: 243), so it might be better to read *zāmîr* as 'singing', similar to its use in 2 Sam. 23:1, Pss 95:2, 119:54, Isa. 24:16, 25:5 and Job 35:10. However, it could possibly be that the poet has used *zāmîr* with intentional ambiguity (Raabe 1991: 214–215; S. M. Paul 1992: 151; Fokkelman 2001: 195), looking backward to the blossoms that have appeared in the land and looking forward to the voice of the turtledove that is heard in the land (Roberts 2007: 113).

13. Abegg, *NIDOTTE* 2:196, argues from Akk. and Aram. cognates that *ḥānat* refers to the ripening process. G. L. Carr (1984: 100) notes that recently discovered Eblaite texts suggest that *sĕmādar* refers to a place from which an especially good variety of grapevine was imported into Israel (cf. Borowski 1987: 104–105). Alternatively, the LXX and Symmachus render it in the sense of the bloom or blooming of the vines, and Rashi says that the stage of *sĕmādar* is when the blossom falls away from the vine and the tender grapes are first visible (Lehrman 1983: 8).

14. 'Cliffs' (*madrēgâ*) in Ezek. 38:20 refers to rock ledges on which doves could be seen only fleetingly (Keel 1994: 106).

'Your appearance' (*mar'ayik*) is a pl. form that may suggest a total view of her appearance rather than a partial glimpse from a distance. To include this nuance, the translation modifies the verb with the adverb 'fully'. Alternatively, GKC 93ss asserts that the pl. suffix may be only an apparent pl., resulting from a contraction of the original sg. form.

Form, structure and setting

The entire lyric in 2:8–14 is spoken by Shulammith, although in vv. 10–14 she quotes the words of Solomon's proposal to her. This section is particularly rich with poetic devices, including nine uses of repeated words or phrases, seven similar terms or expressions, and several contrasts that produce an elevated style appropriate for the occasion. In 2:8–9, the arrival of Solomon is marked by two uses of *hinnēh* (behold) and several participles suggesting his excitement and eagerness. The proposal in 2:10–13 is framed by the inclusio 'Come now, my darling, my fair one,' as Solomon invites Shulammith to come out of the seclusion and safety of her home to join him in the springtime of love. The image of the emergence of spring after winter is changed into the image of a shy dove leaving its hiding places as Solomon in 2:14 invites Shulammith to come to him. Thus the contrast between Solomon's eagerness and Shulammith's reticence is sharply drawn by the use of metaphors.

Comment

8. As this song begins, it is evident that both Shulammith and Solomon have a heightened sense of expectation. Keel (1994: 95) observes well, 'Lovers, whose thoughts and feelings incessantly revolve around each other, are inclined to hear or see the coming of the beloved in every noise or in every person appearing on the horizon. This continuing but often disappointed expectation makes the real event always a happy surprise.' Solomon's love has the same effect on him that Jacob's love for Rachel evoked in Gen. 29:20. In imaginative terms, love enables him to leap over mountains in a single bound. The verb *dālag* is used in 2 Sam. 22:30 for scaling high fortifications, and here it refers to overcoming all obstacles to being with Shulammith. His love motivates and empowers him to do whatever is necessary to get to her. In fact, Solomon's deep love makes this effort seem almost effortless, as is implied by *mĕqappēṣ*.

9. As Shulammith describes the eager approach of Solomon, she uses the explicit comparison *dômeh*, rather than a metaphor or a simple simile with *kĕ*, to liken him to a gazelle or a young stag. The point of reference to these animals is their agility and speed (cf. the similar sense in 2:17 and 8:14), which picture his excitement. As Solomon arrives at her house, he stops to stand behind the wall. He does not barge in uninvited, as though she were his by right, but waits for her to come out to him or to ask him in. Set in the wall are open windows as well as lattice work, perhaps similar to the Mashrabiyya Screen, a traditional Egypt. type of window lattice now displayed in the Victoria and Albert Museum in London. The pl. forms 'gazing at the *windows*, peering through the *lattices*' suggest that Solomon goes from opening to opening in his excited attempt to catch sight of Shulammith. Although it is implied that she is anticipating his arrival, the focus of this verse on Solomon's looking through the window from the outside is an inversion of a familiar OT motif of a woman looking out of the window for the return of a warrior (cf. Judg. 5:28; 2 Kgs 9:30).

10. Apparently, Shulammith responds to Solomon's eager arrival by calling out to him from inside her house, because in v. 10 Solomon answers her verbally. Solomon invites her to come outside to him with a tone of an affirming, tender appeal to her, not by the force of a demand. Much later in the song cycle, Shulammith in 7:11[12] similarly takes the initiative to invite Solomon to go out into the field with her. The pericope in 2:10–13, bracketed by the inclusio 'Come now, my darling, my fair one,' comprises Solomon's proposal of marriage expressed in the time-honoured love language of springtime. *DBI* 806 notes well, 'In pastoral love poetry, nature supplies most of the images by which the lovers express their romantic passions, including their praise of the beloved.'

11. The excitement Shulammith discerns in Solomon as he approaches her house (2:8) and then stands before the wall (2:9) is also evident in his speech, as Solomon states, 'Behold (*hinnēh*), the winter has passed by'. The land of Israel has two main seasons, a rainy winter and a dry summer, with only brief transitional periods between them. After the long winter in which about seventy percent of the annual rainfall falls between November and February (Frick, *ABD* 5:612), the coming of spring at the end of April is welcome relief. In this verse, winter is pictured as a traveller who has passed through the land and is now gone (G. L. Carr 1984: 97). It is significant to contrast Shulammith's words in 1:6, in which she laments her painful past, with Solomon's optimistic anticipation of their bright future in the emerging springtime.

12. Solomon appeals to both sight and sound as evidence that spring has arrived. In using these references, he is speaking in language familiar to Shulammith. As a former vinedresser (cf. 1:6), Shulammith would have been cognizant of these natural indicators of spring. Based on the appearance of the blossoms, Solomon states that now is the time for the singing of the turtledove, a migratory songbird that returns to Israel at its regular time in the beginning of the spring (cf. Jer. 8:7; Bloch and Bloch 1995: 155). The term *'ēt*, which speaks of a suitable time, may also suggest, as in Eccl. 3:1–11, the time sovereignly ordained by God. In this context, the time when nature comes alive with its delights could speak of the divinely planned time for the blossoming of their love.

13. As in the previous two verses, the references here to the early figs and the scent of the grapevines signal the arrival of spring. In Israel, the fig tree blossoms in late March, and the early edible figs develop immediately after that in April (Isa. 28:4; Ringgren, *TDOT* 15:546). In addition to being an indicator of time, these plants in the OT are familiar symbols of prosperity and security (cf. 1 Kgs 4:25[5:5]; 2 Kgs 18:31; Joel 1:12; Amos 4:9; Hab. 3:17; Zech. 3:10). In effect, they picture life that is rich and sweet. Bergant (2001: 30) observes, 'The delicacy of new life and the promise that it extends, the enchantment with which spring invades the senses, both evoke and mirror the splendor of the passion of these lovers. Calling the woman into springtime is really calling her into love.'

14. Apparently, Shulammith initially responds with shyness and hesitation to Solomon's proposal, as a dove that seeks refuge in the cliffs (cf. Jer. 48:28). Emotionally, it is as though she remains in hiding, unseen and silent to him. Solomon, however, desires to find her accessible to him, a sentiment widely expressed in love poetry. Just as nature has awakened to spring (2:12), so Solomon wants Shulammith to awaken to his love. Using the language of sight and sound, Solomon indicates that what he sees and hears in her already delights him, but he wants to know her better. It may be that the language of hiddenness and inaccessibility is another subtle indicator of Shulammith's virginity at this point in the Song (Garrett 2004: 160).

Explanation

8–9. Both Shulammith's description and Solomon's actions in coming to her reflect that their hearts are racing with excitement and joy. It is true that love is not the same as emotion, but love should indeed engage the emotions. Love should not be mere duty, but it should also entail marvellous delight, as the couple in Song of Songs amply demonstrate. Solomon's actions are presented as vivid and fast, for he is eager and excited to catch a glimpse of the woman he loves. His emotions are truly engaged by his love for Shulammith, in contrast to many marriages in the ancient world that were primarily arranged with financial, or, in the case of kings, political, factors in view.

The reference to Solomon standing behind the wall of the house may well be linked with other uses of a wall in 4:12 and 8:8–9 to refer to Shulammith's chastity. If that sense is included here, then 2:9 suggests indirectly that Shulammith is still a virgin at this point in the Song. The eagerness and excitement both of them feel in their love has not caused them to participate in sexual intimacy before the time of their wedding in ch. 4.

10–13. The Song in general, and this section in particular, uses the language of springtime familiar in love poetry throughout history. It is as though up to this point the lovers have experienced only the dullness of winter, but now love is awakening them to the joys of life in all of its vivid colours and fruitfulness. Spring, then, is an apt analogy to the delightful emotions evoked by love.

Hostetter, *NIDOTTE* 3:685, declares accurately that the depiction of spring in this lyric is 'one of the most beautiful songs to nature in the [HB]' and that 'the chapter's picture of springtime love may be among the most exquisite anywhere in literature'. As the winter rains give way to the flowers and songs of spring, the natural world is waking from its long slumber, just as Solomon and Shulammith are being awakened by love. All of nature is poised for new life, so this is the ideal time for the blossoming of their love.

Both Solomon and Shulammith make frequent use of sensual language as they speak of love. Just as Shulammith describes his 'scent' (*rêaḥ*) in 1:3, so Solomon here appeals to the taste of the early figs and the scent of the vines in springtime. By using rustic images that evoke the delights of spring, Solomon speaks in language familiar to her. With his affectionate address 'My darling, my fair one' Solomon frames his proposal in 2:10–13 in the language of the heart. He does not try to force her, but tenderly seeks to draw her into his loving embrace by fervent invitation.

14. As Solomon poetically appeals to Shulammith to emerge from her concealed place in the cliffs, he indicates that love requires openness and accessibility between the lovers; it cannot flourish in the context of emotional distance, but needs genuine connection. Love also does not run roughshod over the feelings of others, but is considerate of one's inner fears and hesitations even as it endeavours to move the relationship along to greater depths of intimacy.

SONG OF SONGS 2:15–17

Translation

SHULAMMITH

[15]Seize for us [the] foxes, little foxes devastating the vineyards,
  Even our vineyards of Semadar.
[16]My beloved is mine, and I am his,
  The one who pastures in the lotuses.
[17]Until the day breathes and shadows flee,
  Turn, my beloved, be like a gazelle or a stag of the deer
  Upon the mountains of spices.

Notes on the text

2:15. 'Foxes', the pl. of *šûʿāl*, often refers to vicious and destructive animals (Ps. 63:10[11]; Lam. 4:18; Neh. 4:3[3:25]), or figuratively of humans who bring destructive consequences (Ezek. 13:4). Bodenheimer, *IDB* 2:249, argues reasonably that the contexts in which *šûʿāl* is used in the OT to describe a carrion-eater would point in the direction of the jackal as the referent. In Song 2:15, however, the *šûʿālîm* are said to devastate plants, so Borowski (1987: 156–157) could possibly be correct in identifying these animals as a species of fruit-eating bat that is commonly known in Israel as the flying fox.

As in 2:13, *sĕmādar* may well refer to a particularly good variety of grapevine. The contrast, then, would be between the high potential of the vineyards and the destruction wrought by the foxes to them.

16. The verb *rāʿâ* can be used for the grazing of animals, and Keel (1994: 114) renders it as a figurative reference to Solomon as a gazelle, resuming the language of 2:9. More probably, it is used here, as elsewhere in the Song, to speak of the human subject Solomon pasturing in the lotuses. Wallis, *TDOT* 13:551, observes:

> The lover pastures his sheep among the lilies (or lotus blossoms; Cant. 2:16; 4:5; 6:30), in the gardens (6:2). There his beloved seeks him as she pastures her kids (1:7) and finds him beside the shepherds' tents (1:8). Here the image of the shepherd and its related imagery appear to have entered the figurative world of 'specialized erotic language'.

17. 'Breathes' (*pûaḥ*) refers to 'the breaking of day when the breezes stir and the protecting shadows (cf. 2:3) of night slip away' (G. L. Carr 1984: 103; cf. Bloch and Bloch 1995: 157; contra Reiterer, *TDOT* 11:505–506). A similar sentiment is expressed in an early Sum. love poem as the woman urges her lover to spend the night with her until dawn (Sefati 1997: 542).

The Hebr. term *beter* has been interpreted in various ways. Some follow Aquila, Symmachus and Jerome in regarding it as a place name Bether, perhaps to be identified with Bettir, a site six miles south-west of Jerusalem (Gold, *IDB* 1:393). Others explain the term as referring to separation, and implying the cleavage of Shulammith's breasts. Keel (1994: 115–117) regards it as an Indian spice, perhaps cinnamon, linking it with 4:6 and 8:14, and this rendering may well be the best.

Form, structure and setting

This short lyric may well be devoted completely to the words of Shulammith, although the speaker in v. 15 is not definite. Although it is closely related to the preceding lyric in 2:8–14, it forms Shulammith's response to the proposal by Solomon, and thus it is best viewed as a discrete unit. The song is dominated by two contrasting images: the foxes in 2:15 represent young men who are sexually predatory, but Solomon is pictured in 2:17 as a gazelle that Shulammith longs to have frolic on the scented mountains of her breasts. As she speaks, Shulammith builds to a climax from the threat of moral ruin by the young men (2:15) to a sense of mutual belonging with Solomon (2:16) to her expressed desire for leisurely intimacy with Solomon (2:17).

Comment

15. The speaker of this verse is ambiguous, and several suggestions have been offered. Bloch and Bloch (1995: 157) propose that Shulammith's brothers are the pl. speakers here because of their expressed concern in 8:8–9 to protect her virginity, but that would be an interpolation into a conversation that otherwise is between Shulammith and Solomon alone. It is possible that Solomon is the speaker, calling upon Shulammith to join with him in overcoming the threats of the foxes (Glickman 1976: 49). Delitzsch (1875: 53–54) regards this as a ditty sung by Shulammith and drawn from her experience as a vinedresser, and Murphy (1990: 141) thinks that it is Shulammith's saucy reply to her lover, indicating that she is not inaccessible as his address to her as a dove in the previous verse would suggest.

In 1:6 and in 8:12, Shulammith refers to her own body as a vineyard, and this metaphor parallels the image of Shulammith as a garden in 4:12 – 5:1. In view of that evidence, it is probably best to view this verse as Shulammith referring primarily to her body as a vineyard, and the pl. 'our vineyards' would then indicate that her situation is a potential predicament shared by the other young women as well. The little foxes that devastate vineyards, then, represent young men who too often attempt to bring the moral ruin of women and who now threaten Shulammith's virginity (cf. Exum 2003b: 148). As in 2:3, where Shulammith likens young men to the inhospitable forest, she is aware of the potential danger they pose to her and her peers. Like the beautiful vines of Semadar, women poised at the onset of their sexual maturity are particularly attractive to men who would compromise their purity. Because foxes are nocturnal, typically attacking under cover of darkness, Shulammith will go on in 2:17 to express her desire that Solomon's pleasurable and protective presence remain with her to guard her throughout the night.

16. In stark contrast to the destructive foxes in v. 15 is Solomon, whom Shulammith pictures as pasturing in the lotuses. The image of a shepherd connotes the traits necessary in caring for sheep in ancient Israel, among which were tenderness, courage, diligence and faithfulness. This verse is the first of three similar, but subtly different, refrains in 2:16, 6:3 and 7:10[11]. Here Shulammith's beloved, whom she first observed from a distance, has now proposed to her, so he is hers. In the Song, lotuses are often used with erotic reference (Bloch and Bloch 1995: 157). In 5:13 lotuses may be a figure for lips, and if this is the case here, then Solomon is kissing Shulammith in this scene, at least in her imagination (cf. her expressed desire in 2:17). Snaith (1993: 42), however, rightly cautions that the reader must be careful to remember that this is poetry, not allegory in which each detail in the language points to a specific reality.

17. This verse provides penetrating insight into the emotions Shulammith feels as her love causes desire for physical intimacy to grow in her heart. Building on the figurative picture of kissing in v. 16, she longs to linger in his embrace. Using again the image of a gazelle (2:9) to speak of Solomon, she declares her desire for Solomon playfully to fondle her breasts throughout the night, until the darkness slips away in the cool of the morning (Garrett 2004: 162). In her imagination, her scented breasts are the mountains on which Solomon her gazelle can frolic. In contrast to the wedding-night scene in 4:6, when Solomon echoes Shulammith's words in 2:17 as he resolves to go his way on the spiced mountains, at this time there is no record that Solomon accepts her invitation. His silence at least suggests that their sexual intimacy is not yet consummated at this point in the Song, but that it awaits their wedding in ch. 4.

Explanation

15. As in the ancient world, moral purity is under attack today, particularly in contemporary culture in which sexual images and messages are prevalent. In addition to the internal drives towards physical intimacy, external threats can damage the progress of love as God intends it. Sexual purity, however, is a treasure worth protecting. To do that requires intentional, resolute effort to combat the powerful forces that threaten to ruin it. Glickman (1976: 49–50) suggests several destructive factors that can ruin relationships in progress, but the problematic issues he cites such as jealousy, pride, selfishness or an unforgiving spirit, as ruinous as they may be, are more applications than the specific meaning of the text in 2:15. This verse with its warnings against immoral men complements the frequent cautions in Prov. 1 – 9 against the enticements of the strange woman, who threatens to lead the young man away from the path of wisdom.

16. Just as the Lord remedied the loneliness of Adam (Gen. 2:18) by creating Eve and bringing her to him so that she became bone of his bone and flesh of his flesh (Gen. 2:22–23), so in the Song there is an emerging sense of mutual connectedness in the couple. Neither the man nor the woman dominates in the Song, but they are connected in an increasingly profound bond of mutuality. Keel (1994: 114) notes, 'The misery of loneliness is overcome by the realization that she is there for him and he is there for her. The human finds fullness, security, peace, and freedom in this happy duality.' Love is nurtured best not by the qualities that impress and dazzle, but by the kind of character that makes one gentle and kind. Love touches the heart, and draws close the one loved in a sense of reciprocal connection.

17. For couples in love, keeping passion and purity in proper perspective can be a formidable challenge. Intense desire is not wrong in itself, but it must be held in check until the right time. The words of Shulammith's invitation to Solomon are strikingly similar to those by which the strange woman in Prov. 7:18 entices the naive youth (cf. Grossberg 1994: 9):

> Let us drink our fill of love till morning,
>   let us delight in amorous embrace.

The sexual desire that love produces can be fulfilled properly only within marriage. When that time arrives, intimacy becomes a good and sacred gift to be enjoyed, but premarital sex subverts the plan of God. Hess (2005: 101) comments on the Song, 'It is erotic love poetry that makes no apology for appealing to all of the senses that God has created. Yet it also affirms that there is an order to this wonderful gift of sex. Its potency and wildness does not mean that there is no restraint.' Intimacy that honours God must overcome both the external threats and the internal drives that could easily compromise its purity.

SONG OF SONGS 3:1–5

Translation

SHULAMMITH

¹Upon my bed night by night I sought him whom my soul loves.
I sought him, but I did not find him.
²I will arise and go around in the city,
In the streets and in the open places;
I will seek him whom my soul loves.
I sought him but I did not find him.
³The guards, the ones going around in the city, found me.
[I asked them,] 'Have you seen him whom my soul loves?'
⁴A short time after I passed away from them,
I found him whom my soul loves.
I clutched him, and I did not let him go,
Until I brought him into the house of my mother,
And into the chamber of her who conceived me.
⁵I adjure you, O daughters of Jerusalem,
By the gazelles or by the does in the field,
Do not incite or excite love until it is pleased.

Notes on the text

3:1. *ballêlôt* is probably used to speak of repeated activity, as in Pss 16:7, 92:2[3] and 134:1, so it may be rendered 'night after night' (Bloch and Bloch 1995: 158). It may well refer to a recurrent dream or nightmare that Shulammith has. Alternatively, Joüon 136b suggests it could mean one night of interrupted sleep.

'Soul' (*nepeš*) stands for Shulammith's whole person, not just for her spiritual aspect. Keel (1994: 121) notes well, 'her whole desire, all her yearnings, her thoughts, her feelings, and her physical needs are directed toward him. It is this kind of longing and passion that the poem wants to portray.'

2. Because Shulammith states in 3:1 that she is upon her bed, the use of *qûm* in this verse probably means 'to arise', rather than being used as an auxiliary verb as in 2:10, 13.

In contrast to an unwalled village, a city (*'îr*) was fortified by a protective wall (McCown, *IDB* 1:633). Thus this scene takes place in an urban context, in contrast to the language of rural nature that dominates the proposal in 2:10–14.

The 'open places' (*rĕḥōbôt*) denote the public square where all sorts of social interactions occurred in the ancient city. Because this was often the site where prostitutes enticed men (Ezek. 16:24, 31; Prov. 7:12), it was a place that was particularly dangerous for a young woman to be alone at night (Judg. 19:15–20; Bartelmus, *TDOT* 13:434).

3. An introductory phrase, 'I asked them', is implied at the beginning of the second line. The absence of the explicit words has the effect of heightening the sense of drama and urgency Shulammith feels (Bloch and Bloch 1995: 158).

4. As in 2:15, the verb *'āḥaz* describes a forceful action, here rendered 'clutched', in contrast to its frequent antonym *rāpâ* (let go).

'The house of my mother' is rendered by Goulder (1986: 27) as a euphemism for welcoming Solomon into her womb in sexual intercourse. In view of the references to her brothers in 1:6 and 8:8–9, Goulder's reading of the language of family in this verse as a reference to sexual intimacy seems to be forced.

5. This verse is identical to 2:7, and the notes on that text apply here as well.

Form, structure and setting

This section is marked off as a unit by the refrain in 2:17 (repeated later in 4:6) that closes the preceding section, and by its culminating refrain in 3:5, which repeats 2:7 and anticipates 8:4. This lyric, totally in the voice of Shulammith, is full of contrasts. It may well be a dream sequence, which would explain its fast changes of scene and its kaleidoscopic portrayals of action. The dominant metaphor of the dream sequence is that of Shulammith's seeking (twice in 3:1 and twice in 3:2) in order to find Solomon (once in each of vv. 1–4). The language of her resolution has clear linguistic links to the previous section, because 'I will arise (*'aqûmâ*)' echoes Solomon's call to her to come with him (*qûmî*) in 2:10, 13, and Shulammith's plan to 'go around' (*'ăsôbĕbâ*) in the city to find him recalls her longing for Solomon to 'turn' (*sōb*) and be like a gazelle upon her breasts in 2:17. When she finds him at last, she clutches him and does not let him go (3:4). In her search, Shulammith leaves the private space of her bed to seek for Solomon in the public spaces of the city, and then brings him into the private space of her mother's chamber. Her dream of leading him into the room of her mother who conceived her, with its undeniable sexual overtones, prompts her again to recognize her vulnerability to sexual temptation at this time when her emotions are so highly aroused, so she calls upon the court girls not to excite her passions. As in 2:7, the sound play in her adjuration imitates the language of an oath in the divine name while employing the dialect of rustic love poetry.

If the Song is read as an impressionistic song cyle with temporal progression, then Shulammith's feelings of separation may be prompted by Solomon's departure after his proposal of marriage in 2:8–14 to prepare for the wedding, introduced with the procession in 3:6–11. This reading would explain the profound change in Shulammith's mood between 2:17 and 3:1. Bergant (2001: 34) observes that 'in the total context of the Song of Songs, it mirrors the emotional tension that lovers experience between the rapture of union and the desolation of separation'.

Comment

1. In 2:15, Shulammith recognized the external threat of young men; here she manifests the internal threat of the fear of being forsaken. Harding (2008: 49) suggests perceptively that the scene in 3:1–4 can be read 'as a moment of crisis in the woman's perception of her relationship, an expression of her perceived vulnerabilities in love and as her attempt to come to terms with these vulnerabilities and deal with them'. As in 2:17, she longs to feel his close presence, but she cannot find him. Her love for Solomon is so powerful that the fear of losing him makes her anxious (Glickman 1976: 51–52; Falk 1990: 148).

The expression 'upon my bed' indicates where Shulammith is when she has the experience of 3:1–5. It is possible that she describes a literal scene, but the abrupt scene changes and her night-time search, which would have been precariously risky for a woman in the ancient world, suggest better that this is a dream or a daydream produced by her subconscious fears and longings (Garrett 2004: 174). Murphy (1990: 145) reasons:

> It is more like 'daydreaming' than a dream, the fantasy of one who yearns to be with an absent lover. Psychologically, this may be only a slight degree removed from the expression of the unconscious in dream. The description internalizes an adventure, a quest, that is always going on within the woman when she is apart from the man.

As in Pss 4:4[5], 6:6[7] and 149:5, the bedroom can refer to the place for the expression of one's most intense emotions (Hamilton, *TWOT* 2:922), although *miškāb* is not always the term for 'bed' used in these contexts. In seeking for her beloved, Shulammith imaginatively exerts intentional, intense effort, but despite her best efforts is unable to find him.

2. In the first part of this verse, Shulammith discloses her internal conversation as she resolves to search for Solomon. In 3:1, she has expressed in general terms that she sought Solomon but did not find him. In 3:2, the particulars of her search are detailed. Missing Solomon in her private space, she goes out into the public space in the centre of the city to locate him. The extended description of her best attempts to find Solomon by extensive search is contrasted with the terse statement of her disappointing failure in her effort. Decidedly different from the adulteress in Prov. 7:12, who goes out into the street at night as she lurks for a victim, and Gomer in Hos. 2:5, who goes after her lovers, Shulammith in seeking her beloved is drawn by the power of love, not by the lust of illicit passion. In this unsuccessful quest, she places herself in considerable danger as she tries to locate Solomon, an indication of the desperate longing she feels for him (Garrett 2004: 171).

3. Shulammith continues to describe her imaginative search for Solomon. The order of the words in the Hebr. text makes a strong contrast with v. 2. The previous verse ends with Shulammith saying, 'I did not find him'. V. 3, referring to the guards, begins with the words 'They found me'. Shulammith 'went around' (*'ăsôbĕbâ*; 3:2) looking for Solomon in the city, and is found by 'the guards who go around' (*hassōbĕbîm*) there. There is a hint of irony, because she 'is unable to find her lover, but the guardians of the city find her' (Murphy 1990: 145). All of Shulammith's resolute effort has come to nought, so, sensing her own inability, she appeals for help in her search. In contrast to the subsequent parallel scene in 5:7, she here regards the guards as a help to her, not a threat. As she speaks to them, she does not give any literal description of Solomon, but rather she refers to him with the language of her heart as 'him whom my soul loves'.

4. Her dream continues in v. 4, because, without receiving directions from the guards, she suddenly finds Solomon. After two statements of disappointment ('I did not find him'; 3:1–2), at last she locates him whom her soul loves. She grasps him and does not relax her grip, for she desperately wants to keep hold of him so that she does not lose him again. In contrast with 1:4, when Solomon brings her into his chambers, and 2:4, when he brings her to the house of wine, Shulammith now takes the initiative as she brings him to the house of her mother. This place is where she learned to love (cf. 8:2). This also is a place of security after her traumatic nightmare of losing Solomon (Glickman 1976: 53). It is the safest and most private place she knows (Munro 1995: 70), and therefore is an apt picture of her great relief. In addition, as Marsman (2003: 164) notes, this is an indication of her desire that Solomon 'become part of the family to whom it was permitted to enter areas that were not accessible to strangers'.

5. In her dream, Shulammith is holding on to Solomon after finding him at last (3:4). This act is similar to the formula of embrace in 2:6 and 8:3 that precedes the other two uses of this refrain in the Song (Murphy 1990: 146). As in 2:7, Shulammith is keenly aware of her strong and increasing desire for Solomon that Exum (1998: 246) aptly describes as 'arousal on the brink of fulfillment'. Because of this real internal threat to her purity before her marriage, she calls on the daughters of Jerusalem not to add external pressure that could arouse her passions prematurely. As Murphy (1990: 147) observes, Shulammith is probably not speaking directly to the court girls physically present with her, but only contemplating the kind of pressure they can exert on her when her emotions are already highly charged. The proper time for sexual intimacy is rapidly approaching, but it is not yet the right time. Until then, love must not be aroused into sexual intimacy.

Explanation

1. For people in love, like Shulammith and Solomon, physical or psychological distance can be intensely painful. Love works to draw people together in intimacy, but many factors can cause a couple to feel separation and pain. Lewis (1960: 169) cautions wisely, 'To love at all is to be vulnerable. Love anything, and your heart will certainly be wrung and possibly be broken. If you want to make sure of keeping it intact, you must give your heart to no one ... It will not be broken; it will become unbreakable, impenetrable, irredeemable.' The feeling of love must be tested to prove if it is real. Time and separation are often painful experiences that serve to demonstrate whether the love one feels is truly genuine. Just as Shulammith expended intense effort in the search for her beloved, Wisdom says that she loves those who love her and those who diligently seek her will find her (Prov. 8:17; cf. Prov. 2:4).

2. The desire and longing prompted by true love can lead one to abandon convenience, comfort, and even safety. Love leads one to think foremost of the beloved and of the relationship, and only secondarily of personal interest. As Shulammith's bold venture into the night illustrates, love must be willing to take risks rather than hold back with undue caution and self-protection.

3. Love directs a couple together into a deep private relationship that is theirs alone. At the same time, it is not independent of other people, because it draws strength from the wider social circle. The demands of love may exhaust personal resources, but the Song reveals that, at times like that, other people in the family or society can step in to provide additional resources which enable intimacy to progress. Love, then, is nurtured by the larger social community. In a comparable way, in both the OT and the NT, the community of believers plays a central role in nurturing love for God and for one another (Ps. 34:3[4]; Heb. 10:24–25).

4. Taking the risk of love has its reward, for it leads to a greater sense of unity and security in the relationship. Love does not seek for what is easy, painless or most convenient. Rather, love persists until it finds its goal, and has sufficient courage and commitment to keep moving towards oneness in a deepening intimacy. In Phil. 3:8–14, Paul reflects the same kind of resolve in his pursuit of knowing Christ as he keeps pressing on towards the goal for which God called him.

5. As love progresses towards marriage, the increasing desire for intimacy that it provokes is both a great delight and a considerable danger. Sexual passion must be kept under control, or else like a river overflowing its banks it can bring devastation. When kept within God-honouring boundaries, passion within the marital bond becomes a source of deep joy. Couples engaged to be married will probably feel the same sexual tension Shulammith and Solomon experienced, and, if they are wise, will follow the example of this ancient couple in waiting until their wedding to taste the fruit of sexual pleasure.

SONG OF SONGS 3:6–11

Translation

NARRATOR

> [6]Who is this coming up from the wilderness like columns of smoke,
>   Perfumed with myrrh and frankincense from all the powders of the
>   merchant!
> [7]Behold, Solomon's couch!
>   Sixty select warriors of Israel are surrounding it.
> [8]All of them are holding a sword, taught in war;
>   Each of them has a sword on his thigh because of danger in the
>   night-time.
> [9]King Solomon has commissioned a palanquin from the trees of
>   Lebanon.
> [10]He made its posts of silver, its support of gold, its seat of purple cloth;
>   Its interior was decorated with erotic scenes by the daughters of
>   Jerusalem.
> [11]O daughters of Zion, go out and see King Solomon
>   With the wreath with which his mother crowned him
>   On the day of his wedding and on the day of his supreme gladness.

Notes on the text

3:6. The interrogative pronoun *mî* is variously translated 'who?' (AV, ASV, NIV) or 'what?' (RSV, JB, NEB). Although *mî* can on rare occasions refer to a thing (GKC 144b), in this case the bed in 3:7–11 (cf. Murphy 1990: 151), an impersonal referent is typically introduced by *mâ*, as in Exod. 13:14. G. L. Carr (1984: 108) notes, 'This same idiom appears in Song 6:10, again with no answer in the text, and in 8:5 where the second half of the colon demands the answer "the girl" (bride).' This is probably not a genuine question, but rather, as in 6:10, 8:5 and Isa. 60:8, a rhetorical device for an exclamation at her dramatic entrance on the scene (Bloch and Bloch 1995: 159).

The f. sg. pronoun *zō't*, as well as the verbal forms *'ōlâ* and *mĕquṭṭeret*, indicates that Shulammith is probably in view, as in the parallels in 6:10 and 8:5 (contra Exum 2003a: 309).

7. As in 1:15, 16, 2:8, 9, 11, 'behold' (*hinnēh*) expresses a strong and excited exclamation.

Waltke 9.7c notes that the use of the rare relative form *šel* after 'his couch' can best be rendered 'Solomon's couch'.

The expression that reads lit. 'sixty warriors from the warriors of Israel' probably has the sense of a superlative construction indicating that the best of the warriors in the realm have been selected to accompany and protect Shulammith.

In echoing Shulammith's search throughout the city in 3:2–3, *sābîb* (surrounding) emphasizes the thoroughness of the protection provided by the sixty select warriors.

8. 'Taught (*mĕlummĕdê*) in war' indicates that these guards are experienced warriors, trained in military skills and tempered in battle (cf. Kapelrud, *TDOT* 8:5).

In the OT, *paḥad* typically means 'fear' or 'dread', but is also used for 'danger' in Pss 53:5[6], 91:5, Job 3:25, 39:22, Prov. 1:26–27, 33 (Müller, *TDOT* 11:519).

9. The Hebr. term *'appiryôn* is used only here in the OT. Bloch and Bloch (1995: 153–164) consider it a stationary structure, similar to the royal pavilion in Esth. 1:6, and suggest it may be the palace Solomon built for Pharaoh's daughter (1 Kgs 7:79). The LXX translation *phoreion* describes a portable sedan chair, the sense in which the Talmud also takes the Hebr. word.

The verb *'āśâ* probably does not indicate that Solomon himself actually built the palanquin, but rather that he commissioned the sedan chair to be made and set out its specifications. The phrase *lô* here is not used reflexively of Solomon making the palanquin for his own use, but it does indicate his direct involvement in its design.

10. The term 'support' (*rĕpîdâ*) refers to the base or covering for the palanquin. Hamilton, *NIDOTTE* 3:1181, observes that it 'may be compared with Arab. *rifadah*, "saddle-blanket," i.e., something spread out and over'.

'ahăbâ can mean either 'love', the tenderness or intricacy with which the daughters of Jerusalem constructed the interior (Roberts 2007: 156), or, perhaps more likely, 'lovemaking', the erotic scenes featured on the interior of the palanquin. G. L. Carr (1984: 112–113) notes, 'Inlay and decoration on beds is familiar from the ancient Near East. At Ugarit, samples of beds inlaid with erotic scenes have been found. Perhaps this is what is being described here.' Less probable, Driver (1950: 135), Hirschberg (1961: 373) and Gordis (1974: 85) argue from an Arab. cognate that the term refers to the interior lining of leather (cf. Hos. 11:4). It is possible, as Grossberg (1981a: 76) contends, that the term is used with an intended double reference, both to luxurious leather and to love.

11. 'Wreath' (*'ăṭārâ*) can indicate a wide variety of head coverings. Here, as in Isa. 61:10, it does not refer to the royal crown of office, but to a festive wreath. G. L. Carr (1984: 113) notes, 'The crowning by his mother indicates that this is a celebratory crowning, for the royal crowning was carried out by the divine representative, the High Priest.'

The expression 'gladness of heart' speaks of 'a gladness that possesses a person completely, extending from the centre to engulf every aspect of the human with happiness (cf. Eccl. 5:20[19]; Isa. 30:29; Jer. 15:16)' (Keel 1994: 137). The Hebr. concept of the heart (*lēb*) encompasses the total person, including the intellect, the emotions and the will (Fabry, *TDOT* 7:412), and in this phrase functions as a sort of superlative.

Form, structure and setting

This lyric is unusual in that it is spoken by the narrator about the couple, rather than being the speech of Solomon or Shulammith, as are the other lyrics in the first section of the Song. Solomon is mentioned three times (3:7, 9, 11), and is twice called King Solomon (3:9, 11). The narrator describes four items, and his descriptions of all of them – the bride (3:6), the bodyguard (3:7–8), the palanquin (3:9–10) and the groom (3:11) – are marked by the highest quality. To accentuate their excellence, the narrator employs a technique by which he looks at them first from a distance, and then zooms in to examine the details. For example, in 3:7–8 he notes that there are sixty warriors surrounding Shulammith, and then specifies them as warriors of Israel, expert with the sword, skilled in war, and with swords on their thighs. In 3:9–10, he calls attention to the palanquin, and then describes it as being made of the wood of Lebanon, silver, gold and purple, and having a luxurious interior. The climax of the section is reached in 3:11, when the narrator describes the festal crowning of Solomon on his wedding day by his mother.

The explicit reference to the wedding in this verse may well be construed as a determinable time marker for the whole Song. If the Song is an impressionistic but sequential depiction of the developing intimacy of Solomon and Shulammith, then the first three chapters of the Song comprise their relationship before their wedding, ch. 4 describes their wedding day and night, and chs. 5–8 reveal aspects of their continued growth in intimacy within their marriage. Hess (2005: 123) observes well, 'It is only within this commitment that all the joys of the male and female lovers come together, for it is only here that they realize the freedom to express those joys without restraint, knowing that the marriage bond seals their love in a lifetime commitment to each other.' By placing this section in the voice of the narrator, the poet signals that the subsequent section beginning in 4:1 finds its setting as the couple celebrate their wedding night.

Comment

6. In ancient Israel, because cities were typically constructed on high elevations for defensive purposes, entering a city would be described as 'going up' (*ʿālâ*) into it (Fuhs, *TDOT* 11:82). Shulammith's movement from the wilderness to the city parallels Solomon's earlier call to her in

2:10–14 to leave behind winter and to join him in the springtime, as well as her relocation from her rural background to the urban court. The 'wilderness' (*midbār*) was noted for its arid and barren condition that made it incapable of sustaining cultivation (cf. Ps. 107:33–36), a stark contrast to the luxuriant garden of love pictured in 4:12 – 5:1. Numerous OT passages also regard the wilderness as the haunt of dangerous and threatening animals, criminals and demons. The wilderness, with its suggestions of humiliation and hardship, could also imply that Shulammith is leaving the precariousness of her singleness (cf. 2:15–17) to dwell within the safety of Solomon's protection in marriage.

The columns of smoke could refer to the dust kicked up by the wedding procession as it travels from the wilderness, or they could represent the scented cloud of burning incense and spices that accompany the procession. In view of 4:6, 14, it could also indicate Shulammith's richly scented body as she approaches Solomon for their wedding. Whatever the specific reference, the senses of both sight and smell are engaged in this description. It may well be that the language is an intentional echo of the visit of the Queen of Sheba to Solomon in 1 Kgs 10:1–10 (Keel 1994: 126). If that is the case, then Shulammith is presented as arriving in a royal caravan laden with the most exquisite spices.

The powders of the merchant reflects the vast international commercial network in the time of Solomon (1 Kgs 9:26–28; 10:14–29; cf. Kjeld Nielsen 1986: 94–100), and the numerous uses of the term 'merchant' (*rôkēl*) in the description of the commercial power Tyre in Ezek. 27 fill out the picture of that trade in luxury items. This is clearly an opulent scene that befits the wedding of a king. The lavish description implies that this is the best wedding procession that a fabulously wealthy king could buy.

7. Although the expression *šellišlōmōh* is ambiguous, the f. referent in the preceding verse indicates that this is probably not the litter in which Solomon rides, but rather the litter that he sends to convey Shulammith to their wedding. Keel (1994: 128) observes, 'Great lords like Solomon did not pick up their wives and concubines themselves but sent an escort party to fetch the bride and bring her to them (cf. Genesis 24). Witnesses to that practice extend from the Hellenistic period (1 Macc. 9:37) back into the Bronze Age.' The 'couch' (*miṭṭâ*) could be used for sleeping or for sitting, and in Amos 6:4 and Esth. 1:6 is used, as here, for luxuriantly ornamented couches. Because ancient roads were not well maintained, the comfort of a high-ranking guest dictated that a hand-carried litter be used.

This lyric is marked by its three mentions of Solomon in 3:7, 9, 11. The only other specific references to the king by name in the Song occur in 1:5 and in 8:11–12.

In the OT, thirty men are listed in the celebratory group that accompanied Samson at his wedding (Judg. 14:11–20) and in the elite cadre of David's mighty men (2 Sam. 23:13, 18–19, 23–37). The sixty select warriors who surround the litter that transports Shulammith constitute a double military honour guard suitable for the occasion of the royal wedding and capable of protecting the bride from all potential dangers on the way. Keel (1978: 283–284) observes that in the thirteenth century BC the Egypt. pharaoh Ramses II sent his entire army to accompany his bride, the daughter of the Hittite king Hattusilis III. Solomon selects his very best men for this important responsibility of bringing Shulammith safely through the wilderness to their wedding.

The collocation of Israel with Solomon suggests that Israel here refers to the united monarchy, rather than to the northern kingdom after the division of 931 BC. This, however, is not necessarily indicative of the date of the writing of the Song (as argued by G. L. Carr 1984: 110), but rather of the time depicted in the literary setting of the poem.

8. It is clear from this verse that the sixty warriors accompanying the bridal procession are not just a ceremonial honour guard, but are a military bodyguard to protect Shulammith. As in 1:8 and 2:2, 14, Solomon has anticipated her fears and responded thoughtfully to them by making suitable provision. In the wilderness through which she passes, bandits and wild animals are prone to attack under the cover of darkness. Solomon realizes that his precious bride must be protected, even more so than a caravan of exotic goods would be. The warriors he selects for this vital responsibility are both capable, for they have been taught in war, and ready to defend her, for they have a sword on their thigh within reach at the moment of need.

The danger in the night-time that prompts Solomon's provision of the bodyguard has been interpreted in several ways. The repeated mention of the swords of the warriors makes it unlikely that the danger in view is that of evil spirits or demons (contra Keel 1994: 129, who cites in support of his view Ps. 91:5; Gen. 32:23ff.; Tob. 3.17; 6.14ff.), because material weapons would not prove adequate against spiritual opponents. It is better to regard *paḥad* as referring to 'some external, objective danger, here either roving bands of outlaws who would relish capturing a wealthy bridal train, or perhaps some wild animals that would attack a lone traveler but not a large party' (G. L. Carr 1984: 110).

9. The focus of this lyric shifts from Shulammith (3:6) to her escort (3:7–8) and now to her luxurious transportation (3:9–10). Every detail speaks of luxury and excellence, as Solomon takes thought of his bride's comfort and pleasure. From the third millennium BC onwards, vehicles of this type were used in Egypt by the wealthy. Ginsburg (1970: 152) describes the kind of canopied litter in view here:

> Palanquins were and are still used in the East by great personages. They are like a couch, sufficiently long for the rider to recline, covered with a canopy resting on pillars at the four corners, hung round with curtains to exclude the sun; they have a door, some-times of lattice-work, on each side. They are borne by four or more

men, by means of strong poles, like those of our sedan-chairs; and in traveling great distances, there are always several sets of men to relieve each other. The materials of which these palanquins are made, and the style of their construction, depend upon the rank and wealth of the owners.

As in the OT historical accounts, Solomon is here connected with the cedars of Lebanon (Mulder, *TDOT* 7:450; Nogalski, *NIDOTTE* 4:901), and as Ezek. 27:5 implies, this wood was prized in the ANE world for its high quality and pleasant scent (Liphschitz and Biger 1991: 168). Solomon uses the finest materials in this palanquin for his bride, and the resulting vehicle for the bridal procession is marked throughout by the highest quality.

10. In the ANE and Mediterranean worlds, purple cloth was usually reserved for the nobility and royalty (cf. Dan. 5:7, 16, 29; Esth. 8:15), because it was very expensive. Purple dye was derived from sea snails, and the great cost of its preparation made it highly valued as a status symbol by the wealthy and powerful from 1500 BC onwards (Jensen 1963: 105–109; Reinhold 1970; Doumet 1980). From the outside, the palanquin speaks of the utmost elegance and luxury. From the inside, what only Shulammith could see in the decorations are scenes of lovemaking, an appropriate theme during the procession to her wedding.

The daughters of Jerusalem, whose culture and beauty were once intimidating to Shulammith (1:5–6; cf. 2:2), now serve as artisans to prepare for her wedding, for she is being elevated to queen, and they function as her ladies in waiting. In 1:11, the court women said that they would make ornaments of gold and silver for Shulammith, but now they are doing for her far more than they realized when they made that offer.

11. Only after the extended description of the bridal procession in 3:6–10 does the bridegroom now come into view (contra Murphy 1990: 152, who argues that the bride is not in view at all in 3:6–11, but he fails to account properly for the f. forms in 3:6–7).

Only in this verse in the Song are the young women referred to as 'daughters of Zion' rather than as the 'daughters of Jerusalem'. Technically, Zion indicated originally the Jebusite citadel that David captured (2 Sam. 5:7), but later came to be used for the whole city of Jerusalem, and even to the nation of Israel in general. It may well be that Zion is used here as an elevated synonym for Jerusalem (Keel 1994: 136), as the courtiers are called to view the king. The festive crowning of brides and grooms on their wedding day was a longstanding custom among the Jews, but the Bab. Talmud, *Soṭah* 49a states that it was abandoned after the destruction of Jerusalem in AD 70 as a sign of mourning.

The OT historical accounts indicate that the queen mother often played an influential role in government, but in the Song the mothers of both Shulammith (3:4; 6:9; 8:2, 5) and Solomon are involved in matters of love. Shulammith's mother provides security in the face of her fears; Solomon's mother leads the public celebration of their union in marriage as she crowns her son with a festal diadem (cf. Ps. 21:3) on this day of his overwhelming joy.

Explanation

6. As the flower of love opens in bloom, it should liberate the heart to be lavish and generous. True love is not reluctant and calculating, offering only what it is required to give, but it should overflow by giving the best it can afford in time, attention, energy and material gifts. It is true that very few people could match the scale of Solomon's costly wedding procession in monetary figures, but all true lovers should equal the generosity of heart that prompted his lavish provision for his bride. Holding back from what one could give is the sign of a heart falling short of full love. In a similar way, in Rev. 19:7–8 at the marriage of the Lamb the bride of Christ is clothed in fine linen.

7–8. Because love highly values the one who is loved, it takes all possible steps to ensure the honour, comfort and protection of the one it cherishes. Love, then, is marked by consideration, even if that entails great cost and effort. It looks at situations from the perspective of the other, rather than in a self-interested way, and then takes action to allay the factors that would bring consternation or threat to the one loved. The ultimate pattern for love is Christ, who gave himself as an offering and a sacrifice to God for sinful humans (Eph. 5:2). Husbands are instructed to love their wives in this kind of self-sacrificing manner (Eph. 5:25–33).

9–10. As Solomon's lavish preparations for his bride demonstrate, love is not grudging in its gifts, but cares enough to give its very best (cf. Christ, who did not grasp his divine prerogatives, but humbled himself to become a human and die on the cross [Phil. 2:5–8; 2 Cor. 8:9]). Love wants to bring the greatest pleasure to one it loves, so it spares no effort to provide all that it possibly can. It seeks to bring delight by its considerate and generous provision.

11. True joy and fulfilment do not find their source in the position one holds or the power one wields, but from love that fills and overflows the heart. As love saturates the heart, it reaches out to enrich and delight the surrounding community, as its blessings spill over to benefit others. In an analogous way, in the praise psalms the grateful worshipper calls upon the community to join him in exulting in the goodness and greatness of Yahweh (cf. Ps. 149:1–3).

SONG OF SONGS 4:1–7

Translation

SOLOMON

> ¹Behold, you are beautiful, my darling!
> Behold, you are beautiful!
> Your eyes are doves from behind your veil;
> Your hair is like a flock of goats that are winding down Mount Gilead.
> ²Your teeth are like a shorn flock that go up from washing,
> For all of them bear twins and none of them is missing.
> ³Your lips are like a scarlet thread, and your mouth is beautiful;
> Your cheek is like a slice of pomegranate from behind your veil.
> ⁴Your neck is like the tower of David, built in courses;
> A thousand shields are hung upon it, all the shields of the warriors.
> ⁵Your two breasts are like two fawns,
> Twins of a gazelle that are grazing in the lotuses.
> ⁶Until the day breathes and the shadows flee,
> I will eagerly go to the mountain of myrrh and the hill of frankincense.
> ⁷All of you is beautiful, my darling,
> And there is no flaw in you.

Notes on the text

4:1. As in 2:8–9, the repeated *hinnāk* with *yāpâ* indicates Solomon's excitement in seeing Shulammith's beautiful appearance.

The term *ṣammâ* is used only four times in the OT: in Isa. 47:2 and in Song 4:1, 3; 6:7. There are several Hebr. words that refer to a veil, and the precise nature of *ṣammâ* is debated (cf. the discussion of three major options by Jenson, *NIDOTTE* 3:815), with some scholars viewing the term as figurative for Shulammith's hair (Bloch 2006: 156, following Rashi and Ibn Ezra), and others accepting the LXX translation *siōpēsis* (silence, taciturnity) as a reference to Shulammith's spirit of quiet expectation (Ceulemans and DeCrom 2007: 511–523). Van der Toorn (1995: 332) concludes, 'It is indeed likely that the Israelite bride wore the veil as an ornament and as a symbol of chastity to be lifted at the consummation of the marriage.'

The verb *gālaš* could mean 'recline', but the descriptive phrase here and in 6:5 suggests the rendering 'descend', or, as Exum (2005: 153) suggests, 'winding down'. Tuell (1993: 103) argues plausibly from a Ug. cognate that the term refers to Shulammith's wavy hair: 'A densely packed herd, viewed from a distance, seems to move downhill with a rippling, wavelike motion, as the animals in the front move forward and others move up to take their place.... The point of the simile now becomes clear: the beloved's hair is wavy.'

2. There is a wordplay between *šĕkkullām* (all of them) and *šakkulâ*. Bloch and Bloch (1995: 170) explain the significance of the latter term: 'A *šakkulāh* here is a ewe that has lost its lamb. Normally in a flock the lambs walk beside their mothers, so the place beside a *šakkulāh* is empty. Here again, the image applies at the same time to the Shulamite's teeth, none of which is missing.'

3. In Judg. 4:21–22, the word *raqqâ* clearly refers to the temple, but the fact that it is here behind Shulammith's veil indicates that her cheek may be in view, and this rendering is supported by the readings in the LXX (*mēlon*) and in Symmachus (*pareiai*). The suggestion by Keel (1994: 146) that this term refers to Shulammith's open mouth assumes that the interior of the pomegranate is the basis for the comparison, but this is unconvincing.

4. The phrase *bānûy lĕtalpiyyôt* is found only here in the OT, and its meaning is much debated. Although Bloch and Bloch (1995: 170–171) raise questions against it on grammatical grounds, the reading by Pope (1977: 465–467; cf. Honeyman 1949: 51–52), 'built in courses', seems to fit better the image of the verse than does the rendering 'built for perfection'.

The two words in this verse for 'shield', *māgēn* and *šelet*, are also used together in 2 Chr. 23:9 and Ezek. 27:11. They seem to be close synonyms rather than referring to two quite different pieces of military equipment.

5. *BHS* suggests without evidence that the final phrase has been added from 2:16, but the Hebr. MS data and the early Gr. translations all support its inclusion in this verse.

6. As in 2:17, 'breathes' (*pûaḥ*) refers to 'the breaking of the day when the breezes stir and the protecting shadows (cf. 2:3) of the night slip away' (G. L. Carr 1984: 103; cf. Bloch and Bloch 1995: 157; contra Reiterer, *TDOT* 11:505–506).

The pronoun and suffix *lî* with the verb 'I will go' has a reflexive sense (cf. Waltke 11.2.10d), as it emphasizes Solomon's strong intention, which here has been rendered 'I will eagerly go'.

7. The term *mûm* (flaw) is used in the OT mostly in the legal literature to refer to the ceremonial perfection of sacrificial animals (e.g. Lev. 22:20–21). Here it speaks of Solomon's perception that Shulammith has 'no physical or moral shortcoming which would detract or mar her beauty' (G. L. Carr 1984: 119; cf. the description of Absalom in 2 Sam. 14:25).

Form, structure and setting

This passage, like 5:10–16, 6:4–10 and 7:1–9[2–10], is a song of description or blazon, 'a poem that praises, by listing, the beautiful features and virtuous qualities of the beloved' (Ryken 1974: 225). In the Near Eastern literature such a song is called a *waṣf*, an Arab. term meaning 'description'. Although songs of description tend to be symbolic, this lyric is much more pictorial in nature. The expression 'you are beautiful, my darling' in vv. 1 and 7 frames the passage as an inclusion, and defines this section as a discrete unit. Within this frame, Solomon's description of Shulammith's beauty begins with her head and proceeds down to her breasts, making extensive use of similes drawn from both her rustic background and his courtly world. Solomon several times (in 4:2, 4–5) states a general description, and then focuses in on the particular details that demonstrate that trait. The arrangement of the comparisons in 4:1–5 from her eyes to her breasts intimates his increasing sexual desire, until in 4:6 he states his resolution to caress her breasts, probably as foreplay to the sexual intercouse that follows in the succeeding section. His final climactic statement in 4:7 proclaims the absolute perfection of Shulammith's beauty, which is greater than the sum of all its parts (Fisch 1988: 83).

Comment

1. The wedding ceremony expected after the detailed description of the procession of Shulammith (3:6–10) and the festive crowning of Solomon (3:11) is not mentioned, although it may plausibly be construed to have occurred before the couple speak intimately in their wedding chamber in this passage. This omission is explained best by recognizing that the focus of the Song is tracing impressionistically the progress of intimacy in their relationship, communicated here by the tender and ardent words by which Solomon speaks to his bride, rather than recording every specific detail of their relationship.

In 4:1–7, Solomon uses extravagant poetic language to express his feelings as he sees the overwhelming beauty of Shulammith on their wedding night. Glickman (1976: 14) notes well:

> Frequently when someone experiences great beauty, he finds that ordinary words are inadequate for expression. He gropes for poetry that may capture something of the beauty he sees. The king had this experience on his wedding night. With his bride before him, he searches for the perfect words of praise for her.

This kind of song of description is known by literary scholars as a blazon, and its longstanding Near Eastern version is called a *waṣf* (Bernat 2004: 328–334). In describing the one loved, the speaker combines pictorial language to represent what is seen with emotive language to reflect what is felt. Soulen (1967: 190) observes:

> The writer is not concerned that his hearers be able to retell in descriptive language the particular qualities or appearance of the woman described; he is much more interested that they share his

joy, awe, and delight. The poet is aware of an emotional congruity between his experience of his beloved's manifold beauty and his experience of the common wonders of life. With this in mind he sets out to convey his discovery in lyrical imagery by creating in his hearers an emotion congruent with his own in the presence of his beloved. (Cf. Brenner 2003: 296.)

The expression with which Solomon begins and ends the *waṣf*, 'You are beautiful, my darling', recalls the same words in his proposal in 2:13. The first line in this verse is the same as in 1:15, but now Solomon goes further in his description of his bride, signalling how the intimacy of their relationship has increased over time.

Although the meaning of the specific term *ṣammâ* is debated, in the OT a veil quite possibly could imply that this is Shulammith's wedding attire (cf. Gen. 29:23–25; Myers, *IDB* 4:747–748). Bloch and Bloch (1995: 167) argue unpersuasively that it is a poetic reference to her hair, for then Solomon would be saying that her hair is over her eyes, which would make them scarcely visible. It is better to construe the language as describing her eyes as partially hidden by her veil, just as doves hide in the concealed places in the cliffs in 2:14.

The comparison of her hair to a flock of goats sounds strange to the modern ear, but G. L. Carr (1984: 114–115) explains the reference: 'The imagery indicates that the beloved does not have her whole head covered with the veil, but that her long black locks ripple and tumble freely. Most Palestinian goats have long wavy black hair. The movement of a large flock on a distant hill makes it appear as if the whole hillside is alive (cf. 1:5; 5:11).' Mount Gilead is the hilly, fertile region east of the Jordan River that was noteworthy for its rich pasturage for livestock. This image, then, speaks of her dark, wavy, glowing, shimmering hair. No doubt, Shulammith's experience with young goats (cf. 1:7) enabled her to accept and appreciate this compliment by analogy.

2. Solomon's description of Shulammith in 4:1–7 proceeds from her head downwards. In this verse, he uses an extended metaphor of sheep to speak of her beautiful teeth. Shearing cuts off the wool that typically is darkened by dust, so shorn sheep that are freshly washed would be clean and usually white. By comparing her teeth to pairs of twin lambs, Solomon indicates that her teeth are perfectly aligned and without a gap in them (Hamilton, *NIDOTTE* 4:267). This image seems to be primarily pictorial, describing her teeth as white and even, which was probably a rarity in a time long before dental hygiene and orthodontia. Probably, this also implies that Shulammith has a lovely smile that highlights the beauty of her face.

3. Apparently, Solomon's description follows the direction of his gaze as he looks from her head downwards. The comparisons in this verse are primarily pictorial, describing the colour of Shulammith's lips and cheeks. Scarlet may well refer to a dye used as lip colouring in the ancient world. The references to scarlet in 2 Sam. 1:24 and Prov. 31:21 indicate that it was a mark of luxury in biblical times. The primary reference of 'mouth', if parallel to her lips and cheeks, is descriptive, but Murphy (1990: 155) suggests plausibly that it may also be a metonymy referring to her voice, the verse then combining visual and auditory features, as in 2:14. The comparison of her cheek to a slice of pomegranate may describe 'the blush-red smoothness of the pomegranate skin' (G. L. Carr 1984: 116–117), but it is also significant that pomegranates were widely regarded as aphrodisiacs in the ANE, and this secondary sense may well be in Solomon's mind.

4. Most of this song of description uses pastoral images, but in 4:4 Solomon speaks out of his own sphere of life as he employs an extended military figure. He compares Shulammith's neck to the tower of David, an edifice unattested in the OT texts or by archaeological discoveries, but which was apparently a significant military defence citadel. He goes on to say that this tower is built in courses. If the image is visual, then it pictures her necklaces that highlight the splendid beauty of her neck (Fox 1985: 130–131; cf. Isserlin 1958: 59). If the image is evocative, then it speaks of the pride and confidence that Shulammith's noble bearing exudes. Glickman (1976: 16–17) comments:

> The tower of David was a military fortress of the nation. The country depended upon the faithfulness and integrity of that fortress. And it must have been very reassuring to look upon that awesome stronghold, displaying as it did all the shields of war. The people had a healthy respect for it. Therefore, when the king likens the neck of his bride to the fortress, he is paying her a great compliment. The way she carries herself reflects an integrity and character that breeds a healthy respect from all who see her.

In a similar way, Prov. 18:10 views the name of Yahweh as a strong and safe tower for the righteous.

In ancient times, warriors fixed their shields to walls during times of great celebration, as Ezek. 27:11 and 1 Macc. 4.57 indicate (Goulder 1986: 33–34), and certainly the king's wedding would be a suitable time for such a glorious display. As in 3:7–8, the 'warriors' (*gibbôrîm*) were the elite troops of Israel, the group from which were drawn the protective guards of the bridal procession. When Solomon gazes upon his bride, he feels the same great pride and confidence as he does when he sees the shields of his best warriors on the citadel.

5. Virtually all of the language in this verse has been used previously in the Song, for Solomon here speaks from the stock language of love poetry. As he sees Shulammith's breasts, or perhaps as he notes the shape of her breasts under her wedding garment, he likens them to two fawns in their tenderness and loveliness, and longs to caress them. This desire is paralleled in 7:7–8[8–9], and is endorsed in Prov. 5:19. Just as fawns are skittish, so Solomon may possibly use this image as well to connote her shyness or nervousness as they prepare to make love on their wedding night.

6. Every word in this verse has been used previously in the Song. Solomon here on their wedding night recalls and responds to Shulammith's previous request in 2:17. When she then asked for him to make love to her all night, it was not yet the right time, but now on the wedding night it is the proper time for them to enjoy sexual intimacy. Exum (2005c: 156) observes astutely, 'In two places in his speech here (4:6 and 10–11) he responds to her urgent desire by picking up words she addressed to him earlier and playing variations on them to show how completely his desire matches hers.' In view of the description of her two breasts in the previous verse, the mountain of myrrh and the hill of frankincense clearly are images for her breasts that Solomon resolves now to caress. In 2:17, Shulammith referred to her breasts as mountains of spices, but Solomon heightens that description by using the exotic perfumes of myrrh and frankincense (cf. van Beek 1960: 70–95) in speaking of them. This language presents 'the beloved hyperbolically as a landscape made up completely of these precious and intoxicating aromatic substances. The decision to hasten to these hills promises experiences of previously unknown divine rapture' (Keel 1994: 153). At last Solomon will fulfil Shulammith's longing as he fondles her perfumed breasts while making love to her.

7. The first line in this verse exactly duplicates words from 4:1, thus forming an inclusio around the lyric in 4:1–7. To Solomon's eyes, every feature of Shulammith is beautiful, a sentiment echoed later by Shulammith as she describes Solomon in 5:16. To reinforce this point, he uses antithetical parallelism. Positively, all of Shulammith is beautiful, and negatively, there is no flaw in her beauty. In speaking of the absence of a flaw, Solomon's primary reference is to her physical appearance, because that is the focus of all the similes in 4:16 and it is also the particular sense of *yāpâ* (Ringgren, *TDOT* 6:218–219). There may, however, be a secondary overtone of her character as well, similar to her praise of his name in 1:3, because in the next section Solomon specifically commends her virginity. In 2:2, Solomon praised Shulammith in comparative terms as more lovely than the other women, but here he uses absolute terms to describe her perfection in loveliness. To him, she is the ideal beauty. Hess (2005: 125) remarks appositely, 'Thus the *waṣf* is a prelude to sexual intimacy, not primarily because it arouses the passions, but because its honesty of expression and detail of observation place the desire within a loving respect for the woman.'

Explanation

1–4. The language of love expresses what it sees as well as what it feels, and in so doing functions as a window into the heart. Solomon's tender words to Shulammith disclose that a heart full of love cannot help but overflow in verbal appreciation to and about the one it loves. It is not content to speak in generalities, but is attentive to the particular features that make the beloved so desirable. It may struggle in finding the right words to express its feelings, so it exploits the full range of experience as it endeavours to communicate what is in the heart.

5. In its delight in its beloved, love prompts the legitimate desire for sexual expression, for in the Song 'joy in sensuous touch is an integral element of their relationship' (*DBI* 880). With the right person at the right time and in the right setting, sexual intimacy is a God-given delight that should be treasured and savoured. This theme in the Song is echoed in the NT, when Heb. 13:4 extols the undefiled marriage bed in contrast to fornication and adultery.

6. The Song of Songs teaches that at the right time sexual intimacy can be enjoyed with great delight and without guilt. Before the time of marriage, however, though the desire for sexual intimacy may probably be strong, that desire must not propel a couple into behaviour that God approves only within the marriage covenant.

7. As Solomon views Shulammith, he regards her as completely beautiful and flawless. In the NT, Eph. 5:25–27 echoes this description as it speaks of Christ's loving work of sacrifice and sanctification by which he presents the church without any spot or wrinkle. Love should not be partial or half-hearted. Rather, it should give itself totally to the beloved, for it finds its complete satisfaction and delight in the one loved.

SONG OF SONGS 4:8 – 5:1

Translation

SOLOMON

> [8]With me from Lebanon, O bride, come with me from Lebanon;
>> Travel from the peak of Amana, from the peak of Senir and Hermon,
>> From the dens of lions and from the mountains of leopards.
> [9]You have excited my heart, my sister, O bride;
>> You have excited my heart by one of your glances,
>> By one piece of your necklace.
> [10]How desirable is your lovemaking, my sister, O bride!
>> How much better is your lovemaking than wine
>> And the scent of your oils than all balsam!
> [11]Your lips are dripping honey;
>> Honey and milk are under your tongue;
>> And the scent of your clothes is like the scent of Lebanon.
> [12]A locked garden is my sister, O bride,
>> A locked spring, a sealed spring.

¹³Your shoots are an enclosed park of pomegranates with excellent fruits,
　Henna plants with nard plants,
¹⁴Nard and saffron, calamus and cinnamon, with all trees of
　　frankincense,
　Myrrh and aloes with all the finest spices.
¹⁵[You are] a garden spring, a well of running water,
　And flowing streams from Lebanon.

SHULAMMITH

¹⁶Awaken yourself, O north wind, and come, O south wind;
　Cause my garden to exhale, let its spices flow down.
　My beloved is coming into his garden,
　And he is eating its excellent fruit.

SOLOMON

⁵:¹I am coming into my garden, O my sister, O bride,
　I am gathering my myrrh with my spice,
　I am eating my honeycomb with my honey,
　I am drinking my wine with my milk.

GOD

　Eat, O friends;
　Drink and become intoxicated, O lovers!

Notes on the text

4:8. The term 'bride' (*kallâ*), used here for the first time in the Song and a total of six times in this passage, could, like 'sister' in 4:9–10, be used in an honorific sense, but may more plausibly indicate that the wedding ceremony has now taken place (Goulder 1986: 37; Keel 1994: 155).

The LXX translates Amana as referring to 'faith' (*pisteōs*), apparently confusing it with the Hebr. noun *'ĕmûnâ*. Aquila, however, rightly translates it as a proper noun, *Amana*.

9. The verb *libbabt* is a pi. from the root *lbb*, from which is derived the noun *lēbāb* (heart). Keel (1994: 162) observes, 'It can be privative ("you have stolen my heart") or intensifying ("you make my heart beat faster," "you excite my heart"). In any case, she affects his heart so that it no longer functions normally. As used in an erotic context, "You drive me crazy," includes both meanings of the verbal form.' Cf. also Waltke 24.4f. Less likely, Waldman (1970: 215–217) argues for a semantic development that leads to the rendering 'you have passionately aroused me'.

The Hebr. text reads lit. 'by one (m. sg.) of your eyes (f. dual)', an unusual construction that may well speak of the action of her eyes rather than being a description of her eyes themselves (G. L. Carr 1984: 121).

10. As in 1:15, 7:6[7], Ezek. 16:13, *yph* includes the sense of desirability in addition to beauty (Keel 1994: 164).

The pl. form *dōdîm* typically refers to physical, sexual lovemaking, as can be seen in Prov. 5:19 and 7:18 (Sanmartin-Ascaso, *TDOT* 3:151).

The Hebr. term *bĕśāmîm*, used also in Song 4:14–15, 5:1, 13, 6:2, 8:14, could be a generic term for 'spices', but more likely refers to a highly prized perfume derived from the balsam bush and found in South Arabia (Murphy 1990: 156). As 1 Kgs 10:2, 10, 25 notes, balsam was included in the gift the Queen of Sheba brought to Solomon, and in Esth. 2:12 was part of Esther's beautification regimen in preparation for being presented to the king.

11. Keel (1994: 165) suggests that in the first phrase, 'Your lips are dripping honey', the combination of *p* and *t* sounds in the Hebr. text enables the hearer to detect 'the thin liquid honey dripping from the honeycomb'.

The term *śalmâ* could be a metathesis for *śimlâ*, and both words are used frequently in the OT as general expressions for clothes (Niehr, *TDOT* 14:158–159). In this case, *śalmâ* probably refers to Shulammith's nightgown.

12. Many Hebr. MSS, followed by the LXX, Syr and Vg translations, read *gan* in place of the MT *gal*, a repetition of the term in the first line (*BHQ* 61). If *gal* is retained as the original reading, then it is used as in Josh. 15:19 and Judg. 1:15 to refer to a 'spring' or 'cistern'. Malul (1997: 249) suggests reasonably that *gal* is a case of Janus parallelism that looks back to the garden in the first line and ahead to the spring in v. 15.

13. The term *šĕlāḥîm* is rare in the OT, although it is derived from the common verb *šālaḥ* (to send). Collins, *NIDOTTE* 4:121, states that it is a passive participle used substantively to refer to 'what is sent or extended, namely, shoots or branches (Isa 16:8)', and that the pl. form in this verse denotes 'shoots' or 'sprouts'. Alternatively, the term could continue the metaphor of the spring from v. 12, and thus refer to watercourses (Exum 2005: 177).

The Hebr. *pardēs* is often regarded as a loanword from Old Pers. that occurs in the OT only here, Neh 2:8 and Eccl. 2:5, to speak of an enclosed garden, although Young (1993: 161–162) argues reasonably for an earlier date for its entry into Hebr. Much later, this term came to mean an orchard (Bloch and Bloch 1995: 177). Eventually, it came into English as 'paradise'.

The pl. forms of 'henna' and 'nard' probably refer back to the pl. 'excellent fruits' in the first line, thus speaking of the bushes rather than the perfume they produce (cf. Keel 1994: 178).

14. The term *rō'š* means lit. 'top, peak, head', but here is used appositionally in an evaluative sense to denote 'finest, best, supreme' (Beuken, *TDOT* 13:257; cf. Joüon 131c).

15. Most commentators render the participle *nōzĕlîm* substantivally as 'flowing streams' (cf. Jer. 18:14), but Bloch and Bloch (1995: 177–178) argue for a possible case for rendering it verbally, which would require reading the verse against the accents.

16. The identity of the speaker in the first half of the verse is debated, with Murphy (1990: 161) arguing that it is a continuation of Solomon's words. However, the reference to '*my* garden' suggests that Shulammith is now speaking and offering herself to Solomon.

The change from imperatives to imperfects in the second half of the verse suggests that Solomon is now entering Shulammith in response to her invitation.

5:1. The four verbs used by Solomon are all perfect tenses. This could be rendered as past action, 'I came into my garden' (Bloch and Bloch 1995: 178), but the final divine word of approval suggests that it is better to translate the verbs as instantaneous perfects, 'I am coming into my garden' (Williams 1976: 30).

The Hebr. term *ya'ar* is rare, and its precise meaning is disputed. The LXX translates it as *arton* (bread), and Symmachus reads *drymon* (thicket), but its connection here with *dĕbaš* supports better a sense of 'sugar cane' or 'honeycomb'. Mulder, *TDOT* 6:211–212, gives a helpful discussion of the interpretative possibilities.

Form, structure and setting

More than any other lyric in the Song, this passage is marked by its extensive use of repetition. Eleven terms are used twice, three terms used three times, six terms used four times, and the term *kallâ* occurs six times. In addition, there are five sets of similar though not specifically repeated expressions. By this means, the poet constructs a clearly framed and unified scene that focuses the attention of the reader.

Furthermore, several times the poet presents a general statement and then as it were zooms the camera in to disclose the particulars that constitute the general point. In 4:8, Solomon calls to Shulammith, 'With me from Lebanon, O bride, come with me from Lebanon', and then says more specifically:

> Travel from the peak of Amana, from the peak of Senir and
> Hermon,
> from the dens of lions and from the mountains of leopards.

In 4:9, Solomon exclaims, 'You have excited my heart', and then says:

> You have excited my heart by one of your glances,
> By one piece of your necklace.

The general description in 4:10a, 'How desirable is your lovemaking', is expounded in 4:10b–11 with detailed sensual images. The general metaphor of Shulammith as a locked garden in 4:12 is followed by an inventory of the exotic plants included in this imaginative site in 4:13–15. Finally, after stating in 5:1a, 'I am coming into my garden', Solomon continues by describing in poetic terms his specific actions as he enters the garden:

> I am gathering my myrrh with my spice,
> I am eating my honeycomb with my honey,
> I am drinking my wine with my milk.

This structural pattern parallels the movement of the passage from the sense of remoteness suggested in 4:8 ('Come with me from Lebanon') to the intimacy in 5:1 ('I am coming into my garden').

It is also significant to note that the lyric begins with distant visual images (Lebanon, Amana, Senir, Hermon, dens of lions, mountains of leopards). Then, under the prominent image of the locked garden, the author uses numerous comparisons, both explicit similes and implicit metaphors, to add to the visual scene the senses of taste, smell and touch. By this powerful artistic strategy, the readers are drawn inexorably into the garden of intimacy, and are invited to experience imaginatively its delights.

Both in its literary structure and in its subject matter, then, the whole scene builds to a climax. As the scene opens, Shulammith is viewed distantly (4:8). Solomon then describes her delights that excite his heart, making use of the senses of taste, smell and touch (4:9–11). Her unmatched potential for lovemaking is portrayed under the extended metaphor of a locked but exotic pleasure garden (4:12–15). Then she opens her garden to her beloved in 4:16, and in 5:1 he responds by entering into her garden of intimacy. The scene is capped by the final words, perhaps by God, that endorse their lovemaking and encourage them to enjoy fully the pleasure of their newfound sexual intimacy within marriage.

Comment

4:8. This section is linked closely to the previous lyric. As Solomon describes the beauty of Shulammith and indicates his desire to make love to her in 4:1–7, he also is aware of the thoughts and emotions that affect her. The repeated call in this verse for her to come with him from Lebanon signals his fervent desire to draw her to him. At the same time, as in 1:9, 2:2, 14, he is alert to her fears. Therefore,

> he calls her imaginatively to come away from the fearful thoughts that like lions and leopards invade her mind before their first intercourse. As he initiates intimacy with her, Solomon is

sensitive to her feelings as she enters a new world that has both powerful allure and palpable risk. He does not rush in merely to satisfy his own drives, but he takes careful thought of her. (Estes 2005: 418)

If the preposition *min* is given its usual sense of 'from', then Lebanon is being used in a figurative rather than literal sense. The place names in this verse all refer to lofty sites in the Anti-Lebanon mountain range north of Israel (Cogan 1984: 255–259). This is a location remote from Israel, and represents the anxious thoughts that fill Shulammith's mind and make her seem inaccessible to Solomon (Murphy 1990: 160; contra Bloch and Bloch 1995: 174), as also previously in 2:14. The mention of lions and leopards evokes the sense of danger and threat (cf. 2:15; Jer. 5:6; Botterweck, *TDOT* 1:387). These predatory wild animals may well symbolize the understandable fears Shulammith has as the couple prepare to make love on their wedding night, a trepidation that may also have been intimated by the image of fawns in 4:5. Glickman (1976: 19) speculates plausibly, 'He realized that his new bride might be fearful and, like most women, more slowly aroused than a man. Yet he wanted to bring her patiently to the fullest experience that was possible for their wedding night. So he calls her from her fears to his arms.'

9. Even as Solomon senses Shulammith's emotional remoteness in 4:8, he is drawn powerfully to her. At this point on their wedding night, their foreplay is progressing at different rates, but by 4:16 Shulammith too is fully ready for sexual intercourse.

His addresses to her connote an increasing sense of intimacy, as he speaks to her first as 'beloved' (4:1), then 'bride' (4:8) and now 'sister'. In the Ug. and Egypt. literature, 'brother' and 'sister' are attested as terms of endearment for lovers (Černy 1954: 2425; Marsman 2003: 135), so these words should not be taken to denote the later Ptolemaic custom of sibling marriage (Keel 1994: 163). The metaphor of sister speaks of the couple's strong emotional bond that makes legitimate the physical expression of their love for one another (cf. 8:1), and could also imply secondarily that Solomon views her as his social equal.

Shulammith's eyes seem to have a ravishing, enchanting effect on Solomon (Murphy 1990: 160), for even the slightest glance of her eyes stimulates him. Just as a glance of her necklace calls attention to her beauty, so a glance of her eyes evokes love in his heart. If her necklace is linked with the previous resolution of the daughters of Jerusalem to make jewellery for her (1:11), then it could imply that she has been assimilated to the upper class, but it could also simply indicate the typical adornment for a time of the celebration of love.

10. The couple on their wedding night are clearly involved in sexual foreplay that is starting to have an overwhelming effect on Solomon. He tells Shulammith of the delight that he is enjoying in their lovemaking, for

he finds their caressing intoxicating. Solomon here echoes and enhances Shulammith's words of longing in 1:2 as he exclaims, 'How much better is your lovemaking than wine'. What he is experiencing in reality is what she longed for in her imagination from the first lyric in the Song.

In the ANE, oils were used primarily for replenishing skin oils lost to the dryness of the air. As Solomon feels and smells Shulammith's softening oils, he finds them more delightful than the best spices. G. L. Carr (1984: 122) notes well, 'The sense of the colon is not that her perfumes are better than any others, but that to her lover even her everyday anointing oils smell better than the most exotic perfumes.' Beyond that, Shulammith herself transcends all the allurements of the cosmetics she employs.

11. As Solomon and Shulammith continue their lovemaking, and begin to kiss ardently, Solomon describes her lips as 'dripping honey'. As in Prov. 24:13, honey seems to be a metaphor for the sweetness of her kisses (G. L. Carr 1984: 122). Solomon then enhances the description by saying that honey and milk are under her tongue. Milk and honey is a common verbal pair in the OT speaking of the lush productivity of the land of Canaan because of the blessing of Yahweh (Caquot, *TDOT* 3:130–131; Olivier, *NIDOTTE* 1:917). Because milk speaks of nutrition, and honey of sweetness, Solomon is indicating by this language that their lovemaking satisfies their deepest needs and desires. In a sense, their love becomes for them a kind of promised land (cf. Exod. 3:8).

The tongue can be used as a metonymy for speech (cf. Prov. 12:18), but in this context refers better to the physical organ as they are kissing. The expression 'under your tongue' suggests that they are kissing deeply (Keel 1994: 166) and savouring the delightful experience (cf. Job 20:12). What Shulammith had desired in the opening scene of the Song (1:2–4), she now comes to enjoy in actual experience (Exum 1999a: 61).

In comparing the scent of her clothes to Lebanon, Solomon is not saying that they smell like cedar. Rather, because of its renowned cedars, Lebanon is used as a symbol of any especially fragrant and pleasant scent (Murphy 1990: 160). It may well be that Solomon becomes particularly aware of the delightful scent of Shulammith's clothes as he or she slips her garment off her as they prepare to make love together.

12. The language of the song, especially when it describes sexual intimacy, is candid but not crude. The poet uses images that communicate the message without straying into explicit descriptions that would transgress into the realm of pornography. Bloch (2006: 153) notes well, 'The suggestive language of metaphor enhances the Song's eroticism, suffusing the entire landscape with eros.'

In the ANE a garden was an enclosed area with plants and a water source, and was protected by a wall or hedge, so that it could be used for the private pleasure of its owner (cf. Cornelius, *NIDOTTE* 1:876). Fox (1985: 283) observes that both in ancient Egypt. love songs and in the Song of Songs 'the garden provides privacy and fresh, natural beauties that appropriately frame the lovemaking and are congruent with the lovers' state of mind'. Consequently, this image was often used in ANE love poetry, as S. M. Paul (1997: 100–108) documents. In the Song, the 'garden' with its spring of water is a constant image for Shulammith's sexual organs, specifically her vagina (G. L. Carr 1984: 123; cf. 4:15–16; 5:1; 6:2, 11; 8:13). Her garden is locked, inaccessible to anyone until she invites Solomon to enter it in 4:16. She has preserved herself as a virgin, so that she can give herself to Solomon alone.

The theme of inaccessibility has been suggested previously in 2:14, where Shulammith is likened to a dove in the concealed places in the cliffs, and in 4:8, where she is pictured as in the remote peaks of Lebanon among the lions and leopards (Keel 1994: 174). In the ANE, water was scarce and precious, so great efforts were taken to secure springs and cisterns from misappropriation by others (cf. 2 Chr. 32:2–4). A seal could also represent a legal mark of ownership that prevented anyone else from entering and using the water source (Ginsburg 1970: 160–161; cf. Song 8:6). The images of the locked garden and the sealed spring, then, both speak of Shulammith's virginity on their wedding night. In the light of her invitation to Solomon to enter her garden in 4:16 and Solomon's statement in 5:1 that he has entered her garden, her virginity has been preserved intact until this moment in their relationship, and this is determinative for interpreting the language of the first half of the Song. Garrett (2004: 196) observes, 'In this verse the notable feature of the metaphor is that she is a "locked" garden and "sealed" fountain. The point is not that she is locked to all others but open to him. Rather, it is that she is as yet still virginal and out of even his reach.' In vv. 13–14, Solomon elaborates on the details of the garden image that he uses to speak of Shulammith, and in v. 15 he expands on the image of her as a spring.

13. The details in 4:13–14 indicate that this is not the description of an actual garden, but rather an idealization, because no ANE garden would have contained the wide variety of plants and trees listed here (Murphy 1990: 160–161). Bloch and Bloch (1995: 177) observe:

> Apart from pomegranates and other delicious fruits, this fantasy orchard also contains an extravagant assortment of exotic spices. Of those mentioned in 4:13–14, only saffron and henna are known for certain to have grown in Palestine. Myrrh, cinnamon, and cane were probably imported, while spikenard, frankincense, and aloes were certainly luxury imports from distant lands, such as India, Arabia, Somalia, and even China.

This garden is replete with taste, colour, quality and scent, indicating the range of sensual delights Solomon finds in Shulammith.

The closer they come to intercourse, the more poetic becomes Solomon's language. His words are not clinical and descriptive, but increasingly evocative and emotional. The repeated motif of this description is 'excellence', for the rare term *meged* is used twice in this passage (4:13, 16). Solomon's primary focus is not on the ecstasy he is feeling, but on the excellence of his beloved.

14. Unlike earlier descriptions in the Song, where Solomon compares Shulammith favourably to the other women, he now speaks of her in terms of the most precious and exotic perfumes and spices. These rare luxury goods were mostly imported from a great distance, and Keel (1994: 178–180) provides an extended and informative discussion of the eight items mentioned in this verse. It is also significant that all of the spices listed here have erotic connotations in the extant ANE love poetry (G. L. Carr 1984: 126). Some of these items are also included in the ingredients of the holy oil in Exod. 30:23–24, in the king's festive wedding garments in Ps. 45:8[9] and in the prostitute's bed in Prov. 7:17, but each of these three cases falls far short of the description of Shulammith in this verse. This extravagant collection, then, is Solomon's poetic enumeration of the varied and appealing delights of his bride, for the garden of her sexuality is beyond all human comparisons. By describing Shulammith in these terms, Solomon reveals how exquisite she is to him.

15. After expounding on Shulammith as a garden now being unlocked to him in 4:13–14, Solomon in this verse describes how the previously sealed spring (4:12) has now opened to him. Unlike a cistern, which holds collected waters, the terms 'spring', 'artesian well' and 'flowing streams' all speak of fresh, running water. Together they present a fit metaphor for the life-giving effect of Shulammith's sexuality. In the ANE, an artesian well of flowing water was especially prized, because it reduced the effort required to draw water (cf. Gen. 26:19).

The running water pictured is confined within the garden, so unlike Prov. 5:16 it is not water dispersed wastefully in the streets. As G. L. Carr (1984: 126) observes, 'The imagery is not of the wide-ranging activities of the girl, but of the abundance of her beauty and fruitfulness when the sealed fountain is opened and the locked garden unbolted.'

The emphasis in this verse on abundant moisture may well suggest that after the verbal and sexual foreplay of 4:1–14 Shulammith is now fully aroused, and her words in the following verse support that implication. Although Shulammith is a virgin on her wedding night, she is full of potential sexual vitality, for she is like the continual streams fed by the melting snows of Lebanon. Previously in 4:8, Lebanon was used as a symbol of her remoteness, but now Solomon adapts the image to make it a symbol of her guarded virginity that is the source of their present sexual delight and their future sexual potential.

16. This verse and the following verse form the exact middle of the Song, both in the number of lines and in its theme. The first half of the book builds towards the moment when the couple first enjoy sexual intercourse on their wedding night, and the second half of the book develops how their intimacy continues to grow within the bond of marriage as the couple start to explore the joys and challenges of intimacy within the marriage relationship.

With Solomon's speech reaching an erotic fervour, Shulammith can remain silent no longer (Exum 2005c: 157). 'Awaken' signals that it is now the proper time for love to be aroused, in contrast to 2:7 and 3:5, when the right time had not yet come. It is now the time for her potential sexuality, which has been preserved for Solomon, to be translated into physical intimacy with him. At last, on their wedding night, Solomon may enter her lush, pristine garden and enjoy the fruit she has reserved for him. Bloch and Bloch (1995: 178) note the parallel between *hāpîḥî* (exhale) here and the related terms in Gen. 2:7 and Ezek. 37:9. They conclude that Shulammith is calling upon the winds to bring her latent sexuality to life.

Shulammith freely gives the garden of her sexuality to Solomon, so that he can now enter *his* garden (cf. Snaith 1993: 69). As she views herself, she now regards her body as *his* garden and *his* fruit, expressions of her total focus on belonging to him. In the OT, going into or coming into a woman is often a euphemism for having sexual intercourse with her (cf. Gen. 16:2). In this passage, the beloved 'coming into his garden' is paralleled with his 'eating its excellent fruit', which also has a similar erotic reference in Prov. 30:20. As Grossberg (2005: 241) observes well, 'Her overture is no less an invitation to him to enjoy the garden than it is an offer of her sexual charms. The nature imagery, however, protects her words from sexual explicitness. The poet prefers delicate indirection.' Solomon now begins to taste the excellent fruit that he described in v. 13.

It may well be, however, that Shulammith's invitation includes even more than her sexuality, for it also implies a call to mutuality. As Linafelt (2002: 327) notes,

> the Song of Songs is full of double entendres, and on one level the garden most certainly represents the woman's sexuality, with her invitation being to the pleasures of carnal love. Yet the garden is also *more* than the woman's sexuality, it is the woman *herself*, and the invitation is to more than the act of consummation. It is an invitation for her lover to become one with her . . .

5:1. Out of sight of the reader, the couple between 4:16 and 5:1 enjoy sexual intercourse for the first time. All that Solomon has desired in anticipation he now comes to enjoy in actuality. The language of this verse draws together the vocabulary of 4:8–16, for their sexual intercourse is the culmination of their verbal and physical foreplay. As Solomon speaks in this verse, he completes the thoughts that Shulammith begins to express in 4:16, for their hearts, minds and bodies are in phase together. For the last time in the Song, Solomon addresses Shulammith as his 'bride' (*kallâ*).

Solomon uses the personal pronoun 'my' eight times as he speaks to Shulammith, for she has now given herself totally to him, and in their love she belongs to him. This pronoun indicates a profound change from 4:12, where Solomon described her as '*a* garden' and '*a* spring'. The four verbs and seven nouns Solomon uses all have erotic reference. For example, 'honey' is often used in the ANE love poetry to speak of the female genitals (G. L. Carr 1984: 129). By this means, Solomon alludes poetically to their sexual intercourse without being crass or pornographic (Whitesell 1995: 98). Song of Songs always treats lovemaking with sublime dignity rather than in a voyeuristic or exploitative spirit.

The final line of the verse seems to be uttered by a voice different from that of the couple, although Keel (1994: 184) argues unconvincingly that this is Solomon urging his companions to enjoy the wedding feast. Various suggestions for the identity of the speaker have been offered (cf. Trible 1978: 163), including the wedding guests (G. L. Carr 1984: 129; Goulder 1986: 39) and the daughters of Jerusalem (Hubbard 1991: 311; Exum 2005c: 182–183). It may well be, however, that this undesignated speaker is God himself (cf. R. M. Davidson 2003: 61–62) expressing his pleasure in their lovemaking and encouraging them to enjoy fully their newfound sexual intimacy within marriage. If this is indeed the case, then God is giving Solomon and Shulammith his 'sanction to enjoy fully the sexual feast that they have just sampled for the first time, just as he gave his approval to Adam and Eve to eat fully from the fruit of the Garden of Eden (Gen. 2:16)' (Estes 2005: 421).

Explanation

4:8–9. The extended verbal and sexual foreplay intimated in this lyric demonstrates that love does not rush selfishly to gratify its own drives and desires, but thinks first of meeting the needs of the other. Love is alert to the feelings and fears of the beloved, and seeks to draw the beloved into intimacy together. It waits, rather than plunging ahead insensitive to what the other person is feeling and fearing.

10. Love does not hide its feelings, but expresses them transparently. It acknowledges honestly the effect love is having, for that is part of the open sharing at the heart of true intimacy. Bergant (1998: 85) describes how Solomon and Shulammith provide an important pattern for intimacy in their lovemaking:

> The man is ravished by the woman, and she is faint with love for him. This is not a one-sided affair where one person dominates the other and the interests of that dominant party are the only ones considered. This is a love relationship where the passion is reciprocal and the pursuits of both parties are addressed.

11. Intimacy brings delights that engages all of the senses, including sight, sound, touch, taste and smell. As the Song demonstrates so well, the total person is enveloped by the powerful effects of love. Hess (2005: 158) notes of this section, 'More than any text in the Bible, these verses reject the suppression of physical pleasures as though in themselves somehow evil or unworthy of God. The poet masters all of the physical senses and their indulgence in magnifying the experiences of physical lovemaking.'

12. Sexual intimacy according to God's design is a treasure to be enjoyed only within the marriage covenant, but in that context is indeed to be enjoyed (cf. Prov. 5:15–20; Heb. 13:4). Untainted virginity is the best wedding gift one can give to his or her spouse.

13–14. The language of love uses all sorts of images to try to express in words what the heart feels. Through sensory language it endeavours to communicate feelings that cannot be defined by prosaic descriptions. By this means, it tries to speak to the heart of the beloved and to evoke a sense of inestimable value.

15–16. When virginity is preserved until marriage, then one can give the full measure of sexual pleasure to the one for whom it has been kept. Sexual pleasure is diluted when it is given prematurely to others, but it is concentrated when it is saved for one's marriage partner, and then given to that one person with a full and open heart. As Prov. 5:15–20 teaches, within the secure boundaries of marriage sexual intimacy is free to be enjoyed in all of its delights (cf. Chisholm 2000: 397–409).

5:1. Within marriage, love brings total satisfaction that is endorsed and celebrated by God. There is no area of life that is beyond God's concern or interest, for even the most intimate moments of lovemaking lie under God's gaze and rule. It is God's intention that humans enjoy with abandon the love he has ordained and designed for their welfare and pleasure. In Gen. 3, eating the forbidden fruit prompted a divine curse; but in the Song, eating the fruit of sexual intimacy within the bonds of marriage is blessed by God.

SONG OF SONGS 5:2–9

Translation

SHULAMMITH

> ^{2}I am sleeping, but my heart is awake.
> I hear my beloved knocking!
> [He says,] 'Open to me, my sister, my darling, my dove, my perfect one,
> Because my head is full of mist,
> My locks [with] the dewdrops of the night.'

³I have stripped off my tunic. Must I put it on?
I have washed my feet. Must I soil them?
⁴My beloved extended his hand from the hole,
And my internal organs were agitated by him.
⁵As I started to open to my beloved,
My hands dripped with myrrh and my fingers with liquid myrrh upon
    the handles of the bolt.
⁶I opened to my beloved, but my beloved had turned away; he had
    passed by.
I swooned when he spoke,
I sought him, but I could not find him,
I called to him but he did not answer.
⁷The watchmen found me, the ones who make a circuit in the city.
They struck me; they bruised me;
The watchmen of the walls took my shawl away from me.
⁸I adjure you, O daughters of Jerusalem,
If you should find my beloved.
What will you tell him?
That I am faint with love.

CHORUS

⁹How is your beloved better than any beloved,
O most beautiful among women?
How is your beloved better than any beloved,
That you are thus adjuring us?

Notes on the text

5:2. Both *yěšēnâ* (sleeping) and *'ēr* (awake) are participles, indicating Shulammith's state of consciousness in this scene. This is a highly vivid mode of speaking that draws the reader imaginatively into her dream. Exum (2005c: 193) states that the language 'captures poetically the transitional moment between sleep and wakefulness that we experience when we are asleep and hear something, and then, in a state of partial wakefulness, are initially unsure whether we actually heard something or dreamed it'.

As in 2:8, *qôl* followed by the genitive can be used as an exclamation, 'I hear my beloved' (Joüon 162e).

The qal form of the verb *dpq*, rather than the hith. as in Judg. 19:22, may suggest a gentle knocking, not that Solomon is trying to break down the door violently (Klingbeil, *NIDOTTE* 1:980).

The absence of the implied introductory formula 'He says' along with the similar feature in 5:3 serves to quicken the pace and heighten the sense of drama (Bloch and Bloch 1995: 180).

3. G. L. Carr (1984: 133) notes that the rare term *'êkākâ* 'here reflects a petulant unwillingness to act rather than the impossibility of action', so here it is best translated 'Must I . . . ?'

Although *regel* can be used as a euphemism for the genitals (cf. 2 Sam. 11:8–11), its use here in parallel with 'tunic' suggests that it is better to take it lit. for her feet that she has washed before going to bed.

4. The common Hebr. word *yād* (hand) seems to be used as a euphemism for the male penis in a few OT texts, such as Isa. 57:8, 10 and Jer. 5:31, 50:15, a sense also found in Ug. and Qumran literature (G. L. Carr 1984: 134; Ackroyd, *TDOT* 5:402–403), but that is not necessarily its sense here.

'Hole' (*ḥōr*) is a rare term in the OT, and its usage here is ambiguous. Some interpreters regard it as a peephole, or a hole giving access to the latch, but neither of these options can be established by the context. Keel (1994: 192) suggests that the hole could be a euphemism for Shulammith's vagina into which Solomon extends his 'hand', or phallus, with the result that she is aroused sexually, but that would constitute rape, which hardly fits the message and tone of the Song. In addition, the preposition *min* is hard to construe as meaning 'into', when its usual meaning is 'from'.

Internal organs can refer to the reproductive organs (cf. Gen. 15:4; 2 Sam. 16:11; Isa. 48:19), but are often used rather as poetic metaphors to speak of human emotions (Bloch and Bloch 1995: 181). Davis (1998: 542) notes that the same expression is used in Jer. 31:20 to speak of Yahweh's deep longing for Ephraim, the northern kingdom that has gone into exile.

The verb *hāmâ* means to be agitated inwardly. Most often this refers to unpleasant responses prompted by anguish, mourning and peril (Baumann, *TDOT* 3:415–416), a negative sense reinforced by the preposition *'al* (Joüon 133f).

5. Dobbs-Allsopp (1995: 43–44) argues convincingly for an ingressive sense of *qwm* as the verb refers to the onset of Shulammith's opening of the door, so that the door is actually opened only in v. 6.

The verbal root *ntp* (dripped) transposes the consonants of *ṭnp* in 5:3, where Shulammith asks if she must soil her feet by opening the door to Solomon.

Keel (1994: 193) argues on metrical grounds that the final phrase 'upon the handles of the bolt' is a gloss, but provides no textual evidence to support his claim, and the Hebr. and LXX texts include it.

The common noun *kap*, here used in the pl. (handles), is capable of several meanings. Ackroyd, *TDOT* 5:405, comments, 'The issue is confused by the use of sexual imagery here, . . . although it seems likely that the phrase was a familiar one referring to part of the door furniture.'

6. The expression *napšî yāṣĕ'â*, lit. 'my soul went out', is used in Gen. 35:18 and Ps. 146:4 for dying. Here it is used hyperbolically to express a surging of her emotions (Bloch and Bloch 1995: 182). Murphy (1990: 165) paraphrases it well as 'I swooned'.

7. G. L. Carr (1984: 137) suggests that 'walls' here can be linked with the same term in 8:9–10, such that the watchmen are stripping off her clothes and gazing on her breasts, but that seems to read more into the text than is warranted. However, Exum (2005c: 197) observes well, 'For men to strip off part of a woman's clothing, even if it is not an essential piece of clothing, is a contemptuous act of exposure.' In the context of the whole verse, 'watchmen of the walls' is a compressed form for the first line of the verse, in which the watchmen are those who make a circuit in the city, and this circuit would probably have been on the casemate walls.

The 'shawl' (rĕdîd) is a light article of clothing listed among the luxury items of the women of Jerusalem in Isa. 3:23. Bloch and Bloch (1995: 182) conclude that it is 'a stylish bit of finery rather than a basic article of clothing'. The LXX reading theristron suggests that it was a light summer garment (Myers, IDB 4:748).

8. The particle 'im (if) after an oath elsewhere in the Song (2:7; 8:4) indicates an emphatic negation, in which case Shulammith would be pleading with the court girls not to tell Solomon that she is worn out by her distraught searching throughout the night for her lover (Fox 1983: 205). The response by the court girls in the next verse, however, seems to suggest better the sense 'I am faint with love' (cf. Joüon 144h).

9. The interrogative pronoun mah is typically used for things, but 'it can be used when reference is made to a person, to ask what that person is' (Joüon 144c).

As in 1:8, the definite adjective hayyāpâ with the preposition bĕ and the pl. noun nāšîm is a comparative superlative meaning 'most beautiful among women' (Waltke 14.5c).

Form, structure and setting

This passage includes many examples of repeated words, and in particular forms of dôd are used eleven times. The verb pātaḥ is significant, as Solomon calls on Shulammith to open to him (5:2), she rises to open to him belatedly (5:5), but when she opens the door he has gone away (5:6). In 5:2, 5–7, similar words and actions are used with reinforcing effect. Some key antitheses include 'I slept but my heart was awake' (5:2), his extravagant address but her excuses (5:3), her opening to her beloved but finding him gone (5:6), and her search for him but failure to find him (5:6). Shulammith begins with a general statement that suggests she is dreaming (5:2a), and then the particulars of her dream are given in 5:2b–8, after which she summarizes her emotion as being faint with love (5:8). V. 9 is a hinge between the dream of 5:2–8 and the song of description in 5:10–16. Some have viewed 5:9 as a later editorial interpolation, but Murphy (1990: 171) notes that 'one cannot rule out the possibility that the experiences related in chapter 5 could have been composed as a unit' (cf. Keel 1994: 197).

Comment

2. The second half of the Song is dominated by Shulammith's perspective, with 80 of the 111 lines coming from her mouth (G. L. Carr 1984: 130). The language of sleeping and awakening used in this verse may well introduce a dream sequence similar to 3:1–4 (Murphy 1990: 165), although Bloch and Bloch (1995: 180) question this. The succeeding verses in this passage leave open the possibility that this could be a poetic rendering rooted in a literal experience in the life of the couple. The contention by Garrett (2004: 204), that this passage represents symbolically Shulammith's anxiety due to the loss of her virginity on their wedding night, however, seems to read an extraneous notion into the text. The description 'asleep' suggests that Shulammith is not thinking lucidly, and her subsequent actions confirm this to be the case. Her heart is awake, but her love is not awake (cf. 2:7; 3:5), for she does not evidence the kind of excitement that animated Solomon on their wedding night (cf. the verb *lbb* in 4:9).

The term *qôl* is an echo of 2:8, where it marks the approach of Solomon as he comes to propose to Shulammith. Here in 5:2 his voice is like a knocking on the door of her heart for her to open to him. Snaith (1993: 72) notes that in classical love poetry Anacreon 3.10 provides a striking parallel to this verse as love begs for admittance with these words: 'Do not fear; for I am drenched from wandering about in the moonlit night.' As Solomon speaks to Shulammith, he brings together in 5:2 the most elaborate collection of terms of affection found anywhere in the Song. This extravagant language is a reflection of the fullness of his heart for her. In assessing her as 'my perfect one' (Kedar-Kopstein, *TDOT* 15:705), he echoes the conclusion of his song of description in 4:7, when he says, 'there is no flaw in her'.

As Gilead and Rosenan (1954: 120–123) and Ashbel (1936: 316–321) document, in Israel dew can be very heavy at night (cf. Judg. 6:33–40). In the OT, dew is typically a symbol of divine blessing (Deut. 33:28; Prov. 3:20).

3. The *kĕttōnet* is a long, often linen, undergarment worn by both men and women (cf. 2 Sam. 13:18–19). Murphy (1990: 165) observes that 'its removal, and also the washing of feet, would indicate preparation to retire'. This undressing and washing would also be preparatory to making love. Shulammith's words of reply form a stark contrast to the response she demonstrated in the earlier dream sequence in 3:1–4 as she went out in the middle of the night to seek Solomon. In addition, they are in a different tone from Solomon's speech in 5:2. Heard in the light of Solomon's extravagant address to her, Shulammith's excuses sound exceptionally flimsy, and manifest a 'failure of desire' (Davis 2006: 182). Some interpreters have taken her words as a tease rather than a rejection (cf. Murphy 1990: 170), because if she has taken off her tunic, then she is probably indicating that she is naked, but Solomon's reaction indicates that he does not hear her in that way. Consequently, her language seems better explained as an indignant refusal to Solomon's passionate request to her. Solomon has come through the night mist to her, but she does not want to be inconvenienced to open the door to him. This seems to be the voice of indifference, which is a great threat to intimacy. Glickman (1976: 61) notes well, 'Often the opposite of love appears not to be hate but indifference. If someone hates you, at least he regards you as a significant person. But if he is indifferent towards you, then he regards you as a zero. And indifference can hurt worse too.' Shulammith's words, then, are windows into her heart. Rather than delighting in the mutuality of intimacy, she seems to place her own convenience ahead of her beloved. The excuses she utters are not how passionate intimacy should speak, but instead represent her desire not to be inconvenienced, even by Solomon. In contrast to her previous response in 3:1–2, she is now putting thoughts of herself ahead of thoughts for him.

4. Some interpreters have suggested that Solomon here is forcing himself sexually upon Shulammith despite her protestation in 5:3. This is not at all certain (cf. Bloch and Bloch 1995: 181; Murphy 1990: 171); but if it were the case, then Solomon also would be manifesting intensely selfish inconsideration for Shulammith. There does seem to be a connection between Solomon's action and Shulammith's emotional response in this verse, but the language is unclear about the nature of the connection. It could possibly be that Solomon's continued sexual advance despite her verbal displeasure causes her to be upset with him. Because his hand is being extended 'from' (*min*) the hole and not into the hole, however, it may better mean that he turns away from her after her words in v. 3, and that Solomon's withdrawal is the action that prompts emotional pain in her. This interpretation would then lead well into the succeeding verses in the passage.

5. After her initial refusal (5:2), Shulammith belatedly arises to open to her beloved. Many interpreters have seen a sexual reference here, especially with the following description of her hands dripping with myrrh, but the dual form of 'hands' is difficult to link with her sexual organs. It seems, then, that *yāday* here is used lit. for her 'hands', and that may also indicate that *yād* in 5:4 should be taken lit. as well. It may well be that in 5:2, 5, 'open' refers to opening a literal door so that the couple can then be together to make love. It is not that *pātaḥ* itself has a sexual referent, but it is preliminary to their sexual intimacy.

The myrrh on the doorbolt has prompted several different interpretations. Glickman (1976: 63) suggests that Solomon leaves some myrrh at the door as a sort of affectionate reminder to indicate that he has been there to see her (cf. also Murphy 1990: 171). On the other hand, Bloch and Bloch (1995: 181–182; cf. Gordis 1974: 90) link the 'liquid myrrh' (*môr 'ōbēr*) with the oil of myrrh in Esth. 2:12, thus arguing that Shulammith is prepared for lovemaking with Solomon and that her words in 5:3 were flirtatious coquetry that Solomon misinterpreted. A straightforward reading of the verse could well indicate that as Shulammith belatedly rises to open the door to admit Solomon, she first anoints her hands with myrrh.

6. This verse completes the action begun in v. 5, as Shulammith rises to open to her beloved. Too late she opens to him because he has already turned away. Too soon Solomon leaves, because at last she does open to him. Whatever Shulammith's intent may have been in 5:3, Solomon takes it as a refusal that causes him to lose interest. As the winter had passed by in 2:11, so now Solomon has quickly departed and disappeared (Bloch and Bloch 1995: 182). While the myrrh is 'passing along' (*'br*) her fingers, Solomon is 'passing by' (*'br*), indicating that this opportunity for love-making has been lost.

As in her earlier dream, Shulammith searches for him, but does not find him. In contrast to her words in v. 3, now she fervently wants to be with him. Although much of the same language is used here as in 3:1–5, this seems to be a more serious breach in their relationship, for in ch. 3 she struggled with separation in her imagination, but now the rift has come in her verbal response to him.

7. In her dream, Shulammith does not find her beloved that she seeks (5:6), but the watchmen of the city find her. Because the watchmen suppose her to be a criminal, probably a prostitute, they treat her badly. Thus this dream turns out much differently from the previous dream in 3:3–4. Instead of assisting her, as in the earlier dream, now the watchmen assault her. No doubt, her nocturnal search in the city was highly unusual, suspicious and very dangerous for a young woman, and this is an implication of how desperate Shulammith feels after she opens to Solomon only to find him gone. Even in her dream, she feels deeply painful emotions.

The guardians of justice misjudge the situation, and as a result become the perpetrators of injustice against Shulammith. Three violent actions, in which they strike, bruise and take her shawl, build to a climax of humiliation, as she is treated as though she were a prostitute. Keel (1994: 195) adduces a Middle Assyrian legal stipulation that directed veiled prostitutes to be arrested and their clothes stripped off. Although the actions in 5:7 are less brutal than the Assyrian practice, this verse is in general parallel to it.

8. Shulammith has not been able to find Solomon in her ill-fated search in the city, so she enlists others to help her. In a similar situation in 3:3 she asked the watchmen for assistance, but they have now humiliated her, so she turns to the court girls. She begs them to be on the lookout for her beloved. Shulammith realizes how much she loves Solomon and how much she longs for him to be with her. She wants Solomon to know her true feelings for him, rather than having him continue in the faulty perception that she is indifferent to him. By requesting them to tell Solomon that she is 'faint with love', Shulammith uses an expression she earlier employed in

2:5 to describe what she knew about herself, but now decides to make this known to him. What has been in her heart all along she now states explicitly, as she discloses her innermost feelings for Solomon. As an antidote to her previous insensitivity, Shulammith refocuses on her love for Solomon. Her reawakened love places her priority upon Solomon rather than upon herself (Estes 2005: 423).

9. The court girls immediately reply to Shulammith's entreaty in the previous verse. They ask her to tell them what superior qualities her beloved has that cause her to be faint with love for him. She has earlier rebuffed him (5:3), so why does she now desire to have him back with her? These questions prod Shulammith to reflect on why she considers Solomon so special, and they compel her to shift her focus away from her own convenience (5:3) and her feelings (5:8) and on to his excellence. In addressing her as 'most beautiful among women', the court girls use the same expression Solomon used earlier in speaking tenderly to her in 1:8. No doubt, this echo serves to jolt her back to a true appraisal of what she really values in him.

Indifference has clouded her perception, but these questions help to clarify the situation for her. Glickman (1976: 66) observes insightfully:

> At the root of indifference is ingratitude. Had she really been grateful for her husband, she would not have been indifferent to him. Thus when the daughters of Jerusalem ask their first question, they give the young wife the encouragement and opportunity to remember and express her appreciation of her husband. And she is poetic about that expression.

She goes on to portray Solomon's excellence in an extravagant song of description in 5:10–16. The court girls may have been asking only for the identifying marks of Solomon, but Shulammith replies with a soaring testimony of her intense admiration of him (cf. Keel 1994: 197).

Explanation

2. As the second half of the Song relates, getting married does not mean that a couple live happily and effortlessly ever after. Just as humans face many challenges prior to marriage, particularly in the area of maintaining purity, so within marriage there are challenges to the continued growth of intimacy. Intimacy can, and should, keep growing throughout the years of the marital relationship, but it will not advance without challenges and effort.

3. In marriage, it is easy to lose sight of how special one's spouse is. The inexorable duties of life can dilute the delight of intimacy, so that what used to provoke excitement now evokes only a yawn. Indifference is a lethal blow to intimacy, because it communicates that the relationship is not as valued as it should be. A similar careless attitude is in view in Matt. 25:1–13, when Jesus contrasts the five wise virgins with the five foolish virgins, who were not prepared for the arrival of the bridegroom for the wedding feast.

4. Insensitivity can have powerful effects on the people we love. Words spoken carelessly or actions taken thoughtlessly can inflict great emotional pain on others. In fact, Jer. 31:20 uses the same kind of language to speak of Yahweh's deep grief when his love for Israel is unrequited by the sinful nation. Real love is careful to anticipate how what is said and what is done will be construed by the one loved. In other words, love should not be impulsive and self-focused, but rather considerate and other-focused.

5–7. When mistakes are made in love, they must be faced honestly so that a move towards reconciliation may begin. To deny or delay will only make the problem fester, so one must be quick to swallow pride and move towards opening to the beloved. In intimacy, poor decisions may well lead to painful consequences. In a comparable way, the psalmist in Ps. 32:3–4 acknowledges that as long as he refused to confess his sin, his body wasted away under Yahweh's heavy hand of conviction.

8. Reconciliation requires that wrongs be admitted, which means pride must often be swallowed. Love takes the risk of revealing what is truly in the heart, rather than hiding behind secrecy that can lead to misperceptions. There is, then, a transparency in intimacy that leads to lovers knowing one another as they alone have known themselves before. In the same way, when sin is confessed to God, that opens the door to renewed delight in him (cf. Ps. 32:1–2, 5).

9. The community in general, and friends in particular, can play an important role in the development or derailment of intimacy. By asking probing questions, others can help to discern whether love is alive and well, or if it is in fact only a mirage. This is true both for human relationships and also for developing a relationship with God.

SONG OF SONGS 5:10–16

Translation

Shulammith

> ^{10}My beloved is dazzling and ruddy,
>   More attractive than a myriad [of men].
> ^{11}His head is gold, pure gold,
>   His locks, date panicles, are black as a raven.
> ^{12}His eyes are like doves over the ravines of water,
>   Bathed in milk, lying down upon the rim.

¹³His cheeks are like a bed of spices, raised beds of perfumes,
   His lips are lotuses dripping with liquid myrrh.
¹⁴His hands are cylinders of gold filled with topaz,
   His abdomen is a plate of ivory set with lapis lazuli.
¹⁵His legs are pillars of marble fixed upon bases of refined gold,
   His appearance is like Lebanon, choice like cedars.
¹⁶His mouth is sweetness, indeed, all of him is delight.
   This is my beloved and this is my friend, O daughters of Jerusalem.

Notes on the text

5:10. The term *ṣaḥ* is often paired with forms of the verb *zkh* to mean 'white', but is also used in Isa. 18:4 and Jer. 4:11 of heat shimmering above the land. Here it can be rendered as 'sparkling' or 'dazzling' (cf. Keel 1994: 198). Although the LXX reads *leukos* (white), Symmachus translates *ṣaḥ* with *lampros*, in the sense of 'bright, radiant'.

As in 2:4, the root *dgl* refers to what is seen or conspicuous, so as a description of Solomon it has the sense of 'attractive'.

The term *rĕbābâ* is used specifically for the number ten thousand in Lev. 26:8, Deut. 32:30 and Judg. 20:10, but can also refer to an undetermined large number (Fabry, *TDOT* 13:278). Here Shulammith uses it to indicate Solomon's absolute superiority in his physical excellence. In her eyes, he is the epitome of true manhood.

11. 'Gold' translates the relatively rare term *ketem*, rather than the common word *zāhāb*. It may well be that *ketem* is an elevated poetic term for pure gold (Wakely, *NIDOTTE* 2:740). The term *paz*, in view of its use in Lam. 4:2, probably refers to refined gold of the finest quality.

The term *taltallîm*, found only here in the OT, refers to the panicles, the loose, irregularly branched flower clusters of the date palm. The date panicles are about twenty inches long, and here they may indicate 'the wild and unruly character of his hair' (Keel 1994: 199).

12. The term *'āpîq* refers to a deep riverbed or ravine that is either dry or, as here, filled with water (Ross, *NIDOTTE* 3:49). LXX paraphrases it as *plērōmata* (abundance).

The second line is interpreted in various ways. Murphy (1990: 172) notes,

> it is usually explained as referring to the eyes set in white ('washing in milk') and in sockets ('sitting in fullness'). The comparison seems to have become an end in itself and is strikingly different from the other lines. There is no certain interpretation of this verse, as can be seen from the diversity among commentators.

13. The term *'ărûgâ* refers to a planting bed (cf. Ezek. 17:7, 10), and could possibly suggest a terrace (Abegg, *NIDOTTE* 3:531). Some Hebr. MSS and the early versions render it as a pl. form, as in 6:2, and this would be a better parallel to the pl. *migdĕlôt*, but the sg. form in the MT is understandable as it is. In either case, the sense is much the same.

As in 5:5, the expression *môr 'ōbēr* refers to liquid myrrh.

14. The Hebr. term *mē'îm* usually refers to the internal organs, such as the bowels, intestines or womb, but here could well speak of Solomon's abdomen (Bloch and Bloch 1995: 186–187).

15. The term *šēš* can be translated 'alabaster', which would be appropriate if it were a visual image speaking of the white colour of Solomon's legs. The following verb *yāsad* makes it more likely, however, that the point of reference is the strength or stability of his legs, in which case the NIV rendering 'marble' is more likely, because alabaster is a soft stone (cf. Ben-Dor, *IDB* 1:75).

16. The pl. abstract nouns *mamtaqqîm* and *maḥămaddîm* are used to refer to the qualities of sweetness and delightfulness or charm that epitomize Solomon (Waltke 7.4.2a; Joüon 136g).

The phrase *kullô maḥămaddîm* is lit. 'his entirety is delight', which Bloch and Bloch (1995: 188) describe as 'a generalizing statement summing up the details of the praise song, paralleling the young man's words to the Shulamite at the end of his praise song, 4:7'.

Form, structure and setting

The section from 5:2 to 6:13 is thematically connected, but within the section 5:10–16 is a defined unit. This passage is Shulammith's response prompted by the question posed by the daughters of Jerusalem in 5:9, in which they ask Shulammith what superior qualities distinguish her beloved. The use of the term 'my beloved' (*dôdî*) in 5:10 and 16 forms an inclusio, and the summary statement in 5:16 explicitly directed to the daughters of Jerusalem clearly demonstrates that this is a literary unit. As in the other songs of description in the Song of Songs, the major literary device is comparison, with many examples of both explicit similes and implicit metaphors being used through the song. Shulammith begins in 5:10 with a general description of Solomon as more attractive than a myriad of men, and then in 5:11–15 details the specific distinguishing attributes that substantiate her general assessment of him. In 5:16, she draws the description to a close with a summary statement that all of him is delight. This is the fine man who is Shulammith's beloved and her friend.

Comment

10. The passage in 5:10–16 is Shulammith's answer to the question posed by the court girls in 5:9. In ANE love literature, songs of description about a woman are comparatively common, but a song of description about a man is seldom attested. As Shulammith has been called 'most beautiful among woman' by Solomon (1:8) and by the daughters of Jerusalem (5:9), so now she describes Solomon as more attractive than a myriad of men. As G. L. Carr (1984: 139) observes, her song 'records what was apparently the epitome of male physical beauty' in ancient Israel. Shulammith begins with a general assessment of his excellence, as the description 'dazzling and ruddy' highlights Solomon in his vigorous and healthy manliness.

11. This song of description, like the song extolling Shulammith in 4:1–7, begins at the head and works downwards as Shulammith indicates her delight in her beloved. If the images in this verse are descriptive, then Solomon is pictured with tan skin and black hair. Some have suggested that the reference to gold could reflect the high value with which Shulammith esteems his noble bearing. For example, Keel (1994: 199) states, 'The metaphor comparing the head to smelted gold, gold that is proved and refined, indicates that the beloved towers over all others in splendor and value.' However, the simile 'black as a raven' is not so easily construed as a statement of value, so it may be better to take both images as having a primarily pictorial reference. The mention of Solomon's hair uses the same term as his statement in 5:2 that his locks are wet with the dewdrops of the night, and Shulammith may be harkening back to that time when she responded with indifference to his eager invitation.

12. In this verse, Shulammith uses several terms in describing Solomon that he previously used in speaking of her beauty, including 'eye' (1:15), 'dove' (1:15; 4:10), 'water' (4:15), 'bathed' (4:2) and 'milk' (4:11). She echoes and expands his description of her eyes as doves in 1:15 and 4:1. As Stendebach, *TDOT* 11:39, suggests, she may well be referring to the enchanting or seductive quality of his gaze at her. In 5:2, Solomon addressed her as 'my dove', and now she uses the same language to describe his eyes. The particular point of association may be the glistening of his eyes, which resemble wet doves with their shining feathers at a water source (Murphy 1990: 166). The imagery also suggests the lush conditions of divine blessing, with ample water and milk as is pictured in the prophecy of Joel 3:18 (cf. Bloch and Bloch 1995: 185–186).

13. The images Shulammith uses in this verse are not visual, as in 5:11–12, but rather evoke the sense of smell, and implicitly indicate the great value she places upon Solomon. Keel (1994: 201) observes, 'His cheeks are compared not merely to balsam but to entire beds of balsam, like the ones planted by the last kings of Judah at Jericho and En-gedi; these beds were jealously guarded by their heirs up to the time of the Roman Empire.' 'Liquid myrrh' is an echo of 5:5, where Shulammith's fingers dripped with the fragrant perfume. Here she uses the image to describe his lips, and more precisely, by metonymy, his kisses. When compared with 4:11, his lips like lotuses dripping with flowing myrrh suggest the fragrant delight she receives as they kiss.

Again, Shulammith draws on Solomon's earlier compliments of her in her praise of him, taking 'spices' (4:10), *migdol*, 'raised bed, tower' (4:4), 'lilies' (2:2), 'lips' (4:3) and verbal forms of nāṭap, 'drip' (4:11), and shifting the descriptions to him. This similarity of language suggests a sense of reciprocity and mutuality essential for the maintenance of intimacy.

14. The imported luxury items Shulammith uses to describe Solomon are primarily indicative of the great value she places on him. In this song of description, she uses gold to speak of Solomon's head (5:11), his hands (5:14) and his feet (5:15). Keel (1994: 205) observes that lapis lazuli is found in passages that describe the decoration of the tabernacle (Exod. 24:10) and the divine throne in Ezekiel's vision of the glory of Yahweh in Ezek. 1:26. Bloch and Bloch (1995: 187) note that in the ancient world ivory was highly valued, and was often carved and decorated with inlays of precious metals and gemstones (Amos 3:15; 6:4; 1 Kgs 22:39; Ps. 45:8[9]; cf. Pritchard, *IDB* 2:773–774).

Longman (2001: 164) proposes that Shulammith is saying that Solomon's 'penis' (mē'āyw) is a 'tusk' ('ešet) of ivory. If that were her meaning, then her graphic sexual language would match some of Solomon's erotic references in his song extolling her beauty in ch. 7, and this would give evidence of the uninhibited nature of their sexual relationship within their marriage. Shulammith's previous use of mē'ay in 5:4, however, points more likely towards an internal and emotional sense of the term. Furthermore, the rest of her descriptions of Solomon in this song are subtle indicators of his appearance and value, and not explicit references to his sexuality (cf. Keel 1994: 205), so it seems best to take this phrase in the sense of 'his abdomen is a plate of ivory'.

15. In this verse, Shulammith uses images such as refined gold, Lebanon and cedars that refer to what is best or most awesome. As she describes Solomon's legs as pillars of marble fixed upon bases of refined gold she does not employ a visual image, but rather an image that evokes his great value to her. Her reference to Lebanon seems to imply the epitome of grandeur and beauty. Bloch and Bloch (1995: 188) remark, 'A hyperbole with Lebanon as the typical symbol of majesty evokes not just the mountain (Judg. 3:3), but also the towering cedar trees, lush vegetation, wine, and sweet fragrance associated with that region.' It could be, however, that as in 4:8 Lebanon refers to what is fearful and intimidating: the emotions she feels in the wake of her self-centred response to Solomon in 5:3. In contrast to Solomon's tender and intimate images of her in 4:10–15, her descriptions of him as a cold and lifeless statue may imply a sense of distant admiration (Brenner 1990: 259), rather than emotional closeness and warmth. Her language, then, could reflect the psychological rift and separation the couple have experienced.

16. In this summary to her song describing Solomon, Shulammith uses abstract nouns rather than adjectives to communicate her overall appreciation of him. In responding to the request of the daughters of Jerusalem in 5:9 to describe her beloved, Shulammith reflects on his good qualities that she values. Her rekindled appreciation is the antidote to her earlier self-centredness, and this opens the door to their reconciliation in ch. 6. The terms *ḥēk*, *mātôq* and the verbal root *ḥmd* all echo 2:3, where Shulammith extols Solomon. She now acknowledges what she has known all along, but which was obscured by her insensitive response to Solomon's invitation in 5:3.

Keel (1994: 206) views *ḥikkô* as referring to Solomon's mouth, for 'love play usually begins with kissing'. The mouth, however, may well be used as a metonymy for speech, for to Shulammith what Solomon says reflects his excellent character. In 5:3, she did not respond positively to his words, but now she has come to acknowledge that what he says is sweetness.

In a statement summarizing her esteem for Solomon, Shulammith says that 'all of him is delight'. She regards Solomon as both her lover and her valued 'friend' (*rēa'*). G. L. Carr (1984: 144) observes well, 'There is refreshing candour in her identifying her lover as also her "friend" – friendship goes far deeper than mere sexual compatibility and excitement. Happy is the husband or wife whose spouse is also a friend.' It is also interesting to note that Shulammith uses for Solomon the m. form *rē'î*, corresponding to his characteristic term of affection for her, *ra'yātî*. By using this language, she may well be implying the mutuality of their love.

Explanation

10–12. Speech is a window into the heart, as it expresses the emotions resident within a person. Complements and affirmations flow freely from an appreciative attitude, and are a measure of the value one places on another. As Jesus said in Luke 6:45, it is out of the overflow of the heart that a person speaks. The psalmic hymns are replete with verbal expressions of gratitude to Yahweh, as the delight that has filled the psalmist's heart overflows into praise that seeks to draw others into worship as well (cf. Ps. 34:3[4]).

13–14. Intimacy does not move in one direction alone, but involves giving and receiving in tender balance. Lovers learn to affirm and compliment each other, and as their hearts come to value the same qualities, they find themselves speaking of and to one another in similar ways. By their speech, they give evidence that they are entering into a world of shared delight.

15. Just as language reveals the joy in a heart, so it can reflect a heart's pains. When a relationship is struggling with misunderstanding or selfishness, then communication is strained as conflicted feelings inevitably affect how one speaks. Restoring a relationship necessarily includes restoring a pattern of speech that is honest, considerate, constructive and tender.

16. Loving relationships are built on appreciation and gratitude, and intimacy within marriage is nurtured by the same factors. Selfishness dulls love, but focusing on the fine qualities of the other person can renew appreciation and revive love. In marriage, a couple must repeatedly return to the touchstone of friendship and admiration as they endeavour to overcome the emotional pain and distance caused by insensitivity towards one another. In a parallel way, sin creates a barrier between the sinner and God (cf. Ps. 66:18; Isa. 59:2). In order for fellowship with God to be restored, one must confess the sin to God and receive cleansing from him, which opens the door to a renewed relationship (1 John 1:7–9).

SONG OF SONGS 6:1–3

Translation

CHORUS

¹Where has your beloved gone, O most beautiful among women?
Where has your beloved turned, that we may help you seek him?

SHULAMMITH

²My beloved has gone down to his garden, to the beds of spices,
In order to pasture in the garden and to gather lotuses.
³I am my beloved's, and my beloved is mine,
He who pastures in the lotuses.

Notes on the text

6:1. G. L. Carr (1984: 145) observes that the NEB reading 'that we may help you to seek him' gives the sense of the final colon of the verse. He remarks, 'Her ardour has convinced them he is worth looking for and they are now willing to join her.'

2. The pl. form *gannîm* may well be a poetic, generalized form equivalent in meaning to the sg. 'garden' (*gan*), as Joüon 136j indicates.

3. The final clause, 'he who pastures in the lotuses', may be a contraction of her fuller description in the previous verse, 'to pasture in the garden and to gather lotuses'. For discussion of this image, see notes on the text of 2:16.

Form, structure and setting

This short passage within the larger section of 5:2 – 6:13 is constructed on the basis of cause and effect. The double question posed by the daughters of Jerusalem in 6:1 prompts Shulammith's answer in 6:2, and the renewed appreciation of Solomon that she reflects in replying to them results in the renewal of intimacy between Shulammith and Solomon (6:3). The language in this section draws heavily on the previous lyrics in the Song, using in particular the term *dôd* to refer to Solomon, the image of the garden to speak of Shulammith, as in 4:12 – 5:1, and the description of Solomon pasturing in the lilies, as in 2:16.

Comment

1. Using the same words of address as in 5:9, 'O most beautiful among women', the court girls ask questions that prompt Shulammith to recall information crucial for her reconciliation with Solomon. In 2:10, Solomon invited her to 'go' (*hlk*) with him, but now has 'gone' (*hlk*) from her. Keel (1994: 208) notes that though the daughters of Jerusalem offer to help Shulammith find Solomon, whom she previously could not locate (5:6), she does not really need their assistance. Keel reasons:

> She did not find him because she did not know where he went – hence the question in 6:1 is a surprise, and even more so the answer in 6:2. Not only does she suddenly know where he went; she knows that he has gone nowhere else than to her, to his beloved, because, as 6:3 says, they belong together.

She does not accept their offer of help, because this would in fact be an interference in the reconciliation of their relationship (cf. Snaith 1993: 85). She realizes that she herself has to seek and find him, for this is not a problem of information, but of intimacy. As Garrett (2004: 224) notes, her question 'allows her to complete the process of transformation through the realization of the full force of her husband's love for her'.

2. Shulammith answers the questions by the court girls in the previous verse. Their questions bring her mind back to the last time she spoke to Solomon, when he came to her and asked her to open up to him. G. L. Carr (1984: 145) observes, 'This unit is more probably her conscience-stricken recollection of her lover's approach to her bed (5:2f.), and her refusal to accept him. Now she remembers their relationship and commitment to each other.' Although there has been a rift in their relationship, she still regards him as her beloved.

Shulammith realizes that she does not need the court girls to search with her for Solomon, because she already knows where to find him. Although Solomon has been absent from her consciousness, he has never really been lost to her (Murphy 1990: 173), for it was only emotional distance, not an actual abandonment. In the ancient world, cities were built on hills for defensive purposes, and gardens were planted in the valleys close by the water source (Mayer, *TDOT* 6:318). Using the language from their wedding night (4:16; 5:1), Shulammith says that Solomon has gone down to 'his garden'; that is, to her. She realizes that his attitude towards her continues to be loving, for he comes in order to pasture in the garden and to gather lotuses. His absence was only in her fears, because despite the insensitivity that had strained their relationship, Solomon's love and commitment to her have remained consistent all the time.

3. There is no specific reference to their coming back together, and there is no explicit time indicator between 6:2 and 6:3, but the implicit sense is that Shulammith's renewed awareness of Solomon results in their reconciliation. In that spirit, she repeats her earlier affirmation of their mutuality in 2:16, but significantly she alters the order of her words. In 2:16, she said, 'My beloved is mine, and I am his', but now she says, 'I am my beloved's, and my beloved is mine'. Murphy (1990: 173) insists that the inversion of 2:16 in this verse does not seem to have any special significance. Poetry, however, typically uses language with great precision, so the change in wording from 2:16 to 6:3 should not be brushed off as inconsequential. It is also noteworthy that a third variant of the mutuality formula is used later in 7:10[11]. In contrast with 2:16, Shulammith now says first that she belongs to her beloved, and then only secondarily that he belongs to her. This focus upon him is a contrast to her self-centred response to Solomon in 5:3, and may well indicate that their reconciliation has resulted from a change in her perspective and from growth in her selflessness. The painful experience she has endured has shifted her focus away from herself and on to her beloved. Now Solomon, not her own convenience, comes first in her heart.

Explanation

1. Love requires personal responsibility. Other people may well provide important assistance, counsel and support, but ultimately intimacy must be nurtured by the lovers themselves. They must be willing to accept personal ownership of the relationship if it is to progress towards maturity.

2. Reconciliation is often very close at hand, even when it does not seem that way. For a couple to be reconciled, at least one party has to be willing to back down from pride and misjudgment. As long as one holds on to personal prerogatives, it will be hard to see things clearly, but when love realizes that it has wrongfully inflicted hurt and pain, it seeks to go back to the touchstone of what it knows of the other person. This knowledge can cause faulty perceptions to dissipate, so that reconciliation can proceed. Throughout the Bible, God reveals himself as eager to forgive and restore his sinful people. In passages such as Isa. 54:5–8 and Jer. 3:11–18, Yahweh speaks of his compassion that reaches out to wayward Judah. Jesus expresses the same longing to gather Jerusalem together as a hen gathers her chicks, but the people were unwilling for him to do so (Matt. 23:37).

3. A loving relationship involves both giving and receiving. At its best, love considers first what it can give, even though all the while realizing that

it will probably receive blessing in return. When love is content to focus primarily on what it receives, then the giving aspect of love can suffer, and that can cause a degeneration into self-centredness. In love, it is truly more blessed to give than to receive. The mutuality of love described in the Song is more than just equality, as Bergant (1998: 106) explains: 'Mutuality respects difference, realizing that the give and take within relationships can be reciprocal without being strictly equal. Partners do not give exactly the same thing to each other, but they must be mutually respectful, attentive, and engaged.'

SONG OF SONGS 6:4–10

Translation

SOLOMON

⁴You, my darling, are fair as Tirzah, beautiful as Jerusalem,
  Brilliant as the stars.
⁵Turn your eyes from before me because they make me crazy;
  Your hair is like a flock of goats that are winding down Mount Gilead.
⁶Your teeth are like a flock of ewes that go up from washing,
  For all of them bear twins, and none of them is missing.
⁷Your cheek is like a slice of pomegranate from behind your veil.
⁸There may be sixty queens and eighty concubines and maidens without
    number,
⁹But my dove, my perfect one – she is unique,
  She is unique to her mother; she is splendid to her who bore her.
  Young women see her and congratulate her,
  Queens and concubines, and they praise her.
¹⁰'Who is this who is looking forth as the dawn, fair as the moon,
  Splendid as the sun, as brilliant as the stars!'

Notes on the text

6:4. Tirzah was the capital of the northern kingdom of Israel from the time of Jeroboam I until Omri built Samaria as his capital in 879 BC (1 Kgs 14:1–20; 16:8–26). In addition to being a site of strategic importance, it was also marked by its natural beauty and lushness (G. L. Carr 1984: 146; cf. Manor, *ABD* 6:573–577). Because the Hebr. term *tirṣâ* means 'beauty', the LXX translated it as the abstract noun *eudokia*, a rendering followed by the Syr, Tg and Vg.

'Brilliant' (*'ăyummâ*) is used in Hab. 1:7 of the Bab. chariots. Here it has been construed as referring to the terrifying view of an approaching army in battle formation (Keel 1994: 215). However, Gordis (1969: 203; cf.

Long 1996: 708–709) argues reasonably that *nidgālôt* both here and in 6:10 may bear the sense of 'these great sights'. The progression in 6:10 of dawn, moon, sun and *nidgālôt* suggests that the term may best be rendered as a poetic reference to the stars. Goitein (1965: 221) concludes plausibly that it is 'a term of popular astronomy designating stars of first class magnitude which are always brilliant and easily to be seen', a sense that fits well in this context in the Song.

BHS asserts without extant textual evidence that the final line of this verse has been added from 6:10. It is, however, more likely that the lines in both 6:4 and 6:10 serve as an inclusio marking the beginning and ending of this song of description.

5. The verb *hirhîbunî* has often been translated in the sense of 'disturb, paralyse', but the use of the term in Ps. 138:3 suggests the meaning 'encourage, excite', as does the LXX translation *anapteroō*. G. L. Carr (1984: 148) argues, 'The Greek word means to raise the feathers (of a bird), and metaphorically is used to mean "put on the tiptoe of expectation" or "to excite" and bring to a state of eager expectation. This is clearly the intent here – her glance "turns him on" and makes him bold in his intentions.' Keel (1994: 215) appropriately paraphrases the verb as 'make crazy', which is the rendering adopted here.

7. For the meaning of *raqqâ*, see the note on the text of 4:3.

The LXX adds the first line from 4:3, but the omission here can be explained by Solomon's avoidance of explicitly sexual descriptions in this scene of reconciliation. He also omits his earlier words of 4:5, which are his description of her breasts.

8. The term *malkâ* (queen) refers either to the king's consort or to an independent female head of state, such as the queen of Sheba (1 Kgs 10:1) or the usurper Athaliah (2 Kgs 11:3). Aside from this passage, in the OT *malkâ* is used exclusively of queens of foreign lands (Culver, *TWOT* 1:509).

A 'concubine' (*pîlegeš*) is an auxiliary wife taken primarily for producing children for the king (Engelken, *TDOT* 11:550). An extensive discussion of concubinage in ancient Israel is found in Epstein 1942: 34–76.

'Maidens' (*'ălāmôt*), as in 1:3, probably refers to adolescent girls who have reached childbearing age, but who have not yet borne a child (Walton, *NIDOTTE* 3:417–418).

9. The sense of *'aḥat* is 'the uniqueness of the woman, not that she is an only child' (Murphy 1990: 175). Fisch (1988: 84) observes well that the effect of *tammātî* is 'to reduce the bride's personality to its primal essence, where all charms have become vain and all that is left is the perfection and wholeness of a unique individual person as that uniqueness is discovered in the direct, dialogic relationship of the lovers to one another'.

The verb *'āšar* in this verse is often translated 'blessed' (cf. AV, ASV, NIV, JB), but, because it takes a human subject, should better be rendered 'congratulate' in the sense of expressing happiness (G. L. Carr 1984: 149;

Hamilton, *TWOT* 1:80). However, Mathys, *TDOT* 15:464, notes that in vv. 8–10 Shulammith is described with godlike features, and in that light is 'blessed' (*'āšar*) and 'praised' (*hālal*) in comparison to all other women.

10. As in 6:9, *bārâ* is not a moral term but an expression indicating the highest quality, so here it is rendered 'splendid'.

The final term, *nidgālôt*, is repeated from 6:4. In this context, when it follows the progression 'dawn, moon, sun', it may well be used metaphorically to speak of the stars (Bloch and Bloch 1995: 191; Murphy 1990: 178; Keel 1994: 220). This would constitute a variation of the familiar 'sun, moon and host of heaven' found in numerous OT passages.

Form, structure and setting

The terms *yāpâ* (beautiful) and *'ăyummâ kannidgālôt* (brilliant as the stars) frame 6:4–10 as an inclusio within the larger section of 5:2 – 6:13. Several structural techniques are used to communicate the excellence of Shulammith's beauty. Similar expressions are combined, as in 6:4, when Shulammith is likened to Tirzah, Jerusalem and the stars. In her uniqueness, she is contrasted to the numerous queens, concubines and maidens of the court in 6:8. The passage is replete with similes and metaphors as the speakers try to find words to describe how beautiful Shulammith is, thus presenting an impression of her incomparability (Hess 2005: 200). The lyric as a whole is built as a climax. First, Solomon extols the physical beauty of Shulammith, then states that she is better than the most esteemed women of the court, and finally the court women express their praise of her transcendent beauty by using comparisons to the celestial bodies.

Comment

4. In her song of description in 5:10–16, Shulammith speaks *about* Solomon to the court girls, but now in his song of description Solomon speaks directly *to* Shulammith. Her insensitive attitude in 5:3 has not made him unresponsive to her. From his words to her, it is clear that he has not let wounded pride get in the way of forgiveness and reconciliation.

In the song of description in 6:4–7, Solomon utters many of the same tender words that he spoke to Shulammith on their wedding night (4:1–7). These familiar words would have communicated to her that his love for her has not changed, despite the rift that came between them, at least in her imagination, in the dream sequence of 5:2–8. Nevertheless, as Snaith (1993: 86–87) notes, this song is strangely pale in its language when compared with the earlier lyric. Solomon seems to avoid the most erotic descriptions from his previous song, probably so as not to give her the false impression that he merely desires her sexually. Glickman (1976: 72) observes astutely, 'here he assures her of his genuine forgiveness by praising her with the same compliments he had given her on their wedding night, and he carefully avoids the sexual aspects of that praise which might lead her to suspect his motives'.

Tirzah and Jerusalem are high standards for describing Shulammith's beauty. The comparison to Tirzah suggests her regal appearance and remarkable beauty (Bloch and Bloch 1995: 188). Jerusalem would have been the pride and joy of Solomon (cf. Pss 48:2[3]; 50:2), so it is an apt measure of his esteem for her. Bergant 2001: 76 suggests that 'in order to concretize his praise, the man simply chose realities from his own experience, realities that were renowned for their commanding splendor'. It may be that Solomon echoes Shulammith's language with a play on words. She said in 5:10 that he is more 'attractive' (dāgûl) than a myriad of men, and now using the same verbal root says that she is as brilliant as the 'stars' (nidgālôt). Solomon finds Shulammith both attractive and awe-inspiring. As he comes to know her better, he realizes how much in her remains a mystery to him. As Keel (1994: 212) observes, she is equally fascinating and frightening to him. Rather than concealing this, Solomon transparently tells her of the powerful effect she has on him.

5. Solomon and Shulammith experience a push-and-pull tension in their relationship. When he asks her to turn her eyes away from him, Solomon uses the same verb (sbb) that Shulammith used in 2:17 when she invited him to love her throughout the night. In 4:1, he said, 'Your eyes are doves from behind your veil', but here he states that her eyes make him crazy (cf. 4:9). Solomon finds Shulammith's beauty, and in particular her eyes, unnerving, and candidly admits the overpowering effect she has on him. It could well be that Solomon's pride tempts him to be angry with her or to nurse the hurt he has absorbed, but when looking into her eyes he is powerless to resist her (Exum 2005a: 88), and cannot help but be moved to love her.

For the sense of the comparison of Shulammith's hair to a flock of goats descending Mount Gilead, see the discussion at 4:1.

6. This verse is identical to 4:2, except that here rĕḥēlîm (ewes) replaces qĕṣûbôt (shorn). For explanation of the sense of the imagery in this verse, see the comment on 4:2.

7. This verse is identical to the second line of 4:3. Solomon omits his earlier description of Shulammith's lips and mouth in 4:3, as well as her breasts in 4:5. Glickman (1976: 72) remarks, 'First their love relationship had to be mended, then the sexual relationship would take care of itself. And as a matter of fact, this is exactly what happened to them. In the next chapter we will see their tenderest, most intimate sexual experience thus far.'

8. In 6:4–7, Solomon speaks to Shulammith in a waṣf as he describes her beauty, but in 6:8–10 speaks about her in a boasting song. Perhaps the rift in ch. 5 has caused Shulammith to doubt her pre-eminent place in

Solomon's heart, so he reassures her that she indeed has first place in his estimation and affection. This would then be parallel to his language in 2:1–2 in which he answers her words of self-deprecation in 1:5–6 by extolling her beauty in comparison with the other women.

In the ancient world, one of the measures of a king's power and prestige was the quality and quantity of his royal harem (Hubbard 1991: 326), and examples of this can be seen in 1 Kgs 11:3, 2 Chr. 11:21 and 2 Chr. 13:21. The historical narratives depict Solomon as having 700 wives and 300 concubines, so some commentators have tried to use the language of this verse to date the writing of this book relatively early in his reign. The contrast between the Solomon of many women in the historical record and the Solomon here who professes that Shulammith is his only one is troubling to many readers. It should be remembered, however, that the Song may well be using Solomon as a literary figure rather than narrating the historical details of the life of Israel's celebrated king. In this verse, it also should be noted that Solomon here states only that these women exist; he does not explicitly say that they belong to him (cf. the similar numerical language in Prov. 30:15, 18, 21, 29). In addition, he seems to use the language of patterned exaggeration, when he refers to sixty queens, eighty concubines and numberless maidens. The pl. 'queens' is very unusual, for in the OT a sg. queen is typically indicated. It may well be that 'queens' here refers to those who are elsewhere called the king's wives (2 Sam. 12:8; Jer. 38:23) or princesses (1 Kgs 11:3) (cf. Keel 1994: 218). Concubines are 'women who performed both sexual and social functions and were held in higher esteem than the rest of the royal entourage except the queens' (Hubbard 1991: 326). The maidens are young court girls, probably identified throughout the Song as the daughters of Jerusalem, who were the girls of the aristocratic families.

9. Solomon's language describing Shulammith as 'my dove, my perfect one' echoes the words of his failed appeal to her in 5:2. His ardour for her has not diminished despite the painful experience they have endured. Solomon values her above all of the other women (6:8), and all of the women agree with his assessment of Shulammith. Ordinarily in the OT it was the birth of a son that brought the greatest joy to a mother, but Shulammith has the first place in her mother's heart. The excellence that her mother perceived in her is affirmed by all of the women. Even among the royalty and nobility, Shulammith stands out as one of a kind, just as she has described Solomon as more attractive than a myriad of men (5:10; cf. Bloch and Bloch 1995: 190). Shulammith, then, is acknowledged as unique by Solomon, by her mother and by all of the court women.

In 1:6, because she was self-conscious about her appearance Shulammith did not want the court girls to look at her, but now all the court women see her and congratulate her. Her esteem, however, is not grounded in her sexual attractiveness to men, but in the qualities of character that the women also appreciate and would desire for themselves (Janzen 1965:

225). In fact, the words by which they extol Shulammith ('congratulate', 'praise') are also used in Prov. 31:28, 31 to speak of the public commendation of the virtuous woman.

10. This verse contains the words that the court women utter in praise of Shulammith. As in 3:6 and 8:5, the f. sg. pronoun zō't indicates that the question refers to Shulammith. Although expressed in the form of a question, in a sense it is a rhetorical question used with the force of an exclamation admiring her overwhelming beauty. The court women, to whom Shulammith had once felt inferior (1:5–6), are now the ones praising her extravagantly. In her superior beauty, she looks down on the other women as though she were gazing at them from the heavens, for the quality of her loveliness far exceeds theirs.

They compare Shulammith to the most beautiful and awesome aspects of nature. Her beauty, then, is not compared to other women, or stated as an abstract quality, but is viewed in terms of the most lovely features in God's world. Shulammith, in her own self-estimation in 1:5, viewed herself as šĕḥôrâ (black), but now the court women liken her to the 'dawn' (šaḥar). They use the language of high poetry in their description, employing the rare terms lĕbānâ for 'moon' and ḥammâ for 'sun'. It may well be that nidgālôt is a verbal echo of Shulammith's description of Solomon in 5:10 as 'more attractive' (dāgûl) than a myriad of men.

Explanation

4–5. The road to love does not always run smoothly. When things get bumpy, as at times they most certainly will, lovers must decide how to respond to each other. Real love chooses not to retaliate, paying back evil for evil, but reaches out towards reconciliation (cf. Rom. 12:17–21). Wounded pride can derail love by focusing its attention on how it has been hurt, but love overcomes evil with good because it values the relationship more than personal ego.

6–7. Contrary to what many people suppose, genuine love cannot be kindled by sex, and neither can wounded love be rekindled by sex. In God's design, sexual intimacy is the overflowing of love. Love is the key that opens the door to sexual pleasure, but sexual activity apart from love and commitment falls far short of genuine intimacy (cf. the tragic example of Amnon and Tamar in 2 Sam. 13:1–19). Once a relationship has been restored through reconciliation, it is liberated to resume the enjoyment of its delights.

8. Fear can creep in from many directions to cast a shadow of doubt over love. To counter this, love must be alert to the factors that can paralyse a relationship, and needs to take the initiative to reassure the fearful or insecure beloved. It makes every effort to communicate that it loves without reserve.

9–10. Love is grounded on good character and fuelled by verbal appreciation. It esteems what is good, not necessarily what is glamorous, and commends these good qualities rather than taking them for granted. Love, then, focuses on what is truly important and valuable, as it seeks to encourage positive attributes by praise.

SONG OF SONGS 6:11–13[6:11 – 7:1]

Translation

SHULAMMITH

> [11]I went down unto the garden of nuts to see the green shoots in the wadi,
>   To see whether the vine had sprouted, whether the pomegranate had
>   blossomed.
> [12]I am beside myself with joy;
>   My soul has set me in chariots of the most noble of my people.

CHORUS

> [13[7:1]]Turn, turn, O Shulammith, turn, turn, that we might inspect you.

SOLOMON

> How you wish to inspect Shulammith as the dancing of the two
>   companies!

Notes on the text

6:11. The term *'ĕgôz* is used only here in the OT. It could possibly refer to the walnut tree, however the walnut was probably not native to Israel (Walker, *NIDOTTE* 1:254). Because its specific identification is uncertain, it is rendered here generically as 'nuts'.

A 'wadi' (*naḥal*) is a deep stream bed that is dry during most of the year, but which can become a raging torrent after rain. During the spring in Israel, a wadi provides moisture for vegetation, but during the hot summer months contains no water (cf. Job 6:15–17).

12. S. M. Paul (1978: 545–547) argues plausibly that the first fragment of this verse is an exact semantic equivalent of an Akk. medical expression for a mental disturbance caused by great joy and exhiliration. His paraphrase 'I am beside myself with joy' has been adopted here.

The Hebr. expression *'ammînādîb* has been construed in various ways, as Pope (1977: 584–592) and Mulder (1992: 104–109) have summarized. The Hebr. variant *'ammînādāb* as a proper name Amminadab is followed by the LXX and the Vg translations. Bloch and Bloch (1995: 194), however, argue reasonably from parallels in Ps. 113:7–8 and 1 Sam. 2:8 that this is a transposition of *nĕdîb ʿammî*, used in a superlative sense for 'most noble of my people'. The MT gives every indication of being corrupt at this point, and the early versions indicate textual confusion at the time when they were produced, so this minor emendation may well be justified here, but the case cannot be proven conclusively. Keel (1994: 228) unconvincingly argues for a proper name, Amminadib, which he says labels the man as a braggart or dandy.

13[7:1]. The imperative *šûbî*, used four times in the first line, is taken by Keel (1994: 228) as a call for Shulammith to return as she turns away, but if it is taken in the sense of the motion of turning (Thompson, *NIDOTTE* 4:56), then it anticipates the next section in which she is portrayed as dancing.

In its form, *haššûlammît* is a gentilic term meaning 'the Shulammite', and this has prompted numerous identifications (Exum 2005c: 225–227; Hess 2005: 209; Huwiler, *ABD* 5:1227). This term is derived from the same *šlm* root as is the name Solomon (Goodspeed 1934: 103; Rowley 1939: 89), so Shulammith may plausibly be regarded as the indicator for the female persona in this Song that idealizes perfect love (cf. Bergant 2001: 81). Consequently, 'it could well be that the author has named the female character Shulammith as the lexical counterpart to Solomon in this poetic picture of intimacy' (Estes 2005: 428). Less convincingly, Goitein (1993: 64) sees here an allusion to Abishag, the lovely maiden from Shunem (later, Shulem) who ministered to the aged David (1 Kgs 1:1–4), and whose name could have become a byword for female beauty; and Terrien (1985: 42) conjectures that the term is the Hebr. equivalent of the Akk. Shulmanitu, one of the titles for Ishtar, the goddess of war and love.

The verb *ḥāzâ* means to observe closely or to inspect (Jepsen, *TDOT* 4:289). It is stronger in sense than the more common verb for seeing, *rāʾâ*, which has been used several times before in the Song.

The particle *mah* can be used to ask 'Why?', but its use in the following verse suggests that it is here used as an exclamation, 'How!'

The term *maḥănāyim* is often interpreted as the proper noun Mahanaim. Its dual form of the term for 'camp, company', however, suggests that it may refer to a dance performed by two groups (Gruber 1981: 342–343; Eising, *TDOT* 4:263). Sendrey (1969: 474–475) argues plausibly that the Hebr. term may be a metaphor for Shulammith's two breasts, and this may well be supported by the following section in which Shulammith is portrayed as dancing before Solomon, and her breasts are specifically mentioned in 7:3[4].

Form, structure and setting

This short lyric is marked by several cases of repetition, including *lir'ôt* (twice in 6:11), *šûbî* (four times in 6:13[7:1]), two forms of the verb *ḥāzâ* in

6:13[7:1] and two references to Shulammith in 6:13[7:1]. Examples of comparison include the intimacy of the couple being pictured as new springtime growth (6:11), their reconciliation being likened to travelling in opulent chariots (6:12), and the scrutiny of Shulammith by the court girls as though they are gazing at a dance of two companies (6:13[7:1]). V. 11 employs a literary climax, as Shulammith looks for new spring growth in the wadi, for budding vines, and for pomegranates in blossom.

Comment

11. This short song is one of the most difficult sections in the book to interpret, and commentators are divided even about the identification of the speaker. Murphy (1990: 178–179) helpfully lays out the conflicting evidence.

It could well be that this lyric fills in the blanks of 6:3 by explaining how the couple came to be reconciled. The text does not provide explicit data to determine whether Shulammith or Solomon is speaking. Bloch and Bloch (1995: 192), Hubbard (1991: 328) and others regard Solomon as the subject and offer textual data and arguments to support their conclusion that this is his song of yearning. If this verse, however, is connected with Shulammith's words in 6:2, then she can be viewed as going back to the garden where she said Solomon could be found. Although 'garden' is often used in the Song as an image for Shulammith's body, here it appears to refer to the garden to which both she and Solomon go. In other words, in this context it represents a place where they fellowship together in their moment of reconciliation. Shulammith goes to the garden in order to see if in their relationship it is still spring, as it was in 2:10–14. As Glickman (1976: 76) observes, 'She went down to the garden to see if their reconciliation might bring that new spring.' Echoing the earlier passage in 2:12 when the blossoms have 'appeared' (r'h) in the land, now she goes down to the garden to 'see' (r'h) if the pomegranates have blossomed.

12. The language used in this verse is very common in the OT, but the syntax is nearly impossible to understand (cf. Mulder 1992: 104–113, who provides a detailed discussion of the ways in which the verse has been rendered by exegetes and translations), because the verse comprises three fragments without conjunctions. Consequently, the interpreter has to infer how the parts of the text link with each other.

In the first fragment, it appears that Shulammith says lit., 'I did not know', which may well indicate that she has lost her composure and is beside herself with joy. This statement could indicate that the reconciliation with Solomon was a surprise to her, but it must be noted that the common verb *yāda'* has such a broad semantic range that this meaning is difficult to prove. It could be that this is an echo of Solomon's earlier words of instruction to her in 1:8 as to how to find him, which begin with the expression 'If you yourself do not know'. It is also possible that this statement of incomplete understanding is an inclusio with Shulammith's description of her dream in 5:2, which she begins with the words 'I am sleeping, but my heart is awake'. If that is the case, then she is bringing to a close the extended passage of 5:2 – 6:13[7:1], in which either literally or imaginatively the couple move from the disastrous consequences of insensitivity through the process of reconciliation to renewed delight in fellowship with one another.

In the second fragment, Shulammith says lit. 'my soul set me'. The term *nepeš* here probably refers to her emotions that have been touched by the reconciliation with Solomon. In her delight, in the third fragment she pictures herself sitting in a privileged and honoured position in an opulent chariot (cf. the elevation of Joseph in Gen. 41:43). Being conveyed in Solomon's chariot, and perhaps with him in his chariot, would demonstrate in a public context that the reconciliation of the couple is complete and they are together again.

13[7:1]. This verse is very difficult, and interpreters have rendered it in many different and conflicting ways. The first line, with its first person pl. form of the verb, seems to be spoken by the chorus of the daughters of Jerusalem, the court girls who desire to gaze at the woman Solomon has described in superlative language in 6:4–10. They want to examine her to verify for themselves that she truly is as beautiful as they have been told (G. L. Carr 1984: 154).

The second line is spoken by a different voice to the chorus. It could be the narrator, but it is unlikely that the narrator who elsewhere addresses the reader would speak here directly to the characters within the Song. Murphy (1990: 185) suggests that it could be Shulammith replying to them in a teasing mood, but then it would be more likely that she would refer to herself as 'me' rather than as Shulammith. If Solomon is the speaker, then he could be asking an indignant question reproving those who want to view Shulammith merely for her beauty or as a sexual object (Keel 1994: 229). It may be best to read this line as an exclamation by Solomon that leads naturally into the highly erotic song of description in 7:1–9[2–10]. Just as in 5:1, their most intimate moments are not the time for others to observe, but for them alone to enjoy together. As Exum (2005c: 230) notes, once again 'the reader is invited to enter the lovers' garden of eroticism yet is excluded from the most intimate moments'. The sensual dancing of Shulammith and Solomon's graphic descriptions of her in the following lyric are sights and words for just the two of them, so the court girls must not think that they will be privileged to witness that scene as though it were a public spectacle.

Explanation

11–12. Fully one-quarter of the Song is devoted to working through the problems caused by insensitivity, for this is a key challenge to the progress of intimacy in marriage. Reconciliation after this kind of rift comes by going back to the roots of the relationship to reaffirm love, appreciation and respect. This retracing of steps requires humility, but that is part of the price of developing true intimacy within a marriage. Intimacy cannot be purchased at bargain rates, but comes at the cost of one's pride. This is true for a marriage, but is also true for every human relationship, as well as for maintaining a relationship with God (cf. 1 Pet. 5:5–6).

13[7:1]. Intimacy draws from other people, but also requires privacy to flourish. As reconciliation overflows into renewed delight, a couple must draw closely together in their exclusive union. There they alone can savour intimacy in its most precious form.

SONG OF SONGS 7:1–10[2–11]

Translation

SOLOMON

1[2]How beautiful are your steps in sandals, O noble daughter!
    The curves of your thighs are like ornaments, the work by a
        craftsman's hand.
2[3]Your navel is a round bowl; may mixed wine not be lacking!
    Your abdomen is a heap of wheat fenced about by lotuses.
3[4]Your two breasts are like two fawns, twins of a gazelle.
4[5]Your neck is like an ivory tower;
    Your eyes are pools in Heshbon by the gate of Bath-Rabbim;
    Your nose is like the tower of Lebanon that looks out towards Damascus.
5[6]Your head upon you is like Carmel,
    And the hair of your head is like purple thread;
    The king is captivated by [your] locks!
6[7]How beautiful you are, and how lovely you are,
    O love, O daughter of pleasures!
7[8]This stature of yours is like a palm tree;
    And your breasts [are like] clusters [of dates].
8[9]I said, 'I will go up into the palm tree;
    I will grasp its blossoms.'
    O may your breasts be like clusters of the vine,
    And the scent of your nose like apricots.
9[10]And your palate is like the best wine.

SHULAMMITH

It is going smoothly for my beloved,
    Gliding over the lips of the sleeping ones.
10[11]I am my beloved's, and his desire is for me.

Notes on the text

7:1[2]. Rather than designating the feet themselves, the pl. of *pa'am* typically refers to feet in motion (Saebø, *TDOT* 12:7), as reflected in the LXX and Vg renderings, 'your steps'.

The use of 'daughter of *nādîb*' probably does not suggest an aristocratic background for Shulammith, because 1:5–6 implies that she came from the lower class, but rather is a statement of the noble quality of her life.

2[3]. The term *beṭen* refers to the lower abdomen, the area of Shulammith's womb (cf. Judg. 13:5, 7). This term is often paired with *reḥem* (womb) in the OT (Freedman/Lundbom, *TDOT* 2:95; Rogers, *NIDOTTE* 1:650). Although several commentators assert that *šōr* be rendered as 'vagina', Hess (2005: 196) argues persuasively for the meaning 'navel'.

3[4]. In place of the MT reading *tā'ŏmê*, the Cairo Genizah reads *tĕ'ômê*, which is in the MT of the parallel verse in 4:5. The two forms are probably identical in meaning, 'twins of', and it is impossible to prove from the textual record whether the readings in the two verses were originally identical or different.

4[5]. The expression *bat-rabbîm* is probably a proper name, perhaps referring to the Ammonite capital city Rabbah (Brenner 1992: 113), and therefore parallel to Heshbon, Lebanon and Damascus. Keel (1994: 236) suggests that it means lit. 'daughter of many', and from this infers that it speaks of the crowds of people who come from the barren steppe to be refreshed by the pools in Heshbon. This renewing effect, he says, is comparable to how Shulammith's eyes bring delight to Solomon. Although this suggestion is interesting and apparently supported by the LXX, it cannot be proven conclusively.

5[6]. Ibn Janah and Ibn Ezra repoint *karmel* to *karmil*, which suggests that Shulammith's hair is crimson, a close parallel to the comparison to purple thread in the second line (Brenner 1990: 268).

The rare word *dallâ* is used elsewhere only in Isa. 38:12 for the 'thrum' (the threads that hang from a weaver's loom), so here it probably refers to Shulammith's loosened hair that hangs freely while she dances.

6[7]. Although *'ahăbâ* is used elsewhere in the song for lovemaking, the structure of this verse seems to support better its use as a vocative as Solomon addresses Shulammith (Hess 2006: 123).

For the final word of the verse, MT reads *batta'ănûgîm* (in pleasures). Aquila's translation *thygatēr tryphōn*, followed by the Syr, presupposes a Hebr. text of *bat ta'ănûgîm* (daughter of pleasures) and Hess (2005: 219) argues persuasively for this reading (cf. *BHQ* 63). As Keel (1994: 242) notes, a daughter of pleasures is 'a woman who provides all the delights and pleasures of love'.

7[8]. The term *qômâ* speaks of stature, often in the sense of height, and sometimes, as here, of erect bearing (cf. Coppes, *TWOT* 2:793).

Bloch and Bloch (1995: 205) argue that the perfect form *dāmĕtâ* is a finite verb referring to past time, but its presence in a song of description is better construed with a stative sense of the verb.

8[9]. The word *sansinnâ* is used only here in the OT. Hostetter, *NIDOTTE* 3:685, states that it refers either to branches, and thus is figurative of Shulammith's hair or arms, or else to the date blossom cluster as a picture of her breasts. The use of *šad* in the previous verse and in the following line suggests that the better reading is 'blossoms', a figurative reference to her breasts.

The term *'ap*, the common word for 'nose', has been rendered in various ways. G. L. Carr (1984: 162–163) suggests that the Ug. parallel *ap* would yield the meaning of 'nipple', and the Akk. *apu* could mean the vulva (cf. Dahood 1976: 109–110). However, the only other use of *'ap* in the Song is in this song of description in 7:4[5], where it clearly refers to Shulammith's nose, and that meaning is probably meant here as well.

9[10]. As GKC 133h and Waltke 14.3.3b note, the cons. form *yên* followed by the adjective *ṭôb* has a superlative force, 'the best wine'.

The RSV and NEB emend the final two lines to f. forms, and regard them as the continued words of Solomon. However, the use of 'my beloved' (*dôdî*), Shulammith's term of endearment for Solomon, strongly supports her as the speaker in the second half of the verse.

Murphy (1990: 184) agrees with the LXX, Syr and Vg translations that the final word *yĕšēnîm* (sleepers) should be emended to *wĕšinnāy* (my teeth). Though this rendering fits the sense of the verse well, it requires several changes from the MT to justify it. The text of the MT can be understood plausibly as it is, so it is probably better to retain it (cf. Keel 1994: 247).

10[11]. The term *tĕšûqâ* is found only three times in the OT: here and in Gen 3:16 and 4:7. The word can have the negative sense of a craving for domination, as in Gen 4:7, or the positive sense of a strong attraction, as it is used in this text (Talley, *NIDOTTE* 4:341). Glickman 2004: 220–223 presents a useful discussion of the interpretative alternatives for this term.

Form, structure and setting

This passage follows the same general progression as seen in the wedding-night scene in ch. 4. Solomon first expresses his delight in Shulammith by means of a song describing her beauty in 7:1–7[2–8] as in 4:1–5, and then he resolves to make love to her in 7:8–9a[9–10a], as also in 4:6. This song of description is marked by more than a dozen similes by which Solomon draws upon elements of the natural world as well as human achievement in order to extol the excellence of Shulammith's body (Alter 1985: 197). The specific descriptions of her body in 7:1–5[2–6] move upwards from her feet to her head and focus particularly on her sexual organs, and culminate in his exclamation in 7:6[7:7] of how beautiful and how pleasing she is (contra Brenner 1990: 251–275, who deconstructs the *wasf* as a ribald and unflattering parody). There is a climax in language from the sense of sight to touch to smell to taste, and then to their implied sexual intercourse in 7:9b[10b], and finally to Shulammith's exclamation of Solomon's desire for her in 7:10[11]).

Comment

1[2]. Compared with Solomon's previous songs of description about Shulammith in 4:1–5 and 6:4–7, this song is by far the most explicitly erotic. Glickman (1976: 82–83) observes, 'the praise of the king is much more sensual and intimate. It reflects a greater knowledge of the physical beauty of his wife'. G. L. Carr (1984: 156) and Hubbard (1991: 332) argue that 7:1–5[2–6] are spoken by the chorus, reflecting their knowledge of female anatomy, but the use of the second person address throughout 7:1–9[2–10] supports Solomon as the sole speaker of the entire lyric. Shulammith appears to be dancing (Sendrey 1969: 474–475; contra Exum 2005c: 231) before her husband either naked or in a light diaphanous garment, so that he can see and describe her most intimate features. Solomon focuses on these parts of her body, in contrast to his careful avoidance of them in the scene of their reconciliation in 6:4–7. By the time of this song in ch. 7, Solomon and Shulammith have been fully reconciled, and it is clear that their intimacy has matured measurably since their wedding.

This description, which begins with her feet and moves upwards, may have been prompted by Solomon's attention being caught by the rapid steps of her dancing (Gordis 1974: 96). As in the wedding-night scene in 4:1, 7, where 'beautiful' (*yāpâ*) was the key term used in describing Shulammith, so now he employs the same word, implying that his former assessment has only been confirmed and has grown over time. The sandals she wears could be regarded as luxury, decorative items as in Ezek. 16:10, but the use of the term in Amos 2:6 and 8:6 demonstrates that sandals do not always or necessarily imply that nuance. It is interesting to note that in Judith 16.9 it was the sandals of Judith that enticed the Assyrian general Holofernes, and here in Song 7:1[2] they may serve the same erotic function. In contrast to Shulammith's humble background (cf. 1:5–6), Solomon implies the excellency of her character as he calls her 'noble daughter'. He soon directs his gaze to her sexual organs as he extols the beauty of the curves of her thighs. This term, which may well be a metonymy for the organs located in that region of her body (cf. the OT description of touching the 'thigh' in swearing an oath in Gen. 24:2, 9, 47:29, which probably is a euphemism for the genitals), refers to the most intimate parts of the body that would be seen only by her husband, or else it would be the most extreme shame for her (cf. Isa. 47:2–3). Reflecting his familiarity with highly artistic craftsmanship, Solomon regards her physical beauty as though she were sculpted by a master.

2[3]. Solomon continues to describe Shulammith by speaking of the region around her sexual organs. Most of the vocabulary he uses in this verse has not been employed before in the Song, for Solomon is breaking new ground in this description. Since their wedding night in 4:1–5, Solomon has had ample opportunity to become knowledgeable about the most intimate features of his wife's body. The highly poetic language he uses is capable of a variety of points of reference, and it is not always possible to prove conclusively his specific intent. In the context of the song of description in 7:1–9a[2–10a], it is unsurprising to find both visual elements and referents of quality.

The metaphor of her navel as a round bowl is primarily visual, but the reference to mixed wine in it must be interpreted in a non-visual way. Keel (1994: 234) suggests that 'wine' requires that the navel be taken as a euphemism for Shulammith's vulva, but the use of a related term to 'navel' in Ezek. 16:4 and Prov. 3:8 to speak of an umbilical cord argues against Keel's rendering (cf. Bloch and Bloch 1995: 201). It might be that Solomon, in describing her navel that he sees while she dances, cannot help but think ahead to the intoxicating delight of their anticipated sexual intercourse, so he exclaims as an aside, 'may mixed wine not be lacking!'

In describing her abdomen as a heap of wheat, he could be implying a visual referent of the tawny colour of her skin (Keel 1994: 235), but it is hard to see that a visual sense would extend to the fence of lotuses that surrounds the wheat. It is possible that wine and wheat are linked in this verse as a reference to the nourishment and pleasure Shulammith provides for Solomon (Štrba 2004: 490). Or wheat, as the staple of the diet and protected by a hedge of lotuses, could speak of the high value Solomon places upon her. Whatever the specific point may be, it is clear that Solomon finds Shulammith supremely delightful.

3[4]. This verse is nearly identical to a line of 4:5. The language Solomon uses of Shulammith is similar to that employed by Shulammith for Solomon in 2:9, which indicates that both of them are speaking in the familiar rhetoric of love poetry. Solomon continues to focus on her most erotic features as he extols her tender and lovely breasts, likening them to twin fawns. By using imagery that clearly recalls their wedding night when he made love to her for the first time, Solomon indicates that they have been fully reconciled after their previous rift.

4[5]. Solomon is enthralled by Shulammith's beauty, and to describe her uses images no doubt familiar in his culture, but difficult for the modern reader to grasp in specific terms. The descriptions in this verse all speak of Shulammith's dignity, elegance and serenity, as they reflect her quality and esteem more than her visual appearance. By means of this imagery, Solomon communicates that he 'values characteristics that suggest a personality at peace with itself and an internal strength of character' (Hess

2005: 217). As in his earlier song of description in 4:4, Solomon uses military language such as 'tower' and 'look out' as comparisons, but here it is a less dominant image. Rather than speaking of her neck as the tower of David, here Solomon refers to it as an ivory tower. Ivory could possibly refer to the light colour of her neck (contra her sunburnt skin in 1:5–6), but more likely it is used similarly to her description of him in 5:14 to speak of Shulammith's noble bearing.

Because of its renown as a site of great fertility (cf. Isa. 16:8–9), the ancient Amorite capital Heshbon (Num. 21:21–30) may be used as an image of beauty and delight, much as Tirzah in 6:4. An excavation in Heshbon has disclosed a large reservoir from the ninth to eighth centuries BC, with a capacity of two million litres (Younker, *ABD* 1:627; Eichner and Scherer 2001: 10–14), which could possibly be one of the pools referred to here (Geraty and Willis 1986: 31). In comparing her eyes to the pools in Heshbon, Solomon may be suggesting 'still, deep calmness rather than the sparkle and shimmer of flowing springs' (G. L. Carr 1984: 158).

The description of her nose like the tower of Lebanon that looks out towards Damascus, the capital of the rival power of Syria, should probably be interpreted similarly to the other images in the verse. This, then, is probably not speaking of the size, shape or prominence of her nose (Keel 1994: 236), but rather the confidence with which she bears herself even in the face of formidable challenges.

5[6]. This song of description proceeds upwards from Shulammith's feet, and at last Solomon describes her head in this verse. In the OT, Mount Carmel is used several times as an image of majestic beauty (Thompson, *ABD* 1:874), and thus functions similarly to other geographical names in the Song. Carmel is a prominent outcropping looking over the Mediterranean Sea, so it is an apt image for Shulammith's regal bearing that distinguishes her above all her peers in beauty and grace. In addition, its perpetual vegetation is an oasis of fertility in a dry land, just as Shulammith's beauty marks her out among all the other women.

The description of her hair as purple thread has been taken literally as an indication that Shulammith used an expensive dye on her hair (Murphy 1990: 186), but the high poetry of this lyric could well point to another rendering. As Solomon gazes at her loosened hair as she dances or as they embrace in the moonlight, purple may speak of the shimmering appearance of the faint light playing on her hair.

The final line of the verse features an ironic use of military language, for the king acknowledges that he is held captive, not by a foreign army, but by the lovely hair of his beloved (Whedbee 1998: 266). Her love and beauty have a powerful control over him, but he considers this a good and desirable predicament into which to fall.

6[7]. This lyric is marked by exclamations that reflect Solomon's heart-felt delight in Shulammith. Many of the terms Solomon uses in this verse, including *yāpâ*, *nāʿēm* and *ʾahăbâ*, have been used since the first chapter of the Song, but have become increasingly rich in their meaning as the relationship between the couple has progressed in intensity and erotic expression. Clearly, Solomon's appreciation of her builds on his earlier admiration for her, as he learns to enjoy personally what he at first valued from a distance.

In contrast to the woman of folly in Prov. 9:17, who claims that stolen water is sweet and bread eaten in secret is 'pleasant' (yin'ām), Shulammith is a continuing source of genuine and legitimate pleasure for Solomon. Consequently, Solomon, who on their wedding night concluded his song of description by saying that Shulammith has no blemish (4:7), now caps his description of her by addressing her as 'daughter of pleasures'. As the parallel use of 'ng in Ps. 37:4 indicates, Shulammith satisfies the deepest desires of her beloved.

7[8]. After addressing Shulammith as the daughter of pleasures in the previous verse, Solomon now resolves to enjoy the pleasures she affords. He uses an extended image of a palm tree, which continues into the next verse, to communicate his intention to make love to her. In the wedding procession in 3:6, Shulammith's approach was compared to 'columns' (tîmărôt) of smoke, but now she is likened to a 'palm tree' (tāmār), probably because of her erect posture and slim form that accentuate her breasts. Her stately bearing that resembles a palm tree is similar to the regal beauty of her head, which Solomon compared to Carmel in 7:5[6]. In the Middle East, the date palm is noted both for its loveliness and its fruitfulness, and is used as a symbol of peace and affluence (Zohary, IDB 2:288; cf. Ps. 92:12–13[14–15]).

8[9]. In the midst of this erotic song of description, Solomon in an aside discloses his inner thoughts as he resolves to make love to Shulammith. As in Prov. 5:19–20, Solomon finds his sexual delight and fulfilment in caressing the breasts of his wife. The language he uses alludes to the process by which date palms are pollenated to produce fruit. In contrast to 2:15, where Shulammith urges that the little foxes be 'grasped' ('ḥz) to remove their damaging effects to their love, Solomon now 'grasps' ('ḥz) her breasts in order to enhance the delightful effect in their lovemaking.

As Solomon refers to the scent of her nose, he may be using 'nose' as a metonymy for her excited breathing as she is being aroused. In this lyric, he finds her pleasing to his various senses, as he uses terms of sight, touch and now smell. Perhaps in contrast to her insensitive response to him in 5:4–5, Solomon desires that she be aroused fully just as he is.

9[10]. Adding to his previous sensual descriptions, Solomon now adds the sense of taste. His use of ḥēk (palate), rather than peh (mouth) or śāpâ (lip), suggests that the couple are kissing deeply. When Shulammith breaks into Solomon's description (contra RSV and NEB), she reflects the sexual and psychological unity they are experiencing. Solomon uses the metaphor of wine to speak of their kissing, and she adopts and extends the word picture by focusing on the delight their lovemaking brings to him. D. M. Carr

(2003: 132) remarks well, 'The poetic device of having her complete his words heightens their mutuality. This is not just male desire of a woman, nor female desire for a man, but mutual desire.' As Solomon has alluded to her delight in the previous verse, so now she notes his enjoyment. They both find joy in the delight of the other.

The term *mêšārîm* (smoothly) may include a secondary ethical overtone of what is right, as it does in 1:4, for this is how intimacy is supposed to be in God's design. In contrast to 5:2, when Shulammith was asleep and did not want to be disturbed, now the couple fall asleep in the ecstasy of love and in each other's embrace. Under God's blessing, when they lie down their sleep is sweet (cf. Ps. 127:2; Prov. 3:24). Reading *yěšēnîm* (sleepers) with the MT and against the LXX, Syr and Vg translations, as in 4:16 – 5:1 their sexual intercourse is now implied without the poet resorting to explicit, voyeuristic language.

10[11]. In this verse, Shulammith utters the third of three similar, but subtly different, refrains. In 2:16a, she said, 'My beloved is mine, and I am his.' Inverting the clauses, she exclaimed in 6:3a, 'I am my beloved's, and my beloved is mine.' Now upon awakening she affirms, 'I am my beloved's, and his desire is for me.' Because the Song is highly poetic, it is reasonable to suppose that the author may well have varied these details with significant conscious intent. With these words, Shulammith no longer focuses on her possession of the beloved, but on his ardent love that has enveloped her with security (R. M. Davidson 2007: 600). Solomon's song of description and words of intention to make love to her in 7:1–9a[2–10a] have evidenced his powerful desire for her. Both of them have come to place the other first, and this provides the secure foundation for their relationship.

The term *těšûqâ* (desire) may well be an echo of Gen. 3:16, one of only two other uses of the word in the OT. If that is indeed the case, then it suggests that their intimacy has progressed to the extent that it functions to counteract the damaging effects on marriage that were introduced by the curse. Lavoie (2000: 79) observes insightfully:

> By electing to use this rare word, this verse in the Song is really redirecting the Genesis text and completely transforming it. The curse of Genesis 3:16 is changed into a blessing. Desire is a joy, not a judgment. The love relationship is no longer unilateral but reciprocal. Moreover, it is no longer the woman who yearns for the man, as in the patriarchal text of Genesis 3:16, but the man for the woman.

In the Song of Songs, then, intimacy within marriage is in part a way back to idyllic Eden (Trible 1978: 160; Terrien 1985: 45; Goitein 1993: 59). Even after the Fall, with its painful consequences, love can provide significant benefits, as it replaces contention for control (Foh 1975: 383) with marital intimacy that focuses on the other rather than upon oneself. Hess (2005: 224) concludes insightfully:

> Thus the Genesis judgment of each person seeking domination is reversed, with each person now seeking mutuality and willingly giving possession of their body to their partner. In the NT this becomes the test of love between a husband and wife, that they give their bodies to one another and love each other as they love their own bodies (1 Cor. 7:2–4; Eph. 5:22–23).

Explanation

1–4[2–5]. Sexual intimacy can and should continue to increase throughout marriage. In contrast to what contemporary culture supposes, sexual intimacy is not just the special prerogative of the young, but should bring increasing delight over time. As a couple come to know one another better, they learn how to enjoy each other more. In other words, true sexual liberation is not found in promiscuity before or outside marriage, but is discovered within the context of an intimate marital relationship, in which a couple can be naked and yet not be ashamed (cf. Gen. 2:25).

5[6]. In contrast with the dominance of the husband that was the painful result of the Fall into sin in Gen. 3:16, in intimacy freedom is linked with being captured. Love binds a couple together in such a way that they find delight in serving one another (cf. the similar exhortation by Paul to Christians to serve one another in love in Gal. 5:13). This is not mere duty, but is freedom within obligation. In God's design, within the bond of marriage there is duty that is freely given and responsibililty that is joyfully accepted.

6[7]. Created in God's image, men and women possess intellect, emotions and will. Intimacy engages the total person. It involves the intellect, because it entails getting to know another person at a profound level. It is also built upon a commitment of the will that chooses to enter into a permanent commitment of marriage. Intimacy, moreover, plumbs the depths of emotions as it draws a couple into a quality of love and delight that cannot be found through any other human experience. Intimacy, then, leads to deep personal knowledge. In a similar way, Paul expresses in Phil. 3:10 his aspiration to know Christ, and Yahweh states in Jer. 9:23–24 that the greatest human achievement is to understand and know him.

7[8]. Sexual intimacy is not the proper way to kindle or rekindle love, but once love has been ignited, it comes into full blaze in sexual union. Within the marriage commitment in a relationship marked by true affection, physical intimacy is more than just satisfying a passionate drive. It is a precious delight to be savoured and enjoyed as God's good gift.

8–10[9–11]. Intimacy produces a sense of joyful mutuality. It does not focus solely or even primarily on what one is expressing and enjoying, but more than that it desires to bring joy to the beloved. In true intimacy, the focus moves more from 'I' to 'we'. Both the husband and the wife grow in spontaneity as they give and receive affection, and as a result both derive pleasure from one another. Intimacy produces a deep and profound longing that counters selfishness as it focuses on the mutual relationship.

SONG OF SONGS 7:11–13[12–14]

Translation

SHULAMMITH

11[12]Come, my beloved, let us go out into the field;
Let us spend the night in the henna bushes.
12[13]Let us start early to the vineyards;
Let us see if the vines have sprouted,
[If] the [vines of] Semadar have opened,
[If] the pomegranates have blossomed.
There I will give my love to you.
13[14]The mandrakes have given a scent,
And all excellent things are over our doors.
New things and old things, my beloved, I have treasured up for you.

Notes on the text

7:11[12]. The term *kĕpārîm* is used for 'villages' in 1 Sam. 6:18, 1 Chr. 27:25 and Neh. 6:2, but in the Song the related term *kōper* refers to henna plants in 1:14 and 4:13. G. L. Carr (1984: 165) observes, 'This shrub, which grows wild in Palestine, is covered in spring with fragrant whitish flowers growing in clusters like grapes.' It seems best in this context, when *kĕpārîm* is parallel to *śādeh* (the field or open country), to accept the NEB reading, 'henna bushes'. The henna bushes that grew wild in ancient Israel would have provided a fragrant setting in which they could delight in lovemaking.

12[13]. As in 2:13, *sĕmādar* probably refers to an especially good variety of grapevines that was imported into Israel.

13[14]. As in Prov. 5:8, *petaḥ* (door) is probably used in a sexual sense.

Form, structure and setting

This short lyric is Shulammith's response to Solomon's 'desire' (*tĕšûqâ*) for her in 7:10[11]. Although Shulammith continues to speak, this section reflects a change of scene from their lovemaking in 7:10[11] to an invitation to spend a night together in the countryside (7:11–13[12–14]). It builds from Shulammith's invitation to Solomon to go with her into the countryside (7:11[12]), to her promise to give her love to him (7:12[13]), to her resolve to bring all sorts of sexual pleasure to him (7:13[14]). The trio of similar images in 7:12[13] – sprouting vines, opened vines, blossoming pomegranates – when read in the light of the familiar metaphor of mandrakes for fertility (7:13[14]) may well be pictures of Shulammith's desire that they conceive a child as the fruit of their love. This sense may also be reinforced by the sound play between *dôdî* (my beloved) and *dûdā'îm* (mandrakes).

Comment

11[12]. Throughout the Song, Shulammith has gradually grown more secure in the warmth of Solomon's love. After the reconciliation of the couple, Shulammith has renewed confidence in their relationship. As on their wedding night in 4:16, she invites Solomon to make love to her. Instead of resisting his invitation, as in 5:2–4, she takes the initiative to urge him to go with her into the field. What she earlier expressed as an inner desire (2:6), now in a sense similar to Solomon's expressed intention in 4:6, Shulammith states verbally her longing to spend the night with him. She expresses her desire in language that echoes Solomon's proposal to her in 2:10–14 to go out into the springtime together. In the mutuality of their love, both Solomon and Shulammith feel free to initiate invitations to lovemaking.

The 'field' (*śādeh*) is the open country outside the settled areas. In the OT it is the site where one can be alone or can meet unobserved with someone else (Gen. 4:8; 1 Sam. 20:5, 11; Ruth 3:14; cf. Keel 1994: 254). Shulammmith wants the two of them to go out into the field, so that they can spend the night together among the fragrant henna bushes. There she will satisfy the desire he has for her (7:10[11]).

12[13]. Continuing the invitation she began in the previous verse, Shulammith echoes the language of Solomon's proposal to her in 2:13, and her own language of 6:11, but now she adds that she will give to him her love. Her image of going to the garden is a common motif in ANE love poetry (Sanmartin-Ascaso, *TDOT* 3:154).

In 1:6, Shulammith did not want to be seen, and in 2:14 Solomon spoke of his desire to see her form and appearance, but here seeing seems to have a deeper significance. The three parallel objects of seeing – the sprouting vine, the opened vines, the blossoming pomegranates – may well be figures for her conception of a child. Borowski (1987: 116–117) observes, 'The pomegranate was always considered a symbol of fertility, probably because of the large number of seeds in each fruit.' Earlier in 5:2, Solomon called her to 'open' (*ptḥ*) to him, probably for sexual intimacy, but she did not. Now she suggests that they use the first light of dawn to look to see if the vines have 'opened' (*ptḥ*) as a result of their sexual activity. In contrast to Judg. 19:25 and Prov. 7:18, where the dawn reveals the tragic results of illicit and shameful sexual activity, for Solomon and Shulammith the light of morning may bring joyful knowledge of the fruit of their lovemaking. Then, she promises, she will freely give her love to him, not under compulsion or out of obligation, but from a full heart.

13[14]. Even at this stage well into their marriage, Shulammith is looking for new ways to bring delight to Solomon as their intimacy continues to grow and thrive over time. Her reference to mandrakes echoes Gen. 30:14–16, where this fruit is considered an aphrodisiac to enhance fertility or to stimulate sexual desire (Grossberg 2005: 239). It may well be, then, that she is implying her desire to conceive children as the natural fruit of their lovemaking (cf. Ps. 45:16[17]). Just as the mandrakes 'give' (*ntn*) their scent, so she will 'give' (*ntn*) her love to him (cf. 7:12[13]). The excellent fruits of her sexuality, which Solomon sensed were in her garden on their wedding night (4:13), they now will enjoy together.

Shulammith's reference to new and old things may well be a merism speaking of the complete range of pleasures she has reserved for him. Keel (1994: 260) notes that this expression may refer to 'erotic pleasures – both those as yet unknown, coming as a surprise, and those that are old and proved'. Particularly significant is that Shulammith has kept all of these sexual pleasures for Solomon, another implication that she was a virgin when they were married, and that she has reserved her body for him alone.

Explanation

11–12[12–13]. Intimacy in God's design overflows into fruitfulness. In addition to enriching the man and woman, it also brings joy to the community. Furthermore, from the marital bond the blessing of children emerges as both the biological and figurative fruit of their love. Through human love, God brings the blessing of children into the world (cf. Gen 17:16; Deut. 7:13).

13[14]. The Song makes clear that sexual pleasure is not just for the young, but can and should continue to increase throughout the course of married life. As a couple keep growing in intimacy, they discover that there is always more to learn, to give, to share and to enjoy. The fruit of intimacy, then, is seen both in the physical conception of children and in the sexual pleasures of lovemaking.

SONG OF SONGS 8:1–4

Translation

SHULAMMITH

¹O that one would make you like a brother to me,
One who sucked the breasts of my mother!
I would find you in the streets; I would kiss you,
And they would not despise me.
²I would lead you, I would bring you into the house of my mother who
taught me.
I would cause you to drink some spiced wine, some of my pomegranate
wine.
³O may his left hand be under my head;
And O may his right hand embrace me.
⁴I adjure you, O daughters of Jerusalem,
Why should you incite or excite love until it is pleased?

Notes on the text

8:1. *mî* has been used before in rhetorical questions in 3:6 and 6:10. Here it seems to bear the nuance 'would that, O that!'

Shulammith says that she would find Solomon in the *ḥûṣ*, probably the public area of the city where she looked for him previously in 3:2 and 5:6. It can be translated 'streets' or 'market'.

2. The verb *nāhag* is elsewhere used in the OT of leading an army into battle (1 Chr. 20:1; 2 Chr. 25:11) and of abducting women (1 Sam. 30:2), but here in an ironic reversal comparable to Song 7:5[6] Shulammith is leading the king into lovemaking.

The term *tĕlammĕdēnî* is ambiguous, for it could be either second person m. sg., referring to Solomon, or third person f. sg., referring to Shulammith's mother, as the LXX translates it. G. L. Carr (1984: 167) observes:

> If the feminine form is assumed, the teacher is the mother who has instructed her daughter in the 'facts of life', and it is to that 'schoolroom' she wants to return to show how well she has learned her lessons. If the masculine form is correct, her request is that her lover teach her the intricacies of love in the place where she had her first intimate contacts. In view of the last part of the verse, the feminine form is preferred: the art of preparing for love is best learned at home.

Bloch and Bloch (1995: 210) aptly note the parallel in Ruth 3:1–5, where Naomi instructs Ruth in preparation for her approach to Boaz.

The rare word '*āsîs* probably refers to stronger wine, comparable to the Gr. *gleukas* in Acts 2:13 (cf. Harris, *TWOT* 2:686). This drink is probably intended by Shulammith to stimulate sexual arousal in Solomon.

3. As in 2:6, the verbal form of 'embrace' (*těḥabběqēnî*) in the second line is a jussive with an optative sense expressing a strong desire. Although no verb is used in the first line, the same optative sense is implied.

4. The Hebr. *mah* is used in place of '*im* that was employed in 2:7 and 3:5, and contra Snaith (1993: 117) and Joüon 144h, who consider it equivalent to a negation, it may well ask 'Why?' Rather than being an insignificant stylistic variation (Murphy 1990: 189; Exum 2005c: 248), the change of term probably changes the tone of the adjuration (Hubbard 1991: 337). It must be remembered that in lyric poetry 'the choice of words is not arbitrary, for the poet selects language that best communicates his message' (Estes 1995: 422). In this case, the prohibitions against arousing sexual passion in 2:7 and 3:5 both came before the wedding scene. After their wedding in 4:1 – 5:1, they have tasted the fruit of sexual intimacy, so further incitement from their peers is redundant (G. L. Carr 1984: 168).

As in 2:7 and 3:5, the prohibition uses wordplay, as the hiph. of '*ûr* (incite) is intensified to the pol. form of the same verb, meaning 'to excite'.

Form and structure

Shulammith continues to speak, and her words in 8:1–4 can plausibly be construed as part of the scene begun in 7:11[12] (Roberts 2007: 312–315). Alternatively, 8:1–3 may look ahead to a different location, her mother's house, in which Shulammith can feel freedom to express her love to Solomon without social sanction. This short lyric traces a climax in intimacy, from Shulammith's desire to kiss Solomon in public (8:1), to leading him to the privacy of her mother's house (8:2), to delighting in his caresses (8:3), and to continued lovemaking without interference (8:4).

Comment

1. Exum (2005c: 246) observes, 'The woman wishes her love were like a brother so that she could kiss him openly in the street without censure. This awareness of social constraints allows the real world to intrude briefly into the world of the lovers.' Shulammith wants to be free to be spontaneous and expressive in her love for Solomon. She desires to be uninhibited by cultural constraints as her feelings overflow in physical intimacy with him. In the ancient world, public affection between lovers was disapproved (cf. Prov. 7:13), but it was considered acceptable if between family members (cf. Gen. 29:11). G. L. Carr (1984: 166) notes, 'What was not in good taste even for husband and wife was perfectly permissible between brother and sister.'

If she were allowed this freedom, she would seek Solomon and find him in the public area of the city (cf. 3:4). Although the language of her desire sounds much like that of the adulteress in Prov. 7:13 (cf. Hos. 2:4–12; Ezek. 16:36–37), Shulammith's intent by contrast is good and honourable, for this intimacy would be with her husband. In the opening scene of the Song, Shulammith privately longed for Solomon to kiss her (1:2), but now she desires to kiss him in public. It is evident that there has been significant progress both in their relationship and in her confidence.

2. In this verse, Shulammith continues to express to Solomon her inner desires, as she clearly initiates lovemaking with him. In 1:4, at the beginning of their relationship she imagined Solomon 'bringing' (*bô'*) her into his chambers, but now resolves to 'bring' (*bô'*) him into the house of her mother. She wants to take him to the safest, most private place she knows (cf. 3:4). In 3:6–11, Solomon conveyed Shulammith to a public place for their wedding, but now she desires to bring him to a private place where they can enjoy sexual intimacy.

Shulammith has learned from her mother about the art of lovemaking, for her mother has been her teacher, fulfilling the pattern of the wisdom tradition in Prov. 1:8 and 6:20. As the imperfect form of *tĕlammĕdēnî* suggests, what her mother taught her has continuing benefits in Shulammith's life. Drawing upon what she has learned from her mother, Shulammith intends to seduce her husband. Garrett (2004: 249) elucidates imaginatively:

> There is something beautiful in this picture. She is not, in entering the world of sexuality, doing something that is alien and abhorrent to her. She is emulating what she has seen and heard all of her life in the person who, up to this time, has been the closest to her. More than that, as her mother made love to her father and so gave birth to daughters and sons, she will do the same and become the teacher of her daughters.

Shulammith plans to cause Solomon to drink spiced wine and strong pomegranate wine. In the Song, drinking wine is an image for kissing (cf. 2:4; 5:1; 7:9[10]) or more general lovemaking. She desires that the sexual enjoyment that they tasted on their wedding night and that was affirmed by the divine voice will continue to enrich their lives. In effect, she wants them to live out Yahweh's command to humans to be fruitful and multiply (Gen. 1:26–28) as she and Solomon follow his exhortation 'Eat, O friends, drink and become intoxicated, O lovers!' (Song 5:1).

3. This strong inner desire of Shulammith follows directly from her words in the previous two verses. Her use of the verb *ḥābaq*, as in 2:6 and Prov. 5:20, indicates that she longs for Solomon to make love to her, as she imagines him sexually fondling her. This verse is virtually identical to 2:6 in its language, but their situation in life has changed significantly. Her previous desire for sexual intimacy could not be honoured at that time, because they were not yet married, but now within the boundaries of marriage the couple can enjoy the delights for which she longs. Her passion for Solomon has not faded due to the routines and stresses of marriage, but continues to burn brightly within her.

4. This verse uses the oath formula of 2:7 and 3:5 (and less directly 5:8) as Shulammith again strongly desires sexual intimacy, although here the words 'by the gazelles or by the hinds of the field' are omitted. She changes the language, however, in a slight but significant way as she now asks rhetorically why their lovemaking should need to be incited or excited. Within the bond of marriage, Shulammith's love has already been completely aroused, so needs no further external encouragement by her peers. The incitement that before marriage would have been destructive is now within marriage redundant. Fokkelman (2001: 206) observes, 'Love, then, is not a force to be toyed with, and we should not be so stupid (the girl tells her friends) as to stir it up prematurely, or manipulate it in some way, since love's authenticity will then be lost and forces released which may swallow you up.'

Explanation

1. As love expresses its inner feelings in physical intimacy, it is also mindful that it functions within social boundaries. Love, then, is not self-absorbed, but situates itself within the community. Love matures beyond self-centredness to consider its effect on others. As love develops, it should draw a couple more closely to the community rather than leading them into their own separate orbit in defiance of others.

2. The community draws boundaries for the expression of intimacy, but also nurtures the enjoyment of intimacy. In the appropriate place and at the appropriate time, love is eager to enjoy the full measure of the delights God has designed for intimacy within the marriage relationship. When marital intimacy is enjoyed to the full, it enriches both the couple and their community around them.

3–4. As love flourishes in marriage, it moves progressively forward in intimacy. Instead of requiring external encouragement, it prospers when it is free from unnecessary, though perhaps well-intentioned, interference.

SONG OF SONGS 8:5–7

Translation

NARRATOR

⁵Who is this who is coming up from the wilderness leaning upon her beloved?

Shulammith

> Under the apricot tree I awakened you.
> There your mother was in labour with you;
> There she was in labour [and] she bore you.
> ⁶Place me as a seal upon your heart, as a seal upon your arm.
> Love is exceedingly strong; ardent passion is completely unyielding;
> Its sparks are fiery sparks, a most powerful flame.
> ⁷Many waters are not able to extinguish love,
> And rivers cannot overflow it.
> If someone were to give all the wealth of his house for love,
> [People] would utterly despise him.

Notes on the text

8:5. As in 2:3 (see note), *tappûaḥ* may possibly best refer to the apricot tree.

The m. sg. pronoun suffixes indicate that 'you' refers to Solomon, so Shulammith here is the speaker. The Syr and several modern translations have construed Solomon as the speaker, but that is unsupported by the Hebr. textual evidence (cf. Tournay 1980: 7).

6. Waltke 14.5b states that absolute superlatives with a negative sense can be formed with *mût* (dying), *māwet* (death) and *šĕ'ōl* (Sheol) (cf. Thomas 1953: 221; Brin 1992: 116). The sense of Shulammith's description of love as 'strong as death', 'unyielding as Sheol' and 'the flame of Yah', then, can be read as 'exceedingly strong', 'completely unyielding' and 'a most powerful flame'. However, it should also be noted that in the OT both Sheol and the grave are often depicted as having an insatiable appetite (Isa. 5:14; Hab. 2:5; Prov. 27:20; 30:15–16; cf. Lewis, *ABD* 2:103).

The term *qin'â* is often translated 'jealousy', but more precisely refers to the 'assertion of the rightful claims of possession' (G. L. Carr 1984: 170). It speaks of an ardent commitment to the exclusivity of the commitment that does not tolerate the violation of the covenant between the two of them (cf. Ps. 69:9[10], where the word is used for the psalmist's intense loyalty for the house of God). Alluding to the use of the term in Exod. 20:5, Garrett (2004: 257) reasons:

> If the jealousy of Yahweh over Israel is the model, the term refers to a proper possessiveness in the setting of a wholesome relationship. Rightly experienced by healthy souls, this exclusivity is part of the glory of love and further indicates the seriousness of entering this relationship.

Similarly, Murphy (1987: 118) states that 'the import of the whole passage is that love pursues its object, the beloved one, with the same finality and tenacity as Death pursues every human being'.

Linafelt (2002: 331) notes perceptively that the sounds in this verse reflect the meaning of the words. The hard k and q sounds in the first two lines emphasize the hardness of love, and then the š sounds in the final line communicate the fiery sparks of passion.

The final word of the verse (šalhebetyâ), 'a most powerful flame', is much disputed. It may be an intensive form of lahab, or it could be read with the BHS apparatus as 'a flame of Yah' (Hausmann, TDOT 7:471; Joüon 141n). If the latter reading is correct, it is probably a Hebr. superlative formed with the divine name, comparable to Jon. 4:11, although R. M. Davidson (2005: 148–154) argues vigorously that the reading 'flame of Yah' points typologically beyond the literal sense to the divine Lover, who is the source of human love.

7. Joüon 147b states that in this verse, as in Gen. 13:16, 'îš is used in the weakened sense of 'someone'.

Form, structure and setting

The final ten verses of the Song are often viewed as a miscellaneous assortment. For example, Murphy (1990: 195) claims that it 'may be a collection of disparate poems or fragments of poems'. On the other hand, it may well be that in the final section the prominent characters and themes of the Song make their final appearances, which brings a sense of literary closure to the song cycle and indirectly supports the unity of the book. As Exum (1973: 74) observes, it 'is really a recapitulation of motifs'.

The lyric in 8:5–7 comprises the climax of the Song, for here Shulammith expresses her desire for love that is unending, unextinguishable and incalculable. The section begins with the chorus asking, 'Who is this who is leaning on her beloved?', in v. 5a, and then in vv. 5b–7 Shulammith expresses the particulars of Solomon's supportive, stable love in the only didactic statement in the Song. She describes the love she experiences and desires in a set of powerful images – it is a seal upon his heart and arm, it is exceedingly strong and completely unyielding, its powerful flame cannot be extinguished by many waters and rivers, and it is beyond the highest price that can be offered for it.

Comment

5. The first line echoes 3:6 and 6:10, with all three of these verses probably referring to Shulammith. Because Shulammith is viewed here leaning against her beloved, this may well be a charming picture of the couple in old age reminiscing about their journey together to intimacy. It has been through long experience that they have learned the true character of love, which will be articulated in 8:6–7.

In contrast to 2:14 and 4:8, Shulammith is no longer inaccessible to Solomon, because she is leaning upon him in love and for support. She reflects in imaginative terms how she awakened Solomon to love, perhaps alluding to a common theme in erotic poetry of love under the trees (Murphy 1990: 191). Her focus, however, is on placing their intimacy within the context of family. In the Song, both of their mothers are presented as deeply involved in the nurture of their love. Shulammith's mother taught her about love (8:2), and Solomon's mother travailed in labour to bear him (8:5; cf. similar language about Shulammith's mother in 6:9). Perhaps Shulammith is suggesting that for love to develop inevitably there is pain, just as there is labour in the process of childbirth. It could also be another allusion to Gen. 3:16 (cf. *těšûqâ* in 7:10[11]), because pain in childbearing is part of the price intimacy must pay in a fallen world if it is to bear the fruit of love.

6. The m. sg. pronoun suffixes indicate that Shulammith continues to speak to Solomon. Nevertheless, Sadgrove (1979: 245) observes well that 'although placed on the lips of the Shulammite, this poem is surely intended to be read as meditating on and universalizing all that has gone before; indeed, this is the only place in the Song where any attempt is made to probe the *meaning* of the love that is its theme; everywhere else it is simply described'. As Solomon was earlier pictured as a sachet of myrrh between Shulammith's breasts (1:13), so now she wants to be like a seal upon his heart. In the ancient world, a seal was either a cylinder or a stamp that was used to show possession of an object (Hallo 1983: 10–13; Kist 2003: 1–14; cf. Hag. 2:23). Tufnell, *IDB* 4:255, observes about seals in Mesopotamia:

> With the development of writing, seals in the form of a cylinder came into use. They were either provided with a loop at the narrow end, or were pierced longways for suspension; the outer face was engraved with patterns and signs in intaglio, worked in reverse; the design therefore read correctly when it was impressed on any flat or curved surface of moist clay, which was then sun-baked to preserve it. The seal could be worn on a necklace or wristlet of beads, or carried attached by a pin to some part of the owner's dress.

Just as she was a sealed spring preserved for him alone (4:12), she now wants to be a seal upon his heart, so that he will be open and available only to her.

Shulammith wants Solomon to place her as a seal upon both his heart (cf. Prov. 3:3) and his arm (cf. Gen. 41:42), so that she may receive both his love and his strength. She wants to be imprinted permanently on the innermost part of his being and to enjoy his full vigour. In other words, she desires his all-consuming love, not just half-hearted affection. As Watson (1995: 263) observes, for love to reach its potential one must value and cherish another with wholehearted esteem that creates a desire for closer intimacy.

Using three superlative expressions, Shulammith, in the only didactic statement in the Song, speaks about the nature of love itself (Exum 2005a: 79). She pictures love as strong as death; that is, 'exceedingly strong', as unyielding as Sheol; that is, 'completely unyielding', and as the flame of Yah; that is, 'a most powerful flame'. An additional, but less likely, superlative has been suggested by Mulder, *TDOT* 14:12, 15, who claims that 'fieriness of Resheph' uses the name of this ANE deity in a way comparable to how the name of Yah is used here. The love Shulammith envisions is as irreversible as death, which may be another intimation of the power of love to counteract the effects of the curse (cf. 7:10[11]). The ardent and exclusive passion she desires is as unyielding as the grave. As a consuming fire, love destroys all that stands in its way, including other relationships, entanglements and selfishness. Tromp (1979: 94) states well, 'Love is represented here as a force which is able to overcome the negative forces which threaten the very existence of world and mankind. In other words, Love gains the victory over chaos and creates wholesome order and life.'

7. The image of fire in v. 6 continues into v. 7, for Shulammith says:

> Many waters are not able to extinguish love,
> And rivers cannot overflow it.

The expression 'many waters' (*mayim rabbîm*) is often used in the Ug. literature to speak of Yam, the rival of Baal, and in the OT refers to the powers of chaos only Yahweh can control (Gen. 1:2; Ps. 93:4; Isa. 51:10; cf. May 1955: 18; Keel 1994: 276). If this phrase does indeed indicate the forces of chaos, then implicitly Yahweh is presented here as the protector of love, for only he is sufficient to thwart that foe. As 7:10[11] 'alludes to love as a partial triumph over the curse on humanity, so also 8:6–7 perhaps suggests that in God's design love functions to counteract the destructive effects of chaos that threaten to extinguish life' (Estes 2005: 436).

In the ancient world, marriages typically entailed financial negotiations between the families, but Shulammith insists counterculturally that love must be given freely, and is not for sale, barter or negotiation. To treat love as a commodity to be purchased is to miss the point entirely, and to try to buy love is in fact to play the fool. Money can no more buy love than it can enable one to avoid death (Ps. 49:7–9[8–10]). Love is not subject to price or negotiation, so any attempt to purchase love would be greeted with the utmost disdain (Murphy 1990: 198).

Explanation

5. The road to intimacy is a long journey over a lifetime. This path to love certainly contains many pleasures, but it also typically entails pain. As in the birth of a child there is labour, so intimacy costs much, but that is true

of anything of high value. In an analogous way, Jas 1:2–4 explains that trials are the means by which endurance is perfected. In addition, there is a social dimension to human intimacy, because it draws from the prior love of parents, and then bears fruit in children.

6. There are high demands for genuine love. True love does not settle for what is convenient or easy, but it is relentless in holding on to the beloved. Just as Yahweh is a jealous God (Exod. 20:3–5; 34:14) who requires exclusive love from his people, so genuine intimacy craves full commitment, and will not be satisfied with anything less (cf. Prov. 5:15–17).

7. Love will probably be tested, and perhaps even threatened, by difficulties in life, but they will not be able to extinguish the flame of true intimacy, a truth Paul echoes in his paean to love in 1 Cor. 13:4–7. As Glickman (1976: 100) notes, 'Love is persevering. It will persevere through the waters of adversity in marriage.' In addition, true love is not for sale. Love cannot be bought by wealth, position or power, because that treats a person as a mere object to be purchased. In the NT, love in its most perfect and persevering form is demonstrated by Christ (Rom. 8:35–39), for nothing can separate God's people from his love.

SONG OF SONGS 8:8–10

Translation

BROTHERS

> [8]We have a little sister, and she has no breasts.
> What should we do for our sister on the day on which she is spoken for?
> [9]If she is a wall, we will build upon her a silver battlement,
> But if she is a door, we will enclose her with a cedar plank.

SHULAMMITH

> [10]I was a wall, and my breasts were like towers;
> Then I was in his eyes like one who finds peace.

Notes on the text

8:8. In the Mishnah, *Yebamot* 62b, *qĕṭannâ* is the legal term for a minor girl: a girl up to twelve years and one day.

Waltke 19.4a observes that the š relative pronoun introduces a resumptive element, so the phrase here may be translated 'on the day on which she is spoken for (on it)'.

9. The term *ṭîrâ* refers to a turret or battlement (cf. Ezek. 46:23). Because the turret here is made of silver, it is probably primarily intended to be decorative rather than protective in function (Murphy 1990: 192–193; Tawil 2006: 42; cf. 1:11).

Bloch and Bloch (1995: 215) note that the parallels in Isa. 1:19–20 and Deut. 20:11–12 support reading the two conditional clauses in this verse in an antithetical sense.

10. The term *môṣĕ'ēt* could be the qal participle of *mṣ'* (to find), the hiph. participle of *yṣ'* (to go out) or perhaps even a f. by-form of *môṣā* (spring) (Gordis 1974: 101). The language of seeking and finding in the Song supports the first of these alternatives as the most likely here (cf. 3:1–4; 5:6–7), and this is also supported by the LXX translation *heuriskousa*.

Form, structure and setting

This short lyric is constructed as a set of before and after pictures. First, the brothers describe Shulammith as a young girl who has no breasts because she has not yet reached puberty (8:8). They set out two contrasting possibilities: if she is sexually inaccessible like a wall, then they will affirm and reward her, but if she is sexually accessible like a door, then they will enclose her to protect her (8:9). Then Shulammith states in 8:10 that when she reached the time of sexual maturity, she was indeed a wall when her breasts matured to become like towers. The climax in v. 10 is in effect a microcosm of the message of the whole Song, for Shulammith says that she was a wall (her virginity), her breasts were like towers (her sexual maturation) and then she found *šālôm* (intimacy with Solomon). In making this statement, she suggests an implicit sound play: Shulammith found *šālôm* when she found Solomon (*Šĕlōmōh*).

Comment

8. This section has received many divergent interpretations (cf. Bloch and Bloch 1995: 214 for a concise survey of the alternatives). It appears that this could be a flashback to Shulammith's childhood, because in real time 8:8–9, in which she has no breasts, must precede her statement in 1:13, when she pictures Solomon as a sachet of myrrh lying between her breasts.

In the OT, customarily the father initiated the marriage negotiations on behalf of his son (Baab, *IDB* 3:283; cf. Judg. 14:2), but brothers were also involved in arranging for marriages in Gen. 24:29–60, 34:6–17 and Judg. 21:22. There is no mention of Shulammith's father in the Song, although her mother and her brothers are mentioned. It is probable that her father had died, so her brothers had the responsibility of arranging for her marriage. Although Shulammith complains in 1:5 about their harsh treatment of her, the brothers do seem to have a sincere, positive concern for her welfare and future prospects. The term 'sister' here is used literally, not as the term of endearment Solomon used in 4:9ff.

At this point in time, Shulammith has not yet reached the age of puberty, marked by the growth of breasts and pubic hair (cf. Ezek. 16:7). In anticipation of that time, which would also be the expected time for her to be spoken for (to receive a proposal of marriage; cf. 1 Sam. 25:39), the brothers discuss together what they need to do to maximize her prospects for a favourable marital match.

9. Shulammith's brothers consider how they will respond to her own disposition about her chastity as she approaches the age of marriage. They want to protect and encourage her virginity in anticipation of her marriage, for they know that sexual impurity on her part would make her less desirable as a potential wife. This could have serious repercussions both for her and for her whole family (M. Burrows 1938: 15). The brothers develop a twofold strategy. They resolve to affirm her commitment to sexual purity, but also to take firm action if they detect in her flirtatious conduct that she is vulnerable to sexual temptation that threatens her virginity. In this, they are not being harsh, but are demonstrating appropriate caution and concern for her welfare. Evidently, 'the brothers take seriously their responsibility to guide and goad their sister toward marriage by doing all they can to protect her from sexual misconduct' (Estes 2005: 436).

Some scholars regard the two conditions as synonymous, with both images stressing the strength of her person (Keel 1994: 279; Garrett 2004: 260; Baumann, *TDOT* 3:233). Hicks (1987: 153–158), however, argues convincingly that the two lines should better be read as a contrast between an immovable wall (Shulammith's sexual inaccessibility) and a movable door (her sexual accessibility). The language of 5:2–5 implies the use of 'door' to speak of sexual activity, as does the open door of the woman of folly in Prov. 9:14. Also, a silver battlement is probably intended for decoration, and has overtones of a festive crowning, but a cedar plank would be used for its durable strength, and thus suggests a military siege (cf. the typical use of *ṣûr*; Thiel, *TDOT* 12:307). Their proposed enclosure of their sister, then, lies in the same semantic field as the descriptions of her as a locked garden and a sealed spring in 4:12–15.

10. Shulammith states that she was a wall (inaccessible and chaste) when she came to the time of her sexual maturity. It was her internal resolve, not just her brothers' external pressure, that caused her to maintain her sexual purity as she saved herself for Solomon alone. She says nothing about being a door, which suggests strongly that 'wall' and 'door' are used antithetically in v. 9. Building upon the image of the wall, Shulammith says that her breasts were like towers. She seems to use 'towers' in a dual sense, both as parts of the fortifications of the wall and also as the most prominent features of the wall.

In the eyes of Solomon, she was like one who finds, or perhaps sues for, 'peace'. The term *šālôm* refers to completeness and wholeness, so

Shulammith is saying that in Solomon she found genuine intimacy. Her brothers offered her protection, but only in Solomon's love did she find peace (cf. Murphy 1990: 193). In fact, the *šālôm* she finds in him is in contrast to the harsh treatment by her brothers (1:5–6), the threats by the little foxes (2:15), the terrors of the night (3:8) and her humiliation by the city watchmen (5:7).

All of the words in this verse are used previously in the Song, as these words recapitulate in brief the message of the song cycle. The whole progress of intimacy that begins in the first verses of the Song comes to fulfilment in this statement that in Solomon Shulammith found her *šālôm*.

Explanation

8–9. Even in the contemporary world, in which men and women take the primary roles in arranging for their own marriages, family and friends still have an important part to play in the development of intimacy. A prominent message from our contemporary culture is 'If it feels good, do it.' As a relationship begins to progress, sexual desires can easily blind a person to the flaws of another, so the perspectives of other people are essential. Because sexual temptations can be so powerful and prevalent, other wise and caring people need to intervene with encouragements toward virtue. They have insights that may well be broader and clearer than those of the person in love. In addition, they can recognize the future implications of present decisions. Caring relatives and friends can encourage in the right direction and deter disasters in the making.

10. The Song of Songs presents intimacy as it can and should be. In God's design, intimacy is not just the immediate satisfaction of sexual drives. It is rather coming to a sense of wholeness and trusting completeness in a marital relationship blessed by God, and thus experiencing what God intended when he said that the man and woman should become one flesh (Gen. 2:24). Shulammith demonstrates why it is crucial to wait for the right time and the right person instead of prematurely tasting the fruit of intimacy before it is ripe.

SONG OF SONGS 8:11–12

Translation

SHULAMMITH

> [11]Solomon owned a vineyard in Baal-hamon.
> He gave the vineyard to keepers;
> Each man must bring from his fruit a thousand [pieces of] silver.

¹²My vineyard is my own before me;
The thousand are for you, O Solomon,
And two hundred are for the ones who keep its fruit.

Notes on the text

8:11. As in Isa. 7:23, the silver pieces here probably refer to shekels, for the shekel was the common measure for weight and later for coinage in ancient Israel (Snaith 1993: 127).

12. Shulammith repeats the phrase *kārmî šellî* from 1:6, and in both cases emphasizes that her body is under her own control.

Form, structure and setting

These two verses are closely linked by the repeated words 'vineyard', 'Solomon', 'keepers', 'fruit' and 'thousand', all of which are found in both v. 11 and v. 12. The most prominent feature of the lyric is the shift from the literal vineyard of Solomon in v. 11 to the figurative vineyard of Shulammith's sexuality that she gives freely to Solomon in v. 12. There are two implicit cause-and-effect constructions: because Solomon let out his vineyard, he requires a payment of one thousand pieces of silver from each of his tenants (v. 11), but because Shulammith's body is hers alone, she freely gives her thousand to Solomon (v. 12). The language in 8:11–12 forms an inclusio with 1:6, suggesting that the Song has been written or edited as a unified composition.

Comment

11. It is difficult to determine the speaker in this verse. In v. 12, clearly Shulammith is speaking, so she may well be the speaker here. Less likely, it could be that the narrator speaks here, but then the words of Shulammith in the next verse would have to build upon what the narrator has started.

If this lyric at the end of the book is viewed as an inclusio with Shulammith's words in 1:5–6, then the implication is that this is the vineyard in which Shulammith laboured at the insistence of her brothers. She was a *nōṭērâ*, just as the tenants are *nōṭĕrîm* in the vineyard. This may give a hint as to how Shulammith came to Solomon's attention, the unspecified background that lies behind the opening lyric in 1:2–4.

The high payment required of the tenant vinedressers indicates that Solomon's vineyard is of the highest quality (Bloch and Bloch 1995: 219; cf. Isa. 7:23). This may well be reinforced by the place name of the unknown site Baal-hamon, which means lit. 'owner of great wealth'. Just as the figurative vineyard of Shulammith's person is abundantly fruitful (4:16; 8:12), so Solomon's vineyard has received the full measure of the blessing of Yahweh (cf. Deut. 28:12; 30:9).

Some scholars try to correlate the thousand pieces of silver with the thousand women in Solomon's harem in 1 Kgs 11:3 (Murphy 1990: 194; Keel 1994: 281–282), but this fails to account for the fact that each of the tenants is required to bring a thousand pieces of silver to Solomon, and also that in v. 12 the tenants are deemed worthy of two hundred pieces of silver for their labour.

12. In contrast to the third person language about Solomon in v. 11, Shulammith now speaks directly to him. As in 1:6, Shulammith shifts from speaking of a literal vineyard to describing her own body under the figure of a vineyard. By stating, 'My vineyard is my own before me', Shulammith insists that she is not the property of another, as was so often the conception in ANE culture, but rather her body is at her own disposal (cf. the parallels cited by Exum 2005a: 278 in Gen. 13:9; 20:15; 24:51; 34:10; 47:6; 1 Sam. 16:16) as she freely and willingly gives herself to Solomon in the spirit of mutuality that is developed throughout the Song (cf. Alden 1988: 277).

At the same time, she is mindful of the role her brothers played in keeping her chaste for Solomon (cf. 8:8–10). She commends them for what they have done in preserving her purity so that she could give her sexuality fully to him, and she wants them to be rewarded for the good they have done for her. There does not seem to be any discernible significance in the specific number two hundred, except that it is a generous level of compensation appropriate to the great service they have rendered. Looking back from the vantage point of maturity, Shulammith expresses her deep appreciation to those who were especially instrumental in protecting her for the kind of intimacy she has come to enjoy in her marriage.

Explanation

11–12. Intimacy is not reluctant or calculating, but freely and willingly gives itself without reserve. It gives heart, soul and body to the one it loves. Anything less is unworthy to be called true love. In the spiritual realm too humans are commanded to love the Lord with all their being (Deut. 6:5; Matt. 22:37; Mark 12:30; Luke 10:27).

The process of protecting others for intimacy may not be pleasant in the short run, but eventually will probably be appreciated and valued. Only a true friend will care enough to stay committed to keeping another on the right track. In time, however, what may be criticized at first as interference will be recognized and appreciated as an important investment in a future marriage.

SONG OF SONGS 8:13–14

Translation

SOLOMON

> ¹³One who sits in the gardens,
>   [Our] companions are listening attentively to your voice;
>   Let me hear you.

SHULAMMITH

> ¹⁴Come quickly, my beloved, and be like a gazelle
>   Or a stag of the deer upon the mountains of spices.

Notes on the text

8:13. The term *ḥăbērîm* is used in 1:7 to refer to Solomon's associates. Here it may be used more generally to speak of other people who observe and learn from the loving relationship between Solomon and Shulammith.
   14. The verb *bāraḥ* (come quickly) usually means to flee *away* from an enemy, but can also mean to flee *to* someone (cf. 1 Sam. 22:20). In this context, Shulammith calls upon Solomon to forsake everything else that might distract or delay him, so that he can give all of his attention to her (Garrett 2004: 265).

Form, structure and setting

The final two verses of the Song feature Solomon and Shulammith one last time. First, Solomon invites her to speak in v. 13, and then in v. 14 Shulammith responds by encouraging him to make love to her. By repeating and adapting language used earlier in the Song in 2:14 and 2:17, both speakers suggest that their love is continuing to grow in intimacy and delight. This brief scene is a fitting climax to the Song, as the final chord of their intimacy lingers and reverberates.

Comment

13. The longing that Shulammith displays in the first lyric in 1:2–4, and which is woven throughout the entire Song, continues right into the final verses (Hubbard 1991: 347). This verse echoes Solomon's invitation to Shulammith in 2:14, when he called her out of her place of seclusion to enjoy fully their love. After many years of marriage, Solomon is still eager to hear her voice, for he finds delight in conversing with the woman he loves. It is clear that their marriage has not settled into a boring routine, because he still eagerly desires and delights in her. As Snaith (1993: 129) observes well, 'the Song never reaches completion, just like love, which is never satisfied: true love is always a quest, a going on, a looking forward'.

In 2:8, Shulammith listened for the *qôl* (sound) of the arrival of Solomon, and now Solomon and their companions are listening for her *qôl* (voice). In Proverbs, the verb *qāšab* is often used for closely attending to the words of wisdom (Mosis, *TDOT* 13:187), and here Shulammith in effect performs the role of a teacher as she communicates to others about love. Just as their relationship has drawn from others (8:2, 8–9), so it contributes to the wider community as well. Other people are enriched and inspired as they observe and learn from this couple that has probed the depths of intimacy. The ripples of their love touch the society around them.

14. In the Song of Songs, Shulammith has both the first and the last word. She ends the Song as she began it, with an expression of her longing for Solomon (Lavoie 2000: 77), but clearly has come to a much deeper level of intimacy with him. In reply to Solomon's request to hear her voice in v. 13, Shulammith invites him to make love to her. For the final time in the song cycle, she addresses him as 'beloved', and then repeats to him her words in 2:17, using nearly identical language. By this means she indicates that she has the same ardent desire for him as she had when they first committed themselves to each other. Her delight in him has not dimmed with time, and she wants him to have the same eager spirit in making love to her as he displayed when they were young (cf. the image of Solomon as a gazelle or a stag in 2:9).

In the last line of the verse, Shulammith synthesizes the language of 2:17 and 4:10 by changing *beter* to *bĕśāmîm* to picture her breasts as mountains of spices. She is, then, asking specifically that Solomon fondle her breasts, for even in their older years, sexual intimacy is still very much an integral feature of their love. Now, however, there need be no limitation by the approach of daybreak, as in her expressed wish in 2:17. Within marriage, intimacy can continue undisturbed until it is fully satisfied.

The Song fades out with the intimation of their lovemaking. Once again, as in 4:16 – 5:1 and 7:9[10], their sexual intimacy, though clearly implied, takes place outside the sight of the reader. Cainion (2000: 256) observes well:

> It may seem a curious manner for the Song to end here in this way, but actually it is the most profound. It is due to this ending that we have revealed to us the understanding that the Shulamite woman will be pursuing her beloved as long as she lives. Her love is so great for him that time is of no consequence, there is no yesterday, there is no tomorrow, there is only the eternal now, and now her desire is towards him.

Explanation

13–14. Love both satisfies and increases desire, because as love grows it enlarges the capacity to enjoy the beloved. In marriage as God has designed it, the best is yet to come. There is much to be learned from those who have drunk deeply of intimacy. People cannot just fall instantly into love, for it takes decades to discover true intimacy. Those who are wise will take care to observe and listen to those who have advanced to maturity in the school of love.

For a loving couple, delight in intimacy does not have to diminish with time, but rather it can and should become richer and deeper over a lifetime. As Bergant (2001: 105) concludes, 'Human love knows no definitive consummation, no absolute fulfillment. Loving relationships are never complete; they are always ongoing, always reaching for more. Regardless of the quality or frequency of lovemaking, there is always a measure of yearning present.'

What the Song teaches of the love between a man and a woman in marriage, the rest of the Bible manifests about the love between God and his people. In the OT, in Jer. 31:3, Yahweh describes the everlasting love by which he has drawn Israel to himself. In the NT, Paul prays in Eph. 3:19 that Christians may be able to know the love of Christ that surpasses knowledge. In God's love, there is always more to learn and experience, for God is continually inviting humans into far deeper intimacy with him.

BIBLIOGRAPHY

COMMENTARIES ON THE SONG OF SONGS

Bergant, Dianne (1998), *Song of Songs: The Love Poetry of Scripture*, Spiritual Commentaries, Hyde Park, N. Y.: New City.

—— (2001), *The Song of Songs*, Berit Olam, Collegeville: Liturgical.

Bloch, Ariel, and Chana Bloch (1995), *The Song of Songs*, New York: Random House.

Brenner, Athalya (1989), *The Song of Songs*, OTG, Sheffield: JSOT Press.

Budde, D. Karl (1898), 'Das Hohelied', in D. Karl Budde, Alfred Bertholet and D. G. Wildeboer, *Die Fünf Megillot*, KHAT 17, Tübingen: Mohr (Siebeck), ix–48.

Carr, G. Lloyd (1984), *The Song of Solomon*, TOTC 17, Leicester: IVP; Downers Grove: IVP.

Davidson, Robert (1986), *Ecclesiastes and the Song of Solomon*, DSB, Philadelphia: Westminster.

Davis, Ellen F. (2000), *Proverbs, Ecclesiastes, and the Song of Songs*, Westminster Bible Companion, Louisville: Westminster John Knox.

Deere, Jack S. (1985), 'Song of Songs', in John F. Walvoord and Roy B. Zuck (eds.), *The Bible Knowledge Commentary*, Wheaton: Victor, 1:1009–1025.

Delitzsch, Franz (1976), *Commentary on the Song of Songs and Ecclesiastes*, ET Edinburgh: T. & T. Clark (German original 1875).

Exum, J. Cheryl (2005c), *Song of Songs*, OTL, Louisville: Westminster John Knox.

Falk, Marcia (1990), *The Song of Songs*, New York: HarperCollins.

Fuerst, Wesley J. (1975), *The Books of Ruth, Esther, Ecclesiastes, the Song of Songs, Lamentations*, CBC, Cambridge: Cambridge University Press.

Garrett, Duane A. (1993), *Proverbs, Ecclesiastes, Song of Songs*, NAC 14, Nashville: Broadman.

—— (2004), 'Song of Songs', in Duane A. Garrett and Paul R. House, *Song of Songs, Lamentations*, WBC 23B, Nashville: Thomas Nelson, 1–265.

Gerleman, Gillis (1965), *Ruth, Das Hohelied*, BKAT 18, Neukirchen-Vluyn: Neukirchener Verlag des Erziehungsvereins.

Gershom, Levi ben (Gersonides) (1998), *Commentary on the Song of Songs*, YJS 28, ET New Haven: Yale University Press (Hebrew original 1325).

Ginsburg, Christian D. (1970), *The Song of Songs and Coheleth*, ET New York: Ktav (German original 1857).

Gledhill, Tom (1994), *The Message of the Song of Songs*, BST, Leicester: IVP.

Gordis, Robert (1974), *The Song of Songs and Lamentations*, rev. ed., New York: Ktav.

Goulder, Michael D. (1986), *The Song of Fourteen Songs*, JSOTSup 36, Sheffield: JSOT.

Hess, Richard S. (2005), *Song of Songs*, BCOTWP, Grand Rapids: Baker Academic.

Hubbard, David A. (1991), *Ecclesiastes, Song of Solomon*, The Communicator's Commentary 15B, Dallas: Word.

Huwiler, Elizabeth (1999), 'Song of Songs', in Roland E. Murphy and Elizabeth Huwiler, *Proverbs, Ecclesiastes, Song of Songs*, NIBCOT 12, Peabody: Hendrickson, 219–290.

Jenson, Robert W. (2005), *Song of Songs*, Interpretation, Louisville: John Knox.

Keel, Othmar (1994), *Song of Songs*, CC, ET Minneapolis: Fortress (German original 1986).

Kinlaw, Dennis F. (1991), 'Song of Songs', in *EBC* 5:1199–1244.

Knight, George A. F. (1988), 'The Song of Songs', in George A. F. Knight and Friedemann W. Golka, *Revelation of God*, ITC, Grand Rapids: Eerdmans, 1–64.

Krinetzki, Leo (= Günter) (1964), *Das Hohe Lied*, KBANT, Düsseldorf: Patmos-Verlag.

——— (1981), *Kommentar zum Hohenlied*, BBET 16, Frankfurt am Main: Peter Lang.

Lamparter, Helmut (1962), *Das Buch der Sehnsucht*, BAT 16.2, Stuttgart: Calwer.

Lehrman, S. M. (1983), 'The Song of Songs', in A. Cohen (ed.), *The Five Megilloth*, Soncino Books of the Bible, London: Soncino, x–32.

Longman III, Tremper (2001), *Song of Songs*, NICOT, Grand Rapids: Eerdmans.

——— (2006), 'Song of Songs', in August H. Konkel and Tremper Longman III, *Job, Ecclesiastes, Song of Songs*, Cornerstone Biblical Commentary 6, Carol Stream, Ill.: Tyndale House, 339–393.

Lys, Daniel (1968), *Le Plus Beau Chant de la Création: Commentaire du Cantique des Cantiques*, LD 51, Paris: Cerf.

Mitchell, Christopher W. (2003), *The Song of Songs*, Concordia Commentary: A Theological Exposition of Sacred Scripture, St. Louis: Concordia.

Müller, Hans-Peter (1992), 'Das Hohelied', in Hans-Peter Müller, Otto Kaiser and James Alfred Loader, *Das Hohelied, Klagelieder, Das Buch Ester*, ATD 16.2, Göttingen: Vandenhoeck & Ruprecht, 1–90.

Murphy, Roland E. (1990), *The Song of Songs*, Hermeneia, Minneapolis: Fortress.

Norris, Richard A. (2003), *The Song of Songs Interpreted by Early Christian and Medieval Commentators*, The Church's Bible, Grand Rapids: Eerdmans.

Ogden, Graham S., and Lynell Zogbo (1998), *A Handbook on Song of Songs*, UBS Handbook Series, New York: United Bible Societies.

Origen (1957), *The Song of Songs Commentary and Homilies*, ACW 27, ET Westminster, Md.: Newman (from Latin translation by Rufinus).

Patterson, Paige (1986), *Song of Solomon*, Everyman's Bible Commentary, Chicago: Moody.

Pope, Marvin H. (1977), *The Song of Songs*, AB 7C, Garden City: Doubleday.

Provan, Iain W. (2001), *Ecclesiastes, Song of Songs*, NIVAC, Grand Rapids: Zondervan.

Reese, James M. (1983), *The Book of Wisdom, Song of Songs*, Old Testament Message 20, Wilmington: Michael Glazier.

Ringgren, Helmer (1958), *Das Hohe Lied*, ATD 16.2, Göttingen: Vandenhoeck & Ruprecht.

Rudolph, Wilhelm (1962), *Das Buch Ruth, Das Hohe Lied, Die Klagelieder*, KAT 17.1–3, Gütersloh: Gerd Mohn.

Schonfield, Hugh J. (1959), *The Song of Songs*, London: Elek.

Snaith, John G. (1993), *Song of Songs*, NCBC, Grand Rapids: Eerdmans.

Stadelmann, Luis (1992), *Love and Politics: A New Commentary on the Song of Songs*, New York: Paulist.

Stoop-van Paridon, P. W. T. (2005), *The Song of Songs: A Philological Analysis of the Hebrew Book Šîr haššîrîm*, Ancient Near Eastern Studies Supplement 17, Louvain: Peeters.

Waterman, Leroy (1948), *The Song of Songs Translated and Interpreted as a Dramatic Poem*, Ann Arbor: University of Michigan Press.

Weems, Renita J. (1997), 'The Song of Songs', in *NIB* 5:363–434.

Wright, J. Robert (ed.) (2005), *Proverbs, Ecclesiastes, Song of Solomon*, ACCSOT 9, Downers Grove: IVP.

Würthwein, Ernst (1969), 'Das Hohelied', in Ernst Würthwein, Kurt Galling and Otto Plöger, *Die Fünf Megilloth*, HAT 18, Tübingen: Mohr (Siebeck), 25–71.

OTHER WORKS

Albrektson, Bertil (1996), 'Singing or Pruning', *BT* 47:109–114.

Albright, William F. (1963), 'Archaic Survivals in the Text of Canticles', in D. Winton Thomas and W. D. McHardy (eds.), *Hebrew and Semitic Studies Presented to Godfrey Rolles Driver*, Oxford: Clarendon, 1–7.

Alden, Robert L. (1988), 'Song of Songs 8:12a: Who Said It?', *JETS* 31: 271–278.

Alexander, Philip S. (1994), 'Tradition and Originality in the Targum of the Song of Songs', in D. R. G. Beattie and M. J. McNamara (eds.), *The Aramaic Bible: Targums in their Historical Context*, JSOTSup 166, Sheffield: JSOT, 318–339.

—— (1996), 'The Song of Songs as Historical Allegory: Notes on the Development of an Exegetical Tradition', in Kevin J. Cathcart and Michael Maher (eds.), *Targumic and Cognate Studies: Essays in Honour of Martin McNamara*, JSOTSup 230, Sheffield: Sheffield Academic Press, 14–29.

—— (2002), *The Targum of Canticles*, ArBib 17A, Collegeville: Liturgical.

Alter, Robert (1985), *The Art of Biblical Poetry*, New York: Basic.

———— (1988), 'The Garden of Metaphor', in Harold Bloom (ed.), *The Song of Songs*, New York: Chelsea House, 121–139.

———— (1998), 'The Poetic and Wisdom Books', in John Barton (ed.), *The Cambridge Companion to Biblical Interpretation*, Cambridge: Cambridge University Press, 226–240.

Angénieux, Joseph (1965), 'Structure du Cantique des Cantiques: En chants encadrés par des refrains alternants', *ETL* 41:96–142.

———— (1966), 'Les trois portraits du Cantique des Cantiques', *ETL* 42:582–596.

———— (1968), 'Le Cantique des Cantiques en huit chants a refrains alternants', *ETL* 44:87–140.

Arbel, Daphna V. (2000), 'My Vineyard, My Very Own, Is for Myself', in Athalya Brenner and Carole R. Fontaine (eds.), *The Song of Songs*, FCBSS 6, Sheffield: Sheffield Academic Press, 90–101.

Archer, Gleason L. (1974), *A Survey of Old Testament Introduction*, rev. ed., Chicago: Moody.

Ashbel, D. (1936), 'On the Importance of Dew in Palestine', *JPOS* 16:316–321.

Audet, Jean-Paul (1956), 'Le Sens du Cantique des Cantiques', *RB* 62:197–221.

———— (1958), 'Love and Marriage in the Old Testament', *Scr* 10:65–83.

Ausloos, Hans, and Bénédicte Lemmelijn (2007), 'Eine neue Interpretation des Hoheliedes 8,5ab', *ZAW* 119:556–563.

Auwers, Jean-Marie (2006), 'Anciens et modernes face au Cantique des Cantiques: Un impossible dialogue?', in André Lemaire (ed.), *Congress Volume Leiden 2004*, VTSup 109, Leiden: Brill, 235–253.

Ayo, Nicholas (1997), *Sacred Marriage: The Wisdom of the Song of Songs*, New York: Continuum.

Baildam, John D. (1999), *Paradisal Love: Johann Gottfried Herder and the Song of Songs*, Sheffield: Sheffield Academic Press.

Baker, John P. (1984), 'Biblical Attitudes to Romantic Love', *TynB* 35:91–128.

Bakon, Shimon (1994), 'Song of Songs', *JBQ* 22:211–220.

Barbiero, Gianni (1995), 'Die Liebe der Töchter Jerusalems: Hld 3,10b MT im Kontext von 3,6–11', *BZ* 39:96–104.

———— (1997), 'Die "Wagen meines edlen Volkes" (Hld 6:12): eine strukturelle Analyse', *Bib* 78:174–189.

Barthelemy, D. (1985), 'Comment le Cantique des Cantiques est-il devenu canonique', in A. Caquot et al. (eds.), *Mélanges bibliques et orientaux en l'honneur de M. Mathias Delcor*, AOAT 215, Neukirchen-Vluyn: Neukirchener Verlag, 13–22.

Barton, John (2005), 'The Canonicity of the Song of Songs', in Anselm C. Hagedorn (ed.), *Perspectives on the Song of Songs*, BZAW 346, Berlin: de Gruyter, 1–7.

Bascom, Robert A. (1994), 'Hebrew Poetry and the Text of the Song of Songs', in Ernst R. Wendland (ed.), *Discourse Perspectives on Hebrew Poetry in the Scriptures*, UBS Monograph Series 7, New York: United Bible Societies, 95–110.

Bauer, Johannes B. (2006), 'Die drei hebräischen Lesarten in Hld 4,8', *BZ*
    50:260–264.
Beek, Gus W. van (1960), 'Frankincense and Myrrh', *BA* 23:70–95.
Bekkenkamp, Jonneke (2000), 'Into Another Scene of Choices: The Theological
    Value of the Song of Songs', in Athalya Brenner and Carole R. Fontaine
    (eds.), *The Song of Songs*, FCBSS 6, Sheffield: Sheffield Academic Press,
    55–89.
Bekkenkamp, Jonneke, and Fokkelien van Dijk (1993), 'The Canon of the Old
    Testament and Women's Cultural Traditions', in Athalya Brenner (ed.),
    A Feminist Companion to the Song of Songs, Sheffield: JSOT, 67–85.
Ben-Yoseph, Jacob (1985), 'The Climate in Eretz Israel During Biblical Times',
    HS 26:225–239.
Bergant, Dianne (1994), ' "My Beloved Is Mine and I Am His" (Song 2:16):
    The Song of Songs and Honor and Shame', *Semeia* 68:23–40.
Bernard of Clairvaux (1971–80), *On the Song of Songs I–IV*, Cistercian Fathers
    Series 4, 7, 31, 40, Spencer, Mass., and Kalamazoo, Mich.: Cistercian
    (Latin original 1135–53).
Bernat, David (2004), 'Biblical *Waṣfs* Beyond Song of Songs', *JSOT* 28:327–349.
Black, Fiona C. (1999), 'What Is My Beloved? On Erotic Reading and the Song
    of Songs', in Fiona C. Black, Roland Boer and Erin Runions (eds.), *The
    Labour of Reading: Desire, Alienation, and Biblical Interpretation*, SBLSS
    36, Atlanta: SBL, 35–52.
—— (2000a), 'Beauty or the Beast? The Grotesque body in the Song of Songs',
    BibInt 8:302–323.
—— (2000b), 'Unlikely Bedfellows: Allegorical and Feminist Readings of Song
    of Songs 7.1–8', in Athalya Brenner and Carole R. Fontaine (eds.), *The
    Song of Songs*, FCBSS 6, Sheffield: Sheffield Academic Press, 104–129.
—— (2001), 'Noctural Egression: Exploring Some Margins of the Song of
    Songs', in A. K. M. Adam (ed.), *Postmodern Interpretations of the Bible –
    A Reader*, St. Louis: Chalice, 93–104.
—— (2006), 'Writing Lies: Autobiography, Textuality, and the Song of Songs',
    in Fiona C. Black (ed.), *The Recycled Bible: Autobiography, Culture, and
    the Space Between*, SBL Semeia Series 51, Atlanta: SBL, 161–183.
Bloch, Chana (2006), 'Translating Eros', in Peter S. Hawkins and Lesleigh
    Cushing Stahlberg (eds.), *Scrolls of Love: Ruth and the Song of Songs*,
    New York: Fordham University Press, 151–161.
Bloom, Harold (ed.) (1988), *The Song of Songs*, Modern Critical Interpretations,
    New York: Chelsea House.
Blumenthal, David R. (1995), 'Where God Is Not: The Book of Esther and Song
    of Songs', *Judaism* 44:80–92.
—— (2005), 'The Images of Women in the Hebrew Bible', in Michael J.
    Broyde and Michael Ausubel (eds.), *Marriage, Sex, and Family in
    Judaism*, Lanham, Md.: Rowman & Littlefield, 15–60.
Boer, Roland (2000), 'The Second Coming: Repetition and Insatiable Desire in
    the Song of Songs', *BibInt* 8:276–301.

Borowski, Oded (1987), *Agriculture in Iron Age Israel*, Winona Lake: Eisenbrauns.

Bosshard-Nepustil, Erich (1996), 'Zur Struktur und Sachprofil des Hohenlieds', *BN* 81:45–71.

Boyarin, Daniel (1990), 'The Song of Songs: Lock or Key? Intertextuality, Allegory and Midrash', in Regina Schwartz (ed.), *The Book and the Text: The Bible and Literary Theory*, Oxford: Basil Blackwell, 214–230.

—— (2007), 'Philo, Origen, and the Rabbis on Divine Speech and Interpretation', in James E. Goehring and Janet A. Timbie (eds.), *The World of Early Egyptian Christianity: Language, Literature, and Social Context: Essays in Honor of David W. Johnson*, Washington: The Catholic University of America Press, 113–129.

Brenner, Athalya (1982), *Colour Terms in the Old Testament*, JSOTSup 21, Sheffield: JSOT.

—— (1983), 'Aromatics and Perfumes in the Song of Songs', *JSOT* 25:75–81.

—— (1985), *The Israelite Woman: Social Role and Literary Type in Biblical Narrative*, Sheffield: JSOT.

—— (1990), ' "Come Back, Come Back the Shulammite" (Song of Songs 7.1–10): A Parody of the *Waṣf* Genre', in Yehuda T. Radday and Athalya Brenner, *On Humour and the Comic in the Hebrew Bible*, JSOTSup 23, Sheffield: Almond, 251–275.

—— (1992), 'A Note on *bat-rabbîm* (Song of Songs VII 5)', *VT* 42:113–115.

—— (ed.) (1993), *A Feminist Companion to the Song of Songs*, Sheffield: JSOT.

—— (1997), *The Intercourse of Knowledge: On Gendering Desire and 'Sexuality' in the Hebrew Bible*, BIS 26, Leiden: Brill.

—— (1999), 'The Food of Love: Gendered Food and Food Imagery in the Song of Songs', *Semeia* 86:101–112.

—— (2000), ' "My" Song of Songs', in Athalya Brenner and Carole R. Fontaine (eds.), *The Song of Songs*, FCBSS 6, Sheffield: Sheffield Academic Press, 154–168.

—— (2003), 'Gazing Back at the Shulammite, Yet Again', *BibInt* 11:295–300.

Brettler, Marc (2006), 'Unresolved and Unresolvable: Problems in Interpreting the Song', in Peter S. Hawkins and Lesleigh Cushing Stahlberg (eds.), *Scrolls of Love: Ruth and the Song of Songs*, New York: Fordham University Press, 185–198.

Brin, Gershon (1992), 'The Superlative in the Hebrew Bible: Additional Cases', *VT* 42:115–118.

Brown, John Pairman (1969a), *The Lebanon and Phoenicia*. Vol. 1: *The Physical Setting and the Forest*, Beirut: American University of Beirut.

—— (1969b), 'The Mediterranean Vocabulary of the Vine', *VT* 19:146–170.

Broyde, Michael J. (1995), 'Defilement of the Hands, Canonization of the Bible, and the Special Status of Esther, Ecclesiastes, and Song of Songs', *Judaism* 44:65–79.

Bullock, C. Hassell (1988), *An Introduction to the Poetic Books of the Old Testament*, rev. ed., Chicago: Moody.

Burns, Camilla (1998), 'Human Love: The Silent Voice of God', *Bible Today* 36:159–163.

Burrows, Mark S. (1998), 'Foundations for an Erotic Christology: Bernard of Clairvaux on Jesus as "Tender Lover"', *ATR* 80:477–491.

—— (2006), 'The Body of the Text and the Text of the Body: Monastic Reading and Allegorical Sub/Versions of Desire', in Peter S. Hawkins and Lesleigh Cushing Stahlberg (eds.), *Scrolls of Love: Ruth and the Song of Songs*, New York: Fordham University Press, 244–254.

Burrows, Millar (1938), *The Basis of Israelite Marriage*, American Oriental Series 16, New Haven: American Oriental Society.

Buss, Martin J. (1996), 'Hosea as a Canonical Problem: With Attention to the Song of Songs', in Stephen Breck Reid (ed.), *Prophets and Paradigms: Essays in Honor of Gene M. Tucker*, JSOTSup 229, Sheffield: Sheffield Academic Press, 79–93.

Butting, Klara (2000), 'Go Your Way: Women Rewrite the Scriptures (Song of Songs 2.8–14)', in Athalya Brenner and Carole R. Fontaine (eds.), *The Song of Songs*, FCBSS 6, Sheffield: Sheffield Academic Press, 142–151.

Byassee, Jason (2006), ' "Roomy Hearts" in a "More Spacious World": Origen of Alexandria and Ellen Davis on the Song of Songs', *ATR* 88:537–555.

Cainion, Ivory J. (2000), 'An Analogy of the Song of Songs and Genesis Chapters Two and Three', *SJOT* 14:219–259.

Calloud, Jean (1992), 'Esquisse: Propositions pour une interprétation raisonnée du Cantique des Cantiques', *Sémiotique et Bible* 65:43–60.

Callow, John (1994), 'Units and Flow in the Song of Songs 1:2–2:6', in Robert D. Bergen (ed.), *Biblical Hebrew and Discourse Linguistics*, Winona Lake: Eisenbrauns, 462–488.

Cantwell, Laurence (1964), 'The Allegory of the Canticle of Canticles', *Scr* 16:76–93.

Carr, David M. (1998a), 'Falling in Love with God', *Bible Today* 36:153–158.

—— (1998b), 'Rethinking Sex and Spirituality: The Song of Songs and Its Readings', *Sound* 81:413–435.

—— (1998c), 'The Song of Songs as a Microcosm of the Canonization and Decanonization Process', in A. Van Der Kooij and K. Van Der Toorn, *Canonization and Decanonization*, SHR 82, Leiden: Brill, 173–189.

—— (2000a), 'Ancient Sexuality and Divine Eros: Rereading the Bible Through the Lens of the Song of Songs', *USQR* 54:1–18.

—— (2000b), 'Gender and the Shaping of Desire in the Song of Songs and Its Interpretation', *JBL* 119:233–248.

—— (2003), *Erotic Word: Sexuality, Spirituality, and the Bible*, Oxford: Oxford University Press.

—— (2006), 'For the Love of Christ: Generic and Unique Elements in Christian Theological Readings of the Song of Songs', in Christine Helmer (ed.), *The Multivalence of Biblical Texts and Theological Meanings*, SBLSymS 37, Atlanta: SBL, 11–35.

Carr, G. Lloyd (1979), 'Is the Song of Songs a "Sacred Marriage" Drama?', *JETS* 22:103–114.

—— (1981), 'The Old Testament Love Songs and Their Use in the New Testament', *JETS* 24:97–105.

—— (1982), 'The Love Poetry Genre in the Old Testament and the Ancient Near East: Another Look at Inspiration, *JETS* 25:489–498.

—— (1993), Song of Songs, in Leland Ryken and Tremper Longman (eds.), *A Complete Literary Guide to the Bible*, Grand Rapids: Zondervan, 281–295.

Černy, J. (1954),Consanguineous Marriages in Pharaonic Egypt, *JEA* 40:23–29.

Ceulemans, Reinhart, and Dries De Crom (2007), 'Greek Renderings of the Hebrew Lexeme in LXX Canticles and Isaiah', *VT* 57:511–523.

Chave, Peter (1998), 'Towards a Not Too Rosy Picture of the Song of Songs', *Feminist Theology* 18:41–53.

Childs, Brevard S. (1979), *Introduction to the Old Testament as Scripture*, Philadelphia: Fortress.

Chisholm, Robert B. (2000), ' "Drink Water from Your Own Cistern": A Literary Study of Proverbs 5:15–23', *BSac* 157:397–409.

Clark, Elizabeth A. (2005), 'Origen, the Jews, and the Song of Songs: Allegory and Polemic in Christian Antiquity', in Anselm C. Hagedorn (ed.), *Perspectives on the Song of Songs*, BZAW 346, Berlin: de Gruyter, 274–293.

Clines, David J. A. (2005), *Interested Parties: The Ideology of Writers and Readers of the Hebrew Bible*, JSOTSup 205, Gender, Culture, Theory 1, Sheffield: Sheffield Academic Press.

Cogan, Mordechai (1984), '. . . From the Peak of Amanah', *IEJ* 34:255–259.

Collon, Dominique (1987), *First Impressions: Cylinder Seals in the Ancient Near East*, Chicago: University of Chicago Press.

Cook, Albert (1968), *The Root of the Thing: A Study of Job and the Song of Songs*, Bloomington: Indiana University Press.

Cooper, Jerrold S. (1971), 'New Cuneiform Parallels to the Song of Songs', *JBL* 90:157–162.

Corney, Richard W. (1998), 'What Does "Literal Meaning" Mean? Some Commentaries on the Song of Songs', *ATR* 80:494–516.

Cotterell, Peter (1996), 'The Greatest Song: Some Linguistic Considerations', *BT* 47:101–108.

Craigie, Peter C. (1979), 'Biblical and Tamil Poetry: Some Further Reflections', *Sciences Religieuses/Studies in Religion* 8:169–175.

Crenshaw, James L. (1986), *Story and Faith*, New York: Macmillan; London: Collier Macmillan.

Crim, Keith R. (1971), ' "Your Neck Is Like the Tower of David" (The Meaning of a Simile in Song of Solomon 4:4)', *BT* 22:70–74.

—— (ed.) (1976), *The Interpreter's Dictionary of the Bible, Supplementary Volume*, Nashville: Abingdon.

Dahood, Mitchell (1976), 'Canticle 7,9 and UT 52,61: A Question of Method', *Bib* 57:109–110.

——— (1982), 'Philological Observations on Five Biblical Texts', *Bib* 63:390–394.

Davidson, Richard M. (2003), 'The Literary Structure of the Song of Songs *Redivivus*', *JATS* 14:44–65.

——— (2005), 'Is God Present in the Song of Songs?', *JATS* 16:143–154.

——— (2007), *Flame of Yahweh: Sexuality in the Old Testament*, Peabody: Hendrickson.

Davis, Ellen F. (1998), 'Romance of the Land in the Song of Songs', *ATR* 80:533–546.

——— (2006), 'Reading the Song Iconographically', in Peter S. Hawkins and Lesleigh Cushing Stahlberg (eds.), *Scrolls of Love: Ruth and the Song of Songs*, New York: Fordham University Press, 172–184.

Deckers, M. (1993), 'The Structure of the Song of Songs and the Centrality of *nepeš* (6.12)', in Athalya Brenner (ed.), *A Feminist Companion to the Song of Songs*, Sheffield: JSOT, 172–196.

Dell, Katharine J. (2005), 'Does the Song of Songs Have Any Connection to Wisdom?', in Anselm C. Hagedorn (ed.), *Perspectives on the Song of Songs*, BZAW 346, Berlin: de Gruyter, 8–26.

Dijk-Hemmes, Fokkelien van (1989), 'The Imagination of Power and the Power of Imagination: An Intertextual Analysis of Two Biblical Love Songs: The Song of Songs and Hosea', *JSOT* 44:75–88.

——— (1993), 'Traces of Women's Texts in the Hebrew Bible', in Athalya Brenner and Fokkelien van Dijk-Hemmes, *On Gendering Texts: Female and Male Voices in the Hebrew Bible*, BIS 1, Leiden: Brill, 17–109.

Dillard, Raymond B., and Tremper Longman III (1994), *An Introduction to the Old Testament*, Grand Rapids: Zondervan.

Dirksen, P. B. (1989), 'Song of Songs III 6–7', *VT* 39:219–225.

Dobbs-Allsopp, F. W. (1995), 'Ingressive *qwm* in Biblical Hebrew', *ZAH* 8:31–54.

——— (2005a), 'The Delight of Beauty and Song of Songs 4:1–7', *Int* 59:260–277.

——— (2005b), 'Late Linguistic Features in the Song of Songs', in Anselm C. Hagedorn (ed.), *Perspectives on the Song of Songs*, BZAW 346, Berlin: de Gruyter, 27–77.

Dorsey, David A. (1990), 'Literary Structuring in the Song of Songs', *JSOT* 46:81–96.

——— (1991), 'Can These Bones Live? Investigating Literary Structure in the Bible', *EJ* 9:11–25.

——— (1999), *The Literary Structure of the Old Testament: A Commentary on Genesis–Malachi*, Grand Rapids: Baker.

Doumet, Joseph (1980), *Étude sur la couleur pourpre ancienne et tentative de reproduction du procédé de teinture de la ville de Tyr décrit par Pline l'Ancien*, Beirut: Imprimerie catholique.

Dove, Mary (1996), 'Sex, Allegory and Censorship: A Reconsideration of Medieval Commentaries on the Song of Songs', *Literature and Theology* 10:317–328.

——— (2000), 'Literal Senses in the Song of Songs', in Philip D. W. Krey and Lesley Smith (eds.), *Nicholas of Lyra: The Senses of Scripture*, Studies in the History of Christian Thought 90, Leiden: Brill, 129–146.

——— (2001), 'Merely a Love Poem?: Common Sense, Suspicion, and the Song of Songs', in Frances Devlin-Glass and Lyn McCredden (eds.), *Feminist Poetics of the Sacred*, AARCCS, Oxford: Oxford University Press, 151–164.

Driver, G. R. (1950), 'Hebrew Notes on Song of Songs and Lamentations', in Walter Baumgartner et al. (eds.), *Festschrift Alfred Bertholet*, Tübingen: Mohr, 134–146.

——— (1974), 'Lice in the Old Testament', *PEQ* 106:159–160.

Dünzl, Franz (1993), *Braut und Bräutigam: Die Auslegung des Canticum durch Gregor von Nyssa*, BGBE 32, Tübingen: Mohr (Siebeck).

Dyrness, William A. (1985), 'Aesthetics in the Old Testament: Beauty in Context', *JETS* 28:421–432.

Edmée, Sister (1998), 'The Song of Songs and the Cutting of Roots', *ATR* 80:547–561.

Eichner, Jens, and Andreas Scherer (2001), ' "Die Teiche von Hesbon": Eine exegetisch-archäologische Glosse zu Cant 7,5ba, *BN* 109:10–14.

Eissfeldt, Otto (1965), *The Old Testament: An Introduction*, ET New York: Harper & Row (German original 1964).

Elliott, M. Timothea (1989), *The Literary Unity of the Canticle*, Europäische Hochschulschriften, Series 23, Theology 371, New York: Peter Lang.

Elliott, Mark W. (1994), 'Ethics and Aesthetics in the Song of Songs', *TynB* 45:137–152.

——— (2000), *The Song of Songs and Christology in the Early Church 381–451*, STAC 7, Tübingen: Mohr (Siebeck).

Emerton, J. A. (1993), 'Lice or a Veil in the Song of Songs 1.7?', in A. Graeme Auld (ed.), *Understanding Poets and Prophets*, JSOTSup 152, Sheffield: JSOT, 127–140.

Emmerson, Grace I. (1994), 'The Song of Songs: Mystification, Ambiguity and Humour', in Stanley E. Porter, Paul Joyce and David E. Orton (eds.), *Crossing the Boundaries: Essays in Biblical Interpretation in Honour of Michael Goulder*, BIS 8, Leiden: Brill, 97–111.

Ena, Jean Emmanuel de (2004), *Sens et interpretations du Cantique des Cantiques*, Paris: Cerf.

Epstein, Louis M. (1942), *Marriage Laws in the Bible and the Talmud*, Harvard Semitic Series 12, Cambridge, Mass.: Harvard University Press.

Erbt, Wilhelm (1906), *Die Hebräer: Kanaan im zeitalter der hebräischen wanderung und hebräischer staatengründungen*, Leipzig: Hinrichs.

Eschelbach, Michael A. (2004), 'Song of Songs: Increasing Appreciation of and Restraint in Matters of Love', *AUSS* 42:305–324.

Estes, Daniel J. (1995), 'The Hermeneutics of Biblical Lyric Poetry', *BSac* 152: 413–430.

—— (2005), *Handbook on the Wisdom Books and Psalms*, Grand Rapids: Baker Academic.

Exum, J. Cheryl (1973), 'A Literary and Structural Analysis of the Song of Songs', *ZAW* 85:47–79.

—— (1981). 'Asseverative *'al* in Canticles 1,6?', *Bib* 62:416–419.

—— (1998), 'Developing Strategies of Feminist Criticism/Developing Strategies for Commentating the Song of Songs', in David J. A. Clines and Stephen D. Moore (eds.), *Auguries: The Jubilee Volume of the Sheffield Department of Biblical Studies*, Sheffield: Sheffield Academic Press, 206–249.

—— (1999a), 'How Does the Song of Songs Mean? On Reading the Poetry of Desire', *SEÅ* 64:47–63.

—— (1999b), In the Eye of the Beholder: Wishing, Dreaming, and *Double Entrendre* in the Song of Songs, in Fiona C. Black, Roland Boer and Eric Runions (eds.), *The Labour of Reading: Desire, Alienation, and Biblical Interpretation*, SBLSS 36, Atlanta: SBL, 71–86.

—— (2000), 'Ten Things Every Feminist Should Know about the Song of Songs', in Athalya Brenner and Carole R. Fontaine (eds.), *The Song of Songs*, FCBSS 6, Sheffield: Sheffield Academic Press, 24–35.

—— (2003a), 'Seeing Solomon's Palanquin (Song of Songs 3:6–11)', *BibInt* 11: 301–316.

—— (2003b), ' "The Voice of My Lover": Double Voice and Poetic Illusion in Song of Songs 2.8–3.5', in J. Cheryl Exum and H. G. M. Williamson (eds.), *Reading from Right to Left: Essays on the Hebrew Bible in Honour of David J. A. Clines*, JSOTSup 373, Sheffield: Sheffield Academic Press, 141–152.

—— (2005a), 'The Little Sister and Solomon's Vineyard: Song of Songs 8:8–12 as a Lovers' Dialogue', in Ronald L. Troxel, Kelvin G. Friebel and Dennis R. Magary (eds.), *Seeking Out the Wisdom of the Ancients: Essays Offered to Honor Michael V. Fox on the Occasion of His Sixty-Fifth Birthday*, Winona Lake: Eisenbrauns, 269–282.

—— (2005b), 'The Poetic Genius of the Song of Songs', in Anselm C. Hagedorn (ed.), *Perspectives on the Song of Songs*, BZAW 346, Berlin: de Gruyter, 78–95.

Falk, Marcia (1982), *Love Lyrics from the Bible: A Translation and Literary Study of the Song of Songs*, Bible and Literature Series 4, Sheffield: Almond.

Feuillet, André (1953), *Le Cantique des Cantiques: Étude de théologie biblique et réflexions sur une méthode d'exégèse*, LD 10, Paris: Cerf.

—— (1961), 'La formule d'appartenance mutuelle (II, 16) et les interprétations divergentes de Cantique des Cantiques', *RB* 68:5–38.

—— (1971), ' "S'asseoir a l'ombre" de l'époux', *RB* 78:391–405.

—— (1987), 'Le drame d'amour du Cantique des Cantiques remis en son contexte prophétique', *Nova et vetera* 49:81–127.

———— (1991), 'La double insertion du Cantique des Cantiques dans la vie de la communauté chrétienne et dans la tradition religieuse de l'Ancien Testament', *Divinitas* 35:5–18.

Fields, Weston W. (1980), 'Early and Medieval Jewish Interpretation of the Song of Songs', *GTJ* 2:221–231.

Fisch, Harold (1988), *Poetry with a Purpose: Biblical Poetics and Interpretation*, Bloomington: Indiana University Press.

Flint, Peter W. (2005), 'The Book of Canticles (Song of Songs) in the Dead Sea Scrolls', in Anselm C. Hagedorn (ed.), *Perspectives on the Song of Songs*, BZAW 346, Berlin: de Gruyter, 96–104.

Foh, Susan T. (1975), 'What Is the Woman's Desire?', *WTJ* 37:376–383.

Fokkelman, J. P. (2001), *Reading Biblical Poetry: An Introductory Guide*, ET Louisville: Westminster John Knox (Danish original).

Fontaine, Carole R. (2004), 'Watching Out for the Watchman (Song 5.7): How I Hold Myself Accountable', in Charles H. Cosgrove (ed.), *The Meanings We Choose: Hermeneutical Ethics, Indeterminacy and the Conflict of Interpretations*, JSOTSup 411, The Bible in the Twenty-First Century Series 5, London: T. & T. Clark, 102–121.

Foster, John L. (1974), *Love Songs of the New Kingdom*, New York: Charles Scribner's Sons.

———— (1995), *Hymns, Prayers, and Songs: An Anthology of Ancient Egyptian Lyric Poetry*, Writings from the Ancient World 8, Atlanta: Scholars Press.

Fox, Michael V. (1981), ' "Love" in the Love Songs', *JEA* 67:181–182.

———— (1983), 'Scholia to Canticles (*i,4b, ii,4, i 4ba, v 8, vi 12*)', *VT* 33:199–206.

———— (1985), *The Song of Songs and the Ancient Egyptian Love Songs*, Madison: University of Wisconsin Press.

Frolov, Serge (1998), 'No Return for Shulammite: Reflections on Cant 7,1', *ZAW* 110:256–258.

Frymer-Kensky, Tikva (1989), 'Law and Philosophy: The Case of Sex in the Bible', *Semeia* 45:89–102.

Gaier, Ulrich (2005), 'Lieder der Liebe: Herders Hohelied-Interpretation', in Anselm C. Hagedorn (ed.), *Perspectives on the Song of Songs*, BZAW 346, Berlin: de Gruyter, 317–337.

Gaster, Theodor H. (1952), 'What "The Song of Songs" Means', *Commentary* 13:316–322.

———— (1960–61), 'Canticles i. 4', *ExpTim* 72:195.

Geraty, Lawrence T., and Lloyd A. Willis (1986), 'The History of Archaeological Research in Transjordan', in Lawrence T. Geraty and Larry G. Herr (eds.), *The Archaeology of Jordan and Other Studies*, Berrien Springs, Mich.: Andrews University Press, 3–72.

Gilead, M., and N. Rosenan (1954), 'Ten Years of Dew Observation in Israel', *IEJ* 4:120–123.

Glazer, Henry (1990–91), 'The Song of Songs: Judaism's Document of Revelation', *Conservative Judaism* 43:55–60.

Glickman, S. Craig (1976), *A Song for Lovers*, Downers Grove: IVP.

—— (2004), *Solomon's Song of Love*, West Monroe, La.: Howard.

Godet, Frederick (1886), *Studies in the Old Testament*, 4th ed., London: Hodder & Stoughton.

—— (1972), 'The Interpretation of the Song of Songs', in Walter C. Kaiser (ed.), *Classical Evangelical Essays in Old Testament Interpretation*, Grand Rapids: Baker, 151–175.

Goitein, S. D. (1965), '*Ayumma Kannidgalot* (Song of Songs VI. 10): "Splendid Like the Brilliant Stars"', *JSS* 10:220–221.

—— (1988), 'Women as Creators of Biblical Genres', *Proof* 8:1–33.

—— (1993), 'The Song of Songs: A Female Composition', in Athalya Brenner (ed.), *A Feminist Companion to the Song of Songs*, FCB 1, Sheffield: JSOT, 58–66.

Gollwitzer, Helmut (1979), *Song of Love: A Biblical Understanding of Sex*, ET Philadelphia: Fortress (German original).

Goodspeed, Edgar J. (1934), 'The Shulammite', *AJSLL* 50:102–104.

Gordis, Robert (1969), 'The Root *dgl* in the Song of Songs', *JBL* 88:203–204.

Görg, Manfred (1982), 'Die "Sänfte Salomos" nach HL 3,9f.', *BN* 18:15–25.

—— (1983a), 'Lexikalisches zu HL 5,11', *BN* 21:26–27.

—— (1983b), 'Travestie im Hohen Lied: Eine kritische Betrachtung am Beispiel von HL 1,5f', *BN* 21:101–115.

—— (1987), 'Eine Selbenbezeichnung in HL 1,3', *BN* 38–39:36–38.

Götz, Ignacio L. (2004), 'Sex and Mysticism', *Crosscurrents* 54:7–22.

Gradwohl, Roland (1963), *Die Farben im Alten Testament*, BZAW 83, Berlin: Alfred Töpelmann.

Green, Arthur (2006), 'Intradivine Romance: The Song of Songs in the Zohar', in Peter S. Hawkins and Lesleigh Cushing Stahlberg (eds.), *Scrolls of Love: Ruth and the Song of Songs*, New York: Fordham University Press, 214–227.

Gregory of Narek (2007), *The Blessing of Blessings: Gregory of Narek's Commentary on the Song of Songs*, tr. Roberta R. Ervine, Cistercian Studies Series 215, Kalamozoo, Mich.: Cistercian.

Grossberg, Daniel (1981a), 'Canticles 3:10 in the Light of a Homeric Analogue and Biblical Poetics', *BTB* 11:74–76.

—— (1981b), 'Sexual Desire: Abstract and Concrete', *Hebrew Studies* 22:59–60.

—— (1989), *Centripetal and Centrifugal Structures in Biblical Poetry*, SBLMS 39, Atlanta: Scholars Press.

—— (1994), 'Two Kinds of Sexual Relationships in the Hebrew Bible', *HS* 35:7–25.

—— (2005), 'Nature, Humanity, and Love in Song of Songs', *Int* 59:229–242.

Gruber, Mayer I. (1981), 'Ten Dance-Derived Expressions in the Hebrew Bible', *Bib* 62:328–346.

Haag, Herbert (1985), 'Das heutige Verständnis des Hohenliedes in der katholischen Exegese', in A. Caquot et al. (eds.), *Mélanges bibliques et*

orientaux en l'honneur de M. Mathias Delcor, AOAT 215, Neukirchen-
Vluyn: Neukirchener Verlag, 209–219.

Hallo, William W. (1983), ' "As the Seal Upon Thine Arm": Glyptic
Metaphors in the Biblical World', in Leonard Gorelick and Elizabeth
Williams-Forte (eds.), *Ancient Seals and the Bible*, Malibu, Calif.:
Undena, 7–17.

———— (1985), ' "As the Seal upon Thy Heart": Glyptic Roles in the Biblical
World', *BRev* 1:20–27.

———— (1993), 'For Love Is Strong as Death', *JANES* 22:45–50.

Hamilton, James M. (2006), 'The Messianic Music of the Song of Songs:
A Non-Allegorical Interpretation', *WTJ* 68:331–345.

Harding, Kathryn (2008), ' "I Sought Him but I Did Not Find Him": The Elusive
Lover in the Song of Songs', *BibInt* 16:43–59.

Harman, A. M. (1978), 'Modern Discussion on the Song of Solomon', *RTR*
37:65–72.

Heinevetter, Hans-Josef (1988), *Komm nun, mein Liebster, Dein Garten ruft
Dich! Das Hohelied als programmatische Komposition*, AMT 69,
Frankfurt am Main: Athenäum.

Hess, Richard S. (2004), 'Equality With and Without Innocence: Genesis 1–3',
in Ronald W. Pierce and Rebecca Merrill Groothuis (eds.), *Discovering
Biblical Equality: Complementarity Without Hierarchy*, Downers Grove:
IVP, 79–95.

———— (2006), 'Single-Word Cola in the Song of Songs?', *JAAS* 9:119–128.

Hicks, R. Lansing (1987), 'The Door of Love', in John H. Marks and Robert M.
Good, *Love and Death in the Ancient Near East: Essays in Honor of
Marvin H. Pope*, Guilford, Conn.: Four Quarters, 117–119.

Hill, Andrew E., and John H. Walton (2000), *A Survey of the Old Testament*,
2nd ed., Grand Rapids: Zondervan.

Hirschberg, Harris H. (1961), 'Some Additional Arabic Etymologies in Old
Testament Lexicography', *VT* 11:373–385.

Holmyard, Harold R. (1998), 'Solomon's Perfect One', *BSac* 155:164–171.

Honeyman, A. M. (1949), 'Two Contributions to Canaanite Topography', *JTS*
50:50–52.

Hopkins, Steven P. (2007), 'Extravagant Beholding: Love, Ideal bodies, and
Particularity', *History of Religions* 47:1–50.

Horbury, William (2003), 'The Books of Solomon in Ancient Mysticism', in
David F. Ford and Graham Stanton (eds.), *Reading Texts, Seeking
Wisdom: Scripture and Theology*, London: SCM, 185–201.

Horst, Friedrich (1961), *Gottes Recht: Gesammelte Studien zum Recht im Alten
Testament*, TB 12, Munich: Chr. Kaiser Verlag.

Hostetter, Edwin C. (1996), 'Mistranslation in Cant 1:5', *AUSS* 34:35–36.

Hunt, Patrick N. (1992), 'Subtle Paronomasia in the Canticum Canticorum:
Hidden Treasures of the Superlative Poet', in Klaus-Dietrich Schunck and
Matthias Augustin (eds.), *Goldene Äpfel in silbernen Schalen: Collected
Communications to the XIIIth Congress of the International*

Organization for the Study of the Old Testament, Leuven 1989, BEATAJ 20, Frankfurt am Main: Peter Lang, 147–154.

—— (1996), 'Sensory Images in Song of Songs 1:12–2:16', in Matthias Augustin and Klaus-Dietrich Schunck (eds.), *Dort zeihen Schiffe dahin...: Collected Communications to the XIVth Congress of the International Organization for the Study of the Old Testament, Paris 1992*, BEATAJ 28, Frankfort am Main: Peter Lang, 69–76.

Hunter, Jannie H. (2000), 'The Song of Protest: Reassessing the Song of Songs', *JSOT* 90:109–124.

Hwang, Andrew (2003), 'The New Structure of the Song of Songs and Its Implications for Interpretation', *WTJ* 65:97–111.

Isserlin, B. S. J. (1958), 'Song of Songs IV,4: An Archaeological Note', *PEQ* 90:59–61.

Janzen, Waldemar (1965), ''ašrê in the Old Testament', *HTR* 58:215–226.

Jensen, Lloyd B. (1963), 'Royal Purple of Tyre', *JNES* 22:104–118.

Jenson, Robert W. (2005), 'Male and Female He Created Them', in Carl E. Braaten and Christopher R. Seitz (eds.), *I am the Lord Your God: Christian Reflections on the Ten Commandments*, Grand Rapids: Eerdmans, 175–188.

Kaiser, Walter C. (2000), 'True Marital Love in Proverbs 5:15–23 and the Interpretation of Song of Songs', in J. I. Packer and Sven K. Soderlund (eds.), *The Way of Wisdom*, Grand Rapids: Zondervan, 106–116.

Kates, Judith A. (2006), 'Entering the Holy of Holies: Rabbinic Midrash and the Language of Intimacy', in Peter S. Hawkins and Lesleigh Cushing Stahlberg (eds.), *Scrolls of Love: Ruth and the Song of Songs*, 201–213, New York: Fordham University Press.

Kearney, Richard (2006), 'The Shulammite's Song: Divine Eros, Ascending and Descending', in Virginia Burrus and Catherine Keller (eds.), *Toward a Theology of Eros*, New York: Fordham University Press, 306–340.

Keel, Othmar (1978), *The Symbolism of the Biblical World: Ancient Near Eastern Iconography and the Book of Psalms*, ET New York: Seabury (German original 1972).

—— (1984), *Deine Blicke sind Tauben*, Stuttgarter Bibelstudien 114.115, Stuttgart: Katholisches Bibelwerk.

Kessler, R. (1965), *Some Poetical and Structural Features of the Song of Songs*, Leeds University Oriental Society Monograph Series 8, Leeds: Leeds University Press.

Kiecker, James G. (2001), 'Comparative Hermeneutics: The *Glossa ordinaria*, Nicholas of Lyra, and Martin Luther on the Song of Songs', in Timothy Maschke et al. (eds.), *Ad Fonts Lutheri: Toward the Recovery of the Real Luther*, Marquette Studies in Theology 28, Milwaukee: Marquette University Press, 104–129.

King, J. Christopher. (2005), *Origen on the Song of Songs as the Spirit of Scripture: The Bridegroom's Perfect Marriage-Song*, Oxford Theological Monographs, Oxford: Oxford University Press.

Kist, Joost (2003), *Ancient Near Eastern Seals from the Kist Collection*, Culture and History of the Ancient Near East 18, Leiden: Brill.

Kramer, Samuel Noah (1969), *The Sacred Marriage Rite: Aspects of Faith, Myth, and Ritual in Ancient Sumer*, Bloomington: Indiana University Press.

Krauss, Samuel (1941–2), 'The Archaeological Background of Some Passages in the Song of Songs', *JQR* 32:115–137.

LaCocque, André (1992), *Subversives: Un Pentateuque de femmes*, Paris: Cerf.

—— (1998), *Romance, She Wrote: A Hermenuetical Essay on Song of Songs*, Harrisburg: Trinity Press International.

—— (2006), 'I am Black and Beautiful', in Peter S. Hawkins and Lesleigh Cushing Stahlberg (eds.), *Scrolls of Love: Ruth and the Song of Songs*, New York: Fordham University Press, 162–171.

Laird, Martin (2002), 'Under Solomon's Tutelage: The Education of Desire in the *Homilies on the Song of Songs*', *Modern Theology* 18:507–525.

—— (2007), 'The Fountain of His Lips: Desire and Divine Union in Gregory of Nyssa's *Homilies on the Song of Songs*', *Spiritus* 7:40–57.

Landsberger, Franz (1954), 'Poetic Units Within the Song of Songs', *JBL* 73:203–216.

Landy, Francis (1979), 'The Song of Songs and the Garden of Eden', *JBL* 98:513–528.

—— (1983), *Paradoxes of Paradise: Identity and Difference in the Song of Songs*, Bible and Literature Series, Sheffield: Almond.

—— (1987), 'The Song of Songs', in Robert Alter and Frank Kermode (eds.), *The Literary Guide to the Bible*, Cambridge, Mass.: Harvard University Press, 305–319.

—— (2001), *Beauty and the Enigma and Other Essays on the Hebrew Bible*, JSOTSup 312, Sheffield: Sheffield Academic Press.

LaSor, William Sanford, et al. (1996), *Old Testament Survey: The Message, Form, and Background of the Old Testament*, 2nd ed., Grand Rapids: Eerdmans.

LaVere, Suzanne (2007), 'From Contemplation to Action: The Role of the Active Life in the *Glossa ordinaria* on the Song of Songs', *Spec* 82:54–69.

Lavoie, Jean-Jacques (1995), 'Festin érotique et tendresse cannibalique dans le Cantique des Cantiques', *Studies in Religion/Sciences Religieuses* 24:131–146.

—— (2000), 'Woman in the Song of Songs', in Gerald Caron (ed.), *Woman Also Journeyed With Him: Feminist Perspectives on the Bible*, Collegeville: Liturgical, 75–81.

Leick, Gwendolyn (1994), *Sex and Eroticism in Mesopotamian Literature*, London: Routledge.

Lemaire, André (1975), *ZĀMÎR* dans la tablette de Gezer et le Cantique des Cantiques', *VT* 25:15–26.

Lewis, Clive Staples (1960), *The Four Loves*, New York: Harcourt & Brace.

Lichtheim, Miriam (1976), *Ancient Egyptian Literature: A Book of Readings.* Vol. 2: *The New Kingdom*, Berkeley: University of California Press.

Linafelt, Tod (2002), 'Biblical Love Poetry (. . . and God)', *JAAR* 70:323–345.
────── (2005), 'The Arithmetic of Eros', *Int* 59:244–258.
────── (2006), 'Lyrical Theology: The Song of Songs and the Advantage of
    Poetry', in Virginia Burrus and Catherine Keller (eds.), *Toward a
    Theology of Eros*, New York: Fordham University Press, 291–305.
Linardou, Kallirroe (2004), 'The Couch of Solomon, a Monk, a Byzantine Lady,
    and the Song of Songs', in R. N. Swanson (ed.), *The Church and Mary*,
    SCH 39, Woodbridge: Boydell, 73–85.
Liphshitz, Nili, and Gideon Biger (1991), 'Cedar of Lebanon (*Cedrus libani*) in
    Israel During Antiquity', *IEJ* 41:167–175.
Loader, James Alfred (1998–2001), 'Exegetical Erotica to Canticles 7:2–6', *JSem*
    10:98–111.
Long, Gary Alan (1996), 'A Lover, Cities, and Heavenly Bodies: Co-Text and the
    Translation of Two Similes in Canticles (6:4c; 6:10d)', *JBL* 115:703–709.
Longman III, Tremper (2008), 'Song of Songs', in Kevin J. Vanhoozer (ed.),
    Theological Interpretation of the Old Testament, Grand Rapids: Baker
    Academic, 186–193.
Loprieno, Antonio (2005), 'Searching for a Common Background: Egyptian Love
    Poetry and the Biblical Song of Songs', in Anselm C. Hagedorn (ed.),
    Perspectives on the Song of Songs, BZAW 346, Berlin: de Gruyter,
    105–135.
Loretz, Oswald (1991), 'Cant 4,8 auf dem Hintergrund ugaritischer und
    assyrischer Beschreibungen des Libanons und Antilibanons', in Dwight R.
    Daniels, Uwe Glessmer and Martin Rösel (eds.), *Ernten, was man sat:
    Festschrift für Klaus Koch zu seinem 65. Geburtstag*, Neukirchen-Vluyn:
    Neukirchener Verlag, 131–141.
────── (2004a), 'Ägyptisierende, mesopotamisierende und ugaritisierende
    Interpretationen der Götter Môt und Eros in Canticum 8,6–7: "Die Liebe
    ist so stark wie Môt" ', *UF* 36:235–282.
────── (2004b), 'Enjambement, versus und "salomonische" Königstravestie im
    Abschnitt Canticum canticorum 3,6–11', in Markus Witte (ed.), *Gott und
    Mensch im Dialog: Festschrift für Otto Kaiser zum 80. Geburtstag*,
    BZAW 345.2, Berlin: de Gruyter, 805–816.
────── (2004c), 'Das pharaonische Wagengespann mit Stute des Canticums
    (1,9–11) in hippologisch-militärgeschichtlicher Sicht', *UF* 36:205–234.
────── (2004d), 'Die ugaritisch-hebräische Gefässbezeichnung *trq/twrq* in
    Canticum 1,3: Liebesdichtung in der westsemitschen Wein- und
    Olivenkultur', *UF* 36:283–289.
Louth, Andrew (1994), 'Eros and Mysticism: Early Christian Interpretation of
    the Song of Songs', in Joel Ryce-Menuhin (ed.), *Jung and the
    Monotheisms*, London: Routledge, 241–254.
Lyke, Larry L. (1999), 'The Song of Songs, Proverbs, and the Theology of Love',
    in Christopher Seitz and Kathryn Greene-McCreight, *Theological
    Exegesis: Essays in Honor of Brevard S. Childs*, Grand Rapids:
    Eerdmans, 208–223.

——— (2007), *I Will Espouse You Forever: The Song of Songs and the Theology of Love in the Hebrew Bible*, Nashville: Abingdon.

Mace, David R. (1953), *Hebrew Marriage: A Sociological Study*, London: Epworth.

McGinn, Bernard (1992), 'With "the Kisses of the Mouth": Recent Works on the Song of Songs', *JR* 72:269–275.

Malena, Sarah (2007), 'Spice Roots in the Song of Songs', in Sarah Malena and David Miano (eds.), *Milk and Honey: Essays on Ancient Israel and the Bible in Appreciation of the Judaic Studies Program at the University of California, San Diego*, Winona Lake: Eisenbrauns, 165–184.

Malul, Meir (1997), 'Janus Parallelism in Biblical Hebrew: Two More Cases (Canticles 4,9.12)', *BZ* 41:246–249.

Mariaselvam, Abraham (1988), *The Song of Songs and Ancient Tamil Love Poems: Poetry and Symbolism*, AnBib 118, Rome: Pontificio Istituto Biblico.

Marsman, Hennie J. (2003), *Women in Ugarit and Israel: Their Social and Religious Position in the Context of the Ancient Near East*, OtSt 49, Leiden: Brill.

Matter, E. Ann (1990), *The Voice of My Beloved: The Song of Songs in Western Medieval Christianity*, Philadelphia: University of Pennsylvania.

——— (2006), 'The Love Song of the Millennium: Medieval Christian Apocalyptic and the Song of Songs', in Peter S. Hawkins and Lesleigh Cushing Stahlberg (eds.), *Scrolls of Love: Ruth and the Song of Songs*, New York: Fordham University Press, 228–243.

May, Herbert G. (1955), 'Some Cosmic Connotations of *MAYIM RABBÎM*, "Many Waters"', *JBL* 74:9–21.

Mazor, Yair (1990), 'The Song of Songs or the Story of Stories? *The Song of Songs*: Between Genre and Unity', *SJOT* 1:1–29.

Meek, Theophile James (1922), 'Canticles and the Tammuz Cult', *AJSLL* 39:1–14.

——— (1924), 'Babylonian Parallels to the Song of Songs', *JBL* 43:245–252.

Menn, Esther M. (2000), '*Targum of the Song of Songs* and the Dynamics of Historical Allegory', in Craig A. Evans (ed.), *The Interpretation of Scripture in Early Judaism and Christianity*, JSPSup 33, Sheffield: Sheffield Academic Press, 423–445.

——— (2003), 'Sexuality in the Old Testament: Strong as Death, Unquenchable as Fire', *CurTM* 30:37–45.

Merkin, Daphne (1994), 'The Woman in the Balcony: On Rereading the Song of Songs', in Christina Büchman and Celina Spiegel (eds.), *Out of the Garden: Woman Writers on the Bible*, New York: Fawcett Columbine, 238–251.

Meyers, Carol (1987), 'Gender Imagery in the Song of Songs', *HAR* 10:209–223.

——— (1988), *Discovering Eve: Ancient Israelite Women in Context*, New York: Oxford University Press.

———— (1991), '"To Her Mother's House": Considering a Counterpart to the Israelite *Bêt 'āb*', in David Jobling et al. (eds.), *The Bible and the Politics of Exegesis: Essays in Honor of Norman K. Gottwald on His Sixty-fifth Birthday*, Cleveland: Pilgrim, 39–51.

Moor, Johannes C. de (1993), 'The Love of God in the Targum to the Prophets', *JSJ* 24:257–265.

Moore, Stephen D. (2000), 'The Song of Songs in the History of Spirituality', *CH* 69:328–349.

Moye, Jerry (1990), '*Song of Songs* – Back to Allegory? Some Hermeneutical Considerations', *AJT* 4:120–125.

Mulder, Martin J. (1992), 'Does Canticles 6,12 Make Sense?', in F. Garcia Martinez, A. Hilhorst and C. J. Labuschague (eds.), *The Scriptures and the Scrolls: Studies in Honour of A. S. van der Woude on the Occasion of His 65th Birthday*, 104–113, VTSup 49, Leiden: Brill.

Müller, Hans-Peter (1984), *Vergleich und Metapher im Hohenlied*, OBO 56, Göttingen: Vandenhoeck & Ruprecht.

———— (1988a), 'Begriffe menschlicher Theomorphie', *ZAH* 1:112–121.

———— (1988b), 'Hld 4,12–5,1: ein althebräisches Paradigma poetischer Sprache', *ZAH* 1:191–201.

———— (1994), 'Menschen, Landschaften und religiöse Erinnerungsreste: Anschlusserörterungen zum Hohenlied', *ZTK* 91:375–395.

———— (1996), 'Kohelet und Amminadab', in Anja A. Diesel et al. (eds.), '*Jedes Ding hat seine Zeit...*': *Studien zur israelitischen und altorientalischen Weisheit: Diethelm Michel zum 65. Geburtstag*, BZAW 241, Berlin: de Gruyter, 149–165.

———— (1997), 'Travestien und geistige Landschaften: Zum Intergrund einiger Motive bei Kohelet und im Hohenlied', *ZAW* 109:557–574.

———— (2004), 'Zur Frage nach dem "Wesen" früher Lyrik: Am Beispiel des Hohenliedes', in Markus Witte (ed.), *Gott und Mensch im Dialog: Festschrift für Otto Kaiser zum 80. Geburtstag*, BZAW 345.2, Berlin: de Gruyter, 817–832.

Munro, Jill M. (1995), *Spikenard and Saffron: The Imagery of the Song of Songs*, JSOT 203, Sheffield: Sheffield Academic Press.

Murphy, Roland E. (1949), 'The Structure of the Canticle of Canticles', *CBQ* 11:381–391.

———— (1954), 'Recent Literature on the Canticle of Canticles', *CBQ* 16:1–11.

———— (1973), 'Form-Critical Studies in the Song of Songs', *Int* 27:413–422.

———— (1977), 'Towards a Commentary on the Song of Songs', *CBQ* 39:482–496.

———— (1979), 'Interpreting the Song of Songs', *BTB* 9:99–105.

———— (1981), 'Patristic and Medieval Exegesis – Help or Hindrance?', *CBQ* 43:505–516.

———— (1985), 'Cant 2:8–17 – A Unified Poem?', in Ed. A. Caquot et al. (eds.), *Mélanges bibliques et orientaux en l'honneur de M. Mathias Delcor*, AOAT 215, Neukirchen-Vluyn: Neukirchener Verlag, 305–310.

———— (1986), 'History of Exegesis as a Hermeneutical Tool: The Song of Songs', *BTB* 16:87–91.

———— (1987), 'Dance and Death in the Song of Songs', in John H. Marks and Robert M. Good (eds.), *Love and Death in the Ancient Near East: Essays in Honor of Marvin H. Pope*, Guilford, Conn.: Four Quarters, 117–119.

Ndoga, S. S., and H. Viviers (2000), 'Is the Woman in the Song of Songs Really That Free?', *HTS* 56:1286–1307.

Neusner, Jacob (1988), *The Mishnah: A New Translation*, New Haven: Yale University Press.

———— (1989), *Song of Songs Rabbah: An Analytical Translation*, 2 vols., BJS 197–198, Atlanta: Scholars Press.

———— (1993), *Israel's Love Affair With God: Song of Songs*, The Bible of Judaism Library, Valley Forge: Trinity Press International.

Nichols, Aidan (2007), *Lovely, Like Jerusalem: The Fulfillment of the Old Testament in Christ and the Church*, San Francisco: Ignatius.

Nielsen, Kirsten (1998), 'Song of Songs', in Steven L. McKenzie and M. Patrick Graham (eds.), *The Hebrew Bible Today*, Louisville: Westminster John Knox, 179–185.

Nielsen, Kjeld (1986), *Incense in Ancient Israel*, VTSup 38, Leiden: Brill.

Nissinen, Martti (1998), 'Love Lyrics of Nabû and Tašmetu: An Assyrian Song of Songs?', in Manfred Dietrich and Ingo Kottsieper (eds.), *'Und Mose schrieb dieses Lied auf': Studien zum Alten Testament und zum alten Orient: Festschrift für Oswald Loretz zur Vollendung seines 70. Lebensjahres mit Beiträgen von Freunden, Schülern und Kollegen*, AOAT 250, Münster: Ugarit-Verlag, 585–634.

Norris, Richard A. (1998), 'The Soul Takes Flight: Gregory of Nyssa and the Song of Songs', *ATR* 80:517–532.

Ogden, Graham (1996), ' "Black But Beautiful" (Song of Songs 1.5)', *BT* 47:443–445.

Ostriker, Alicia Suskin (2000), 'A Holy of Holies: The Song of Songs as Countertext', in Athalya Brenner and Carole R. Fontaine, *The Song of Songs*, FCBSS 6, Sheffield: Sheffield Academic Press, 36–54.

———— (2007), *For the Love of God: The Bible as an Open Book*, New Brunswick: Rutgers University Press.

Pardes, Ilana (1992), *Countertraditions in the Bible: A Feminist Approach*, Cambridge, Mass.: Harvard University Press.

Parsons, Greg W. (1999), 'Guidelines for Understanding and Utilizing the Song of Songs', *BSac* 156:399–422.

Patmore, Hector (2006), ' "The Plain and Literal Sense": On Contemporary Assumptions about the Song of Songs', *VT* 56:239–250.

Patterson, Richard D. (2008), 'Metaphors of Marriage as Expressions of Divine–Human Relations', *JETS* 51:689–702.

Paul, Martin (2001), 'Die *fremde Frau* in Sprichwörter 1–9 und die *Geliebte* des Hohenliedes: Ein Beitrag zur Intertextualität', *BN* 106:40–46.

Paul, Shalom M. (1978), 'An Unrecognized Medical Idiom in Canticles 6, 12 and Job 9, 21', *Bib* 59:545–547.

——— (1992), 'Polysensuous Polyvalency in Poetic Parallelism', in Michael Fishbane and Emanuel Tov (eds.), *Sha'arei Talmon: Studies in the Bible, Qumran, and the Ancient Near East Presented to Shemaryahu Talmon*, Winona Lake: Eisenbrauns, 147–163.

——— (1995), 'The Plural of Ecstasy, in Mesopotamian and Biblical Love Poetry', in Ziony Zevit, Seymour Gitin and Michael Sokoloft (eds.), *Solving Riddles and Untying Knots: Biblical, Epigraphic, and Semitic Studies in Honor of Jonas C. Greenfield*, Winona Lake: Eisenbrauns, 585–597.

——— (1997), 'A Lover's Garden of Verse: Literal and Metaphorical Imagery in Ancient Near Eastern Love Poetry', in Mordechai Cogan, Barry L. Eichler and Jeffrey H. Tigay (eds.), *Tehillah le-Moshe: Biblical Judaic Studies in Honor of Moshe Greenberg*, Winona Lake: Eisenbrauns, 99–110.

Payne, Robin (1996), 'The Song of Songs: Song of Woman, Song of Man, Song of God', *ExpTim* 107:329–333.

Pecknold, C. C. (2003), 'The Readable City and the Rhetoric of Excess', *Crosscurrents* 52:516–520.

Pelletier, Anne-Marie (1989), *Lectures du Cantique des Cantiques*, AnBib 121, Rome: Pontificio Istituto Biblico.

Perry, T. A. (2005), 'The Coordination of KY/'L KN in Cant. I 1–3 and Related Texts', *VT* 55:528–541.

Pertile, Lino (2006), 'The Harlot and the Giant: Dante and the Song of Songs', in Peter S. Hawkins and Lesleigh Cushing Stahlberg (eds.), *Scrolls of Love: Ruth and the Song of Songs*, New York: Fordham University Press, 268–280.

Petersen, David L., and Kent Harold Richards (1992), *Interpreting Hebrew Poetry*, GBS, Minneapolis: Fortress.

Phipps, William E. (1975), *Recovering Biblical Sensuousness*, Philadelphia: Westminster.

——— (1988), 'The Plight of the Song of Songs', in Harold Bloom (ed.), *The Song of Songs*, Modern Critical Interpretations, New York: Chelsea House, 5–23.

Polaski, Donald C. (1997), 'What Will Ye See in the Shulammite? Women, Power and Panopticism in the Song of Songs', *BibInt* 5:64–81.

Pope, Marvin H. (1970), 'A Mare in Pharaoh's Chariotry', *BASOR* 200:56–61.

——— (1980), 'Response to Sasson on the Sublime Song', *Maarav* 2:207–214.

——— (1988), 'Metastases in Canonical Shapes of the Super Song', in Gene M. Tucker et al. (eds.), *Canon, Theology, and Old Testament Interpretation: Essays in Honor of Brevard S. Childs*, Philadelphia: Fortress, 312–328.

Provan, Iain W. (2000), 'The Terrors of the Night: Love, Sex, and Power in Song of Songs 3', in J. I. Packer and Sven K. Soderlund (eds.), *The Way of Wisdom: Essays in Honor of Bruce K. Waltke*, Grand Rapids: Zondervan, 150–167.

Raabe, Paul R. (1991), 'Deliberate Ambiguity in the Psalter', *JBL* 110:213–227.

Rabin, Chaim (1979), 'The Song of Songs and Tamil Poetry', *SR* 3:205–219.

Rainbow, Jesse (2007), 'The Song of Songs and the *Testament of Solomon*: Solomon's Love Poetry and Christian Magic', *HTR* 100:249–274.

Reines, C. W. (1975), 'Beauty in the Bible and in the Talmud', *Judaism* 24:100–107.

Reinhold, Meyer (1970), *History of Purple as a Status Symbol in Antiquity*, Collection Latomus 116, Brussels: Latomus.

Richardson, John P. (1997), 'Preaching from the *Song of Songs*, Allegory Revisited', *ERT* 21:250–257.

Robert, A. (1948), 'Les appendices du Cantique des Cantiques', *RB* 55:161–183.

Roberts, D. Phillip (2007), *Let Me See Your Form: Seeking Poetic Structure in the Song of Songs*, Studies in Judaism, Lanham, Md.: University Press of America.

Rochettes, Jacqueline des, et al. (2001), 'Les Mots du Cantique: Une Polysémie Symphonique', *BLE* 102:167–180.

Rowley, H. H. (1939), 'The Meaning of "The Shulammite"', *AJSLL* 56:84–91.

———(1965), 'The Interpretation of the Song of Songs', in *The Servant of the Lord and Other Essays on the Old Testament*, 2nd rev. ed., Oxford: Basil Blackwell, 195–245.

Rundgren, Frithiof (1962), "*pryon* "Tragsessel, Sänfte"', *ZAW* 74:70–72.

Ryan, Thomas F. (2001), 'Sex, Spirituality, and Pre-Modern Readings of the Song of Songs', *Hor* 28:81–104.

Ryken, Leland (1974), *The Literature of the Bible*, Grand Rapids: Zondervan.

———(1992), *Words of Delight: A Literary Introduction to the Bible*, 2nd ed., Grand Rapids: Baker.

Sadgrove, M. (1979), 'The Song of Songs as Wisdom Literature', in E. A. Livingstone (ed.), *Studia Biblica 1978*, JSOTSup 11, Sheffield: JSOT Press, 245–248.

Saebø, Magne (1996), 'On the Canonicity of the Song of Songs', in Michael V. Fox et al. (eds.), *Texts, Temples, and Traditions: A Tribute to Menahem Haran*, Winona Lake: Eisenbrauns, 267–277.

Salvesen, Alison (2005), 'Pigs in the Camps and the Breasts of My Lambs: Song of Songs in the Syriac Tradition', in Anselm C. Hagedorn (ed.), *Perspectives on the Song of Songs*, BZAW 346, Berlin: de Gruyter, 260–273.

Sasson, Jack M. (1973), 'A Further Cuneiform Parallel to the Song of Songs?', *ZAW* 85:359–360.

Sasson, Victor (1989), 'King Solomon and the Dark Lady in the Song of Songs', *VT* 39:407–414.

Schenker, A., et al. (eds.) (2004), *Biblia Hebraica Quinta*, Stuttgart: Deutsche Bibelgesellschaft.

Schwab, George M. (2002), *The Song of Songs' Cautionary Message Concerning Human Love*, Studies in Biblical Literature 41, New York: Peter Lang.

Scott, Mark S. M. (2006), 'Shades of Grace: Origen and Gregory of Nyssa's Soteriological Exegesis of the "Black and Beautiful" Bride in Song of Songs 1:5', *HTR* 99:65–83.

Sefati, Yitschak (1997), 'Dumuzi-Inanna Songs', in William W. Hallo (ed.), *The Context of Scripture*. Vol. 1: *Canonical Compositions from the Biblical World*, Leiden: Brill, 540–543.

——— (1998), *Love Songs in Sumerian Literature: Critical Edition of the Dumuzi-Inanna Songs*, Bar-Ilan Studies in Near Eastern Languages and Culture, Ramat Gan: Bar-Ilan University Press.

Segal, Benjamin J. (1987–8), 'Double Meanings in the Song of Songs', *Dor le Dor* 16:249–255.

Segal, M. H. (1962), 'The Song of Songs', *VT* 12:470–490.

Sendrey, Alfred (1969), *Music in Ancient Israel*, New York: Philosophical Library.

Shea, William H. (1980), 'The Chiastic Structure of the Song of Songs', *ZAW* 92:378–396.

——— (1993), 'The Song of Seedtime and Harvest from Gezer', in Johannes C. de Moor and Wilfred G. E. Watson (eds.), *Verse in Ancient Near Eastern Prose*, AOAT 42, Neukirchen-Vluyn: Neukirchener Verlag, 243–250.

Shehadeh, Lamia Rustum (1991), 'Lebanon in Ancient Texts', in S. Seikaly et al. (eds.), *Quest for Understanding: Arabic and Islamic Studies in Memory of Malcolm H. Kerr*, Beirut: American University of Beirut, 3–13.

Sivan, Daniel, and Shamir Yona (1998), 'Pivot Words or Expressions in Biblical Hebrew and in Ugaritic Poetry', *VT* 48:399–407.

Soulen, Richard N. (1967), 'The *Wasfs* of the Song of Songs and Hermeneutic', *JBL* 86:183–190.

Sparks, Kenton L. (2005), *Ancient Texts for the Study of the Hebrew Bible: A Guide to the Background Literature*, Peabody: Hendrickson.

——— (2008), 'The Song of Songs: Wisdom for Young Jewish Women', *CBQ* 70:277–299.

Stephan, St. H. (1922), 'Modern Palestinian Parallels to the Song of Songs', *JPOS* 2:199–278.

Stone, Michael E. (2007), 'The Interpretation of Song of Songs in 4 Ezra', *JSJ* 38:226–233.

Štrba, Blažeg (2004), '*šošnh* of the Canticle', *Bib* 85:475–502.

Suarès, Carlo (1972), *The Song of Songs: The Canonical Song of Solomon Deciphered According to the Original Code of the Qabala*, Berkeley: Shambala.

Suderman, W. Derek (2005), 'Modest or Magnificent? Lotus versus Lily in Canticles', *CBQ* 67:42–58.

Sviri, Sara (1995), '*The Song of Songs* – Eros and the Mystical Quest', in Jonathan Magonet (ed.), *Jewish Explorations of Sexuality*, Providence, R. I.: Berghahn, 41–50.

Tanner, J. Paul (1997a), 'The History of Interpretation of the Song of Songs', *BSac* 154:23–46.

——— (1997b), 'The Message of the Song of Songs', *BSac* 154:142–161.

Tawil, Hayim (2006), 'Two Biblical Architectural Images in Light of Cuneiform Sources', *BASOR* 341:37–52.

Terrien, Samuel (1985), *Till the Heart Sings: A Biblical Theology of Manhood and Womanhood*, Grand Rapids: Eerdmans.

Thomas, D. Winton (1953), 'A Consideration of Some Unusual Ways of Translating the Superlative in Hebrew', *VT* 3:209–224.

Toorn, Karel van der (1995), 'The Significance of the Veil in the Ancient Near East', in David P. Wright, David Noel Freedman and Avi Hurvitz (eds.), *Pomegranates and Golden Bells: Studies in Biblical, Jewish, and Near Eastern Ritual, Law, and Literature in Honor of Jacob Milgrom*, Winona Lake: Eisenbrauns, 327–339.

Tournay, Raymond Jacques (1959), 'Les Chariots D'Aminadab (Cant. vi 12): Israël, Peuple Théophore', *VT* 9:288–309.

——— (1980), 'The Song of Songs and Its Concluding Section', *Imm* 10:5–14.

——— (1988), *Word of God, Song of Love*, ET New York: Paulist (French original 1982).

Toy, John (2007), 'God and Eroticism', *Theology* 110:323–331.

Trible, Phyllis (1978), *God and the Rhetoric of Sexuality*, OBT, Philadelphia: Fortress.

Tromp, Nicolas J. (1979), 'Wisdom and the Canticle: Ct 8, 6c–7b: Text, Character, Message and Import', in M. Gilbert (ed.), *La Sagesse de l'Ancien Testament*, BETL 51, Leuven: Leuven University Press, 88–95.

Tuell, Steven S. (1993), 'A Riddle Resolved by an Enigma: Hebrew *glš* and Ugaritic *GLT*', *JBL* 112:99–104.

Turner, Denys (1995), *Eros and Allegory: Medieval Exegesis of the Song of Songs*, Cistercian Studies Series 156, Kalamazoo, Mich.: Cistercian.

Urbach, Ephraim E. (1971), 'The Homiletical Interpretations of the Sages and the Expositions of Origen on Canticles, and the Jewish–Christian Disputation', in Joseph Heinemann and Dov Noy (eds.), *Studies in Aggadah and Folk-Literature*, ScrHier 22, Jerusalem: Magnes, 247–275.

Vernus, Pascal (2005), 'Le *Cantique des Cantiques* et l'Egypte pharaonique. Etat de la question', in Anselm C. Hagedorn (ed.), *Perspectives on the Song of Songs*, BZAW 346, Berlin: de Gruyter, 150–162.

Villiers, D. W de, and J. J. Burden (1989), 'Function and Translation: A Twosome in the Song of Songs', *OTE* 2:1–11.

Viviers, Hendrik (2002), 'The Rhetoricity of the "Body" in the Song of Songs', in Stanley E. Porter and Dennis L. Stamps (eds.), *Rhetorical Criticism and the Bible*, JSNTSup 195, London: Sheffield Academic Press, 237–254.

Volfing, Annette (2005), 'Middle High German Appropriations of the Song of Songs: Allegorical Interpretation and Narrative Extrapolation', in Anselm C. Hagedorn (ed.), *Perspectives on the Song of Songs*, BZAW 346, Berlin: de Gruyter, 294–316.

Wagner, Andreas (2007), 'Das Hohe Lied – theologische Implikationen seines literarischen Charakters als Sammlung von Liebesliedern', *ZAW* 119:539–555.

Waldman, Nahum M. (1970), 'A Note on Canticles 4 9', *JBL* 89:215–217.

Walsh, Carey Ellen (1999), 'A Startling Voice: Woman's Desire in the Song of Songs', *BTB* 28:129–134.

—— (2000), *Exquisite Desire: Religion, the Erotic, and the Song of Songs*, Minneapolis: Fortress.

Watson, Wilfred G. E. (1994), *Traditional Techniques in Classical Hebrew Verse*, JSOTSup 170, Sheffield: Sheffield Academic Press.

—— (1995), 'Some Ancient Near Eastern Parallels to the Song of Songs', in Jon Davies, Graham Harvey and Wildred G. E. Watson (eds.), *Words Remembered, Texts Renewed: Essays in Honour of John F. A. Sawyer*, JSOTSup 195, Sheffield: Sheffield Academic Press, 253–271.

—— (1997), 'Love and Death Once More (Song of Songs VIII 6)', *VT* 47:385–387.

—— (1998), 'Parallel Word Pairs in the Song of Songs', in Manfried Dietrich and Ingo Kottsieper (eds.), *Und Mose schrieb dieses Lied auf*, SATAO, Münster: Ugarit-Verlag, 785–808.

Webb, Barry G. (1990), 'The Song of Songs: A Love Poem and as Holy Scripture', *RTR* 49:91–99.

—— (2000), *Five Festal Garments: Christian Reflections on the Song of Songs, Ruth, Lamentations, Ecclesiastes and Esther*, NSBT 10, Downers Grove: IVP.

Webster, Edwin C. (1982), 'Pattern in the Song of Songs', *JSOT* 22:73–93.

Wendland, Ernst R. (1995), 'Seeking the Path Through a Forest of Symbols: A Figurative and Structural Survey of the Song of Songs', *JTT* 7:13–59.

Wenham, Gordon J. (1972), '*BeTÛLĀH* "A Girl of Marriageable Age" ', *VT* 22:326–348.

Westenholz, Joan Goodnick (1995), 'Love Lyrics from the Ancient Near East', in Jack M. Sasson (ed.), *Civilizations of the Ancient Near East*, 4:2471–2482, New York: Charles Scribner's Sons.

Wetzstein, J. G. (1873), 'Die syrische Dreschtafel', *Zeitschrift für Ethnologie* 5:270–302.

Whedbee, J. William (1993), 'Paradox and Parody in the Song of Solomon: Towards a Comic Reading of the Most Sublime Song', in Athalya Brenner (ed.), *A Feminist Companion to the Song of Songs*, FCB 1, Sheffield: JSOT, 266–278.

—— (1998), *The Bible and Comic Vision*, Cambridge: Cambridge University Press.

White, John B. (1978), *A Study of the Language of Love in the Song of Songs and Ancient Egyptian Poetry*, SBLDS 38, Missoula: Scholars Press.

Whitesell, Connie J. (1995), 'Behold, Thou Art Fair, My Beloved', *Parab* 20:92–99.

Williams, Ronald J. (1976), *Hebrew Syntax: An Outline*, 2nd ed., Toronto: University of Toronto Press.

Winandy, Jacques (1965), 'La Litière de Salomon (Ct. III 9–10)', *VT* 15:103–110.

Wirt, Sherwood Eliot (1990), 'Some New Thoughts about the Song of Solomon', *JETS* 33:433–436.

Wright, John (1981), 'Sexuality Within the Old Testament', *St. Mark's Review* 106:3–12.

Yamauchi, Edwin M. (1978), 'Cultural Aspects of Marriage in the Ancient World', *BSac* 135:241–252.

Young, Ian (1993), *Diversity in Pre-Exilic Hebrew*, FAT 5, Tübingen: Mohr (Siebeck).

INDEX OF SCRIPTURE REFERENCES

INDEX OF AUTHORS

INDEX OF SUBJECTS: ECCLESIASTES

INDEX OF SUBJECTS:
THE SONG OF SONGS

under the sun

" " cruise